MyManagementLab™: Improves Student Engagement Before, During, and After Class

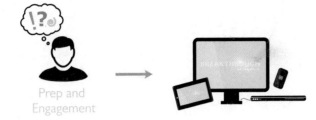

Prep and Engagement

- **Learning Catalytics**—A "bring your own device" student engagement, assessment, and classroom intelligence system helps instructors analyze students' critical-thinking skills during lectures.

- **Dynamic Study Modules (DSMs)**—Through adaptive learning, students get personalized guidance where and when they need it most, creating greater engagement, improving knowledge retention, and supporting subject-matter mastery. Also available on mobile devices.

- **MediaShare for Business**—A curated collection of business videos tagged to learner outcomes helps students understand why they are learning key concepts and how they will apply those in their careers. Instructors can assign customizable, auto-scored assignments and upload their favourite YouTube clips or original content.

Decision Making

- **Personal Inventory Assessment**—A collection of online exercises promotes self-reflection and engagement in students, enhancing their ability to connect with concepts taught in principles of management, organizational behaviour, and human resources management classes.

- **Decision-making Simulations**—Simulations put your students in the role of a key decision maker. The simulations change and branch according to the decisions students make, providing a variation of scenario paths. Upon completion of each, students receive a grade and a detailed report of the choices they made and the consequences.

- **Writing Space**—Better writers make great learners, who perform better in their courses. The Writing Space—providing a single location to develop and assess concept mastery and critical thinking—offers assisted-graded and create-your-own writing assignments, allowing you to exchange personalized feedback with students quickly and easily.

- **Additional Features**—Included with the MyLab are a powerful homework and test manager, robust gradebook tracking, and comprehensive online course content.

ESSENTIALS OF ORGANIZATIONAL BEHAVIOUR

STEPHEN P. ROBBINS
San Diego State University

TIMOTHY A. JUDGE
University of Notre Dame

KATHERINE E. BREWARD
University of Winnipeg

CANADIAN EDITION

EDITORIAL DIRECTOR: Claudine O'Donnell
ACQUISITIONS EDITOR: Karen Townsend
MARKETING MANAGER: Leigh-Anne Graham
PROGRAM MANAGER: Steven Lee
SENIOR PROJECT MANAGER: Jessica Hellen
SENIOR DEVELOPMENTAL EDITOR: Keriann McGoogan
MEDIA EDITOR: Rachel Stuckey
MEDIA DEVELOPER: Kelli Cadet

PRODUCTION SERVICES: iEnergizer Aptara®, Ltd.
PERMISSIONS PROJECT MANAGER: Joanne Tang
PHOTO PERMISSIONS RESEARCH: Mike Lackey, Integra
TEXT PERMISSIONS RESEARCH: Renae Horstman, Integra
INTERIOR AND COVER DESIGNER: Anthony Leung
COVER IMAGE: © alotofpeople - Fotolia.com
VICE-PRESIDENT, CROSS MEDIA AND PUBLISHING
SERVICES: Gary Bennett

Pearson Canada Inc., 26 Prince Andrew Place, Don Mills, Ontario M3C 2T8.

ISBN-13: 978-0-13-418297-1

1 16

Library and Archives Canada Cataloguing in Publication
Robbins, Stephen P., 1943-, author
    Essentials of organizational behaviour / Stephen P. Robbins
(San Diego State University), Timothy A. Judge (University of
Notre Dame), Katherine E. Breward (University of Winnipeg).
—Canadian edition.

Includes bibliographical references and index.
Electronic monograph in PDF format.
ISBN 978-0-13-418297-1 (pdf)

    1. Organizational behavior. I. Judge, Tim, author II. Breward,
Katherine, author III. Title.

HD58.7.R6 2016   658.3   C2016-906216-3

This book is dedicated to our friends and colleagues in the Organizational Behavior Teaching Society who, through their teaching, research, and commitment to the leading process, have significantly improved the ability of students to understand and apply OB concepts. It is also dedicated to the many leaders, managers, and workers who agreed to share their stories for use as examples and mini cases throughout the text. Their willingness to reflect on their experiences and share their triumphs, mistakes, and hard-won insights improves the learning experience for all.

Brief Contents

Part 1 Prologue 1

Chapter 1   What Is Organizational Behaviour?   1

Part 2 Understanding Yourself and Others 19

Chapter 2   Diversity in Organizations   19

Chapter 3   Attitudes and Job Satisfaction 46

Chapter 4   Emotions and Moods   63

Chapter 5   Personality and Values   82

Part 3 Making and Implementing Decisions 106

Chapter 6   Perception and Individual Decision Making   106

Chapter 7   Motivation Theories   126

Chapter 8   Motivation: From Concepts to Applications   147

Part 4 Communicating in Groups and Teams 166

Chapter 9   Foundations of Group Behaviour   166

Chapter 10   Understanding Work Teams   186

Chapter 11   Communication   203

Part 5 Negotiating Power and Politics 223

Chapter 12   Leadership   223

Chapter 13   Power and Politics   245

Part 6 Leading, Understanding, and Transforming the Organization System 266

Chapter 14   Conflict and Negotiation   266

Chapter 15   Foundations of Organization Structure   288

Chapter 16   Organizational Culture   309

Chapter 17   Organizational Change and Stress Management   327

Contents

Preface xv

Acknowledgments xviii

About the Authors xix

1 What Is Organizational Behaviour? 1

LEARNING OBJECTIVES 1

The Importance of Interpersonal Skills 1

Enter Organizational Behaviour 2

Complementing Intuition with Systematic Study 3
  Big Data 4

Disciplines That Contribute to the OB Field 4
  Psychology 5
  Social Psychology 6
  Sociology 6
  Anthropology 6
  Political Science 6
  Neuroscience 7

A Brief History of OB 7

There Are Few Absolutes in OB 7

Challenges and Opportunities for OB 9
  Responding to Economic Pressures 11
  Responding to Globalization 11
  Managing Workforce Diversity 12
  Improving Customer Service 12
  Improving People Skills 12
  Working in Networked Organizations 13
  Enhancing Employee Well-Being at Work 13
  Creating a Positive Work Environment 13
  Improving Ethical Behaviour 14

Coming Attractions: Developing an OB Model 14
  An Overview 14

Summary 15

Implications for Managers 15

Breakout Question for Group Discussion 15

Personal Inventory Assessment 16

Self-Reflection Activity 16

Mini Case   Managing Group Behaviour Without Formal
Power 16

Mini Case   The People Side of Target's Canadian
Catastrophe 17

2 Diversity in Organizations 19

LEARNING OBJECTIVES 19

Diversity 19
  Diversity in the Canadian Context: Multiculturalism as
  a Guiding Principle and Formal Policy 20
  Demographic Characteristics of the Canadian
  Workforce 20
  Levels of Diversity 23

How Do Employees Differ? Biographical Characteristics 24
  Age 24
  Gender 26
  Sexual Orientation and Gender Identity 27
  Race, Ethnicity, and Immigration Status 27
  Cultural Identity 31
  Disability 31
  Religion 33
  Ability 34

Intellectual Abilities 34

Physical Abilities 35
  Disabilities in the Context of Job Specification 36
  Discrimination 36

Implementing Diversity Management Strategies 38
  Attracting, Selecting, Developing, and Retaining
  Diverse Employees 38
  Diversity in Groups 40
  Effective Diversity Programs 40

Summary 42

Implications for Managers 42

Breakout Question for Group Discussion 42

Personal Inventory Assessment 42

Self-Reflection Activity 43

Mini Case   Disability-Based Discrimination 43

Mini Case   Classroom Diversity and Groups 44

3 Attitudes and Job Satisfaction 46

LEARNING OBJECTIVES 46

Attitudes 46
  What Are the Main Components of
  Attitudes? 47
  Does Behaviour Always Follow from Attitudes? 48
  Moderating Variables 49

What Are the Major Job Attitudes? 49
  Job Satisfaction 50
  Job Involvement 50
  Organizational Commitment 50
  Perceived Organizational Support 50
  Employee Engagement 51

Job Satisfaction 52
  Measuring Job Satisfaction 52
  How Satisfied Are People in Their Jobs? 53
  What Causes Job Satisfaction? 54

**The Impact of Satisfied and Dissatisfied Employees on the
Workplace 55**
  Job Satisfaction and Job Performance 56
  Job Satisfaction and OCB 57
  Job Satisfaction and Customer Satisfaction 57
  Job Satisfaction and Absenteeism 57
  Job Satisfaction and Turnover 57

        Job Satisfaction and Workplace Deviance 58
        Managers Often "Don't Get It" 58

    Summary 59
    Implications for Managers 59
    Breakout Question for Group Discussion 59
    Personal Inventory Assessment 59
    Self-Reflection Activity 59
    Mini Case   The Promotion 60
    Mini Case   Work Attitudes, Recognition, Feedback, and
    Fairness 61

4   Emotions and Moods   63

    LEARNING OBJECTIVES   63

    What Are Emotions and Moods? 64
        The Basic Emotions 64
        The Basic Moods: Positive and Negative
        Affect 65
        Experiencing Moods and Emotions 65
    The Function of Emotions and Moods 66
        Do Emotions Make Us Irrational? 66
        Do Emotions Make Us Ethical? 66
    Sources of Emotions and Moods 67
        Potential Influences on Moods and Emotions 67
    Emotional Labour 71
    Affective Events Theory 72
    Emotional Intelligence 73
        The Case for EI 73
        The Case Against EI 73
    Emotion Regulation 74
    OB Applications of Emotions and Moods 75
        Selection 75
        Decision Making 75
        Creativity 76
        Motivation 76
        Leadership 76
        Negotiation 77
        Customer Service 77
        Job Attitudes 77
        Deviant Workplace Behaviours 78
        Safety and Injury at Work 78

    Summary 78
    Implications for Managers 78
    Breakout Question for Group Discussion 79
    Personal Inventory Assessment 79
    Self-Reflection Activity 79
    Mini Case   Emotional Labour at the Call Centre 79
    Mini Case   Emotional Contagion Unleashed 80

5   Personality and Values   82

    LEARNING OBJECTIVES   82

    Personality 83
        What Is Personality? 83
    Dominant Personality Frameworks 84

        The Myers-Briggs Type Indicator 84
        The Big Five Personality Model 85
    Other Personality Frameworks 87
        The Dark Triad 88
        Approach–Avoidance 90
    Other Personality Traits Relevant to OB 90
        Core Self-Evaluations 91
        Self-Monitoring 91
        Proactive Personality 91
    Personality and Situations 92
        Situation Strength Theory 92
        Trait Activation Theory 94
    Values 94
        The Importance and Organization of Values 95
        Terminal Versus Instrumental Values 95
    **Linking an Individual's Personality and Values to the
    Workplace 95**
        Person–Job Fit 95
        Person–Organization Fit 97
    International Values 97
        Hofstede's Framework 97
        The GLOBE Framework 99
        Comparison of Hofstede's Framework and the GLOBE
        Framework 100
        Our Primary Trading Partner: Key U.S./Canadian
        Differences 100
        Nations Within Nations: Aboriginal Values in the
        Canadian Context 101
        Acculturation and Biculturalism: Immigrant
        Adjustment and Changes in Values 101

    Summary 101
    Implications for Managers 102
    Break-Out Question for Group Discussion 102
    Personal Inventory Assessment 102
    Self-Reflection Activity 102
    Mini Case   The Personality Problem 103
    Mini Case   Interview Expectations and Cultural
    Confusion 104

**6   Perception and Individual Decision
    Making   106**

    LEARNING OBJECTIVES   106

    What Is Perception? 107
        Factors That Influence Perception 107
    **Social Perception: Making Judgments About
    Others 107**
        Attribution Theory 107
        Common Shortcuts in Judging Others 109
    **The Link Between Perception and Individual Decision
    Making 111**
    Decision Making in Organizations 112
        The Rational Model, Bounded Rationality, and
        Intuition 112
    Common Biases and Errors in Decision Making 113
        Overconfidence Bias 113

Anchoring Bias 114
Confirmation Bias 115
Availability Bias 115
Escalation of Commitment 115
Risk Aversion 115
Hindsight Bias 116

Organizational Constraints on Decision Making 116
Performance Evaluation 116
Reward Systems 117
Formal Regulations 117
System-Imposed Time Constraints 117
Historical Precedents 117

What About Ethics in Decision Making? 117
Three Ethical Decision Criteria 118

Creativity in Organizations 119
Creative Behaviour 119
Causes of Creative Behaviour 120
Creative Outcomes (Innovation) 121

Summary 121
Implications for Managers 122
Breakout Question for Group Discussion 122
Personal Inventory Assessment 122
Self-Reflection Activity 122
Mini Case   Hiring School Bus Drivers 123
Mini Case   Career Planning as Decision Making 124

7   Motivation Theories   126
LEARNING OBJECTIVES   126

Defining Motivation 127
Early Theories of Motivation 127
Hierarchy of Needs Theory 127
Theory X and Theory Y 128
Two-Factor Theory 129
McClelland's Theory of Needs 130

Contemporary Theories of Motivation 131
Self-Determination Theory 131
Goal-Setting Theory 132

Other Contemporary Theories of Motivation 135
Self-Efficacy Theory 135
Equity Theory and Linkages to Perceptions of Organizational Justice 136
Expectancy Theory 141

Fostering Workplace Motivation 142
Creating Job Engagement 142

Summary 143
Implications for Managers 143
Breakout Question for Group Discussion 144
Personal Inventory Assessment 144
Self-Reflection Activity 144
Mini Case   What Does "Fair" Mean? 144
Mini Case   Goals, Revisited 145

8   Motivation: From Concepts to Applications   147
LEARNING OBJECTIVES   147

Motivating by Job Design: The Job Characteristics Model 148
The Job Characteristics Model 148

How Can Jobs Be Redesigned? 149
Job Rotation 149
Job Enrichment 150
Relational Job Design 151

Alternative Work Arrangements 151
Flextime 151
Job Sharing 153
Telecommuting 153

Employee Involvement 155
Examples of Employee Involvement Programs 155
Linking Employee Involvement Programs and Motivation Theories 156

Using Pay to Motivate Employees 156
What to Pay: Establishing a Pay Structure 157
How to Pay: Rewarding Individual Employees Through Variable-Pay Programs 157

Using Benefits to Motivate Employees 160
Flexible Benefits: Developing a Benefits Package 161

Using Intrinsic Rewards to Motivate Employees 161
Employee Recognition Programs 161

Summary 162
Implications for Managers 162
Breakout Question for Group Discussion 163
Personal Inventory Assessment 163
Self-Reflection Activity 163
Mini Case   Getting the Best from Your Salesforce 163
Mini Case   Enriching Jobs at the Construction Site 165

9   Foundations of Group Behaviour   166
LEARNING OBJECTIVES   166

Defining and Classifying Groups 167
The Five-Stage Model 167
An Alternative Model for Temporary Groups with Deadlines 168

Group Roles 169
Role Perception 169
Role Expectations 169
Role Conflict 169

Group Norms 170
Norms and Behaviour 170
Conformity 170
Deviant Workplace Behaviour 172

Group Status 173
What Determines Status? 174
Status and Norms 174
Status and Group Interaction 174

Group Size 174
Groups and Work Attitudes: More on Social Loafing 175

Group Cohesiveness **175**

Group Diversity **176**

Faultlines 177

Group Decision Making **177**

Groups Versus the Individual 177

Groupthink and Groupshift 178

Group Decision-Making Techniques **180**

Summary 181

Implications for Managers 182

Breakout Question for Group Discussion 182

Personal Inventory Assessment 182

Self-Reflection Activity 182

Mini Case   Accepting New Norms? A Harassed Reporter Fights Back 183

Mini Case   Canada's (Biased?) Guide to Healthy Eating 184

10 Understanding Work Teams **186**

LEARNING OBJECTIVES 186

Why Have Teams Become So Popular? **187**

Differences Between Groups and Teams **187**

Types of Teams **188**

Problem-Solving Teams 188

Self-Managed Work Teams 188

Cross-Functional Teams 189

Virtual Teams 190

Multiteam Systems 191

Creating Effective Teams **192**

Context 192

Team Composition 193

Team Processes 195

Turning Individuals into Team Players **197**

Selecting: Hiring Team Players 197

Training: Creating Team Players 197

Rewarding: Providing Incentives to Be a Good Team Player 198

Beware! Teams Aren't Always the Answer **198**

Summary 199

Implications for Managers 199

Breakout Question for Group Discussion 199

Personal Inventory Assessment 200

Self-Reflection Activity 200

Mini Case   Lifelong Learning and Teamwork 200

Mini Case   Team Incentives and Unintended Consequences 201

11 Communication **203**

LEARNING OBJECTIVES 203

The Communication Process **204**

Direction of Communication **204**

Downward Communication 205

Upward Communication 205

Lateral Communication 205

Organizational Communication **206**

Formal Small-Group Networks 206

The Grapevine 207

Modes of Communication **208**

Oral Communication 208

Written Communication: Traditional Print and Electronic Forms 208

Nonverbal Communication 210

Choice of Communication Channel **211**

Channel Richness 211

Choosing Communication Methods 211

Information Security 213

Persuasive Communication **213**

Automatic and Controlled Processing 213

Interest Level 213

Prior Knowledge 214

Personality 214

Message Characteristics 214

Barriers to Effective Communication **214**

Filtering 214

Selective Perception 215

Information Overload 215

Emotions 215

Language 215

Silence 216

Communication Apprehension 216

Lying 217

Global Implications **217**

Cultural Barriers 217

Cultural Context 218

A Cultural Guide 218

Summary 219

Implications for Managers 220

Breakout Question for Group Discussion 220

Personal Inventory Assessment 220

Self-Reflection Activity 220

Mini Case   The Informal Communication Network 221

Mini Case   Voicing and Being a "Team Player" 221

12 Leadership **223**

LEARNING OBJECTIVES 223

What Is Leadership? **223**

Trait Theories **224**

Behavioural Theories **224**

Summary of Trait Theories and Behavioural Theories 226

Contingency Theories **226**

The Fiedler Model 226

Other Contingency Theories 228

Charismatic Leadership and Transformational Leadership **229**

Charismatic Leadership 229

Transformational Leadership 232

Authentic Leadership: Ethics and Trust **235**

What Is Authentic Leadership? 235

Ethical Leadership 235
Servant Leadership 235
Trust and Leadership 236
What Are the Consequences of Trust? 237
Leading for the Future: Mentoring 237
Mentoring 237
Challenges to the Leadership Construct 238
Leadership as an Attribution 238
Substitutes for and Neutralizers of Leadership 239
Finding and Creating Effective Leaders 240
Selecting Leaders 240
Training Leaders 240

Summary 240
Implications for Managers 241
Breakout Question for Group Discussion 241
Personal Inventory Assessment 241
Self-Reflection Activity 241
Mini Case   A Study of Leadership Style 242
Mini Case   Situational Leadership Comes Clean 243

13 Power and Politics 245

LEARNING OBJECTIVES 245

A Definition of Power 245
Contrasting Leadership and Power 246
Bases of Power 246
Formal Power 247
Personal Power 247
Which Bases of Power Are Most Effective? 248
Power Tactics 248
How Power Affects People 251
Politics: Power in Action 252
Definition of Organizational Politics 252
The Reality of Politics 252
Causes and Consequences of Political Behaviour 253
Factors Contributing to Political Behaviour 253
How Do People Respond to Organizational Politics? 255
Impression Management 256
The Ethics of Behaving Politically 259
Mapping Your Political Career 260

Summary 261
Implications for Managers 262
Breakout Question for Group Discussion 262
Personal Inventory Assessment 262
Self-Reflection Activity 262
Mini Case   Power Abused—Celebrity and Harassment 263
Mini Case   Power in Academe 264

14 Conflict and Negotiation 266

LEARNING OBJECTIVES 266

A Definition of Conflict 267
The Traditional View of Conflict 267
The Interactionist View of Conflict 267
Types and Loci of Conflict 268

Types of Conflict 268
Loci of Conflict 269
The Conflict Process 270
Stage I: Potential Opposition or Incompatibility 271
Stage II: Cognition and Personalization 271
Stage III: Intentions 272
Stage IV: Behaviour 273
Stage V: Outcomes 274
Negotiation 275
Bargaining Strategies 276
The Negotiation Process 278
Steps in the Negotiation Process 278
Individual Differences in Negotiation Effectiveness 280
Personality Traits in Negotiation 280
Moods/Emotions in Negotiation 280
Culture in Negotiations 281
Gender Differences in Negotiations 282

Summary 283
Implications for Managers 283
Breakout Question for Group Discussion 283
Personal Inventory Assessment 284
Self-Reflection Activity 284
Mini Case   Win–Lose Negotiation Tactics Lead to Corporate Humiliation 284
Mini Case   Coming Back from Conflict 285

15 Foundations of Organization Structure 288

LEARNING OBJECTIVES 288

What Is Organizational Structure? 289
Work Specialization 289
Departmentalization 290
Chain of Command 291
Span of Control 291
Centralization and Decentralization 292
Formalization 293
Common Organizational Designs 293
The Simple Structure 293
The Bureaucracy 294
The Matrix Structure 295
New Design Options 296
The Virtual Organization 296
The Boundaryless Organization 297
The Leaner Organization: Downsizing 298
Why Do Structures Differ? 300
Organizational Strategies 301
Organization Size 301
Technology 301
Environment 302
Organizational Designs and Employee Behaviour 302

Summary 304
Implications for Managers 304
Breakout Question for Group Discussion 305
Personal Inventory Assessment 305

Self-Reflection Activity 305
Mini Case   Structured for Service 305
Mini Case   Structuring for Multiple Purposes—Finding the Right Balance 306

16 Organizational Culture   309

LEARNING OBJECTIVES   309

What Is Organizational Culture?   310
A Definition of Organizational Culture 310
Culture Is a Descriptive Term 310
Do Organizations Have Uniform Cultures? 310
Strong Versus Weak Cultures 311
Culture Versus Formalization 311

What Do Cultures Do?   311
The Functions of Culture 312
Culture Creates Climate 312
Culture as a Liability 313

Creating and Sustaining Culture   314
How a Culture Begins 314
Keeping a Culture Alive 314
Summary: How Cultures Form 317

How Employees Learn Culture   318
Stories 318
Rituals 318
Symbols 318
Language 319

Creating an Ethical Organizational Culture   319

Creating a Positive Organizational Culture   320
Building on Employee Strengths 320
Rewarding More Than Punishing, and the Value of the "Small" Stuff 321
Emphasizing Vitality and Growth 321
Limits of Positive Culture 322

Global Implications   322

Summary 323
Implications for Managers 324

Breakout Question for Group Discussion 324
Personal Inventory Assessment 324
Self-Reflection Activity 324
Mini Case   Developing and Maintaining a Safety Culture 325
Mini Case   Culture Change at the RCMP 325

17 Organizational Change and Stress Management   327

LEARNING OBJECTIVES   327

Forces for Change   327

Resistance to Change   329
Overcoming Resistance to Change 329

Approaches to Managing Organizational Change   332
Lewin's Three-Step Model 332
Kotter's Eight-Step Plan for Implementing Change 333
Organizational Development 334

Creating a Culture for Change   335
Stimulating a Culture of Innovation 336

Work Stress and Its Management   337
What Is Stress? 337
Consequences of Stress 338
Managing Stress 339

Summary 341
Implications for Managers 341
Breakout Question for Group Discussion 342
Personal Inventory Assessment 342
Self-Reflection Activity 342
Mini Case   Stressed in Software 342
Mini Case   Make Way For Innovation 344

Epilogue 345
Endnotes 347
Glossary 393
Index 401

Preface

This book was created as an alternative to the usual 600-or-700-page comprehensive textbook in organizational behaviour (OB). It attempts to provide balanced coverage of all the key elements making up the discipline of OB in a style that readers will find both informative and interesting. We're pleased to say that this text has achieved a wide following in short courses and executive programs and in traditional courses as a companion volume with experiential, skill development, case, and readings books. It is currently used at more than 500 colleges and universities in the United States, Canada, Latin America, Europe, Australia, and Asia. It has also been translated into Spanish, Portuguese, Japanese, Chinese, Dutch, Polish, Turkish, Danish, and Bahasa Indonesian.

What do people like about this book? Surveys of users have found general agreement about the following features. Needless to say, they've all been retained in this edition.

- *Balanced topic coverage.* Although short in length, this book continues to provide balanced coverage of all the key concepts in OB. This includes not only traditional topics, such as personality, motivation, and leadership, but also cutting-edge issues such as emotions, diversity, negotiation, and teamwork.

- *Writing style.* This book is frequently singled out for its fluid writing style and extensive use of examples. Users regularly tell us that they find this book "conversational," "interesting," "student friendly," and "very clear and understandable."

- *Practicality.* This book has never been solely about theory. It's about using theory to better explain and predict the behavior of people in organizations. In each edition of this book, we have focused on making sure that readers see the link between OB theories, research, and implications for practice.

- *Integration of globalization, diversity, and ethics.* The topics of globalization and cross-cultural differences, diversity, and ethics are discussed throughout this book. Rather than being presented only in separate chapters, these topics have been woven into the context of relevant issues. Users tell us they find that this integrative approach makes these topics more fully part of OB and reinforces their importance.

- *Comprehensive supplements.* This book may be short, but not on supplements. It comes with a complete, high-tech support package that includes a comprehensive Instructor's Manual and Test Bank and PowerPoint Slides. See below for access information.

KEY FEATURES OF THE CANADIAN EDITION

- Includes extensive Canadian demographic information about workforce participation rates, labour market outcomes, work attitudes, and other organizational trends.

- Examples throughout the textbook reflect balanced coverage of contemporary Canadian issues such as the implementation of multicultural ideals, the Temporary Foreign Worker Program, harassment and culture change within the RCMP, rights of transsexual workers, emerging standards for psychologically safe workplaces, changing regulations regarding marijuana possession and usage, and insights gained from recent human rights tribunal decisions.

- First Nations, Métis, and Inuit perspectives and examples are included throughout, particularly in the chapters discussing diversity, work attitudes, leadership, organizational culture, and motivation.

- The experiences and varied perspectives of immigrant workers are reflected in pervasive examples, particularly in chapters discussing diversity, work attitudes, organizational culture, and motivation.

- Two short mini cases and a group discussion activity are included in each chapter to encourage reflection and applied learning.

- Coverage of electronic communication has been increased, with specific tips for maximizing the effectiveness of communication strategies.

- Personal Inventory Assessments (PIAs) and the associated self-reflection activities allow students to assess their own skills and abilities and reflect upon the impact of their scores, and provide tips for further development. In the self-reflection activities, students are asked to carefully consider the scores they received in their PIA assessments and the effect those traits and characteristics might have on their working lives. The likely impact on workplace behaviours, performance, and effectiveness are explored by either using hypothetical scenarios or asking students to reflect on past events in their lives. This practice personalizes the content and helps students transition from memorization of theory to applied learning.

- A new "Implications for Managers" section was created to bring chapter topics together with practical advice for managers.

RESOURCES FOR STUDENTS

MyManagementLab™

We have created an outstanding supplements package for *Essentials of Organizational Behaviour*, Canadian Edition. In particular, we have provided access to MyManagementLab, which provides students with an assortment of tools to help enrich and expedite learning. MyManagementLab is an online study tool for students and an online homework and assessment tool for faculty. It lets students assess their understanding through auto-graded tests and assignments, develop a personalized study plan to address areas of weakness, and practise a variety of learning tools to master management principles. New and updated MyManagementLab resources include the following:

- *Personalized study plan.* As students work through MyManagementLab's new Study Plan, they can clearly see which topics they have mastered—and, more importantly, which they need to work on. Each question has been carefully written to match the concepts, language, and focus of the text, so students can get an accurate sense of how well they've understood the chapter content.

- *Personal Inventory Assessment (PIA).* Students learn better when they can connect what they are learning to their personal experience. PIA is a collection of online exercises designed to promote self-reflection and engagement in students, enhancing their ability to connect with concepts taught in principles of management, organizational behaviour, and human resources management classes. Assessments can be assigned by instructors, who can then track students' completions. Student results include a written explanation along with a graphic display that shows how their results compare to the class as a whole. Instructors will also have access to this graphic representation of results to promote classroom discussion.

- *Assignable mini-cases.* Instructors have access to a variety of case-based assessment material that can be assigned to students, with multiple-choice assessment.

- *Learning Catalytics.* Learning Catalytics is a "bring your own device" student engagement, assessment, and classroom intelligence system. It allows instructors to engage students in class with a variety of question types designed to gauge student understanding.

- *Dynamic Study Modules (DSMs).* Through adaptive learning, students get personalized guidance where and when they need it most, creating greater engagement, improving knowledge retention, and supporting subject-matter mastery. Also available on mobile devices.

- *MediaShare for Business*. MediaShare for Business helps students understand why they are learning key concepts and how they will apply those in their careers. Consisting of a curated collection of business videos tagged to learning outcomes, instructors can assign customizable, auto-scored assignments. Instructors can also upload their favourite YouTube clips or original content and employ MediaShare's powerful repository of tools to maximize student accountability and interactive learning, and provide contextualized feedback for students and teams who upload presentations, media, or business plans.

- *Decision-making Simulations*. Simulations help students analyze and make decisions in common business situations; they assess student choices and include reinforcement quizzes, outlines, and glossaries.

- *Writing Space*. Better writers make great learners—who perform better in their courses. The Writing Space, providing a single location to develop and assess concept mastery and critical thinking, offers assisted-graded and create-your-own writing assignments, allowing you to exchange personalized feedback with students quickly and easily. Students can use Writing Space to complete the Self-Reflection Activities from the text.

- *Pearson eText*. The Pearson eText gives students access to their textbook anytime, anywhere. In addition to note taking, highlighting, and bookmarking, the Pearson eText offers interactive and sharing features. Instructors can share their comments or highlights, and students can add their own, creating a tight community of learners within the class.

INSTRUCTOR RESOURCES

Most of the instructor supplements listed here are available for download from a password-protected section of Pearson Canada's online catalogue (http://www.pearsoncanada.ca/highered). Navigate to your book's catalogue page to view a list of the supplements available. See your local Pearson Canada sales representative for details and access. The following supplements are available with this text:

- *Instructor's Resource Manual*. This extensive manual, written to ensure close coordination with the book, includes a chapter overview, chapter objectives, a suggested lecture outline, answers to all of the text cases, additional discussion questions, exercises, and suggested assignments.

- *Computerized Test Bank*. Pearson's computerized test banks allow instructors to filter and select questions to create quizzes, tests, or homework. Instructors can revise questions or add their own, and may be able to choose print or online options. These questions are also available in Microsoft Word format.

- *PowerPoint® Presentations*. Ready-to-use PowerPoint slideshows are designed for classroom presentation. Use them as is, or edit content to fit your classroom needs.

- *Image Library*. This package provides instructors with images to enhance their teaching.

- *Learning Solutions Managers*. Pearson's Learning Solutions Managers work with faculty and campus course designers to ensure that Pearson technology products, assessment tools, and online course materials are tailored to meet your specific needs. This highly qualified team is dedicated to helping schools take full advantage of a wide range of educational resources, by assisting in the integration of a variety of instructional materials and media formats. Your local Pearson Canada sales representative can provide you with more details on this service program.

Acknowledgments

We owe a debt of gratitude to all those at Pearson Canada who have worked so hard on the development of this Canadian edition. We want to thank Editorial Director Claudine O'Donnell, Acquisitions Editor Loree Buchan, Program Manager Karen Townsend, Senior Developmental Editor Keriann McGoogan, Senior Project Manager Jessica Hellen, Permissions Project Manager Joanne Tang, Associate Art Director Anthony Leung, Copy Editor Rodney Rawlings, and Media Developer Kelli Cadet. The authors would also like to acknowledge the following contributors for their hard work in providing content for the MyLab activities: Nicole M. Coomber, University of Maryland; Pamela DeLotell, Kaplan University; Ryan D. Lowe, University of Delaware; Sarah Shepler, Ivy Tech Community College; Richard Michalski, McMaster University; and Chris Roubecas, Southern Alberta Institute of Technology. The Canadian author and publisher would like to thank the following reviewers, and others who have chosen to remain anonymous, for their feedback on this project:

Starr Allaby, Douglas College
Clifford Blake, University of Waterloo
N. Sue Bruning, University of Manitoba
Karen Case, NSCC, Strait Area Campus
Craig Dyer, Red River College
Wenlu Feng, Centennial College
Charles Keim, MacEwan University
Mary Marier, SAIT Polytechnic
Jody Merritt, St. Clair College

Susan Milton, Mohawk College
Murray Moman, Red River College, Exchange District Campus
Cynthia A. Riley, Georgian College
Roberta Sawatzky, Okanagan College
Zina Suissa, McGill School of Continuing Education
Russell Turner, Fleming College
Nicole Vincic, Mohawk College

Last but not least, we would like to thank the people who promote the book to the market, Director of Marketing Leigh-Anne Graham and Senior Marketing Manager Lisa Gillis. Thank you, everyone, for the attention you've given this book.

About the Authors

Stephen P. Robbins
Ph.D., University of Arizona

Stephen P. Robbins is professor emeritus of management at San Diego State University and the world's best-selling textbook author in the areas of both management and organizational behaviour. His books are used at more than a thousand U.S. colleges and universities, have been translated into 19 languages, and have appeared in adapted editions for Canada, Australia, South Africa, and India. Dr. Robbins is also the author of the best-selling books *The Truth About Managing People*, 2nd ed. (Financial Times/Prentice Hall, 2008) and *Decide & Conquer* (Financial Times/Prentice Hall, 2004).

In his "other life," Dr. Robbins actively participates in masters' track competitions. Since turning 50 in 1993, he's won 18 national championships and 12 world titles, and set numerous U.S. and world age-group records at 60, 100, 200, and 400 metres. In 2005, Dr. Robbins was elected into the USA Masters' Track & Field Hall of Fame.

Timothy A. Judge
Ph.D., University of Illinois at Urbana-Champaign

Timothy A. Judge is currently the Franklin D. Schurz Professor of Management at the Mendoza College of Business, University of Notre Dame; and Visiting Professor, Division of Psychology & Language Sciences, University College London. He has held academic positions at the University of Florida, University of Iowa, Cornell University, Charles University in the Czech Republic, Comenius University in Slovakia, and University of Illinois at Urbana-Champaign. Dr. Judge's primary research interests are in (1) personality, moods, and emotions; (2) job attitudes; (3) leadership and influence behaviors; and (4) careers (person–organization fit, career success). Dr. Judge has published more than 150 articles on these and other major topics in journals such as the *Academy of Management Journal* and the *Journal of Applied Psychology*. He is a fellow of several organizations, including the American Psychological Association and the Academy of Management. Among the many professional acknowledgments of his work, most recently Dr. Judge was awarded the Academy of Management Human Resources Division's Scholarly Achievement Award for 2014. Dr. Judge is a co-author of *Organizational Behavior*, 16th ed., with Stephen P. Robbins, and *Staffing Organizations*, 8th ed., with Herbert G. Heneman III. At Notre Dame, Judge teaches undergraduate and MBA classes in management skills, organizational behaviour, leadership, and staffing. He is married and has three children—a daughter who is a healthcare social worker, a daughter who is currently studying abroad, and a son in middle school.

Katherine E. Breward
Ph.D., Richard Ivey School of Business, Western University

Katherine E. Breward worked for over 14 years in the Kitchener-Waterloo high-tech sector before returning to academe, complementing her extensive academic understanding of workplace dynamics with applied professional experience. Dr. Breward is currently at the University of Winnipeg, where her primary research interests include non-conscious prejudice, workplace discrimination, disability accommodation, and best practices in diversity management. Dr. Breward's work has appeared in the *Canadian Journal of Disability Studies*; the *Journal of Immigrant and Minority Health*; the *British Journal of Management*; *Equality, Diversity, and Inclusion: An International Journal*; and the *Case Research Journal*. Her award-winning teaching cases are known for helping students make strong connections between abstract theory and real-world workplaces.

Dr. Breward lives on a working farm and orchard outside Winnipeg with her husband, daughter, three cats, an overgrown Alaskan Malamute, and an ever-expanding library of science fiction and fantasy novels. When not working on her latest research project, she enjoys planting new tree hybrids, photographing wildlife, and hunting for fossils.

Chapter 1
What Is Organizational Behaviour?

Gregory Holmgren/Alamy Stock Photo

LEARNING OBJECTIVES

After studying this chapter, you should be able to:

1. Discuss the importance of interpersonal skills in the workplace.

2. Define *organizational behaviour* (OB).

3. Assess the importance of using a scientific approach to OB.

4. Identify the major behavioural science disciplines that contribute to OB.

5. Explain why few absolutes apply to OB.

6. Describe the challenges and opportunities managers face when applying OB concepts in their workplaces.

7. Compare the three levels of analysis in this text's OB model.

You've probably made many observations about people's behaviour in your life. In a way, you are already proficient at seeing some of the major themes in organizational behaviour (OB). At the same time, you probably have not had the tools to make these observations in a systematic, scientific manner. This is where OB comes into play. And, as we'll learn, OB is much more than common sense, intuition, and soothsaying.

THE IMPORTANCE OF INTERPERSONAL SKILLS

Until the late 1980s, business school curricula emphasized the technical aspects of management, focusing on economics, accounting, finance, and quantitative techniques. Course work in human behaviour and people skills received relatively less attention. Since then, however, business schools have realized the significant role understanding human behaviour plays in determining a manager's effectiveness. As Sylvie Albert, Dean of the Department of Business and Economics at the University of Winnipeg, stated, "business programs these days are striving to provide a combination of technical and soft skills at the request of employers. Although a multidisciplinary understanding is beneficial for advancement in most careers, workplaces are looking for employees with demonstrated emotional intelligence, leadership and critical thinking skills. The expectation is that the development of these skills will be incorporated in coursework."[1]

Incorporating OB principles into the workplace can yield many important organizational outcomes. For one, companies known as good places to work have been found (http://www.canadastop100.com) to generate superior performance from their employees.[2] Canadian Tire, Great West Life, 3M Canada, the Aboriginal People's Television Network, Labatt Breweries, SaskTel, and RBC have all won "Best Employer in Canada" awards for having worker-friendly programs such as formal mentoring, flexible work hours, telecommuting programs, and tuition reimbursement. Some of them, including Canadian Tire headquarters and select RBC facilities, even have free onsite health and fitness activities. These companies excel at what they do and part of their success can be attributed to their supportive environments. Second, developing managers' interpersonal skills helps organizations attract and keep high-performing employees, which is important because outstanding employees are always in short supply and costly to replace. These skills are especially relevant in highly diverse workplaces because interpersonal skills are needed to work effectively with people who may be quite different from oneself. Canada is one of the most diverse nations on Earth, making these skills particularly important. New managers in Canada and elsewhere are far more likely to fail due to a lack of people skills as opposed to a lack of technical or strategic thinking skills. Even workers without management responsibilities have smoother workplace interactions when aware of key aspects of human behaviour. Third, there are strong associations between the quality of workplace relationships and employee job satisfaction, stress, and turnover. One large survey of hundreds of workplaces and more than 200,000 respondents showed that social relationships among coworkers and supervisors were strongly related to overall job satisfaction. Positive social relationships were also associated with lower stress at work and lower intentions to quit.[3] Further research indicates that employees who relate to their managers with supportive dialogue and proactivity find that their ideas are endorsed more often, which improves workplace satisfaction.[4] Finally, increasing the OB element in organizations can foster social responsibility awareness. Accordingly, universities and colleges have begun to incorporate social entrepreneurship education into their curriculum in order to train future leaders to use interpersonal skills to address social issues within their organizations.[5] This curriculum reflects a growing awareness of the need for understanding the means and outcomes of corporate social responsibility.[6]

We know that in today's competitive and demanding workplace, managers can't succeed on their technical skills alone. They also have to exhibit good people skills and be comfortable dealing with ambiguity. There are few absolute truths in human behaviour in general and organizational behaviour in particular, but OB knowledge combined with situation-specific critical assessment and judgment can help both managers and potential managers to better understand their workers. This is turn helps develop meaningful people skills that are informed by validated scientific knowledge about human behaviour.

ENTER ORGANIZATIONAL BEHAVIOUR

OB's goal is to understand and predict human behaviour in organizations. The complexities of human behaviour are not easy to predict, but neither are they random—certain fundamental consistencies underlie the behaviour of all individuals.

We've made the case for the importance of "people skills." But the discipline on which this text is based does not use that term, but rather *organizational behaviour*.

Organizational behaviour (OB) is a field of study that investigates the impact individuals, groups, and structure have on behaviour within organizations, for the purpose of applying such knowledge toward improving an organization's effectiveness. That's a mouthful, so let's break it down.

Organizational behaviour is a field of study, meaning that it is a distinct area of expertise with a common body of knowledge. It studies three determinants of behaviour in organizations: individuals, groups, and structure. In addition, OB applies the knowledge gained about individuals, groups, and the effect of structure on behaviour in order to make organizations work more effectively.

To sum up our definition, OB is the study of what people do in an organization and how their behaviour affects the organization's performance. And because OB is concerned specifically with employment-related situations, it emphasizes behaviour as related to concerns such as jobs, work, absenteeism, employment turnover, productivity, human performance, and management. Although debate exists about the relative importance of each, OB includes these core topics:

- Motivation
- Leader behaviour and power
- Interpersonal communication
- Group structure and processes
- Attitude development and perception
- Change processes
- Conflict and negotiation
- Work design[7]

COMPLEMENTING INTUITION WITH SYSTEMATIC STUDY

Each of us is a student of behaviour. Whether or not you've explicitly thought about it before, you've been "reading" people almost all your life, watching their actions and trying to interpret what you see or to predict what people might do under different conditions. Unfortunately, the casual or commonsense approach to reading others can often lead to erroneous predictions. However, you can improve your predictive ability by supplementing intuition with a more scientific approach.

The systematic, scientific approach in this text will uncover important facts and provide a base from which to make more accurate predictions of behaviour. Underlying this approach is the belief that behaviour is not random. Rather, we can identify fundamental consistencies underlying the behaviour of all individuals and modify them to reflect individual differences. It is important to note that most of the studies that form the basis for OB have been conducted in North America. From a scientific perspective that means we are less certain that the findings apply across other cultures; members of those cultures may have different values and behavioural expectations. (In this book, you will find comments in each chapter highlighting behaviour that may be heavily influenced by culture.) However, this important limitation is being actively corrected with expanded and more diverse research. And even now, OB is able to provide insight into some fundamental consistencies; they just have to be viewed with caution when operating in non–North American contexts.

These fundamental consistencies are very important. Why? Because they allow predictability. Behaviour is generally predictable, and the *scientific study* of behaviour is a means to making reasonably accurate predictions. When we use the term **scientific study**, we mean looking at relationships, attempting to attribute causes and effects, and basing our conclusions on scientific evidence—that is, on data gathered under controlled conditions, and rigorously measured and interpreted.

Evidence-based management (EBM) complements systematic study by basing managerial decisions on the best available scientific data. For example, we want doctors to make decisions about patient care on the basis of the latest available knowledge, and EBM argues that managers should do the same, becoming more scientific in how they think about management problems. A manager might pose a managerial question, search for the best available evidence, and apply the relevant information to the question or case at hand. You might think it difficult to argue against this (what manager would say decisions shouldn't be based on evidence?), but the vast majority of management decisions are made "on the fly," with little systematic study of available evidence.[8] It is also worth noting that managers aren't the only ones who benefit from a more scientific interpretation of behaviour. Average workers can also use these insights to better manage their workplace relationships, resolve conflicts, and seek influence.

Scientific study and EBM add to **intuition**, or those gut feelings about what makes others (and ourselves) tick. Of course, the things you have come to believe in an unsystematic way are not necessarily incorrect. Jack Welch (former CEO of GE) has noted: "The trick, of course, is to know when to go with your gut." But if we make *all* decisions with intuition or gut instinct, we're working with incomplete information—it's like making an investment decision with only half the data about the potential for risk and reward.

Big Data

It is good news for the future of business that researchers, the media, and company leaders have identified the potential of data-driven management and decision making. While "big data"—the extensive use of statistical compilation and analysis—has been applied to many areas of business, increasingly it is applied to making effective decisions and managing human resources. This has been enabled because companies increasingly keep information on human resources management matters such as absenteeism and productivity in large databases, allowing the comparison of hundreds or thousands of records across time from multiple companies. This process results in the recognition of broad trends and patterns that would otherwise be difficult to detect. For example, Xerox used big data to reduce employee turnover at their call centre. Analysis of employment data demonstrated that certain personality traits were more strongly associated with staying on the job than prior call centre experience. As a result, human resource managers changed their hiring criteria, deemphasizing experience and testing personality instead. In six months turnover was reduced by one-fifth.

The use of big data for managerial practices, though relatively new, holds much promise. A manager who uses data to define objectives, develop theories of causality, and test those theories can determine which employee activities are relevant to the objectives.[9] However, we're not advising you to throw your intuition, or all the business press, out the window. In dealing with people, leaders often rely on hunches, and sometimes the outcomes are excellent. Other times, hunches are informed by biases that get in the way. Research findings indicate we are likely to be biased toward information that we've heard most recently, that has been frequently repeated, or that is of personal relevance. While research findings should be viewed with the same discernment as data output, the prudent use of big data, along with an understanding of human behavioural tendencies, can contribute to sound decision making and ease natural biases. What we are advising is to use evidence as much as possible to inform your intuition and experience. That is the promise of OB.

DISCIPLINES THAT CONTRIBUTE TO THE OB FIELD

Several social science disciplines contribute to OB, but none are more important than psychology.

Organizational behaviour is an applied behavioural science built on contributions from a number of behavioural disciplines, mainly psychology and social psychology, sociology, anthropology, and, increasingly, political science and neuroscience. Psychology's contributions have been principally at the individual or micro level of analysis, while the other disciplines have contributed to our understanding of macro concepts such as group processes and organization. Neuroscience has contributed to our understanding at the individual and group level of analysis. Exhibit 1-1 gives an overview of the major contributions to the study of organizational behaviour.

Psychology

Psychology seeks to measure, explain, and sometimes change the behaviour of humans and other animals. Contributors who add to the knowledge of OB are learning theorists, personality theorists, counselling psychologists, and, most importantly, industrial and organizational psychologists.

Early industrial/organizational psychologists studied the problems of fatigue, boredom, and other working conditions that might impede efficient work performance. More recently, their contributions have expanded to include learning, perception, personality, emotions, training, leadership effectiveness, needs and motivational forces, job satisfaction, decision-making

EXHIBIT 1-1 Toward an OB Discipline

processes, performance appraisals, attitude measurement, employee-selection techniques, work design, and job stress.

Social Psychology

Social psychology, generally considered a branch of psychology, blends concepts from both psychology and sociology to focus on peoples' influence on one another. One major study area is *change*—how to implement it and how to reduce barriers to its acceptance. Social psychologists also contribute to measuring, understanding, and changing attitudes; identifying communication patterns; and building trust. They have made important contributions to our study of group behaviour, power, and conflict.

Sociology

While psychology focuses on the individual, **sociology** studies people in relation to their social environment or culture. Sociologists have contributed to OB through their study of group behaviour in organizations, particularly formal and complex organizations. Perhaps most importantly, sociologists have studied organizational culture, formal organization theory and structure, organizational technology, communications, power, and conflict.

Anthropology

Anthropology is the study of societies to learn about human beings and their activities. Anthropologists' work on cultures and environments has helped us understand differences in fundamental values, attitudes, and behaviour between people in different countries and within different organizations. Much of our current understanding of organizational culture, organizational environments, and differences among national cultures is a result of the work of anthropologists or those using their methods.

Political Science

Political science is the study of systems of government but also political behaviours and activities. As such, it provides insight into the distribution of power and resources, and how those distribution decisions are influenced. Political scientists contribute to our understanding of the government regulation of industry, strategic mergers and acquisitions, group behaviour and decision making, public relations, and the use of personal-influence tactics and power plays within organizations.

Neuroscience has recently begun making important contributions to our understanding of organizational behaviour.

anekoho/Fotolia

Neuroscience

Neuroscience is the study of the structure and function of the nervous system and brain. Neuroscientists have recently begun contributing to OB by studying topics such as the impact of hormone levels on risk-taking in business contexts, the influence of pheromones on team behaviours, and the underlying cognitive structures and neural processes that contribute to inadvertent prejudice and associated skill discounting and underutilization of workers.[10]

A BRIEF HISTORY OF OB

Organizational behaviour as a distinct discipline started when scientific approaches to management began to indicate that behavioural considerations were important predictors of productivity. The famous Hawthorne studies were conducted between 1924 and 1932 at Hawthorne Electrical Company. The scientists involved were trying to discover the optimal temperature, lighting levels, and work pace to maximize productivity. Instead, they discovered that being observed and having people pay attention to the efforts of workers increased productivity regardless of temperature, lighting, etc. This helped launch an entire area of study devoted to motivation and teams.[11]

In the 1950s the Carnegie School headquartered at Carnegie Mellon University was influential in directing attention to the integration of decision analysis, management science, and psychology.[12] This resulted in the development of important concepts such as bounded rationality, which states that decision making is influenced not only by rational assessment but also by cognitive limitations that can result in subconscious biases and inaccurate risk assessments. This insight helped practitioners understand why suboptimal decisions are frequently made by managers and leaders, and further research brought better understanding of some of those problems and better decision making.

The 1960s and 1970s saw many developments in organizational behaviour, with important discoveries being made in the areas of motivation, team behaviour, and leadership. Systems approaches that considered the influence of broader social structures also emerged— such as institutional theory, which focused on norms, rules, and routines, and contingency theory, which looked at the influence of the broader environment on management practice.

The 1980s and 1990s saw more focus on organizational culture and organizational change. This change was partly driven by new insights emerging from anthropology and psychology but also influenced by economic changes that led to increased globalization and widespread corporate downsizing, making understanding of culture and change more immediately relevant.

More recently, research inspired by the anthropological approach has focused on, among other things, situational models of leadership. Systems theories have offered new insights about optimizing the effectiveness of diversity management programs. Scholars in the Carnegie tradition have examined bounded rationality in the context of attitudes about mental health in the workplace and the influence of those attitudes on policy formulation. Each of these schools of thought continues to be developed today, making organizational behaviour an exciting and innovative area of ongoing research.

THERE ARE FEW ABSOLUTES IN OB

Laws in the physical sciences—chemistry, astronomy, physics—are consistent and apply in a wide range of situations. They allow scientists to generalize about the pull of gravity or to be confident about sending astronauts into space to repair satellites. Human beings are complex, and few, if any, simple and universal principles explain organizational behaviour. Because we are not all alike, our ability to make simple, accurate, and sweeping generalizations is limited. For example, not everyone is motivated by money, and people may behave differently at a religious service than they do at a party.

"Next time, don't start the presentation by asking, 'Can you tolerate ambiguity?'!"

Cartoonresource/Shutterstock

That doesn't mean, of course, that we can't offer reasonably accurate explanations of human behaviour or make valid predictions. It does mean that OB concepts must reflect situational, or contingency, conditions. We can say x leads to y, but only under conditions specified in z—the **contingency variables**. The science of OB was developed by applying general concepts to a particular situation, person, or group. For example, OB scholars would avoid stating that everyone likes complex and challenging work (the general concept). Why? Because not everyone wants a challenging job. Some people prefer routine over varied work, or simple over complex tasks. A job attractive to one person might not be to another; its appeal is contingent on the person who holds it.

As mentioned earlier, there are particular challenges when OB research that was conducted in one country or culture is applied in another country or culture. Cultures differ significantly from one part of the world to the next. These differences are often subtle. For example, individual accomplishment is very important in Canadian society, while people from many Asian and Latin American cultures tend to focus on group achievement.[13] This simple difference has a profound impact on things like leadership style, organizational culture, motivational strategies, and the structure of work tasks. There are other cultural differences, such as the perceived appropriateness of maintaining a strict power hierarchy, which make it problematic to make assumptions about the applicability of research findings when working across cultures. Sites like the Hofstede Centre can help you assess these cultural differences and their impact on workplace practice (http://geert-hofstede.com).

Imagine China/Newscom

CHALLENGES AND OPPORTUNITIES FOR OB

Understanding organizational behaviour has never been more important for managers. Take a quick look at the dramatic changes in organizations. The typical employee is getting older; the workforce is becoming increasingly diverse; corporate downsizing and the heavy use of temporary workers are severing the bonds of loyalty that tied many employees to their employers; and global competition requires employees to become more flexible and cope with rapid change.

As a result of these changes and others such as the rising use of technology, employment options have adapted to include new opportunities for workers. Exhibit 1-2 details some of the types of options individuals may find offered to them by organizations or for which they would like to negotiate. Under each heading in the exhibit, you will find a grouping of options from which to choose—or combine. For instance, at one point in your career you might find yourself

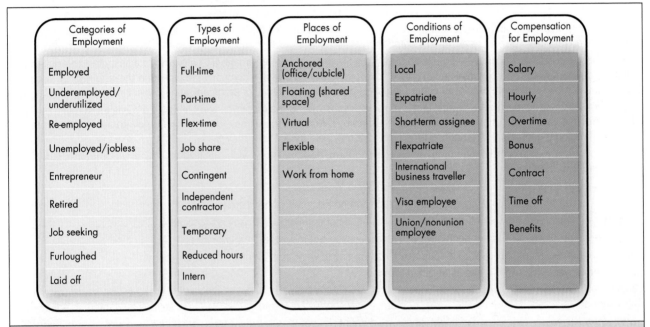

Categories of Employment	Types of Employment	Places of Employment	Conditions of Employment	Compensation for Employment
Employed	Full-time	Anchored (office/cubicle)	Local	Salary
Underemployed/ underutilized	Part-time	Floating (shared space)	Expatriate	Hourly
Re-employed	Flex-time	Virtual	Short-term assignee	Overtime
Unemployed/jobless	Job share	Flexible	Flexpatriate	Bonus
Entrepreneur	Contingent	Work from home	International business traveller	Contract
Retired	Independent contractor		Visa employee	Time off
Job seeking	Temporary		Union/nonunion employee	Benefits
Furloughed	Reduced hours			
Laid off	Intern			

Employed—working for a for-profit or nonprofit company, an organization, or an individual, either for money and/or benefits, with established expectations for performance and compensation

Underemployed/underutilized—working in a position or with responsibilities that are below one's educational or experience attainment level, or working less than full-time when one wants full-time employment

Re-employed—refers to either employees who were dismissed by a company and rehired by the same company, or to employees who left the workforce (were unemployed) and found new employment

Unemployed/jobless—currently not working; may be job-seeking, either with or without government benefits/assistance, either with or without severance pay from a previous job, either new to the workforce or terminated from previous employment, either short-term unemployed (months) or long-term/chronic unemployed (years)

Entrepreneur—one who runs his or her own business, either as a sole worker or as the founder of a company with employees

Retired—one who has ended his or her career in a profession, either voluntarily by choice or involuntarily by an employer's mandate

Job-seeking—currently unemployed; actively looking for a job, either with or without government benefits from previous job or from disability/need, either with or without severance pay from previous job, either new to the workforce or terminated from previous employment

Furloughed—similar to a layoff; an employer-required work stoppage, temporary (weeks up to a month, usually); pay is often suspended during this time, though the person retains employment status with the company

EXHIBIT 1-2   Employment Options

Sources: J. R. Anderson Jr. et al., "Action Items: 42 Trends Affecting Benefits, Compensation, Training, Staffing and Technology," *HR Magazine* (January 2013), p. 33; M. Dewhurst, B. Hancock, and D. Ellsworth, "Redesigning Knowledge Work," *Harvard Business Review* (January–February 2013), pp. 58–64; E. Frauenheim, "Creating a New Contingent Culture," *Workforce Management* (August 2012), pp. 34–39; N. Koeppen, "State Job Aid Takes Pressure off Germany," *The Wall Street Journal* (February 1, 2013), p. A8; and M. A. Shaffer, M. L. Kraimer, Y.-P. Chen, and M. C. Bolino, "Choices, Challenges, and Career Consequences of Global Work Experiences: A Review and Future Agenda," *Journal of Management* (July 2012), pp. 1282–1327.

(Continued)

Laid off—can be a temporary employer-required work stoppage, usually without pay, but is more often a permanent termination from the company in which the employee is recognized to be not at fault

Full-time—hours for full-time employment are established by companies, generally more than 30 hours per week in a set schedule, sometimes with salary pay and sometimes with hourly pay, often with a benefit package greater than that for the part-time employment category

Part-time—hours for full-time employment are established by companies, generally less than 30 hours per week in a set schedule, often with hourly pay, often with a benefit package less than that for the full-time employment category

Flex-time—an arrangement in which the employee and employer create nonstandard working hours, which may be a temporary or permanent schedule; may be an expectation for a number of hours worked per week

Job share—an arrangement in which two or more employees fill one job, generally by splitting the hours of a full-time position that do not overlap

Contingent—the workforce of outsourced workers (including professional service firms, specialized experts, and business consultants), these employees are paid hourly or by the job and do not generally receive any company benefits and are not considered as part of the company; contingent workers may be also temporary employees or independent contractors

Independent contractor—an entrepreneur in essence, but often a specialist professional who does not aspire to create a business but who provides services or goods to a company

Temporary—individuals who may be employed directly by the organization or through an employment agency/temporary agency; their hours may be fixed per week or vary, they do not generally receive any company benefits, and they are not considered part of the company; they are employed either for a short duration or as a trial for an organization's position openings

Reduced-hours—reduction in the normal employee's work schedule by the employer, sometimes as a measure to retain employees/reduce layoffs in economic downturns as in Germany's *Kurzarbeit* program, which provides government subsidies to keep workers on the job at reduced hours; employees are only paid for the time they work

Intern—short-term employment, often with an established term, designed to provide practical training to a pre-professional, either with or without pay

Anchored—an employee with an assigned office, cubicle, or desk space

Floating—an employee with a shared space workplace and no assigned working area

Virtual—an employee who works through the Internet and is not connected with any office location

Flexible—an employee who is connected with an office location but may work from anywhere

Work from home—an employee who is set up by the company to work from an office at home

Local—employees who work in one established location

Expatriate—employees who are on extended international work assignments with the expectation that they will return (repatriate) after an established term, usually a year or more; either sent by corporate request or out of self-initiated interest

Short-term assignee—employees on international assignments longer than business trips yet shorter than typical corporate expatriate assignments, usually 3 to 12 months

Flexpatriate—employees who travel for brief assignments across cultural or national borders, usually 1 to 2 months

International business traveller—employees who take multiple short international business trips for 1 to 3 weeks

Visa employee—an employee working outside of his or her country of residence who must have a work visa for employment in the current country

Union/nonunion employee—an employee who is a member of a labour union, often by trade, and subject to its protections and provisions, which then negotiates with management on certain working condition issues; or an employee who works for a nonunion facility or who sometimes elects to stay out of membership in a unionized facility

Salary—employee compensation based on a full-time workweek, in which the hours are generally not kept on a time clock but where it is understood that the employee will work according to job needs

Hourly—employee compensation for each hour worked, often recorded on time sheets or by time clocks

Overtime—for hourly employees, compensation for hours worked that are greater than the standard workweek and paid at an hourly rate determined by law

Bonus—compensation in addition to standard pay, usually linked to individual or organizational performance

Contract—prenegotiated compensation for project work, usually according to a schedule as the work progresses

Time off—either paid or unpaid; negotiated time off according to the employment contract (including vacation time, sick leave, and personal days) and/or given by management as compensation for time worked

Benefits—generally stated in the employment contract or the Human Resources Employee Handbook; may include health insurance plans, savings plans, retirement plans, discounts, and other options available to employees at various types of employment

EXHIBIT 1.2 Employment Options (*Continued*)

employed full time in an office in a localized, nonunion setting with a salary and bonus compensation package, while at another point you might wish to negotiate for a flextime, virtual position and choose to work from overseas for a combination of salary and extra paid time off.

In short, today's challenges bring opportunities for managers to use OB concepts. In this section, we review some of the most critical issues confronting managers for which OB offers solutions—or at least meaningful insights toward solutions.

Responding to Economic Pressures

In early 2015 the Canadian economy experienced major challenges. Dropping oil prices severely impacted oilsands production and profitability. Since this industry represents a significant component of the Canadian economy, everything from the dollar to average housing prices was negatively impacted.[14] Layoffs and job losses were widespread, especially in Alberta. When things like this happen managers are on the front lines with the employees who must be fired, who are asked to make do with less, and who worry about their futures. The difference between good and bad management can be the difference between profit and loss or, ultimately, between survival and failure.

Managing employees well when times are good can be just as hard, if not harder, than when times are bad. But the OB approaches sometimes differ. In good times, understanding how to reward, satisfy, and retain employees is at a premium. In bad times, issues like stress, decision making, and coping come to the fore.

There are many reasons why it is more important than ever to learn OB concepts.

Responding to Globalization

Organizations are no longer constrained by national borders. McCain Foods, headquartered in Florenceville, New Brunswick, has 19,000 employees and 50 production facilities spanning six continents. The Vancouver-based franchise 1-800-GOT-JUNK licenses their business model in Canada, the United States, and Australia. Toronto-based custom broker Livingston International has over 3,200 employees located at more than 125 border points, seaports, airports, and other locations across in North America, Europe, and Asia. Montreal's Bombardier sells their planes and trains all over the world and they have facilities on all continents except Antarctica.

The world has indeed become a global village. In the process, the manager's job has changed. Effective managers will anticipate and adapt their approaches to the global issues we discuss next.

Increased Foreign Assignments   If you're a manager, you are increasingly likely to find yourself in a foreign assignment—transferred to your employer's operating division or subsidiary in another country. Once there, you'll have to manage a workforce very different in needs, aspirations, and attitudes from those you are accustomed to back home. To be effective, you will need to understand everything you can about your new location's culture and workforce—and demonstrate your cultural sensitivity—before introducing alternative practices.

Working with People from Different Cultures   Even in your own country, you'll find yourself working with bosses, peers, and other employees born and raised in different cultures.

What motivates you might not motivate them. Or your communication style might be straightforward and open, which others might find uncomfortable and threatening. To work effectively with people from different cultures, you need to understand how their culture, geography, and religion have shaped them, and how to adapt your management style to their differences.

Overseeing Movement of Jobs to Countries with Low-Cost Labour   It is increasingly difficult for managers in advanced nations, where minimum wages are typically $10 or more an hour, to compete against firms that rely on workers from Bangladesh and other developing nations, where labour is available for 30 cents an hour. In a global economy, jobs tend to flow to where lower costs give businesses a comparative advantage, though labour groups, politicians, and local community leaders see the exporting of jobs as undermining the job market at home. Managers face the difficult task of balancing the interests of their organizations with their responsibilities to the communities in which they operate.

Adapting to Differing Cultural and Regulatory Norms   "Going global" for a business is not as simple as typing in an overseas e-mail address, shipping goods off to a foreign port, or building facilities in other countries. To be successful, managers need to know the cultural norms of the workforce in each country where they do business. For instance, in some countries a large percentage of the workforce enjoys long holidays. There will be country and local regulations to consider, too. Managers of subsidiaries abroad need to be aware of the unique financial and legal regulations applying to "guest companies" or else risk violating them. Violations can have implications for their operations in that country and also for political relations between countries. Managers also need to be cognizant of differences in regulations for competitors in that country; many times, the laws will give national companies significant financial advantages over foreign subsidiaries.

Managing Workforce Diversity

One of the most important challenges for organizations is *workforce diversity*, the concept that organizations are becoming more heterogeneous in terms of gender, age, race, ethnicity, sexual orientation, ability, and inclusion of other diverse groups. Whereas globalization focuses on differences among people *from* different countries, workforce diversity addresses differences among people *within* given countries.

Workforce diversity acknowledges a workforce of women, men, and transgendered persons, many racial and ethnic groups, individuals with a variety of physical or psychological abilities, and people who differ in age and sexual orientation. Managing diversity is a global concern. Though we have more to say about workforce diversity later, suffice it to say here that diversity presents great opportunities and poses challenging questions for managers and employees in all countries. How can we leverage differences within groups for competitive advantage? Should we treat all employees alike? Should we recognize individual and cultural differences? How can we foster cultural awareness in employees without lapsing into stereotyped political correctness? What are the legal requirements in each country? Does diversity even matter?

Improving Customer Service

Service employees include technical support representatives, fast-food counter workers, sales clerks, nurses, automobile repair technicians, consultants, financial planners, and flight attendants. The shared characteristic of their jobs is substantial interaction with an organization's customers. OB can help managers increase the success of these interactions by showing how employee attitudes and behaviour influence customer satisfaction.

Many an organization has failed because its employees failed to please customers. OB can provide considerable guidance in helping managers create customer-friendly cultures in which employees are friendly and courteous, accessible, knowledgeable, prompt in responding to customer needs, and willing to do what's necessary to please the customer.[15]

Improving People Skills

As you proceed through the chapters of this text, we'll present relevant concepts and theories that can help you explain and predict the behaviour of people at work. You'll also gain insight into specific people skills you can use on the job. For instance, you'll learn ways to design motivating jobs, techniques for improving your management skills, and skills to create more effective teams.

Working in Networked Organizations

Networked organizations allow people to communicate and work together even though they may be thousands of miles apart. Independent contractors can telecommute via computer to workplaces around the globe and change employers as the demand for their services changes. Software programmers, graphic designers, systems analysts, technical writers, photo researchers, book and media editors, and medical transcribers are just a few examples of people who can work from home or other nonoffice locations.

The manager's job is different in a networked organization. Motivating and leading people and making collaborative decisions online require techniques different from those required when individuals are physically present at a single location. As more employees do their jobs by linking to others through networks, managers must develop new skills. OB can provide valuable insights for honing those skills.

Enhancing Employee Well-Being at Work

The typical employee in the 1960s or 1970s showed up at a specified workplace Monday through Friday and worked for clearly defined 8- or 9-hour chunks of time. That's no longer true for a large segment of today's workforce; even the definition of the workplace has been expanded to include anywhere a laptop or smartphone can go. Even if employees work at home or from half a continent away, managers need to consider their well-being at work.

One of the biggest challenges to maintaining employee well-being is that organizations are asking employees to put in longer hours, either in the office or online. Employees are increasingly complaining that the line between work and nonwork time has blurred, creating personal conflicts and stress. Second, employee well-being is challenged by heavy outside commitments. Millions of single-parent households and employees with dependent parents are significantly challenged in balancing work and family responsibilities, for instance.

As a result of their increased responsibilities in and out of the workplace, recent studies suggest employees want jobs that give them flexibility in their work schedules so they can better manage work–life conflicts.[16] Organizations that don't help their people achieve work–life balance will find it increasingly difficult to attract and retain the most capable and motivated employees. As you'll see in later chapters, the field of OB offers a number of suggestions to guide managers in designing workplaces and jobs that can help employees reduce such conflicts.

Creating a Positive Work Environment

A significant growth area in OB research is **positive organizational scholarship** (also called *positive organizational behaviour*), which studies how organizations develop human strengths, foster vitality and resilience, and unlock potential. Researchers in this area say too much OB research and management practice has been targeted toward identifying what's wrong with organizations and their employees. In response, they try to study what's *good* about them.[17] Some key independent variables in positive OB research are engagement, hope, optimism, and resilience in the face of strain.

Positive organizational scholars have studied a concept called "reflected best self"— asking employees to think about when they were at their "personal best" in order to understand how to exploit their strengths. The idea is that we all have things at which we are unusually good, yet we too often focus on addressing our limitations and too rarely think about how to exploit our strengths.[18]

Although positive organizational scholarship does not deny the value of the negative (such as critical feedback), it does challenge researchers to look at OB through a new lens and pushes organizations to exploit employees' strengths rather than dwell on their limitations.

Improving Ethical Behaviour

In an organizational world characterized by cutbacks, expectations of increasing productivity, and tough competition, it's not surprising many employees feel pressured to cut corners, break rules, and engage in other questionable practices.

Increasingly, employees face **ethical dilemmas and ethical choices**, in which they are required to identify right and wrong conduct. Should they blow the whistle if they uncover illegal activities in their company? Do they follow orders with which they don't personally agree? Do they play politics to advance their career?

What constitutes ethical behaviour has never been clearly defined, and in recent years it has showed. Everywhere we see elected officials pad expense accounts or take bribes, corporate executives inflate profits so they can cash in lucrative stock options, and university administrators look the other way when winning coaches encourage scholarship athletes to take easy courses. When caught, these people make excuses such as "Everyone does it" or "You have to seize every advantage nowadays."

Determining the ethically correct way to behave is especially difficult in a global economy, because different cultures have different perspectives on certain ethical issues.[19] Fair treatment of employees in an economic downturn varies considerably across cultures, for instance. As we'll see, perceptions of religious, ethnic, and gender diversity differ across countries. Is it any wonder employees are expressing increasing uncertainty about what is appropriate ethical behaviour in their organizations?[20]

Today's manager must create an ethically healthy climate for employees in which they can do their work productively with minimal ambiguity about right versus wrong behaviours. Companies that promote a strong ethical mission, encourage employees to behave with integrity, and provide strong leadership can influence employee decisions to behave ethically.[21] In upcoming chapters, we'll discuss the actions managers can take to create an ethically healthy climate and help employees sort through ambiguous situations.

COMING ATTRACTIONS: DEVELOPING AN OB MODEL

We conclude this chapter by presenting a general model that defines the field of OB and stakes out its parameters, concepts, and relationships. Studying the model, you will get a good picture of how the topics in this text can inform your approach to management issues and opportunities.

An Overview

A **model** is an abstraction of reality, a simplified representation of some real-world phenomenon. Exhibit 1-3 presents the skeleton of our OB model. It proposes three types of variables (inputs, processes, and outcomes) at three levels of analysis (individual, group, and organizational). In the chapters to follow, we will proceed from the individual level (Chapters 2 through 8) to group behaviour (Chapters 9 through 14) to the organizational level (Chapters 15 through 17). The model illustrates that inputs lead to processes which lead to outcomes; we will discuss these interrelationships for each level of analysis. Notice that the model also shows that outcomes can influence inputs in the future, which highlights the broad-reaching effect OB initiatives can have on an organization's future.

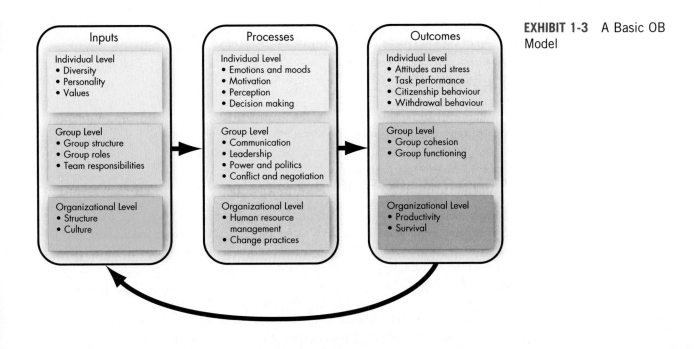

EXHIBIT 1-3 A Basic OB Model

Inputs

Individual Level
• Diversity
• Personality
• Values

Group Level
• Group structure
• Group roles
• Team responsibilities

Organizational Level
• Structure
• Culture

Processes

Individual Level
• Emotions and moods
• Motivation
• Perception
• Decision making

Group Level
• Communication
• Leadership
• Power and politics
• Conflict and negotiation

Organizational Level
• Human resource management
• Change practices

Outcomes

Individual Level
• Attitudes and stress
• Task performance
• Citizenship behaviour
• Withdrawal behaviour

Group Level
• Group cohesion
• Group functioning

Organizational Level
• Productivity
• Survival

SUMMARY

Managers need to develop their interpersonal, or people, skills to be effective in their jobs. Organizational behaviour (OB) investigates the impact that individuals, groups, and structure have on behaviour within an organization, and it applies that knowledge to make organizations work more effectively.

IMPLICATIONS FOR MANAGERS

- Use scientifically validated information about human behaviour to help improve your interpersonal skills in the workplace. This will increase your leadership potential.

- Use metrics and situational variables rather than "hunches" to explain cause-and-effect relationships.

- Improve your technical skills and conceptual skills through training and staying current with organizational behaviour trends like big data.

- Organizational behaviour can improve your employees' work quality and productivity by showing you how to empower your employees, design and implement change programs, improve customer service, and help your employees balance work–life conflicts.

- Use caution when applying OB research in international contexts; some of the underlying cultural norms and expectations may vary, altering results.

- Recognize that human behaviour in the workplace is influenced by factors at three different levels: individual, group, and organizational. Paying attention to relevant factors at all three levels rather than focusing on just one can improve management effectiveness.

BREAKOUT QUESTION FOR GROUP DISCUSSION

When supervising others in a workplace, how might you effectively combine intuition and scientifically validated information to arrive at optimal decisions? What might that process look like?

In the Personal Inventory Assessment found in MyManagementLab, take the assessment: Multicultural Awareness Scale.

SELF-REFLECTION ACTIVITY

Being a multicultural nation has important consequences for Canada and for Canadians. Part of being a multicultural nation is accepting cultural differences and ensuring that cultural factors do not pose barriers to full participation in all aspects of society, including the labour market. Of course, multiculturalism is an ideal, one implemented with varying degrees of success. Take the Personal Inventory Assessment found in MyManagementLab. Once you have your score, think carefully about what it means. If you got a high score, congratulations—you have good insight into the day-to-day behaviours and attitudes that support multicultural ideals. If you got a low score, you might wish to enhance your understanding of cultural differences and their impacts.

Take a few moments to reflect on what your result means for you personally and for the people around you. In a multicultural society, what happens when some people have a poor understanding of cultural differences? How does that compare to what happens when there is heightened understanding? In the workplace, what sort of management and policy-based decisions might emerge if people do not understand cultural differences? Would they be different from management techniques used in settings where diversity is acknowledged? Which approach would support social equity the most?

You can improve your score and enhance your understanding by engaging in conversations with people from other cultures who live in your community—knowledge, empathy, and understanding go hand in hand.

MINI CASE | MANAGING GROUP BEHAVIOUR WITHOUT FORMAL POWER

Chiamara recently began taking business classes at her local university, because, tired of working for others in the retail sector, she wanted to learn enough to start her own business. She felt she had very strong leadership skills and really wanted to run a company her way.

She was surprised, and a little dismayed, to discover that her introductory course on organizational behaviour involved a great deal of group work—in fact, 35 percent of her grade depended on it. That made Chiamara anxious for several reasons. First of all, she would be randomly assigned to her group by the instructor and so would have no control over who she would work with. Second, she had been hoping to become eligible for scholarships in her second year of studies and was especially concerned about getting good grades, but she had had some very negative group experiences in the past that might create challenges in that regard. For example, whether it was high school or workplace training, she was usually the most driven person in a group and would often redo all the work at the end to make sure it was up to her own high standards; but groupmates had accused her of being overbearing and condescending, The truth was she just didn't know why they couldn't work together to produce high-quality work in the first place.

Chiamara's worries were all the greater because she had moved to Canada from Nigeria three years previously, and despite the fact that English was the official language in her home country she still had a strong spoken accent. (She herself could not hear it but others told her about it.) In the past she had found that some people in Canada, when they had trouble understanding her, treated her differently—almost as though she had nothing to contribute.

She wondered how best to make sure she got off on the right foot with her group. If her new colleagues did stereotype her, what might help? Even if they didn't, how might she more diplomatically motivate everyone to do their best, hand in assignments on time, and generally contribute fully? How might she make sure the team members had the common goal of getting A+ and worked efficiently toward that goal?

Chiamara looked over the first chapter of her organizational behaviour textbook. She was especially interested in the information about levels of analysis. The textbook highlighted the fact that human behaviour is influenced at three different levels: individual, group, and organizational. Each level contributes something a little different. She started to wonder how this understanding might help her influence her group.

Looking at each level separately, what sorts of things would influence behaviour while completing team-based tasks? As a person with no formal authority or power, how might she use this knowledge to steer her group in a positive, socially healthy, and productive direction?

Discussion Questions

1. What insights might Chiamara gain about group functioning by looking at individual levels of analysis? (Remember to consider what she might be able to learn about herself and the impact of her own behaviours!)

2. Which of the disciplines that contribute to OB help us to better understand individual behaviour? Justify your answer.

3. What insights might Chiamara gain about group functioning at the group level? Be specific about how organizational behaviour insights at this level of analysis can improve group functioning.

4. Is the organizational level of analysis relevant to this case? Why or why not? Explain your answer.

MINI CASE THE PEOPLE SIDE OF TARGET'S CANADIAN CATASTROPHE

U.S. discount retailer Target Corporation learned some very hard lessons when they attempted to launch their brand in Canada, a launch that ultimately became a high-profile and humiliating failure.

Target began by acquiring 189 failing Zeller's stores in early 2011. By 2013's end, 124 of those locations had been converted into Target stores and other outlets were being built in communities across the country. Despite enormous excitement and significant media coverage when these stores opened, things rapidly began to go badly. In January 2015 Target announced their complete withdrawal from Canada and the Canadian division filed for bankruptcy. About 17,600 workers lost their jobs. While the reasons for the failure were complex, human behaviour was a big part of it all.

Target Corporation had been confident at the outset because Canadian consumers were already familiar with their brand. Target was a popular destination for cross-border shoppers, a common phenomenon in more southern communities. Since they were already attracting Canadian consumers, the corporation made assumptions about their ability to satisfy this new market. But complaints rapidly emerged about poor product selection and a lack of desirable brands. Canadian consumers were also surprised and angered to discover that prices on some items were much higher than in U.S. outlets. The prices reflected duties, tariffs, and transport costs, but of course the consumers did not care about Target Canada's expense structure; they cared about having their expectations violated and about perceived inequities as compared to American consumers.

Communications and the management of important change initiatives were also problematic, as evidenced by the many supply chain problems that were reported. Target Canada did launch a brand-new information system to manage inventory in their Canadian operations, but their failure to transition effectively to this new tool led to communication errors throughout the supply chain—and ultimately empty shelves and frustrated consumers.

The resentment only worsened when Target Canada announced their withdrawal from Canada. Target offered all employees 16 weeks of severance pay, well exceeding minimum legal requirements, yet they were still heavily criticized. This was in part because the total value of the compensation package for all 17,600 employees was approximately $70 million while the total severance package (including stock options and benefits) received by ex-CEO Gregg Steinhafel the previous May had been $61 million. Canadians, generally less tolerant of huge discrepancies in pay than Americans, were shocked. Online forums were filled with comments trashing the Target brand and reiterating the importance of "buying Canadian." If anything, Target's foray into Canada seemed to have made Canadians less likely to buy from American retailers, the exact opposite of the stated intent.

Sources: J. Sturgeon, "Target's Exit from Canada Will Be Rapid," *Global News*, January 20th, 2015, http://globalnews.ca/news/1782357/targets-exit-from-canada-will-be-rapid; Trefis Team, "Target Canada Story: Origin, Fall, and Restoration," *Forbes* (December 31, 2014), http://www.forbes.com/sites/greatspeculations/2014/12/31/target-canada-story-origin-fall-restoration; Staff reporter, "Target's Package for Ex-CEO Matches Package for All 17,600 Canadian Workers," *CBC News*, January 22, 2015, http://www.cbc.ca/news/business/target-s-package-for-ex-ceo-matches-package-for-all-17-600-canadian-workers-1.2927893.

Discussion Questions

1. Business decisions are often assessed in purely financial rather than human terms. How might the study of people in general and organizational behaviour in particular have helped Target with some of the challenges they faced when entering the Canadian market?

2. Outline some of the problems associated with using "gut feel" when entering a new country to do business. Is there any evidence that overreliance on "gut feel" might have occurred in this case? How might scientifically validated information help a company enter a new country more successfully?

PERSONAL INVENTORY ASSESSMENT

MyManagementLab

Study, practise, and explore real management situations with these helpful resources:
- **Interactive Lesson Presentations:** Work through interactive presentations and assessments to test your knowledge of management concepts.
- **PIA (Personal Inventory Assessments):** Enhance your ability to connect with key concepts through these engaging self-reflection assessments.
- **Study Plan:** Check your understanding of chapter concepts with self-study quizzes.
- **Simulations:** Practise decision making in simulated management environments.

Chapter 2
Diversity in Organizations

Martin Barraud/AGE Fotostock

LEARNING OBJECTIVES

After studying this chapter, you should be able to:

1. Describe the demographic characteristics of the Canadian labour force.

2. Explain the relevance of the Multiculturalism Act and other equity-focused legislation to Canadian diversity practices.

3. Assess the business benefits and management challenges associated with a diverse workforce.

4. Evaluate how stereotyping and workplace discrimination undermine equity goals.

5. Identify the key biographical characteristics that are prone to workplace stereotyping and describe how intersectionality influences the lived experiences of workers with these characteristics.

6. Contrast intellectual and physical ability.

7. Recommend best practices for managing diversity effectively within the organization.

Diversity in society and in organizations is complex. In this chapter, we look at how organizations work to maximize the potential contributions of a diverse workforce. We also show how demographic characteristics such as ethnicity and individual differences in the form of ability affect employee performance and satisfaction.

DIVERSITY

Canada was the first country in the world to adopt multiculturalism as an official policy, thereby affirming the value and dignity of all citizens regardless of their ethnic origins, language, or religious beliefs. We aren't all the same. This is obvious enough, but managers sometimes forget they need to recognize and capitalize on differences to get the most from their employees. Valuing differences helps to minimize discrimination, which occurs when job candidates or employees experience differential treatment based on characteristics unrelated to work performance such as gender, ethnicity, or religious beliefs. Beyond that, however, effective diversity management also increases an organization's access to the widest possible pool of skills, abilities, and ideas. This can help companies innovate more effectively, address diverse customer needs more appropriately, and have other positive benefits. That said, while diversity can be a great asset, managers also need to recognize that differences among people can lead to miscommunication, misunderstanding, and conflict. In this chapter, we'll learn about how individual characteristics like age, gender, race, ethnicity, and abilities can influence employee performance. We'll also see how managers can develop awareness about these characteristics and manage a diverse workforce effectively.

Diversity in the Canadian Context: Multiculturalism as a Guiding Principle and Formal Policy

The 1971 Multiculturalism Policy of Canada confirmed the rights of Aboriginal peoples and the formal status of Canada's two official languages, English and French. In 1988, this policy was supplemented by the Multiculturalism Act, which aimed to be even more inclusive. Some of the changes introduced in the Act include: (1) formal statements of support for the maintenance of languages other than Canada's two official languages, (2) mandating programs and practices that enhance community participation for all citizens, (3) mandating programs and practices that enhance understanding and respect for diversity, and (4) requiring the collection of statistical data measuring the outcomes of these initiatives.[1]

Multiculturalism as a policy ensures that all citizens can maintain their identities, acknowledge and celebrate their ancestry, and still have a sense of belonging in Canada. As a result, it encourages harmony and cross-cultural understanding and supports efforts to integrate all citizens and enable them to take an active part in Canada's social, cultural, economic, and political affairs. Multiculturalism has led to a higher percentage of newcomers eventually becoming Canadian citizens. With less pressure to give up their home culture, immigrants will usually choose dual citizenship. This allows them to contribute fully to Canadian society while acknowledging and honouring their family history and roots.[2]

Multiculturalism legislation has been criticized on various grounds. Some critics claim that it encourages people to focus on their differences rather than their similarities. Others say that the legislation represents a shallow commitment not backed up with the resources necessary to genuinely foster cultural maintenance. The latter critics state that in practice multiculturalism has focused on things like festivals while failing to address underlying systemic barriers to true cross-cultural acceptance and inclusion.

Demographic Characteristics of the Canadian Workforce

In the past, OB textbooks noted that rapid change was occurring as the predominantly white, male managerial workforce gave way to a gender-balanced, multiethnic one. Today, that change is well under way and progress continues, although things are certainly not fully equal yet. The substantial progress so far is increasingly reflected in the makeup of managerial and professional jobs. For example, between 1976 and 2012 the employment rate among women in Canada rose from 41.9 to 57.9 percent while at the same time the employment rate for men fell from 72.7 to 65.8 percent.[3] Gender-based employment discrimination has not been completely eliminated, as we can see in the gender-gap table of Exhibit 2-1. Each subindex looks at a different category in order to assess women's

Measure	1993	1994	1995	1996	1997	1998	1999	2000	2001	2002	2003	2004	2005
Economic Participation and Opportunity Sub-Index													
Labour Force Participation[26]	0.809	0.810	0.817	0.819	0.823	0.832	0.836	0.843	0.848	0.855	0.865	0.868	0.867
Wage Equality Between Women and Men for Similar Work[27]	0.729	0.702	0.729	0.728	0.699	0.718	0.683	0.706	0.698	0.702	0.701	0.700	0.705
Average Earned Income[28]	0.642	0.620	0.643	0.636	0.617	0.627	0.626	0.617	0.623	0.628	0.628	0.633	0.640
Legislators, Senior Officials and Managers[29]	.522	.542	.525	.570	.582	.619	.543	.550	.537	.516	.556	.574	.560
Professional and Technical Workers[30]	1.050	1.062	1.079	1.154	1.389	1.362	1.374	1.348	1.358	1.478	1.451	1.468	1.447
Sub-Index Score	*0.728*	*0.718*	*0.730*	*0.735*	*0.725*	*0.740*	*0.718*	*0.726*	*0.724*	*0.724*	*0.732*	*0.736*	*0.737*
Educational Attainment Sub-index													
Literacy Rate[31]	1.048	1.048	1.048	1.048	1.048	1.048	1.048	1.048	1.048	1.048	1.022	1.022	1.022
Net Primary Level Enrolment[32]	1.0	1.0	1.0	1.0	1.0	1.0	1.0	1.0	1.0	1.0	1.0	1.0	1.0
Net Secondary Level Enrolment[33]	1.0	1.0	1.0	1.0	1.0	1.0	1.0	1.0	1.0	1.0	1.0	.99	.98
Gross Tertiary Level Enrolment[34]	1.0	1.0	1.0	1.0	1.0	1.0	1.0	1.0	1.0	1.0	1.0	1.0	1.0
Sub-Index Score	*1*	*1*	*1*	*1*	*1*	*1*	*1*	*1*	*1*	*1*	*1*	*0.999*	*0.996*
Health and Survival Sub-Index													
Healthy Life Expectancy[35]	1.06	1.06	1.06	1.06	1.06	1.06	1.06	1.06	1.06	1.06	1.06	1.06	1.06
Sex Ratio at Birth[36]	.945	.946	.946	.953	.939	.954	.952	.947	.950	.947	.952	.947	.951
Sub-Index Score	*0.980*	*0.980*	*0.980*	*0.980*	*0.976*	*0.980*	*0.980*	*0.980*	*0.980*	*0.980*	*0.980*	*0.980*	*0.980*
Political Empowerment Sub-Index													
Seats in Parliament[37]	.219	.219	.219	.219	.259	.259	.259	.259	.259	.259	.259	.267	.267
Women at Ministerial Level[38]	0.333	0.333	0.235	0.235	0.235	0.235	0.321	0.321	0.345	0.345	0.345	0.310	0.310
Number of Years of a Female Head of State (Last 50 Years) Over Male Value[39]	.02	.02	.02	.02	.02	.02	.02	.02	.02	.02	.02	.02	.02
Sub-Index Score	*0.155*	*0.155*	*0.130*	*0.130*	*0.143*	*0.143*	*0.164*	*0.164*	*0.170*	*0.170*	*0.170*	*0.164*	*0.164*
Overall Gender Gap Score	**0.715**	**0.713**	**0.710**	**0.711**	**0.711**	**0.716**	**0.715**	**0.717**	**0.718**	**0.718**	**0.720**	**0.720**	**0.719**

EXHIBIT 2-1 Gender Gap and Employment, Education, and Political Participation (*Continued*)

EXHIBIT 2-1 Gender Gap and Employment, Education, and Political Participation (*Continued*)

Notes:

[26] "Table 1.a: Labour force participation rate (ILO estimates; by sex and age group)." Key Indicators of the Labour Market, 7th Edition. Geneva: International Labour Organization. http://kilm.ilo.org/kilmnet/

[27] "CANSIM Table 202-0102: Average female and male earnings, and female-to-male earnings ratio, by work activity, 2010 constant dollars." Ottawa: Statistics Canada.

[28] "CANSIM Table 202-0101: Distribution of earnings, by sex, 2010 constant dollars, annual." Ottawa: Statistics Canada.

[29] "Employment—Total Employment by Occupation." LABORSTA. Geneva: International Labour Organization. http://laborsta.ilo.org/STP/guest

[30] "Employment—Total Employment by Occupation." LABORSTA. Geneva: International Labour Organization. http://laborsta.ilo.org/STP/guest

[31] Adult Literacy Survey Database. Ottawa: Statistics Canada (2011). "Table 2.8.2: Standard score differences in mean skills proficiencies between men and women on the prose, document, numeracy and problem solving scales, 2003 and 2008." Literacy for Life: Further Results from the Adult Literacy and Life Skills Survey. OECD Publishing. Based on latest available year of data.

[32] Human Development Report. New York: United Nations *Development Programme.*

[33] Human Development Report. New York: United Nations *Development Programme.*

[34] Human Development Report. New York: United Nations *Development Programme.*

[35] CANSIM Table 102-0511: "Life expectancy, abridged life table, at birth and at age 65, by sex, Canada, provinces and territories." Ottawa: Statistics Canada. CANSIM Table 102-0025: "Life expectancy, abridged life table, at birth and at age 65, by sex, Canada, provinces and territories." Ottawa: Statistics Canada. Ratio truncated at 1.06 value.

[36] CANSIM Table 102-4509: "Live births, by birth weight and sex, Canada, provinces and territories." Ottawa: Statistics Canada; CANSIM Table 051-0013: "Estimates of births, by sex, Canada, provinces and territories." Ottawa: Statistics Canada.

[37] "Members of Parliament." Parliament of Canada. http://www.parl.gc.ca/MembersOfParliament/MainMPsCompleteList.aspx?TimePeriod=Current&Language=E

[38] "The Canadian Ministry (Cabinet)." Parliament of Canada. http://www.parl.gc.ca/MembersOfParliament/MainCabinetCompleteList.aspx?TimePeriod=Historical&Language=E. Based on latest available year of data.

[39] Author's own calculations.

Source: Kate McInturff, "Closing Canada's Gender Gap," Table 1, *Behind the Numbers*, April 2013. © Canadian Centre for Policy Alternatives. This work is protected by copyright and the making of this copy was with the permission of Access Copyright. Any alteration of its content or further copying in any form whatsoever is strictly prohibited unless otherwise permitted by law.

---

overall well-being. The Economic Participation and Opportunity Sub-Index is of particular interest, as it deals with variables related to employment and job type. It illustrates the degree to which women are underpaid and underrepresented in certain types of occupations and how much progress they have made over the years. For example, the ratio of women to men who work as legislators, senior officials, and managers has remained nearly unchanged (from .522 in 1993 to .560 in 2012). This means men outnumber women in these professions 2 to 1. As you can see in many of the index categories, despite continued and meaningful disadvantage some progress is being made. Women today are more likely to be employed full time, have an advanced education, occupy positions of authority, and earn wages closer to those of men.[4]

Similarly, while other groups continue to experience labour market disadvantages, their employment rates indicate ongoing improvement to diversity levels in the workplace. Workers with disabilities, for example, had a 46.4 percent labour force participation rate in 2001. That increased to 51.3 percent by 2006.[5] Labour force surveys conducted in 2011 found that recent immigrants had a labour force participation rate of 82.9 percent, while immigrants who had been in Canada more than five years and domestic-born Canadians had rates of approximately 87 percent.[6] Workers over the age of 65 represent an increasingly large portion of the workforce as well, 12 percent of them reporting as employed in 2012.[7] This shift toward a diverse workforce means Canadian organizations need to make diversity management a central component of their policies and practices.

Data collected by Ontario's Human Resources Professional Association (HRPA) shows major employer concerns and opportunities resulting from the demographic makeup of the Canadian workforce.[8] The aging of the workforce is consistently one of the most significant concerns of HR managers, along with the loss of skills resulting from the retirement of many baby boomers, increased medical costs, and the need to enhance cross-cultural understanding. Other issues include increased global competition for talent and the complexity of meeting legal HR requirements.

Levels of Diversity

Although much has been said about diversity in age, race, gender, ethnicity, religion, and disability status, experts now recognize that these demographic characteristics are just the tip of the iceberg.[9] Demographics mostly reflect **surface-level diversity**, not thoughts and feelings, and can lead employees to perceive one another through stereotypes and assumptions. However, evidence has shown that as people get to know one another, they become less concerned about demographic differences if they see themselves in terms of more important characteristics, such as personality and values, that represent **deep-level diversity**.[10] This type of diversity is much more subtle, and can be difficult to recognize at first because it relates to invisible patterns of thought and unstated (often non-conscious) cultural assumptions. For example, people from some parts of the world may consider it improper to question their manager if they think he or she is making a mistake, while others may believe it expected and required of them. Since these types of differences tend to go unrecognized, deep-level diversity can be responsible for persistent conflicts and misunderstandings. But it can also lead to profoundly different modes of thought that can heighten creativity and innovation in team settings.

To better understand the difference between surface- and deep-level diversity, consider a couple of examples. Luis and Carol are managers who seem to have little in common at first glance. Luis is a young Mexican who emigrated to Canada three years ago. He is a university graduate with a business degree. Carol is an older, long-tenured employee raised in rural Manitoba, who started as a customer service trainee after high school and worked her way up the hierarchy. At first, these coworkers may notice their surface-level differences in education, ethnicity, regional background, and gender. However, as they get to know one another, they may find they are both deeply committed to their families, have a common way of thinking about important work problems, like to work collaboratively, and are interested in international assignments in the future. Such similarities will overshadow the more superficial differences, and research suggests that after an initial period of familiarization the two people will work well together.

As a second example, Steve and Dave are two unmarried, White, male college graduates from Ontario who recently started working together. Superficially, they seem well matched. But Steve is highly introverted, prefers to avoid risks, solicits the opinions of others before making decisions, and likes the office quiet. Dave is extroverted, risk-seeking, and assertive, and likes an active, energetic work environment. Their surface-level similarity will not necessarily lead to positive interactions, because they have fundamental, deep-level differences. It will be a challenge for them to collaborate regularly at work, and they'll have to make some compromises to get things done together.

Throughout this text, we will encounter differences between deep- and surface-level diversity in various contexts. Individual differences in personality and culture shape preferences for rewards, communication styles, reactions to leaders, negotiation styles, and many other aspects of behaviour in organizations.

When people first meet, they are usually perceptive of surface-level diversity characteristics, but when they get to know one another more, they become aware of deep-level diversity characteristics.

HOW DO EMPLOYEES DIFFER? BIOGRAPHICAL CHARACTERISTICS

OB recognizes the factors contributing to discrimination that affect the organization.

Biographical characteristics such as age, gender, ethnicity, disability, and immigration status are some of the most obvious ways employees differ. Having various points of view represented in the workforce is considered a strength for many reasons, including a better understanding of diverse customers' needs, more creativity and innovation, and broader social justice through inclusion.

However, despite the strengths diversity brings, variations in surface-level characteristics may still be the basis for discrimination against classes of employees, so it is worth knowing how closely related these surface-level characteristics actually are to important work outcomes. Many are not as important as people believe, and far more variation in work outcomes occurs *within* groups sharing biographical characteristics than between them.

Age

The relationship between age and job performance is likely to be an issue of increasing importance during the next decade for many reasons. For one, the workforce is aging worldwide; by projections, 93 percent of the growth in the labour force from 2006 to 2016 will be from workers over age 54.[11] The graph shown here as Exhibit 2-2 demonstrates the reasons for this: it shows the ratio of working-age persons (aged 15 to 64) for each person aged 65 and over. This ratio is an indicator of the changes occurring to the age structure of the Canadian population, and it shows us that our population is aging.

The impact of this population profile is not entirely certain, as Canadian human rights legislation has, for all intents and purposes, outlawed mandatory retirement because it amounts to age discrimination. Most workers today no longer have to retire at age 65, although there are some exceptions for jobs in which extreme physical demands are a bona fide occupational requirement. (Firefighters are one example.) A 2015 poll of

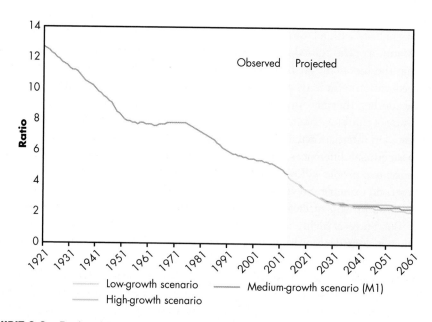

EXHIBIT 2-2 Ratio of Number of Persons Aged 15 to 64 for Each Person Aged 65 and Over

Source: Statistics Canada. "Population Projections for Canada, Provinces and Territories 2009 to 2036," 2010, Catalogue No. 91-520-XPE.

3,000 Canadians between the ages of 30 and 65 indicated that 60 percent planned to work past age 65, an increase from 48 percent when the same poll was conducted in 2008.[12]

Employers express mixed feelings about the older worker.[13] They see a number of positive qualities that many (but not all) older workers bring to their jobs, such as experience, judgment, a strong work ethic, and commitment to quality. But older workers are also stereotyped as lacking flexibility and resisting new technology. When organizations are actively seeking individuals who are adaptable and open to change, the perceived negatives associated with age hinder the initial hiring of older workers.

Now let's take a look at the evidence. What effect does age actually have on turnover, absenteeism, productivity, and satisfaction? The relationships may surprise you. Based on studies of the age–turnover relationship, the older you get, the less likely you are to quit your job.[14] This shouldn't be too surprising. As workers get older, they may have fewer alternative job opportunities because their skills may have become more specialized to certain types of work. There is also an incentive for older workers to stay in their current jobs: Longer tenure tends to provide higher wage rates, longer paid vacations, and more attractive pension benefits.

It may seem likely that age is positively correlated to absenteeism, but this isn't true. Most studies show that older employees have lower rates of avoidable absence versus younger employees and equal rates of unavoidable absence, such as sickness absence.[15] In general, the older working population is healthier than you might expect. Recent research indicates that, worldwide, older workers do not have more psychological problems or day-to-day physical health problems than younger workers.[16]

Many people believe productivity declines with age. It is often assumed that skills like speed, agility, strength, and coordination decay over time and that prolonged job boredom and lack of intellectual stimulation contribute to reduced productivity. The evidence, however, contradicts those assumptions. Reviews of the research find that age and job task performance are unrelated and that older workers are more likely to engage in organization-helping behaviour.[17]

Our final concern is the relationship between age and job satisfaction, where the evidence is mixed. A review of more than 800 studies found that older workers tend to be more satisfied with their work, report better relationships with coworkers, and are more committed to their employing organizations.[18] Other studies, however, have found a U-shaped relationship, meaning that job satisfaction increases up to middle age, at which point it begins to drop off (see Exhibit 2-3). It may well be that the relationship is complex and depends on job type. When we separate the results by job type, we find that satisfaction tends to continually increase among professionals as they age, whereas it falls among nonprofessionals during middle age and then rises again in the later years. Thus an employee's enjoyment of a service-industry position or one involving manual labour may be affected by age differently than her satisfaction with a professional position.

If age has some positive and few negative effects on work effectiveness, what are the effects of discrimination against individuals on the basis of age? The indications are that age discrimination negatively affects organizational culture and overall company performance. One study of more than 8,000 employees in 128 companies found that an organizational climate favouring age discrimination was associated with lower levels of overall employee commitment to the company. This, in turn, was related to lower levels of organizational performance.[19] Such results suggest that combating age discrimination may help achieve higher levels of organizational performance.

In sum, we can see that the surface-level characteristic of an employee's age is an unfounded basis for discrimination, and that a workforce of age-diverse employees is a benefit to an organization.

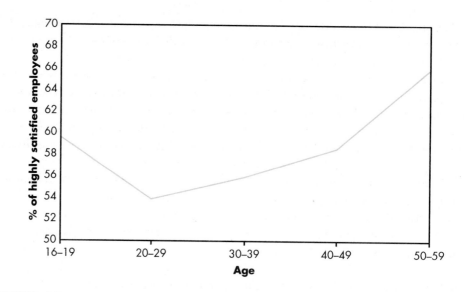

EXHIBIT 2-3   Job Satisfaction Curve

Source: Data from Andrew Clark, Andrew Oswald, and Peter Warr, "Is Job Satisfaction U-Shaped in Age?" *Journal of Occupational and Organizational Psychology Journal of Occupational and Organizational Psychology* 69, no. 1 (March 1996), pp. 57–81.

Gender

Few issues initiate more debates, misconceptions, and unsupported opinions than whether women perform as well on jobs as men do.

The best place to begin to consider this is with the recognition that few, if any, important differences between men and women affect job performance. In fact, a 2012 meta-analysis of job performance studies found that women scored slightly higher than men on performance measures (although, pertinent to our discussion on discrimination, men were *rated* as having higher promotion potential).[20] There are no consistent male–female differences in problem-solving ability, analytical skills, competitive drive, motivation, sociability, or learning ability.[21]

Unfortunately, stereotypic sex roles still have a detrimental effect on both men and women. Statistics Canada data from 2011 showed that the gender wage gap was 26 percent for full-time workers. This meant that for every $1 earned by a male, a female earned 74 cents.[22] Similarly, while women hold 53.7 percent of the bachelor's degrees in the working age Canadian population,[23] one recent study found that science professors still view their female undergraduate students as less competent than males with the same accomplishments and skills.[24] Research also indicates that female students are unfortunately prone to accept occupational stereotypes and often perceive a lack of fit between themselves and traditionally male roles.[25] Males are not immune, either; men working in traditionally feminine occupations such as nursing and daycare have reported experiencing skill discounting, social shunning, and unfair treatment similar to that sometimes experienced by women in traditionally masculine roles.[26]

In the hiring realm, research indicates that managers are still influenced by gender bias when selecting candidates for certain positions.[27] A recent study reported that once on the job, men and women may be offered a similar number of developmental experiences, but females are less likely to be assigned challenging positions by men, assignments that may help them achieve higher organizational positions.[28] Women who succeed in traditionally male domains are perceived as less likeable, more hostile, and less desirable as supervisors,[29] although women at the top have been reporting that this perception can be countered by effective interpersonal skills.[30] Research also suggests that women believe sex-based discrimination is more prevalent than do male employees, and these beliefs are especially pronounced among women who work with a large proportion of men.[31]

Research has shown that workers who experience the worst form of overt discrimination, sexual harassment, have higher levels of psychological stress, and these feelings in turn are related to lower levels of organizational commitment and job satisfaction, and higher intentions to leave.[32] As with age discrimination, the evidence suggests that combating sex discrimination may be associated with better performance for the organization as a whole, partly because employees discriminated against are more likely to leave. Research continues to underline that although the reasons for employee turnover are complex, sex discrimination is detrimental to organizational performance particularly for intellectual positions, for managerial employees, in the United States, and in medium-size firms.[33]

As with the surface-level characteristic of employee age, we can see that there are many misconceptions about male and female workers. Discrimination is still an issue, but there is strong support among many organizations for a diverse workforce.

Sexual Orientation and Gender Identity

In 2012 a researcher at Harvard University conducted an interesting field experiment. Fictitious but realistic résumés were sent applying for 1,700 actual entry-level job openings. The applications were identical, except that half mentioned the applicant's involvement in gay organizations during college and half did not.

The experiment found that, while much has changed, the full acceptance and accommodation of gay, lesbian, bisexual, and transgender employees remains a work in progress. Those applications without the mention of involvement in gay organizations received 60 percent more callbacks than the ones with it.[34] This study was conducted in the United States, where legal protections based on sexual orientation are much weaker than in Canada, but it still suggests the existence of bias in the broader corporate culture.

Federal law prohibits discrimination against employees based on sexual orientation. This protection extends to all aspects of employment, including the provision of benefits to same-sex spouses and common-law partners. The unique workplace needs of transgendered individuals have also received increased attention, especially as regards respectful pronoun usage and access to safe and harassment-free washroom facilities. In 2001, only eight companies in the Fortune 500 had policies on gender identity. By 2013, that number had increased to roughly half. Ken Disken, former senior vice-president of defence contractor Lockheed Martin (one of the top companies in the Fortune 500), justified the firm's pro-tolerance policies as follows: "Lockheed Martin is committed to providing the most supportive and inclusive environment for all employees. Ensuring a positive, respectful workplace and robust set of benefits for everyone is critical to retaining employees and helping them develop to their fullest potential."[35] In concrete terms, simple **accommodations** like gender-neutral washrooms and change rooms can make the workplace more welcoming for transgendered persons, contributing to a culture of respect.

Race, Ethnicity, and Immigration Status

Race is a controversial issue in society and in organizations. We define *race* as the biological heritage people use to identify themselves. It is worth noting, however, that recent genetic analysis of global populations by Princeton researchers Cavalli-Sforza, Manozzi, and Piazza has created serious doubt about the very existence of distinct races. Their research shows that there is a continuum of genetic traits and you cannot identify someone's race just from their genes, suggesting race is a social not a biological construct. This social reality is readily observable; for example, people of mixed race such as actress Halle Berry or musician Bobby Dreadfull are commonly referred to as African-American or African-Canadian rather than

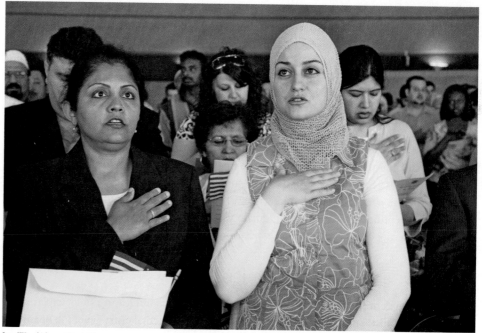

The wearing of the hijab during citizenship swearing-in ceremonies became a controversial topic of discussion after Prime Minister Stephen Harper questioned the practice in early 2015, resulting in a mix of support, backlash, and accusations of systematic racism.

Jim West/Alamy Stock Photo

being called mixed-race. *Ethnicity* is the additional set of cultural characteristics that often overlaps with race. These definitions allow every individual to define his or her race and ethnicity. In addition to race and ethnicity, immigration status also impacts people's individual workplace experiences in ways that will be investigated shortly.

Race and ethnicity have been studied as they relate to outcomes such as hiring decisions, performance evaluations, pay, and experiences of workplace discrimination. Research has consistently shown that in employment settings, individuals tend to slightly favour colleagues of their own race in performance evaluations, promotion decisions, and pay raises, although such differences are not found consistently, especially when highly structured methods of decision making reduce the opportunity for discrimination.[36] Most research also shows that members of racial and ethnic minorities report higher levels of discrimination and social exclusion in the workplace.[37]

While many racial and ethnic groups experience labour market challenges in Canada, Aboriginal people have experienced some of the most negative outcomes. In 2012 the general unemployment rate across Canada was 7.2 percent, while for Aboriginals it was 14.8 percent.[38] When employed, Aboriginal people also tend to earn less than other Canadians, even when education and geographical location are taken into account. For example, in 2006 the median income in Canada for non-Aboriginals was $27,097, while among First Nations workers it was $18,962. Non-Aboriginals working on urban reserves earned on average 34 percent more than their First Nations counterparts. On rural reserves that income discrepancy increased to 88 percent.[39]

The picture becomes even more complex when immigration status is considered. First of all, many Canadians have a poor understanding of immigration policy, and they frequently confuse refugees and immigrants. Refugees (also termed *humanitarian-class immigrants*) are brought into Canada on compassionate grounds to satisfy obligations under the UN Convention for Refugees, international legislation signed by the government in 1951. Refugees do receive significant financial support from the Canadian government during their first year in Canada, but their numbers are few. In 2013 only 12,200 refugees were permitted to come to Canada.[40] More recently, 25,000 Syrians were allowed in; however, this was an exceptional event related to the Syrian war and the associated migrant crisis in Europe. Most refugees accepted into Canada are families with young children who had been living in desperate conditions in squalid refugee camps, sometimes enduring there for more than a decade. Canada also gives preferential access to gay and lesbian refugees who face persecution and torture in their home countries/refugee camps due to their sexual orientation.

In the same year that the 12,200 refugees came, approximately 250,000 immigrants were admitted. These were required to be employable with skills needed in Canada or financially self-sufficient entrepreneurs (termed *economic-class immigrants*), or have family members in Canada who signed documents guaranteeing their financial support for a minimum of 10 years as a condition of entry (termed *family-class immigrants*). Recently fewer and fewer family-class immigrants have been permitted in Canada, as can be seen in Exhibit 2-4. Both family-class and economic-class migrants do not in any way put a burden on Canadian taxpayers; rather, they bring money into the country. They are frequently confused with refugees, though, a confusion often politically leveraged to create the false impression that immigrants are a drain on society. These attitudes unfairly and negatively impact the day-to-day workplace experiences and career outcomes of immigrants, who make up a substantial portion of the Canadian labour pool and population. Exhibit 2-5 shows the percentage of our population that is foreign-born as compared to the percentage in other countries. This emphasizes the importance of immigrant success to the overall economy.

Recently arrived immigrants often experience skill discounting and discrimination when attempting to enter the Canadian labour market. The degree to which this is experienced is influenced by a concept known as *intersectionality*, which the United Nations defines as an "attempt to capture the consequences of the interaction between two or more forms of subordination ... and address the manner in which systems create inequalities that structure the relative position of persons."[41] Basically this means that when it comes to identity, the whole is not the sum of the parts. A simple mental exercise demonstrates this effect: Close your eyes and visualize a mother. Then visualize a teenager. Finally visualize a single person. The mental pictures (stereotypes) that you generated in your head are probably quite different from the mental picture generated if you were to visualize a teenage single mother. Similarly, the stereotypes and forms of bias experienced by individuals are influenced by several different aspects of their identity in combination. Their race and ethnicity, for example, combine with their immigration status and gender such that the

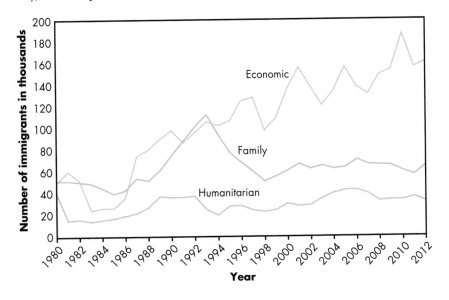

EXHIBIT 2-4 Number of Immigrants by Category of Admission

Data available as of October 2013. A small number of immigrants in other categories of admission are not shown in this figure. Most immigrants admitted to Canada in 2012 were part of the economic category of the immigration policy.

Source(s): Citizenship and Immigration Canada.

EXHIBIT 2-5 Proportion of Foreign-Born Population

Source(s): Statistics Canada 2013. *Immigration and Ethnocultural Diversity in Canada*, National Household Survey 2011, Catalogue No. 99-010-x, Figure 1.

experiences of a newly arrived, Christian, Caucasian British male would be profoundly different from those of a newly arrived woman of colour from Ghana who wore a hijab.

This difference is evidenced in unemployment rates when the data are presented separately on the basis of group membership. Labour market statistics from 2007 indicate that in Ontario the immigrant unemployment rate was 6.8 percent compared to 4.4 percent for Canadian-born workers. Very recent arrivals to Canada, meaning immigrants who had arrived within the last five years, had unemployment rates nearly double those of the general population. Even within that group, however, differences were evident on the basis of ethnicity and home region. Recent arrivals who were African-born experienced unemployment rates as high as 20.8 percent, while recently arrived Asian-born immigrants had rates much closer to those of domestic-born workers.[42] These discrepancies remained even when education and prior work experience were taken into account, meaning that the different outcomes were not due to systematic differences in skill and education levels, but related to the intersection of race, ethnicity, and immigration status.

As we discussed before, discrimination—for any reason—leads to increased turnover, which is detrimental to organizational performance. Better representation of all equity-seeking groups in organizations remains an important goal. When organizations fall short of that goal, recent research indicates that an individual of minority status is much less likely to leave his or her organization if there is a feeling of inclusiveness—that is, a positive diversity climate.[43] Some research suggests that having a positive climate for diversity overall can also lead to increased sales, suggesting that there are organizational performance gains associated with reducing racial and ethnic discrimination.[44]

We can thus conclude that discrimination based on any non-job-related traits is ungrounded and destructive to individuals and organizations. How do we move beyond discrimination? The answer is in understanding one another's viewpoint. Evidence suggests that some people find interacting with other racial groups uncomfortable unless there are clear behavioural scripts to guide them;[45] therefore, creating diverse work groups focused on mutual goals might be helpful, along with developing a positive diversity climate.

People need to be aware of the prevalence of non-conscious discrimination and maintain personal mindfulness to try and avoid stereotypical thinking.

Cultural Identity

We have seen that people define themselves in terms of race and ethnicity. Many people, both immigrants and domestic-born, also carry a strong cultural identity as well. This link with the culture of their ancestry or youth lasts a lifetime, no matter where the individual may live in the world. People choose their cultural identity, and they also choose how closely they observe the norms of that culture. Cultural norms influence the workplace, sometimes resulting in clashes. Organizations must adapt.

Thanks to global integration and changing labour markets, today's global companies would do well to understand and respect the cultural identities of their employees, both as groups and as individuals. A U.S. company looking to do business in, say, Latin America, needs to understand that employees there expect long summer holidays. Differences can be more subtle. For example, some cultures have a formalized attitude to hierarchy and power such that questioning one's leaders is seen as highly disrespectful. Organizational change initiatives that rely on collecting constructive criticism about managerial practices from employees may pose a challenge in this environment. Other cultures focus on group achievements rather than individual achievements, influencing expectations about reward and incentive structures.[46] A company that violates local cultural norms will find that resistance among employees is strong, even if that resistance is not always overt.

A company seeking to be sensitive to the cultural identities of its employees should look beyond accommodating its majority groups and instead create as much of an individualized approach to practices and norms as possible. Often, managers can provide the bridge of workplace flexibility to meet both organizational goals and individual needs.

Disability

Workers with disabilities have traditionally experienced many challenges and barriers in the labour force. People with physical or mental disabilities are more likely to be unemployed or underemployed, they are more likely to experience turnover, work part-time hours, be in entry-level jobs, and experience job insecurity.[47] These outcomes are especially unfortunate because two-thirds of people with disabilities want to and can work.[48] Employer-provided accommodations can assist those individuals in their efforts to maximize their participation. Receipt of accommodations has been associated with job retention, increased morale, and productivity.[49]

A sociopolitical model has become part of the human rights paradigm in Canadian legal thinking on disability. This change in perceptions of disability was part of a larger rights-based movement that included calls for greater government oversight and enforcement of basic human rights. Disablement, it maintains, is not a deviation from an individual bodily norm so much as a naturally occurring and enduring feature in every society.[50] As perspectives on disability have evolved, numerous political resources have been devoted to maximizing rates of labour force participation and the provision of employer-sponsored accommodations among workers with disabilities as one component of reaching equity goals. Examples of Canadian legislation enacted to improve labour force participation of persons with disabilities include the Canadian Charter of Rights and Freedoms, the Human Rights Act, and the Employment Equity Act in Canada. The Charter prohibits discrimination based on disability; the latter two both prohibit discrimination and mandate reasonable accommodation.

These federal acts are supplemented by provincial ones. For example, Ontario has passed the Ontarians with Disability Act (1997), updated most recently under Bill 125; it is enforced by the Ontario Human Rights Commission. Its original purpose was to achieve a barrier-free Ontario for persons with disabilities. Compliance requires the timely removal of barriers when this can be accomplished within reasonable cost parameters. The Act applies to employment, public transit, education, and provincial and municipal government service settings. The Human Rights Commission, while able to award damages for noncompliance, works primarily within a paradigm of reform through education and mediation.

Exceptions to the "duty to accommodate" under human rights and equity legislation include situations in which doing so creates undue hardship or when *bona fide occupational requirements (BFOR)* are unable to be fulfilled, which means that the position cannot be modified without creating genuine safety risk. The case of Alberta Dairy Pool versus the Alberta Human Rights Commission (1990, 2.S.C.R. 489) established the following criteria for undue hardship used to determine if an employer is required to provide a specific accommodation, which have since been used more broadly in courts across the country:[51]

- Excessive expenses will be incurred.
- It will disrupt existing collective agreements.
- It will create morale problems with other employees.
- The employer has highly interchangeable workforce/facilities.
- The employer has a very small operation.
- The employer has legitimate safety concerns.

While this list can guide accommodation granting decisions, employers often need to be reminded that most accommodations are simple to provide and are either free or low-cost. One study found that the average direct cost associated with accommodations that were not free was only $600.[52] Examples of common accommodations for physical disabilities are technical devices such as Braille readers, software such as voice recognition, assistive devices such as special chairs or railings in washrooms, human support in the form of personal assistants, scheduling flexibility, and special parking spaces. Common accommodations for mental, sensory, and psychiatric disabilities include being able to work in a quiet, private workspace without distractions (for people with attention deficit disorder), scheduling flexibility, social accommodation (creating understanding among coworkers about communication-style differences associated with autism, for example), and darkened rooms (as sensitivity to florescent lighting is a common side effect of medications taken for mood disorders and schizophrenia).

Workers with disabilities have many skills and qualifications, but they are often overlooked due to stereotypes about disability.

Maskot/Alamy Stock Photo

Huntstock/Brand X Pictures/Getty Images

Fotosearch/Getty Images

Refusal of accommodation should be an extraordinary circumstance. Providing accommodations benefits not only the individual and the employer, but also signals to other workers that the organizational culture is inclusive and supports diverse needs.

The impact of disabilities on employment outcomes has been explored from a variety of perspectives. On the one hand, when disability status is randomly assigned to hypothetical candidates, disabled individuals are rated as having superior personal qualities like dependability and potency.[53] Another review suggested workers with disabilities receive higher performance evaluations; however, it also found that individuals with disabilities tend to encounter lower performance expectations and are less likely to be hired.[54] People with disabilities are much more likely to be stereotyped in ways that negatively impact long-term employment prospects, often being unfairly perceived as less capable or even infantile. These effects impact all workers with disabilities, but are strongest for people with psychiatric and neurological impairments, and for people with invisible disabilities or disabilities such as obesity or addiction that are perceived as being one's own fault.[55] Workers with psychiatric disabilities in particular experience very high levels of discrimination and are often stereotyped as unpredictable and violent. This occurs despite the fact that violence is not typical of psychiatric conditions such as depression, bipolar disorder, and schizophrenia—contrary to the media-driven stereotype reinforced on crime shows. Psychiatric conditions are treatable and people who have them can be fully engaged, productive workers.

In sum, the treatment of the disabled workforce has long been problematic, but the recognition of the talents and abilities of disabled individuals has made a difference, reducing workplace discrimination. In addition, technology aids and the reduction of stereotyping have greatly increased the scope of available jobs for those with all types of disabilities. Managers need to be attuned to the true requirements of employee jobs and match the skills of the individual with the requirements of the job, providing accommodations when needed for all qualified individuals.

Religion

Not only do religious and nonreligious people question each other's belief systems, often people of different religious faiths conflict. There are few—if any—countries in which religion is a nonissue in the workplace. The Canadian Charter of Rights and Freedoms and the Human Rights Act prohibit employers from discriminating against employees on the basis of their religion. Other countries have similar regulations, but many do not and those that do, do not always enforce them effectively.

Perhaps the greatest religious diversity issue in Canada today revolves around Islam. Across the world Islam is one of the most popular religions. Yet there is evidence that people are discriminated against for their Islamic faith in the Canadian job market. Experiences range from having skills discounted and being denied interviews to social exclusion and spurious safety complaints as a result of wearing hijabs.[56] The Quebec Charter of Values, which was proposed in 2014 but failed to pass when the party supporting it lost the election, sought to ban religious attire in government workplaces. Although all religious attire was included, the widespread public opinion was that this represented an attack on the hijab and Muslim women in particular.[57] This incident highlights the need for ongoing protection of religious freedoms in our multicultural society.

Faith can be an employment issue wherever religious beliefs prohibit or encourage certain behaviours. The behavioural expectations can be informal, such as a common practice of employees leaving early on Christmas Eve. Or they may be systemic, such as the Monday-to-Friday workweek, which accommodates a Christian belief of not working on Sundays and a Jewish belief of not working on Saturdays. Religious individuals may also feel they have an obligation to express their beliefs in the workplace.

Simple steps can often be taken to accommodate this, such as having rooms available for daily prayers or installing ventilation systems to manage smoke from First Nations smudging ceremonies.

Before the election, when it appeared that the proposed Quebec Charter of Values might pass, some Ontario hospitals recognized the discomfort of Muslim Quebecers and saw a recruiting opportunity. They offered employment in more tolerant and hospitable surroundings. One recruitment advertisement by Lakeridge hospital featured a Muslim women wearing a hijab, a lab coat, and a stethoscope. The ad proudly proclaimed "we care what's in your head, not what's on it".

Ability

We've so far covered surface characteristics unlikely, on their own, to directly relate to job performance. Now we turn to deep-level abilities that *are* closely related to job performance. Contrary to what we were taught in grade school, we weren't all created equal in our abilities. Most people are to the left or the right of the median on some normally distributed ability curve. For example, regardless of how motivated you are, you may not be able to act as well as Scarlett Johansson, play basketball as well as LeBron James, or write as well as Stephen King. Of course, just because we aren't all equal in abilities does not imply that some individuals are inherently inferior. Everyone has strengths and weaknesses that make him or her relatively superior or inferior to others in performing certain tasks or activities. From management's standpoint, the issue is not whether people differ in terms of their abilities. They clearly do. The issue is using the knowledge that people differ to increase the likelihood an employee will perform her job well.

What does *ability* mean? As we use the term, **ability** is an individual's current capacity to perform the various tasks in a job. Overall abilities are essentially made up of two sets of factors: intellectual and physical.

INTELLECTUAL ABILITIES

Intellectual abilities are those needed to perform mental activities—thinking, reasoning, and problem solving. Most societies put a high value on intelligence, and for good reason. Smart people generally earn more money and attain higher levels of education. They are also more likely to emerge as leaders of groups. However, assessing and measuring intellectual ability is not always simple. People aren't consistently capable of correctly assessing their own cognitive ability.[58] IQ (intelligence quotient) tests are designed to ascertain a person's general intellectual abilities, but the origins, influence factors, and testing of IQ are controversial.[59]

The seven most frequently cited dimensions making up intellectual abilities are number aptitude, verbal comprehension, perceptual speed, inductive reasoning, deductive reasoning, spatial visualization, and memory.[60] Exhibit 2-6 describes these dimensions.

Intelligence dimensions are positively related, so if you score high on verbal comprehension, for example, you're more likely to also score high on spatial visualization. The correlations aren't perfect, meaning people do have specific abilities that predict important work-related outcomes when considered individually.[61] However, the correlations are high enough that researchers also recognize a general factor of intelligence, **general mental ability (GMA)**. Evidence strongly supports the idea that the structures and measures of intellectual abilities generalize across cultures. Someone in Venezuela or Sudan, for instance, does not have a different set of mental abilities from those of a U.S. or Czech individual.

Dimension	Description	Job Example
Number aptitude	Ability to do speedy and accurate arithmetic.	Accountant: Computing the sales tax on a set of items.
Verbal comprehension	Ability to understand what is read or heard and the relationship of words to each other.	Plant manager: Following corporate policies on hiring.
Perceptual speed	Ability to identify visual similarities and differences quickly and accurately.	Fire investigator: Identifying clues to support a charge of arson.
Inductive reasoning	Ability to identify a logical sequence in a problem and then solve the problem.	Market researcher: Forecasting demand for a product in the next time period.
Deductive reasoning	Ability to use logic and assess the implications of an argument.	Supervisor: Choosing between two different suggestions offered by employees.
Spatial visualization	Ability to imagine how an object would look if its position in space were changed.	Interior decorator: Redecorating an office.
Memory	Ability to retain and recall past experiences.	Salesperson: Remembering the names of customers.

EXHIBIT 2-6 Dimensions of Intellectual Ability

Jobs differ in the demands they make on intellectual abilities. The more complex a job is in terms of information-processing demands, the more general intelligence and verbal abilities will be necessary to perform successfully.[62] When employee behaviour is highly routine and there are few or no opportunities to exercise discretion, a high IQ is not as important to performing well. However, that does not mean people with high IQs cannot have an impact on traditionally less complex jobs. Research consistently indicates a correlation between cognitive ability and task performance.[63]

It might surprise you that the intelligence test most widely used in hiring decisions takes only 12 minutes to complete. It's the Wonderlic Cognitive Ability Test. There are different forms of the test, but each has 50 questions and the same general construct.

The Wonderlic measures both speed (almost nobody has time to answer every question) and power (the questions get harder as you go along), so the average score is quite low—about 21 of 50. Because the Wonderlic is able to provide valid information cheaply (for $5 to $10 per applicant), more companies are using it in hiring decisions.

While intelligence is a big help in performing a job well, it doesn't make people happier or more satisfied with their jobs. The correlation between intelligence and job satisfaction is about zero. Why? Research suggests that although intelligent people perform better and tend to have more interesting jobs, they are also more critical when evaluating their job conditions. Thus, smart people have it better, but they also expect more.[64]

PHYSICAL ABILITIES

Though the changing nature of work suggests intellectual abilities are increasingly important for many jobs, **physical abilities** have been and will remain valuable. Research on hundreds of jobs has identified nine basic abilities needed in the performance of physical tasks,[65] described in Exhibit 2-7. Individuals differ in the extent to which they have each.

EXHIBIT 2-7 Nine Basic
Physical Abilities

Strength Factors	
1. Dynamic strength	Ability to exert muscular force repeatedly or continuously over time.
2. Trunk strength	Ability to exert muscular strength using the trunk (particularly abdominal) muscles.
3. Static strength	Ability to exert force against external objects.
4. Explosive strength	Ability to expend a maximum of energy in one or a series of explosive acts.
Flexibility Factors	
5. Extent flexibility	Ability to move the trunk and back muscles as far as possible.
6. Dynamic flexibility	Ability to make rapid, repeated flexing movements.
Other Factors	
7. Body coordination	Ability to coordinate the simultaneous actions of different parts of the body.
8. Balance	Ability to maintain equilibrium despite forces pulling off balance.
9. Stamina	Ability to continue maximum effort requiring prolonged effort over time.

Not surprisingly, there is also little relationship among them: a high score on one is no assurance of a high score on others. High employee performance is likely to be achieved when management has ascertained the extent to which a job requires each of the nine abilities and then ensures that employees in that job have those abilities.

Disabilities in the Context of Job Specification

The importance of ability at work obviously creates problems when we attempt to formulate workplace policies that recognize diversity in terms of disability status. As we have noted, recognizing that individuals have different abilities that can be taken into account when making hiring decisions is not problematic. However, it is discriminatory to make blanket assumptions about people on the basis of a disability. It is also possible to make accommodations for disabilities. Employers should carefully consider the bona fide occupational requirements associated with their job descriptions and job specifications. Ensuring the accuracy of job descriptions and considering alternative ways to complete tasks can go a long way toward removing inadvertent barriers for workers with disabilities.

Discrimination

Although diversity presents many opportunities for organizations, effective diversity management also means working to eliminate unfair **discrimination**. To discriminate is to note a difference between things, which in itself isn't necessarily bad. Noticing one employee is more qualified than another is necessary for making hiring decisions; noticing an employee is taking on leadership responsibilities exceptionally well is necessary for making promotion decisions. Usually when we speak of discrimination, though, we mean allowing our behaviour to be unduly influenced by stereotypes about *groups* of people. Rather than looking at individual characteristics, unfair discrimination assumes everyone in a group is the same. This discrimination is often very harmful to organizations and employees.

Exhibit 2-8 provides definitions and examples of some forms of discrimination in organizations. Although many of these actions are prohibited by law, and therefore aren't

Type of Discrimination	Definition	Examples from Organizations
Discriminatory policies or practices	Actions taken by representatives of the organization that deny equal opportunity to perform or unequal rewards for performance.	Older workers may be targeted for layoffs because they are highly paid and have lucrative benefits.
Sexual harassment	Unwanted sexual advances and other verbal or physical conduct of a sexual nature that create a hostile or offensive work environment.	Salespeople at one company went on company-paid visits to strip clubs, brought strippers into the office to celebrate promotions, and fostered pervasive sexual rumours.
Intimidation	Overt threats or bullying directed at members of specific groups of employees.	Workers with psychiatric disabilities have reported being threatened and bullied by coworkers. Their bullies are sometimes reacting out of fear since they mistakenly assume that people with conditions like schizophrenia or bipolar disorder are more likely to be violent. That is simply not true.
Mockery and insults	Jokes or negative stereotypes; sometimes the result of jokes taken too far.	Arab-Americans have been asked at work whether they were carrying bombs or were members of terrorist organizations.
Exclusion	Exclusion of certain people from job opportunities, social events, discussions, or informal mentoring; can occur unintentionally.	Many women in finance claim they are assigned to marginal job roles or are given light workloads that don't lead to promotion.
Incivility	Disrespectful treatment, including behaving in an aggressive manner, interrupting the person, or ignoring varying opinions.	Female lawyers note that male attorneys frequently cut them off or do not adequately address their comments.

EXHIBIT 2-8 Forms of Discrimination

Source: J. Levitz and P. Shishkin, "More Workers Cite Age Bias After Layoffs," *Wall Street Journal* (March 11, 2009), pp. D1–D2; W. M. Bulkeley, "A Data-Storage Titan Confronts Bias Claims," *Wall Street Journal* (September 12, 2007), pp. A1, A16; D. Walker, "Incident with Noose Stirs Old Memories," *McClatchy-Tribune Business News* (June 29, 2008); D. Solis, "Racial Horror Stories Keep EEOC Busy," *Knight-Ridder Tribune Business News*, July 30, 2005, p. 1; H. Ibish and A. Stewart, *Report on Hate Crimes and Discrimination Against Arab Americans: The Post–September 11 Backlash, September 11, 2001–October 11, 2001* (Washington, DC: American-Arab Anti-Discrimination Committee, 2003); A. Raghavan, "Wall Street's Disappearing Women," *Forbes* (March 16, 2009), pp. 72–78; and L. M. Cortina, "Unseen Injustice: Incivility as Modern Discrimination in Organizations," *Academy of Management Review* 33, no. 1 (2008), pp. 55–75.

part of almost any organization's official policies, the practices persist. Thousands of cases of employment discrimination are documented every year, and many are forwarded to provincial human rights commissions for mediation and, if necessary, formal adjudication. Many more go unreported. As discrimination has increasingly come under both legal scrutiny and social disapproval, most overt forms have faded, which may have resulted in an increase in more covert forms like incivility or exclusion (see Exhibit 2-8 for definitions of these terms).[66]

It is also important to recognize that discrimination can often occur on a non-conscious level, meaning that the people engaged in discriminatory behaviours may not be aware that they are discriminating. This occurs because stereotypes are often triggered below the level of conscious awareness.[67] A recent meta-study looked at non-conscious (or implicit) associations commonly linked to various minorities using a tool developed at Harvard called the implicit association test. They used data from 184 studies, which were conducted in Germany, the Netherlands, Italy, the United Kingdom, Australia, Canada, Poland and the United States. All the studies verified the existence of non-conscious prejudices and confirmed that those biases impact social, consumer, and political behaviours. Ironically this tends to occur more often among people who are trying to avoid prejudice.[68] For example, a hiring manager may intend to be fair but subconsciously associate women with mediation skills and men with more aggressive conflict resolution styles. Although they would not be consciously aware of stereotyping, that hiring manager may perceive female candidates as being more likely to get along with others, leading to biased assessments of male candidates. Under Canadian law employers are responsible for inadvertent discrimination, so it is important to be aware of these implicit effects and address them before they result in adverse impact.

As you can see, discrimination can occur in many ways, and its effects can be varied depending on the organizational context and the personal biases of its members. Some forms, like exclusion or incivility, are especially hard to root out because they are difficult to observe and may occur simply because the actor isn't aware of the effects of her actions. Intentional or not, discrimination can lead to serious negative consequences for employers, including reduced productivity, reductions in helpful behaviours, negative conflicts, and increased turnover. Discrimination also leaves qualified job candidates out of initial hiring and promotions. Even if an employment discrimination lawsuit is never filed, a strong business case can be made for aggressively working to eliminate unfair discrimination.

Discrimination is one of the primary factors that prevent companies from realizing the benefits of diversity, whether the discrimination is deliberate or non-conscious. On the other hand, recognizing diversity opportunities can lead to an effective diversity management program and ultimately to a better organization. *Diversity* is a broad term, and the phrase *workplace diversity* can refer to any characteristic that makes people different from one another. The following section outlines how to implement diversity management strategies in order to make your organization more inclusive and productive.

IMPLEMENTING DIVERSITY MANAGEMENT STRATEGIES

A diversity management strategy is necessary to realize the potential benefits of a diverse workforce and to minimize discrimination.

Having discussed a variety of ways in which people differ, we now look at how a manager can and should manage these differences. **Diversity management** makes everyone more aware of and sensitive to the needs and differences of others. This definition highlights the fact that diversity programs include and are meant for everyone. Diversity is much more likely to be successful when we see it as everyone's business than if we believe it helps only certain groups of employees.

Attracting, Selecting, Developing, and Retaining Diverse Employees

One method of enhancing workforce diversity is to target recruiting messages to specific demographic groups underrepresented in the workforce. This means placing advertisements in publications geared toward specific demographic groups; recruiting at colleges, universities, and other institutions with significant numbers of underrepresented minorities; posting job ads in community centres and social venues where underrepresented groups gather; and forming partnerships with associations like the Justicia Project (supporting female lawyers) or the Society of Women Engineers. For example, if Aboriginal workers are underrepresented, a company may choose to advertise job opening on the Aboriginal People's Television Network, in band offices, or in the specialist newspaper titled First Nations Drum.

Research has shown that women and minorities do have greater interest in employers that make special efforts to highlight a commitment to diversity in their recruiting materials. Diversity advertisements that fail to show women and minorities in positions of organizational leadership send a negative message about the diversity climate at an organization.[69] Of course, in order to show the pictures, organizations must have diversity in their management ranks. Some companies have been actively working toward recruiting less-represented groups. Google, for instance, has been making sure female candidates meet other women during interviews and offering family benefits that may appeal to them.[70] Etsy, an online retailer, hosts engineering classes and provides grants for aspiring women coders, then hires the best.[71]

The selection process is one of the most important places to apply diversity efforts. Managers who hire need to value fairness and objectivity in selecting employees and focus on the productive potential of new recruits. When managers use a well-defined protocol for assessing applicant talent and the organization clearly prioritizes nondiscrimination policies, qualifications become far more important in determining who gets hired than demographic characteristics.[72] In concrete terms this would mean the following:

- Make sure that job criteria are established using valid job analysis processes.
- Confirm that interview questions and selection tests are free from subtle cultural or gender biases.
- Have multiple interviewers to minimize the impact of individual biases (both conscious and non-conscious).
- Ask all candidates exactly the same interview questions in the same order and have a predetermined scoring sheet to assess their responses.
- Use statistical (mathematical) scoring sheets to rank job candidates instead of subjective approaches.
- Ensure that the same level of training and support is offered to all new hires.
- Ensure that coworkers treat all newcomers in a friendly and respectful manner.
- Confirm that performance criteria are clearly communicated and objectively measured.

Benefits are another area to apply diversity efforts. The typical Canadian benefit package may include things that are unnecessary or culturally inappropriate for some workers. For example, a single person working in his or her first job may have less need for life insurance than a single parent with two dependent children. A childless couple may value travel health insurance benefits while parents may value access to childcare. In Canada eldercare benefits often refer to assistance finding an institution in which to place your elderly relative. This service may not be desirable to people from cultures in which living with elderly relatives and caring for them personally is the norm. Flexible benefit plans that allow people to select from a wide range of benefits based on a points system are both cost-effective and useful for addressing the disparate needs of a diverse group of workers.

Individuals who are demographically different from their coworkers may be more likely to feel low commitment and to turn over, but a positive diversity climate can be helpful. Many diversity training programs are available to employers, and research efforts are focusing on identifying the most effective initiatives. It seems that the best programs are inclusive of all employees in their design and implementation, rather than targeted to special groups of employees.[73] The training should focus on behaviours rather than attitudes, creating concrete connections to day-to-day communication and interactions. For example, rather than tell people "Be respectful to all others," which is an attitude, you might outline specific behaviours they are expected to engage in, such as listening without interrupting and openly acknowledging all members' contributions. A positive diversity climate based on mutual respect should be the goal. Workers appear to prefer an organization that values diversity.

Diversity in Groups

Most contemporary workplaces require extensive work in group settings. When people work in groups, they need to establish a common way of looking at and accomplishing the major tasks, and they need to communicate with one another often. If they feel little sense of membership and cohesion in their groups, all group attributes are likely to suffer.

Does diversity hurt or help group performance? The answer is yes. In some cases, diversity in traits can hinder team performance, whereas in others diversity can facilitate performance.[74] Whether diverse or homogeneous teams are more effective depends on the characteristic of interest. Demographic diversity (in gender, race, and ethnicity) does not appear to either hurt or help team performance in general. On the other hand, teams of individuals who are highly intelligent, conscientious, and interested in working in team settings are more effective. Thus, diversity on these variables is likely to be a bad thing—it makes little sense to try to form teams that mix in members who are lower in intelligence, lower in conscientiousness, and uninterested in teamwork. In other cases, differences can be a strength. Groups of individuals with different types of expertise and education are more effective than homogeneous groups. Similarly, a group made up entirely of assertive people who want to be in charge, or a group whose members all prefer to follow the lead of others, will be less effective than one that mixes leaders and followers.

The impact of diversity on groups is complex. In general, diversity leads to better performance when innovation and creativity are required because many different views are represented. When there are time pressures, however, diverse groups may struggle because it takes longer to come to conclusions when there is variation in opinions and approaches. That said, regardless of the composition of the group, differences can be leveraged to achieve superior performance. The most important factor is to emphasize the similarities among members.[75] Groups of diverse individuals will be much more effective if leaders can show how members have a common interest in the group's success. Evidence also shows leaders who emphasize goals and values in their leadership style are more effective in managing diverse teams.[76]

Effective Diversity Programs

Effective, comprehensive workforce programs encouraging diversity have three distinct components. First, they teach managers about the legal framework for equal employment opportunity and encourage fair treatment of all people regardless of their demographic characteristics. Second, they teach managers how a diverse workforce will be better able to serve a diverse market of customers and clients. Third, they foster personal development practices that bring out the skills and abilities of all workers, acknowledging how differences in perspective can be a valuable way to improve performance for everyone.[77]

Much concern about diversity has to do with fair treatment.[78] Most negative reactions to diversity programs are based on the idea that discriminatory treatment of any kind is unfair, even if it seeks to redress historical inequities. Regardless of race or gender, people are generally in favour of diversity-oriented programs if they believe the policies ensure everyone a fair opportunity to show their skills and abilities. There are significant differences in how this issue is handled in the United States and Canada and they can create confusion. Americans use a quota-based approach called *affirmative action*, under which a specific percentage of jobs must be filled by minority candidates and there are concrete penalties, such as fines, for having a workforce not representative of the local population. This creates significant incentive for employers to hire historically disadvantaged workers; but it might be perceived as unfair in circumstances in which a slightly less qualified candidate is given a job preferentially over a more qualified candidate due to minority status. As a result these programs can be controversial, although they have measurably improved labour market outcomes for minorities.

Canadian approaches to diversity management focus on process rather than outcomes. They are not quota-based but focused on providing fair opportunity, so they are called *employment equity programs* rather than affirmative action programs. These programs focus on ensuring that recruitment and selection processes are fair, training is inclusive, and performance management is free from bias. Canadian employers need to prove, for example, that their interview questions and selection tests are free of cultural or gender bias and their promotion criteria are objective, valid, and fair. This approach is usually better received by members of the dominant culture, since it lessens fears that more qualified candidates who are not minorities will be denied employment. Some critique the approach, however, arguing that it results in less accountability overall. Despite these criticisms the employment equity method has also measurably improved outcomes for historically disadvantaged workers, usually with much less political resistance and between-group tension than when using affirmative action. A major study of the consequences of diversity programs concluded that organizations with diversity training were not consistently more likely to have women and minorities in upper management positions than organizations without diversity training.[79] Why might this be? Experts have long known that one-shot training sessions without strategies to encourage diversity management back on the job are not likely to be very effective. Ongoing diversity strategies should include measuring the representation of women and minorities in managerial positions, and holding managers accountable for achieving more demographically diverse management teams. Researchers also suggest that diversity experiences are more likely to lead to positive adaptation for all parties if (1) the diversity experience undermines stereotypical attitudes, (2) the perceiver is motivated and able to consider a new perspective on others, (3) the perceiver engages in stereotype suppression and generative thought in response to the diversity experience, and (4) the positive experience of stereotype undermining is repeated frequently.[80] Diversity programs based on these principles are likely to be more effective than traditional classroom learning.

Organizational leaders should examine their workforce to determine whether target groups have been underutilized. If groups of employees are not proportionally represented in top management, managers should look for any hidden barriers to advancement. Managers can often improve recruiting practices, make selection systems more transparent, and provide training for those employees who have not had adequate exposure to certain material in the past. The organization should also clearly communicate its policies to employees so they can understand how and why certain practices are followed. Communications should focus as much as possible on qualifications and job performance; emphasizing certain groups as needing more assistance might well backfire. Research indicates a tailored approach will be needed for international companies. For instance, a case study of the multinational Finnish energy company TRANSCO found it was possible to develop a consistent global philosophy for diversity management. However, differences in legal and cultural factors across nations forced TRANSCO to develop unique policies to match the cultural and legal framework of each country in which it operated.[81] For example, in a small number of countries in Southeast Asia and the Middle East, compensation is tied to family status, married people with children being paid more than single people without dependents for the same work. If this system is part of the culture and history of the nation, a foreign company is unlikely to be able to change local expectations or regulations.

SUMMARY

- There is an official policy of multiculturalism in Canada, enabling people to feel free to express their cultural traditions and heritage while also being committed to their Canadian identity.

- The Canadian workforce is highly diverse, creating both opportunities and challenges for managers.

- Differences in age, gender, sexual orientation, race, ethnicity, immigration status, religious affiliation, and ability all impact workplace experiences. These identity markers combine, or intersect, in complex ways that influence individual outcomes.

- Stereotyping and associated discrimination can occur on a conscious or a nonconscious basis. Either way there are negative repercussions for both individuals and organizations.

- Organizations should engage in a range of diversity management practices to ensure equitable, ethical, and legally defensible staffing decisions.

IMPLICATIONS FOR MANAGERS

- Understand your organization's antidiscrimination and diversity management policies thoroughly and share them with all employees.

- Assess and challenge your stereotype beliefs to increase your objectivity.

- Look beyond readily observable biographical characteristics and consider the individual's capabilities before making management decisions.

- Fully evaluate what accommodations a person with disabilities will need and then fine-tune the job to that person's abilities.

- Seek to understand and respect the unique biographical characteristics of each individual; a fair but individualistic approach yields the best performance.

BREAKOUT QUESTION FOR GROUP DISCUSSION

There has been a long-running debate about the reasons why certain professions (such as computer scientist, engineer, nurse, and daycare worker) are dominated by one gender, much of it centred around whether people are attracted to occupations considered suitable for their gender due to natural gender-based preferences or socialized (learned) roles. We now know that most stereotypes operate on a subconscious level. How does that insight influence our understanding of this classic nature/nurture debate?

PERSONAL INVENTORY ASSESSMENT

 P I A PERSONAL INVENTORY ASSESSMENT

In the Personal Inventory Assessment found in MyManagementLab, take the assessment: Intercultural Sensitivity Scale.

SELF-REFLECTION ACTIVITY

Canada, as a multicultural country, has a much higher level of ethnic diversity than most countries. It is almost inevitable that you will end up interacting with people from different cultures at school, at work, and in the community. Blended families with members from several different cultures are also becoming more common. Assess your own comfort level with intercultural communication by taking the Personal Inventory Assessment found in MyManagementLab self-assessment titled Intercultural Sensitivity Scale. Once you see your score, think carefully about what it means. If you are not comfortable, where did this discomfort come from? What do you do when given an opportunity to "practise" by interacting with others different from yourself? Is that behaviour helping you to develop your skills or holding you back? What are the potential career impacts associated with poor intercultural communication?

You can continue to develop your skills in this area by actively seeking out opportunities to communicate with people different from yourself. You may find that gaining more knowledge about different cultures helps you feel more comfortable. People who scored very low on this scale may be prone to anxiety when communicating across cultures, and this anxiety itself makes communication more difficult. Avoidance is tempting but it is not the answer. You can lessen anxiety by using relaxation techniques such as meditation or yoga breathing. You may also find it helpful to practise cross-cultural communication in an understanding environment in which you feel less pressure. Social-cultural events provide opportunities for interaction without the pressure of work deadlines and task-related expectations.

MINI CASE   DISABILITY-BASED DISCRIMINATION

People can make biased decisions with the best of intentions. In 2014, this reality hit home for the Brandon Police Services when the Manitoba Human Rights Commission awarded damages to Billy-Jo Nachuk for discrimination that he experienced at the hands of three on-duty police officers. Discrimination, even when inadvertent, can compromise the ethics that organizations represent with their mandate, mission, vision, and values. How and why do these types of incidents occur?

On April 16, 2011, Billy-Jo Nachuk, a decorated veteran suffering from posttraumatic stress disorder, made a courageous decision. The anxiety associated with his condition had kept him out of public spaces for two full years but now he had Gambler, a service dog specifically trained to help him manage his symptoms. With Gambler accompanying him, Mr. Nachuk felt comfortable enough to socialize at the local Keystone Motor Inn's restaurant and bar. Unfortunately, Keystone management felt his service dog was merely a pet. Despite explanations and the provision of official service dog certification papers, Keystone management complained about the presence of the dog to three on-duty police officers who were also patronizing the restaurant. The formal decision released from the Human Rights Commission of Manitoba states that the following exchange then took place:

> Mr. Nachuk alleges that one officer asked, "So what's with the dog?" to which he replied "it is a service dog." Mr. Nachuk describes the officer as responding "aggressively," "Why? You're not blind!" Mr. Nachuk tried to explain his situation but was interrupted by the same officer who said, "You're not going to be doing a search with that dog tonight, either." He continued to try and explain what kind of dog his service dog was but the officers "refused to listen." A second officer told him that the manager wanted the dog out and that Mr. Nachuk "was very close to being thrown in jail." At this point, "feeling totally degraded" he took his coat and he and his dog Gambler were escorted out of the bar by the police.

Mr. Nachuk filed a human rights complaint for discrimination based on disability as a result of this incident. In April 2014 the Commission agreed that discrimination had taken place and awarded him damages. The Brandon Police Services have since improved their training standards regarding disability rights. But the question remains: How could three officers working together make the mutual decision that Mr. Nachuk's dog was not a "legitimate" service dog in the face of clear evidence otherwise, most notably his official service dog papers? Is it possible that the fact that Mr. Nachuk is an Aboriginal influenced the officers? First Nations people are often unfairly stereotyped and some bands have a history of conflict with legal officials resulting from ongoing rights and land disputes. This conflict has led to tension and mistrust between some Aboriginal people and police services.

Discussion Questions

1. Did the history of conflict between First Nations people and legal officials influence what happened here?

2. What does the situation experienced by Billy-Jo Nachuk tell us about our own capacity for bias and decision-making errors?

3. Do you think providing training in the workplace about disability rights will be adequate to prevent similar incidents in the future? Why or why not? If not, what else should Brandon Police Services consider doing?

MINI CASE CLASSROOM DIVERSITY AND GROUPS

This case is fictional, but it is inspired by similar events that occurred on a university campus in Canada in 2014. **The opinions presented here represent the viewpoints of an individual student and should not be considered reflective of Muslim males or Muslim immigrants in general.**

Amy Liu was profoundly confused about how best to support the equality rights of her students. Amy was an instructor teaching an introductory class in organizational behaviour. A group presentation and associated group paper was an important component of the course. Together the presentation and paper were worth 30 percent of the course grade.

Amy randomly assigned students to groups at the beginning of the semester, because it forced students to work with people who were unfamiliar and different from themselves. The student population at her institution was very diverse—random group assignment practically guaranteed that each group would be a mix of ethnicities, gender and sexual orientations, and cultures. Because diversity management and cross-cultural communication were components of her course, Amy considered these mixed groups to be excellent practice for applying skills learned in class. She was accustomed to mentoring groups that were struggling; in fact she considered those discussions to be key tools to help illustrate important course concepts such as effective conflict resolution. But Amy had never encountered a group problem quite like this.

When Amy randomly assigned groups this term, one of her groups consisted of four women from various backgrounds and one man. Most of the women were in their late teens, but one was a mature student in her 40s. The other member was a 23-year-old Muslim man who had recently immigrated to Canada from Pakistan. He had been raised in a particularly traditional household by very conservative parents. While many other Pakistani Muslim students had no problems being in a mixed group, he felt that it was profoundly inappropriate to have close contact with females who were not related to him. He had respectfully requested that he be reassigned to a group consisting of male students only, or permitted to complete a presentation and project alone.

The university did encourage accommodation of religious needs. They had, for example, set up a prayer room in several of the main campus buildings so that Muslim students could attend to their daily prayers. They had also built conference facilities with ventilation systems for First Nations smudging ceremonies and they sold kosher and halal food in all cafeterias. The university also prioritized gender equality. Amy did not see how she could accommodate the male student's request while also maintaining gender equity for female students. She agonized over what to do for a couple of days.

Discussion Questions

1. What should Amy Liu do?

2. What types of resources could and should be used to help make good decisions in ambiguous situations like this?

3. What diversity management policies and procedures could help decision makers to make fair and defensible decisions when rights seem to be in conflict with each other?

MyManagementLab

Study, practise, and explore real management situations with these helpful resources:

• **Interactive Lesson Presentations:** Work through interactive presentations and assessments to test your knowledge of management concepts.

• **PIA (Personal Inventory Assessments):** Enhance your ability to connect with key concepts through these engaging self-reflection assessments.

• **Study Plan:** Check your understanding of chapter concepts with self-study quizzes.

• **Simulations:** Practise decision making in simulated management environments.

PERSONAL INVENTORY ASSESSMENT

Chapter 3
Attitudes and Job Satisfaction

Hey, congratulations on getting that promotion. You beat me fair and square.

Of course I beat you! I am much better than you after all.

Pearson Education

LEARNING OBJECTIVES

After studying this chapter, you should be able to:

1. Describe and contrast the three components of an attitude.

2. Summarize the relationship between attitudes and behaviour.

3. Compare and contrast the major job attitudes.

4. Define *job satisfaction*.

5. Recommend best practices for measuring job satisfaction.

6. Assess potential employee responses to dissatisfaction.

We seem to have attitudes toward everything, whether it's about our leaders, our college or university, our families, or ourselves. In this chapter, we look at attitudes, their link to behaviour, and how employees' satisfaction or dissatisfaction with their jobs affects the workplace.

ATTITUDES

Attitudes are evaluative statements—either favourable or unfavourable—about objects, people, or events. They reflect how we feel about something. When you say "I like my job," you are expressing your attitude about work.

Attitudes are complex. If you ask people about their attitude toward religion, Rona Ambrose, Prime Minister Justin Trudeau, or the organization they work for, you might get a simple response, but the underlying reasons are probably complicated. To fully understand attitudes, we must consider their fundamental properties or components.

What Are the Main Components of Attitudes?

Typically, researchers have believed that attitudes have three components: cognition, affect, and behaviour.[1] Let's look at each.

The statement "My pay is low" is the **cognitive component** of an attitude—a description of or belief in the way things are. It sets the stage for the more critical part of an attitude—its **affective component**. Affect is the emotional or feeling segment of an attitude and is reflected in the statement "I am angry over how little I'm paid." Finally, affect is often an immediate precursor to behaviour. The **behavioural component** of an attitude describes an intention to behave in a certain way toward someone or something—to continue the example, "I'm going to look for another job that pays better."

Viewing attitudes as having three components—cognition, affect, and behaviour—is helpful in understanding the complexity and potential relationship between attitudes and behaviour. Keep in mind that these components are closely related, and cognition and affect in particular are inseparable in many ways. For example, imagine you realize that someone has just treated you unfairly. Aren't you likely to have feelings about that, occurring virtually instantaneously with the realization? Thus, cognition and affect are intertwined.

Exhibit 3-1 illustrates how the three components of an attitude are related. In this example, an employee didn't get a promotion he thought he deserved; a coworker got it instead. The employee's attitude toward his supervisor is illustrated as follows: The employee thought he deserved the promotion (cognition), he strongly dislikes his supervisor (affect), and he has complained and taken action (behaviour). Although we often think cognition causes affect, which then causes behaviour, in reality these components are difficult to separate. In addition, as we saw in Chapter 2 when discussing implicit association tests, sometimes affect and behaviour can occur as a result of non-conscious forms of cognition. To put it another way, we don't always fully understand our own attitudes and actions, and the explanations we come up with for our own behaviour might sometimes be inaccurate as a result.

In organizations, attitudes are important for their behavioural component. If workers believe, for example, that supervisors, auditors, bosses, and time-and-motion engineers are all in conspiracy to make employees work harder for the same or less money, it makes sense to try to understand how these attitudes formed, how they relate to actual job behaviour, and how they might be changed.

EXHIBIT 3-1 The Components of an Attitude

Does Behaviour Always Follow from Attitudes?

A week ago Jana had interviewed for her dream job. She wanted to work for a resort chain as a quality control expert, which would mean travelling to their resorts around the world and evaluating the facilities and service. Before the interview she had told all her friends how exciting and exotic the work would be. But two days after the interview, Jana was told another candidate had been selected. Discussing it with her friends later, she said, "Well, it would have been a lousy job anyway, because you'd never be home long enough to spend time with family. Plus all the travel makes it likely that you'll pick up colds and other illnesses all the time. I'm sure it isn't that great."

Early research on attitudes assumed they were causally related to behaviour—that is, the attitudes people hold determine what they do. Common sense, too, suggests a relationship. Isn't it logical that people watch television programs they like, or that employees try to avoid assignments they find distasteful?

However, in the late 1960s, a review of the research challenged this assumed effect of attitudes on behaviour.[2] One researcher—Leon Festinger—argued that attitudes *follow* behaviour. Subsequent researchers have agreed that attitudes predict future behaviour and confirmed Festinger's idea that moderating variables can strengthen the link.[3]

Did you ever notice how people change what they say so it doesn't contradict what they do? Perhaps a friend of yours consistently argued that his apartment complex was better than yours until another friend in your complex asked him to move in with him; once he moved to your complex, you noticed his attitude toward his former apartment became more critical. Festinger proposed that cases of attitude following behaviour illustrate the

It is surprisingly common for people to give advice that they themselves do not follow.

Pearson Education

effects of **cognitive dissonance**,[4] any incompatibility an individual might perceive between two or more attitudes or between behaviour and attitudes.

Research has generally concluded that people do seek consistency among their attitudes and between their attitudes and their behaviour.[5] As Festinger argued, any form of inconsistency is uncomfortable and individuals will therefore attempt to reduce it. People will seek a stable state, which is a minimum of dissonance. They either alter the attitudes or the behaviour, or they develop a rationalization for the discrepancy.

No individual, of course, can completely avoid dissonance. You know texting and driving is unsafe, but you do it anyway and hope nothing bad happens. Or you give someone advice you have trouble following yourself.

Festinger proposed that the desire to reduce dissonance depends on three factors, including the *importance* of the elements creating it and the degree of *influence* we believe we have over them. The third factor is the *rewards* of dissonance; high rewards accompanying high dissonance tend to reduce the tension inherent in the dissonance (the dissonance is less distressing if accompanied by something good, such as a higher pay raise than expected). Individuals will be more motivated to reduce dissonance when the attitudes are important or when they believe the dissonance is due to something they can control.

In Jana's case she experienced cognitive dissonance when she discovered that her best efforts were not adequate to land her dream job. Since she couldn't have the job, her attitude toward it changed significantly. She told herself she had never really wanted it anyway and that it was in fact undesirable.

Moderating Variables

The most powerful moderators of the attitudes relationship are the *importance* of the attitude, its *correspondence to behaviour*, its *accessibility*, the presence of *social pressures*, and whether a person has *direct experience* with the attitude.[6] Let's review each of these in turn.

Important attitudes reflect our fundamental values, self-interest, or identification with individuals or groups we value. These attitudes tend to show a strong relationship to our behaviour.

Specific attitudes tend to predict specific behaviours, whereas general attitudes tend to predict general behaviours. For instance, asking someone about her intention to stay with an organization for the next six months is likely to better predict turnover for that person than asking her how satisfied she is with her job overall. On the other hand, overall job satisfaction would better predict a general pattern of behaviour, such as whether the individual was engaged in her work or motivated to contribute to her organization.[7]

You're more likely to remember attitudes you frequently express, and attitudes that our memories can easily access are more likely to predict our behaviour. Discrepancies between attitudes and behaviours tend to occur when social pressures to behave in certain ways hold exceptional power, as in most organizations. Finally, the attitude–behaviour relationship is likely to be much stronger if an attitude refers to something with which we have direct personal experience.

WHAT ARE THE MAJOR JOB ATTITUDES?

We each have thousands of attitudes, but OB focuses on a very limited number of work-related attitudes that tap positive or negative evaluations employees hold about their work environments. Much of the research has looked at three attitudes: job satisfaction, job involvement, and organizational commitment.[8] Other important attitudes include perceived organizational support and employee engagement.

Individuals have many kinds of attitudes about their jobs. Of the main job attitudes, organizational commitment and job satisfaction are the most widely studied.

Job Satisfaction

When people speak of employee attitudes, they usually mean **job satisfaction**, which describes a positive feeling about a job, resulting from an evaluation of its characteristics. A person with a high level of job satisfaction holds positive feelings about his job, while a person with a low level holds negative feelings. Because OB researchers give job satisfaction high importance, we'll review this attitude in detail later.

Job Involvement

Related to job satisfaction is **job involvement**,[9] which measures the degree to which people identify psychologically with their jobs and consider their perceived performance levels important to self-worth.[10] Employees with a high level of job involvement strongly identify with and really care about the kind of work they do. Another closely related concept is **psychological empowerment**, employees' beliefs in the degree to which they influence their work environments, their competencies, the meaningfulness of their jobs, and their perceived autonomy.[11] Research suggests that empowerment initiatives need to be tailored to the culture and desired behavioural outcomes. One study of nursing managers in Singapore found that good leaders empower their employees by fostering their self-perception of competence—through involving them in decisions, making them feel their work is important, and giving them discretion to "do their own thing."[12] Another study found, however, that for teachers in India, the self-perception of competence does not affect innovative behaviour.[13]

As with job satisfaction, high levels of both job involvement and psychological empowerment are positively related to citizenship behaviour, discussed later in this chapter, and job performance.[14]

Organizational Commitment

An employee with **organizational commitment** identifies with a particular organization and its goals and wishes to remain a member. Most research has focused on emotional attachment to an organization and belief in its values as the "gold standard" for employee commitment.[15]

A positive relationship appears to exist between organizational commitment and job productivity, but it is a modest one.[16] A review of 27 studies suggested the relationship between organizational commitment and performance is strongest for new employees and considerably weaker for more experienced employees.[17] Research indicates that employees who feel their employers fail to keep promises to them feel less committed, and these reductions in commitment, in turn, lead to lower levels of creative performance.[18] And, as with job involvement, the research evidence demonstrates negative relationships between organizational commitment and both absenteeism and turnover.[19]

Theoretical models propose that employees who are committed will be less likely to engage in work withdrawal even if they are dissatisfied, because they have a sense of organizational loyalty or attachment. On the other hand, employees who are not committed, who feel less loyal to the organization, will tend to show lower levels of attendance at work across the board. Research confirms this theoretical proposition.[20] It does appear that even if employees are not currently happy with their work, they are willing to make sacrifices for the organization if they are committed enough.

Perceived Organizational Support

When John Greene was diagnosed with leukemia, CEO Marc Benioff and 350 fellow Salesforce.com employees covered all out-of-pocket costs for his care, staying in touch with him throughout his recovery. Stories like this are part of the reason Salesforce.com is on

Fortune's 100 Best Companies to Work For list.[21] The organization is demonstrating strong organizational support.

Perceived organizational support (POS) is the degree to which employees believe the organization values their contributions and cares about their well-being. Research shows that people perceive their organizations as supportive when rewards are deemed fair, when employees have a voice in decisions, and when they see their supervisors as supportive.[22] Employees with strong POS perceptions have been found more likely to have higher levels of citizenship behaviours, lower levels of tardiness, and better customer service.[23] This seems to hold true mainly in countries where the power distance, the degree to which people in a country accept that power in institutions and organizations is distributed unequally, is lower. In low-power-distance countries like the United States, people are more likely to view work as an exchange than as a moral obligation, so employees look for reasons to feel supported by their organizations. In high-power-distance countries like China, employee POS perceptions are not so based on demonstrations of fairness, support, and encouragement. POS can be a predictor anywhere on a situation-specific basis, of course. One study found POS predicted the job performance and citizenship behaviours of Chinese employees who were untraditional or low-power-distance in their orientation.[24] For Salesforce.com's John Greene, living in a low-power-distance culture, the support he received created a sense of community and a desire to reciprocate by being a stellar employee.

Employee Engagement

John Greene's motivation to be a good employee and work as hard as possible is an example of **employee engagement**. This is a relatively new concept that refers to an individual's involvement with, satisfaction with, and enthusiasm for, the work she does. To evaluate engagement, we might ask employees whether they have access to resources and the opportunities to learn new skills, whether they feel their work is important and meaningful, and whether their interactions with coworkers and supervisors are rewarding.[25] Highly engaged employees have a passion for their work and feel a deep connection to their companies; disengaged employees have essentially checked out—putting time but not energy or attention into their work. Engagement becomes a real concern for most organizations because surveys indicate that few employees—between 17 percent and 29 percent—are highly engaged by their work.

Engagement levels determine many measurable outcomes. A study of nearly 8,000 business units in 36 companies found that units whose employees reported high average levels of engagement achieved higher levels of customer satisfaction, were more productive, brought in higher profits, and experienced lower levels of turnover and accidents than other business units.[26] Molson Coors, for example, found that engaged employees were five times less likely to have safety incidents, and when an accident did occur it was much less serious and less costly for an engaged employee than for a disengaged one ($63 per incident versus $392). Caterpillar set out to increase employee engagement and recorded a resulting 80 percent drop in grievances and a 34 percent increase in highly satisfied customers.[27]

Such promising findings have earned employee engagement a following in business organizations and management consulting firms. However, the concept is relatively new and still generates active debate about its usefulness. Part of the reason for this is the difficulty of identifying what creates job engagement. For instance, two top reasons for job engagement that participants gave in a recent study were (1) having a good manager they enjoy working for and (2) feeling appreciated by their supervisor. Because both factors relate to work relationships, it would be easy to conclude that this proves the case for job engagement. Yet, in this same study, individuals ranked "liking and respecting my coworkers" lower on the list, below career advancement concerns.[28]

One review of the job engagement literature concluded, "The meaning of employee engagement is ambiguous among both academic researchers and among practitioners who use it in conversations with clients." Another reviewer called engagement "an umbrella term for whatever one wants it to be."[29] More recent research has set out to clarify the dimensions of employee engagement. For instance, a study in Australia found that emotional intelligence is linked to job satisfaction and well-being, and to employee engagement.[30] Another recent study suggested that engagement fluctuates partially due to daily challenge-seeking and demands.[31]

It is clear that the debate about the determinants and dimensions of job engagement is far from settled, but it is also clear that job engagement yields important organizational outcomes.

Are These Job Attitudes Really All That Distinct?   You might wonder whether the preceding job attitudes are really distinct. If people feel deeply engaged by their job (high job involvement), isn't it probable they like it, too (high job satisfaction)? Won't people who think their organization is supportive (high perceived organizational support) also feel committed to it (strong organizational commitment)? Evidence suggests these attitudes *are* highly related, perhaps to a troubling degree that makes one wonder whether there are useful distinctions to be made among them.

There is some distinctiveness among attitudes, but they overlap greatly for various reasons, including the employee's personality. If you as a manager know someone's level of job satisfaction, you know most of what you need to know about how that person sees the organization. Recent research suggests that managers tend to identify their employees as belonging to one of four distinct categories: enthusiastic stayers, reluctant stayers, enthusiastic leavers (planning to leave), and reluctant leavers (not planning to leave but should leave).[32]

JOB SATISFACTION

We have already discussed job satisfaction briefly. Now let's dissect the concept more carefully. How do we measure job satisfaction? What causes an employee to have a high level of job satisfaction? How do dissatisfied and satisfied employees affect an organization? Understanding the inputs and outcomes of job satisfaction is an important tool toward managing your best organizational asset, your employees.

Measuring Job Satisfaction

Our definition of **job satisfaction**—a positive feeling about a job resulting from an evaluation of its characteristics—is clearly broad. Yet that breadth is appropriate. A job is more than shuffling papers, writing programming code, waiting on customers, or driving a truck. Jobs require interacting with coworkers and bosses, following organizational rules and policies, meeting performance standards, living with less than ideal working conditions, and the like.[33] An employee's assessment of his satisfaction with the job is thus a complex summation of many discrete elements. How, then, do we measure it?

Two approaches are popular. The *single global rating* is a response to one question, such as "All things considered, how satisfied are you with your job?" Respondents circle a number between 1 and 5 on a scale from "highly satisfied" to "highly dissatisfied." The second method, the *summation of job facets*, is more sophisticated. It identifies key elements in a job such as the nature of the work, supervision, present pay, promotion opportunities, and relationships with coworkers.[34] Respondents rate these on a standardized scale, and researchers add the ratings to create an overall job satisfaction score.

Is one of these approaches superior? Intuitively, summing up responses to a number of job factors seems likely to achieve a more accurate evaluation of job satisfaction. Research, however, doesn't support the intuition.[35] This is one of those rare instances in which simplicity seems to work as well as complexity, making one method essentially as valid as the other. The best explanation is that the concept of job satisfaction is so broad, a single question captures its essence. The summation of job facets may also leave out important facets encompassed in the broader question.

Both methods are helpful, and the choice of which to use should be determined by the organization's reason for collecting the data. The single-global-rating method isn't very time-consuming, it provides a quick snapshot, freeing time for other tasks. This efficiency means that the data can be collected multiple times in relatively quick succession, enabling identification of changes over time. The summation-of-job-facets method helps managers zero in on specific problems and deal with them faster and more accurately since it identifies the areas that are driving the most dissatisfaction.

How Satisfied Are People in Their Jobs?

Are most people satisfied with their jobs? The answer seems to be a qualified yes in Canada and most other developed countries. A survey conducted in 2013 with 8,000 workers in Canada, France, Germany, India, Netherlands, the United Kingdom, and the United States, indicated that Canadians had the highest job satisfaction rates. Fully 64 percent of Canadians reported loving or liking their job and only 7 percent reported hating it.[36] Among the other countries studied, Germany had the lowest number reporting loving or liking their jobs (34 percent), while the United States had the highest reporting hating their jobs (15 percent). Immigrants in Canada, who currently make up one in five of all workers in the country, have lower job satisfaction rates than domestic-born Canadians. Their job attitudes are associated with the length of time they have been in Canada. Immigrants who have been here more than 40 years actually have higher satisfaction rates than domestic-born employees, but recently arrived immigrants' satisfaction is substantially lower,[37] perhaps due to widespread underutilization and underemployment among this population. Young workers in Canada also report consistently lower satisfaction than mature workers, possibly due to current economic difficulties that result in similar widespread underutilization.[38]

Research shows satisfaction levels vary a lot, depending on which facet of job satisfaction you're talking about. As shown in Exhibit 3-2, people have typically been more satisfied with their jobs overall, with the work itself, and with their supervisors and coworkers than they have been with their pay and with promotion opportunities. It's not really clear why people dislike their pay and promotion possibilities more than other aspects of their jobs.[39]

As we have already seen, there are observable cultural differences in job satisfaction levels. Evidence suggests employees in Western cultures have higher levels of job satisfaction

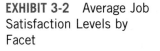

EXHIBIT 3-2 Average Job Satisfaction Levels by Facet

EXHIBIT 3-3 Average Levels of Employee Job Satisfaction by Country

Source: J. H. Westover, "The Impact of Comparative State-Directed Development on Working Conditions and Employee Satisfaction," *Journal of Management & Organization* (July 2012), pp. 537–554.

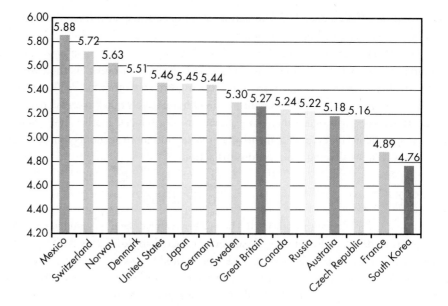

than those in Eastern cultures.[40] (See Chapter 5 content on Hofstede for more information about the influence of cultural values on work attitudes.) Exhibit 3-3 provides the results of a global study of job satisfaction levels of workers in 15 countries. As the exhibit shows, the highest levels appear in Mexico and Switzerland. Do employees in these cultures have better jobs? Or are they simply more positive (and less self-critical)? Conversely, the lowest score in the study was for South Korea. There is a lack of autonomy in the South Korean culture and their businesses tend to be rigidly hierarchical in structure. Does this in itself make for low job satisfaction? Other research suggests that cultural compatibility may be a more important predictor of satisfaction than working conditions per se. For example, a study of 70,000 workers in 48 nations found that people from collectivist cultures tended to focus on harmonious teamwork as a driver of satisfaction, whereas people from more individualistic cultures focused on work–life balance. Similarly, workers from cultures that tend to avoid uncertainty became more satisfied when there was strong communication from managers, whereas workers from countries that tend to be more comfortable with ambiguity were more concerned with training opportunities.[41] This highlights the need to avoid making assumptions when working with employees from around the world. Asking people about their satisfaction levels is always important, but especially when working in an unfamiliar cultural context.

What Causes Job Satisfaction?

Think about the best job you've ever had. What made it so? Chances are you liked the work you did and the people with whom you worked. Interesting jobs that provide training, variety, independence, and control satisfy most employees.[42] There is also a strong correspondence between how well people enjoy the social context of their workplace and how satisfied they are overall. Interdependence, feedback, social support, and interaction with coworkers outside the workplace are strongly related to job satisfaction, even after accounting for characteristics of the work itself.[43]

You've probably noticed that pay comes up often when people discuss job satisfaction. For people who are poor or who live in poor countries, pay does correlate with job satisfaction and overall happiness. But that changes once an individual reaches a standard level of comfortable living. A meta-analysis of the research literature found little relationship between pay levels and satisfaction, and subsequent research generally concurs with this conclusion. Satisfaction does rise incrementally with pay, but the effect is very small. People who earn $80,000 are, on average, no happier with their jobs than those who earn closer to $40,000.[44] The job satisfaction–pay relationship is a complex matter of perspective. For example, recent research indicates that job satisfaction may be higher for employees who enter the workforce during lean economic times, even when they earn less pay. This higher job satisfaction appears to last throughout the individual's career, no matter what pay and economic conditions ensue.[45] This suggests that other factors, such as equity perceptions, interact with pay levels to determine job satisfaction. Equity theory, further explored in Chapter 7, suggests that job satisfaction is based on comparing out efforts and rewards with the efforts and rewards of others. If we feel we are being treated fairly in comparison to others, we tend to be satisfied regardless of our absolute pay levels.

Money does motivate people, as we will discover in Chapter 6. But what motivates us is not necessarily what makes us happy. One study found that many factors other than money led to employee job satisfaction, including the nature of the work (employees whose jobs involved caregiving, and those who worked in skilled trades, were more satisfied), structural characteristics of the job (people who worked for companies with fewer than 100 employees, and people whose jobs involved supervising others, were more satisfied), and even demographics (employees were least job-satisfied when in their 40s).[46] Other studies have found that the working relationship between employees and their immediate supervisors predicts job satisfaction such that workers with good relationships characterized by respectful communication are much more satisfied.[47] Even access to training and development opportunities can have a positive impact.[48] Personality also plays a role. Research has shown that people who have positive **core self-evaluations (CSEs)**—who believe in their inner worth and basic competence—are more satisfied with their jobs than those with negative core self-evaluations. Finally, expectancy theory, explored in more detail in Chapter 7, highlights the importance of perceived justice in determining job satisfaction. People who believe that there is a positive correlation between their effort, their performance, and the rewards they earn are generally much more satisfied than workers who perceive a poor connection between these things.

THE IMPACT OF SATISFIED AND DISSATISFIED EMPLOYEES ON THE WORKPLACE

What happens when employees like their jobs, and when they dislike their jobs? One theoretical model—the exit–voice–loyalty–neglect framework—is helpful in understanding the consequences of dissatisfaction. Exhibit 3-4 illustrates the framework's four responses, which

EXHIBIT 3-4 Responses to Dissatisfaction

The degree to which someone likes their job can influence not only their workplace experiences but the experiences of other coworkers too.

Andersen Ross/Stockbyte/Getty Images

differ along two dimensions: constructive/destructive and active/passive. The responses are as follows:[49]

- **Exit.** The **exit response** directs behaviour toward leaving the organization, including looking for a new position as well as resigning. To measure the effects of this response to dissatisfaction, researchers study individual terminations and *collective turnover*, the total loss to the organization of employee knowledge, skills, abilities, and other characteristics.[50]

- **Voice.** The **voice response** includes actively and constructively attempting to improve conditions, including suggesting improvements, discussing problems with superiors, and undertaking some forms of union activity.

- **Loyalty.** The **loyalty response** means passively but optimistically waiting for conditions to improve, including speaking up for the organization in the face of external criticism and trusting the organization and its management to "do the right thing."

- **Neglect.** The **neglect response** passively allows conditions to worsen and includes chronic absenteeism or lateness, reduced effort, and increased error rate.

Exit and neglect behaviours encompass our performance variables—productivity, absenteeism, and turnover. But this model expands employee response to include voice and loyalty—constructive behaviours that allow individuals to tolerate unpleasant situations or revive satisfactory working conditions. It helps us understand situations, such as we sometimes find among unionized workers. Union members often express dissatisfaction through the grievance procedure or formal contract negotiations. These voice mechanisms allow them to continue in their jobs while convincing themselves they are acting to improve the situation.

As helpful as this framework is, it's quite general. We now discuss more specific outcomes of job satisfaction and dissatisfaction in the workplace.

Job Satisfaction and Job Performance

As several studies have concluded, happy workers are more likely to be productive workers. Some researchers used to believe the relationship between job satisfaction and job performance was a myth. But a review of 300 studies suggested the correlation is quite strong.[51]

As we move from the individual to the organizational level, we also find support for the satisfaction–performance relationship.[52] When we gather satisfaction and productivity data for the organization as a whole, we find, organizations with more satisfied employees tend to be more effective than organizations with fewer satisfied employees.

Job Satisfaction and OCB

It seems logical to assume job satisfaction should be a major determinant of an employee's *organizational citizenship behaviour* (OCB; also discussed as simply *citizenship behaviour*).[53] Satisfied employees would seem more likely to talk positively about their organizations, help others, and go beyond the normal expectations, perhaps because they want to reciprocate their positive experiences. Consistent with this thinking, evidence suggests job satisfaction *is* moderately correlated with OCB; people who are more satisfied with their jobs are more likely to engage in OCB.[54] Why? Fairness perceptions help explain the relationship.[55] Individuals who feel their coworkers support them are more likely to engage in helpful behaviours, whereas those who have antagonistic relationships with coworkers are less likely to do so.[56] Individuals with certain personality traits are also more satisfied with their work, which in turn leads them to engage in more OCB.[57] Finally, research shows that when people are in a good mood, they are more likely to engage in OCB.[58]

Job Satisfaction and Customer Satisfaction

As we noted in Chapter 1, employees in service jobs often interact with customers. Because service organization managers should be concerned with pleasing customers, it is reasonable to ask: Is employee satisfaction related to positive customer outcomes? For frontline employees who have regular customer contact, the answer seems to be yes; satisfied employees do appear to increase customer satisfaction and loyalty.[59]

A number of companies are acting on this evidence. WestJet, for instance, is well known for allowing their employees to have a little fun on the job and empowering them to make their own decisions. The satisfaction the employees derive from this organizational culture translates into better customer care. In fact the airline is famous for their lighthearted and humorous flight attendants, who are known for enhancing the customer experience with their warmly positive attitude, jokes, and silly mid-flight games.[60]

Job Satisfaction and Absenteeism

We find a consistent negative relationship between satisfaction and absenteeism, but the relationship is moderate to weak.[61] While it certainly makes sense that dissatisfied employees are more likely to miss work, other factors affect the relationship. Organizations that provide liberal sick leave benefits are encouraging all their employees—including those who are highly satisfied—to take days off. You can find work satisfying yet still want to enjoy a three-day weekend if the extra break comes free with no penalties. When numerous alternative jobs are available, dissatisfied employees have high absence rates, but when there are few alternatives, dissatisfied employees have the same (low) rate of absence as satisfied employees.[62]

Job Satisfaction and Turnover

The relationship between job satisfaction and turnover is stronger than between satisfaction and absenteeism.[63] Recent research suggests that managers looking to determine who might be likely to leave should focus on employees' job satisfaction levels over time, because levels do change. A pattern of lowered job satisfaction is a predictor of possible intent to leave. Job satisfaction has an environmental connection too. If the climate within an employee's immediate workplace is one of low job satisfaction, there will be a "contagion effect." This research suggests managers should consider the job satisfaction patterns of coworkers when assigning new workers to a new area.[64]

The satisfaction–turnover relationship also is affected by alternative job prospects. If an employee is presented with an unsolicited job offer, job dissatisfaction is less predictive of turnover because the employee is more likely leaving in response to "pull" (the lure of the other job) than "push" (the unattractiveness of the current job). Similarly, job dissatisfaction is more likely to translate into turnover when employment opportunities are plentiful because employees perceive that it is easy to move. Also, when employees have high "human capital" (high education, high ability), job dissatisfaction is more likely to translate into turnover because they have, or perceive, many available alternatives.[65] Finally, employees' embeddedness in their jobs and communities can help lower the probability of turnover, particularly in collectivist cultures.[66] Embedded employees seem less likely to want to consider alternative job prospects.

Job Satisfaction and Workplace Deviance

Job dissatisfaction and antagonistic relationships with coworkers predict a variety of behaviours organizations find undesirable, including incivility and bullying, substance abuse, stealing at work, excessive socializing, passive resistance to new initiatives, and tardiness. Sandra Robinson and Rebecca Bennett pioneered the initial work in this area, defining these behaviours collectively as "workplace deviance."[67] Researchers argue these behaviours are indicators of a syndrome called *counterproductive behaviour* or *employee withdrawal*.[68] If employees don't like their work environment, they'll respond somehow, though it is not always easy to forecast exactly *how*. One worker might quit. Another might use work time to surf the Internet or take work supplies home for personal use. In short, workers who don't like their jobs "get even" in various ways. Because those ways can be quite creative, controlling only one behaviour such as with an absence policy leaves the root cause untouched. To effectively control the undesirable consequences of job dissatisfaction, employers should attack the source of the problem—the dissatisfaction—rather than try to control the different responses.

Managers Often "Don't Get It"

Given the evidence we've just reviewed, it should come as no surprise that job satisfaction can affect the bottom line. One study by a management consulting firm separated large organizations into high morale (more than 70 percent of employees expressed overall job satisfaction) and medium or low morale (fewer than 70 percent). The stock prices of companies in the high-morale group grew 19.4 percent, compared with 10 percent for the medium- or low-morale group. Despite these results, many managers are unconcerned about employee job satisfaction. Still others overestimate how satisfied employees are with their jobs, so they don't think there's a problem when there is. In one study of 262 large employers, 86 percent of senior managers believed their organization treated its employees well, but only 55 percent of employees agreed. Another study found 55 percent of managers thought morale was good in their organization, compared to only 38 percent of employees.[69]

Regular surveys can reduce gaps between what managers *think* employees feel and what they *really* feel. This can impact the bottom line in small franchise sites as well as large companies. For instance, Jonathan McDaniel, manager of a KFC restaurant, surveyed his employees every three months. Some results led him to make changes, such as giving employees greater say about which workdays they have off. However, McDaniel believed the process itself was valuable. "They really love giving their opinions," he said. "That's the most important part of it— that they have a voice and that they're heard." Surveys are no panacea, but if job attitudes are as important as we believe, organizations need to find out how job attitudes can be improved.[70]

SUMMARY

- Attitudes consist of three components: cognitive, affective, and behavioural.
- Managers should be interested in their employees' attitudes, especially their job satisfaction, because attitudes give warnings of potential problems and influence behaviour.
- It is important to measure job satisfaction accurately. The measurement tool used will depend on the reason for collecting the data.
- Creating a satisfied workforce is not a guarantee of successful organizational performance, but evidence strongly suggests that whatever managers can do to improve employee attitudes will likely result in positive outcomes including greater organizational effectiveness, higher customer satisfaction, and increased profits.
- Job satisfaction is related to organizational effectiveness—a large study found that business units whose employees had high-average levels of engagement had higher levels of customer satisfaction and lower levels of turnover and accidents. All else equal, it clearly behooves organizations to have a satisfied workforce.

IMPLICATIONS FOR MANAGERS

- Recognize that attitudes have cognitive, affective, and behavioural components. Managers looking to foster attitudinal change should focus on behaviours but also address cognition and affect.
- Pay attention to your employees' job satisfaction levels as determinants of their performance, organizational citizenship, turnover, absenteeism, and withdrawal behaviours.
- Measure employee job attitudes objectively and at regular intervals in order to determine how employees are reacting to their work.
- Consider the fact that high pay alone is unlikely to create a satisfying work environment. Pay attention to social, justice, and equity concerns to maximize workers' satisfaction.

BREAKOUT QUESTION FOR GROUP DISCUSSION

Based on what you've learned in this chapter, explain how coworkers (peers, not supervisors) influence job satisfaction. What can the average employee do on his or her own to make the workplace a more satisfying and engaging place?

PERSONAL INVENTORY ASSESSMENT

In the Personal Inventory Assessment found in MyManagementLab, take the assessment: Core Self Evaluation Scale.

SELF-REFLECTION ACTIVITY

Your core self-evaluation provides a snapshot in time of your levels of self-esteem, self-confidence, perceived life control, and emotional state. It is important to recognize that levels of each of these variables change over time and change according to context. When completing the assessment think about your work life right now.

Once you have your score, reflect carefully about what it means. Are there problems associated with high core self-evaluations? How might that high self-esteem and confidence be perceived by others? Is a low core self-evaluation always a bad thing? When, if ever, might a lower core self-evaluation prove functional?

In addition, think about how to improve your core self-evaluation. That process is very personal, but some concrete suggestions are offered online by taking the Personal Inventory Assessment found in MyManagementLab.

MINI CASE THE PROMOTION

Fred Blogs stared at the phone receiver in disbelief. He was too stunned to be disappointed. The disappointment would come later, once he had fully processed what had just happened.

The light for line 2, the customer line, blinked as his phone began to ring. Fred knew he should really answer; it was probably a customer needing help with his or her new photocopier equipment. Normally Fred did everything he could to help customers, including staying late, going in person to their office when phone support wouldn't suffice, and even letting them call him on his cellphone on evenings and weekends. But now, after what had just happened—well, let's just say it was time to take an hour or two off and go for a walk. The customer calling would just have to solve his own problem this time.

Fred had begun working for Encre Office Machines in Toronto 14 months ago, immediately after completing his MBA at the age of 36. Prior to his return to school, he had worked 14 years in field sales in the software sector. Fred had sold large, complex database and enterprise resource planning solutions to corporate clients. The products allowed clients to automate business processes from inventory control and accounting to human resources management. Selling these tools meant spending a great deal of time with C-level executives analyzing business processes and communication flow. Fred had been very successful in that role, but after 14 years he grew tired of having a sales quota hanging over his head every month. He saw the MBA as a way to transition to a new, less stressful career.

Unfortunately, Fred's master plan had not included a recession. After taking two years off for his MBA, he found himself newly graduated, in debt, and unemployed with few immediate job prospects. Unwilling to go back into direct sales field, Fred started applying for jobs in other functional areas. His undergraduate degree had been in education. Although he'd long ago decided that looking after a classroom full of kids all day wasn't for him now, he thought he might leverage his combined education degree and MBA to get a corporate trainer role. He thought he could do a great job of staff training and education, especially for sales, presentation, and customer service skills.

After almost six weeks of sending out résumés, Fred finally landed an interview with Encre Office Machines. The interview went well but both he and the human resources person interviewing him admitted that he was overqualified for the entry-level training role they had available. It wasn't what he had hoped for—instead of training managers and new hires he would be training customers who had just bought new photocopiers. Customers needed lessons on how to maintain the machine and use advanced copy features. It seemed like a comedown. But one thing encouraged Fred. The human resources manager had said, "We understand that this job is a little simple for someone with your experience and background but we are really interested in getting you on our team and this is the only job available right now. Within a year to 18 months something more suitable should open up and we can promote you, but for now we just want you on board." Under the circumstances, with his bank account dwindling, Fred accepted the job.

Fred proceeded to do truly excellent work for the next 14 months, which he considered a trial period during which he would prove he was promotion material. He enjoyed the challenge. He went above and beyond for his customers. He also examined the processes Encre used to manage and monitor customer inquiries, and made some process-related suggestions that improved communication between the training team and technical support. The accolades he got for that felt great! He took on tasks other trainers balked at due to their difficulty, most notably helping high-maintenance clients known to be bad-tempered and difficult. He smiled inside every time he helped out, sure his actions were being noticed. Fred did all this and bided his time, waiting for his opportunity.

After 14 months it happened. A new job was created at Encre in response to excessive turnover among sales personnel. A Director of Training role was created to oversee, manage, and improve the new-hire orientation and sales training process. The internal job ad that went around the company stated that key qualifications included a business degree, demonstrated knowledge of the training function, a minimum of five years' success in field sales, and a proven record of innovation. Fred felt very confident when he sent in his application. His confidence was further bolstered when he got a call the next day setting up an interview.

On the day of the interview Fred prepared carefully, picking out his best tie and adding extra shine to his shoes. He had reviewed the corporate strategic objectives and even talked to several sales reps to get their perspective on training needs. He was ready to blow the interview out of the water! That's when he got the call he couldn't believe, the call cancelling his interview. "I am sorry," the assistant said, "but the VP has decided that only someone with sales experience at Encre should be considered for the job." "That is ludicrous," thundered Fred, "I have 14 years of experience selling technology, doesn't that count for anything?"

Fred went home early that day, deflated and angry at the same time. That weekend he turned his cell phone off. Let the customer wait until Monday, he thought to himself bitterly. He continued like this for a week, heading out the door. He probably would have continued like that for some time but then he heard the news.

The promotion to Director of Training had been working 9 to 5 and then given to someone currently in sales at Encre, Tom Fields. Tom had no formal education credentials, had a BBA rather than an MBA, and only 8 years' experience in sales. What truly infuriated Fred, however, was that Tom was the life partner of Jim Guenther, Encre's VP of Operations. It had actually been the VP of Sales who had made the decision, but she was known to be friends with Jim.

The whole thing seemed very suspicious, and even in this bad economy Fred had no patience for unfairness. He considered his options: stay and work hard for another promotion, stay and do the bare minimum, or move on. He decided to . . .

Discussion Questions

1. Despite the fact that he was underemployed, Fred seemed to enjoy his job at first. What conditions contributed to Fred's job satisfaction when he was first hired?

2. Explain why Fred's workplace behaviour changed so dramatically. What could have prevented the behavioural change?

3. Is this a process or an outcome related issue? Explain your answer.

4. What could a manager do now, after these events occurred, to improve Fred's job satisfaction?

MINI CASE WORK ATTITUDES, RECOGNITION, FEEDBACK, AND FAIRNESS

Elisa looked around her new office in mid-August and felt excited. She had recently graduated with her PhD in business and was eager to begin her first full-time academic role. She was determined to be the best professor she could possibly be.

Elisa was particularly enthusiastic about her new teaching responsibilities. She had taught as a sessional instructor at other institutions while completing her studies but had been fulfilling short-term contracts where she had had little control over the course content and teaching approach. Now, as an assistant professor, Elisa could be more creative when deciding how to approach her classes.

She worked very hard in her first term to create the best educational experience possible for her students. She recorded each of her lectures and watched them again later to see where she could improve. She held extra office hours to be more available to her students. Experiential learning techniques and hands-on activities were introduced and seemed to help her students to better understand course content.

All in all, Elisa felt that she had really excelled and she looked forward to seeing her efforts reflected in her course evaluations. Her evaluations when she was a sessional instructor had always been excellent, and she felt that with her new academic freedom there was no place to go but up. Elisa secretly coveted the recognition of a teaching award and wondered if the evaluations might be her first steps in that direction. Other than test results, the evaluations were her sole means of getting feedback on her effectiveness.

But Elisa had never seen the forms before, and when she did see them for the first time she was dismayed to say the least.

She had been accustomed to getting detailed student feedback at her previous institution, when working as a sessional. Those forms had asked a series of 12 questions about the instructor's knowledge, teaching style, approachability, and fairness of evaluations. This being so, it was easy to determine where one was lacking and how to improve. But these forms were nothing like that. There was an open area to write in feedback, but that section was optional and she feared that many students would not bother filling it in. Only two formal questions were asked: (1) Is this course an elective or required? and (2) Select from the following two choices: Was the instructor satisfactory or unsatisfactory?

The second question distressed her most ... satisfactory or unsatisfactory? What about excellence? Was it actually impossible to earn "excellent?" She had strived for excellence her entire life. Now that formally achieving it wasn't even an option, she began looking back on all those hours spent perfecting her lectures and providing one-on-one help to students. She was still glad the students were supported, but suddenly she didn't feel the same way about all that extra work. She looked over her newly purchased book of experiential learning exercises. A part of her couldn't help asking: Is the extra effort I'm putting in really worth it?

Discussion Questions

1. What seems to be important to Elisa? Put another way, what seems to drive job satisfaction for her?

2. Use expectancy and equity perspectives to explain why Elisa's job attitudes changed so dramatically after she saw the student evaluations.

3. If you were Elisa's manager (department chair) how would you address this issue? What might help improve Elisa's job satisfaction?

MyManagementLab

Study, practise, and explore real management situations with these helpful resources:
- **Interactive Lesson Presentations:** Work through interactive presentations and assessments to test your knowledge of management concepts.
- **PIA (Personal Inventory Assessments):** Enhance your ability to connect with key concepts through these engaging self-reflection assessments.
- **Study Plan:** Check your understanding of chapter concepts with self-study quizzes.
- **Simulations:** Practise decision making in simulated management environments.

PERSONAL INVENTORY ASSESSMENT

Chapter 4
Emotions and Moods

Stockerteam/Fotolia

After studying this chapter, you should be able to:

1. Differentiate between emotions and moods.

2. Discuss whether emotions are rational and what functions they serve.

3. Assess the validity of potential sources of emotions and moods.

4. Describe the impact emotional labour has on employees.

5. Apply affective events theory in a workplace context.

6. Evaluate the evidence for and against the existence of emotional intelligence.

7. Identify and implement strategies for emotion regulation and assess their likely effects.

8. Apply your understanding of emotions and moods to better evaluate specific OB issues.

Given the obvious role emotions play in our lives, it might surprise you that the field of OB has not given the topic of emotions much attention.[1] Why? Generally, because emotions in the workplace were historically thought to be detrimental. Both managers and researchers rarely viewed emotions as constructive or contributing to performance. Although managers knew emotions were an inseparable part of everyday life, they tried to create organizations that were emotion-free. Researchers tended to focus on strong negative emotions—especially anger—that interfered with an employee's ability to work effectively.

Thankfully, this thinking is changing. Certainly some emotions, particularly exhibited at the wrong time, can hinder performance. Other emotions are neutral, and some are constructive. Employees bring their emotions to work every day, so no study of OB would be comprehensive without considering their role in workplace behaviour.

WHAT ARE EMOTIONS AND MOODS?

In our analysis, we'll need three terms that are closely intertwined: *affect*, *emotions*, and *moods*.

Affect is a generic term that covers a broad range of feelings people experience, including both emotions and moods.[2] **Emotions** are intense feelings directed at someone or something.[3] **Moods** are less intense feelings than emotions that often arise without a specific event acting as a stimulus.[4] Exhibit 4-1 shows the relationships among affect, emotions, and moods.

First, as the exhibit shows, *affect* is a broad term that encompasses emotions and moods. Second, there are differences between emotions and moods. Emotions are more likely to be caused by a specific event, and emotions are more fleeting than moods. Also, some researchers speculate that emotions may be more action-oriented—they may lead us to some immediate action—while moods may be more cognitive, meaning they may cause us to think or brood for a while.[5] Finally, as the exhibit shows, emotions and moods are closely connected and can influence each other. A specific emotion may lead to a generally bad or good mood, and moods can influence how particular events stimulate specific emotions.

Affect, emotions, and moods are separable in theory; in practice the distinction isn't always crystal clear. When we review the OB topics on emotions and moods, you may see more information about emotions in one area and about moods in another. This is simply the state of the research. Let's start with a review of the basic emotions.

The Basic Emotions

How many emotions are there? There are dozens, including anger, contempt, enthusiasm, envy, fear, frustration, disappointment, embarrassment, disgust, happiness, hate, hope, jealousy, joy, love, pride, surprise, and sadness. Numerous researchers have tried to limit them to a fundamental set.[6] But some scholars argue that it makes no sense to think in terms of "basic" emotions because even emotions we rarely experience, such as shock, can have a powerful effect on us.[7]

Psychologists have tried to identify the basic emotions by studying facial expressions but have found the process difficult.[8] One problem is that some emotions are too complex to be easily represented on our faces. Cultures also have norms that govern emotional expression, so the way we *experience* an emotion isn't always the same as the way we *show* it. People in the United States and Canada recognize a smile as indicating happiness, for

EXHIBIT 4-1 Affect, Emotions, and Moods

example, but in the Middle East a smile is more likely to be seen as a sign of sexual attraction, so women have learned not to casually smile at men. In collectivist countries, people are more likely to believe another's emotional displays have something to do with the relationship between them, while people in individualistic cultures don't necessarily think others' emotional expressions are directed at them.

It's unlikely that psychologists or philosophers will ever completely agree on a set of basic emotions, or even on whether there is such a thing. Still, many researchers agree on six essentially universal emotions—anger, fear, sadness, happiness, disgust, and surprise.[9] Some even plot them along a continuum: happiness–surprise–fear–sadness–anger–disgust.[10] The closer two emotions are to each other on this continuum, the more likely people will confuse them. We sometimes mistake happiness for surprise, but rarely do we confuse happiness and disgust.

Emotions can be fleeting, but moods can endure … quite a while. Because moods can last longer and be more durable, they are studied differently than are emotions. In order to understand the impact of emotions and moods in organizations, we next classify the many distinct emotions into broader mood categories.

The Basic Moods: Positive and Negative Affect

As a first step toward studying the effects of moods and emotions in the workplace, it will be helpful to classify emotions into two categories: positive and negative.[11] Positive emotions—such as joy and gratitude—express a favourable evaluation or feeling. Negative emotions—such as anger or guilt—express the opposite. Keep in mind that emotions can't be neutral. Being neutral is being nonemotional.[12]

The two categories of emotions now represent overall mood states, known as positive and negative affect. We can think of **positive affect** as a mood dimension consisting of positive emotions such as excitement, enthusiasm, and elation at the high end (high positive affect), and boredom, depression, and fatigue at the low end (low positive affect, or lack of positive affect). **Negative affect** is a mood dimension consisting of nervousness, stress, and anxiety at the high end (high negative affect), and contentedness, calmness, and serenity at the low end (low negative affect, or lack of negative affect).

Experiencing Moods and Emotions

As if it weren't complex enough to consider the many distinct emotions and moods a person can identify, the reality is that we all experience moods and emotions differently. Our broader categorizations (positive and negative) can thus be helpful in finding commonalities. For most people, for instance, positive moods are somewhat more common than negative moods. Indeed, research finds a **positivity offset**, meaning that at zero input (when nothing in particular is going on), most individuals experience a mildly positive mood.[13] This appears to be true for employees in a wide range of job settings. One study of customer-service representatives in a British call centre revealed that people reported experiencing positive moods 58 percent of the time.[14] Another research finding is that negative emotions are likely to become negative moods. Perhaps this happens because people think about events that created strong negative emotions five times as long as they do about events that created strong positive ones.[15]

Does the degree to which people experience positive and negative emotions vary across cultures? Yes. In China, people report experiencing fewer positive and negative emotions than people in other cultures, and the emotions they experience are less intense. Compared with Mainland Chinese, Taiwanese are more like U.S. workers in their experience of emotions: in one study, they reported more positive and fewer negative emotions than their Chinese counterparts.[16] This isn't because people of different cultures are inherently different: People in most cultures appear to have certain positive and negative emotions in common, and people interpret negative and positive emotions in much the same way worldwide. We all view negative emotions such as hate, terror, and rage as dangerous and destructive, and we desire positive emotions such as joy, love, and happiness. However, an individual's experience of emotions appears to be culturally shaped. Some cultures value certain emotions more than others, which leads individuals to change their perspective on experiencing those emotions. There is much to be learned in exploring the value differences. For instance, Canadian culture values enthusiasm, while the Chinese consider negative emotions—while not always pleasant—as potentially more useful and constructive in workplace settings than do people in Canada.

> In this value, the Chinese may be right. Recent research has suggested that negative affect has many benefits. Visualizing the worst-case scenario often allows people to accept present circumstances and cope, for instance.[17] Negative affect can allow managers to think more critically and fairly, other research indicates.[18]

Now that we've identified the basic emotions, the basic moods, and our experience of them, we will next explore the function of emotions and moods, particularly in the workplace.

THE FUNCTION OF EMOTIONS AND MOODS

In some ways, emotions are a mystery. What function do they serve? As we discussed, researchers and managers determined for many years that emotions serve no purpose in the workplace. Psychologists have always said otherwise, insisting that emotions serve a function in any human situation. Organizational behaviourists have been finding that emotions can be critical to an effectively functioning workplace. Let's discuss two critical areas—rationality and ethicality—in which emotions can enhance performance.

Do Emotions Make Us Irrational?

How often have you heard someone say, "Oh, you're just being emotional"? You might have been offended. Observations like this suggest that rationality and emotion are in conflict and that if you exhibit emotion, you are likely to act irrationally. The perceived association between emotionality and irrationality is so strong that some researchers argue that displaying emotions such as sadness to the point of crying is toxic to a career and we should leave the room rather than allow others to witness it.[19] This perspective suggests the demonstration or even experience of emotions can make us weak, brittle, or irrational. However, this is wrong.

Research is increasingly indicating that emotions are critical to rational thinking. Brain injury studies in particular suggest we must have the ability to experience emotions to be rational. Why? Because our emotions provide a context for how we understand the world around us. For instance, a recent study indicated that individuals in a negative mood are better able to discern truthful information than people in a happy mood.[20] Therefore, if we have a concern about someone telling the truth, shouldn't we conduct an inquiry while we are actively concerned, rather than wait until we cheer up? There may be benefits to this, or maybe not, depending on all the factors including the range of our emotions. The keys are to acknowledge the effect that emotions and moods are having on us, and to not automatically discount our emotional responses as irrational or invalid.

Do Emotions Make Us Ethical?

A growing body of research has begun to examine the relationship between emotions and moral attitudes.[21] It was previously believed that, like decision making in general, most ethical decision making was based on higher-order cognitive processes, but research on moral emotions increasingly questions this perspective. Examples of moral emotions include sympathy for the suffering of others, guilt about our own immoral behaviour, anger about injustice done to others, contempt for those who behave unethically, and disgust at violations of moral norms. Numerous studies suggest that moral judgments are largely based on feelings rather than on cognition, although assessments of fairness (which frequently influence moral judgments), do have a cognitive component. We tend to see our moral boundaries as logical and reasonable, not as emotional. We therefore must be careful to objectively analyze our ethical decisions.

When we study emotions and moods in relation to ethics and organizational behaviour, it is tempting to focus on the categorization and work outcome aspects, which might lead us to some useful conclusions for managers. However, the sources of emotions and moods should not be overlooked, because when we identify sources, we are better able to predict behaviour and manage people well.

SOURCES OF EMOTIONS AND MOODS

Have you ever snapped at a coworker or family member for no particular reason? Have you ever felt like being silly even when in a serious situation? If you have, you probably wonder where emotions and moods come from. Here we discuss some of the primary influences. They can be grouped into two main types: influences based on who you are (such as age and personality) and influences based on your circumstances at the time (such as time of day, your blood sugar level, etc.)

Potential Influences on Moods and Emotions

The first three that we will examine are influencers that are based on who you are. They include personality, age, and gender; although the latter is considered controversial due to disputes about whether emotional differences are ingrained or learned.

Personality   Moods and emotions have a personality trait component: Most people have built-in tendencies to experience certain moods and emotions more frequently than others do. People also experience the same emotions with different intensities, which is called **affect intensity**.[22] Affectively intense people experience both positive and negative emotions more deeply: when they're sad, they're really sad, and when they're happy, they're really happy.

Trueffelpix/Shutterstock

Our personality impacts mood and emotion. For example some people tend to take a pessimistic view of things, heightening negative emotions. They tend to see their glass as half-empty. Others are generally more optimistic, with a tendency towards the positive and seeing the glass as half-full.

Age   Do young people experience more extreme positive emotions (so-called youthful exuberance) than older people? If you answered yes, you were wrong. One study of people ages 18 to 94 revealed that negative emotions seem to occur less as people get older. Periods of highly positive moods lasted longer for older individuals, and bad moods faded more quickly.[23]

Sex   Many people believe women are more emotional than men. Is there any truth to this? Evidence does confirm women are more emotionally expressive than men,[24] experience emotions more intensely, tend to "hold onto" emotions longer, and display more frequent expressions of both positive and negative emotions, except anger.[25] Many of these findings may, however, be due to differences in socialization and gender roles rather than sex.

The remaining influences on mood relate more to the circumstances of the moment and include time of day, day of the week, weather, stress level, the nature of the activity, amount of sleep and exercise the person has had, and blood sugar levels. We will examine each in more detail. While some, such as day of the week, are not under our control, others, such as getting adequate sleep and eating regularly, are. Controlling them may allow for better emotional regulation during the workday.

Time of Day   People vary in their moods by the time of day. However, research suggests most of us actually follow the same pattern, and the nature of this pattern may surprise you. Exhibit 4-2 illustrates moods analyzed from 509 million Twitter messages posted by 2.4 million individuals across 84 countries.[26] As you see, levels of positive affect are greatest in the evening, and lowest in the early morning, on most days of the week. Levels of negative affect are also highest in the overnight hours, but the lowest point is later in the morning than for positive affect.

Day of the Week   Are people in their best moods on the weekends? In most cultures that is true—for example, U.S. adults tend to experience their highest positive affect on Friday, Saturday, and Sunday, and their lowest on Monday.[27] As shown in Exhibit 4-3, the trend tends to be true in several other cultures as well.

Weather   Many people believe their mood is tied to the weather. However, a fairly large and detailed body of evidence conducted by multiple researchers suggests weather has little effect, at least for most people.[28] Some people do experience a medical condition called *seasonal affect disorder*, in which depressive moods are associated with the lowered light levels of the winter months. This occurs most frequently at northern latitudes and can often be addressed with the use of special lights.[29] For others, however, the link between weather and mood is an **illusory correlation**, which occurs when we associate two events that in reality have no connection. This phenomenon explains why people tend to *think* nice weather improves their mood.

Stress   As you might imagine, stressful events at work (a nasty e-mail, an impending deadline, loss of a big sale, a reprimand from the boss) negatively affect moods. Even positive changes, such as planning a wedding or getting a promotion, can substantially increase overall stress levels. The effects of stress also build over time. Mounting stress can worsen our moods such that we experience more negative emotions. Although sometimes we thrive on stress, most of us find stress takes an emotional toll.

Social Activities   For most people, social activities increase positive moods and have little effect on negative moods. The type of social interaction does appear to matter. Research suggests activities that are physical (skiing or hiking with friends), informal (going to a party), or epicurean (eating with others) are more strongly associated with increases in positive mood than events that are formal (attending a meeting) or sedentary (watching TV with friends).[30] The personality of the individual is also relevant. Introverts, for example, may find large parties stress-inducing rather than stress relieving. They often prefer quieter social venues and interacting with fewer people, sometimes as few as two or three, at one time.[31]

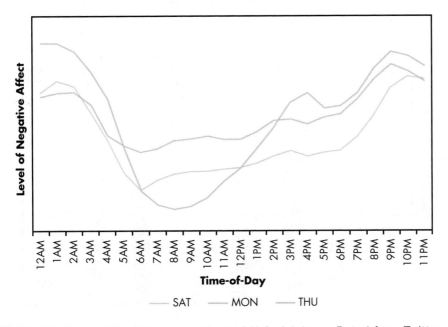

EXHIBIT 4-2 Time-of-Day Effects on Mood of U.S. Adults as Rated from Twitter Postings

Note: Based on analysis of U.S. Twitter postings and coding of words that represent positive feelings (delight, enthusiasm) and negative feelings (fear, guilt). Lines represent percent of total words in Twitter post that convey these moods.

Sources: Based on S. A. Golder and M. W. Macy, "Diumal and Seasonal Mood Vary with Work, Sleep, and Daylength Across Diverse Cultures," *Science* 333 (2011), pp. 1878–1881; and A. Elejalde-Ruiz, "Seize the Day," *Chicago Tribune* (September 5, 2012), accessed June 20, 2013 at http://articles.chicagotribune.com.

Sleep   Sleep quality affects mood, and increased fatigue puts workers at health risks of disease, injury, and depression.[32] According to one study, poor sleep impairs job satisfaction because people feel fatigued, irritable, and less alert.[33] This is a big problem, since according to researchers and public health specialists, 41 million U.S. workers are able to sleep less than six hours per night. Interestingly, Canadians seem somewhat better off. Data collected

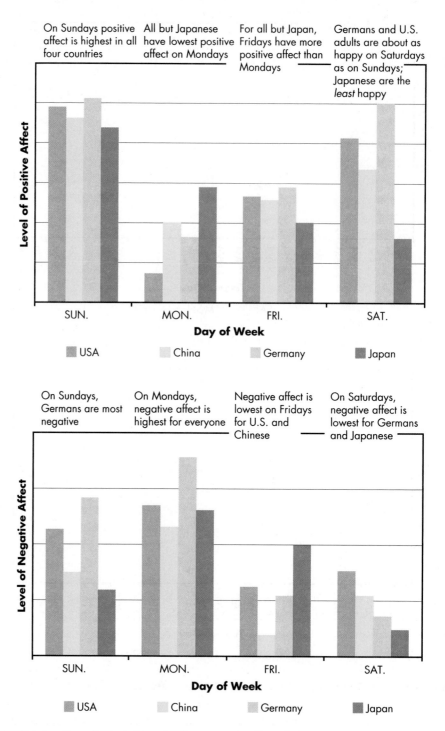

EXHIBIT 4-3 Day-of-Week Mood Effects across Four Cultures

Sources: Based on S. A. Golder and M. W. Macy, "Diurnal and Seasonal Mood Vary with Work, Sleep, and Daylength Across Diverse Cultures," *Science* 333 (2011), pp. 1878–1881; and A. Elejalde-Ruiz, "Seize the Day," *Chicago Tribune* (September 5, 2012), accessed June 20, 2013 at http://articles.chicagotribune.com.

by Statistics Canada in 2005 indicated that adult men averaged 8 hours and 7 minutes of sleep while women average 8 hours, 18 minutes.[34]

Exercise   You often hear that people should exercise to improve their mood. Does "sweat therapy" really work? Apparently. Research consistently shows exercise enhances people's positive mood.[35] While not terribly strong overall, the effects are strongest for those who are depressed.

Blood Sugar Levels Low blood sugar occurs when someone has not eaten for too long. It has been strongly associated with irritability, disagreeableness, and even combative behaviours. Excessively high blood sugar, too, most common among untreated diabetics, has been linked to depression.[36] Avoiding long periods without food, monitoring health, and keeping small snacks such as dried fruits and nuts handy can head off disruptive behaviour that is due to blood sugar levels.

It might seem by now that we all—leaders, managers, and employees alike—operate as unwitting slaves to our emotions and moods. On an internal experiential level, this may be true. Yet we know from our workplace experiences that people aren't expressing every brief emotion that flits through their consciousness. On the way toward applying what we've discussed to specific OB applications, let's put together what we've learned about emotions and moods with workplace behaviours, beginning with emotional labour.

EMOTIONAL LABOUR

Natasha works at a Tim Hortons summer camp as a rock climbing instructor. The camps, provided free to underprivileged kids, focus on providing a positive summer experience for children who otherwise would have few opportunities for outdoor recreation. Being upbeat and enthusiastic is part of the job. Normally this is no problem for Natasha, but this week she just found out her grandmother is ill and requires surgery. She is so worried that she finds it very hard to be upbeat and encouraging. But she knows the kids deserve her best so she forces herself to do it anyway.

Employees expend physical and mental labour by putting body and mind, respectively, into the job. But jobs also require **emotional labour**, an employee's expression of organizationally desired emotions during interpersonal transactions at work. Emotional labour is a key component of effective job performance. We expect flight attendants to be cheerful, funeral directors to be sad, and doctors emotionally neutral. But emotional labour is relevant to almost every job. At the least your managers expect you to be courteous, not hostile, in your interactions with coworkers and customers.

The way we experience an emotion is obviously not always the same as the way we show it. To analyze emotional labour, we divide emotions into *felt* or *displayed emotions*.[37] **Felt emotions** are our actual emotions. In contrast, **displayed emotions** are those that the organization requires workers to show and considers appropriate in a given job. They're not innate; they're learned, and they may or may not coincide with felt emotions. For instance, research suggests that in U.S. workplaces, it is expected that workers should typically display positive emotions like happiness and excitement, and suppress negative emotions like fear, anger, disgust, and contempt.[38] The same is true for Canadian workers. Effective managers have learned to be serious when giving an employee a negative performance evaluation and to hide their anger when they've been passed over for promotion.

Displaying fake emotions requires us to suppress real ones. **Surface acting** is hiding inner feelings and emotional expressions in response to display rules. A worker who smiles at a customer even when he doesn't feel like it is surface acting. **Deep acting** is trying to modify our true inner feelings based on display rules. Surface acting deals with *displayed* emotions, and deep acting deals with *felt* emotions.

Displaying emotions we don't really feel can be exhausting. When employees have to project one emotion while feeling another, this disparity is called **emotional dissonance**. Emotional dissonance is like cognitive dissonance (discussed in Chapter 3), except that it concerns feelings rather than thinking. Bottled-up feelings of frustration, anger, and resentment can lead to emotional exhaustion. Long-term emotional dissonance is a predictor for job burnout, declines in job performance, and lower job satisfaction.[39]

Circumstances and the attitudes of those around us can impact our ability to cope with emotional labour and associated dissonance. In Natasha's case she probably finds it easier to "put on happy face" because the children she is working with at her summer camp are generally well behaved and happy to be there. She might find it more difficult to do the same if she worked at a customer service desk in a grocery store, where many customers come because they are angry or frustrated and need help.

It is important to counteract the effects of emotional labour and emotional dissonance. Research in the Netherlands and Belgium has indicated that surface acting is stressful to employees, while *mindfulness* (learning to objectively evaluate our emotional situation in the moment, akin to deep acting) is beneficial to employee well-being.[40] It is also important to give employees who engage in surface displays a chance to relax and recharge. A study that looked at how cheerleading instructors spent their breaks from teaching found those who used the time to rest and relax were more effective after their breaks. Instructors who did chores during their breaks were only about as effective after their break as they were before.[41]

The concept of emotional labour makes intuitive and organizational sense. Affective events theory, discussed in the next section, fits a job's emotional labour requirements into a construct that leads to work events, emotional reactions, and, finally, to job satisfaction and job performance.

AFFECTIVE EVENTS THEORY

We've seen that emotions and moods are an important part of our personal lives and our work lives. But how do they influence our job performance and satisfaction? A model called **affective events theory (AET)** demonstrates that employees react emotionally to things that happen to them at work, and this reaction influences their job performance and satisfaction.[42]

Exhibit 4-4 summarizes AET. The theory begins by recognizing that emotions are a response to an event in the work environment. The work environment includes everything surrounding the job—the variety of tasks and degree of autonomy, job demands, and requirements for emotional labour. This environment creates work events that can be hassles, uplifting events, or both. Examples of hassles are colleagues who refuse to carry their share of work, conflicting directions from different managers, and excessive time pressures. Uplifting events include meeting a goal, getting support from a colleague, and receiving recognition for an accomplishment.[43]

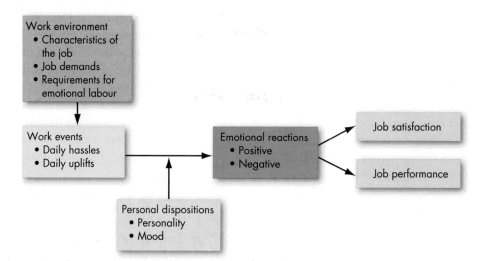

EXHIBIT 4-4 Affective Events Theory

Source: Based on N. M. Ashkanasy and C. S. Daus, "Emotion in the Workplace: The New Challenge for Managers," *Academy of Management Executive* (February 2002), p. 77.

Work events trigger positive or negative emotional reactions, to which employees' personalities and moods predispose them to respond with greater or lesser intensity. People who score low on emotional stability are more likely to react strongly to negative events, and our emotional response to a given event can change depending on mood. Finally, emotions influence a number of performance and satisfaction variables, such as organizational citizenship behaviour, organizational commitment, level of effort, intention to quit, and workplace deviance.

AET provides us with valuable insights into the role emotions play in primary organizational outcomes of job satisfaction and job performance. Employees and managers therefore shouldn't ignore emotions or the events that cause them.[44] Emotional intelligence is another framework that helps us understand the impact of emotions on job performance, so we will look at that next.

EMOTIONAL INTELLIGENCE

Emotional intelligence (EI) is a person's ability to (1) perceive emotions in the self and others, (2) understand the meaning of these emotions, and (3) regulate his or her emotions accordingly in a cascading model, as shown in Exhibit 4-5. People who know their own emotions and are good at reading emotional cues—for instance, knowing why they're angry and how to express themselves without violating norms—are most likely to be effective.[45]

People who know their own emotions and are good at reading others' emotions may be more effective in their jobs.

Several studies suggest EI plays an important role in job performance. However, EI has been a controversial concept in OB, with supporters and detractors. In the following sections, we review the arguments for and against its viability.

The Case for EI

The arguments in favor of EI include its intuitive appeal, the fact that it predicts criteria that matter, and the idea that it is biologically based.

EI Is Intuitively Appealing   Intuition suggests that people who can detect emotions in others, control their own emotions, and handle social interactions well have an advantage in the business world.

EI Predicts Criteria That Matter   Evidence suggests a high level of EI means a person will perform well on the job.

EI Is Biologically Based   There is evidence that EI is genetically influenced, further supporting the idea that it measures a real underlying biological factor.[46]

The Case Against EI

For all its supporters, EI has just as many critics who say it is vague and impossible to measure, and they question its validity.

EI Researchers Do Not Agree on Definitions   To many researchers, it's not clear what EI is, because researchers use different definitions of it.[47]

EI Can't Be Measured   The measures of EI are diverse, and researchers have not subjected them to as much rigorous study as they have measures of personality and general intelligence.[48]

EI Is Nothing but Personality with a Different Label   Some critics argue that because EI is so closely related to intelligence and personality, once you control for these factors, it has nothing unique to offer. To some extent, researchers have resolved this issue by noting that EI is a construct partially determined by traits like cognitive intelligence, conscientiousness, and neuroticism, so it makes sense that EI is correlated with these characteristics.[49]

EXHIBIT 4-5 A Cascading Model of Emotional Intelligence

Although the field is progressing in its understanding of EI, many questions have not been answered. EI is wildly popular among consulting firms and in the popular press, and while it has accumulated some support in the research literature, critics remain. Love it or hate it, one thing is for sure—EI is here to stay. So may be our next topic, emotion regulation, which is part of the EI literature but is increasingly studied as an independent concept.[50]

EMOTION REGULATION

Alex drives a city bus and sometimes feels very frustrated with traffic and the foolish driving errors made by others on the road. On bad days Alex envisions screaming at other drivers and is sometimes even tempted to throw something at them as the bus goes by. He never does it, though; instead he deliberately slows down his breathing and thinks soothing thoughts until the anger passes. On those days Alex is heavily involved in *emotion regulation*.

The central idea behind emotion regulation is to identify and modify the emotions you feel. Recent research suggests that emotion management ability is a strong predictor of task performance for some jobs and organizational citizenship behaviours.[51] Researchers of emotion regulation often study the strategies people employ to change their emotions. One strategy we have discussed in this chapter is surface acting, or putting on a face of appropriate response to a given situation. Surface acting doesn't change the emotions, though, so the regulation effect is minimal. Deep acting, another strategy we have covered, is less

Have you ever tried to cheer yourself up when you're feeling down, or calm yourself when you're feeling angry?

airdone/Shutterstock

psychologically costly than surface acting, because the employee is actually trying to experience the emotion. Though less "false" than surface acting, however, it might still be difficult because it represents acting nonetheless.

Although the research is ongoing, studies indicate that effective emotion regulation techniques include acknowledging rather than suppressing our emotional responses to situations, and reevaluating events after they occur.[52] Another technique with potential is *venting*, or expressing negative emotions outwardly. Research shows that open expression of emotions can be helpful to the individual, as opposed to keeping them bottled up. Caution must be exercised, though, because venting touches other people.

As you might suspect, not everyone is equally good at regulating emotions. Individuals higher in the personality trait of neuroticism have more trouble with emotion regulation and often find their moods beyond their ability to control. Individuals with lower levels of self-esteem are less likely to try to improve their sad moods, perhaps because they are less likely than others to feel they deserve to be in a good mood.[53]

Alex, our city bus driver, finds that some days he is better able to regulate his emotions than others. The information in the above section "Sources of Emotions and Moods" may give some indication why this task can be more difficult under certain circumstances. Although emotion regulation techniques can help us cope with difficult workplace situations, research indicates that the effect varies.

For example, a recent study in Taiwan found that participants who worked for abusive supervisors reported emotional exhaustion and work withdrawal tendencies, but to different degrees according to the emotion regulation strategies they employed. This suggests that more research on the application of techniques needs to be done to help employees.[54]

Thus, while there is much promise in emotion regulation techniques, the best route to creating a positive workplace is to recruit positive-minded individuals and train leaders to manage their moods, job attitudes, and performance.[55] The best leaders manage emotions as much as they do tasks and activities.

Now that we have studied the role of emotions and moods in organizational behaviour, let's consider the opportunities for more specific applications that our understanding provides.

OB APPLICATIONS OF EMOTIONS AND MOODS

Our understanding of emotions and moods can impact the selection process, decision making, creativity, motivation, leadership, negotiation, customer service, job attitudes, deviant workplace behaviour, and safety.

Positive emotions can increase problem-solving skills and help us understand and analyze new information.

Selection

Research indicates that employers should consider EI in selecting employees, especially for jobs that demand a high degree of social interaction. More employers have started to use EI measures in their hiring processes and are finding high-scoring EI employees outperform low-scoring employees for recruiting and sales positions. It also makes sense for managers to select members who are predisposed to positive moods for teamwork, because positive moods transmit from team member to team member. One study of professional cricket teams, for instance, found players' happy moods affected the moods of their team members and positively influenced their performance.[56]

Decision Making

Moods and emotions have effects on decision making that managers should understand. Positive emotions and moods seem to help people make sound decisions. Positive emotions furthermore enhance problem-solving skills, so positive people find better solutions to problems.[57]

OB researchers continue to debate the role of negative emotions and moods in decision making. Although one major study suggested that depressed people reach more accurate judgments,[58] more recent evidence hints that they make poorer decisions. Why? Because depressed people are slower at processing information and tend to weigh all possible options rather than the most likely ones.[59] They search for the perfect solution, when there rarely is one.

Creativity

As we see throughout this text, one goal of leadership is to maximize employee productivity. Creativity is influenced by emotions and moods, but there are two schools of thought on the relationship. Much research suggests that people in good moods tend to be more creative than people in bad moods.[60] People in good moods produce more ideas and more options, and others think their ideas are original.[61] They are more flexible and open in their thinking, which may explain why they're more creative.[62] This research suggests that supervisors should try to keep employees happy, because doing so creates more good moods, which in turn leads people to be more creative.[63] Other researchers do not believe a positive mood enhances creativity. They argue that when people are in positive moods, they may relax ("If I'm in a good mood, things must be going okay, and I must not need to think of new ideas") and not engage in the critical thinking necessary for some forms of creativity.[64]

The research findings may not be as conflicting as they seem. Rather than looking at positive or negative affect, it's possible to conceptualize moods as active feelings like anger, fear, or elation, and contrast these with deactivating moods like sorrow, depression, or serenity. All the activating moods, whether positive *or* negative, seem to lead to more creativity, whereas deactivating moods lead to less.[65] This would suggest managers should try to increase the energy in the workplace rather than focus on enhancing positive moods.

Motivation

Several studies have highlighted the importance of moods and emotions on motivation. One study found that a group in a good mood was more motivated in a problem-solving task than a group in a neutral mood.[66] Another study found that giving people performance feedback—whether real or fake—influenced their mood, which then influenced their motivation.[67] One other study in Taiwan found that employees in a good mood were more helpful and felt better about themselves, which led to superior performance.

So a cycle can be created in which positive moods cause people to be more creative, which leads to positive feedback from those observing their work. This positive feedback further reinforces the positive mood, which may make people perform even better, and so on. Overall, the findings suggest a manager may enhance employee motivation—and performance—by encouraging good moods. That is exactly what was done at the Googleplex, the Google headquarters located in Mountain View, California. Workplace tools were deployed to reduce stress, improve mood, and foster happiness. Managers reported increases in creativity and intrinsic motivation as a result of these initiatives.

Leadership

Research indicates that in leadership, putting people in a good mood makes good sense. Leaders who focus on inspirational goals generate greater optimism and enthusiasm in employees, which leads to more positive social interactions with coworkers and customers.[68] A study with Taiwanese military participants further indicates that by sharing emotions, leaders can inspire positive emotions in their followers that lead to higher task performance.[69]

Research indicates that when leaders are in a good mood, group members are more positive; as a result, they cooperate better.[70] But what about when leaders are sad? A recent study found that leader displays of sadness increased the analytic performance of followers through emotional contagion, perhaps because followers attended more closely to the tasks at hand. This study also indicated that leaders are perceived as more effective when they share positive emotions, and followers are more creative in a positive emotional environment.[71]

Corporate executives, who set the tone for an organizational culture, know emotional content is critical for employees to buy into their vision of the company's future and accept change. When higher-ups offer new visions, especially with vague or distant goals, it is often difficult for employees to accept the changes they'll bring. By arousing emotions and linking them to an appealing vision, leaders increase the likelihood that managers and employees alike will accept change.[72]

Negotiation

Negotiation is more of an emotional process than we may care to admit, but have you considered the potential of using emotions and moods to enhance your negotiation skills? For example, several studies suggest that a negotiator who feigns anger has an advantage over her opponent. Why? Because when a negotiator shows anger, the opponent concludes the negotiator has conceded all she can and so he gives in.[73] However, anger should be used selectively in negotiation: angry negotiators who have less information or less power than their opponents have significantly worse outcomes.[74]

Like the use of any emotion, context matters. Displaying a negative emotion (such as anger) can be effective, but feeling bad about your performance appears to impair future negotiations. Individuals who do poorly in a negotiation experience negative emotions, develop negative perceptions of their counterparts, and are less willing to share information or be cooperative in future negotiations.[75]

Altogether, the best negotiators are probably the ones who remain emotionally detached. One study of people who had suffered damage to the emotional centres in their brains suggested that unemotional people may be the best negotiators, because they're not likely to overcorrect when faced with negative outcomes.[76]

Customer Service

Workers' emotional states influence customer service, which influences levels of repeat business and customer satisfaction.[77] This is primarily due to **emotional contagion**—the "catching" of emotions from others. When someone experiences positive emotions and laughs and smiles at you, you tend to respond positively. Of course, the opposite is true as well.

Studies indicate a matching effect between employee emotions and customer emotions.[78] In the employee-to-customer direction, research finds that customers who catch the positive emotions of employees shop longer. In the other direction, when an employee feels unfairly treated by a customer, it's harder for him to display the positive emotions his organization expects of him.[79] High-quality customer service makes demands on employees because it often puts them in a state of emotional dissonance, which can be deleterious to the employee and the organization. Managers can interrupt negative contagion by fostering positive moods.

Job Attitudes

There is good news and bad news about the relationship between moods and job attitudes. The good news is that it appears that a positive mood at work can spill over to your off-work hours, and a negative mood at work can be restored to a positive mood after a break. Several studies have shown people who had a good day at work tend to be in a better mood at home that evening, and vice versa.[80] Other research has found that although people do emotionally take their work home with them, by the next day the effect is usually gone.[81]

The bad news is that the moods of your household may interfere. As you might expect, one study found if one member of a couple was in a negative mood during the workday, the negative mood spilled over to the spouse at night.[82] Thus, the relationship between moods and job attitudes is reciprocal—how our workday goes colours our moods, but our moods also affect how we see our job.

Deviant Workplace Behaviours

Anyone who has spent much time in an organization realizes people sometimes behave in ways that violate established norms and threaten the organization, its members, or both. As we saw in Chapter 3, these actions are called *deviant workplace behaviours*.[83] Many can be traced to negative emotions.

Evidence suggests that people who feel negative emotions are more likely than others to engage in short-term deviant behaviour at work such as gossiping or searching the Internet.[84] Nevertheless, a recent study in Pakistan found that anger correlated with more aggressive counterproductive behaviours such as abuse against others and production deviance, while sadness did not. Neither anger nor sadness predicted workplace withdrawal, which suggests that managers need to take employee expressions of anger seriously because employees may stay with an organization and continue to act aggressively toward others.[85] Managers therefore need to stay connected with their employees to gauge emotions and their intensity.

Safety and Injury at Work

Research relating negative affectivity to increased injuries at work suggests employers might improve health and safety (and reduce costs) by ensuring workers aren't engaged in potentially dangerous activities when they're in a bad mood. Bad moods can contribute to injury at work in several ways.[86] Individuals in negative moods tend to be more anxious, which can make them less able to cope effectively with hazards. A person who is always fearful will be more pessimistic about the effectiveness of safety precautions, because she feels she'll just get hurt anyway, or she might panic or freeze up when confronted with a threatening situation. Negative moods also make people more distractible, and distractions can lead to careless behaviours.

SUMMARY

- Emotions and moods are similar in that both are affective in nature. But they're also different—moods are more general than emotions.
- Events impact emotions and moods. The time of day, stressful situations, blood sugar levels, and sleep patterns are some of the factors that influence emotions and moods.
- OB research on emotional labour, affective events theory, and emotional regulation helps us understand how people deal with emotions.
- Emotional intelligence, although controversial, is a competency that can be developed in anyone, helping them better understand their own emotions and the emotions of others.
- Emotions and moods have proven relevant for virtually every work outcome, with implications for effective managerial practices.

IMPLICATIONS FOR MANAGERS

- Recognize that emotions are a natural part of the workplace and good management does not mean creating an emotion-free environment.
- To foster effective decision making, creativity, and motivation in employees, model positive emotions and moods as much as is authentically possible.

- Provide positive feedback to increase the positivity of the workplace.
- In the service sector, encourage positive displays of emotion, which make customers feel more positive and thus improve customer service interactions and negotiations.
- Managers who understand the role of emotions and moods will significantly improve their ability to explain and predict their coworkers' and employees' behaviour.

BREAKOUT QUESTION FOR GROUP DISCUSSION

Imagine that you have a very sensitive subject to discuss with an employee who you supervise. For example, perhaps you need to correct poor performance or discuss a problem with their personal hygiene. Based on what we know about the various influences on emotions and moods, when would be the optimal time to arrange a meeting? What else could be done to lessen the potential for an extremely negative emotional response during your discussion?

PERSONAL INVENTORY ASSESSMENT

In the Personal Inventory Assessment found in MyManagementLab, take the assessment: Emotional Intelligence Assessment.

SELF-REFLECTION ACTIVITY

As we've seen, emotional intelligence is an important tool in every worker's toolkit. This is especially true for people in service-oriented jobs, managers, and supervisors. Take the Personal Inventory Assessment found in MyManagementLab to assess your own level of emotional intelligence. Many of us overestimate our own EI. Are you surprised by your score? Why or why not? Do you think your friends and family would agree with the score that you received? Why or why not? If nothing changes, would your current skill level be likely to positively or negatively impact your career?

There are several ways to improve your EI. Think about the people who you consider emotionally intelligent. What behaviours do they engage in? You may find that putting yourself in the role of the other person can help create more empathy. This process might involve asking them to explain their experience, using active listening techniques to carefully process their response, and generally being mindful of changes in mood or behaviour. If empathy is difficult for you, reading both fiction and nonfiction that allows you to see the world from another person's perspective can help develop your ability to be empathetic. Other ways to increase EI are educating yourself about body language and facial expression interpretation and using introspection and journalling to gain greater insight into your own emotions.

MINI CASE   EMOTIONAL LABOUR AT THE CALL CENTRE

After working a four-hour shift, Paul readied himself to leave his call centre station and go home. As usual, he was thoroughly exhausted. He worked as a customer service representative for an online flower retailer. Customers who had problems with their orders would call in for help. Common issues he had to deal with were missed deliveries, delivery of the wrong flowers or flowers in poor condition, and billing errors.

Today had been an especially stressful day. He'd had two particularly difficult customers and it had been almost impossible to come up with a solution that would satisfy either of them. In one case some flowers had been sent to the wrong funeral home. The daughter of the deceased was very distressed that their mother's funeral had to proceed without the blooms. The other customer, a man, had sent red roses to two different women—a surprisingly common occurrence. The cards, with their respective intimate messages, had been mixed up accidentally. That customer had yelled at Paul for "ruining his life" for almost five minutes before Paul could even get a word in to respond.

At the end of the day all he could do for either of them was offer a partial refund and a discount on their next purchase, which did not satisfy the customers at all and just led to more yelling and some name-calling before they hung up on him in frustration. Yes, it had definitely been a tough day.

When Paul got on the bus to go home, he noticed that there was one seat left but a young woman next to it had left her backpack there. Normally Paul was a polite person, but today he was in no mood for nonsense. "Can't you see the bus is full," he snapped at her, "have a bit of common courtesy." The woman blushed, apologized quickly, and moved the bag. Paul immediately felt even worse and was trying to decide how best to word an apology but he ran out of time. She got off on the next stop.

He sighed and wondered what was wrong with him. Lately he always seemed to be in a bad mood after work. The customers were rude, often he couldn't really solve their problems in the way they wanted, his supervisor only cared about how many calls he answered per hour, and since he was on the phone all the time and worked short shifts with no formal breaks he never really got to know his colleagues. The only good thing about the job was the paycheque. If he could find another job, he would quit, but until then he was stuck. How, he asked himself, can I make this job tolerable? And what can help me to manage these moods once I leave the office and head home?

Discussion Questions

1. If this situation does not change, what consequences might there be for Paul's well-being and work performance?

2. What might Paul do to help himself better deal with the emotional labour required for his job?

3. What might the employer do differently in this scenario to minimize the negative impact of emotional labour on their workers?

MINI CASE EMOTIONAL CONTAGION UNLEASHED

Paloma Dupries could not believe her eyes. "Are they serious?" she said out loud to nobody in particular. "This is ridiculous!"

She has just received a message from her union in response to a job sharing request she had made. She had been working as a nurse in a small hospital in New Brunswick for five months, fulfilling a paternity-leave contract. Now the new father, Victor Patel, had announced that, although he did want to return to his job, he also wanted to fully participate in raising his twin sons. Therefore he wished to return on a part-time basis, working only three days per week. Paloma has been thrilled to hear the news, because it meant she might be able to keep her job for the other two days a week. Since she had been planning to pursue a master's degree at the local university, a part-time job would be ideal. She discussed it with Victor and they both agreed it was a great solution.

Victor and Paloma went to their immediate manager with the proposal. The manager also thought it a great idea, but cautioned them that since this represented a nonstandard work arrangement the union would have to approve it. Despite these cautions, Victor and Paloma felt somewhat giddy. It was such a good solution for them both, they were excited about seeing an ideal lifestyle developing in which each could balance personal goals with their need for income. Then the response from the union came.

It stated that job sharing could only occur if both parties shared the job exactly equally, meaning each would work for 2.5 days a week. The union felt that any other arrangement would be disadvantageous to the person with the reduced work hours and they were unwilling to support that inequity.

"But that makes no sense," opined Victor, "as long as we both agree to the work split that should be all that matters." "I agree," said Paloma, "and I tried to explain that to them, but they won't listen to me. Is there any way we could just do the 2.5-day split?" "Unfortunately not," replied Victor. "My wife is an accountant and she has looked carefully at the numbers. We can only afford to do this if I can get three days a week. Losing that half-day tips us over into a financially nonviable situation." "How frustrating," commented Paloma, "because while I am in school, two days a week is all I could really handle anyway."

After further conversations with management and their union steward, the two workers realized the situation was futile and they abandoned their attempt at job sharing. Word got around, as it always does, and Paloma found that many sympathetic coworkers came over on her last day to express their regrets about her leaving. Victor, for his part, felt stressed out about returning full-time but felt he had little choice.

Six months later, Paloma ran into Victor at the local Tim Hortons. "How are things going at the hospital?" she asked curiously. "Pretty much business as usual," replied Victor, "I've been looking for other work, but no luck yet so I am still there. The oddest thing is happening though. Everyone is copping attitude with the union steward and he is probably going to get thrown out at the next election. He hasn't really done anything wrong. A few bad decisions were made, like the one about our job sharing proposal, but those were made by committees, not just him personally. Still, the negativity seems to have rubbed off on him; nobody likes him or wants him to represent them anymore. To be honest, I feel a little sorry for him." "Not me," said Paloma, "If you ask me he got what he deserved, committees or not!"

Discussion Questions

1. What emotional responses should the union have anticipated as a result of refusing this request? Could those responses have been better managed somehow?

2. What emotional responses could the union have anticipated as a result of granting this request? How might those responses have been leveraged to help drive positive workplace outcomes?

3. Discuss the role emotional contagion may have had in influencing perceptions about the union steward.

MyManagementLab

Study, practise, and explore real management situations with these helpful resources:
- **Interactive Lesson Presentations:** Work through interactive presentations and assessments to test your knowledge of management concepts.
- **PIA (Personal Inventory Assessments):** Enhance your ability to connect with key concepts through these engaging self-reflection assessments.
- **Study Plan:** Check your understanding of chapter concepts with self-study quizzes.
- **Simulations:** Practise decision making in simulated management environments.

PERSONAL INVENTORY ASSESSMENT

Chapter 5
Personality and Values

Leon Switzer/ZUMA Press, Inc./Alamy Stock Photo

LEARNING OBJECTIVES

After studying this chapter, you should be able to:

1. Describe personality, the way it is measured, and the factors that shape it.

2. Explain the Myers-Briggs Type Indicator (MBTI) personality framework and the Big Five model, and compare their relative strengths and weaknesses.

3. Identify the three traits of the Dark Triad, and describe the contrasting ideas of the approach–avoidance framework.

4. Discuss how the concepts of core self-evaluation (CSE), self-monitoring, and proactive personality contribute to the understanding of personality.

5. Assess how context (the specific situation) affects the degree to which personality predicts behaviour.

6. Contrast terminal and instrumental values.

7. Describe the differences between person–job fit and person–organization fit.

8. Evaluate how differences in value scores across Hofstede's five dimensions of national culture may impact behaviour.

We all have different personalities. In the first half of this chapter, we review the research on personality and its relationship to behaviour. People also differ in their values. In the latter half of the chapter, we look at how values shape many of our work-related behaviours, and how values tend to vary by national culture.

PERSONALITY

Why are some people quiet and passive, others loud and aggressive? Are certain personality types better adapted for certain jobs? Before we can answer these questions, we need to address a more basic one: What is personality?

What Is Personality?

When psychologists speak of personality, they don't mean a person has charm or is constantly smiling; they mean a dynamic concept of the growth and development of a person's whole psychological system. First we will define personality, and then discuss personality measurement methods and determinants.

Defining Personality   Personality is commonly defined as a persistent set of characteristics, qualities, and traits that taken together form a unique person.[1] For our purposes, you should think of **personality** as the sum total of the ways an individual reacts to and interacts with others.

Measuring Personality   The most important reason managers need to know how to measure personality is that research has shown personality tests are useful in hiring decisions and help managers forecast who is best for a job.[2] The most common means of measuring personality is through self-report surveys in which individuals evaluate themselves on a series of factors, such as "I worry a lot about the future." Though self-report measures work when well constructed, the respondent might lie or practice impression management to create a good impression. When people know their personality scores are going to be used for hiring decisions, they rate themselves as about half a standard deviation more conscientious and emotionally stable than if they are taking the test to learn more about themselves.[3] Another problem is accuracy; a candidate who is in a bad mood when taking the survey may have inaccurate scores.

Personality Determinants   An early debate in personality research centred on whether an individual's personality is the result of heredity or environment. Personality appears to be a result of both; however, research tends to support the importance of heredity over the environment.

Personality—the sum total of the ways an individual reacts to and interacts with others—is partly genetic in origin; yet, personality can be easily measured by various survey methods, including self-report surveys.

Heredity refers to factors determined at conception. Physical stature, facial features, gender, temperament, muscle composition and reflexes, energy level, and biological rhythms are generally considered to be either completely or substantially influenced by parentage—by your biological parents' genetic, physiological, and psychological makeup. The heredity approach argues that the ultimate explanation of an individual's personality is the molecular structure of the genes, located in the chromosomes.

Researchers in many different countries have studied thousands of sets of identical twins who were separated at birth and raised apart.[4] If heredity played little or no part in determining personality, you would expect to find few similarities between separated twins. Researchers have found, however, that genetics accounts for about 50 percent of the personality similarities between twins and more than 30 percent of shared occupational and leisure interests. In an unusually extreme example, one set of twins who were separated for 39 years and raised more than 70 kilometres apart were found to drive the same model and colour car. Although they had never met, they chain-smoked the same brand of cigarette, owned dogs with the same name, and regularly vacationed within three blocks of each other in a beach community 2,400 kilometres away.

Interestingly, twin studies have suggested parental behaviour doesn't add much to personality development. The personalities of identical twins raised in different households were far more similar to each other than to the personalities of siblings with whom the twins were raised. Ironically, the most important contribution our parents may make to our personalities is giving us their genes!

This is not to suggest that personality never changes. People's scores on dependability tend to increase over time, as when young adults start families and establish careers. However, strong individual differences in dependability remain; everyone tends to change by about the same amount, so their rank order stays roughly the same.[5] An analogy to intelligence may make this clearer. Children become smarter as they age, so nearly everyone is smarter at age 20 than at age 10. Still, if Sahkyo is smarter than Siwili at age 10, she is likely to be smarter than he is at age 20, too. Research has shown that personality is more changeable in adolescence and more stable among adults.[6]

Early work on personality tried to identify and label enduring characteristics that describe an individual's behaviour, including shy, aggressive, submissive, lazy, ambitious, loyal, and timid. When someone exhibits these characteristics in a large number of situations, we call them the **personality traits** of that person.[7] The more consistent the characteristic over time, and the more frequently it occurs in diverse situations, the more important that trait is in describing the individual.

Early efforts to identify and classify the primary traits that govern behaviour[8] often produced long lists that were difficult to generalize from and provided little practical guidance to organizational decision makers. Two exceptions are the Myers-Briggs Type Indicator and the Big Five Model, now the dominant frameworks for assessing an individual's personality traits. Let's discuss each of them in turn.

DOMINANT PERSONALITY FRAMEWORKS

Throughout history, people have sought to understand what makes individuals behave in myriad ways. Many of our behaviours stem from our personalities, so understanding the components of personality helps us predict behaviour. Important theoretical frameworks and assessment tools, discussed next, help us categorize and study the dimensions of personality.

The Myers-Briggs Type Indicator

The **Myers-Briggs Type Indicator (MBTI)** is the most widely used personality-assessment instrument in the world.[9] It is a 100-question personality test that asks people how they usually feel or act in situations. Respondents are classified as extraverted or introverted (E or I), sensing or intuitive (S or N), thinking or feeling (T or F), and judging or perceiving (J or P):

- *Extraverted (E) Versus Introverted (I).* Extraverted individuals are outgoing, sociable, and assertive. Introverts are quiet and shy.

- *Sensing (S) Versus Intuitive (N).* Sensing types are practical, prefer routine and order, and focus on details. Intuitives rely on unconscious processes and look at the "big picture."

- *Thinking (T) Versus Feeling (F).* Thinking types use reason and logic to handle problems. Feeling types rely on their personal values and emotions.

- *Judging (J) Versus Perceiving (P).* Judging types want control and prefer order and structure. Perceiving types are flexible and spontaneous.

These classifications describe personality types by identifying one trait from each of the four pairs. For example, Introverted/Intuitive/Thinking/Judging (INTJ) people are visionaries with original minds and great drive. They are skeptical, critical, independent, determined, and often stubborn. ENFJs are natural teachers and leaders. They are relational, motivational, intuitive, idealistic, ethical, and kind. ESTJs are organizers. They are realistic, logical, analytical, and decisive, perfect for business or mechanics. The ENTP type is innovative, individualistic, versatile, and attracted to entrepreneurial ideas. This person tends to be resourceful in solving challenging problems but may neglect routine assignments.

According to the Research Department at Psychometrics Canada, introverts account for 48.1 percent of the E/I responses in the English-speaking Canadian population. The three most common types are ISTJ (14.8 percent), ESTJ (11.4 percent), and ENFP (9.6 percent).[10]

The MBTI has been widely used by organizations, including Apple Computer, AT&T, Citigroup, GE, and 3M Co.; many hospitals and educational institutions; and even the Canadian. Armed Forces. It is used as a recruitment and selection tool, allowing companies to hire new employees who have personality traits that are associated with success on the job. It is also used as a career planning tool, allowing the employee and employer to work together to plan a career path that more likely to have good job–person fit since it is aligned with their personality. For example, a highly introverted person might choose to increase his or her technical skills rather than seeking promotion to a socially demanding management role. Some organizations use the MBTI to form project teams, reducing the likelihood of conflicts by assigning compatible personalities to work together. Finally, some use it to better understand and mediate existing interpersonal conflicts. The MBTI is especially useful for this purpose because it highlights differences in decision-making style that can cause persistent conflict. At the University of Saskatchewan, Dwayne Docken, career development coordinator with the university's Aboriginal Student Centre, recommends the test highly. He says, "[T]he MBTI assessment is helpful because it presents similar messages [as traditional Medicine Wheels], but in a language and context that can help to bridge the generation gap between students and Elders. Like the complementary and balanced elements of the Medicine Wheel, the MBTI type table represents aspects of personality and preference that are different but equal in value—and all vital to a truly successful balance, whether in school, work or life."[11]

The MBTI is taken by over 2.5 million people each year and 89 of the Fortune 100 companies use it.[12] Evidence is mixed about its validity as a measure of personality, however; most of the evidence is against it.[13] One problem is that the model forces a person into one type or another; that is, you're either introverted or extraverted. There is no in-between, though most people are both extraverted and introverted to some degree. Another problem is with the reliability of the measure. When people retake the assessment, they often receive different results. An additional problem is in the difficulty of interpretation. There are levels of importance for each of the MBTI facets, and separate meanings for certain combinations of facets, all of which require trained interpretation that can leave room for error. Finally, results from the MBTI tend to be unrelated to job performance. The MBTI can thus be a valuable tool for increasing self-awareness and providing career guidance, but managers should consider using the Big Five Personality Model, discussed next, as the personality selection test for job candidates instead.

The Big Five Personality Model

The MBTI may lack strong supporting evidence, but an impressive body of research supports the thesis of the **Big Five Model**—that five basic dimensions underlie all others and encompass most of the significant variation in human personality.[14] Test scores of the Big Five traits do a very good job of predicting how people behave in a variety of real-life situations.[15] These are the Big Five factors:

The Big Five personality traits are related to many OB criteria; each of the five traits has proven its usefulness to understanding individual behaviour in organizations.

- **Extraversion.** The **extraversion** dimension captures our comfort level with relationships. Extraverts tend to be gregarious, assertive, and sociable. Introverts tend to be reserved, timid, and quiet. This dimension also refers to preferred stimulation levels. Introverts tend to become overwhelmed when there are a lot of stimuli in the environment (such as a large, busy party), and they may seek a quiet place to recover from the excess sensory input, while extroverts are energized and excited by busy environments.

- **Agreeableness.** The **agreeableness** dimension refers to an individual's propensity to defer to others. Highly agreeable people are cooperative, warm, and trusting. People who score low on agreeableness are cold, disagreeable, and antagonistic.

- *Conscientiousness.* The **conscientiousness** dimension is a measure of reliability. A highly conscientious person is responsible, organized, dependable, and persistent. Those who score low on this dimension are easily distracted, disorganized, and unreliable.

- *Emotional stability.* The **emotional stability** dimension—often labelled by its converse, *neuroticism*—taps a person's ability to withstand stress. People with positive emotional stability tend to be calm, self-confident, and secure. Those with high negative scores tend to be nervous, anxious, depressed, and insecure.

- *Openness to experience.* The **openness to experience** dimension addresses range of interests and fascination with novelty. Open people are creative, curious, and artistically sensitive. Those at the other end of the category are conventional and find comfort in the familiar.

How Do the Big Five Traits Predict Behaviour at Work?

Research has found relationships between the Big Five personality dimensions and job performance.[16] As the authors of the most-cited review observed, "The preponderance of evidence shows that individuals who are dependable, reliable, careful, thorough, able to plan, organized, hardworking, persistent, and achievement-oriented tend to have higher job performance in most if not all occupations."[17] Employees who score higher in conscientiousness develop higher levels of job knowledge, probably because highly conscientious people learn more (a review of 138 studies revealed conscientiousness was related to GPA).[18] Higher levels of job knowledge contribute to higher levels of job performance. There can be "too much of a good thing," however, as extremely conscientious individuals typically do not perform better than those who are simply above average in conscientiousness.[19]

Conscientiousness is important to organizational success. A study of the personality scores of 313 CEO candidates in private equity companies (of whom 225 were hired; their company's performance was later correlated with their personality scores) found conscientiousness—in the form of persistence, attention to detail, and setting of high standards—was more important than other traits.

Interestingly, conscientious people live longer; they take better care of themselves and engage in fewer risky behaviours like smoking, drinking and drugs, and unsafe sexual or driving behaviours.[20] They don't adapt as well to changing contexts, however. They are generally performance-oriented and may have more trouble learning complex skills early in the training process, because their focus is on performing well rather than on learning. Finally, they are often less creative than less conscientious people, especially artistically.[21]

Although conscientiousness is most consistently related to job performance, the other Big Five traits are also related to aspects of performance and have other implications for work and for life. Let's look at them one at a time. Exhibit 5-1 summarizes these traits.

Of the Big Five traits, emotional stability is most strongly related to life satisfaction, job satisfaction, and low stress levels. High scorers are more likely to be positive and optimistic and experience fewer negative emotions; they are generally happier than low scorers. Low scorers are hypervigilant (looking for problems or impending signs of danger) and are vulnerable to the physical and psychological effects of stress.

Extraverts tend to be happier in their jobs and in their lives. They experience more positive emotions than do introverts, and they more freely express these feelings. Extraverts also tend to perform better in jobs with significant interpersonal interaction. They usually have more social skills and friends. Finally, extraversion is a relatively strong predictor of leadership emergence in groups; extraverts are more socially dominant, "take charge" people and usually more assertive than introverts.[22] Extraverts are more impulsive than introverts; they are more likely to be absent from work and engage in risky behaviours such as

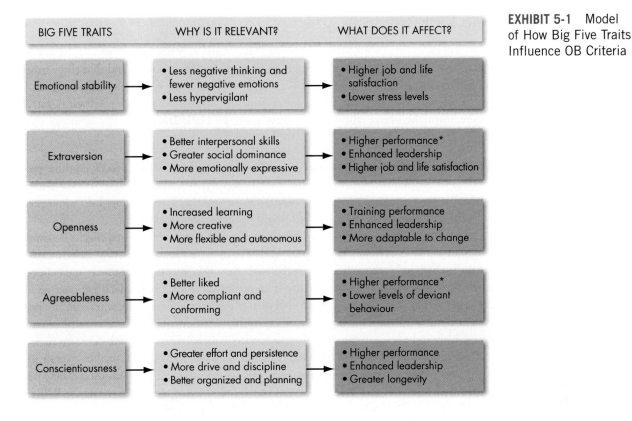

BIG FIVE TRAITS	WHY IS IT RELEVANT?	WHAT DOES IT AFFECT?
Emotional stability	• Less negative thinking and fewer negative emotions • Less hypervigilant	• Higher job and life satisfaction • Lower stress levels
Extraversion	• Better interpersonal skills • Greater social dominance • More emotionally expressive	• Higher performance* • Enhanced leadership • Higher job and life satisfaction
Openness	• Increased learning • More creative • More flexible and autonomous	• Training performance • Enhanced leadership • More adaptable to change
Agreeableness	• Better liked • More compliant and conforming	• Higher performance* • Lower levels of deviant behaviour
Conscientiousness	• Greater effort and persistence • More drive and discipline • Better organized and planning	• Higher performance • Enhanced leadership • Greater longevity

EXHIBIT 5-1 Model of How Big Five Traits Influence OB Criteria

unprotected sex, drinking, and other sensation-seeking acts.[23] One study also found extraverts were more likely than introverts to lie during job interviews.[24]

High scorers for openness to experience are more creative in science and art than low scorers. Because creativity is important to leadership, open people are more likely to be effective leaders—and more comfortable with ambiguity. They cope better with organizational change and are more adaptable in varying contexts. As for the downside, evidence suggests they are susceptible to workplace accidents.[25]

You might expect agreeable people to be happier than disagreeable people. They are, but only slightly. When people choose romantic partners, friends, or organizational team members, agreeable individuals are usually first choice. Agreeable individuals are better liked than disagreeable people; they tend to do better in interpersonally oriented jobs such as customer service. Agreeable people also are more compliant and rule abiding, less likely to get into accidents, and more satisfied in their jobs. They contribute to organizational performance by engaging in citizenship behaviour[26] and are less likely to engage in organizational deviance. Agreeableness, however, is associated with lower levels of career success (especially earnings), perhaps because agreeable people are less willing to promote their self-interests.

The Big Five personality factors appear in almost all cross-cultural studies,[27] including China, Israel, Germany, Japan, Spain, Nigeria, Norway, Pakistan, and the United States. Generally, the findings corroborate what has been found in U.S. research: Of the Big Five traits, conscientiousness is the best predictor of job performance.

OTHER PERSONALITY FRAMEWORKS

Research indicates the Big Five traits have the most verifiable linkages to important organizational outcomes, but they are neither the only traits a person exhibits nor the only ones with organizational behaviour implications. Let's discuss some other traits, known collectively as the Dark Triad, and the approach–avoidance framework, which describes personality traits in terms of motivation.

The Dark Triad

With the exception of neuroticism, the Big Five traits are what we call socially desirable, meaning we might be glad to score high on them. Researchers have found that three other socially *undesirable* traits, which we all have in varying degrees, are relevant to organizational behaviour: Machiavellianism, narcissism, and psychopathy. Owing to their negative nature, researchers have labelled these three traits the **Dark Triad**—though, of course, they do not always occur together.[28]

Machiavellianism　Hao is a young bank manager in Shanghai. He's received three promotions in the past four years and makes no apologies for the aggressive tactics he's used to propel his career upward. "My name means clever, and that's what I am—I do whatever I have to do to get ahead," he says. Hao would be termed Machiavellian.

The personality characteristic of **Machiavellianism** (often abbreviated *Mach*) is named after Niccolo Machiavelli, who wrote in the 16th century on how to gain and use power. An individual high in Machiavellianism is pragmatic, maintains emotional distance, and believes ends can justify means. "If it works, use it" is consistent with a high-Mach perspective. A considerable amount of research has found high Machs manipulate more, win more, are persuaded less, and persuade others more than do low Machs.[29] They are more likely to act aggressively and engage in other counterproductive work behaviours as well. A recent review of the literature revealed that Machiavellianism does not significantly predict overall job performance.[30] High-Mach employees, by manipulating others to their advantage, may win in the short term, but they lose those gains in the long term because they are not well liked.

The effects of Machiavellianism depend somewhat on the context. The reason, in part, is that individuals' personalities affect the situations they choose. One study showed that high-Mach job seekers were less positively affected by knowing an organization engaged in a high level of corporate social responsibility (CSR).[31] Another study found that Machs' ethical leadership behaviours were less likely to translate into followers' work engagement because followers "see through" these behaviours and realize it is a case of surface acting.[32]

Narcissism　Sabrina likes to be the centre of attention. She often looks at herself in the mirror, has extravagant dreams, and considers herself a person of many talents. Sabrina is a narcissist. The trait is named for the Greek myth of Narcissus, a youth so vain and proud he fell in love with his own image. In psychology, **narcissism** describes a person who has a grandiose sense of self-importance, requires excessive admiration, has a sense of entitlement, and is arrogant. Evidence suggests narcissists are more charismatic than others.[33] Both leaders and managers tend to score higher on narcissism, suggesting that a certain self-centeredness is needed to succeed. Some evidence suggests that narcissists are more adaptable and make better business decisions than others when the decision is complex.[34] One study of Norwegian bank employees found that those scoring high on narcissism enjoyed their work more.[35]

Some people believe that camera phones and social media encourage narcissism. Among people who believe that, the "selfies" trend is considered a sign of widespread, excessive, narcissism.

While narcissism seems to have little relationship with overall job performance, it is fairly strongly related to increased counterproductive work behaviours and is linked to other negative outcomes. A study found that while narcissists thought they were *better* leaders than their colleagues, their supervisors rated them as *worse*. In highly ethical contexts, narcissistic leaders are likely to be perceived as ineffective and unethical.[36] A study of Swiss Air Force officers found that narcissists were particularly likely to be irritated by feeling under-benefited, meaning that when narcissists don't get what they want, they are more stressed by that than others.[37]

Pearson Education

Some people believe that camera phones and social media encourage narcissism. Among people who believe that, the "selfies" trend is considered a sign of widespread, excessive, narcissism.

Special research attention has been paid to the narcissism of CEOs. An executive described Oracle's CEO Larry Ellison as follows: "The difference between God and Larry is that God does not believe he is Larry."[38] A study of narcissistic CEOs revealed that they make more acquisitions, pay higher premiums for those acquisitions, respond less clearly to objective measures of performance, and respond to media praise by making even more acquisitions.[39] Research using data compiled over 100 years has shown that narcissistic CEOs of baseball organizations generate higher levels of manager turnover, although members of external organizations see them as more influential.[40]

Narcissism and its effects are not confined to CEOs or celebrities. Like the effects of Machiavellianism, those of narcissism vary by context, but are represented in all areas of life. For example, narcissists are more likely to post self-promoting material on their Facebook pages.[41]

Psychopathy   Psychopathy is part of the Dark Triad, but in organizational behaviour it does not connote insanity. In the OB context, **psychopathy** is defined as a lack of concern for others, and a lack of guilt or remorse when their actions cause harm.[42] Measures of psychopathy attempt to assess the person's motivation to comply with social norms; willingness to use deceit to obtain desired ends and the effectiveness of those efforts; impulsivity; and disregard, that is, lack of empathic concern, for others.

The literature is not consistent about whether psychopathy or other aberrant personality traits are important to work behaviour. One review found little correlation between measures of psychopathy and job performance or counterproductive work behaviours. A recent study found that antisocial personality, which is closely related to psychopathy, was positively related to advancement in the organization but unrelated to other aspects of career success and effectiveness.[43] Still other research suggests that psychopathy is related to the use of hard influence tactics (threats, manipulation) and bullying work behaviour (physical or verbal threatening).[44] The cunning displayed by people who score high on psychopathy may help them gain power in an organization, but keep them from using that power toward healthy ends for themselves or their organizations.

Given the relative newness of research on the Dark Triad, using psychopathology scores for employment decisions may carry more risks for now than rewards. Organizations wishing to assess psychopathy or other aberrant traits need to exercise caution. Human rights legislation prohibits discrimination against individuals with "a physical or mental impairment." It is unclear whether psychiatric diagnoses that relate to personality disorders would qualify. Other psychiatric conditions such as schizophrenia or bipolar disorder clearly fall into the protected disability category, but the legal status of biologically based personality disorders are unclear at best. This does not mean organizations must hire every person who applies, or that they cannot consider mental makeup in hiring decisions. However, if they do, federal human rights and provincial employment rights legislation should be used as a guideline on when it is permissible to consider this factor. Avoidance is permitted when the mental condition prevents or severely restricts effective performance, and when it cannot be reasonably accommodated without creating undue hardship.[45] As the name implies, the Dark Triad represents three traits that can present significant downsides for individuals and organizations. It would be easy to make quick conclusions on them as managers, but it is important to keep discussions on personality in perspective. The degrees of each trait—the Big Five, the Dark Triad, and other traits—in a person, and the combination of the traits, matter a great deal to organizational outcomes. So does the person's approach–avoidance motivation, which we discuss next.

Approach–Avoidance

The MBTI, the Big Five, and the Dark Triad are not the only theoretical frameworks for personality. Recently, the **approach–avoidance framework** has cast personality traits as motivations. Approach and avoidance motivation represent the degree to which we react to stimuli whereby approach motivation is our attraction to positive stimuli, and avoidance motivation is our aversion to negative stimuli.

The approach–avoidance framework organizes traits and may help explain how they predict work behaviour. One study showed, for instance, that approach and avoidance motivation can help explain how core self-evaluations affect job satisfaction.[46] The framework also addresses our multiple motives when we act. For example, competitive pressures tend to invoke both approach motivation (people work harder to win) and avoidance motivation (people are distracted and demotivated by fear of losing). The way an individual performs depends on which of these motivations dominates.[47] Another study found that when newcomers joined IT companies in India, they received support from their supervisor (who helped the newcomer by doing a special favour), but also verbal aggression (the supervisor made fun of new ideas). The support they received provoked approach behaviour (the newcomer asked the supervisor for feedback on performance). The aggression provoked avoidance behaviour (the newcomer avoided speaking with the supervisor unless absolutely necessary). The net effect on performance depended on which of these dominated.[48]

While the approach–avoidance framework has provided some important insights into behaviour in organizations, there are several unresolved issues. First, is the framework simply a way of categorizing positive and negative traits, such as conscientiousness and neuroticism? Second, what traits fit into the framework? Nearly all the traits reviewed in this text do—including the Big Five, the Dark Triad, and others—yet these traits are quite different. Do we gain enough from aggregating them to make up for possibly missing other insights into behaviour that are unique to each? Further research and evaluation are needed. For now, it is helpful to consider our approach–avoidance tendencies while we explore some other relevant personality traits in the next section.

OTHER PERSONALITY TRAITS RELEVANT TO OB

As we've discussed, studies of the Big Five traits, the Dark Triad, and approach–avoidance tendencies have much to offer to the field of OB. Now we'll look at other attributes that are powerful predictors of behaviour in organizations: core self-evaluations, self-monitoring, and proactive personality.

Core Self-Evaluations

People who have positive a **core self-evaluation (CSE)** like themselves and see themselves as effective, capable, and in control of their environment. Those with negative CSE tend to dislike themselves, question their capabilities, and view themselves as powerless over their environment.[49] We discussed in Chapter 3 that core self-evaluations relate to job satisfaction, because people positive on this trait see more challenge in their jobs and actually attain more complex jobs.

People with positive CSE perform better than others because they set more ambitious goals, are more committed to their goals, and persist longer in attempting to reach them. One study of life insurance agents found core self-evaluations were critical predictors of performance. In fact, this study showed the majority of successful salespersons did have positive CSE.[50] Ninety percent of life insurance sales calls end in rejection, so an agent has to believe in herself to persist. People who have high CSE provide better customer service, are more popular coworkers, and have careers that begin on better footing and ascend more rapidly over time.[51] They perform especially well if they feel their work provides meaning and is helpful to others.[52]

What happens when someone thinks he is capable but is actually incompetent? One study found that many Fortune 500 CEOs are overconfident, and their perceived infallibility often causes them to make bad decisions.[53] These CEOs may be *over*confident and have high CSE, but people with lower CSE may sell themselves short and be less happy and effective than they might be because of it. If people decide they can't do something, they might not try, reinforcing their self-doubt.

Self-Monitoring

Zoe is always in trouble at work. Although she's competent, hardworking, and productive, she is rated no better than average in performance reviews, and she seems to have made a career of irritating her bosses. Zoe's problem is that she's politically inept. She's unable to adjust her behaviour to fit changing situations. As she said, "I'm true to myself. I don't remake myself to please others." In psychological terms, Zoe is a low *self-monitor*.

Self-monitoring describes an individual's ability to adjust her behaviour to external, situational factors.[54] High self-monitors show considerable adaptability in adjusting their behaviour to external situational factors. They are highly sensitive to external cues and can behave differently in varying situations, sometimes presenting striking contradictions between their public persona and their private self. Low self-monitors like Zoe can't disguise themselves in that way. They tend to display their true dispositions and attitudes in every situation; hence, there is high behavioural consistency between who they are and what they do.

Evidence indicates high self-monitors pay closer attention to the behaviour of others and are more capable of conforming than are low self-monitors.[55] High self-monitors also receive better performance ratings, are more likely to emerge as leaders, and show less commitment to their organizations.[56] In addition, high self-monitor managers tend to be more mobile in their careers, receive more promotions (both internal and cross-organizational), and be more likely to occupy central positions in organizations.[57]

Proactive Personality

Did you ever notice that some people actively take the initiative to improve their current circumstances or create new ones? These are proactive personalities.[58] Those with a **proactive personality** identify opportunities, show initiative, take action, and persevere until meaningful change occurs, compared to others who passively react to situations. Proactive individuals have many desirable behaviours that organizations covet. They also have higher levels of job performance and career success.[59]

Proactive personality may be important for work teams. One study of 95 research and development teams in 33 Chinese companies revealed that teams with high-average levels of proactive personality were more innovative.[60] Like other traits, proactive personality is affected by context. One study of bank branch teams in China found that if a team's leader was not proactive, the potential benefits of the team's proactivity will lie dormant or, worse, be suppressed by the leader.[61]

A recent study of 231 Flemish unemployed individuals found that proactive individuals abandoned their job searches sooner. It may be that proactivity includes knowing when to step back and reconsider alternatives in the face of failure.[62]

In short, while proactive personality may be important to individual and team performance, like all traits it may have downsides, and its effectiveness may depend on the context. This brings us to the study of context and personality. Do you think personality changes in various situations? Let's explore this possibility.

PERSONALITY AND SITUATIONS

Earlier we discussed how research shows that heredity is more important than environment in developing our personalities. The environment is not irrelevant, though. Some personality traits like the Big Five tend to be effective in almost any environment or situation. For example, research indicates that conscientiousness is helpful in the performance of most jobs, and extraversion is related to emergence as a leader in most situations.

Increasingly, we are learning that the effect of particular traits on organizational behaviour depends on the situation. Two theoretical frameworks, situation strength and trait activation, help explain how this works.

Situation Strength Theory

Imagine you are in a meeting with your department. How likely are you to walk out in the middle of the meeting, shout at someone, turn your back on the group, or fall asleep? It's probably highly unlikely. Now imagine working from home. You might work in your pajamas, listen to loud music, or take a catnap.

Situation strength theory proposes that the way personality translates into behaviour depends on the strength of the situation. By *situation strength*, we mean the degree to which norms, cues, or standards dictate appropriate behaviour. Strong situations pressure us to exhibit the right behaviour, clearly show us what that behaviour is, and discourage the wrong behaviour. In weak situations, conversely, "anything goes," and thus we are freer to express our personality in our behaviours. Thus, research suggests that personality traits better predict behaviour in weak situations than in strong ones. Swearing is a simple example of this theory in action. Aspects of personality including attention seeking, conservatism, and risk tolerance will influence the degree to which an individual tends to swear. Their behaviour, however, will also be constrained by the situation such that they will be more likely to swear when casually hanging around with friends and less likely to when in a classroom or in a meeting with their boss.

Researchers have analyzed situation strength in organizations in terms of four elements.[63]

1. **Clarity**, or the degree to which cues about work duties and responsibilities are available and clear. Jobs high in clarity produce strong situations because individuals can readily determine what to do. For example an actor or cameraman's duties are clear and unambiguous, while a movie producer's role is less well defined and may include a range of activities from simply providing money to making casting and editing choices.
2. **Consistency**, or the extent to which cues regarding work duties and responsibilities are compatible with one another. Jobs with high consistency represent strong situations

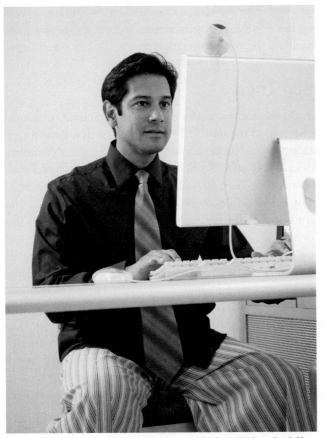
RubberBall/Alamy Stock Photo

The situation we find ourselves in will encourage, or discourage, displaying certain personality traits and other characteristics, at least for those able to self-monitor.

because all the cues point toward the same desired behaviour. The job of manager often lacks consistency due to incompatible goals such as maximizing employee well-being while reducing staff and associated costs.

3. **Constraints**, or the extent to which individuals' freedom to decide or act is limited by forces outside their control. Jobs with many constraints represent strong situations because an individual has limited discretion. Accountants, for example, are constrained by international accounting regulations, while sales representatives are free to use a wide range of strategies, tactics, and techniques.

4. **Consequences**, or the degree to which decisions or actions have important implications for the organization or its members, clients, supplies, and so on. Jobs with important consequences represent strong situations because the environment is probably heavily structured to guard against mistakes. A surgeon's job, for example, has higher consequences than a foreign-language teacher's.

Some researchers have speculated that organizations are, by definition, strong situations because they impose rules, norms, and standards that govern behaviour. These constraints are usually appropriate. For example, we would not want an employee to feel free to engage in sexual harassment, to follow questionable accounting procedures, or to come to work only when the mood strikes. But that does not mean it is always desirable for organizations to create strong situations for their employees. First, jobs with myriad rules and tightly controlled processes can be dull or demotivating. Most of us prefer having some freedom to decide how to do our work. Second, people do differ, so what works well for one person might work poorly for another. Third, strong situations might suppress the creativity, initiative, and discretion prized by some cultures. One recent study, for example, found that in weak organizational situations, employees were more likely to behave proactively in accordance with their values.[64] Finally, work is increasingly complex and interrelated globally.

Creating strong rules to govern complex, interrelated, and culturally diverse systems might be not only difficult but unwise. Managers need to recognize the role of situation strength in the workplace and find the appropriate balance.

Trait Activation Theory

Another important theoretical framework toward understanding situational activators for personality is **trait activation theory (TAT)**. TAT predicts that some situations, events, or interventions "activate" a trait more than others. For example, a commission-based compensation plan would likely activate individual differences in extraversion because extraversion is more reward-sensitive, than, say, openness to new experiences. Conversely, the performance level of marketers developing new online advertising techniques would be more likely to be correlated with their openness to new experiences than their extraversion scores.

A recent study applying TAT found that individual differences in the tendency to behave prosocially mattered more when coworkers were not supportive. In other words, in a supportive environment, everyone behaves prosocially, but in an environment that is not so nice, whether an individual has the personality to behave prosocially makes a major difference.[65]

Together, situation strength and trait activation theories show that the debate over nature versus nurture might best be framed as nature *and* nurture. Not only does each affect behaviour, but they interact with one another. Put another way, personality affects work behaviour and the situation affects work behaviour, but when the situation is right, the power of personality to predict behaviour is even higher.

Having discussed personality traits—the enduring characteristics that describe a person's behaviour—we now turn to values. Values are often very specific and describe belief systems rather than behavioural tendencies. Some beliefs or values say little about a person's personality, and we don't always act consistently with our values.

VALUES

Is assisted suicide right or wrong? Is a desire for power good or bad? The answers to these questions are value-laden.

Values represent basic convictions that "a specific mode of conduct or end-state of existence is personally or socially preferable to an opposite or converse mode of conduct or end-state of existence."[66] Values contain a judgmental element because they carry an individual's ideas about what is right, good, or desirable. We all have a hierarchy according to the relative importance we assign to values such as freedom, pleasure, self-respect, honesty, obedience, and equality.

Values tend to be relatively stable and enduring.[67] Many of the values we hold are established in our early years—by parents, teachers, friends, and others. As children, we are told certain behaviours or outcomes are *always* desirable or *always* undesirable, with few grey areas. You were never taught to be just a little bit honest or a little bit respectful toward elders, for example. It is this absolute, black-or-white characteristic of values that ensures their stability and endurance. (That does not imply that we always act on our values in an absolute manner. We may choose to lie, for example, but we are aware that we are doing something wrong when we do it and most people will feel some level of guilt or anxiety about compromising their values.) If we question our values, they may change, but more often they are reinforced. There is also evidence linking personality to values.[68] Open people, for example, may be more politically liberal, whereas conscientious people may place a greater value on rules ensuring safe or ethical conduct. To explore the topic further, we will discuss the importance and organization of values next.

The Importance and Organization of Values

Values lay the foundation for our understanding of people's attitudes and motivation, and they influence our perceptions. We enter an organization with preconceived notions of what "ought" and "ought not" to be. These notions are not value-free; on the contrary, they contain our interpretations of right and wrong and our preference for certain behaviours or outcomes over others. While values can sometimes augment decision making, at times they can also cloud objectivity and rationality.[69] Regardless of whether they clarify or bias our judgment, our values do influence our attitudes and behaviours at work.

Suppose you enter an organization with the view that allocating pay on the basis of performance is right, while allocating pay on the basis of seniority is wrong. How will you react if you find the organization you've just joined rewards seniority and not performance? You're likely to be disappointed—this can lead to job dissatisfaction and a decision not to exert a high level of effort because "It's probably not going to lead to more money anyway." Would your attitudes and behaviour be different if your values aligned with the organization's pay policies? Most likely.

Terminal Versus Instrumental Values

How can we organize values? One researcher—Milton Rokeach—argued that we can separate values into two categories. One set, called **terminal values**, refers to desirable end-states. These are the goals a person would like to achieve during his lifetime. The other set, called **instrumental values**, refers to preferable modes of behaviour, or means of achieving the terminal values. Some examples of terminal values are prosperity and economic success, freedom, health and well-being, world peace, and meaning in life. Examples of instrumental values are autonomy and self-reliance, personal discipline, kindness, and goal-orientation. Each of us places value on both the ends (terminal values) and the means (instrumental values). A balance between the two is important, as well as an understanding of how to strike this balance. Which terminal and instrumental values are especially key vary by the person.

So far, we've discussed personality and values separately, including some organizational implications for each. As you can see, finding a fit between an individual person and an optimal work situation is complex. A few theories we discuss in the next section help link an individual's personality and values to jobs and organizations.

LINKING AN INDIVIDUAL'S PERSONALITY AND VALUES TO THE WORKPLACE

Thirty years ago, organizations were concerned only with personality because their primary focus was to match individuals to specific jobs. That concern has expanded to include how well the individual's personality *and* values match the organization. Why? Because managers today are less interested in an applicant's ability to perform a *specific* job than with the applicant's *flexibility* to meet changing situations and commitment to the organization.

We'll now discuss person–job fit and person–organization fit in more detail.

Person–Job Fit

The effort to match job requirements with personality characteristics is best articulated in John Holland's **personality–job fit theory**.[70] Holland presents six personality types and proposes that satisfaction and the propensity to leave a position depend on how well individuals match their personalities to a job. Exhibit 5-2 describes the six types, their personality characteristics, and examples of the congruent occupations for each.

Type	Personality Characteristics	Congruent Occupations
Realistic: Prefers physical activities that require skill, strength, and coordination.	Shy, genuine, persistent, stable, conforming, practical	Mechanic, drill press operator, assembly line worker, farmer
Investigative: Prefers activities that involve thinking, organizing, and understanding.	Analytical, original, curious, independent	Biologist, economist, mathematician, news reporter
Social: Prefers activities that involve helping and developing others.	Sociable, friendly, cooperative, understanding	Social worker, teacher, counselor, clinical psychologist
Conventional: Prefers rule-regulated, orderly, and unambiguous activities.	Conforming, efficient, practical, unimaginative, inflexible	Accountant, corporate manager, bank teller, file clerk
Enterprising: Prefers verbal activities in which there are opportunities to influence others and attain power.	Self-confident, ambitious, energetic, domineering	Lawyer, real estate agent, public relations specialist, small business manager
Artistic: Prefers ambiguous and unsystematic activities that allow creative expression.	Imaginative, disorderly, idealistic, emotional, impractical	Painter, musician, writer, interior decorator

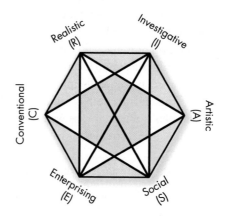

EXHIBIT 5-3 Relationships Among Occupational Personality Types

Source: Reprinted by special permission of the publisher, Psychological Assessment Resources, Inc., from *Making Vocational Choices,* copyright 1973, 1985, 1992 by Psychological Assessment Resources, Inc. All rights reserved.

Holland developed the Vocational Preference Inventory questionnaire, which contains 160 occupational titles. Respondents indicate which they like or dislike, and their answers form personality profiles. Research supports the resulting hexagonal diagram shown in Exhibit 5-3.[71] The closer two fields or orientations are in the hexagon, the more compatible they are. Adjacent categories are quite similar, whereas diagonally opposite ones are highly dissimilar.

What does all this mean? Personality–job fit theory argues that satisfaction is highest and turnover lowest when personality and occupation are in agreement. A realistic person in a realistic job is in a more congruent situation than a realistic person in an investigative job. A realistic person in a social job is in the most incongruent situation possible. The key point of this model is that people in jobs congruent with their personality should be more satisfied and less likely to voluntarily resign than people in incongruent jobs.

Person–Organization Fit

We've noted that researchers have looked at matching people to organizations and jobs. If an organization faces a dynamic and changing environment and needs employees able to readily change tasks and move easily between teams, it's more important that employees' personalities fit with the overall organization's culture than with the characteristics of any specific job.

The *person–organization fit* theory essentially argues that people are attracted to and selected by organizations that match their values, and they leave organizations that are not compatible with their personalities.[72] Using the Big Five terminology, for instance, we could expect that people high on extraversion fit well with aggressive and team-oriented cultures, people high on agreeableness match up better with a supportive organizational climate than one focused on aggressiveness, and people high on openness to experience fit better in organizations that emphasize innovation rather than standardization.[73] Following these guidelines at the time of hiring should identify new employees who fit better with the organization's culture, which should, in turn, result in higher employee satisfaction and reduced turnover. Research on person–organization fit has also looked at whether people's values match the organization's culture. This match predicts job satisfaction, commitment to the organization, and low turnover.[74]

Are person–job fit and person–organization fit more applicable in some countries than others? Apparently yes. Research indicated that person–job fit was a strong predictor of lower turnover in the United States, but a combination of person–organization fit and other factors strongly predicted lower turnover in India.[75] These findings may be generalizable for individualistic countries like the United States, and collectivistic countries like India, but more research is needed to understand the exact relationship.

INTERNATIONAL VALUES

Unlike personality, which as we have seen is largely genetically determined, values are learned from our environments. Values are also shared between people and passed down from one generation to the next. For these reasons, different value systems have developed over time in each national culture. As researchers have sought to understand the national value system differences, two important frameworks that have emerged are from Geert Hofstede and the GLOBE studies.

Values do appear to vary across cultures, meaning that, on average, people's values in one nation tend to differ from those in another; however, there is substantial variability in values within a culture.

Hofstede's Framework

One of the most widely referenced approaches for analyzing variations among cultures was done in the late 1970s by Geert Hofstede.[76] Hofstede surveyed more than 116,000 IBM employees in 40 countries about their work-related values and found that managers and employees vary on five value dimensions of national culture:

- *Power distance.* **Power distance** describes the degree to which people in a country accept that power in institutions and organizations is distributed unequally. A high rating on power distance means that large inequalities of power and wealth exist and are tolerated in the culture, as in a class or caste system that discourages upward mobility. A low power distance rating characterizes societies that stress equality and opportunity.

- *Individualism versus collectivism.* **Individualism** is the degree to which people prefer to act as individuals rather than as members of groups and believe in individual rights above all else. **Collectivism** emphasizes a tight social framework in which people expect others in groups of which they are a part to look after them and protect them.

- **Masculinity versus femininity.** Hofstede's construct of **masculinity** is the degree to which the culture favours stereotypically masculine values such as achievement, power, and control, as opposed to stereotypically feminine values such as social harmony. A high masculinity rating indicates the culture has separate roles for each gender and endorses competitive, assertive behaviours, particularly among men. A high **femininity** rating means the culture sees little differentiation between gender roles and endorses communal, nurturing behaviours.

- **Uncertainty avoidance.** The degree to which people in a country prefer structured over unstructured situations defines their **uncertainty avoidance**. In cultures that score high on uncertainty avoidance, people have an increased level of anxiety about uncertainty and ambiguity and use laws and controls to reduce uncertainty. People in cultures low on uncertainty avoidance are more accepting of ambiguity, are less rule-oriented, take more risks, and more readily accept change.

- **Long-term versus short-term orientation.** This newer addition to Hofstede's typology measures a society's devotion to traditional values. People in a culture with **long-term orientation** look to the future and value thrift, persistence, and tradition. In a **short-term orientation**, people value the here and now; they accept change more readily and don't see commitments as impediments to change.

How do different countries score on Hofstede's dimensions? The variation is immense. For example, power distance is higher in Malaysia than in any other country, and lowest in Austria. The United States is the most individualistic nation of all (closely followed by Australia and Great Britain). Guatemala is the most collectivistic nation. The country with the highest masculinity rank by far is Japan, and the country with the highest femininity rank is Sweden. Greece scores the highest in uncertainty avoidance, while Singapore scores the lowest. Hong Kong has one of the longest-term orientations; Pakistan has the shortest-term orientation. To see the full value profiles of some of Canada's key trading partners and the nations that provide large numbers of immigrants to Canada refer to Exhibit 5-4. Profiles for other nations are available online.

English-speaking Canada has a profile similar to many other wealthy Commonwealth nations, including Australia, Great Britain, and New Zealand. Anglophone Canadians score high in individualism and relatively high in masculinity, indicating a society focused on personal achievement, material wealth, competition, and prestige. Anglophone Canadians tend to score in the lower middle range in uncertainty avoidance and the lower end in power distance, indicating an equity-focused society willing to take responsible risks. Francophone Canadians have a similar profile, with some subtle differences. French-Canadians score higher in power distance and lower in individualism; As a result they tend to be more formal and hierarchical. They score lower in masculinity and higher in uncertainty avoidance, indicating that Francophones as a group tend to be more relationship-focused, emotionally expressive, and risk-averse than Anglophone Canadians. Hofstede did not collect data from First Nations peoples, so their cultural value profile is not included here. Some insights into their cultural values appear later in this chapter.

Hofstede's culture dimensions have been enormously influential on OB researchers and managers, and he has been one of the most widely cited social scientists ever. Nevertheless, his research has been criticized. First, although the data has been updated, the original work is more than 40 years old and was based on a single company (IBM). A lot has happened on the world scene since then. Some of the most obvious changes include the fall of the Soviet Union, the transformation of central and eastern Europe, the end of apartheid in South Africa, the rise of China as a global power, and the advent of a worldwide recession. These changes would more than likely shift some of the cultural values that Hofstede's framework assesses. Second, few researchers have read the details of Hofstede's methodology closely and they are therefore unaware of the many decisions and

Country	Power Distance		Individualism Versus Collectivism		Masculinity Versus Femininity		Uncertainty Avoidance		Long-versus Short-Term Orientation	
	Index	Rank	Index	Rank	Index	Rank	Index	Rank	Index	Rank
Anglo Canada	39	39	80	4–5	52	24	48	41–42	23	30
Franco Canada	54	32–33	73	9	45	32–33	60	32–33	n/a	n/a
Germany	35	42–44	67	15	66	9–10	65	29	31	22–24
Hong Kong	68	15–16	25	37	57	18–19	29	49–50	96	2
India	77	10–11	48	21	56	20–21	40	45	61	7
Indonesia	78	8–9	14	47–48	46	30–31	48	41–42		
Jamaica	45	37	39	25	68	7–8	13	52		
Japan	54	32–33	46	22–23	95	1	92	7	80	4
Korea (South)	60	27–28	18	43	39	41	85	16–17	75	5
Mexico	81	5–6	30	32	69	6	82	18		
Pakistan	55	32	14	47–48	50	25–26	70	24–25	0	34
Philippines	94	4	32	31	64	11–12	44	44	19	31–32
United States	40	38	91	1	62	15	46	43	29	27
Regions:										
East Africa	64	21–23	27	33–35	41	39	52	36	25	28–29
West Africa	77	10–11	20	39–41	46	30–31	54	34	16	33

EXHIBIT 5-4   Hofstede's Cultural Values by Nation: A Sampling of Country Profiles

Notes: Scores range from 0 = extremely low on dimension to 100 = extremely high. 1 = highest rank. LTO ranks: 1 = China; 15–16 = Bangladesh; 21 = Poland; 34 = lowest.

Source: Copyright Geert Hofstede BV, hofstede@bart.nl. Reprinted with permission.

judgment calls he had to make (for example, reducing the number of cultural values to just five).

Research across 598 studies with more than 200,000 respondents investigated the relationship between Hofstede's cultural values and a variety of organizational criteria at both the individual and national level of analysis.[77] Overall, the five original culture dimensions were found to be equally strong predictors of relevant outcomes. The researchers also found that measuring individual scores resulted in much better predictions of most outcomes than assigning all people in a country the same cultural values. In sum, this research suggests that Hofstede's framework may be a valuable way of thinking about differences among people, but we should be cautious about assuming all people from a country have the same values.

The GLOBE Framework

Begun in 1993, the Global Leadership and Organizational Behaviour Effectiveness (GLOBE) research program is an ongoing cross-cultural investigation of leadership and national culture. Using data from 825 organizations in 62 countries, the GLOBE team has identified nine dimensions on which national cultures differ.[78] Some dimensions—such as power distance, individualism/collectivism, uncertainty avoidance, and future orientation (similar to long-term versus short-term orientation)—resemble the Hofstede dimensions. The main difference is that the GLOBE framework added dimensions, such as humane orientation (the degree to which a society rewards individuals for being altruistic, generous, and kind to others) and performance orientation (the degree to which a society encourages and rewards group members for performance improvement and excellence). The GLOBE studies also separated out Hofstede's masculinity dimension into two distinct values: gender equality, meaning the support for equality between men and women in society, and assertiveness, meaning the social acceptability of dominant, forceful behaviours.

Comparison of Hofstede's Framework and the GLOBE Framework

Which framework is better, Hofstede's or GLOBE's? That's hard to say, and each has its supporters. It is important to note that both frameworks result in similar profiles. Put another way, you will get similar results and country value groupings regardless of which one you use. The only two countries whose scores differed markedly between the Hofstede and GLOBE studies were Brazil and Israel. In the former case the subpopulations studied were from different cultural groups within Brazil and in the latter case immigration significantly changed the ethnic profile of the nation in the intervening years, from a primarily European Jewish population to a more diverse population including many Middle Eastern and Northern African Jewish people.

Overall we give more emphasis to Hofstede's dimensions here, because they have stood the test of time and the GLOBE study confirmed them. For example, a review of the organizational commitment literature found that the Hofstede and the GLOBE individualism/collectivism dimensions operated similarly. Specifically, both frameworks suggest that organizational commitment (discussed earlier) tends to be lower in individualistic countries.[79] Both frameworks thus have a great deal in common, and each has something unique to offer.

Our Primary Trading Partner: Key U.S./Canadian Differences

It is important to learn about many different cultures; but the United States is Canada's largest trading partner, so it is especially important to be aware of cultural differences between that country and Canada. The following table summarizes some key cultural differences identified by the Environics Institute for Survey Research.[80] These differences will influence negotiating tactics, compensation system design, motivational strategies, and day-to-day workplace behaviours in various ways. For example, the disparity in pay between the top earner in a company, such as the CEO, and the bottom earner, such as a labourer, will generally be much greater in an American firm than a Canadian firm. See Exhibit 5-5.

Canadian Culture	American Culture
Generally more risk-averse.	Generally values risk-taking.
Focus on accommodation of difference.	Focus on goals and desire for achievement.
Money is suspect.	Money is everything.
Income should be distributed relatively equally.	Income inequality is okay, winner takes all.
Seeks best quality of life.	Seeks highest standard of living.
Self-effacing humour.	Putdown-based humour.
Poverty is primarily due to social ills.	Poverty is primarily due to lack of individual effort.
Somewhat indirect communication, focus on tact.	Direct communication, focus on being forthright or blunt.
Calm demeanor is expected during negotiation.	Some aggressiveness is acceptable during negotiation.
Religion is private and seldom discussed in casual social situations.	Religion is a key part of one's identity and may be discussed in casual social situations.

EXHIBIT 5-5 Comparison of Canadian Versus American Culture

Nations Within Nations: Aboriginal Values in the Canadian Context

Canada includes many different Aboriginal cultures, none of which were examined in the Hofstede and GLOBE studies. There is immense cultural variation across bands. Most notably, some bands are matrilineal and emphasize communal behaviours while others are patrilineal and emphasize a warrior ethos similar to what Hofstede termed "masculinity." Even with these differences, however, there are common cultural themes. Aboriginal cultures tend to be more collectivist, with an emphasis on participative decision-making processes. This is often described as having "power with" rather than "power over." Relationship building and reaching consensus are more important than efficiency. Direct personal confrontation is avoided; in fact, noninterference in the lives of others is a key cultural value. Formalized respect for elders is also an important part of most Aboriginal cultures.[81]

Acculturation and Biculturalism: Immigrant Adjustment and Changes in Values

Cultural value profiles become more complex when individuals are exposed to multiple cultures. There is evidence that our core values are formed early in life and stabilize between the ages of 11 to 14. Children routinely exposed to two or more cultures from a very early age are likely to adopt a blended value system, or be truly bicultural or even multicultural.[82] There is evidence that older people, however, go through *acculturation*. Acculturation is defined as the process by which individuals change as a result of being influenced by contact with another culture.[83] Early conceptualizations of acculturation focused on the immigrant's receptiveness to the social norms and values of the host country, which were impacted by personal characteristics such as language ability, age at time of migration, and duration of stay in the host country.[84] A researcher named Berry extended the concept of acculturation by defining it on the basis of the degree to which immigrants are willing to adapt to the dominant culture/values and the degree to which they want to maintain their own ethnic culture and values. This conceptualization led to the identification of four possible acculturation orientations: integration, marginalization, assimilation, and separation. Members of the host culture will also have expectations regarding the degree to which immigrants will integrate or maintain their home culture and values, which influence outcomes.[85] If the expectations of the immigrants and the members of the host culture both support assimilation then immigrants are more likely to change their value orientations over time as a result of exposure to the new culture. Those focused on integration will maintain some of their old values and adopt some new ones. Groups who experience separation generally maintain the values of their prior culture, as do marginalized individuals and groups.

SUMMARY

- Personality matters to organizational behaviour. It does not explain all behaviour, but it sets the stage.

- Emerging theory and research reveal how personality matters more in some situations than in others.

- The Big Five has been a particularly important advancement in our understanding of personality; it, along with the Dark Triad and other traits impact workplace behaviours and attitudes.

- Every trait has advantages and disadvantages for work behaviour, and there is no perfect constellation of traits that is ideal for every situation.

- Personality can help you to understand why people (including you!) act, think, and feel the way we do, and the astute manager can put that understanding to use by taking care to place employees in situations that best fit their personality.
- Values often underlie and explain attitudes, behaviours, and perceptions. Values tend to vary internationally along dimensions that can predict organizational outcomes; however, an individual may or may not hold values that are consistent with the values of the national culture.

IMPLICATIONS FOR MANAGERS

- Consider screening job candidates for high conscientiousness—as well as the other Big Five traits, depending on the criteria your organization finds most important. Other traits, such as core self-evaluation or narcissism, may be relevant in certain situations.
- Although the MBTI has faults, you can use it in training and development to help employees better understand themselves, help team members better understand each other, and open up communication in work groups and possibly reduce conflicts.
- You need to evaluate your employees' jobs, their work groups, and your organization to determine the optimal personality fit.
- Take into account employees' situational factors when evaluating their observable personality traits, and lower the situation strength to better ascertain personality characteristics.
- The findings from Hofstede's work and the GLOBE program underscore the need for managers to understand the cultural values of their employees. The more you take into consideration people's different cultures, the better you will be able to determine their work behaviour and create a positive organizational climate that performs well.

BREAK-OUT QUESTION FOR GROUP DISCUSSION

When hiring do you think it is more important to focus on person–job fit or person–organization fit? Defend your answer.

PERSONAL INVENTORY ASSESSMENT

In the Personal Inventory Assessment found in MyManagementLab, take the assessment: Personality Style Indicator.

SELF-REFLECTION ACTIVITY

Since the fit between personality and job type is an important driver of job satisfaction, it is important to know as much about your own personality as possible when making career management decisions. Take the Personal Inventory Assessment found in MyManagementLab to find out more about your own personality.

Once you have seen your personality profile, it is time to think about what it means. Remember that personality traits are not good or bad per se, but alignment between your personality and your job can help increase performance and satisfaction levels. Think carefully about your combination of traits. Do they suggest that you would be better off in a boisterous, fast-paced, and competitive job like field sales or public relations? Or perhaps you would be better suited to quiet, detail-oriented work, like accounting or programming? How sociable are you? Some people may enjoy work that makes extensive social demands, such as teaching, while others prefer to minimize social interaction, emphasizing technical and mechanical work. The key is not to try and fight your personality but to find the best fit that allows you to use your natural strengths to their best effect.

If you are unsure what personality type is best suited to a particular job, you can read research available from organizations such as the Canadian Human Resources Management Professional Association and you can talk with people already working in the occupation of interest.

MINI CASE THE PERSONALITY PROBLEM

Jasmine Patel, Director of Human Resource Management at Vertical Horizon, sat at her desk feeling completely perplexed. She was at a loss about how to handle a high-performing but socially disruptive employee, Rhett Stark.

Vertical Horizon was a software company in the Kitchener-Waterloo high tech corridor. They had originally been known for their programming tools, tools that helped large teams of software developers work together effectively. Now, however, they were moving into other areas such as web content management. Since the company was in the midst of changing their focus and their product lines, it was critically important to have experienced, high-performing sales representatives supporting the transition. If their new product line failed, it might well take the entire company down with it.

The sales team consisted of 12 outside (field) sales representatives and 6 inside representatives who supported the outside reps. Each inside rep was responsible for lead generation and otherwise supporting the two outside sales reps assigned to them. In addition there was a sales manager who could be consulted on a day-to-day basis for advice and a VP Sales who was responsible for strategic initiatives. Most of the sales reps had been with the company for less than two years. In fact, even the Sales Manager and the VP Sales were relatively new to the organization, and as a result they frequently consulted with Rhett to access his tacit knowledge about their products, customers, and strategies.

Rhett was an outside sales rep who had been with the company for over eight years, an extremely long time in the software world. He was the undisputed master of the sale. His natural charisma combined with strong product knowledge and excellent customer references helped him exceed his quota quarter after quarter. Unfortunately, Rhett's success came with a significant downside. He was charming, brash, and confident, a natural leader who drew people to him like a magnet. People felt special around him, and would frequently comment that "when he talks to you he makes you feel like you are the most important and interesting person in the world." It was what he did with those people afterwards that was the problem.

Rhett was the ringleader of a group of sales reps who would frequently work late, then go out drinking and partying together. This behaviour was supported and at times even funded by the VP Sales, who felt that this kind of behaviour made for a strong team. The nights spent clubbing and bar hopping together did seem to create a lot of cohesion within the work group, but it also had some negative effects.

Jasmine had overheard two male members of the sales team talking in the cafeteria. They were discussing stressful marital difficulties that had arisen as a result of their late nights out drinking. "What kind of bothered me," one said to the other, "is that when I told Rhett this was causing problems at home he just laughed. He was the one who kept convincing me to stay out late! I know it is my own responsibility but you would think he would be more sympathetic." In addition, a high-performing sales rep named Malcolm had come to talk with Jasmine. "It is pretty clear that Rhett has a lot of informal power around here," he said, "everyone, even management, listens to him and does what he says. I'm worried because I'm not part of his 'pack.' I don't drink or go out with everyone; my church doesn't believe in that sort of thing. Besides, I'd rather be home with my family. But Rhett makes fun of me behind my back all the time for being lame. Some other employees have told me how he gets everyone to laugh at me. The teasing and insults I could live with, what really bothers me is something else. Given his informal power in this department, how can I ever expect a fair chance at promotion?"

Most worrisome, however, was Rhett's behaviour with female staff. Jasmine could not verify all the reports, but rumour had it that Rhett had slept with more than a dozen women in the office over the past eight years. Jasmine could verify two affairs, both with inside sales reps; one of them reported directly to Rhett. However, neither woman was interested in submitting a complaint. Jasmine had found out about the situation in another way. She had gone into the women's washroom one day to find the two women crying together. It seems that they had just discovered that (1) Rhett was married with one child and his wife was pregnant with their second and (2) both of them had been dating him without knowing about the wife (Rhett kept his marriage quiet and had no family pictures on his desk and no wedding ring), or about each other. Making matters worse, one of the women was now pregnant with Rhett's child. She was in extreme distress; she was a Catholic and already raising two children alone, and could not conceive of either aborting or raising three kids by herself. The second woman was more annoyed and angry than distressed, but, like Malcolm, she was extremely anxious about Rhett's influence over her later career progression.

Nothing Rhett had done was illegal, and in the absence of formal complaints and evidence he could not be effectively disciplined for having personal relationships with direct reports. Jasmine had no authority to tell Rhett how to live his personal life, but it was clear that he was causing a lot of damage in the department. He also appeared to be completely unconcerned, even amused, by the swath of destruction left in his wake. Jasmine suspected he was a narcissist, perhaps even highly Machiavellian. But he was their best sales rep by far. How could she manage this difficult personality and still maintain a healthy working environment?

Discussion Questions

1. Do you agree with Jasmine's assessment that Rhett is Machiavellian and a narcissist? Why or why not?

2. Assuming that Rhett is Machiavellian and a narcissist, what is the most effective way to minimize the damage he can do to other employees?

3. Assuming that you knew ahead of time that Rhett's personality included the Dark Triad. Would you still hire him for a sales role? Why or why not?

MINI CASE   INTERVIEW EXPECTATIONS AND CULTURAL CONFUSION

Bao-Zhi walked home feeling disappointed yet again. He was sure the interviewer would not be calling him back for a second interview. He could tell she had been disappointed with his responses. But he was not sure why. The same thing had happened twice before, and he had trouble understanding it.

Bao-Zhi had immigrated to Calgary with credentials as a mining engineer. He had earned a master's degree in engineering from the second-highest-ranked school in China and had worked for a Chinese mining company for over a decade. During that time he had received excellent performance ratings and three promotions, an unusually fast career progression in his firm.

Once he had arrived in Canada, it had taken a full two years for his engineering credentials to be recognized. During that time he had taken on a series of temporary jobs doing simple tasks like packing orders in warehouses and cleaning offices. Now, his credentials recognized, he was eager to get back to his real career. He found it easy to get interviews; people with his skills were in high demand. But at the interviews, though, things seldom went well.

Bao-Zhi thought back to the questions he had been asked today. The interviewer had wanted to know about his achievements as a mining engineer back in China. Bao-Zho knew it would be rude to brag about how quickly he had been promoted, instead he talked about a team he had worked on. The entire team had reengineered some processes in a manner that had reduced pollution by 12.3 percent. Some of the key ideas had originally been Bao-Zhi's, but since modesty was important he had talked about the performance of the whole team and did not single himself out. The interviewer had not seemed as impressed by their remarkable achievement as Bao-Zhi thought she would be.

Next the interviewer asked what he would do if he saw his manager making a mistake on some paperwork. This question concerned Bao-Zhi. Didn't they hire competent managers? It seemed a strange thing to ask, but Bao-Zhi reiterated how important it was to support a manager. The mistake, if not crucial, could be ignored in order to save face. Once again the interviewer did not seem impressed. Bao-Zhi felt defeated. He thought getting his engineering credentials recognized would launch a great career in Canada, but there were barriers he never expected. The interviews were so different from what he expected. Would he ever give answers that made them want to hire him?

Discussion Questions

1. Why is Bao-Zhi struggling in his interviews?

2. Using Hofstede's cultural values as a frame of reference, what cross-cultural communication barriers do you see operating here? Be specific.

3. Is there a way the interviewer might phrase her questions that would minimize cultural misunderstandings or biases? Explain your answer.

MyManagementLab

Study, practise, and explore real management situations with these helpful resources:

- **Interactive Lesson Presentations:** Work through interactive presentations and assessments to test your knowledge of management concepts.
- **PIA (Personal Inventory Assessments):** Enhance your ability to connect with key concepts through these engaging self-reflection assessments.
- **Study Plan:** Check your understanding of chapter concepts with self-study quizzes.
- **Simulations:** Practise decision making in simulated management environments.

PERSONAL INVENTORY ASSESSMENT

Chapter 6

Perception and Individual Decision Making

PBNJ Productions/Blend Images/Getty Images

LEARNING OBJECTIVES

After studying this chapter, you should be able to:

1. Define *perception*, and explain the factors that influence it.

2. Explain attribution theory, and describe the common shortcuts used in judging others.

3. Explain the link between perception and decision making.

4. Contrast the rational model of decision making with bounded rationality and intuition.

5. Recognize common decision biases or errors and discuss how to avoid them.

6. Evaluate how individual differences and organizational constraints affect decision making.

7. Contrast the three ethical decision-making criteria and apply those criteria to day-to-day workplace decisions.

8. Define *creativity*, and describe the three-stage model of creativity.

Any discussion of individual decision making must take into account the role of how we perceive people and situations. In this chapter, we will discuss various factors in the individual decision-making process—factors like perception and biases that shape how we are likely to make decisions, and factors like ethics and creativity that we should consider in order to make the best decisions.

WHAT IS PERCEPTION?

Perception is a process by which individuals organize and interpret sensory impressions in order to give meaning to their environment. However, what we perceive can be substantially different from objective reality. For example, all employees in a firm may view it as a great place to work—favourable working conditions, interesting job assignments, good pay, excellent benefits, understanding and responsible management—but, as most of us know, it's very unusual to find such agreement. More commonly, people have very different impressions of their workplace even when their job tasks and working conditions are similar.

Why is perception important in the study of OB? Simply because people's behaviour is based on their perception of what reality is, not on reality itself. As you've surely found in your own experiences, what we perceive can be substantially different from objective reality. *The world as it is perceived is the world that is behaviourally important.* To understand what we have in common in our interpretations of reality, we need to begin with the factors that influence our perceptions.

Factors That Influence Perception

A number of factors shape and sometimes distort perception. These factors can reside in the *perceiver*; in the object, or *target*, being perceived; or in the *situation* in which the perception is made.

When you look at a target, your interpretation of what you see is influenced by your personal characteristics—attitudes, personality, motives, interests, past experiences, and expectations. For instance, if you expect police officers to be authoritative, you may perceive them as such, regardless of their actual traits.

The characteristics of the target also affect what we perceive. Loud people are more likely to be noticed than quiet ones. So, too, are extremely attractive or unattractive individuals. Because we don't look at targets in isolation, the relationship of a target to its background influences perception, as does our tendency to group close things and similar things together. We often perceive women, men, immigrants, Caucasians, Aboriginal people, Asians, or members of any other group that has clearly distinguishable characteristics as alike in other, unrelated ways as well. We also have a broad tendency to perceive people who we think are similar to us in positive ways and people who we think are different from us in negative ways.

Context matters, too. The time at which we see an object or event can influence our attention, as can location, light, heat, or situational factors. For instance, at a club on Saturday night you may not notice someone "decked out." Yet that same person so attired for your Monday morning management class would certainly catch your attention. Neither the perceiver nor the target has changed between Saturday night and Monday morning, but the situation is different.

People have inherent biases in how they see others (perception) and in how they make decisions (decision making). We can better understand people by understanding these biases.

SOCIAL PERCEPTION: MAKING JUDGMENTS ABOUT OTHERS

Now we turn to the application of perception concepts most relevant to OB—*social perception*, or the perceptions people form about each other. We begin with a discussion of attribution theory, a construct that helps to explain how we form perceptions of other people.

Attribution Theory

Nonliving objects such as desks, machines, and buildings are subject to the laws of nature, but they have no beliefs, motives, or intentions. People do. When we observe people, we attempt to explain their behaviour. Our perception and judgment of a person's actions are influenced by the assumptions we make about that person's state of mind.

Attribution theory tries to explain the ways we judge people differently, depending on the meaning we attribute to a behaviour.[1] It suggests that when we observe an individual's behaviour, we attempt to determine whether it was internally or externally caused. That determination depends largely on three factors: (1) distinctiveness, (2) consensus, and (3) consistency. Let's clarify the differences between internal and external causation, and then we'll discuss the determining factors.

Internally caused behaviours are those an observer believes to be under the personal control of another individual. *Externally* caused behaviour is what we imagine the situation forced the individual to do. For example, if one of your employees is late for work, you might attribute that to his overnight partying and subsequent oversleeping. This is an internal attribution. But if you attribute his tardiness to an automobile accident that tied up traffic, you are making an external attribution.

Now let's discuss the three determining factors. *Distinctiveness* refers to whether an individual displays different behaviours in different situations. Is the employee who arrives late today also one who regularly blows off other kinds of commitments? What we want to know is whether this behaviour is unusual. If it is, we are likely to give it an external attribution. If it's not, we will probably judge the behaviour to be internal.

If everyone who faces a similar situation responds in the same way, the behaviour shows *consensus*. The behaviour of our tardy employee meets this criterion if all employees who took the same form of transportation or route were also late. From an attribution perspective, if consensus is high, you would probably give an external attribution to the employee's tardiness, whereas if other employees who took the same route made it to work on time, you would attribute his lateness to an internal cause.

Finally, an observer looks for *consistency* in a person's actions. Does the person respond the same way over time? Coming in 10 minutes late for work is not perceived in the same way for an employee who hasn't been late for several months as it is for an employee who is late three times a week. The more consistent the behaviour, the more we are inclined to attribute it to internal causes.

Exhibit 6-1 summarizes the key elements in attribution theory. It tells us, for instance, that if an employee, Katelyn, generally performs at about the same level on related tasks as she does on her current task (low distinctiveness); other employees frequently perform differently—better or worse—than Katelyn on that task (low consensus); and Katelyn's performance on this current task is consistent over time (high consistency), anyone judging Katelyn's work will likely hold her primarily responsible for her task performance (internal attribution).

EXHIBIT 6-1 Attribution Theory

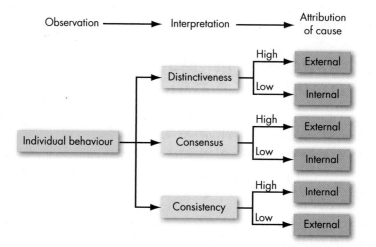

One of the findings from attribution theory research is that errors or biases distort attributions. When we make judgments about the behaviour of other people, we tend to underestimate the influence of external factors and overestimate the influence of internal or personal factors.[2] This **fundamental attribution error** can explain why a sales manager is prone to attribute the poor performance of her sales agents to laziness rather than to a competitor's innovative product line. Individuals and organizations tend to attribute their own successes to internal factors such as ability or effort, while blaming failure on external factors such as bad luck or unproductive coworkers. People also tend to attribute ambiguous information as relatively flattering, accept positive feedback, and reject negative feedback. This is **self-serving bias**.[3]

The evidence on cultural differences in perception is mixed, but most suggests there *are* differences across cultures in the attributions people make.[4] One study found Korean managers were less prone to self-serving bias—they tended to accept responsibility for group failure "because I was not a capable leader" instead of attributing failure to group members.[5] On the other hand, in other research Asian managers are more likely to blame institutions or whole organizations, whereas Western observers believe individual managers should get blame or praise.[6] That probably explains why U.S. newspapers feature the names of individual executives when firms do poorly, whereas Asian media cover how the firm as a whole has failed. This tendency to make group-based attributions also explains why individuals from Asian cultures are more likely to make group-based stereotypes.[7] Attribution theory was developed based on experiments with U.S. and Western European workers. But the studies suggest caution in making attribution theory predictions in non-Western societies, especially in countries with strong collectivist traditions.

Differences in attribution tendencies don't mean the basic concepts of attribution completely differ across cultures, though. Self-serving biases may be less common in East Asian cultures, but evidence suggests they still operate across cultures.[8] Studies indicate Chinese managers assess blame for mistakes using the same distinctiveness, consensus, and consistency cues Western managers use.[9] They also become angry and punish those deemed responsible for failure, a reaction shown in many studies of Western managers. This means the basic process of attribution applies across cultures, but that it takes more evidence for Asian managers to conclude that someone else should be blamed.

The concept of attribution theory significantly advances our understanding of people perception by helping us identify why we may draw certain conclusions from people's behaviour. Having discussed social perception in particular, now let's take a more general look at the common shortcuts we use to simplify our processing of others' behaviour.

Common Shortcuts in Judging Others

The shortcuts for judging others often allow us to form perceptions rapidly and provide valid data for making predictions. However, shortcuts can and do sometimes result in significant distortions.

Selective Perception   Any characteristic that makes a person, an object, or an event stand out will increase the probability that we will perceive it. Why? Because it is impossible for us to assimilate everything we see; we can take in only certain stimuli. Thus, you are more likely to notice cars like your own, and your boss may reprimand some people and not others doing the same thing. Because we can't observe everything going on around us, we use **selective perception**. But we don't choose randomly. We select according to our interests, background, experience, and attitudes. Selective perception allows us to speed-read others, but not without the risk of drawing an inaccurate or incomplete picture. Seeing what we want to see, we can draw unwarranted conclusions from an ambiguous situation.

Halo Effect   When we draw an impression about an individual on the basis of a single characteristic, such as intelligence, sociability, or appearance, a **halo effect** is operating.[10] The halo effect was confirmed in a classic study in which subjects were given a list of traits such as intelligent, skillful, practical, industrious, determined, and warm and asked to evaluate the person to whom those traits applied.[11] With these qualities in mind, subjects also then judged the person to be wise, humorous, popular, and imaginative. When the same list substituted the word "cold" for "warm," a completely different picture emerged; subjects did not judge the person as holding positive qualities. Clearly, the subjects were allowing a single trait to influence their overall impression of the person they were judging. As managers, we need to be careful not to draw inferences from small clues.

Contrast Effects   An adage among entertainers is "Never work with kids or animals." Why? Audiences love children and animals so much that you'll look bad in comparison. This example demonstrates how a **contrast effect** can distort perceptions. We don't evaluate a person in isolation. Our reaction is influenced by other persons we have recently encountered.

Social Identity Effects   Social identity theory is a psychological theory of the social self, intergroup relations, and group processes. It was originally developed by Tajfel and Turner, and has since been validated in hundreds of studies.[12] The basic premise is that social category membership defines the individual, at least in part. People belong to many social categories that vary in importance to them (for example, ethnic, professional, religious, special-interest), and each comes with norms defining how one should think, feel, and behave. Since social identities are evaluative, there is a profound need for the individual to feel that their in-group(s) are superior to the relevant out-group(s). Out-group members are depersonalized to maximize the difference between in-group members and out-group members.[13] For example, students living in one residence may come to feel that their residence is the "best" and may believe that the smartest and most socially engaging students live there. Members of one department, such as sales or production, may believe that they work harder and contribute more to the company than the other departments. Members of a particular faith may feel that their religion is superior to all others. Thus, social identities encourage the type of categorization and self-enhancement that leads to stereotyping and the discounting of those perceived as different.

Stereotyping   When we judge someone on the basis of our perception of the group to which he belongs, we are **stereotyping**.[14]

We deal with an unmanageable number of stimuli from our complex world by using *heuristics* or stereotypes to make decisions quickly. For example, it does make sense to assume that Allison from finance will be able to help you figure out a forecasting problem. The problem occurs when we generalize inaccurately or too much. In organizations, we frequently hear comments that represent stereotypes based on gender, age, race, religion,

Social identity effects can be observed all around us. Notice, for example, that although ethnic groups are mingling in this cafeteria, people still tend to sit with others from their own ethnic group.

Ariel Skelley/Blend Images/Getty Images

ethnicity, and even weight (see Chapter 2):[15] "Men aren't interested in childcare," "Older workers can't learn new skills," "Aboriginals are lazy and do not want to work," "Asian immigrants are hardworking and conscientious." Research suggests stereotypes operate emotionally and often below the level of conscious awareness, making them particularly hard to challenge and change.[16]

Stereotypes can be deeply ingrained and powerful enough to influence life-and-death decisions. In one infamous recent example, Brian Sinclair, an Aboriginal and a 45-year-old double amputee confined to a wheelchair, was ignored for 34 hours in a Winnipeg emergency room. He died while waiting, an entirely preventable death given the nature of the health condition he sought treatment for. An inquest found that neglect of his healthcare needs was influenced in part by stereotypes about Aboriginals, homeless people, and their usage of health services.[17] One study found that students who read scenarios describing leaders tended to assign higher scores for leadership potential and effective leadership to Whites than to minorities even though the content of the scenarios was equivalent, supporting the idea of a stereotype of Whites as better leaders.[18]

One problem of stereotypes is that they *are* widespread generalizations, though they may not contain a shred of truth when applied to a particular person or situation. We have to monitor ourselves to make sure we're not unfairly applying a stereotype in our evaluations and decisions. Stereotypes are an example of the warning "The more useful, the more danger from misuse."

It should be obvious by now that our perceptions, many of which are near-instantaneous and without conscious deliberation, colour our outlook. Sometimes our perceptions have little impact on anyone, but more often our perceptions greatly influence our decisions. The first step toward increasing the effectiveness of organizational decision making is to understand the process on an individualized level, discussed next.

THE LINK BETWEEN PERCEPTION AND INDIVIDUAL DECISION MAKING

Individuals make **decisions**, choices from among two or more alternatives. Ideally, decision making would be an objective process, but the way individuals make decisions and the quality of their choices are largely influenced by their perceptions. Individual decision making is an important factor of behaviour at all levels of an organization. Top managers determine their organization's goals, what products or services to offer, how best to finance operations, or where to locate a new manufacturing plant. Middle- and lower-level managers set production schedules, select new employees, and decide how to allocate pay raises. Organizations sometimes give their nonmanagerial employees decision-making authority historically reserved for managers alone, but even in traditional settings, nonmanagerial employees make decisions that affect the organization.

Decision making occurs as a reaction to a **problem**.[19] That is, a discrepancy exists between the current state of affairs and some desired state, requiring us to consider alternative courses of action. If your car breaks down and you rely on it to get to work, you have a problem that requires a decision on your part. Unfortunately, most problems do not come neatly labeled as such. One person's *problem* is another person's *satisfactory state of affairs*. One manager may view her division's 2 percent decline in quarterly sales to be a serious problem requiring immediate action on her part. Her counterpart in another division, who also had a 2 percent sales decrease, might consider that quite acceptable. So awareness that a problem exists and that a decision might or might not be needed is a perceptual issue.

Every decision requires us to interpret and evaluate information. We typically receive data from multiple sources we need to screen, process, and interpret. Which data are relevant to the decision, and which are not? Our perceptions will answer that question. We also need to develop alternatives and evaluate their strengths and weaknesses. Again, our perceptual process will affect the final outcome. Throughout the decision-making process, perceptual errors often surface that can bias analyses and conclusions.

DECISION MAKING IN ORGANIZATIONS

Business schools train students to follow rational decision-making models. While such rationalistic models have merit, they don't always describe how people actually make decisions. OB improves the way we make decisions in organizations by addressing the decision-making errors people commit in addition to the perception errors we've discussed. First, we will describe some decision-making constructs, and then we will describe a few of the most common errors.

The Rational Model, Bounded Rationality, and Intuition

In OB, there are generally accepted constructs of decision making each of us employ to make determinations: rational decision making, bounded rationality, and intuition. Though their processes make sense, they may not lead to the most accurate (or best) decisions. More importantly, there are times when one strategy may lead to a better outcome than another in a given situation.

Rational Decision Making We often think the best decision maker is **rational** and makes consistent, value-maximizing choices within specified constraints.[20] These decisions often follow a six-step **rational decision-making model**.[21] The six steps are listed in Exhibit 6-2.

The rational decision-making model assumes that the decision maker has complete information, is able to identify all the relevant options in an unbiased manner, and chooses the option with the highest utility.[22] In reality, though, most decisions don't follow the rational model; people are usually content to find an acceptable or reasonable solution to a problem rather than an optimal one. We tend to limit our choices to the neighbourhood of the problem's symptom and the current alternative at hand. As one expert in decision making put it, "Most significant decisions are made by judgment, rather than by a defined prescriptive model."[23] Unfortunately, people are remarkably unaware of making suboptimal decisions.[24]

Bounded Rationality Often, we don't follow the rational decision-making model because our limited information-processing capability makes it impossible to assimilate all the information necessary to optimize.[25] Many problems don't have an optimal solution because they are too complicated to fit the rational decision-making model, so people *satisfice*—they seek solutions that are "satisfactory and sufficient." We tend to reduce complex problems to a level we can readily understand. When you considered which college or university to attend, did you look at every viable alternative? Did you carefully identify all the criteria that were important in your decision? Did you evaluate each alternative against the criteria in order to find the optimal college? The answers are probably no. Don't feel bad; few people make their college choice this way. Instead of optimizing, you probably satisficed.

EXHIBIT 6-2
Steps in Rational
Decision-Making Model

1. Define the problem.
2. Identify the decision criteria.
3. Allocate weights to the criteria.
4. Develop the alternatives.
5. Evaluate the alternatives.
6. Select the best alternative.

Because the human mind cannot formulate and solve complex problems with full rationality, we operate within the confines of **bounded rationality**. We construct simplified models that extract the essential features from problems without capturing all their complexity.[26] We can then behave rationally within the limits of the simple model.

How does bounded rationality work for the typical individual? Once we've identified a problem, we begin to search for criteria and alternatives. The criteria are unlikely to be exhaustive. We identify alternatives that are highly visible and that usually represent familiar criteria and tried-and-true solutions. Next, we begin reviewing the alternatives, focusing on choices that differ little from the current state until we identify one that is "good enough"—that meets an acceptable level of performance. Thus ends our search. Therefore, the solution represents a satisficing choice—the first *acceptable* one we encounter—rather than an optimal one.

Satisficing is not always bad—a simple process may frequently be more sensible than the traditional rational decision-making model.[27] To use the rational model, you need to gather a great deal of information about all the options, compute applicable weights, and then calculate values across a huge number of criteria. All these processes can cost time, energy, and money. If there are many unknown weights and preferences, the fully rational model may not be any more accurate than a best guess. Sometimes a fast-and-frugal process of solving problems might be your best option.

Intuition Perhaps the least rational way of making decisions is **intuitive decision making**, a non-conscious process created from distilled experience.[28] Intuitive decision making occurs outside conscious thought; relies on holistic associations, or links between disparate pieces of information; is fast; and is *affectively charged*, meaning it engages the emotions.[29]

While intuition isn't rational, it isn't necessarily wrong. Nor does it always contradict rational analysis; the two can complement each other. Nor is intuition superstition, or the product of some magical or paranormal sixth sense. Intuition is complex and based on years of experience and learning.

Does intuition help effective decision making? Researchers are divided, but most experts are skeptical, in part because intuition is hard to measure and analyze. Probably the best perspective is what one expert has offered: "Intuition can be very useful as a way of setting up a hypothesis but is unacceptable as 'proof.'" Use hunches derived from your experience to speculate, yes, but always make sure to test those hunches with objective data and rational, dispassionate analysis.[30]

As you can see, the more objective processes for decision making we use may correct some of the problems with our perceptual process. Just as there are biases and errors in the perceptual process, it stands to reason there are identifiable biases and errors in our decision making, which we will outline next.

COMMON BIASES AND ERRORS IN DECISION MAKING

Decision makers engage in bounded rationality, but they also allow systematic biases and errors to creep into their judgments.[31] To minimize effort and avoid trade-offs, people tend to rely too heavily on experience, impulses, gut feelings, and rules of thumb. Shortcuts can be helpful; however, they can distort rationality. Following are the most common biases in decision making. Exhibit 6-3 provides some suggestions for how to avoid falling into these biases and errors.

Perceptual and decision-making biases and heuristics are not necessarily bad. They allow us to process information more quickly and efficiently. The key is to be self-aware enough to see when a bias or shortcut may be counterproductive.

Overconfidence Bias

Recent research continues to conclude that we tend to be overconfident about our abilities and about the abilities of others, and that we are usually not aware of this bias.[32]

EXHIBIT 6-3

Reducing Bias and Errors

Source: Robbins, Stephen P.,
*Decide And Conquer: Make Winning
Decisions And Take Control Of Your
Life,* 1st Ed., © 2004, pp.164–168.
Reprinted and Electronically repro-
duced by permission of Pearson
Education, Inc., New York, NY.

Focus on goals.

Without goals, you can't be rational, you don't know what information you need, you don't know which information is relevant and which is irrelevant, you'll find it difficult to choose between alternatives, and you're far more likely to experience regret over the choices you make. Clear goals make decision making easier and help you eliminate options that are inconsistent with your interests.

Look for information that disconfirms your beliefs.

One of the most effective means for counteracting overconfidence and the confirmation and hindsight biases is to actively look for information that contradicts your beliefs and assumptions. When we overtly consider various ways we might be wrong, we challenge our tendencies to think we're smarter than we actually are.

Don't try to create meaning out of random events.

The educated mind has been trained to look for cause-and-effect relationships. When something happens, we ask why. And when we can't find reasons, we often invent them. You have to accept that there are events in life outside your control. Ask yourself whether patterns can be meaningfully explained or whether they are merely coincidence. Don't attempt to create meaning out of coincidence.

Increase your options.

No matter how many options you've identified, your final choice can be no better than the best of the option set you've selected. This argues for increasing your decision alternatives and for using creativity in developing a wide range of diverse choices. The more alternatives you can generate, and the more diverse those alternatives, the greater your chance of finding an outstanding one.

It's been said that "no problem in judgment and decision making is more prevalent and more potentially catastrophic than overconfidence."[33] When we're given factual questions and asked to judge the probability that our answers are correct, we tend to be overly optimistic. When people say they're 90 percent confident about the range a certain number might take, their estimated ranges contain the correct answer only about 50 percent of the time—and experts are no more accurate than novices in setting up confidence intervals.[34]

Individuals whose intellectual and interpersonal abilities are *weakest* are most likely to overestimate their performance and ability.[35] There's also a negative relationship between entrepreneurs' optimism and performance of their new ventures: the more optimistic, the less successful.[36] The tendency to be too confident about their ideas might keep some from planning how to avoid problems that arise.

Anchoring Bias

Anchoring bias is a tendency to fixate on initial information and fail to adequately adjust for subsequent information.[37] In other words, our mind appears to give a disproportionate amount of emphasis to the first information it receives. Anchors are widely used by people in professions in which persuasion skills are important—advertising, management, politics, real estate, and law. Anytime a negotiation takes place, so does anchoring. When a prospective employer asks how much you made in your prior job, your answer typically anchors the employer's offer. (Remember this when you negotiate your salary, but set the anchor only as high as you truthfully can.) The more precise your anchor, the smaller the adjustment. Some research suggests people think of making an adjustment after an anchor is set as rounding off a number: If you suggest a salary of $55,000, your boss will consider $50,000 to

$60,000 a reasonable range for negotiation, but if you mention $55,650, your boss is more likely to consider $55,000 to $56,000 the range of likely values.[38]

Confirmation Bias

The rational decision-making process assumes we objectively gather information. But we don't. We *selectively* gather it. **Confirmation bias** represents a case of selective perception: we seek out information that reaffirms our past choices, and we discount information that contradicts them.[39] We also tend to accept at face value information that confirms our preconceived views, while we are skeptical of information that challenges them. Therefore, the information we gather is typically biased toward supporting views we already hold. We even tend to seek sources most likely to tell us what we want to hear, and we give too much weight to supporting information and too little to contradictory. We are most prone to confirmation bias when we believe we have good information and have strong opinions. Fortunately, those who feel there is a need to be accurate in making a decision are less prone to confirmation bias.

Availability Bias

More people fear flying than fear driving in a car. But if flying on a commercial airline were as dangerous as driving, the equivalent of two 747s filled to capacity would crash every week, killing all aboard. Because the media give more attention to air accidents, we tend to overstate the risk of flying and understate the risk of driving.

Availability bias is our tendency to base judgments on information readily available. Recent research indicates that a combination of readily available information and our previous direct experience with similar information is particularly impactful to our decision making. Events that evoke emotions, that are particularly vivid, or that are more recent tend to be more available in our memory, leading us to overestimate the chances of unlikely events such as being in an airplane crash, suffering complications from medical treatment, or getting fired.[40] Availability bias can also explain why managers give more weight in performance appraisals to employee behaviours on which they took notes—even if those notes represent a small sample of all the employee's actions.

Escalation of Commitment

Another distortion that creeps into decisions is a tendency to escalate commitment, often for increasingly nonrational reasons.[41] **Escalation of commitment** refers to our staying with a decision even if there is clear evidence it's wrong. Consider a friend who has been dating someone for several years. Although he admits things aren't going too well, he says he is still going to marry her. His justification: "I have a lot invested in the relationship!"

When is escalation most likely to occur? Evidence indicates that it occurs when individuals view themselves as responsible for the outcome. The fear of personal failure even biases the way we search for and evaluate information so that we choose only information that supports our dedication. We might, for example, weight opinions in favour of reinvestment as more credible than opinions for divestment.[42]

Risk Aversion

Mathematically, we should find a 50–50 flip of the coin for $100 to be worth as much as a sure promise of $50. After all, the expected value of the gamble over a number of trials is $50. However, nearly everyone but committed gamblers would rather have the sure thing than a risky prospect.[43] For many people, a 50–50 flip of a coin even for $200 might not be worth as much as a sure promise of $50, even though the gamble is mathematically worth twice as much! This tendency to prefer a sure thing over a risky outcome is **risk aversion**.

Risk aversion can be harmful or beneficial depending on the context. Being risk-averse is considered a form of bias when our risk perceptions are substantially misaligned with objective reality. Risk aversion has important implications for management practice. To offset the risks inherent in a commission-based wage, companies pay commissioned employees considerably more than they do those on straight salaries. Risk-averse employees will stick with the established way of doing their jobs, rather than taking a chance on innovative methods. Sticking with a strategy that has worked in the past minimizes risk, but it will lead to stagnation. Ambitious people with power that can be taken away (most managers) appear to be especially risk-averse, perhaps because they don't want to lose on a gamble everything they've worked so hard to achieve.[44] CEOs at risk of termination, too, are especially risk-averse, even when a riskier investment strategy is in their firms' best interests.[45]

Hindsight Bias

Hindsight bias is the tendency to believe falsely, after the outcome is known, that we would have accurately predicted it.[46] When we have feedback on the outcome, we seem good at concluding it was obvious.

For instance, the home video rental industry collapsed when online distribution outlets ate away at the market.[47] Hollywood Video declared bankruptcy in May 2010 and began liquidating its assets; Blockbuster filed for bankruptcy in September 2010. Some have suggested that if these organizations had leveraged their brand and distribution resources effectively, developed web-based delivery sooner, as Netflix did, and added low-cost distribution in grocery and convenience stores, which Redbox offers, they could have avoided failure. While that seems obvious now in hindsight, tempting us to think we would have predicted it, many experts with good information failed to predict these two major trends that would upend the industry. After the fact, it is easy to see that a combination of automated and mail-order distribution would outperform the traditional brick-and-mortar movie rental business. Though criticisms of decision makers may have merit, as Malcolm Gladwell, author of *Blink* and *The Tipping Point*, writes, "What is clear in hindsight is rarely clear before the fact."[48]

We are all susceptible to biases like hindsight bias, but are we all susceptible to the same degree? Much of OB research centres on answering this type of question. Our individual differences do play a significant role in our decision-making processes, while our organizations constrain the range of our available decision choices.

ORGANIZATIONAL CONSTRAINTS ON DECISION MAKING

Having examined the rational decision-making model, bounded rationality, and some of the most salient biases and errors in decision making, we turn now to a discussion of organizational constraints. Organizations can constrain decision makers, creating deviations from the rational model. Managers shape decisions to reflect the organization's performance evaluation and reward systems, to comply with formal regulations, and to meet organizationally imposed time constraints. Precedent can also influence decisions.

Performance Evaluation

Managers are influenced by the criteria on which they are evaluated. If a division manager believes the manufacturing plants under her responsibility are operating best when she hears nothing negative, we would find her plant managers spending a good part of their time ensuring that negative information doesn't reach her.

Reward Systems

The organization's reward system influences decision makers by suggesting which choices have better personal payoffs. If the organization rewards risk aversion, managers are more likely to make conservative decisions. For instance, for over half a century (the 1930s through the mid-1980s), General Motors consistently gave promotions and bonuses to managers who kept a low profile and avoided controversy. Their executives became adept at dodging tough issues and passing controversial decisions on to committees, which detrimentally influenced the organization over time.

Formal Regulations

David, a shift manager at a Taco Bell restaurant in Halifax, describes constraints he faces on his job: "I've got rules and regulations covering almost every decision I make—from how to make a burrito to how often I need to clean the restrooms. My job doesn't come with much freedom of choice." David's situation is not unique. All but the smallest organizations create rules and policies to program decisions and get individuals to act in the intended manner. In doing so, they limit decision choices.

Government regulations also impact the decisions made by individuals within organizations. For example, federal equity legislation may limit an organization's ability to determine individual salaries as they see fit. Both federal human rights and provincial employment standards legislation influence recruitment and selection processes. Many Aboriginal bands have also complained about legislated constraints put on their treaty rights and ability to self-govern, which in some cases limits their ability to leverage economic opportunities and choose culturally appropriate ways to deal with social problems.[49]

System-Imposed Time Constraints

Almost all important decisions come with explicit deadlines. A report on new-product development may have to be ready for executive committee review by the first of the month. Such conditions often make it difficult, if not impossible, for managers to gather all the information before making a final choice.

Historical Precedents

Decisions aren't made in a vacuum; they have a context. Individual decisions are points in a stream of choice; those made in the past are like ghosts that haunt and constrain current choices. It's common knowledge that the largest determinant of the size of any given year's budget is last year's budget. Choices made today are largely a result of choices made over the years.

WHAT ABOUT ETHICS IN DECISION MAKING?

Ethical considerations should be an important criterion in all organizational decision making. In this section, we present three ways to frame decisions ethically.[50] Managers also need to understand the important role creativity should play in the decision process; the best managers employ strategies to increase the creative potential of their employees and harvest the ideas for organizational application.

Three Ethical Decision Criteria

The first ethical yardstick is **utilitarianism**, which proposes making decisions solely on the basis of their *outcomes*, ideally to provide the greatest good for the greatest number. This view dominates business decision making. It is consistent with goals such as efficiency, productivity, and high profits.

Another ethical criterion is to make decisions consistent with fundamental liberties and privileges, as set forth in documents such as the Canadian Charter of Rights and Freedoms. An emphasis on *rights* in decision making means respecting and protecting the basic rights of individuals, such as the right to religious freedom, free speech, and equal treatment. This criterion protects **whistle-blowers** when they reveal an organization's unethical practices to the press or government agencies using their right of free speech.

A third criterion is to impose and enforce rules fairly and impartially to ensure *justice* or an equitable distribution of benefits and costs. Union members typically favour this view, because it justifies paying people the same wage for a given job regardless of performance differences, and using seniority as the primary determination in layoff decisions.

Each criterion has advantages and liabilities. A focus on utilitarianism promotes efficiency and productivity, but it can sideline the rights of some individuals, particularly those with minority representation. The use of rights protects individuals from injury and is consistent with freedom and privacy, but it can create a legalistic environment that hinders productivity and efficiency. A focus on justice protects the interests of the underrepresented and less powerful, but it can encourage a sense of entitlement that reduces risk taking, innovation, and productivity.

Decision makers, particularly in for-profit organizations, often feel comfortable with utilitarianism. The "best interests" of the organization and its stockholders can justify a lot of questionable actions, such as large layoffs or polluting production practices. But many critics feel this perspective needs to change. Public concern about individual rights and social justice suggests managers should develop ethical standards based on nonutilitarian criteria. This presents a challenge, because satisfying individual rights and social justice creates far more ambiguities than utilitarian effects on efficiency and profits. However, while raising prices, selling products with questionable effects on consumer health, closing down inefficient plants, laying off large numbers of employees, and moving production overseas to cut costs can be justified in utilitarian terms, there may no longer be a single measure by which good decisions are judged.

Increasingly, researchers are turning to **behavioural ethics**—an area of study that analyzes how people behave when confronted with ethical dilemmas. Their research tells us that while ethical standards exist collectively (society and organizations) and individually

Human rights tribunals are an interesting place to evaluate ethical decision-making behaviours. Investigating a few past cases can help you identify how social identity effects and stereotyping often contribute to the kind of discrimination that gives rise to complaints. You can also see the detailed criteria used by the tribunal members when making their ruling—a decision with lasting impact on multiple parties.

Darryl Dyck/CP/AP Images

(personal ethics), individuals do not always follow ethical standards promulgated by their organizations, and we sometimes violate our own standards. Our ethical behaviour varies widely from one situation to the next.

CREATIVITY IN ORGANIZATIONS

Although the rational decision-making model will often improve decisions, a decision maker also needs **creativity**, the ability to produce novel and useful ideas. Novel ideas are different from what's been done before but are appropriate for the problem.

Although all aspects of organizational behaviour have complexities, that is especially true for creativity. To simplify, Exhibit 6-4 provides a **three-stage model of creativity** in organizations. The core of the model is *creative behaviour*, which has both *causes* (predictors of creative behaviour) and *effects* (outcomes of creative behaviour). In this section, we discuss the three stages of creativity, starting with the centre, creative behaviour.

Creative Behaviour

Creative behaviour occurs in four steps, each of which leads to the next:

1. *Problem formulation.* Any act of creativity begins with a problem that the behaviour is designed to solve. Thus, **problem formulation** is defined as the stage of creative behaviour in which we identify a problem or opportunity that requires a solution as yet unknown. For example, artist/entrepreneur Marshall Carbee and businessperson John Bennett founded Eco Safety Products after discovering that even paints declared safe by the U.S. Environmental Protection Agency (EPA) emit hazardous chemical compounds. Thus, Bennett's development of artist-safe soy-based paint began with identifying a safety problem with paints currently on the market.[51]

2. *Information gathering.* Given a problem, the solution is rarely directly at hand. We need time to learn more and to process that learning. Thus, **information gathering** is the stage of creative behaviour when possible solutions to a problem incubate in an individual's mind. Niklas Laninge of Hoa's Tool Shop, a Stockholm-based company that helps organizations become more innovative, argues that creative information gathering means thinking beyond usual routines and comfort zones. For example, have lunch with someone outside your field to discuss the problem. "It's so easy, and you're forced to speak about your business and the things that you want to accomplish in new terms. You can't use buzzwords because people don't know what you mean," Laninge says.[52]

3. *Idea generation.* Once we have collected the relevant information, it is time to translate knowledge into ideas. Thus, **idea generation** is the process of creative behaviour

EXHIBIT 6-4 Three-Stage Model of Creativity in Organizations

in which we develop possible solutions to a problem from relevant information and knowledge. Increasingly, idea generation is collaborative. For example, technology company HeroX is currently working with the accounting firm MNP LLP and a panel of Canadian healthcare experts to crowdsource ideas to improve health among Aboriginal populations, particularly those living on remote reserves. MNP LLP have funded $30,000 in prizes, to be awarded for the best and most workable ideas. While they anticipate that most ideas will come from industry professionals and established researchers, the public and in particular members of Aboriginal communities who are not among those experts will also be encouraged to participate because they bring a different and important set of knowledge to the table—including first-hand knowledge of conditions and processes at the sites of interest.[53]

4. **Idea evaluation.** Finally, it's time to choose from the ideas we have generated. Thus, **idea evaluation** is the process of creative behaviour in which we evaluate potential solutions to identify the best one. Sometimes the method of choosing can be innovative. When Dallas Mavericks owner Mark Cuban was unhappy with the team's uniforms, he asked fans to help design and choose the best uniform. Cuban said, "What's the best way to come up with creative ideas? You ask for them. So we are going to crowd source the design and colours of our uniforms."[54] Generally, you want those who evaluate ideas to be different from those who generate them, to eliminate the obvious biases.

Causes of Creative Behaviour

Having defined creative behaviour, the main stage in the three-stage model, we now look back to the causes of creativity: creative potential and creative environment.

Creative Potential Is there such a thing as a creative personality? Indeed. While creative genius—whether in science (Albert Einstein), art (Pablo Picasso), or business (RIM's Jim Balsillie)—is scarce, most people have some of the characteristics shared by exceptionally creative people. The more of these characteristics we have, the higher our creative potential.

Intelligence is related to creativity. Smart people are more creative because they are better at solving complex problems. However, intelligent individuals may also be more creative because they have greater "working memory"; that is, they can recall more information related to the task at hand.[55]

The Big Five personality trait of openness to experience (see Chapter 5) correlates with creativity, probably because open individuals are less conformist in action and more divergent in thinking.[56] Other traits of creative people are proactive personality, self-confidence, risk taking, tolerance for ambiguity, and perseverance.[57]

Expertise is the foundation for all creative work, and is thus the single most important predictor of creative potential. Film writer, producer, and director Quentin Tarantino spent his youth working in a video rental store, where he built up an encyclopedic knowledge of movies. The potential for creativity is enhanced when individuals have abilities, knowledge, proficiencies, and similar expertise to their field of endeavour. For instance, you wouldn't expect someone with minimal knowledge of programming to be very creative as a software engineer.

Creative Environment Most of us have creative potential we can learn to apply, but as important as creative potential is, by itself it is not enough. We need to be in an environment in which creative potential can be realized. What environmental factors affect whether creative potential translates into creative behaviours?

First and perhaps most important is *motivation*. If you aren't motivated to be creative, it is unlikely you will be. A review of 26 studies revealed that intrinsic motivation, or the desire to work on something because it's interesting, exciting, satisfying, and challenging (discussed in more detail in Chapter 7), correlates fairly strongly with creative outcomes. This link is true regardless of whether we are talking about student creativity or employee creativity.[58]

It is also valuable to work in an environment that rewards and recognizes creative work. The organization should foster the free flow of ideas, including providing fair and constructive judgment. Freedom from excessive rules encourages creativity; employees should have the freedom to decide what work is to be done and how to do it. One study of 385 employees working for several drug companies in China revealed that both structural empowerment (in which the structure of the work unit allows sufficient employee freedom) and psychological empowerment (which lets the individual feel personally empowered) were related to employee creativity.[59]

Creative Outcomes (Innovation)

The final stage in our model of creativity is the outcome. Creative behaviour does not always produce a creative or innovative outcome. An employee might generate a creative idea and never share it. Management might reject a creative solution. Teams might squelch creative behaviours by isolating those who propose different ideas. One study showed that most people have a bias against accepting creative ideas because ideas create uncertainty. When people feel uncertain, their ability to see any idea as creative is blocked.[60]

We can define *creative outcomes* as ideas or solutions judged novel and useful by relevant stakeholders. Novelty itself does not generate a creative outcome if it isn't useful. Thus, "off-the-wall" solutions are creative only if they help solve the problem. The usefulness of the solution might be self-evident (the iPad), or it might be considered successful by stakeholders before the actual success can be known.[61]

Creative ideas do not implement themselves; translating them into creative outcomes is a social process that requires utilizing other concepts addressed in this text, including power and politics, leadership, and motivation.

SUMMARY

- Individuals base their behaviour not on the way their external environment actually is, but rather on the way they see it or believe it to be.

- Individuals often make errors in perception due to common biases and mental short-cuts including self-serving biases, social identity effects, and stereotyping.

- An understanding of the way people make decisions can help us explain and predict behaviour, and also avoid common decision-making errors.

- Few important decisions are simple or unambiguous enough for the rational model's assumptions to fully apply. We find individuals looking for solutions that satisfice rather than optimize, injecting biases and prejudices into the decision-making process, and relying on intuition.

- Given the difficulties of making optimal decisions it becomes especially important to consider the ethics of our decisions: utilitarian, rights-based, and justice approaches can help with this.

- Managers should encourage creativity in employees and teams to create a route to innovative decision making.

IMPLICATIONS FOR MANAGERS

- Behaviour follows perception, so to influence behaviour at work, assess how people perceive their work. Often behaviours we find puzzling can be explained by understanding the initiating perceptions.

- Make better decisions by recognizing perceptual biases and decision-making errors we tend to commit. Learning about these problems doesn't always prevent us from making mistakes, but it does help.

- Adjust your decision-making approach to the national culture you're operating in and to the criteria your organization values. If you're in a country that doesn't value rationality, don't feel compelled to follow the decision-making model or to try to make your decisions appear rational. Adjust your decision approach to ensure compatibility with the organizational culture.

- Combine rational analysis with intuition. These are not conflicting approaches to decision making. By using both, you can actually improve your decision-making effectiveness.

- Try to enhance your creativity. Actively look for novel solutions to problems, attempt to see problems in new ways, use analogies, and hire creative talent. Try to remove work and organizational barriers that might impede your creativity.

BREAKOUT QUESTION FOR GROUP DISCUSSION

What personal habits might you adopt today that would help increase the accuracy of your perceptions and minimize perceptual bias when meeting new people? Make sure you explain *why* your proposed strategies would be effective.

PERSONAL INVENTORY ASSESSMENT

In the Personal Inventory Assessment found in MyManagementLab, take the assessment: How Creative Are You?

SELF-REFLECTION ACTIVITY

Do you consider yourself a creative person? To assess your own level of creativity try taking the Personal Inventory Assessment found in MyManagementLab "How Creative Are You?" Once you see your score, think carefully about what it means for your future career. Are some careers contraindicated for you due to very high or very low levels of creativity? Should that information help to guide your career decisions or not? Also consider: Are there downsides to high creativity? What benefits might be associated with low creativity?

You can enhance your own creative abilities if you do want to improve your score. Get into the mental habit of trying to look at things in new ways. Try to think in metaphors and analogies, as this can heighten creativity. Most importantly, don't be afraid of looking silly. New ideas require some risk taking and the anxiety created by risk can interfere with creative processes.

Etienne's pen abruptly stopped scratching across his notepad. He took a long sip of cold, too-bitter coffee. "Umm," he said to his interviewee, "I'm not sure I heard that correctly, could you repeat what you said?" "Sure," replied Duane, the large middle-aged man sitting across from him, "For fun on weekends I like to dress up in women's clothes and go to the bars as my alter ego, Diane." For the first time in years, Etienne found himself speechless. "Well, you are very honest," he finally managed to squeak out. "I figure I may as well be," commented Duane. "After all, this is a small town, and it's only a matter of time until you find out anyway. If something like that would impact my employment here, I would rather it come up now." Etienne took another gulp of coffee and moved on to the next question.

He had worked for a school bussing company as an HR specialist for nine years. One of his primary responsibilities was hiring and training school bus drivers. Key qualifications included a clean driving record, clean criminal record, responsible and safe driving habits, and an ability to calm, manage, and tolerate children from frightened kindergarteners on their first day of school to unruly teenagers going through rebellious fazes. Bus drivers also had to be sensitive to public perceptions. They were cautioned, for example, not to hug or otherwise touch any of the children, even if the child was very young and upset, to avoid the appearance of impropriety. One driver had been fired because over lunch he had parked the school bus at a local bar. Although he had drunk only one beer at 12:00 and he was not due to drive until 2:45, the reputational damage of having a school bus seen at that location was sufficient to result in his dismissal.

The company had a group of dedicated bus drivers who had been with the company for a long time, but turnover was still relatively high. Many parents with young children chose to drive a school bus for a few years to spend time with their children before returning to full-time employment. In addition, new immigrants with advanced degrees often worked there while waiting for their foreign credentials to go through the recognition process. These types of employees seldom lasted more than two years, so hiring was an ongoing task.

Duane had responded to the ad for new drivers and in all respects had seemed a strong candidate. He had driven city busses in Guelph, Ontario for 16 years before moving north to be primary caregiver to his aging parents. He had a clean and reliable driving record and had been highly recommended by his former employer. He had lots of experience with children: from the time he was 5 to when he was 14, he had coached his nephew's soccer team; it was his way of helping support his sister, a single parent, since she had wanted a positive male role model in her son's life.

There was no reason not to hire Duane. Throughout the rest of the interview he had performed well. That said, the cross-dressing thing made Etienne feel weird. He had grown up in a small, conservative rural community and had never before met anyone who would admit to cross-dressing. He couldn't help but feel it might be a problem. Would parents worry about their kids having contact with such a person? He couldn't explain why, but he felt "wriggly in his guts" about it.

He began to wonder if he was just being silly. He decided to talk about it with someone else. Since he was the only HR employee there, Etienne went to Heather, the vice-president for their area, to get a second opinion.

He described the situation to her the next day in her office. "What are your specific concerns?" asked Heather. "Well, I am worried about how parents will react if they learn one of our school bus drivers is a cross-dresser." "How would that be relevant?" "People might worry about their kids," replied Etienne. "I don't see why. He is a cross-dresser, not a pedophile. The two have nothing to do with each other. Sure, some parents might be upset, but are we really going to cater to other people's biases? Not that long ago, people would have been upset to see women drivers too. That doesn't mean we pander to it. … Ultimately, the decision is yours. You know I want to keep our company out of the press, that is the most important thing. But we also have to consider who we are as a company and the messages we send."

Etienne went home and gave the matter a lot of thought. Finally he decided to …

Discussion Questions

1. What perceptual biases might be influencing Etienne's perspective about Duane as a job candidate?

2. In theory, how might perceptual biases and decision-making biases influence Etienne's decision making?

3. What might help Etienne make the optimal decision in this situation? Explain your answer.

4. Using each of the three ethical decision-making models, determine what Etienne should do. Do you arrive at different answers according to which ethical model you are using? What might the implication of that be?

MINI CASE   CAREER PLANNING AS DECISION MAKING

Maria sat in the bright sunshine on the patio of her favourite Montreal deli waiting for her friend to join her for lunch. While waiting, she thought about her career options.

Maria had finished her last exam for her honours business degree only five weeks earlier. She was graduating at a time when downturns in the energy and manufacturing sectors impacted both the overall economy and the job market. In addition, parts of the economy had yet to recover from the worldwide financial crisis of 2008 and consumer spending was down. The trickle-down effects impacted hiring of entry-level workers in industries from consumer packaged goods to insurance, banking, natural resource extraction, even the retail sector. Many new business graduates struggled to find work of any kind.

She had originally planned to go into international development after completing her degree. She was especially interested in programs that helped develop entrepreneurship skills in economically disadvantaged areas. She had spent the last six months of her degree sending letters to aid agencies and educational organizations, and discovered it was much more difficult to enter the field than she had imagined. She found herself competing with job candidates who spoke four or five languages, had worked as entrepreneurs themselves, and had extensive volunteer experience in the developing world. She only spoke two languages and had never run a business or travelled abroad.

While pondering that, Maria found out her mother had been diagnosed with ovarian cancer. Treatment would be lengthy and difficult, and Maria wanted to be home in Montreal for the next year or two to help out. She decided to try and find a job that would help her to develop skills that would let her realize her ultimate career goals while also supporting herself and her mother.

After an intensive five-week search (well, more like four weeks—she had been a zombie for a week after finally finishing her last exam), Maria was pleasantly surprised to find that she had gotten three different job offers. None were exactly what she had envisioned herself doing, but she couldn't really afford to be picky.

The first job offer was from a call centre that handled customer care for a large cell and Internet service provider. She would answer calls and help resolve customer complaints about service and billing. The job didn't pay very well, just minimum wage, but she could earn more by selling extra services and upgrades to people calling in. The hours were also flexible, which would allow her to take some free language classes offered at her local recreation centre and go to medical appointments with her mother. It seemed okay, although the work would be boring and the call centre itself was loud and chaotic. Just the same, she had an felt an unaccountable unease just walking into the place. To add to her discomfort, during the interview process she had not been able to meet the person who would be her supervisor.

The second job offered was selling seafood and frozen beef products door to door. The pay was entirely commission-based, which Maria felt made the job entrepreneurial in nature. She had never been outgoing, and in fact was rather shy sometimes. She wasn't sure door-to-door sales was really her thing. When she had gone for the job interview, however, she had been happy to see a successful-looking woman interviewing her. This interviewer explained how she herself had started out selling door to door but had been quickly promoted and given an opportunity to develop other business skills. She also mentioned that other sales reps did not always work out, and about 35 percent were let go after their first few months due to non-performance. The woman had pictures on her desk of her travels in Tanzania and Kenya, where she had done volunteer work several summers ago. She even had a Spanish heritage, just like Maria. Maria thought the woman was amazing and came out of the interview thinking, Well, if she could succeed here surely I can too!

The third offer was for a job as general office assistant in a small, family-run plumbing business. Her duties would include answering phones, invoicing customers, updating their website, scheduling the plumber's calls, and maintaining their inventory of parts. It paid $2.50 more per hour than minimum wage, but the hours were strict; she needed to be there from 8:00 to 4:00 every day. It was also made clear to her that overtime was common and she would be expected to work extra hours on short notice without complaint. Maria had found the office atmosphere pleasant, if task-focused, and she liked the idea of doing a number of tasks instead of just one thing all the time, but she also realized that advancement in such a small, family firm was extremely unlikely. She wasn't sure how her experience would be viewed by aid agencies either. Doing routine office work didn't seem very entrepreneurial to her, although entrepreneurs did have to know about running a business.

As her friend finally rounded the corner to meet her for lunch, Maria decided to ask her opinion. Which job would best serve her short-term and long-term goals?

Discussion Questions

1. What would be the best way for Maria to go about making this important decision? Please explain your answer.

2. Do you see any evidence of perceptual biases influencing Maria's thinking about each job opportunity? Put another way, is she being objective when she evaluates each option? If not, which perceptual biases are impacted her thought process?

3. What decision-making errors might Maria be especially prone to under these circumstances? How might she best avoid them?

MyManagementLab

Study, practise, and explore real management situations with these helpful resources:
- **Interactive Lesson Presentations:** Work through interactive presentations and assessments to test your knowledge of management concepts.
- **PIA (Personal Inventory Assessments):** Enhance your ability to connect with key concepts through these engaging self-reflection assessments.
- **Study Plan:** Check your understanding of chapter concepts with self-study quizzes.
- **Simulations:** Practise decision making in simulated management environments.

PERSONAL INVENTORY ASSESSMENT

Chapter 7
Motivation Theories

Clynt Garnham Technology/Alamy Stock Photo

LEARNING OBJECTIVES

After studying this chapter, you should be able to:

1 Describe the three key elements of motivation.

2 Evaluate the applicability of early theories of motivation.

3 Contrast the elements of self-determination theory and goal-setting theory.

4 Demonstrate the differences between self-efficacy theory, equity theory, and expectancy theory, and be able to apply each theory in a workplace setting.

5 Discuss organizational justice and the four types of justice that influence it.

6 Assess the implications of employee job engagement for management.

Motivating employees is one of the most important, and one of the most challenging, aspects of management. As we will see, there is no shortage of advice about how to do it. Motivation is not simply about working hard—it also reflects your view of your own abilities.

Motivation is one of the most frequently researched topics in OB.[1] According to the Canadian Human Resources Centre, 60 percent of Canadian employees responding to a semiannual survey reported a lack of engagement at work. A further 15 percent reported being actively disengaged while

only 25 percent felt actively engaged.[2] In another survey, 69 percent of workers reported wasting time at work every day, and nearly a quarter said they waste between 30 and 60 minutes every day. How? Usually by surfing the Internet (checking the news and visiting social network sites) and chatting with coworkers.[3] So, though times change, the problem of motivating a workforce stays the same.

In this chapter, we'll review the basics of motivation, assess motivation theories, and provide an integrative model that fits theories together.

DEFINING MOTIVATION

Some individuals seem driven to succeed. The same student who struggles to read a textbook for more than twenty minutes may devour a *Harry Potter* book in a day or two. The difference is the situation. As we analyze the concept of motivation, keep in mind that the level of motivation varies both between individuals and within individuals at different times.

We define **motivation** as the processes that account for an individual's *intensity*, *direction*, and *persistence* of effort toward attaining a goal.[4] While general motivation is concerned with effort toward *any* goal, we'll narrow the focus to *organizational* goals toward work-related behaviour.

Intensity describes how hard a person tries. This is the element most of us focus on when we talk about motivation. However, high intensity is unlikely to lead to favourable job-performance outcomes unless the effort is channelled in a *direction* that benefits the organization. Therefore, we consider the quality of effort as well as its intensity. Effort directed toward, and consistent with, the organization's goals is the kind of effort we should be seeking. Finally, motivation has a *persistence* dimension. This measures how long a person can maintain effort. Motivated individuals stay with a task long enough to achieve their goals, even when they encounter difficulties.

EARLY THEORIES OF MOTIVATION

The idea that motivation is a key factor in worker productivity was first highlighted by early studies examining the relationship between the physical environment and productivity. These studies, which took place between 1927 and 1932, are collectively referred to as the "Hawthorne studies." The researchers originally intended to find the best temperature, lighting levels, and work pace to maximize productivity. The results were surprising. For example, when they increased the light level for the experimental group of workers, output rose for that unit and for the control group. But as they dropped the light level in the experimental group, productivity continued to increase in both groups. In fact, productivity in the experimental group decreased only when the light intensity had been reduced to that of moonlight, leading researchers to believe that something else influenced behaviour.

The researchers next isolated a small group of women assembling telephone relays from the main work group so their behaviour could be more carefully observed. Over the next several years, this small group's output increased steadily, and the number of personal and sick absences was approximately one-third that of the regular production department. It became evident this group's performance was significantly influenced by its "special" status. The members thought they were in an elite group, and that management showed concern about their interests by engaging in experimentation. In essence, workers in both the illumination and assembly experiments were really reacting to the increased attention they received. That attention made them feel special and valued, motivating them to work harder. It was a radical insight at the time and it led to much more theorizing and research on worker motivation.

Four theories of employee motivation formulated during the 1950s, although now of questionable validity, are probably the best known. We discuss more valid explanations later, but these four represent a foundation, and practising managers still use their terminology.

Hierarchy of Needs Theory

The best-known theory of motivation is Abraham Maslow's **hierarchy of needs**.[5] Maslow hypothesized that within every human being, there exists a hierarchy of five needs:

1. *Physiological.* Related to hunger, thirst, shelter, sex, and other bodily needs.
2. *Safety.* Security and protection from physical and emotional harm.

3. **Social.** Affection, belongingness, acceptance, and friendship.
4. **Esteem.** Internal factors such as self-respect, autonomy, and achievement, and external factors such as status, recognition, and attention.
5. **Self-actualization.** Drive to become what we are capable of becoming; includes growth, achieving our potential, and self-fulfillment.

According to Maslow, as each need becomes substantially satisfied, the next one becomes dominant. If a need is not satisfied, however, people become "stuck" on that level and cannot be motivated by tactics that address higher levels of the pyramid. So if you want to motivate someone, you need to understand what level of the hierarchy that person is currently on and focus on satisfying that need, moving up the steps in Exhibit 7-1. For example, Maslow would suggest that workers who are under the poverty line would be unlikely to be motivated by challenging work because their basic security and physiological needs are not yet being met.

Maslow's theory has received wide recognition, particularly among practising managers. It is intuitively logical and easy to understand. Unfortunately, however, research does not validate it. Maslow provided no empirical substantiation, and several studies that sought to validate it found no support for it.[6] But old theories, especially intuitively logical ones, die hard.

Some researchers have attempted to revive components of the needs hierarchy concept using principles from evolutionary psychology.[7] They propose that lower-level needs are the chief concern of immature animals or those with primitive nervous systems, whereas higher needs are more frequently observed in mature animals with more developed nervous systems. They also note distinct underlying biological systems for different types of needs. Time will tell whether revisions to Maslow's hierarchy will be useful for practising managers.

Theory X and Theory Y

One theory consistent with the needs hierarchy is Douglas McGregor's dichotomy of Theory X and Theory Y.[8] Under **Theory X**, managers believe employees inherently dislike work and must therefore be directed or even coerced into performing it (thus assuming that lower-order needs dominate). Under **Theory Y**, in contrast, managers assume employees can view work as being as natural as rest or play, and therefore the average person can learn to accept, and even seek, responsibility (thus assuming that higher-order needs dominate). McGregor believed Theory Y assumptions were more valid, and thus proposed motivating through participative decision making, challenging work, and good group relations. Unfortunately, like the needs hierarchy, little evidence confirms that *either* set of assumptions is valid or that acting on Theory Y assumptions will always lead to more motivated workers.

EXHIBIT 7-1 Maslow's Hierarchy of Needs

Source: A. H. Maslow, *Motivation and Personality*, 3rd ed., R. D. Frager and J. Fadiman (eds.). © 1997. Adapted by permission of Pearson Education, Inc., Upper Saddle River, New Jersey.

Two-Factor Theory

Believing an individual's relationship to work is basic, and that the attitude toward work can determine success or failure, psychologist Frederick Herzberg wondered, "What do people want from their jobs?" He asked people to describe, in detail, situations in which they felt exceptionally *good* or *bad* about their jobs. The responses differed significantly and led Herzberg to his **two-factor theory**—also called *motivation-hygiene theory*.[9]

As shown in Exhibit 7-2, intrinsic factors such as advancement, recognition, responsibility, and achievement seem related to job satisfaction. Respondents who felt good about their work tended to attribute these factors to themselves, while dissatisfied respondents tended to cite extrinsic factors such as supervision, pay, company policies, and working conditions.

To Herzberg, the data suggest that the opposite of satisfaction is not dissatisfaction, as was traditionally believed. Removing dissatisfying characteristics from a job does not necessarily make the job satisfying. Herzberg proposed a dual continuum: The opposite of "satisfaction" is "no satisfaction," and the opposite of "dissatisfaction" is "no dissatisfaction."

According to Herzberg, the factors that lead to job satisfaction are separate and distinct from those that lead to job dissatisfaction. Therefore, managers who seek to eliminate factors that can create job dissatisfaction may bring about peace, but not necessarily motivation. They will be placating rather than motivating their workers. As a result, Herzberg characterized conditions such as quality of supervision, pay, company policies, physical working conditions, relationships with others, and job security as **hygiene factors**. When they're adequate, people will not be dissatisfied; neither will they be satisfied. If we want to *motivate* people in their jobs, Herzberg suggested emphasizing factors associated with the work itself or with outcomes directly derived from it, such as promotional opportunities, personal growth opportunities, recognition, responsibility, and achievement. These are the characteristics people find intrinsically rewarding.

Like Maslow's needs hierarchy and McGregor's Theory X and Theory Y, the two-factor theory has not been well supported in research and has many detractors.[10] Criticisms centre

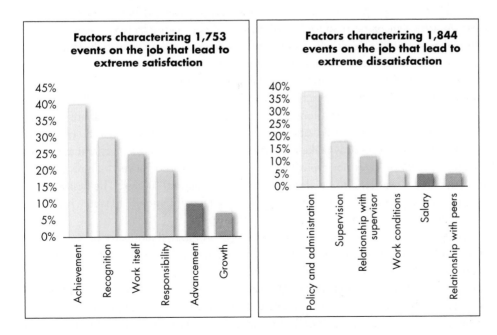

EXHIBIT 7-2   Comparison of Satisfiers and Dissatisfiers

on Herzberg's original methodology, and his assumptions such as the statement that satisfaction is strongly related to productivity. Subsequent research has tended to show that if hygiene and motivational factors are equally important to a person, both are capable of motivating people.

Regardless of the criticisms, Herzberg's theory has been quite influential, and few managers are unfamiliar with its recommendations.

McClelland's Theory of Needs

You have one beanbag and five targets set up in front of you, each farther away than the last. Target A sits almost within arm's reach. If you hit it, you get $2. Target B is a bit farther out, but about 80 percent of the people who try can hit it. It pays $4. Target C pays $8, and about half the people who try can hit it. Very few people can hit Target D, but the payoff is $16 for those who do. Finally, Target E pays $32, but it's almost impossible to achieve. Which would you try for? If you selected C, you're likely to be a high achiever. Why? Read on.

McClelland's theory of needs was developed by David McClelland and his associates.[11] It looks at three needs:

- **Need for achievement (nAch)** is the drive to excel, to achieve in relationship to a set of standards.

- **Need for power (nPow)** is the need to make others behave in a way they would not have otherwise.

- **Need for affiliation (nAff)** is the desire for friendly and close interpersonal relationships.

McClelland and subsequent researchers focused most of their attention on nAch. High achievers perform best when they perceive their probability of success as .5—that is, a 50–50 chance. They dislike gambling with high odds, because they feel no achievement satisfaction from success that comes by pure chance. Similarly, they dislike low odds (high probability of success), because then there is no challenge to their skills. They like to set goals that require stretching themselves a little.

Relying on an extensive amount of research, we can predict some relationships between achievement need and job performance. First, when jobs have a high degree of personal responsibility, feedback, and an intermediate degree of risk, high achievers are strongly motivated. They are successful in entrepreneurial activities such as running their own businesses, for example, and managing self-contained units within large organizations.[12] Second, a high need to achieve does not necessarily make someone a good manager, especially in large organizations. People with a high achievement need are interested in how well they do personally, and not in influencing others to do well. High-nAch salespeople do not necessarily make good sales managers, and the good general manager in a large organization does not typically have a high need to achieve.[13] Third, needs for affiliation and power tend to be closely related to managerial success. The best managers are high in their need for power and low in their need for affiliation.[14] In fact, a high power motive may be a requirement for managerial effectiveness.[15]

The view that a high achievement need acts as an internal motivator presupposes two cultural characteristics—willingness to accept a moderate degree of risk (which excludes countries with strong uncertainty-avoidance characteristics) and concern with performance (which applies to countries with strong achievement characteristics). This combination is found in Anglo-American countries such as the United States, Canada, and Great Britain,[16] and much less in more collectivistic societies like Chile and Portugal.

Among the early theories of motivation, McClelland's has garnered the best research support. Unfortunately, it has less practical effect than the others. Because McClelland argued that the three needs are subconscious—we may rank high on them but not know it—measuring them is not easy. In the most common approach, a trained expert presents pictures to individuals, asks them to tell a story about each, and then scores the responses in terms of the three needs. However, the process is time-consuming and expensive, and few organizations have been willing to invest in employing McClelland's concept.

CONTEMPORARY THEORIES OF MOTIVATION

Early theories of motivation either have not held up under close examination or have fallen out of favour. In contrast, contemporary theories have one thing in common: Each has a reasonable degree of valid supporting documentation. This doesn't mean they are unquestionably right. We call them "contemporary theories" because they represent the current state of thinking in explaining employee motivation.

Self-Determination Theory

"It's strange," said Marcia. "I started work at the humane society as a volunteer. I put in 15 hours a week helping people adopt pets. And I loved coming to work. Then, three months ago, they hired me full-time at $12 an hour. I'm doing the same work I did before. But I'm not finding it nearly as much fun."

Does Marcia's reaction seem counterintuitive? There's an explanation for it. It's called **self-determination theory**, which proposes that people prefer to feel they have control over their actions, so anything that makes a previously enjoyed task feel more like an obligation than a freely chosen activity will undermine motivation.[17] Much research on self-determination theory in OB has focused on **cognitive evaluation theory**, a complementary theory that hypothesizes that extrinsic rewards will reduce intrinsic interest in a task. When people are paid for work, it feels less like something they *want* to do and more like something they *have* to do. Self-determination theory proposes that in addition to being driven by a need for autonomy, people seek ways to achieve competence and positive connections to others. A large number of studies support self-determination theory.[18] Its major implications relate to work rewards.

When organizations use extrinsic rewards as payoffs for superior performance, employees feel they are doing a good job less because of their own intrinsic desire to excel than because that's what the organization wants. Eliminating extrinsic rewards can shift an individual's perception of why he works on a task from an external to an internal explanation. If you're reading a novel a week because your English literature instructor requires you to, you can attribute your reading behaviour to an external source. However, if you find yourself continuing to read a novel a week after the course is over, your natural

Many parents pay their kids for good grades. Self-determination theory suggests this may be counterproductive.

Monkey Business Images/Shutterstock

inclination is to say, "I must enjoy reading novels, because I'm still reading one a week." What does self-determination theory suggest for providing rewards? It suggests some caution in the use of extrinsic rewards to motivate. Rewards and deadlines diminish motivation if people see them as coercive or controlling. More specifically, self-determination theory suggests that pursuing goals out of intrinsic motives (such as a strong interest in the work itself) is more sustaining to human motivation than extrinsic rewards. Similarly, cognitive evaluation theory suggests that providing extrinsic incentives may, in many cases, undermine intrinsic motivation.

A more recent outgrowth of self-determination theory is **self-concordance**, which considers how strongly people's reasons for pursuing goals are consistent with their interests and core values. Across cultures, if individuals pursue goals because of intrinsic interest, they are more likely to attain goals, are happier when they do, and are happy even if they do not.[19] Why? Because the process of striving for goals is fun whether or not the goal is achieved.[20] The opposite appears true as well. Recent research reveals that when people do *not* enjoy their work for intrinsic reasons, those who work because they feel obligated to do so can still perform well, though they experience higher levels of strain as a result.[21] What does all this mean? For individuals, it means: Choose your job for reasons other than extrinsic rewards. For organizations, it means: Managers should provide intrinsic as well as extrinsic incentives. Managers need to make the work interesting, provide recognition, and support employee growth and development. Employees who feel what they do is within their control and a result of free choice are likely to be more motivated by their work and committed to their employers.[22]

Goal-Setting Theory

In general, managers should make goals specific and difficult—managers should set the highest goals to which employees will commit.

Gene Broadwater, former coach of the Hamilton High School cross-country team, gave his squad these last words before they approached the starting line for the league championship race: "Each one of you is physically ready. Now, get out there and do your best. No one can ever ask more of you than that."

You've heard the sentiment a number of times yourself: "Just do your best. That's all anyone can ask." But what does "Do your best" mean? Do we ever know whether we've achieved that vague goal? Would the cross-country runners have recorded faster times if Coach Broadwater had given each a specific goal? Research on **goal-setting theory** reveals impressive effects of goal specificity, challenge, and feedback on performance.

In the late 1960s, Edwin Locke proposed that intentions to work toward a goal are a major source of work motivation.[23] That is, goals tell an employee what needs to be done and how much effort is needed.[24] Evidence strongly suggests that specific goals increase performance; that difficult goals, when accepted, result in higher performance than do easy goals; and that feedback leads to higher performance than does nonfeedback.[25]

In general, specific goals produce a higher level of output than the generalized goal "Do your best." Why? Specificity itself seems to act as an internal stimulus. When a trucker commits to making 12 round-trip hauls between Toronto and Buffalo, New York each week, this intention gives him a specific objective to attain. Other things being equal, he will outperform a counterpart with no goals or the generalized goal "Do your best."

If factors such as acceptance of goals are held constant, the more difficult the goal, the higher the level of performance. Of course, it's logical to assume easier goals are more likely to be accepted. But once a hard task is accepted, we can expect the employee to exert a high level of effort to try to achieve it.

Why are people motivated by difficult goals?[26] First, they get our attention and help us focus. Second, they energize us because we have to work harder to attain them. Do you study as hard for an easy exam as you do for a difficult one? Probably not. Third, when goals are difficult, people persist in trying to attain them. Finally, difficult goals lead us to discover strategies that help us perform the job or task more effectively. If we have to struggle to solve a difficult problem, we often think of a better way to go about it.

People do better when they get feedback on how well they are progressing toward their goals because it helps identify discrepancies between what they have done and what they want to do next—that is, feedback guides behaviour. But all feedback is not equally potent. Self-generated feedback—with which employees are able to monitor their own progress or receive feedback from the task process itself—is more powerful than externally generated feedback.[27]

If employees can participate in setting their own goals, will they try harder? The evidence is mixed. In some cases, participatively set goals yielded superior performance; in others, individuals performed best when assigned goals by their boss. But a major advantage of participation may be that it increases acceptance of the goal as a desirable one toward which to work.[28] Without participation, the individual pursuing the goal needs to clearly understand its purpose and importance.[29]

In addition to feedback, three other factors influence the goals–performance relationship: *goal commitment, task characteristics*, and *national culture*. Goal-setting theory assumes an individual is *committed* to the goal and determined not to lower or abandon it. The individual (1) believes he can achieve the goal and (2) wants to achieve it.[30] Goal commitment is most likely to occur when goals are made public, when the individual has an internal locus of control, when the goals are self-set rather than assigned, and when goals are based at least partly on individual ability.[31]

Goals seem to affect performance more strongly when *tasks* are simple rather than complex, well learned rather than novel, independent rather than interdependent, and on the high end of achievability.[32] On interdependent tasks, group goals are preferable.

Setting specific, difficult, individual goals may have different effects in different *cultures*. Most goal-setting research has been done in the United States and Canada, where individual achievement and performance are most highly valued. Research has not shown that group-based goals are more effective in collectivist than in individualist cultures. In collectivistic and high power-distance cultures, achievable moderate goals can be more highly motivating than difficult ones.[33] Finally, assigned goals appear to generate greater goal commitment in high than in low power-distance cultures.[34] More research is needed to assess how goal constructs might differ across cultures.

Although goal setting has positive outcomes, it is not unequivocally beneficial. For example, some goals may be *too* effective.[35] When learning something is important, goals related to performance undermine adaptation and creativity, because people become too focused on outcomes and ignore changing conditions. A goal to learn and generate alternative solutions will be more effective than a goal to perform. In addition, some authors argue that goals can lead employees to focus on a single standard and exclude all others. For example, a goal to boost short-term stock prices may lead organizations to ignore long-term success and even to engage in unethical behaviour such as cooking the books to meet the goal. Other studies show that employees low in conscientiousness and emotional stability experience greater emotional exhaustion when their leaders set goals.[36] Finally, individuals may fail to give up on an unattainable goal, even when it might be beneficial to do so. Despite differences of opinion, most researchers agree that goals are powerful in shaping behaviour although they also highlight that managers should make sure goals are aligned with company objectives.

Research has found that people differ in the way they regulate their thoughts and behaviours during goal pursuit. Generally, people fall into one of two categories, though they could belong to both. Those with a **promotion focus** strive for advancement and accomplishment, and they approach conditions that move them closer toward desired goals. Those with a **prevention focus** strive to fulfill duties and obligations and avoid conditions that pull them away from desired goals. Although you would be right in noting that both strategies are in the service of goal accomplishment, the manner in which they get there is quite different.

As an example, consider studying for an exam. You might engage in promotion-focused activities such as reading class materials and notes, or in prevention-focused activities such as refraining from things that would get in the way of studying, such as playing video games or going out with friends. Or you could do both. Ideally, it's probably best to be both promotion- *and* prevention-oriented.[37]

Implementing Goal-Setting Theory How do managers make goal-setting theory operational? That's often left up to the individual. Some set aggressive performance targets—what General Electric called "stretch goals." Some Canadian employers, such as Kruger Products and Fidelity Investments, are known for demanding performance goals. But many companies and individual managers don't set goals. Asked whether their jobs had clearly defined goals, only a minority of employees in a survey said yes.[38]

A more systematic way to utilize goal setting is with **management by objectives (MBO)**, an initiative most popular in the 1970s, but still used today. MBO emphasizes participatively set goals that are tangible, verifiable, measurable, and relate to the broader organizational mission and strategies. As shown in Exhibit 7-3, the organization's overall objectives are translated into specific objectives for each level (divisional, departmental, individual). But because lower-unit managers jointly participate in setting their own goals, MBO works from the bottom up as well as the top down. The result is a hierarchy that links objectives from one level to those at the next. For the individual employee, MBO provides specific personal performance goals and helps workers see how their job, no matter what level they are at, influences attainment of broader corporate objectives.

Four ingredients are common to MBO programs: goal specificity, participation in decision making (including the setting of goals or objectives), an explicit time period, and performance feedback.[39] Many elements in MBO programs match propositions of goal-setting theory. For example, having an explicit time period to accomplish objectives matches goal-setting theory's emphasis on goal specificity. Similarly, we noted earlier that feedback about goal progress is a critical element of goal-setting theory. The only area of possible disagreement between MBO and goal-setting theory is participation: MBO strongly advocates participation, whereas goal-setting theory demonstrates that managers' assigned goals are usually just as effective.

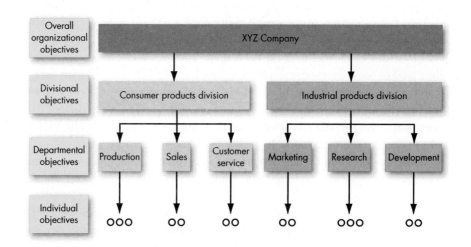

EXHIBIT 7-3 Cascading of Objectives

OTHER CONTEMPORARY THEORIES OF MOTIVATION

Self-Efficacy Theory

Self-efficacy theory, also known as *social cognitive theory* or *social learning theory*, refers to an individual's belief that he is capable of performing a task.[40] The higher your self-efficacy, the more confidence you have in your ability to succeed. So, in difficult situations, people with low self-efficacy are more likely to lessen their effort or give up altogether, while those with high self-efficacy will try harder to master the challenge.[41]

Self-efficacy can create a positive spiral in which those with high efficacy become more engaged in their tasks and then, in turn, increase their performance, which increases efficacy further.[42] Changes in self-efficacy over time are related to changes in creative performance as well.[43] Individuals high in self-efficacy also seem to respond to negative feedback with increased effort and motivation, while those low in self-efficacy are likely to lessen their effort after negative feedback.[44] How can managers help their employees achieve high levels of self-efficacy? By bringing goal-setting theory and self-efficacy theory together.

Goal-setting theory and self-efficacy theory don't compete; they complement each other. As Exhibit 7-4 shows, employees whose managers set difficult goals for them will have a higher level of self-efficacy and set higher goals for their own performance. Why? Setting difficult goals for people communicates your confidence in them. Imagine you learn that your boss sets a higher goal for you than for your coworkers. How would you interpret this? As long as you didn't feel you were being picked on, you would probably think, "Well, I guess my boss thinks I'm capable of performing better than others." This sets in motion a psychological process in which you're more confident in yourself (higher self-efficacy) and you set higher personal goals, performing better both inside and outside the workplace.

> Managers will increase employees' motivation by increasing their confidence in successfully completing the task (self-efficacy).

The researcher who developed self-efficacy theory, Albert Bandura, proposes four ways self-efficacy can be increased:[45]

1. Enactive mastery
2. Vicarious modelling
3. Verbal persuasion
4. Arousal

According to Bandura, the most important source of increasing self-efficacy is *enactive mastery*—that is, gaining relevant experience with the task or job. If you've been able to do the job successfully in the past, you're more confident you'll be able to do it in the future.

The second source is *vicarious modelling*—becoming more confident because you see someone else doing the task. If your friend studies hard and improves their grade point average, it increases your confidence that you can improve your grade point average, too.

honeyflavour/Fotolia

> The children's fable about the "little engine that could" is a good example of high perceived self-efficacy. In the story a small train engine struggles to make it up a steep hill, yet he succeeds by persistent effort and by saying "I think I can" to himself repeatedly. In the story it is his belief in himself and his abilities that leads directly to success.

EXHIBIT 7-4 Joint Effects of Goals and Self-Efficacy on Performance

Source: Based on E. A. Locke and G. P. Latham, "Building a Practically Useful Theory of Goal Setting and Task Motivation: A 35-Year Odyssey," *American Psychologist* (September 2002), pp. 705–717.

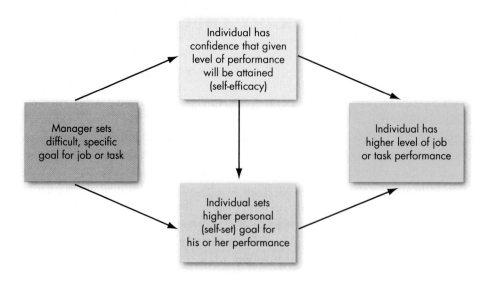

Vicarious modelling is most effective when you see yourself as similar to the person you are observing. Watching Canadian team captain Christine Sinclair score an amazing goal in the Women's World Cup might not increase your confidence in being able to play the ball yourself, but if you watch an ordinary person in your local adult recreational league do the same thing, it's more persuasive.

The third source is *verbal persuasion*: becoming more confident because someone convinces you that you have the skills necessary to be successful. Motivational speakers use this tactic.

Finally, Bandura argues that *arousal* increases self-efficacy. Arousal leads to an energized state, so the person gets "psyched up" and performs better. But if the task requires a steady, lower-key perspective (say carefully editing a manuscript), arousal may in fact hurt performance.

The best way for a manager to use verbal persuasion is through the *Pygmalion effect*—a form of self-fulfilling prophecy in which believing something can make it true. In some studies, teachers were told their students had very high IQ scores, when in fact they spanned a range from high to low. Consistently with the Pygmalion effect, the teachers spent more time with the students, gave them more challenging assignments, and expected more of them—all of which led to higher student self-efficacy and better grades.[46] This strategy has been used successfully in the workplace.[47] In one example, sailors who were told convincingly that they would not get seasick were in fact much less likely to do so.[48]

What are the OB implications of self-efficacy theory? Well, it's a matter of applying Bandura's sources of self-efficacy to the work setting. Training programs often make use of enactive mastery by having people practise and build their skills. In fact, one reason training works is that it increases self-efficacy.[49] Individuals with higher levels of self-efficacy also appear to reap more benefits from training programs and are more likely to use their training on the job.[50]

Equity Theory and Linkages to Perceptions of Organizational Justice

Ainsley is a student at Queens University working toward a bachelor's degree in finance. In order to gain some work experience and increase her marketability, she has accepted a summer internship in the finance department at a pharmaceutical company. She is quite pleased at the pay: $18 an hour is more than other students in her cohort were receiving for their summer internships. At work she meets Josh, a recent graduate of Queens University working as a middle manager in the same finance department. Josh makes $30 an hour.

On the job, Ainsley might be described as a go-getter. She's engaged, satisfied, and always willing to help others. Josh is quite the opposite. He often seems disinterested in his job and even has thoughts of quitting. Pressed one day about why he is unhappy, Josh cites his pay as the main reason. Specifically, he tells Ainsley that he makes much less than managers at other pharmaceutical companies. "It isn't fair," he complains. "I work just as hard as they do, yet I don't make as much. Maybe I should go work for the competition."

How could someone making $30 an hour be less satisfied with his pay and less motivated than someone making $18 an hour? The answer lies in **equity theory** and, more broadly, in principles of organizational justice. According to equity theory, employees compare what they get from their job (their "outcomes," such as pay, promotions, recognition, or having the corner office) to what they put into it (their "inputs," such as effort, experience, and education). People seek fairness. They expect a reasonable balance (or equity) between their effort and their rewards. When assessing fairness, people will compare their efforts (inputs) to the efforts of others and to the level of effort that was required in previous jobs at other organizations. They will then compare their rewards (outputs), taking the ratio of their outcomes to their inputs and comparing it to the same ratios in their previous job(s) and of their current coworkers. This is shown in Exhibit 7-5. If we believe our ratio to be equal to those with whom we compare ourselves, a state of equity exists and we perceive the situation as fair.

Based on equity theory, employees who perceive inequity will make one of six choices:[51]

1. Change inputs (exert less effort if underpaid or more if overpaid).
2. Change outcomes (individuals paid on a piece-rate basis can increase their pay by producing a higher quantity of units of lower quality).
3. Distort perceptions of self ("I used to think I worked at a moderate pace, but now I realize I work a lot harder than everyone else.").
4. Distort perceptions of others ("Mike's job isn't as desirable as I thought.").
5. Choose a different referent ("I may not make as much as my brother-in-law, but I'm doing a lot better than my DAD did when he was my age.").
6. Leave the field (quit the job).

The relevance of equity theory to employee motivation has been supported, with some interesting exceptions.[52] First, inequities created by overpayment do not seem to significantly affect behaviour in most work situations. So don't expect an employee who feels overpaid to give back part of her salary or put in more hours to make up for the inequity. Although individuals may sometimes perceive that they are over-rewarded, they restore equity by rationalizing their situation ("I'm worth it because I work harder than everyone else.").

Ratio Comparisons*	Perception
$\dfrac{O}{I_A} < \dfrac{O}{I_B}$	Inequity due to being underrewarded
$\dfrac{O}{I_A} = \dfrac{O}{I_B}$	Equity
$\dfrac{O}{I_A} > \dfrac{O}{I_B}$	Inequity due to being overrewarded

*Where $\dfrac{O}{I_A}$ represents the employee; and $\dfrac{O}{I_B}$ represents relevant others.

O = outcomes and I = Inputs

EXHIBIT 7-5   Equity Theory

Second, not everyone is equity-sensitive.[53] A few actually prefer outcome–input ratios lower than the referent comparisons. Predictions from equity theory are not likely to be very accurate about these "benevolent types."

Although equity theory is not applicable to every situation, the hypothesis served as an important precursor to the study of **organizational justice**, or more simply, applied fairness, in the workplace.[54] Equity theory helps to inform what we should do to foster motivation, organizational justice tells us how to actually go about doing it. Organizational justice is concerned with how employees feel authorities and decision makers treat them. For the most part, employees evaluate how fairly they are treated along four dimensions, shown in Exhibit 7-6.

Distributive justice is concerned with the fairness of the outcomes, such as pay and recognition, that employees receive. Outcomes can be allocated in many ways. For example, we could distribute raises equally among employees, or we could base them on which employees need money the most. However, as we discussed about equity theory, employees tend to perceive their outcomes are fairest when they are distributed equitably.

Does the same logic apply to teams? At first glance, it would seem that distributing rewards equally among team members is best for boosting morale and teamwork—that way, no one is favoured more than another. A recent study of National Hockey League teams suggests otherwise. Differentiating the pay of team members on the basis of their inputs (how well they performed in games) attracted better players to the team, made it more likely they would stay, and increased team performance.[55]

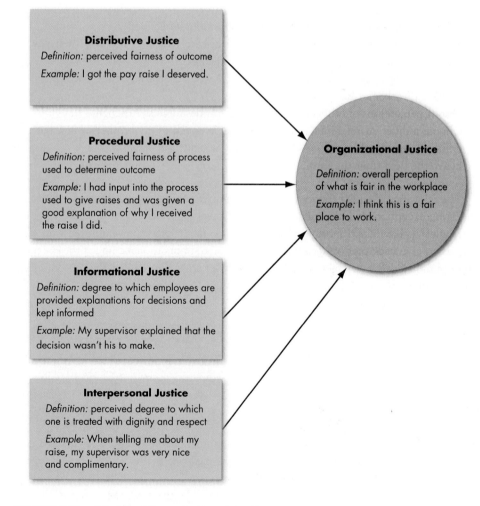

EXHIBIT 7-6 Model of Organizational Justice

The way we have described things so far, it would seem that distributive justice and equity are gauged in a rational, calculative way as individuals compare their outcome–input ratios to others. But the experience of justice, and especially injustice, is often not so cold and calculated. Instead, people base distributive judgments on a feeling or an emotional reaction to the way they think they are being treated relative to others, and their reactions are often "hot" and emotional rather than rational.[56]

Although employees care a lot about *what* outcomes are distributed (distributive justice), they also care a lot about *how* outcomes are distributed. While distributive justice looks at *what* outcomes are allocated, **procedural justice** examines *how* outcomes are allocated.[57] What makes procedures more or less fair? There are several factors. For one, employees perceive that procedures are fairer when they are given a say in the decision-making process. Having direct influence over how decisions are made, or at the very least being able to present your opinion to decision makers, creates a sense of control and makes us feel empowered (we discuss empowerment more in Chapter 8). Employees perceive that procedures are fairer when decision makers follow several "rules." These include making decisions in a consistent manner (across people and over time), avoiding bias (not favouring one group or person over another), using accurate information, considering the groups or people their decisions affect, acting ethically, and remaining open to appeals or correction.

It turns out that procedural and distributive justice combine to influence people's perceptions of fairness. If outcomes are favourable and individuals get what they want, they care less about the process, so procedural justice doesn't matter as much when distributions are perceived to be fair. It's when outcomes are unfavourable that people pay close attention to the process. If the process is judged to be fair, then employees are more accepting of unfavourable outcomes.[58] Why is this the case? It's likely that employees believe that fair procedures, which often have long-lasting effects, will eventually result in a fair outcome, even if the immediate outcome is unfair. Think about it. If you are hoping for a raise and your manager informs you that you did not receive one, you'll probably want to know how raises were determined. If it turns out that your manager allocated raises based on merit, and you were simply outperformed by a coworker, then you're more likely to accept your manager's decision than if raises were based on favouritism. Of course, if you get the raise in the first place, then you'll be less concerned with how the decision was made.

Beyond outcomes and procedures, research has shown that employees care about two other types of fairness that have to do with the way they are treated during interactions with others. The first type is **informational justice**, which reflects whether managers provide employees with explanations for key decisions and keep them informed of important organizational matters. The more detailed and candid managers are with employees, the more fairly treated those employees feel.

Though it may seem obvious that managers should be honest with their employees and not keep them in the dark about organizational matters, many managers are hesitant to share information. This is especially the case with bad news, which is uncomfortable for both the manager delivering it and the employee receiving it. For example, managers may fail to provide an adequate explanation for bad news such as a layoff or temporary pay cut out of a fear of being blamed, worries about making the situation worse, or concerns about triggering legal action.[59] In fact, research has linked the *absence* of explanations to increased litigation intentions by employees who have been laid off.[60] Explanations for bad news are beneficial when they take the form of post hoc excuses ("I know this is bad, and I wanted to give you the office, but it wasn't my decision") rather than justifications ("I decided to give the office to Sam, but having it isn't a big deal").[61]

The second type of justice relevant to interactions between managers and employees is **interpersonal justice**, which reflects whether employees are treated with dignity and

To promote fairness in the workplace, managers should consider openly sharing information on how allocation decisions are made. Fair and open procedures are especially important when the outcome is likely to be viewed negatively by some or all employees.

respect. Compared to the three other forms of justice we've discussed, interpersonal justice is unique in that it can occur in everyday interactions between managers and employees.[62] This quality allows managers to take advantage of (or miss out on) opportunities to make their employees feel fairly treated. Many managers may view treating employees politely and respectfully as too "soft," choosing more aggressive tactics out of a belief that doing so will be more motivating. Although displays of negative emotions such as anger may be motivating in some cases,[63] managers sometimes take this too far. Consider the backlash experienced by the information technology firm Fiserv when CEO Jeffrey Yabuki's angry and dismissive behaviour toward employees, including frequent comments that it is "my way or the highway" were exposed on the employer review website Glassdoor. Employees who encountered these behaviours reported feeling intimidated, diminished, and disrespected rather than motivated. Many reported leaving the company to avoid being exposed to Yabuki's behaviour any further.[64]

After all this talk about types of justice, how much does justice really matter to employees? A great deal, as it turns out. When employees feel fairly treated, they respond in a number of positive ways. All four types of justice discussed in this section have been linked to higher levels of task performance and citizenship behaviours such as helping coworkers, as well as lower levels of counterproductive behaviours such as shirking job duties. Distributive and procedural justice are more strongly associated with task performance, while informational and interpersonal justice are more strongly associated with citizenship behaviour. Even physiological outcomes, such as how well employees sleep and the state of their health, have been linked to fair treatment.[65]

Why does justice have these positive effects? First, fair treatment enhances commitment to the organization and makes employees feel it cares about their well-being. In addition, employees who feel fairly treated trust their supervisors more, which reduces uncertainty and fear of being exploited by the organization. Finally, fair treatment elicits positive emotions, which in turn prompt citizenship behaviours.[66]

Studies suggest that managers are motivated to foster employees' perceptions of justice because they wish to ensure compliance, maintain a positive identity, and establish fairness at work.[67] To enhance perceptions of justice, managers should realize that employees are especially sensitive to unfairness in procedures when bad news has to be communicated (that is, when distributive justice is low). Thus, it's important to openly share information about how allocation decisions are made, follow consistent and unbiased procedures, and engage in practices to increase the perception of procedural justice. However, it may be that managers are constrained in how much they can affect distributive and procedural justice because of formal organizational policies or cost constraints. Interpersonal and informational justice are less likely to be governed by these mechanisms because providing information and treating employees with dignity are practically "free." In such cases, managers wishing to promote fairness could focus their efforts more on informational and interpersonal justice.[68]

In terms of cultural differences, meta-analytic evidence shows individuals in both individualistic and collectivistic cultures prefer an equitable distribution of rewards over an equal division (everyone gets paid the same regardless of performance).[69] Across nations, the same basic principles of procedural justice are respected, and workers around the world prefer rewards based on performance and skills over rewards based on seniority.[70] However, in collectivist cultures employees expect rewards to reflect their individual needs as well as their performance.[71] Other research suggests that inputs and outcomes are valued differently in various cultures.[72] Some cultures emphasize status over individual achievement as a basis for allocating resources. Materialistic cultures are more likely to see cash compensation and rewards as the most relevant outcomes of work, whereas relational cultures will see social rewards and status as important outcomes. International managers must consider the cultural preferences of each group of employees when determining what is "fair" in different contexts.

Expectancy Theory

One of the most widely accepted explanations of motivation is Victor Vroom's **expectancy theory**.[73] Although it has its critics, most of the evidence supports the theory.[74]

Expectancy theory argues that the strength of our tendency to act a certain way depends on the strength of our expectation of a given outcome and its attractiveness. In practical terms, employees will be motivated to exert a high level of effort when they believe it will lead to a good performance appraisal; that a good appraisal will lead to organizational rewards, such as salary increases and/or intrinsic rewards; and that the rewards will satisfy the employees' personal goals. The theory, therefore, focuses on three relationships (see Exhibit 7-7).

1. **Effort–performance relationship.** The probability perceived by the individual that exerting a given amount of effort will lead to performance.
2. **Performance–reward relationship.** The degree to which the individual believes performing at a particular level will lead to the attainment of a desired outcome.
3. **Rewards–personal goals relationship.** The degree to which organizational rewards satisfy an individual's personal goals or needs and the attractiveness of those potential rewards for the individual.[75]

Expectancy theory helps explain why a lot of workers aren't motivated on their jobs and do only the minimum necessary to get by. Let's frame the theory's three relationships as questions employees need to answer in the affirmative if their motivation is to be maximized.

First: *If I give a maximum effort, will it be recognized in my performance appraisal?* For many employees, the answer is no. Why? Their skill level may be deficient, which means no matter how hard they try, they're not likely to be high performers. The organization's performance appraisal system may be designed to assess non-performance factors such as loyalty, initiative, or courage, which means more effort won't necessarily result in a higher evaluation. Another possibility is that employees, rightly or wrongly, perceive the boss doesn't like them. As a result, they expect a poor appraisal, regardless of effort. These examples suggest that people will be motivated only if they perceive a link between their effort and their performance.

Second: *If I get a good performance appraisal, will it lead to organizational rewards?* Many organizations reward things besides performance. When pay is based on factors such as having seniority, being cooperative, or "kissing up" to the boss, employees are likely to see the performance–reward relationship as weak and demotivating.

Finally: *If I'm rewarded, are the rewards attractive to me?* The employee works hard in the hope of getting a promotion but gets a pay raise instead. Or the employee wants a more interesting and challenging job but receives only a few words of praise. Unfortunately, many managers are limited in the rewards they can distribute, which makes it difficult to tailor rewards to individual employee needs. Some managers incorrectly assume that all employees want the same thing, thus overlooking the motivational effects of differentiating rewards. Whenever the offered rewards are not attractive to the employee, employee motivation suffers.

1. Effort–performance relationship
2. Performance–reward relationship
3. Rewards–personal goals relationship

EXHIBIT 7-7 Expectancy Theory

As a vivid example of how expectancy theory can work, consider stock analysts. They make their living trying to forecast a stock's future price; the accuracy of their buy, sell, or hold recommendations is what keeps them in work or gets them fired. But it's not quite that simple. Analysts place few sell ratings on stocks, although in a steady market, by definition, as many stocks are falling as are rising. Expectancy theory provides an explanation: Analysts who place a sell rating on a company's stock have to balance the benefits they receive by being accurate against the risks they run by drawing that company's ire. What are these risks? Risks include public rebuke, professional blackballing, and exclusion from information. When analysts place a buy rating on a stock, they face no such trade-off, because, obviously, companies love it when analysts recommend that investors buy their stocks. So the incentive structure suggests the expected outcome of buy ratings is higher than the expected outcome of sell ratings, and that's why buy ratings vastly outnumber sell ratings.[76]

Does expectancy theory work? Some critics suggest it has only limited use and is more valid where individuals clearly perceive effort–performance and performance–reward linkages.[77] Because few individuals do, the theory tends to be idealistic. If organizations actually rewarded individuals for performance rather than seniority, effort, skill level, and job difficulty, expectancy theory might be much more valid. However, rather than invalidating it, this criticism can explain why a significant segment of the workforce exerts low effort on the job.

FOSTERING WORKPLACE MOTIVATION

Creating Job Engagement

When Joseph reports to his job as a hospital nurse, it seems that everything else in his life goes away, and he becomes completely absorbed in what he is doing. His emotions, thoughts, and behaviour are all directed toward patient care. In fact, he can get so caught up in work that he isn't even aware of how long he's been there. As a result of this total commitment, he is more effective in providing patient care and feels uplifted by his time at work.

Joseph has a high level of **job engagement**, the investment of an employee's physical, cognitive, and emotional energies into job performance.[78] Practising managers and scholars have become interested in facilitating job engagement, believing factors deeper than liking a job or finding the work interesting drive performance. Studies attempt to measure this deeper level of commitment.

The Gallup organization has been using 12 questions to assess the extent to which employee engagement is linked to positive work outcomes for millions of employees over the past 30 years.[79] There are far more engaged employees in highly successful than in average organizations, and groups with more engaged employees have higher levels of productivity, fewer safety incidents, and lower turnover. Academic studies have also found positive outcomes. One study examined multiple business units for their level of engagement and found a positive relationship with a variety of practical outcomes.[80] Another study reviewed 91 distinct investigations and found higher levels of engagement associated with task performance and citizenship behaviour.[81]

What makes people more likely to be engaged in their jobs? One key is the degree to which an employee believes it is meaningful to engage in work. This is partly determined by job characteristics and access to sufficient resources to work effectively.[82] Another factor is a match between the individual's values and those of the organization.[83] Leadership behaviours that inspire workers to a greater sense of mission also increase employee engagement.[84]

One of the critiques of engagement theory is that the construct is partially redundant with job attitudes like satisfaction or stress.[85] Other critics note there may be a dark side to engagement, as evidenced by a positive relationship between engagement and work–family conflict.[86] For instance, individuals might grow so engaged in their work roles that family responsibilities become an unwelcome intrusion. An overly high level of engagement can lead to a loss of perspective and, ultimately, burnout. Further research exploring how engagement relates to negative outcomes may help clarify whether some highly engaged employees might be getting too much of a good thing.

SUMMARY

- The motivation theories in this chapter differ in their predictive strength.

- Maslow's hierarchy, Theory X and Theory Y, Two-Factor Theory, and McClelland's Theory focus on needs. None has found widespread support, although McClelland's is the strongest, particularly regarding the relationship between achievement and productivity.

- Self-determination theory and cognitive evaluation theory have merits to consider. Goal-setting theory can be helpful but does not cover absenteeism, turnover, or job satisfaction. Reinforcement theory can be helpful, but not regarding employee satisfaction or the decision to quit.

- Equity theory's strongest legacy is that it provided the spark for research on organizational justice, which has more support in the literature.

- Expectancy theory can be helpful, but assumes employees have few constraints on decision making, such as bias or incomplete information, and this limits its applicability.

- Organizational justice is influenced by distributive, procedural, informational, and interpersonal justice. The relevance of each form of justice varies by situation.

- Job engagement goes a long way toward explaining various degrees of employee commitment, although the outcomes of high engagement may not all be desirable.

IMPLICATIONS FOR MANAGERS

- Make sure extrinsic rewards for employees are not viewed as coercive, and recognize the importance of intrinsic motivators that appeal to employees' desires for autonomy, relatedness, and competence.

- Consider goal-setting theory: Within reason, clear and difficult goals often lead to higher levels of employee productivity.

- In accordance with self-efficacy theory, efforts you make to help your employees feel successful in completing tasks will result in their increased motivation.

- As suggested by justice theory, ensure that employees feel fairly treated; sensitivity to processes and interactions are particularly important when rewards are distributed unequally.

- Expectancy theory offers a partial means of enhancing employee productivity, absenteeism, and turnover: Employees are more motivated to engage in behaviours they think they can perform, which in turn lead to valued rewards.

Discuss goal setting strategies that you currently use to help you study effectively and hand in assignments on time. How are those strategies working for you now? Based on what you've learned about motivation, how might you improve them?

PERSONAL INVENTORY ASSESSMENT

In the Personal Inventory Assessment found in MyManagementLab, take the assessment: Work Motivation Indicator.

SELF-REFLECTION ACTIVITY

What does work mean to you? Is your job a means to end, allowing you to support a desired lifestyle? Is it a way to seek power and prestige? Is it a calling, a central part of who you are? The Personal Inventory Assessment found in MyManagementLab "Work Motivation Indicator" helps to evaluate what you really want out of your working life. Think carefully about what the result means for future career and lifestyle planning. What is important to your identity? What personal sacrifices, if any, are you prepared to make for your job? What are you willing to trade (money, prestige, time, etc.) in order to have time for other interests? The answers to these questions should guide your career decisions. People with a calling, for example, may be willing to earn lower wages at less prestigious jobs in order to reach their goals. Social workers who try to improve lives in underprivileged communities are a commonly cited example. People looking to maintain a certain lifestyle standard, by contrast, may be less willing to make material sacrifices to achieve their career goals.

MINI CASE   WHAT DOES "FAIR" MEAN?

As Sophia walked past the cubicles of the production-related office staff, she tried to ignore the occasional low, muttered complaint. The resentment over summer hours had simmered this long, a few more days wouldn't make any difference. As Director of Finance and Information Technology, it was not Sophia's direct responsibility to manage production staff, but since she was the most senior executive located at their company's rural packaging plant she felt a certain responsibility to attend to employee morale, even if it was somewhat outside of her formal job description. Now she wondered how to address this mess before it became toxic.

Sophia worked for the Canadian subsidiary of an American consumer packaged goods company who made skin care and personal hygiene products. Their facility in rural Ontario packaged products for the Canadian market, which had unique requirements, such as French and English labelling. The Canadian operations were responsible for their own sales and marketing campaigns. The sales branch focused on placing their products in retail outlets such as grocery stores and pharmacies, while the marketing team focused on reaching end consumers through television and magazine ads. The sales and marketing teams had offices in Toronto, but other functions, such as accounting and information technology, were located in the more affordable rural offices. The rural facility had about 250 employees who worked on the packaging assembly line in two shifts and 35 office employees. Of those 35, six were considered production employees, responsible for taking customer orders, handling customer service inquiries, and ensuring quality control and proper inventory management within the plant.

Ironically, their problems had begun precisely because Sophia was trying to improve employee morale. Several office employees had been asking for summer hours, meaning they would come in half an hour earlier each morning and then get Friday afternoons off. Stephen, the accounting supervisor responsible for a staff of seven bookkeepers and analysts, had been particularly adamant. "Everyone enjoys a long weekend," he said to Sophia, "and the accounting employees deserve it even more than most because every single month-end they are here until midnight two or three nights in a row while we get the monthly financial statement and reports wrapped up. Offering summer hours is the least we can do." Sophia had agreed, and had instituted the summer hours for office staff. It was not possible to do the same for production staff, since the packaging assembly line had to keep running through the full two shifts to keep up with demand. That meant that the six production-related office employees also had to stay, just in case they were needed by either customers or the plant staff.

It wasn't long before one of the most senior production-office employees, an operations expert named Bianca, started to object. It was difficult to watch all her colleagues leaving early to enjoy the Friday sunshine while she and her team were stuck behind their desks just in case they were needed (which they often weren't). The offices had always had a family feel—most employees had been there over 10 years. Bianca tried not to take it personally, but it was hard. It just didn't seem fair to her. She had expressed that opinion at a staff meeting last week only to have Stephen in Accounting confront her. "So what exactly is fairness to you anyway?" Stephen asked. "Because I never see you complain when we are staying late for month end and you are out the door by 5:00 or 5:30!"

Sophia hated to see that kind of infighting developing. She had also noticed that a couple of production employees had called in sick on Fridays recently and some of their reports had been late. That wasn't a good sign. How could she make everyone feel they were fairly treated? And what exactly was fairness anyway?

Discussion Questions

1. Using what you know about equity theory, expectancy theory, and organizational justice, explain why Stephen and Bianca have different perceptions of what fairness means when it comes to implementing summer hours.

2. Assume that Sophia makes no changes to the summer hours program. What long-term motivational impacts do you anticipate for office staff? How about production staff? Explain your reasoning.

3. Imagine you are Sophia. What do you do now to maintain the highest possible motivation among the greatest number of employees? Explain your reasoning.

MINI CASE   GOALS, REVISITED

In 2010 the CBC's *The Fifth Estate* profiled Peter Nygard, founder and CEO of Nygard, a successful clothing retailer catering largely to working-age women. The documentary, titled *Larger Than Life*, presented an unflattering portrait of an abusive, egotistical sexual predator who had difficulty reigning in his prodigious temper. Although Peter Nygard himself disputes some of the content presented in the documentary, several different people reported that he was fond of telling employees "I am God here" while making difficult and sometimes impossible demands.

Peter Nygard owns a large estate in the Bahamas that is used to entertain. In one example of goal setting "Nygard style," the CBC reported that Nygard had asked that groundskeepers ensure mosquitos were controlled in the resort through fogging and other chemical controls. The tennis courts were especially prone to mosquitos, and Peter had instituted a simple system: Every time a guest was bitten by a mosquito while playing tennis he would fine the groundkeeper on shift at the time. Fines ranged from $5 to $15 per incident. This incentive system was ultimately deemed illegal, because multiple fines might easily result in employees making little to nothing for their work. In interviews collected by the CBC, some employees commented that the complex system of fines (of which the mosquito fines were just one example), combined with the vulnerability of the workers and Peter's frequent rages and abusive behaviour, created working conditions comparable to slavery.

Discussion Questions

1. Using goal-setting theory as your framework, explain why Nygard's "mosquito fine" policy would be ineffective at motivating desirable job task behaviours.

2. Using goal-setting theory as your framework, devise an incentive system that would maximize performance—in this case meaning careful attention to mosquito control. Explain and justify your strategy.

3. What impact would abusive behaviour and frequent temper tantrums by the CEO be likely to have on short-term employee motivation? What about long-term motivation and engagement? Explain your answer using motivational theory to justify your perspective.

PERSONAL INVENTORY ASSESSMENT

MyManagementLab

Study, practise, and explore real management situations with these helpful resources:

• **Interactive Lesson Presentations:** Work through interactive presentations and assessments to test your knowledge of management concepts.

• **PIA (Personal Inventory Assessments):** Enhance your ability to connect with key concepts through these engaging self-reflection assessments.

• **Study Plan:** Check your understanding of chapter concepts with self-study quizzes.

• **Simulations:** Practise decision making in simulated management environments.

Chapter 8
Motivation: From Concepts to Applications

designpics/123RF, Stock-Asso/Shutterstock, Robert Byron/123RF, Riccardo Piccinini/Fotolia

LEARNING OBJECTIVES

After studying this chapter, you should be able to:

1 Explain the job characteristics model and the way it motivates by changing the work environment.

2 Compare the main ways jobs can be redesigned.

3 Assess how specific alternative work arrangements may motivate employees.

4 Explain how employee involvement measures can motivate employees.

5 Evaluate how different types of variable-pay programs can contribute to increased employee motivation.

6 Demonstrate how flexible benefits turn benefits into motivators.

7 Describe the motivational benefits of intrinsic rewards and use that knowledge to assess employee engagement and recognition programs.

Pay is not the only motivator for working individuals. Pay is a central means of motivation, but what you're actually doing for the money matters, too. In Chapter 7, we focused on motivation theories. In this chapter, we apply motivation concepts to practices. While it's important to understand the foundational concepts, it's even more important to see how, as a manager, you can use them.

MOTIVATING BY JOB DESIGN: THE JOB CHARACTERISTICS MODEL

Increasingly, research on motivation focuses on approaches that link motivational concepts to the way work is structured. Research in **job design** suggests that the way the elements of a job are organized can influence employee effort. We'll discuss the job characteristics model and investigate ways jobs can be redesigned. We'll then explore alternative work arrangements.

The Job Characteristics Model

Developed by J. Richard Hackman and Greg Oldham, the **job characteristics model (JCM)** describes jobs by five core dimensions:[1]

Although there are individual differences, most people respond well to intrinsic job characteristics; the job characteristics model summarizes what intrinsic job characteristics might be altered to make the work more interesting and intrinsically motivating for employees.

1. **Skill variety** is the degree to which a job requires different activities using specialized skills and talents. The work of a garage owner-operator who does electrical repairs, rebuilds engines, does bodywork, and interacts with customers scores high on skill variety. The job of a body shop worker who sprays paint eight hours a day scores low on this dimension
2. **Task identity** is the degree to which a job requires completion of a whole and identifiable piece of work. A cabinetmaker who designs furniture, selects the wood, builds the object, and finishes it has a job that scores high on task identity. A job scoring low on this dimension is operating a lathe to make table legs.
3. **Task significance** is the degree to which a job is perceived to affect the lives or work of other people. The job of a nurse helping patients in a hospital intensive care unit scores high on task significance. Sweeping floors in a hospital scores low because, although cleanliness is very important to minimize disease transmission, many people do not think about how much sweeping floors contributes to that important outcome. In another example, a lawyer who actively prosecutes cases may feel more task significance than the clerk who merely checks court documents for spelling and grammar errors before they are submitted.
4. **Autonomy** is the degree to which a job provides the worker freedom, independence, and discretion in scheduling work and determining the procedures for carrying it out. A sales manager who schedules his own work and the sales approach for each customer without supervision has a highly autonomous job. An account representative who is required to follow a standardized sales script with potential customers while under supervision has a job low in autonomy.
5. **Feedback** is the degree to which carrying out work activities generates direct and clear information about your own performance. A job with high feedback is testing and inspecting iPads. Assembling components of an iPad as they move down an assembly line would provide low feedback.

Exhibit 8-1 presents the job characteristics model (JCM). Note how the first three dimensions—skill variety, task identity, and task significance—combine to create meaningful work the employee will view as important, valuable, and worthwhile. Jobs with high autonomy give employees a feeling of personal responsibility for results; feedback will show employees how effectively they are performing. The JCM proposes that individuals obtain internal rewards when they learn (knowledge of results) that they personally have performed well (experienced responsibility) on a task they care about (experienced meaningfulness).[2] The more these three psychological states are present, the greater will be employees' motivation, performance, and satisfaction, and the lower their absenteeism and

EXHIBIT 8-1 The Job Characteristics Model

Source: J. Richard Hackman & Greg R. Oldham, *Work Redesign*, 1st Ed., © 1980, p. 90. Reprinted and Electronically reproduced by permission of Pearson Education, Inc., New York, NY.

likelihood of leaving. As Exhibit 8-1 indicates, individuals with a high growth need are likely to experience the critical psychological states when their jobs are enriched—and respond to them positively.

In general, research concurs with the factors of the JCM, although studies have introduced potential modifiers. One study suggested that when employees were "other-oriented" (concerned with the welfare of others at work), the relationship between intrinsic job characteristics and job satisfaction was weaker. A few studies have tested the JCM in different cultures, but the results aren't consistent. The fact that the JCM is relatively individualistic (it considers the relationship between the employee and her work) suggests job enrichment strategies may not have the same effects in collectivistic cultures as in individualistic cultures (such as Canada).[3] However, another study suggested the degree to which jobs offered intrinsic motivators predicted job satisfaction and job involvement equally well for U.S., Japanese, and Hungarian employees.[4] Since these countries score differently on the individualism scale, this study suggests that the relevance of intrinsic motivators may be more strongly influenced by other, as yet unidentified, factors.

HOW CAN JOBS BE REDESIGNED?

"Every day was the same thing," Frank said. "Stand on that assembly line. Wait for an instrument panel to be moved into place. Unlock the mechanism and drop the panel into the Jeep Liberty as it moved by on the line. Then I plugged in the harnessing wires. I repeated that for eight hours a day. I don't care that they were paying me 24 dollars an hour. I was going crazy. Finally, I just said . . . this isn't going to be the way I'm going to spend the rest of my life. My brain was turning to Jell-O . . . so I quit. Now I work in a print shop and I make less than 15 dollars an hour. But let me tell you, the work I do is really interesting. The job changes all the time, I'm continually learning new things, and the work really challenges me!"

The repetitive tasks in Frank's job at the Jeep plant provided little variety, autonomy, or motivation. In contrast, his job in the print shop is challenging and stimulating. Let's look at some of the ways to put the JCM into practice to make jobs more motivating.

Job Rotation

If employees suffer from over-routinization of their work, one alternative is **job rotation**, or the periodic shifting of an employee from one task to another with similar skill requirements at the same organizational level (also called *cross-training*). Many manufacturing firms have adopted job rotation as a means of increasing flexibility and avoiding layoffs. Managers at these companies train workers on all their equipment so they can move around as needed in response to incoming orders. International evidence from Italy, Britain, and Turkey shows that job rotation is associated with higher levels of organizational performance in manufacturing settings.[5] Although job rotation was originally conceptualized for assembly line and manufacturing employees, many organizations use job rotation for new managers and others to help them get a picture of the whole business.[6]

At Singapore Airlines, for instance, a ticket agent may take on the duties of a baggage handler. Extensive job rotation is among the reasons Singapore Airlines is rated one of the best airlines in the world.[7]

The strengths of job rotation are that it reduces boredom, increases motivation, and helps employees understand how their work contributes to the organization, which increases task significance. However, it has drawbacks. Work done repeatedly may become habitual and routine, which makes decision making more automatic and "efficient." Training costs increase as each rotation necessitates a round of training, and moving a worker into a new position reduces productivity for that role. Job rotation also creates disruptions when members of the work group have to adjust to new employees. And supervisors may have to spend more time answering questions and monitoring the work of recently rotated employees.

Job Enrichment

Job enrichment expands jobs by increasing the degree to which the worker controls the planning, execution, and evaluation of the work. An enriched job allows the worker to do a complete activity, increases the employee's freedom and independence, increases responsibility, and provides feedback so individuals can assess and correct their own performance.[8]

How does management enrich an employee's job? Exhibit 8-2 offers suggested guidelines based on the JCM. *Combining tasks* puts fractionalized tasks back together to form a new and larger module of work. *Forming natural work units* makes an employee's tasks an identifiable and meaningful whole. *Establishing client relationships* increases the direct relationships between workers and their clients (clients can be internal as well as outside the organization). *Expanding jobs vertically* gives employees responsibilities and control formerly reserved for management. *Opening feedback channels* lets employees know how well they are doing and whether their performance is improving, deteriorating, or remaining constant.

Another method for improving the meaningfulness of work is providing employees with mutual assistance programs.[9] Employees who can help each other directly through their work come to see themselves, and the organizations for which they work, in more positive, prosocial terms. This, in turn, can increase employee commitment to the organization.

EXHIBIT 8-2 Guidelines for Enriching a Job

Source: Hackman, J.R., *Improving Life At Work*, 1st Ed., © 1977, p. 138. Reprinted and Electronically reproduced by permission of Pearson Education, Inc., New York, NY.

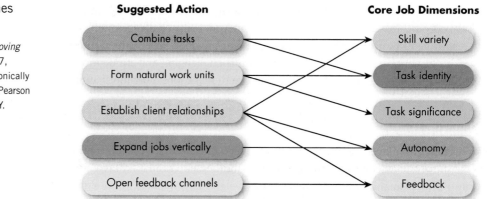

The evidence on job enrichment indicates that it reduces absenteeism and turnover costs and increases satisfaction, but not all programs are equally effective.[10] A review of 83 organizational interventions designed to improve performance management found that frequent, specific feedback on solving problems was linked to consistently higher performance, but infrequent feedback that focused more on past problems than future solutions was much less effective.[11] Thus, job enrichment can be effective when accompanied by practices—such as feedback—that support it. To some degree, its effectiveness also depends on the person. One study found employees with a higher preference for challenging work experienced larger reductions in stress following job redesign than individuals who did not prefer challenging work.[12]

Relational Job Design

While redesigning jobs on the basis of job characteristics theory is likely to make work more intrinsically motivating, contemporary research is focusing on how to make jobs more prosocially motivating to people. In other words, how can managers design work so employees are motivated to promote the well-being of the organization's beneficiaries (customers, clients, patients, and employees)? This view of job design shifts the spotlight from the employee to those whose lives are affected by the job that employee performs.[13]

One way to make jobs more prosocially motivating is to better connect employees with the beneficiaries of their work by relating stories from customers who have found the company's products or services to be helpful. This also increases task significance. The medical device manufacturer Medtronic invites people to describe how its products have improved, or even saved, their lives and shares these stories with employees during annual meetings, providing a powerful reminder of the impact of their work. One study found that radiologists who saw photographs of patients whose scans they were examining made more accurate diagnoses of their medical problems. Why? Seeing the photos made it more personal, which elicited feelings of empathy in the radiologists.[14]

Even better, in some cases managers may be able to connect employees directly with beneficiaries. Researchers found that when university fundraisers briefly interacted with the undergraduates who would receive the scholarship money they raised, they persisted 42 percent longer in their fundraising, and raised nearly twice as much money, as those who didn't interact with potential recipients.[15] The positive impact was apparent even when fundraisers met with just a single scholarship recipient.

ALTERNATIVE WORK ARRANGEMENTS

Another approach to motivation is to consider alternative work arrangements such as flextime, job sharing, or telecommuting. These are likely to be especially important for a diverse workforce of dual-earner couples, single parents, workers with ongoing health needs and/or disabilities, and employees caring for a sick or aging relative.

Flextime

Susan is the classic "morning person." She rises at 5:00 a.m. sharp each day, full of energy. However, as she puts it, "I'm usually ready for bed right after the 7:00 p.m. news."

Susan's work schedule as a claims processor at Great West Life Assurance is flexible. Her office opens at 6:00 a.m. and closes at 7:00 p.m., and she schedules her eight-hour day within this thirteen-hour period. Because Susan is a morning person whose seven-year-old son gets out of school at 3:00 p.m., she opts to work from 6:00 a.m. to 3:00 p.m. "My work hours are perfect. I'm at the job when I'm mentally most alert, and I can be home to take care of my son after he gets out of school."

Susan's schedule is an example of **flextime**, short for "flexible work time." Employees must work a specific number of hours per week but may vary their hours of work within limits. As in Exhibit 8-3, each day consists of a common core, usually six hours, with a flexibility band surrounding it. The core may be 9:00 a.m. to 3:00 p.m., with the office opening at 6:00 a.m. and closing at 6:00 p.m. Employees must be at their jobs during the common core period, but they may accumulate their other two hours around that. Some flextime programs allow employees to accumulate extra hours and turn them into a free day off each month.

Flextime has become extremely popular. According to a recent survey, 53 percent of U.S. organizations now offer some form of flextime.[16] In Canada a similar survey found that 35% of organizations offered it. This is not just a North American phenomenon. In Germany, for instance, 73 percent of businesses offer flextime, and flextime is becoming more widespread in Japan as well.[17] In Germany, Belgium, the Netherlands, and France, by law employers are not allowed to refuse an employee's request for either a part-time or a flexible work schedule as long as the reason is reasonable, such as to care for an infant.[18]

Claimed benefits include reduced absenteeism, increased productivity, reduced overtime expenses, reduced hostility toward management, reduced traffic congestion around work sites on commute paths, elimination of tardiness, and increased autonomy and responsibility for employees—any of which may increase employee job satisfaction.[19]

EXHIBIT 8-3

Possible Flextime Staff Schedules

Schedule 1	
Percent Time:	100% = 40 hours per week
Core Hours:	9:00 A.M.–5:00 P.M., Monday through Friday (1-hour lunch)
Work Start Time:	Between 8:00 A.M. and 9:00 A.M.
Work End Time:	Between 5:00 P.M. and 6:00 P.M.
Schedule 2	
Percent Time:	100% = 40 hours per week
Work Hours:	8:00 A.M.–6:30 P.M., Monday through Thursday (1/2-hour lunch)
	Friday off
Work Start Time:	8:00 A.M.
Work End Time:	6:30 P.M.
Schedule 3	
Percent Time:	90% = 36 hours per week
Work Hours:	8:30 A.M.–5:00 P.M., Monday through Thursday (1/2-hour lunch)
	8:00 A.M.–Noon Friday (no lunch)
Work Start Time:	8:30 A.M. (Monday–Thursday); 8:00 A.M. (Friday)
Work End Time:	5:00 P.M. (Monday–Thursday); Noon (Friday)
Schedule 4	
Percent Time:	80% = 32 hours per week
Work Hours:	8:00 A.M.–6:00 P.M., Monday through Wednesday (1/2-hour lunch)
	8:00 A.M.–11:30 A.M. Thursday (no lunch)
	Friday off
Work Start Time:	Between 8:00 A.M. and 9:00 A.M.
Work End Time:	Between 5:00 P.M. and 6:00 P.M.

As for flextime's actual record, most of the evidence stacks up favourably. It tends to reduce absenteeism and frequently improves worker productivity,[20] probably for several reasons. Employees can schedule their work hours to align with personal demands, reducing tardiness and absences, and they can work when they are most productive. Flextime can also help employees balance work and family lives; it is a popular criterion for judging how "family-friendly" a workplace is. Finally, employees with ongoing health needs find that flextime enables them to schedule medical appointments and follow-up care without needing to take time off. It may thus make workplaces more approachable for people with disabilities, an underemployed and frequently financially disadvantaged group in Canada.

Flextime's major drawback is that it's not applicable to every job or every worker. It works well with clerical tasks in which an employee's interaction with people outside his or her department is limited. It is often not a viable option for receptionists or sales personnel in retail stores—any whose jobs require them to be at their workstations at predetermined times. It also appears that people who have a strong desire to separate their work and family lives are less motivated to use flextime.[21] Overall, employers need to consider the appropriateness of both the work and the workers before implementing flextime schedules.

Job Sharing

Job sharing allows two or more individuals to split a traditional 40-hour-a-week job. One employee might perform the job from 8:00 a.m. to noon and another from 1:00 p.m. to 5:00 p.m., or they could work full but alternate days. For example, top Ford engineers Julie Levine and Julie Rocco engaged in a job-sharing program that allowed both to spend time with their families while redesigning the Explorer crossover. Typically, one of them would work late afternoons and evenings and the other worked mornings. They agreed that the program worked well, although making the job-share work required a great deal of time and preparation.[22]

Only 12 percent of large organizations offer job sharing, a significant decline from 18 percent in 2008.[23] Reasons it is not more widely adopted include the difficulty of finding compatible partners to job-share and the historically negative perceptions of individuals not completely committed to their jobs and employers. However, decreasing job sharing for these reasons may be shortsighted. Job sharing allows an organization to draw on the talents of more than one individual for a given job. It opens the opportunity to acquire skilled workers—for instance, parents with young children and retirees—who might not be available on a full-time basis. From the employee's perspective, job sharing can increase motivation and satisfaction.

An employer's decision to use job sharing is sometimes based on economics and national policy. Two part-time employees sharing a job can be less expensive than one full-time employee, but some experts suggest this is not the case because training, coordination, and administrative costs can be high. Between 2009 and 2012 the Canadian federal government encouraged job sharing in order to minimize layoffs. During that period the number of federal workers engaged in job sharing increased from 27,000 to 165,104.[24] Many German and Japanese[25] firms have been using job sharing for the same reason. Germany's Kurzarbeit program, now close to 100 years old, has kept employment levels from plummeting throughout the economic crisis by switching full-time workers to part-time job-sharing work.[26]

Ideally, employers should consider each employee and job separately, seeking to match up the skills, personalities, and needs of each employee with the tasks required for the job to look for potential job-sharing matches.

Telecommuting

It might be close to the ideal job for many people: no rush hour traffic, flexible hours, freedom to dress as you please, and fewer interruptions. It's called **telecommuting**, or working at home at least two days a week on a computer linked to the employer's office.[27] (A closely related term—the *virtual office*—describes working from home on a relatively permanent basis.) While telecommuting would seem to mesh with a transition to knowledge work (which often can be performed anywhere), it has been a popular topic lately not for its potential, but rather for reconsideration. Recently, large companies such as Yahoo and Best Buy have eliminated this form of flexible work.[28] Yahoo CEO Marissa Mayer has discussed how telecommuting may undermine corporate culture, noting: "People are more productive when they're alone, but they're more collaborative and innovative when they're together."[29]

While the movement away from telecommuting for some companies like Yahoo has made the headlines, it appears that for most, the movement continues to grow.

Statistics Canada reported that in 2008, the most recent year for which statistics are available, 11.2 percent of employees and 60 percent of the self-employed worked from home at least one day a week. Taken together that means that 19 percent of the Canadian working population works from home some of the time.[30] One recent survey of nearly 500 organizations found that 57 percent of organizations offered telecommuting, with 36 percent allowing employees to telecommute at least part of the time and 20 percent allowing employees to telecommute full-time, and these percentages have remained relatively stable since 2008.[31] Organizations that actively encourage telecommuting are the Bank of Canada, Molson Coors, IBM, L'Oréal Canada, the City of Calgary, Resource Conservation Manitoba, the National Ballet of Canada, and a number of government agencies.[32]

What kinds of jobs lend themselves to telecommuting? There are three categories: routine information-handling tasks, mobile activities, and professional and other knowledge-related tasks.[33] Writers, attorneys, analysts, and employees who spend the majority of their time on computers or the telephone—including telemarketers, customer-service representatives, reservation agents, and product-support specialists—are candidates. As telecommuters, they can access information on their computers at home as easily as in the office.

Telecommuting has several potential benefits: a larger labour pool from which to select, higher productivity, improved morale, and reduced office-space costs. A positive relationship exists between telecommuting and supervisor performance ratings, but the anticipated relationship between telecommuting and lower turnover intentions has not been substantiated in research.[34]

Beyond the benefits to employees and organizations, telecommuting has potential benefits to society. It can help people living in isolated and disadvantaged communities to more fully participate in the workforce. This improved access to paid work has broader economic and social justice implications, particularly for First Nations and Inuit people living in remote Northern communities. It can also help reduce the environmental impact of business activities, making telecommuting socially responsible. One study estimated that, in the United States, if people telecommuted half the time, carbon emissions would

Teleworking is not an all-or-nothing issue. Fully 67 percent of Canadian teleworkers who were profiled in the 2008 Statistics Canada study worked 10 hours or less a week from home and came into the office for "face-time" on other days.

michaeljung/Fotolia

be reduced by approximately 51 metric tons per year. Environmental savings could come about from lower office energy consumption, reduced gas usage, fewer traffic jams that emit greenhouse gasses, and fewer road repairs.[35] In addition it could lessen the need for some dual-earning couples to have two cars, reducing personal household expenses and resource wastage even further.

Telecommuting has several downsides. The major one for management is less direct employee supervision. In today's team-focused workplace, telecommuting may make it more difficult to coordinate teamwork and can reduce knowledge transfer in organizations.[36] From the employee's standpoint, telecommuting can increase feelings of isolation and reduce job satisfaction. Telecommuters are also vulnerable to the "out of sight, out of mind" effect.[37] Employees who aren't at their desks, who miss meetings, and who don't share in day-to-day informal workplace interactions may be at a disadvantage when it comes to raises and promotions because they're perceived as not putting in the requisite "face-time."

Telecommuting is a contemporary reality, particularly in the minds of employees. Telecommuting certainly does appear to make sense given changes in technology, the nature of work, and preferences of younger workers. Yet as the Yahoo experience shows, some leaders do not think those benefits outweigh the costs.

EMPLOYEE INVOLVEMENT

Employee involvement is a participative process that uses employees' input to increase their commitment to organizational success. If workers are engaged in decisions that increase their autonomy and control over their work lives, they will become more motivated, more committed to the organization, more productive, and more satisfied with their jobs. These benefits don't stop with individuals—when teams are given more control over their work, morale and performance increase as well.[38]

To be successful, employee involvement programs should be tailored to country norms.[39] The average Canadian worker is generally receptive to participative approaches as long as they perceive that management is sincere when seeking their involvement. Newcomers to Canada, however, may find the practice unfamiliar and uncomfortable. Recent immigrants from countries with a high power-distance may require additional reassurances about cultural appropriateness before embracing participative management styles. This idea is reinforced by a study of four countries, including the United States and India, that confirmed the importance of modifying practices to reflect national culture.[40] While U.S. employees readily accepted employee involvement programs, managers in India who tried to empower their employees were rated low by those employees. These reactions are consistent with India's high power-distance culture, which accepts and expects differences in authority. Similarly, Chinese workers who were very accepting of traditional Chinese values showed few benefits from participative decision making, but workers who were less traditional were more satisfied and had higher performance ratings under participative management.[41] Another study conducted in China found that involvement increased employees' thoughts and feelings of job security, enhancing their well-being.[42]

Examples of Employee Involvement Programs

Let's look at two major forms of employee involvement—participative management and representative participation—in more detail.

Participative Management Common to all **participative management** programs is joint decision making, in which subordinates share a significant degree of decision-making power with their immediate superiors. Participative management has, at times, been considered a panacea for poor morale and low productivity. In reality, for participative management to be effective, followers must have trust and confidence in their leaders. Leaders should refrain from coercive techniques and instead stress the organizational consequences of decisions to their followers.[43]

Studies of the participation–performance relationship have yielded mixed findings.[44] Organizations that institute participative management report higher stock returns, lower turnover rates, and higher labour productivity, although these effects are typically not large.[45] Research at the individual level indicates participation has only a modest influence on employee productivity, motivation, and job satisfaction. This doesn't mean participative management isn't beneficial. However, it is not a sure means of improving performance.

Representative Participation   Most countries in western Europe require companies to practice **representative participation**, called "the most widely legislated form of employee involvement around the world."[46] Representative participation redistributes power within an organization, putting labour on a more equal footing with the interests of management and stockholders by letting workers be represented by a small group of employees who participate in decision making.

The two most common forms of representation are works councils and board representatives.[47] Works councils are groups of nominated or elected employees who must be consulted when management makes decisions about employees. Board representatives are employees who sit on a company's board of directors and represent employees' interests.

The influence of representative participation on working employees seems to be minimal.[48] Works councils are dominated by management and have little impact on employees or the organization. While participation might increase the motivation and satisfaction of employee representatives, there is little evidence that this trickles down to the employees they represent. Overall, "the greatest value of representative participation is symbolic. If one is interested in changing employee attitudes or in improving organizational performance, representative participation would be a poor choice."[49]

Linking Employee Involvement Programs and Motivation Theories

In contrast to research on the job characteristics model and work redesign, which is mostly favourable, the evidence on employee involvement programs is decidedly mixed. It is not clear that employee involvement programs have lived up to their promise.

Employee involvement draws on a number of the motivation theories we discussed in Chapter 7. Theory Y is consistent with participative management and Theory X with the more traditional autocratic style of managing. In terms of two-factor theory, employee involvement programs could provide intrinsic motivation by increasing opportunities for growth, responsibility, and involvement in the work itself. The opportunity to make and implement decisions—and then see them work out—can help satisfy an employee's needs for responsibility, achievement, recognition, growth, and enhanced self-esteem. Extensive employee involvement programs have the potential to increase intrinsic motivation. And giving employees control over key decisions, along with ensuring that their interests are represented, can augment feelings of procedural justice.

USING PAY TO MOTIVATE EMPLOYEES

As we saw in Chapter 3, pay is not a primary factor driving job satisfaction. However, it does motivate people, and companies often underestimate its importance. Comparative pay rates are closely related to perceived justice, meaning that pay can impact motivation directly through acquired spending power (a reward), and indirectly via justice perceptions. One study found that while 45 percent of employers thought pay was a key factor in losing top talent, 71 percent of top performers called it a strong reason.[50]

Given that pay is so important, will the organization lead, match, or lag the market in pay? How will individual contributions be recognized? In this section, we consider (1) what to pay employees (decided by establishing a pay structure), (2) how to pay individual employees (decided through variable-pay plans and skill-based pay plans), (3) what benefits and choices to offer (such as flexible benefits), and (4) how to construct employee recognition programs.

What to Pay: Establishing a Pay Structure

There are many ways to pay employees. The process of initially setting pay levels entails balancing *internal equity*—the worth of the job to the organization (usually established through a technical process called job evaluation)—and *external equity*—the competitiveness of an organization's pay relative to pay in its industry (usually established through pay surveys). Obviously, the best system pays what the job is worth, while also paying competitively relative to the labour market.

Some organizations prefer to pay above the market, while some may lag the market because they can't afford to pay market rates, or they are willing to bear the costs of paying below market (namely higher turnover as people are lured to better-paying jobs). Some companies who have realized impressive gains in income and profit margins have done so partly by holding down employee wages, such as Comcast, Walt Disney, McDonald's, and AT&T.[51]

Pay more, and you may get better-qualified, more highly motivated employees who will stay with the organization longer. A study covering 126 large organizations found employees who believed they were receiving a competitive pay level had higher morale and were more productive, and customers were more satisfied as well.[52] But pay is often the highest single operating cost for an organization, which means paying too much can make the organization's products or services too expensive.

Establishing a pay structure thus has broad implications for employees and for the organization as a whole. Finding the right balance can be an art and a science, handled best when leaders understand the implications of pay decisions.

How to Pay: Rewarding Individual Employees Through Variable-Pay Programs

"Why should I put any extra effort into this job?" asked Anne, a fourth-grade elementary schoolteacher in Thunder Bay, Ontario. "I can excel or I can do the bare minimum. It makes no difference. I get paid the same. Why do anything above the minimum to get by?" While many schoolteachers are intrinsically motivated to perform well, comments like Anne's have been voiced by some teachers for decades because pay increases are tied to seniority.[53] Many organizations, public and private, are moving away from pay based on seniority because of this motivational limitation. It is worth noting that this objection to seniority-based pay is actually based on justice and equity concerns. As equity theory suggests, there is a reluctance to put in more work than others for the same reward. It also relates to expectancy theory: Why work harder when you get the same reward either way?

Piece-rate, merit-based, bonus, skill-based, profit-sharing, gain-sharing, and employee stock ownership plans are all forms of a **variable-pay program**, which bases a portion of an employee's pay on some individual and/or organizational measure of performance.[54] Variable-pay plans have long been used to compensate salespeople and executives, but the scope of variable-pay jobs has broadened. Recent research indicates that 26 percent of U.S. companies have either increased or plan to increase the proportion of variable pay in

Variable-pay plans focus on performance rather than seniority. Properly designed and administered, these plans do appear to enhance employee motivation. When they are poorly designed, however, they can have damaging unintended consequences, as we will see shortly.

employee pay programs, and another 40 percent have already recently increased the proportion of variable pay.[55]

Globally, around 80 percent of companies offer some form of variable-pay plan. In Latin America, more than 90 percent of companies offer some form of variable-pay plan. Latin American companies also have the highest percentage of total payroll allocated to variable pay, at nearly 18 percent. European and U.S. companies are relatively lower, at about 12 percent.[56] When it comes to executive compensation, Asian companies are outpacing Western companies in their use of variable pay.[57]

A recent study of 415 companies in South Korea suggested that group-based pay-for-performance plans can have a strong, positive effect on organizational performance.[58] Unfortunately, not all employees see a strong connection between pay and performance. Therefore, the results of pay-for-performance plans are mixed; the context and the receptivity of the individual to the plans play a large role.

Let's examine the different types of variable-pay programs in more detail.

Piece-Rate Pay

The **piece-rate pay plan** has long been popular as a means of compensating production workers with a fixed sum for each unit of production. A pure piece-rate plan provides no base salary and pays the employee only for what he or she produces. Ballpark workers selling peanuts are frequently paid piece-rate. If they sell 40 bags of peanuts at $2.50 each for their earnings, their take is $40. The more peanuts they sell, the more they earn. The limitation of these plans is that they're not feasible for many jobs. An emergency room (ER) doctor and nurse can earn significant salaries regardless of the number of patients seen or their patients' outcomes. Would it be better to pay them only if their patients fully recover? It seems unlikely that most would accept such a deal, and it might cause unanticipated consequences as well (such as ERs avoiding patients with chronic or terminal conditions). So, although piece-rate incentives are motivating and relevant for some jobs, it is unrealistic to think they can constitute all employees' pay.

Merit-Based Pay

A **merit-based pay plan** pays for individual performance based on performance appraisal ratings. A main advantage is that high performers can get bigger raises. If designed correctly, merit-based plans let individuals perceive a strong relationship between their performance and their rewards.[59]

Although you might think a person's average level of performance is the key factor in merit pay decisions, recent research indicates that the projected level of future performance also plays a role. Managers may unknowingly be basing merit pay decisions on how they *think* employees will perform, which may result in overly optimistic (or pessimistic) pay decisions.[60]

Despite their intuitive appeal, merit pay plans have several limitations. One is that they are typically based on an annual performance appraisal and thus are only as valid as the performance ratings. Poor choices about which aspects of job performance to focus on can have negative consequences. For example, call centre employees who are compensated on the basis of the number of calls they take each day may sacrifice call quality, rushing customers or leaving their issues unresolved. They may even hang up on customers with difficult and time-consuming problems! Another limitation is that the pay-raise pool of available funds fluctuates on economic or other conditions that have little to do with individual performance. For instance, a colleague at a top university who performed very well in teaching and research was given a pay raise of only $300. Why? Because the pay-raise pool was very small. Yet that is hardly pay-for-performance. Lastly, a move away from merit pay is coming from organizational leaders who don't feel it separates high and low performers enough.

The concept and intention of merit pay—that employees are paid for performance—is sound. For employee motivation purposes, however, merit pay should be only one part of a performance recognition program.

Bonuses An annual **bonus** is a significant component of total compensation for many jobs. The incentive effects of performance bonuses should be higher than those of merit pay because, rather than paying for performance years ago that has rolled into current base pay, bonuses reward recent performance. When times are bad or when performance deteriorates, firms can cut bonuses to reduce compensation costs. The CEO of Canadian National Railway Co., for example, recently saw his eligible (or possible) bonus drop significantly and get capped due to concerns the board of directors had about increased numbers of derailments and injuries.[61] In another example, several major Canadian banks have bonus structures and total amounts of available bonus dollars that fluctuate annually to reflect earnings levels.[62]

Although admittedly a bit manipulative-sounding, taking rewards and bonuses and splitting them into multiple categories—even if those categories are meaningless—may increase motivation.[63] Why? Because, research indicates, people are more likely to feel they missed out on a reward if they don't receive all from each category.

Skill-Based Pay **Skill-based pay** (also called *competency-based* or *knowledge-based pay*) is an alternative to job-based pay that centres pay levels on how many skills employees have or how many jobs they can do.[64] Under these plans improving skills by taking courses or tackling new types of assignments results in predictable raises. For employers, the lure of skill-based pay plans is increased workforce flexibility: Staffing is easier when employees possess a wide range of usable skills. Skill-based pay also facilitates communication, because people gain a better understanding of the skills used for other organizational jobs. One study found that across 214 different organizations, skill-based pay was related to higher levels of workforce flexibility, positive attitudes, membership behaviours, and productivity.[65] Another study found that over five years, a skill-based pay plan was associated with higher levels of individual skill change and skill maintenance.[66] These results suggest that skill-based pay plans are effective.

What about the downsides? Employees who are constantly upgrading their skills may be more attractive in the labour market, resulting in turnover when they receive offers from other companies. People can also "top out"—that is, they can learn all the skills the program calls for them to learn. This can be frustrating after they've been challenged by an environment of learning, growth, and continual pay raises. Plus, skill-based plans don't address overall performance but only whether someone can manage the skills. Perhaps reflecting these weaknesses, one study of 97 North American companies using skill-based pay plans found that 39 percent had switched to a more traditional market-based pay plan seven years later.[67] A skill-based pay plan may thus help an organization increase the scope of skills of its workforce, but may be limited to a prescribed number of development years. A skill-based plan would rarely be a good overall motivational strategy.

Profit-Sharing Plans A **profit-sharing plan** distributes compensation according to some established formula designed around a company's profitability. Compensation can be direct cash outlays or, particularly for top managers, allocations of stock options. When you read about executives like Research in Motion's Jim Balsillie, earning millions per year, much of it comes from stock options previously granted on the basis of company profit performance.[68] Or take Facebook's Mark Zuckerberg, who despite accepting a $1 salary made $2.3 billion in 2012 after cashing out 60,000 stock options.[69]

Of course, the vast majority of profit-sharing plans are not so grand in scale. Jao started his own snow removal business at age 13. He employed his friends, Ibrahim and Marissa, and paid them each 25 percent of the profits he made on each property. Profit-sharing plans at the organizational level appear to have positive impacts on employee attitudes; employees report a greater feeling of psychological ownership.[70] Obviously, profit sharing does not work when there is no reported profit per se, such as in nonprofit organizations, or often in the public sector. However, it may make sense for many organizations, large or small.

Gainsharing   Gainsharing[71] is a formula-based group incentive plan that uses improvements in group productivity or reductions in waste from one period to another to determine the total amount of money allocated. Its popularity seems narrowly focused among large manufacturing companies, although some healthcare organizations have experimented with it as a cost-saving mechanism. Gainsharing differs from profit sharing in tying rewards to productivity gains and waste reduction rather than profits, so employees can receive incentive awards even when the organization isn't profitable. Because the benefits accrue to groups of workers, high performers pressure weaker ones to work harder, improving performance for the group as a whole.[72]

Employee Stock Ownership Plans   An **employee stock ownership plan (ESOP)** is a company-established benefit plan in which employees acquire stock, often at below-market prices, as part of their benefits. Research on ESOPs indicates they increase employee satisfaction and innovation.[73] Their impact on performance is less clear. ESOPs have the potential to increase employee job satisfaction and work motivation, but employees need to psychologically experience ownership.[74] That is, in addition to their granted financial stake in the company, they need to be kept regularly informed of the status of the business and have the opportunity to influence its performance.[75]

ESOPs for top management can reduce unethical behaviour. CEOs are less likely to manipulate firm earnings reports to make themselves look good in the short run when they have an ownership share.[76] Of course, ESOPs are not wanted by all companies, and they won't work in all situations, but they can be an important part of an organization's motivational strategy.

Evaluation of Variable Pay   Do variable-pay programs increase motivation and productivity? Studies generally support the idea that organizations with profit-sharing plans have higher levels of profitability than those without them.[77] Profit-sharing plans have also been linked to higher levels of employee commitment to the organization, especially in small organizations.[78] Thus, economist Ed Lazear was generally right when he said, "Workers respond to prices just as economic theory predicts. Claims by sociologists and others that monetizing incentives may actually reduce output are unambiguously refuted by the data." But that doesn't mean everyone responds positively to variable-pay plans.[79] One study found that whereas piece-rate pay plans stimulated higher levels of productivity, this positive effect was not observed for risk-averse employees.

You'd probably think individual pay systems such as merit pay or pay-for-performance work better in individualistic cultures such as Canada or that group-based rewards such as gainsharing or profit sharing work better in collectivistic cultures. Unfortunately, there isn't much research on the issue. One study did suggest that employee beliefs about the fairness of a group incentive plan were more predictive of pay satisfaction in the United States than in Hong Kong. One interpretation is that North American employees are more critical in appraising group pay plans, and therefore it's more important that the plans are communicated clearly and administered fairly.[80]

USING BENEFITS TO MOTIVATE EMPLOYEES

As with pay, benefits are both an employee provision and an employee motivator. Whereas organizations of yesteryear took a "one size fits all" approach to benefits, meaning a standard package was issued to every employee, contemporary leaders understand that each individual employee values the components of a benefits package differently. A flexible program turns the benefits package into a motivational tool.

Flexible Benefits: Developing a Benefits Package

Consistently with expectancy theory's thesis that organizational rewards should be linked to each employee's goals, **flexible benefits** individualize rewards by allowing individuals to choose the compensation package that best satisfies his current needs and situation. These plans replace the "one benefit plan fits all" programs designed for a male with a wife and two children at home that dominated organizations for more than 50 years.[81] Fewer than 10 percent of employees now fit this image: About 25 percent are single, and one-third are part of two-income families with no children. Flexible benefits can accommodate differences in employee needs on the basis of age, marital status, partner's benefit status, and the number and age of dependants.

Today, most major corporations in Canada offer flexible benefits. A recent survey of 211 Canadian organizations found that 60 percent offer flexible benefits, up from 41 percent in 2005.[82] Flexible benefits are becoming the norm in other countries and in small companies, too. A similar survey of firms in the United Kingdom found that nearly all major organizations were offering flexible benefits programs, with options ranging from private supplemental medical insurance to holiday trading (with coworkers), discounted bus travel, and child care assistance.[83] Almost all major U.S. firms also offer this form of benefit package.

USING INTRINSIC REWARDS TO MOTIVATE EMPLOYEES

We have discussed motivating employees through job design and by the extrinsic rewards of pay and benefits. On an organizational level, are those the only ways to motivate employees? Not at all! We would be remiss to overlook intrinsic rewards organizations can provide such as employee recognition programs, discussed next.

Employee Recognition Programs

Desna makes $10.50 per hour working at her fast-food job in Iqaluit, Nunavut, and the job isn't very challenging or interesting. Yet she talks enthusiastically about the job, her boss, and the company that employs her. "What I like is the fact that Guy [her supervisor] appreciates the effort I make. He compliments me regularly in front of the other people on my shift, and I've been chosen Employee of the Month twice in the past six months. Did you see my picture on that plaque on the wall?"

Organizations are increasingly recognizing what Desna knows: Work rewards can be both intrinsic and extrinsic. Rewards are intrinsic in the form of employee recognition programs and extrinsic in the form of compensation systems. Employee recognition programs range from a spontaneous and private thank-you to widely publicized formal programs in which specific types of behaviour are encouraged and the procedures for attaining recognition are clearly identified.

As companies and government organizations face tighter budgets, nonfinancial incentives become more attractive. The Fairmont Group, a Canadian chain of luxury hotels, has a well-known "Star" program that allows managers, peers, and even customers to recognize service excellence when they see it. Winners are acknowledged at monthly receptions held in their honour.[84] Multinational corporations like Symantec Corporation have also increased their use of recognition programs. Centralized programs across offices in different countries can help ensure that all employees, regardless of where they work, can be recognized for their contribution to the work environment.[85] Recognition programs are common in American and Australian firms as well as Canadian companies.[86]

Some research suggests that financial incentives may be more motivating in the short term, but in the long run nonfinancial incentives motivate best.[87] A few years ago, 1,500 employees were surveyed in a variety of work settings to find out what they considered the most powerful workplace motivator. Their response? Recognition, recognition, and more recognition.

An obvious advantage of recognition programs is that they are inexpensive, because praise is free.[88] Recognition programs with or without financial rewards can be highly motivating to employees. Despite the increased popularity of recognition programs, critics argue they are highly susceptible to political manipulation by management. When applied to jobs for which performance factors are relatively objective, such as sales, recognition programs are likely to be perceived by employees as fair. However, in most jobs, the criteria for good performance aren't self-evident, which allows managers to manipulate the system and recognize their favourites. Abuse can undermine the value of recognition programs and demoralize employees.

Virtual managers, meaning those who manage employees who work in disparate physical locations, may experience particular challenges motivating their workers. This occurs in part because recognition is more challenging in environments where you don't actually see your employees perform each day. Virtual managers, even more so than others, need to clearly communicate their performance expectations and devise effective measurement tools. Finding ways to monitor and recognize performance without an ongoing physical presence requires creativity. Options can include peer recognition programs, client surveys, and the use of highly objective (often mechanical or software-driven) measurement of performance outputs.

Where formal recognition programs are used, care must be taken to ensure fairness. Where they are not used, it is important to motivate employees by recognizing their performance efforts.

SUMMARY

- Understanding what motivates individuals is key to organizational performance.
- Employees whose differences are recognized, who feel valued, and who have the opportunity to work in jobs tailored to their strengths and interests will be motivated to perform at the highest levels.
- The job characteristics model is a tool to help make jobs more engaging by being attentive to task identity, task significance, skill variety, autonomy, and feedback.
- Compensation plans, when well designed, can enhance motivation. When poorly designed, however, they can encourage negative and counterproductive workplace behaviours.
- Employee participation and recognition can increase employee productivity, commitment to work goals, motivation, and job satisfaction.

IMPLICATIONS FOR MANAGERS

- *Recognize individual differences.* Spend the time necessary to understand what's important to each employee. Design jobs to align with individual needs and maximize their motivation potential.
- *Use goals and feedback.* You should give employees firm, specific goals, and they should receive feedback on how well they are faring in pursuit of those goals.

- *Allow employees to participate in decisions that affect them.* Employees can contribute to setting work goals, choosing their own benefits packages, and solving productivity and quality problems.
- *Link rewards to performance.* Rewards should contain a performance component, and employees must find the process to be fair. Recognize the power of both extrinsic and intrinsic rewards.
- *Check the system for equity.* Employees should perceive that experience, skills, abilities, effort, and job requirements explain differences in pay, job assignments, and other rewards.

BREAKOUT QUESTION FOR GROUP DISCUSSION

Employee recognition programs often work, but sometimes they are not taken seriously by employees. Based on what you know about applied motivation, what might make a program more or less effective at motivating pride and high performance?

PERSONAL INVENTORY ASSESSMENT

In the Personal Inventory Assessment found in MyManagementLab, take the assessment: Diagnosing the Need for Team Building.

SELF-REFLECTION ACTIVITY

Are teams being used effectively in your current workplace? The above Personal Inventory Assessment found in MyManagementLab about diagnosing the need for team building can help you determine the answer. Once you have seen your overall score, review your answers again and look for patterns. Some questions focus on information flow, others on collegiality, trust, and the vision and mission of the organization. Is there a pattern in your answers? For example, did you consistently rate communication effectiveness as low, or collegiality?

Assessing the pattern of responses can help you diagnose what specifically you need to do to improve team functioning. Consider how you would approach team building if top-down communication was the primary problem. What would a good solution look like? What if the primary problem was a lack of team spirit and social engagement among workers? Would your solution look the same? Why or why not?

MINI CASE   GETTING THE BEST FROM YOUR SALESFORCE

Safi manages a team of elite sales representatives at a mid-sized software company. Due to technological changes their main document management product has become largely redundant. The old product helped companies manage complex libraries of data such as their patents, the technical specifications of their products, and policy and procedure manuals. The new content management product handles similar tasks, but with an important innovation: it also helps companies manage the largest and most complex websites, websites that have many authors contributing simultaneously. It even permits companies to tailor their websites to different audiences on the basis of individuals' browsing histories and their relationship to the organization (customer, supplier, or partner).

Since these software systems are complex and customized to each organization, it usually takes 7–9 months to close a deal—that is, from the first contact with the customer to the end, when the system is installed and the client receives training.

Safi has noticed that the sales reps aren't really pushing the new product and sales are sluggish. The sales reps get a small salary (about $22,000), but on average 65–85 percent of their total income comes from commission. The old product has commission rates of 6 percent for new sales and 15 percent for annual maintenance contract renewals. The new product has a commission rate of 6 percent for new-product sales and 10 percent for annual maintenance contract renewals. Renewals for both products are required for ongoing access to technical support services and are therefore considered mandatory by the overwhelming majority of their customer base. The existing customer base is quite large; it is possible to achieve the minimum acceptable sales quota by selling only renewals in some territories. Achieving quota is the single most important thing, and is what sales representatives receive public recognition for at their quarterly sales meetings. New deals are considered much more prestigious than contract renewals, but they are also more risky. The average new deal is worth anywhere from $100,000 to $450,000, but such deals can take months to close and some fall through at the last minute. Renewal prices are based on the value of the original contract and range from 5 percent of the original purchase price to 12 percent, depending on the level of service desired.

Sales territories are reviewed and changed annually on the basis of the organization's strategic goals. For instance, in the previous year the CEO had decided that federal government was a key target client. This resulted in all federal sales leads being reassigned to a single government sales specialist rather than being assigned based on geographic territory, as had been done in the past. The geographic territories were sometimes reshuffled as well to reflect changes in demand. Silicon Valley, for example, had been made its own territory two years previously, much to the chagrin of the California sales rep. The maritime provinces were lumped with Quebec at the same time, creating one territory where there had previously been two.

Reviewing the sluggish sales, Safi began to wonder whether there was something wrong with her compensation and recognition system. She knew she had an elite and capable team with a proven track record. They had been thoroughly trained and coached, so the poor sales of the new product probably had more to do with motivation than knowledge or ability. Looking over the existing incentive package Safi decided that she needed to . . .

Discussion Questions

1. Using motivational theory as your guideline, identify strengths and weaknesses of the existing compensation system. Could the compensation and recognition system be contributing to poor sales of the new product? If so, explain how.

2. How might you alter the existing compensation system to help the organization better realize their goals? Be sure to explain why your system would be effective.

3. Are there any organizational justice issues with the current compensation process? If so, what are they? How might they impact employee attitudes and performance?

ENRICHING JOBS AT THE CONSTRUCTION SITE

Jean-Claude sighed as he looked at the page in his organizational behaviour textbook for the sixth time. He was very interested in the job characteristics model, but he wasn't sure how best to put it into practice.

Jean-Claude was a construction site supervisor who had been working with the same team of construction professionals for several years. Each individual had his or her own specialty and would come on-site when needed. Some were experts in framing, others were electricians, plumbers, drywall installers, and so on. For some reason, however, Jean-Claude found it especially difficult to keep roofing experts on his team. He wondered if enriching the job would help.

Roofers installed shingles, which was particularly hot, repetitive, and physically demanding work. Unlike with some other tasks, roofers did not need to be licensed. There were few, if any, opportunities for independent decision making, and feedback only arrived at the very end of the job in the form of a quick "It's okay" or "It's not okay" from the site supervisor. Pay tended to be lower than that of other construction professionals, and the work less prestigious. Some of the other workers, particularly those with journeyman credentials, considered them low-skill "grunts" rather than professionals like themselves. In addition to all of that, some people disliked working on steep, high roofs even with appropriate safety gear. All in all, roofing was considered a tedious, strenuous, hazardous job that few really enjoyed. It was not surprising, therefore, that it was the one job he consistently had problems staffing.

He thought the job characteristics model might help him make the roofer's job more engaging, and staffing it easier. He thought carefully about each and every component of the model and what it might mean in the context of construction in general and roofing in particular. But it was a pretty routine job, and Jean-Claude struggled to find ways to apply the model.

Giving up, he decided to go to a movie and think about something else. As often happens, halfway through the movie it came to him. He knew exactly how to improve skill variety, task significance, task identity, even autonomy and feedback! Jean-Claude started writing down his plan. He was going to make the following changes to the roofing job . . .

Discussion Questions

1. What, specifically, makes the roofing job less engaging?

2. How might Jean-Claude adjust the roofing job to make it more engaging? Use the job characteristics model as a guide when responding.

3. Is the job characteristics model universally applicable? Can you think of any jobs it might not apply to? If so, why would it not apply? If not, why do you think that is?

MyManagementLab

Study, practise, and explore real management situations with these helpful resources:

- **Interactive Lesson Presentations:** Work through interactive presentations and assessments to test your knowledge of management concepts.
- **PIA (Personal Inventory Assessments):** Enhance your ability to connect with key concepts through these engaging self-reflection assessments.
- **Study Plan:** Check your understanding of chapter concepts with self-study quizzes.
- **Simulations:** Practise decision making in simulated management environments.

PERSONAL INVENTORY ASSESSMENT

Chapter 9
Foundations of Group Behaviour

Pearson Education

LEARNING OBJECTIVES

After studying this chapter, you should be able to:

1 Define *group*, and identify the five stages of group development.

2 Discuss how the punctuated equilibrium model helps us to better understand group behaviours.

3 Show how role requirements change in different situations.

4 Demonstrate how norms exert influence on an individual's behaviour.

5 Discuss the dynamics of status in group behaviour.

6 Assess how group size may impact group performance.

7 Contrast the benefits and disadvantages of high levels of group cohesion.

8 Discuss the impact of diversity on group effectiveness.

9 Contrast the strengths and weaknesses of group decision making.

10 Compare the effectiveness of interacting, brainstorming, and the nominal group technique.

Groups have their place—and their pitfalls. The objectives of this chapter and of Chapter 10 are to introduce you to basic group concepts, provide you with a foundation for understanding how groups work, and show you how to create effective teams. Let's begin by defining a *group* and explaining why people join groups.

DEFINING AND CLASSIFYING GROUPS

A **group** is two or more individuals, interacting and interdependent, who have come together to achieve particular objectives. Groups can be either formal or informal; both types affect employee behaviour and performance. A **formal group** is defined by the organization's structure, with designated work assignments and established tasks. In formal groups, the behaviours team members should engage in are stipulated by and directed toward organizational goals. The six members of an airline flight crew are a formal group, for example. Other examples could include a Band Council, a board of directors, a sports team, or a project team. In contrast, an **informal group** is neither formally structured nor organizationally determined. Informal groups in the work environment meet the need for social contact. Four employees from different departments who regularly have lunch together or who meet to play squash on weekends are an informal group. These types of interactions among individuals, though informal, deeply affect their behaviour and performance.

Groups generally pass through a predictable sequence in their evolution. In this section, we describe the five-stage model and an alternative model for temporary groups with deadlines.

Groups can be either formal or informal; regardless of the type of group, group norms, roles, and identities have powerful effects on individuals' behaviour.

The Five-Stage Model

As shown in Exhibit 9-1, the **five-stage group-development model** characterizes groups as proceeding through the distinct stages of forming, storming, norming, performing, and adjourning.[1]

The first stage, the **forming stage**, is characterized by uncertainty about the group's purpose, structure, and leadership. Members determine acceptable behaviour for themselves in the group by trial and error. This stage is complete when members have begun to think of themselves as part of a group.

The **storming stage** is one of intragroup conflict. Members accept the group but resist the constraints it imposes on individuality. There is conflict over who will control the group. When this stage is complete, there will be a relatively clear hierarchy of leadership.

In the third stage, close relationships develop and the group demonstrates cohesiveness. There is a strong sense of group identity and camaraderie. This **norming stage** is complete when the group structure solidifies and the group has assimilated a common set of expectations of what constitutes correct member behaviour.

The fourth stage is **performing**. The structure is now fully functional. Group energy has advanced from understanding each other to performing the task at hand.

For permanent work groups, performing is the last stage in development. For committees, teams, task forces, and similar groups that have a limited scope of work, the **adjourning stage** is for wrapping up activities and preparing to disband. Some group members are upbeat, basking in the group's accomplishments. Others may be depressed over the loss of camaraderie sustained during the work group's life. Still others may feel alienated or angry and happy to move on, particularly if the group did not function well together.

Prestage I   Stage I Forming   Stage II Storming   Stage III Norming   Stage IV Performing   Stage V Adjourning

EXHIBIT 9-1 Stages of Group Development

Many interpreters of the five-stage model have assumed that a group becomes more and more effective as it progresses through the first four stages. Although this may be generally true, what makes a group effective is actually more complex.[2] First, groups proceed through the stages of group development at different rates. Some may even get stuck in a particular stage, such as storming, for extended periods of time. Groups with a strong sense of purpose and strategy tend to rapidly reach the performing stage and improve over time, whereas those with less sense of purpose see their performance worsen over time. Similarly, groups that begin with a positive social focus achieve the performing stage more rapidly. It's also true that groups do not always proceed clearly from one stage to the next. Storming and performing can occur simultaneously, and groups can regress to previous stages.

An Alternative Model for Temporary Groups with Deadlines

Temporary groups with finite deadlines,[3] such as classmates preparing a presentation for a semester-long class, don't seem to follow the usual five-stage model. Studies indicate they have their own unique sequencing of actions (or inaction): (1) Their first meeting sets the group's direction; (2) the first phase of group activity is one of inertia and thus slower progress; (3) a transition takes place exactly when the group has used up half its allotted time;[4] (4) this transition initiates major changes; (5) a second phase of inertia follows the transition; and (6) the group's last meeting is characterized by markedly accelerated activity.[5] This is called the **punctuated-equilibrium model**, as shown in Exhibit 9-2. The pattern may sound familiar, especially when you think back to past high school and postsecondary courses with group work components. As you read more about the model, reflect about those past experiences. When did your groups' meet and most importantly, when did the bulk of the work get done? Did your experiences reflect this pattern?

The first meeting sets the group's direction, and then a framework of behavioural patterns and assumptions through which the group will approach its project emerges, sometimes in the first few seconds of the group's existence. Once set, the group's direction is solidified and is unlikely to be reexamined throughout the first half of its life. This is a period of inertia—the group tends to stand still or become locked into a fixed course of action even if it gains new insights that challenge initial patterns and assumptions.

One of the most interesting discoveries in work team studies[6] was that groups experienced their transition precisely halfway between the first meeting and the official deadline—whether members spent an hour on their project or six months. The midpoint appears to work like an alarm clock, heightening members' awareness that their time is limited and they need to get moving. This transition ends phase 1 and is characterized by a concentrated burst of changes, dropping of old patterns, and adoption of new perspectives.

EXHIBIT 9-2 The Punctuated-Equilibrium Model

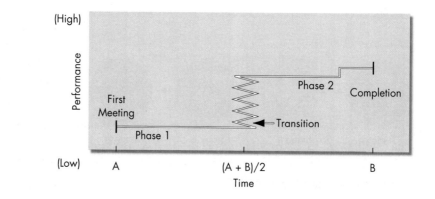

The transition sets a revised direction for phase 2, a new equilibrium or period of inertia in which the group executes plans created during the transition period.

The group's last meeting is characterized by a final burst of activity to finish its work. In summary, the punctuated-equilibrium model characterizes groups as exhibiting long periods of inertia interspersed with brief revolutionary changes triggered primarily by members' awareness of time and deadlines. Keep in mind, however, that this model doesn't apply to all groups but is suited to the finite quality of temporary task groups working under a time deadline.[7]

GROUP ROLES

Work groups shape members' behaviour and help explain individual behaviour as well as the performance of the group itself. Some of the defining group properties are roles, norms, status, size, cohesiveness, and diversity. Let's begin with the first group property, roles.

Shakespeare said, "All the world's a stage, / And all the men and women merely players." Using the same metaphor, all group members are actors, each playing a **role**, a set of expected behaviour patterns attributed to someone occupying a given position in a social unit. We are required to play a number of diverse roles, both on and off our jobs. As we'll see, one of the tasks in understanding behaviour is grasping the role a person is currently playing.

Biyen is a plant manager with Wesco, an electrical equipment manufacturer in Vancouver. At his job, Biyen fulfills a number of roles—employee, member of middle management, electrical engineer, and primary company spokesperson in the community. Off the job, Biyen holds more roles: husband, father, spirit drum maker, tennis player, community elder, and president of his homeowners' association. Many of these roles are compatible; some create conflicts. For example, how does Biyen's spiritual commitment and status as an elder influence his managerial decisions regarding layoffs, expense padding, and provision of training opportunities to employees? A recent offer of promotion requires Biyen to relocate, yet his family wants to stay in Vancouver. Can the role demands of his job be reconciled with the demands of his husband, father, and community elder roles?

Different groups impose different role requirements on individuals. Like Biyen, we all play a number of roles, and our behaviour varies with each.

Role Perception

Our view of how we're supposed to act in a given situation is a **role perception**. We get role perceptions from stimuli all around us—for example, friends, books, films, and television, such as when we form an impression of the work of doctors from watching *Grey's Anatomy*. Apprenticeship programs allow beginners to watch an expert so they can learn to act as they should.

Role Expectations

Role expectations are the way others believe you should act in a given context. A federal judge is viewed as having propriety and dignity, a band elder is viewed as having wisdom and insight, while a hockey coach is seen as aggressive, dynamic, and inspiring to his players.

Role Conflict

When compliance with one role requirement may make it difficult to comply with another, the result is **role conflict**.[8] At the extreme, two or more role expectations can be completely contradictory. For example, if you were to provide a performance evaluation on a person you mentored, your roles as evaluator and mentor may conflict.

GROUP NORMS

Did you ever notice that golfers don't speak while others are taking their turn or that employees very seldom criticize their bosses in public? Why not? The answer is norms.

All groups have established **norms**—acceptable standards of behaviour shared by their members that express what they ought and ought not to do under certain circumstances. Norms are distinct from rules, policies, and laws, which are formally enforced by the legitimate hierarchy within an organization. Norms, by contrast, emerge more naturally and influence behaviour with a minimum of external controls. Different groups, communities, and societies have different norms, but they all have them.[9]

Norms can cover any aspect of group behaviour.[10] Probably the most common is a *performance norm*, providing explicit cues about how hard members should work, how to do the job, what level of tardiness is appropriate, and the like. These norms are capable of greatly affecting behaviour and performance, if they are internalized. Other norms include *appearance norms* (dress codes, unspoken rules about when to look busy), *social arrangement norms* (with whom to eat lunch, whether to form friendships with coworkers off the job, whether to offer tobacco to an community elder before requesting their advice), and *resource allocation norms* (assignment of difficult jobs, distribution of resources like pay or equipment).

Norms and Behaviour

As we've mentioned, norms in the workplace significantly influence employee behaviour. This may seem intuitive, but full appreciation of the influence of norms on worker behaviour did not occur until the famous "Hawthorne studies" undertaken between 1924 and 1932 at the Western Electric Company's Hawthorne Works in Chicago[11] (see Chapter 7). Basically the studies verified that employees respond positively, improving their performance, when management pays attention to them. There was an interesting nuance to the employee's behaviours in these studies, however; they were clearly influenced by group norms.

As part of the Hawthorne studies, a wage incentive plan was introduced to a group of workers in the bank wiring observation room. The most important finding was that employees did not individually maximize their output. Rather, their role performance became controlled by a group norm. Members were afraid that if they significantly increased their output, the unit incentive rate might be cut, the expected daily output might be increased, layoffs might occur, or slower workers might be reprimanded. So the group established its idea of a fair output—neither too much nor too little. Members helped each other ensure their reports were nearly level, and the norms the group established included a number of behavioural "don'ts." *Don't* be a rate-buster, turning out too much work. *Don't* be a chiseller, turning out too little work. *Don't* squeal on any of your peers. The group enforced their norms with name-calling, ridicule, ostracism, and even punches to the upper arm of violators. The group thus operated well below its capability, using norms that were tightly established and strongly enforced. Similar "rules" have been anecdotally reported by many people working in manufacturing environments today.[12]

Conformity

Julien hates wearing suits and he never wears them to class. Today he has a big presentation to make in his Introduction to Business class and he knows that all the other members of his group plan to wear suits so they look professional. Even though he personally thinks it is silly, Julien dutifully puts on his suit that morning.

As a member of a group, you desire acceptance by the group. Thus, you are susceptible to conforming to the group's norms. Considerable evidence suggests that groups can put

EXHIBIT 9-3   Examples of Cards Used in Asch's Study

strong pressure on individual members to change their attitudes and behaviours to conform to the group's standard.[13] There are numerous reasons for conformity, with recent research highlighting the importance of a desire to develop meaningful social relationships with others or to maintain a favourable self-concept.

While conformity can help foster group cohesion, it also has its downsides. It can be a problem within groups because it may limit idea generation and creativity. To avoid issues managers should encourage group leaders to actively seek input from all members and they should avoid expressing their own opinions too soon, especially in the early stages of deliberation. This may be especially important when working with people from collectivist cultures, especially if their cultures are also characterized by high power-distance and high uncertainty avoidance. Countries with this profile include Mexico, Turkey, Columbia, Peru, and Iran. People from cultures with this profile will be more likely to conform than people from individualistic cultures with low power-distance and low uncertainty avoidance, such as Canada, the United States, and South Africa.

The impact group pressures for **conformity** can have on an individual member's judgment was demonstrated in studies by Solomon Asch.[14] Asch made up groups of seven or eight people who were asked to compare two cards held by the experimenter. One card had one line, and the other had three lines of varying length, one of which was identical to the line on the one-line card, as Exhibit 9-3 shows. The difference in line length was quite obvious; in fact, under ordinary conditions, subjects made fewer than 1 percent errors in announcing aloud which of the three lines matched the single line. But what happens if members of the group begin giving incorrect answers? Would pressure to conform cause an unsuspecting subject (USS) to alter an answer? Asch arranged the group so only the USS was unaware the experiment was rigged. The seating was prearranged so the USS was one of the last to announce a decision.

The experiment began with several sets of matching exercises. All the subjects gave the right answers. On the third set, however, the first subject gave an obviously wrong answer—for example, saying "C" in Exhibit 9-3. The next subject gave the same wrong answer, and so did the others. Now the dilemma confronting the USS was this: Publicly state a perception that differs from the announced position of the others in the group, or give an incorrect answer in order to agree with the others.

The results over many experiments and trials showed 75 percent of subjects gave at least one answer that conformed—that they knew was wrong but was consistent with the replies of other group members—and the average conformer gave wrong answers 37 percent of the time. What meaning can we draw from these results? They suggest group norms press us toward conformity. There is some evidence that levels of conformity are decreasing slowly over time,[15] but it is still a powerful force. Much like Julien, putting on his hated suit for his class presentation, we desire to be one of the group and therefore we avoid being visibly different.

Do individuals conform to the pressures of all groups to which they belong? Obviously not, because people belong to many groups, and their norms vary and sometimes are

Conformity serves a purpose but can also be non-functional.

Pearson Education

contradictory. People conform to the important groups to which they belong or hope to belong. These important groups are **reference groups**, in which a person is aware of other members, defines himself as a member or would like to be a member, and feels group members are significant to him. A member of the Nisichawayasihk Cree Nation who works for a nearby hydroelectric company is a group member within their Band and their company; however, if a conflict ever arose between the Band and the company, they would likely side with the Band, as that group is probably much more central to their overall identity—it is their primary reference group. The implication, then, is that all groups do not impose equal conformity pressures on their members, since their importance is in the eye of the perceiver.

Deviant Workplace Behaviour

LeBron is frustrated by a coworker who constantly spreads malicious and unsubstantiated rumours about him. Debra is tired of a member of her work team who, confronted with a problem, takes out his frustration by yelling and screaming at her and other members. And Mi-Cha recently quit her job as a dental hygienist after being constantly sexually harassed by her employer.

What do these three illustrations have in common? They represent employees exposed to acts of deviant workplace behaviour.[16] **Deviant workplace behaviour** (also called *antisocial behaviour* or *workplace incivility*) is voluntary behaviour that violates significant organizational norms and, in doing so, threatens the well-being of the organization or its members. Exhibit 9-4 provides a typology of deviant workplace behaviours, with examples of each.

Few organizations will admit to creating or condoning conditions that encourage and maintain deviant norms. Yet they exist. Employees report an increase in rudeness and disregard toward others by bosses and coworkers in recent years. And nearly half of employees

Category	Examples
Production	Leaving early
	Intentionally working slowly
	Wasting resources
Property	Sabotage
	Misusing equipment
	Stealing from the organization
Political	Showing favouritism
	Gossiping and spreading rumors
	Blaming coworkers
Personal aggression	Sexual harassment
	Verbal abuse
	Stealing from coworkers

EXHIBIT 9-4   Typology of Deviant Workplace Behaviour

Sources: Based on S. L. Robinson and R. J. Bennett, "A Typology of Deviant Workplace Behaviours: A Multidimensional Scaling Study," *Academy of Management Journal* (April 1995), p. 565. Copyright 1995 by Academy of Management (NY); S. H. Appelbaum, G. D. Iaconi, and A. Matousek, "Positive and Negative Deviant Workplace Behaviours: Causes, Impacts, and Solutions," *Corporate Governance* 7, no. 5 (2007), pp. 586–598; and R. W. Griffin and A. O'Leary-Kelly, *The Dark Side of Organizational Behaviour* (New York: Wiley, 2004).

who have suffered this incivility say it has led them to think about changing jobs; 12 percent actually quit because of it.[17] A study of nearly 1,500 respondents found that in addition to increasing turnover intentions, incivility at work increased reports of psychological stress and physical illness.[18] Recent research also suggests that lack of sleep, which hinders a person's ability to regulate emotions and behaviours, can lead to deviant behaviour. As organizations have tried to do more with less, pushing their employees to work extra hours, they may indirectly be facilitating deviant behaviour.[19]

Like norms in general, individual employees' antisocial actions are shaped by the group context within which they work. Evidence demonstrates deviant workplace behaviour is likely to occur when supported by group norms.[20] For example, workers who socialize either at or outside work with people who are frequently absent from work are more likely to be absent themselves as they begin to identify with that possible group norm.[21] Thus, when deviant workplace norms surface, employee cooperation, commitment, and motivation are likely to suffer.

What are the consequences of workplace deviance for teams? Some research suggests a chain reaction occurs in groups with high levels of dysfunctional behaviour.[22] The process begins with negative behaviours like shirking, undermining coworkers, or being generally uncooperative. As a result, the team collectively starts to experience negative moods. These negative moods result in poor coordination of effort and lower levels of group performance.

GROUP STATUS

Status—a socially defined position or rank given to groups or group members by others—permeates every society. Even the smallest group will show differences in member status over time. Status is a significant motivator and has major behavioural consequences when individuals perceive a disparity between what they believe their status is and what others perceive it to be.

What Determines Status?

According to **status characteristics theory**, status tends to derive from one of three sources:[23]

1. *The power a person wields over others.* Because they likely control the group's resources, people who control the group outcomes tend to be perceived as high status.
2. *A person's ability to contribute to group goals.* People whose contributions are critical to the group's success tend to have high status. Some thought NBA star Kobe Bryant had more say over player decisions than his coaches (though not as much as he wanted!).
3. *An individual's personal characteristics.* Someone whose personal characteristics are positively valued by the group (good looks, intelligence, money, being an elder in Aboriginal communities, or simply having a friendly personality) typically has higher status than someone with fewer valued attributes.

Status and Norms

Status has some interesting effects on the power of norms and pressures to conform. High-status individuals are often given more freedom to deviate from norms than are other group members.[24] For instance, physicians resist administrative decisions made by lower-ranking insurance company employees.[25] High-status people are also better able to resist conformity pressures than their lower-status peers. Research indicates an individual who is highly valued by a group but doesn't need or care about the group's social rewards is particularly able to disregard conformity norms.[26] This can sometimes observed at executive meetings, where everyone except for one key player (such as Bill Gates at Microsoft, for instance) will be dressed in suits. In this hypothetical example Bill Gates would have no need to dress up since his status in that context would be higher than that of every other person in the room. He could wear shorts or a jogging suit and still command respect. In general, bringing high-status members into a group may improve performance, but only up to a point, perhaps because they may introduce counterproductive norms.[27]

Status and Group Interaction

High-status people tend to be more assertive group members.[28] They speak out more often, criticize more, state more commands, and interrupt others more often. Lower-status members tend to participate less actively in group discussions. When they possess expertise and insights that could aid the group, failure to fully utilize these members reduces the group's overall creativity and performance. Perhaps this is partly why large differences in status within groups are associated with poorer individual performance, lower health, and higher intentions to leave the group.[29]

GROUP SIZE

Does the size of a group affect the group's overall behaviour? Yes, but the effect depends on what dependent variables we examine. Groups with a dozen or more members are good for gaining diverse input. If the goal is fact-finding, larger groups should be more effective. Smaller groups of about seven members are better at producing something concrete within deadlines.

One of the most important findings about the size of a group concerns **social loafing**, the tendency for individuals to expend less effort when working collectively than alone.[30] Social loafing directly challenges the assumption that the productivity of the group as a whole should at least equal the sum of the productivity of the individuals in it.

Does team spirit spur individual effort and enhance a group's overall productivity? German psychologist Max Ringelmann compared the results of individual and group performance on a rope-pulling task.[31] He expected that three people pulling together should exert three times as much pull on a rope as one person, and eight people eight times as much. One person pulling on a rope alone exerted an average of 63 kilograms of force. But in groups of three, the per-person force dropped to 53 kilograms. And in groups of eight, it fell to only 31 kilograms per person.

Replication of Ringelmann's research with similar tasks has been generally successful.[32] Total group performance increases with group size, but the addition of new members has diminishing returns on individual productivity. So more might be better, in that total productivity of a group of four is greater than that of three, but the individual productivity of each member declines. More is not always better when it comes to getting the most out of every individual.

GROUPS AND WORK ATTITUDES: MORE ON SOCIAL LOAFING

What causes social loafing? It may be a belief that others in the group are not carrying their fair share. If you see others as lazy or inept, you can reestablish equity by reducing your effort. But simply failing to contribute may not be enough to be labelled a "free rider." Instead, the group must believe the social loafer is acting in an exploitive manner (benefitting at the expense of other team members).[33] Another explanation for social loafing is the diffusion of responsibility. Because group results cannot be attributed to any single person, the relationship between an individual's input and the group's output is clouded. Individuals may then be tempted to become free riders and coast on the group's efforts. The implications for OB are significant. When managers use collective work situations to enhance morale and teamwork, they must also be able to identify individual efforts. Otherwise, they must weigh the potential losses in productivity from using groups against the possible gains in worker satisfaction.[34]

Social loafing appears to have a Western bias. It occurs more consistently within individualist cultures, such as the United States and Canada, which are dominated by self-interest. It does *not* occur consistently in collectivist societies, in which individuals are motivated by in-group goals. In studies comparing U.S. employees with employees from the People's Republic of China and Israel (both collectivist societies), the Chinese and Israelis showed no propensity to engage in social loafing and actually performed better in a group than alone.

Recent research indicates that the stronger an individual's work ethic is, the less likely that person is to engage in social loafing.[35] There are ways to prevent social loafing, useful in many work contexts but especially helpful for group projects in educational settings: (1) Set group goals, so the group has a common purpose to strive toward; (2) increase intergroup competition, which focuses on the shared outcome; (3) engage in peer evaluation, so each person evaluates each other person's contribution; (4) select members who have high motivation and prefer to work in groups; and (5) if possible, base group rewards in part on each member's unique contributions.[36] Although no magic bullet will prevent social loafing in all cases, these steps should help minimize its effect.

GROUP COHESIVENESS

Groups differ in their **cohesiveness**—the degree to which members are attracted to each other and motivated to stay in the group. Some work groups are cohesive because the members have spent a great deal of time together, the group's small size or purpose facilitates high interaction, or external threats have brought members close together.

Cohesiveness affects group productivity. Studies consistently show that the relationship between cohesiveness and productivity depends on the group's performance-related norms.[37] If norms for quality, output, and cooperation with outsiders are high, for instance, a cohesive group will be more productive than will a less cohesive group. But if cohesiveness is high and performance norms are low, productivity will be low. If cohesiveness is low and performance norms are high, productivity increases, but less than in the high-cohesiveness/high-norms situation. When cohesiveness and performance-related norms are both low, productivity tends to fall into the low-to-moderate range.

What can you do to encourage group cohesiveness? (1) Make the group smaller; (2) encourage agreement with group goals; (3) increase the time members spend together; (4) increase the group's status and the perceived difficulty of attaining membership; (5) stimulate competition with other groups; (6) give rewards to the group rather than to individual members; and (7) physically isolate the group.[38]

GROUP DIVERSITY

The final property of groups we consider is **diversity** in the group's membership, or the degree to which members of the group are similar to, or different from, one another. A great deal of research focuses on how diversity influences group performance. Some research looks at cultural diversity and some at racial, gender, and other differences. Overall, studies identify both costs and benefits from group diversity.

Diversity appears to increase group conflict, especially in the early stages of a group's tenure, which often lowers group morale and raises dropout rates. One study compared groups that were culturally diverse (composed of people from different countries) and homogeneous (composed of people from the same country). On a wilderness survival exercise, the groups performed equally well, but the members from the diverse groups were less satisfied with their groups, were less cohesive, and had more conflict.[39] Another study examined the effect of differences in tenure on the performance of 67 engineering research and development groups.[40] When people had roughly the same level of tenure, performance was high, but as tenure diversity increased, performance dropped off. There was an important qualifier: Higher levels of tenure diversity were not related to lower performance for groups when there were effective team-oriented human resources practices. Teams in which members' values or opinions differ tend to experience more conflict, but leaders who can get the group to focus on the task at hand and encourage group learning are able to reduce these conflicts and enhance discussion of group issues.[41] It seems diversity can be bad for performance even in creative teams, but appropriate organizational support and leadership might offset the problems.

Culturally and demographically diverse groups may perform better over time—if they can get over their initial conflicts. Why might this be so?

Surface-level diversity—in observable characteristics such as national origin, race, and gender—alerts people to possible deep-level diversity—in underlying attitudes, values, and opinions. One researcher has argued, "The mere presence of diversity you can see, such as a person's race or gender, actually cues a team that there's likely to be differences of opinion."[42] Although those differences can lead to conflict, they also provide an opportunity to solve problems in unique ways.

One study of jury behaviour found diverse juries more likely to deliberate longer, share more information, and make fewer factual errors when discussing evidence. Two studies of MBA student groups found surface-level diversity led to greater openness. Surface-level diversity may subconsciously cue team members to be more open-minded in their views.[43]

The impact of diversity on groups is mixed. It is difficult to be in a diverse group in the short term. However, if members can weather their differences, over time diversity may help them be more open-minded, creative, and to do better. But even positive effects are unlikely to be especially strong. As one review stated, "The business case (in terms of demonstrable financial results) for diversity remains hard to support based on the extant research."[44]

Faultlines

One possible side effect of diverse teams—especially those that are diverse in terms of surface-level characteristics—is **faultlines**, or perceived divisions that split groups into two or more subgroups based on individual differences such as sex, race, age, work experience, and education.

Say group A is composed of three men and three women. The three men have approximately the same amount of work experience and backgrounds in marketing. The three women have about the same amount of work experience and backgrounds in finance. Group B also has three men and three women, but they all differ in terms of their experience and backgrounds. Two of the men are relatively experienced, while the other is new. One of the women has worked at the company for several years, while the other two are new. In addition, two of the men and one woman in group B have backgrounds in marketing, while the other man and the remaining two women have backgrounds in finance. It is thus likely that a faultline will result in subgroups of males and females in group A but not in group B based on the differentiating characteristics.

Research on faultlines has shown that splits are generally detrimental to group functioning and performance. Subgroups may wind up competing with each other, which takes time away from core tasks and harms group performance. Groups that have subgroups learn more slowly, make more risky decisions, are less creative, and experience higher levels of conflict. Subgroups are less likely to trust each other. Finally, although the overall group's satisfaction is lower when faultlines are present, satisfaction with subgroups is generally high.[45]

Are faultlines ever a good thing? One study suggested that faultlines based on differences in skill, knowledge, and expertise could be beneficial when the groups were in organizational cultures that strongly emphasized results. Why? A results-driven culture focuses people's attention on what's important to the company rather than on problems arising from subgroups.[46] Another study showed that problems stemming from strong faultlines based on gender and educational major were counteracted when their roles were cross-cut and the group as a whole was given a common goal to strive for. Together, these strategies force collaboration between members of subgroups and focus their efforts on accomplishing a goal that transcends the boundary imposed by the faultline.[47]

Overall, although research on faultlines suggests that diversity in groups can be a double-edged sword, recent work indicates they can also be strategically employed to improve performance.

GROUP DECISION MAKING

The belief—embodied in juries—that two heads are better than one has long been accepted as a basic component of the Canadian legal system and those of many other countries. Many decisions in organizations are made by groups, teams, or committees. We'll discuss the advantages of group decision making, along with the unique challenges group dynamics bring to the decision-making process. Finally, we'll offer some techniques for maximizing the group decision-making opportunity.

Groups Versus the Individual

Decision-making groups may be widely used in organizations, but are group decisions preferable to those made by an individual alone? The answer depends on a number of factors. Let's begin by looking at the strengths and weaknesses of group decision making.[48]

Group decision making is not always better than individual decision making.

Strengths of Group Decision Making   Groups generate *more complete information and knowledge*. By aggregating the resources of several individuals, groups bring more input as well as heterogeneity into the decision process. They offer *increased diversity of views*. This

bikeriderlondon/Shutterstock

Juries are a great example of using group decision making in an attempt to minimize bias.

opens up the opportunity to consider more approaches and alternatives. Finally, groups lead to increased *acceptance of a solution*. Group members who participated in making a decision are more likely to enthusiastically support and encourage others to accept it.

Weaknesses of Group Decision Making   Group decisions are time-consuming because groups typically take more time to reach a solution. There are *conformity pressures*. The desire by group members to be accepted and considered an asset to the group can squash any overt disagreement. Group discussion can be *dominated by one or a few members*. If they're low- and medium-ability members, the group's overall effectiveness will suffer. Finally, group decisions suffer from *ambiguous responsibility*. In an individual decision, it's clear who is accountable for the final outcome. In a group decision, the responsibility of any single member is diluted.

Effectiveness and Efficiency   Whether groups are more effective than individuals depends on how you define effectiveness. Group decisions are generally more *accurate* than the decisions of the average individual in a group, but less accurate than the judgments of the most accurate person.[49] In terms of *speed*, individuals are superior. If *creativity* is important, groups tend to be more effective. And if effectiveness means the degree of *acceptance* the final solution achieves, the nod again goes to the group.[50]

But we cannot consider effectiveness without also assessing efficiency. With few exceptions, group decision making consumes more work hours than an individual tackling the same problem alone. The exceptions tend to be instances in which, to achieve comparable quantities of diverse input, the single decision maker must spend a great deal of time reviewing files and talking to other people. In deciding whether to use groups, then, managers must assess whether increases in effectiveness are more than enough to offset the reductions in efficiency.

Groupthink and Groupshift

Two by-products of group decision making, groupthink and groupshift, can affect a group's ability to appraise alternatives objectively and achieve high-quality solutions.

Groupthink relates to norms and describes situations in which group pressures for conformity deter the group from critically appraising unusual, minority, or unpopular views. Groupthink afflicts many groups and can dramatically hinder their performance. **Groupshift** describes the way group members tend to exaggerate their initial positions when discussing alternatives and arriving at a solution. In some situations, caution dominates and there is a conservative shift, while in other situations groups tend toward a risk-taking shift.

Let's look at groupthink and groupshift in detail.

Groupthink   Have you ever felt like speaking up in a meeting, a classroom, or an informal group but decided against it? One reason may have been shyness. Or you may have been a victim of groupthink. The individual's mental efficiency, reality testing, and moral judgment deteriorate as a result of group pressures.[51]

We have all seen the symptoms of groupthink:

1. Members rationalize any resistance to the assumptions they've made. No matter how strongly the evidence may contradict their basic assumptions, they reinforce them.
2. Members apply direct pressure on those who express doubts about any of the group's shared views, or who question the validity of arguments supporting the alternative favoured by the majority.
3. Members who have doubts or differing points of view seek to avoid deviating from what appears to be group consensus by keeping silent about misgivings and even minimizing to themselves the importance of their doubts.
4. There is an illusion of unanimity. If someone doesn't speak, it's assumed she is in full accord. Abstention becomes a "yes" vote.[52]

Groupthink appears closely aligned with the conclusions Solomon Asch drew in his experiments with a lone dissenter. Individuals who hold a position different from that of the dominant majority are under pressure to suppress, withhold, or modify their true feelings and beliefs. As members, we find it more pleasant to be in agreement—to be a positive part of the group—than to be a disruptive force, even if disruption would improve effectiveness. Groups more focused on performance than learning are especially likely to fall victim to groupthink and to suppress the opinions of those who do not agree with the majority.[53]

Does groupthink afflict all groups? No. It seems to occur most often when there is a clear group identity, when members hold a positive image of their group that they want to protect, and when the group perceives a collective threat to this positive image.[54] So it is not a dissenter-suppression mechanism as much as a means for a group to protect its positive image. One study showed that those influenced by groupthink were more confident about their course of action early on.[55] Groups that believe too strongly in the correctness of their course of action are more likely to suppress dissent and encourage conformity than are groups that are more skeptical about it.

What can managers do to minimize groupthink?[56] First, they can monitor group size. People grow more intimidated and hesitant as group size increases, and although there is no magic number that will eliminate groupthink, individuals are likely to feel less personal responsibility when groups get larger than about 10 members. Managers should also encourage group leaders to play an impartial role. Leaders should actively seek input from all members and avoid expressing their own opinions, especially in the early stages of deliberation. In addition, managers should appoint one group member to play the role of devil's advocate, overtly challenging the majority position and offering divergent perspectives. Yet another suggestion is to use exercises that stimulate active discussion of diverse alternatives without threatening the group or intensifying identity protection. Have group members delay discussion of possible gains so they can first talk about the dangers or risks inherent in a decision. Requiring members to initially focus on the negatives of an alternative makes the group less likely to stifle dissenting views and more likely to gain an objective evaluation.

Groupshift or Group Polarization   There are differences between group decisions and the individual decisions of group members.[57] As discussed previously, what appears to happen in groups is that the discussion leads members toward a more extreme view of the position they already held. Conservatives become more cautious, and more aggressive types take on more risk. The group discussion tends to exaggerate the initial position of the group.

We can view group polarization as a special case of groupthink. The group's decision reflects the dominant decision-making norm that develops during discussion. Whether the shift in the group's decision is toward greater caution or more risk depends on the dominant pre-discussion norm.

The shift toward polarization has several explanations.[58] It's been argued, for instance, that discussion makes members more comfortable with each other and thus more willing to express extreme versions of their original positions. Another argument is that the group diffuses responsibility. Group decisions free any single member from accountability for the group's final choice, so a more extreme position can be taken. It's also likely that people take on extreme positions because they want to demonstrate how different they are from the outgroup.[59] People on the fringes of political or social movements take on ever-more-extreme positions just to prove they are really committed to the cause, whereas those who are more cautious tend to take moderate positions to demonstrate how reasonable they are.

So how should you use the findings on groupshift? Recognize that group decisions exaggerate the initial position of the individual members, that the shift has been shown more often to be toward greater risk, and that which way a group will shift is a function of the members' pre-discussion inclinations.

We now turn to the techniques by which groups make decisions. These reduce some of the dysfunctional aspects of group decision making.

GROUP DECISION-MAKING TECHNIQUES

The most common form of group decision making takes place in **interacting groups**. Members meet face to face and rely on both verbal and nonverbal interaction to communicate. The manner in which a decision is ultimately taken within these groups can vary. In Canada and other democratic countries, for instance, disagreements are often settled with a vote, with the majority getting their way. Among Aboriginal groups in Canada, however, consensus-based models are more common. In some of those communities, most notably Inuit communities, discussion continues until there is consensus among all parties even if that process takes days. Regardless of how the decision is ultimately made, and as our discussion of groupthink demonstrated, interacting groups often censor themselves and pressure individual members toward conformity of opinion. Brainstorming and the nominal group technique can reduce problems inherent in the traditional interacting group.

Brainstorming can overcome the pressures for conformity that dampen creativity[60] by encouraging any and all alternatives while withholding criticism. In a typical brainstorming session, a half-dozen to a dozen people sit around a table. The group leader states the problem in a clear manner so all participants understand. Members then freewheel as many alternatives as they can in a given length of time. To encourage members to "think the unusual," no criticism is allowed, even of the most bizarre suggestions, and all ideas are recorded for later discussion and analysis.

Brainstorming may indeed generate ideas—but not in a very efficient manner. Research consistently shows individuals working alone generate more ideas than a group in a brainstorming session. One reason for this is "production blocking." When people are generating ideas in a group, many are talking at once, which blocks the thought process and eventually impedes the sharing of ideas.[61] The nominal group technique goes further than brainstorming by helping groups arrive at a preferred solution.[62]

The **nominal group technique** restricts discussion or interpersonal communication during the decision-making process, hence the term *nominal*. Group members are all physically present, as in a traditional committee meeting, but they operate independently. Specifically, a problem is presented and then the group takes the following steps:

1. Before any discussion takes place, each member independently writes down ideas on the problem.
2. After this silent period, each member presents one idea to the group. No discussion takes place until all ideas have been presented and recorded.
3. The group discusses the ideas for clarity and evaluates them.
4. Each group member silently and independently rank-orders the ideas. The idea with the highest aggregate ranking determines the final decision.

The chief advantage of the nominal group technique is that it permits a group to meet formally but does not restrict independent thinking, as does an interacting group. Research generally shows nominal groups outperform brainstorming groups.[63]

Each of the group-decision techniques has its own set of strengths and weaknesses. The choice depends on what criteria you want to emphasize and the cost–benefit trade-off. As Exhibit 9-5 indicates, an interacting group is good for achieving commitment to a solution, brainstorming develops group cohesiveness, and the nominal group technique is an inexpensive means for generating a large number of ideas.

Effectiveness Criteria	Type of Group		
	Interacting	Brainstorming	Nominal
Number and quality of ideas	Low	Moderate	High
Social pressure	High	Low	Moderate
Money costs	Low	Low	Low
Speed	Moderate	Moderate	Moderate
Task orientation	Low	High	High
Potential for interpersonal conflict	High	Low	Moderate
Commitment to solution	High	Not applicable	Moderate
Development of group cohesiveness	High	High	Moderate

EXHIBIT 9-5 Evaluating Group Effectiveness

SUMMARY

- Norms control behaviour by establishing standards of right and wrong. The norms of a given group can help explain members' behaviours for managers.

- Status inequities create frustration and can adversely influence productivity and willingness to remain with an organization.

- The impact of size on a group's performance depends on the type of task. Larger groups are associated with lower satisfaction.

- Cohesiveness may influence a group's level of productivity, depending on the group's performance-related norms.

- Diversity appears to have a mixed impact on group performance, with some studies suggesting that diversity can help performance and others suggesting it can hurt it.

- Role conflict is associated with job-induced tension and job dissatisfaction.[64]

- People generally prefer to communicate with others at their own status level or a higher one, rather than with those below them.[65]

- Using techniques such as brainstorming and the nominal group technique can lessen bias and member silencing when engaging in group decision-making.

IMPLICATIONS FOR MANAGERS

- Recognize that groups can dramatically affect individual behaviour in organizations, to either positive or negative effect. Therefore, pay special attention to roles, norms, and cohesion—to understand how these are operating within a group is to understand how the group is likely to behave.

- To decrease the possibility of deviant workplace activities, ensure that group norms do not support antisocial behaviour.

- Pay attention to the organizational status levels of the employee groups you create. Because lower-status people tend to participate less in group discussions, groups with high status differences are likely to inhibit input from lower-status members and reduce their potential.

- When forming employee groups, use larger groups for fact-finding activities and smaller groups for action-taking tasks. When creating larger groups, you should also provide measures of individual performance.

- To increase employee satisfaction, work on making certain your employees perceive their job roles the same way you perceive their roles.

BREAKOUT QUESTION FOR GROUP DISCUSSION

Based on what you've learned about group norms and social loafing, what would help minimize social loafing when you are assigned group projects in class? How could you make sure everyone contributes their fair share to the group project?

PERSONAL INVENTORY ASSESSMENT

In the Personal Inventory Assessment found in MyManagementLab, take the assessment: Communicating Supportively.

SELF-REFLECTION ACTIVITY

Communication is used to convey information but also to convey social support. The Personal Inventory Assessment found in MyManagementLab "Communicating Supportively" helps you assess your ability to convey supportiveness, engage in coaching behaviours, and provide negative feedback in a respectful and productive manner. You may find that you excel in one area (such as communicating supportively) but that you need work in another (such as providing negative feedback). At the end of the quiz you will find concrete tips for improving in each distinct area.

You may find it insightful to reflect back on the communication styles and patterns that you learned as a child. These habits often persist throughout our lives, sometimes on a subconscious level. Are there any negative family patterns that you need to break to help foster better communication skills? Are there positive patterns that you should be sure to retain? In addition, think about other people who have supported you in the past. What communication behaviours did they use and what can you learn from them?

ACCEPTING NEW NORMS? A HARASSED REPORTER FIGHTS BACK

Perceived groups norms, role fulfillment, and status can combine in toxic ways, as a Hydro employee discovered when he was fired in May 2015 for behaviour that occurred off the job at a Toronto sporting event.

Sports news reporter Shauna Hunt was attempting to interview Toronto Football Club (TFC) fans after a game. Television cameras were rolling and a small group of men could be seen huddling in the background, giggling. Eventually one of the men interrupted Ms. Hunt's interview by grabbing the microphone and shouting a vulgar and sexually aggressive phrase that has been abbreviated in the media as FHRITP.

The "FHRITP" phenomenon started in response to a staged video that went viral online. It featured actors playing the roles of interviewer and interviewee when their interview is interrupted by someone yelling "FHRITP." Many people did not realize the original video was faked. A toxic norm quickly developed in which real reporters at real sporting events, particularly female reporters, were targeted with the offensive phrase while they were working. Reporters in places as varied as England, the United States, and Canada all reported frequent interruptions, with some female routinely reporting several instances a day.

This is the environment Shauna Hunt worked in and one day she said "enough." Instead of ignoring the interruption and starting her interview again she turned to the group cheering on her harasser and asked them if they also planned to harass her and why they thought the behaviour was acceptable. The television camera, meanwhile continued to roll. Sean Simoes responded to her questions, laughing and defending the FHRITP practice. He told Ms. Hunt that she was lucky she was not experiencing even more aggressive and physical forms of harassment and said that FHRITP was "awesome."

The footage was posted on the Internet and went viral. The harassers were quickly shamed online, the story received widespread mainstream news coverage, and within days Hydro Ontario announced that they were firing Simoes for violating the company's ethical guidelines. Simoes later send a private message to Shauna Hunt apologizing for his behaviour.

Males have historically enjoyed a privileged status in Western society, one that still echoes today. Norms around sexual harassment have changed significantly in the past 40 years and many things that used to be considered harmless or common, such as catcalling or casually touching women in public places, are now recognized as inappropriate harassment that is part of a wider rape culture. Elements of patriarchal privilege still remain embedded in society, though, especially in contexts that are stereotypically considered highly masculine, such as professional sporting events. It is worth noting that the FHRITP phenomenon overwhelmingly targeted women reporters in general and sports reporters in particular—women infringing on traditionally male domains.

Simoes clearly felt that his defence of FHRITP was socially acceptable. He endorsed the practice loudly and vigorously in a crowded public place, when he knew television cameras were recording him. Yet clearly he misjudged. Once the video went viral, it became clear that a large part of society, including his employer, did not in fact support this norm.

Simoes's apology, which gained him little political traction due to its private nature, suggests that he himself may have found his behaviour inappropriate on reflection. It seems unlikely that Simoes would have indulged in similar behaviour at work, with family, or in other social contexts. For example, if he saw a reporter covering a traffic accident it is unlikely he would attempt to grab the microphone or defend interruptions and sexual harassment. What was so different about the TFC game?

Sources: J. Armstrong, "MLSE Willing to Ban Anyone Yelling FHRITP near Facilities," *Global News* (May 12, 2015), http://globalnews.ca/news/1993793/mlse-willing-to-ban-anyone-yelling-fhritp-near-facilities; R. Levinson King, "Bystander Calls FHRITP Incident at TFC Offensive," *Toronto Star* (May 13, 2015), accessed July 25, 2015 at http://www.thestar.com/news/gta/2015/05/13/bystander-calls-fhritp-incident-at-toronto-fc-match-offensive.html; J. Hathaway, article in Gawker, January 2, 2015, accessed July 25, 2015 at http://gawker.com.

Discussion Questions

1. How might group norms and role fulfillment have led Simoes to believe that his behaviour during this incident was okay?

2. Discuss how power and status influenced norm development for the FHRITP "community." Put another way, how might being a male sports fan in 2015 have influenced Simoes's perceptions of acceptable behaviour?

3. Discuss how power and status influenced norm development for the reporting community. Put another way, how might being a female sports reporter in 2015 have influenced Shauna Hunt's decision to publically shame her harassers? What does this decision tell us about evolving gender norms?

MINI CASE CANADA'S (BIASED?) GUIDE TO HEALTHY EATING

What happens when members of a group have interests that may conflict with the stated goals of the group? What sort of norms might develop in that context? And how will those norms impact group decision making? The story of the development of *Canada's Food Guide* provides some interesting insights into these questions.

The *Guide* is published by Health Canada and is intended to be a guideline to healthy eating for teachers, healthcare workers, and everyday people. It influences everything from grade-school health class curriculum development to food choices in hospitals and other institutions. It is the second most frequently downloaded federal document after income tax forms.

The most recent version of *Canada's Food Guide* was released in 2007 to widespread criticism from medical practitioners, health researchers, and academics. The *Guide* has been criticized for being scientifically unsound, biased toward foods important for Canada's agriculture and food science industries, and overly focused on individual nutrients rather than whole foods.

For example, the *Guide* recommends consuming larger amounts of red meat and dairy products than scientific studies suggest are warranted. Both of these industries are important throughout Canada, particularly in Quebec and the Prairies. The *Guide* implies that juice and whole fruit are equivalent, which is not true, as the former does not include dietary fibre and lacks other important nutrients. The *Guide* also recommends daily serving quantities that, if followed, would be highly likely to lead to excess calorie consumption and obesity.

How does something like this happen? There are many contributing factors.

The development of the *Canada's Food Guide* is heavily influenced by a 12-member Food Guide Advisory Committee. Fully 25 percent of the people on that committee were employed (at the time they sat on the committee) by corporations whose financial interests would be affected by the *Guide*'s recommendations. Both the dairy industry and the grain/cereals industry have been perceived as influencing the *Guide*'s recommendations, which continue to include milk and grain consumption in quantities and forms not supported by nutrition research. For example, research clearly indicates that whole grains are superior to refined grains, yet the *Guide* recommends that only half of the daily recommended servings of grain come from whole-grain sources. It recommends refined grains due to the inclusion of added supplements such as folic acid, despite the need for such supplements being questionable in the general population (although they are important for childbearing women). Similarly, the *Guide* recommends large quantities of dairy products largely for their calcium, while underplaying alternative calcium sources such as leafy greens.

Canada's Food Guide remains controversial, and its recommendations are often discussed in the press. Perhaps it would be better to change how the Advisory Committee is structured, in favour of something more likely to lead to unbiased decision making. Specifically, the *Guide*'s compilers might ...

Sources: M. Wente, "A Big Fat Surprise for Dietary Dogma," *Globe and Mail* (March 14, 2015), accessed July 24, 2015 at http://www.theglobeandmail.com/globe-debate/a-big-fat-surprise-for-dietary-dogma/article23440389; Y. Freedhoff, "Canada's Food Guide to Unhealthy Eating," *Weighty Matters* (November, 2006), accessed July 22, 2015 at http://www.weightymatters.ca/2006/11/canadas-food-guide-to-unhealthy-eating.html; Y. Freedhoff, "Canada's Food Guide Is Broken," *Globe and Mail* (April 26, 2015), accessed July 20, 2015 at http://www.theglobeandmail.com/life/health-and-fitness/health-advisor/canadas-food-guide-is-broken-and-no-one-wants-to-fix-it/article24111642.

Discussion Questions

1. Outline the main reasons that the existing *Guide* might reflect biased decision making. Refer to group size, composition, status, role conflict, and potential for norm development when answering.

2. What might be changed about the Advisory Committee or the associated development process to minimize the chances of biased or poor decision making?

3. Is the Advisory Committee's decision making an example of group polarization? Defend your answer.

MyManagementLab

Study, practise, and explore real management situations with these helpful resources:

- **Interactive Lesson Presentations:** Work through interactive presentations and assessments to test your knowledge of management concepts.
- **PIA (Personal Inventory Assessments):** Enhance your ability to connect with key concepts through these engaging self-reflection assessments.
- **Study Plan:** Check your understanding of chapter concepts with self-study quizzes.
- **Simulations:** Practise decision making in simulated management environments.

PERSONAL INVENTORY ASSESSMENT

Chapter 10
Understanding Work Teams

VectorLifestylepic/Shutterstock

LEARNING OBJECTIVES

After studying this chapter, you should be able to:

1 Analyze the growing popularity of teams in organizations.

2 Contrast groups and teams.

3 Contrast the five types of teams.

4 Identify the characteristics of effective teams.

5 Show how organizations can create team players.

6 Decide when to use individuals instead of teams.

Teams are increasingly the primary means for organizing work in contemporary business firms. In fact, there are few more damaging insults than "not being a team player." Do you think you're a team player?

Decades ago, when companies such as W. L. Gore, Volvo, Toyota, and General Foods introduced teams into their production processes, it made news because no one else was doing it. Today, the organization that *doesn't* use teams has become newsworthy. Teams are everywhere.

WHY HAVE TEAMS BECOME SO POPULAR?

How do we explain the popularity of teams? As organizations have restructured to compete more efficiently, they have turned to teams as a way to optimize employee talents. Teams are more flexible and responsive to changing events than traditional departments or other forms of permanent groupings. They can quickly assemble, deploy, refocus, and disband. Another explanation for the popularity of teams is that they are an effective means for management to democratize organizations, facilitate employee participation in operating decisions, and increase employee involvement. Diverse teams can even enhance creativity and innovation under the right circumstances.

The fact that organizations have turned to teams doesn't necessarily mean they're always effective. Team members, as humans, can be swayed by fads, peer pressure, and herd mentality that can lead to biased decisions. Teams can also diffuse responsibility to the point of becoming passive and can foster discounting and dismissal of important alternate voices. Are teams truly effective? What conditions affect their potential? How do members work together? These are some of the questions we'll answer in this chapter.

DIFFERENCES BETWEEN GROUPS AND TEAMS

Groups and teams are not the same thing. In this section, we define and clarify the difference between work groups and work teams.[1]

Previously, we defined a *group* as two or more individuals, interacting and interdependent, who have come together to achieve particular objectives. A **work group** is a group that interacts primarily to share information and make decisions to help each member perform within that member's area of responsibility.

Work groups have no need or opportunity to engage in collective work with joint effort, so the group's performance is merely the summation of each member's individual contribution. There is no positive synergy to create an overall level of performance greater than the sum of the inputs. A work group is a collection of individuals doing their work, albeit with interaction and/or interdependency.

A **work team**, on the other hand, generates positive synergy through coordinated effort. The individual efforts result in a level of performance greater than the sum of those individual inputs.

In both work groups and work teams, there are often behavioural expectations of members, collective normalization efforts, active group dynamics, and some level of decision making (even if just informally about the scope of membership). Both work groups and work teams may generate ideas, pool resources, or coordinate logistics such as work schedules; for the work group, however, this effort will be limited to information gathering for decision makers outside the group. Whereas we can think of a work team as a subset of a work group, the team is constructed to be purposeful (symbiotic) in its member interaction. The distinction between a work group and a work team should be kept even when the terms are mentioned interchangeably in differing contexts. Exhibit 10-1 highlights the differences between work groups and work teams

The definitions help clarify why organizations structure work processes by teams. Management is looking for positive synergy that will allow the organizations to increase performance. The extensive use of teams creates the *potential* for an organization to generate greater outputs with no increase in employee head count. Notice, however, that we said *potential*. There is nothing magical that ensures the achievement of positive synergy in the creation of teams. Merely calling a *group* a *team* doesn't automatically improve its performance. As we show later in this chapter, effective teams have certain common characteristics. If management hopes to gain increases in organizational performance through the use of teams, its teams must possess these characteristics.

EXHIBIT 10-1 Comparing Work Groups and Work Teams

Work Groups		Work Teams
Share information	← Goal →	Collective performance
Neutral (sometimes negative)	← Synergy →	Positive
Individual	← Accountability →	Individual and mutual
Random and varied	← Skills →	Complementary

TYPES OF TEAMS

Teams can make products, provide services, negotiate deals, coordinate projects, offer advice, and make decisions.[2] In this section, first we describe four common types of teams in organizations: *problem-solving teams*, *self-managed work teams*, *cross-functional teams*, and *virtual teams* (see Exhibit 10-2). Then we will discuss *multiteam systems*, a "team of teams."

Problem-Solving Teams

In the past, teams were typically composed of 5 to 12 hourly employees from the same department who met for a few hours each week to discuss ways of improving quality, efficiency, and the work environment.[3] These **problem-solving teams** rarely have the authority to unilaterally implement any of their suggestions, but if their recommendations are paired with implementation processes, some significant improvements can be realized. For instance, brokerage firm Merrill Lynch used a problem-solving team to brainstorm ways to reduce the number of days needed to open a new cash management account.[4] By finding ways to cut the number of steps from 46 to 36, the team—and eventually the firm—reduced the average number of days from 15 to 8. The Canadian military is undertaking a similar process on a larger scale in an effort to address widespread sexual harassment in the forces. Newly appointed top general Jonathan Vance scheduled a summit of military leaders in August 2015 to begin to discuss the problem and find workable solutions. Part of their efforts will include extensive consultation with smaller, more localized problem-solving teams in various areas of the military.[5]

Self-Managed Work Teams

As we discussed, problem-solving teams only make recommendations. Some organizations have gone further and created teams that also implement solutions and take responsibility for outcomes.

Self-managed work teams are groups of employees (typically 10 to 15 in number) who perform highly related or interdependent jobs; these teams take on some supervisory

EXHIBIT 10-2 Four Types of Teams

Problem-solving   Self-managed   Cross-functional   Virtual

Xinhua/Alamy Stock Photo

General Jonathan Vance's efforts to eradicate sexual harassment in the Canadian military will require the help of problem-solving teams.

responsibilities.[6] Typically, the responsibilities include planning and scheduling work, assigning tasks to members, making operating decisions, taking action on problems, and working with suppliers and customers. Fully self-managed work teams even select their own members and evaluate each other's performance. When self-managed work teams are established, former supervisory positions take on decreased importance and are sometimes eliminated.

Research on the effectiveness of self-managed work teams has not been uniformly positive.[7] Some research indicates that they may be more or less effective based on the degree to which team-promoting behaviours are rewarded. One study of 45 self-managing factory teams found that when members perceived that economic rewards such as pay were dependent on input from their teammates, performance improved for both individuals and the team as a whole.[8]

A second area of research focus has been the effect of conflict on self-managed work team effectiveness. Some research indicates that self-managed teams are not effective when there is conflict. When disputes arise, members often stop cooperating and power struggles ensue, which leads to lower group performance.[9] However, other research indicates that when members feel confident they can speak up without being embarrassed, rejected, or punished by other team members—in other words, when they feel psychologically safe—conflict can be beneficial and boost team performance.[10]

Thirdly, research has explored the effect of self-managed work teams on member behaviour. Here again the findings are mixed. Although individuals on teams report higher levels of job satisfaction than other individuals, studies indicate they sometimes have higher absenteeism and turnover rates. One large-scale study of labour productivity in British establishments found that although using teams improved individual (and overall) labour productivity, no evidence supported the claim that *self-managed* teams performed better than traditional teams with less decision-making authority.[11] On the whole, it appears that for self-managing teams to be advantageous, a number of facilitating factors must be in place. Kraft Foods Inc., for example, uses self-managed work teams in 62 different manufacturing plants in Canada, the United States, and Mexico. They observe, however, that "it is important that the company be connected throughout, from top to bottom, with a common, uniform database, and that all units operate with a single set of user-friendly, information and work-practice systems (for the team system to work effectively)."[12]

Cross-Functional Teams

Starbucks created a team of individuals from production, global PR, global communications, and U.S. marketing to develop the Via brand of instant coffee. The team's suggestions resulted in a product that was cost-effective to produce and distribute, and marketed with a tightly integrated, multifaceted strategy.[13] Michael Coupland, President and Chief Operating Officer of the Canadian Football League, uses similar teams of coaches, marketers, player representatives, financial experts, public relations specialists, and even fashion designers to help launch an entertaining and attractive sporting brand. These examples illustrate the use of **cross-functional teams**, made up of employees from about the same hierarchical level but different work areas who come together to accomplish a task.

Cross-functional teams are an effective means of allowing people from diverse areas to exchange information, develop new ideas, solve problems, and coordinate complex projects. Due to the high need for coordination, cross-functional teams are not simple to manage. Their early stages of development are often long, as members learn to work with the diversity and complexity. And it takes time to build trust and teamwork, especially among people from varying backgrounds with different experiences and perspectives.

Organizations have used horizontal, boundary-spanning teams for decades, and we would be hard pressed to find a major organization or product launch that did not employ cross-functional teams. Most of the major automobile manufacturers—Toyota, Honda, Nissan, BMW, GM, Ford, and Chrysler—use these teams to coordinate complex projects. Network equipment corporation Cisco Systems relies on cross-functional teams to identify new business opportunities in the field and then implement them from the bottom up.[14]

In sum, the strength of traditional cross-functional teams is the face-to-face collaborative efforts of individuals with diverse skills from a variety of disciplines. When the unique perspectives of these members is considered, these teams can be very effective.

Virtual Teams

Cross-functional teams do their collaborative work primarily face-to-face, whereas **virtual teams** use computer technology to unite physically dispersed members to achieve a common goal.[15] Virtual teams collaborate online—using communication links such as wide area networks, corporate social media, videoconferencing, and e-mail—whether members are nearby or continents apart. Virtual teams are so pervasive that it's a bit of a misnomer to call them "virtual." Nearly all teams today do at least some of their work remotely, including many classroom-based teams working on group assignments and projects.

For virtual teams to be effective, management should ensure that (1) trust is established among members (one inflammatory remark in an e-mail can severely undermine trust), (2) team progress is monitored closely (so the team doesn't lose sight of its goals and no team member "disappears"), and (3) the efforts and products of the team are publicized throughout the organization (so the team does not become invisible).[16] As we saw in Chapters 7 and 8, justice and recognition foster positive work attitudes. These practices help maintain positive justice perceptions since it is more likely that all members will contribute on an ongoing basis and their efforts will be recognized. When there is no manager, peers need to fulfill these roles for each other, mutually reinforcing trust and effective communication. A team contract that spells out expectations for communication format and frequency and provides a timeline for contribution submissions can be a good tool for peer-based groups including teams working on school projects.

Virtual teams face special challenges. They may suffer because there is less social rapport and direct interaction among members, leaving some members feeling isolated. One study showed that team leaders can reduce the feeling of isolation, however, by communicating frequently and consistently with team members so none feel unfairly disfavoured.[17] As discussed in Chapter 8, this creates a sense of relational justice that helps maintain positive work attitudes. Another challenge is to correctly disperse information. Evidence from 94 studies involving more than 5,000 groups found that virtual teams are better at sharing unique information (information held by individual members, not the entire group), but they tend to share less information overall.[18] A further challenge is finding the best amount of communication. Low levels of virtual communication in teams result in higher levels of information sharing, but high levels of virtual communication (meaning almost all communication is done online) hinder it.

Thus, it is a mistake to think that virtual teams are an easy substitute for face-to-face teams. While the geographical reach and immediacy of virtual communication makes virtual teams a natural development, managers must make certain this type of team is the optimal choice for the desired outcome and then maintain an oversight role throughout the collaboration.

Multiteam Systems

The types of teams we've described so far are typically smaller, standalone teams, though their activities relate to the broader objectives of the organization. As tasks become more complex, teams often grow in size. Increases in team size are accompanied by higher coordination demands, creating a tipping point at which the addition of another member does more harm than good. To solve this problem, organizations are employing **multiteam systems**, collections of two or more interdependent teams that together have a higher, shared goal. In other words, multiteam systems are a "team of teams."[19]

To picture a multiteam system, imagine the coordination of response needed after a major car accident. There is the emergency medical services team, which responds first and transports the injured to the hospital. An emergency room team then takes over, providing medical care, followed by a recovery team. Although the emergency services team, the emergency room team, and the recovery team are technically independent, their activities are interdependent, and the success of one depends on the success of the others. Why? Because they all share the higher goal of saving lives.

Some factors that make smaller, more traditional teams effective do not necessarily apply to multiteam systems and can even hinder their performance. One study showed that multiteam systems performed better when they had "boundary spanners" whose job was to coordinate with members of the other subteams. This reduced the need for some team member communication. Restricting the lines of communication was helpful because it reduced coordination demands.[20] Research on smaller, standalone teams tends to find that opening up all lines of communication is better for coordination, but when it comes to multiteam systems, the same rules do not always apply.

In general, a multiteam system is the best choice when either a team has become too large to be effective or teams with distinct functions need to be highly coordinated.

xtock/Shutterstock

Multiteam systems can basically be thought of as teams of teams. This lessens communication and coordination problems while still inviting participation from as many relevant parties as necessary.

CREATING EFFECTIVE TEAMS

Many researchers have tried to identify factors related to team effectiveness. To help, some studies have organized what was once a large list of characteristics into a relatively focused model.[21] Exhibit 10-3 summarizes what we currently know about what makes teams effective. As you'll see, the model builds on many of the group concepts introduced earlier.

In considering the team effectiveness model, keep in mind three points. First, teams differ in form and structure. The model attempts to generalize across all varieties of teams, but avoids rigidly applying its predictions to all teams.[22] Use it as a guide. Second, the model assumes teamwork is preferable to individual work. Creating "effective" teams when individuals can do the job better is like perfectly solving the wrong problem. Third, let's consider what *team effectiveness* means in this model. Typically, team effectiveness includes objective measures of the team's productivity, managers' ratings of the team's performance, and aggregate measures of member satisfaction. One commonly used set of criteria that is compatible with the model presented above is referred to as the Hackman Criteria (for Harvard researcher and creator Richard Hackman).[23] It measures effectiveness on the basis of output, social processes, and learning. In practice that would mean that the final outputs produced by the team must meet the standards set by key stakeholders, the internal social processes should enhance or maintain the group's ability to work together in the future, and the experience of working in the team environment should act to satisfy the personal needs of team members.

We can organize the key components of effective teams into three general categories. First are the resources and other *contextual* influences that make teams effective. The second relates to the team's *composition*. Finally, *process* variables are events within the team that influence effectiveness. We will discuss each of these components next.

Context

The four contextual factors most significantly related to team performance are adequate resources, effective leadership and structure, a climate of trust, and performance evaluation and reward systems that reflect team contributions.

EXHIBIT 10-3 Team Effectiveness Model

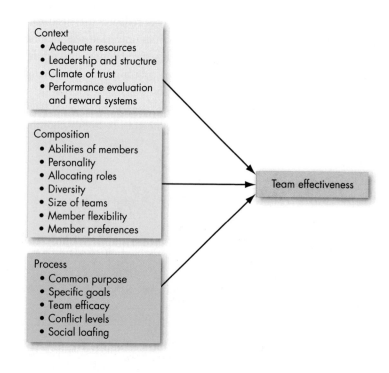

Adequate Resources Teams are part of a larger organization system; every work team relies on resources outside the group to sustain it. A scarcity of resources directly reduces the ability of a team to perform its job effectively and achieve its goals. As one study concluded after looking at 13 factors related to group performance, "perhaps one of the most important characteristics of an effective work group is the support the group receives from the organization."[24] This support includes timely information, proper equipment, adequate staffing, encouragement, and administrative assistance.

Effective Leadership and Structure Teams can't function if they can't agree on who is to do what and ensure all members share the workload. Agreeing on the specifics of work and how they fit together to integrate individual skills requires leadership and structure, either from management or from the team members themselves. It's true in self-managed teams that team members absorb many of the duties typically assumed by managers, but a manager's job then becomes managing *outside* (rather than inside) the team.

Leadership is especially important in multiteam systems. Here, leaders need to empower teams by delegating responsibility to them, and management plays the role of facilitator, making sure teams work together rather than against one another.[25] Teams that establish shared leadership by effectively delegating it are more effective than teams with a traditional single-leader structure.[26]

A Climate of Trust Members of effective teams trust each other. They also exhibit trust in their leaders.[27] Interpersonal trust among team members facilitates cooperation, reduces the need to monitor each other's behaviour, and bonds individuals by the belief that members won't take advantage of them. Members are more likely to take risks and expose vulnerabilities when they trust others on their team. Trust is the foundation of leadership; it allows a team to accept and commit to the leader's goals and decisions.

The overall level of trust in a team is important, but how trust is dispersed among team members also matters. Trust levels that are asymmetric and imbalanced between team members can diminish the performance advantages of a high overall level of trust—in such cases, coalitions form that often undermine the team as a whole.[28]

Performance Evaluation and Reward Systems Individual performance evaluations and incentives may interfere with the development of high-performance teams. So, in addition to evaluating and rewarding employees for their individual contributions, management should utilize hybrid performance systems that incorporate an individual member component and a group reward to recognize positive team outcomes.[29] Group-based appraisals, profit sharing, gain sharing, small-group incentives, and other system modifications can reinforce team effort and commitment as long as those incentives are well designed.

Team Composition

The team composition category includes variables that relate to how teams should be staffed—the abilities and personalities of team members, allocation of roles, diversity, size of the team, and members' preference for teamwork.

Team composition matters—the optimal way to construct teams depends on the ability, skill, and other traits of team members.

Abilities of Members Part of a team's performance depends on the knowledge, skills, and abilities of individual members.[30] It's true we occasionally read about an athletic team of mediocre players who, because of excellent coaching, determination, and precision teamwork, beat a far more talented group. But such cases make the news precisely because they are unusual. A team's performance is not merely the sum of its individual members' abilities. However, these abilities influence what members can do and how effectively they will perform on a team.

When the task entails solving a complex problem such as reengineering an assembly line, high-ability teams—composed of mostly intelligent members—do better than lower-ability teams. High-ability teams are also more adaptable to changing situations; they can more effectively apply existing knowledge to new problems.

Of course, the ability of the team's leader matters as well. Smart team leaders help less intelligent team members when they struggle with a task. A less intelligent leader can actually neutralize the effect of a high-ability team.[31]

Personality of Members

We demonstrated in Chapter 5 that personality significantly influences individual behaviour. Some dimensions identified in the Big Five personality model are relevant to team effectiveness.[32] Specifically, teams that rate higher on mean levels of conscientiousness and openness to experience tend to perform better, and the minimum level of team member agreeableness also matters: teams do worse when they include one or more highly disagreeable members. This relates to the concept of emotional contagion you read about in Chapter 4. Perhaps one bad apple *can* spoil the whole bunch!

Research provides us with a good idea about why personality traits are important to teams. Conscientious people are good at backing up other team members, and they're good at sensing when their support is truly needed. Conscientious teams also have other advantages—one study found that specific behavioural tendencies such as personal organization, achievement orientation, and endurance were all related to higher levels of team performance.[33] Open team members communicate better with one another and throw out more ideas, which makes teams composed of open people more creative and innovative.[34]

By matching individual preferences with team role demands, managers increase the likelihood that the team members will work well together.

Team composition can be based on individual personalities to good effect. Suppose an organization needs to create 20 teams of 4 people each and has 40 highly conscientious people and 40 who score low on conscientiousness. Would the organization be better off (1) forming 10 teams of highly conscientious people and 10 teams of members low on conscientiousness, or (2) "seeding" each team with 2 people who scored high and 2 who scored low on conscientiousness? Perhaps surprisingly, evidence suggests option 1 is best; performance across the teams will be higher if the organization forms 10 highly conscientious teams and 10 teams low in conscientiousness. The reason is that a team with varying conscientiousness levels will not work to the peak performance of the highly conscientious members. Instead, a group normalization dynamic (or simple resentment) will complicate interactions and force the highly conscientious members to lower their expectations, reducing the group's performance. In cases like this, it does appear to make sense to put conscientious team members into teams with other conscientious members."[35]

Allocation of Roles

Members should be selected to ensure all the various team roles are filled. A study of 778 major league baseball teams over a 21-year period highlights the importance of assigning roles appropriately.[36] As you might expect, baseball teams with more experienced and skilled members performed better. However, the experience and skill of players in core roles who handled more of the workflow of the team, and who were central to all work processes (pitchers and catchers), were especially vital. Based on this study and many other research findings, managers should assign the most able, experienced, and conscientious workers to the central roles in a team.

Diversity of Members

In Chapter 9, we discussed research on the effect of diversity on groups. How does *team* diversity affect *team* performance? The degree to which members of a work unit (group, team, or department) share a common demographic attribute, such as age, sex, race, educational level, or length of service in the organization, is the subject of **organizational demography**. This is closely related to the social identity–based perceptual biases described in Chapter 6. You may recall that social identity effects mean that we tend to think people like us (in-groups members) are inherently superior and more trustworthy than people different from us (out-group members). Organizational demography combined with social identity suggests that diversity in attributes such as age or the date of joining should help us predict turnover within groups. The logic goes like this: Turnover will be greater among those with dissimilar backgrounds because communication is more difficult and conflict is more likely. Increased conflict makes membership less attractive, so employees are more likely to quit. Similarly, the losers of a conflict are more apt to leave voluntarily or be forced out.[37] The conclusion would be that diversity, at least on these two characteristics, negatively affects team performance. On the other hand, people with diverse perspectives are likely to be more creative and innovative as a team, because they will have a broader range of knowledge, information, and life experience to draw on when considering alternatives and proposing solutions. This positive influence is more likely to occur when the members respect each other's viewpoints and have strong communication skills.

We have discussed research on team diversity in race or gender. But what about diversity created by national differences? Like the aforementioned research, evidence here indicates elements of national diversity interfere with team processes, at least in the short term.[38] Cultural diversity does seem to be an asset for tasks that call for a variety of viewpoints. But culturally heterogeneous teams have more difficulty learning to work with each other and solving problems. The good news is that these difficulties seem to dissipate with time. Although newly formed culturally diverse teams underperform newly formed culturally homogeneous teams, the differences disappear after about three months.[39] Once again, if respectful communication protocols are followed, cultural diversity can also increase creativity and innovation on teams, especially those creating products and services for diverse customer bases.

Size of Teams   Most experts agree that keeping teams small is key to improving group effectiveness.[40] Generally speaking, the most effective teams have five to nine members. Experts suggest using the smallest number of people who can do the task. Unfortunately, managers often err by making teams too large. It may require only four or five members to develop an array of views and skills, while coordination problems can increase exponentially as team members are added. When teams have too many members, cohesiveness and mutual accountability decline, social loafing increases, and people communicate less. Large teams have trouble coordinating, especially under time pressure. When a natural working unit is somewhat large and you want a team effort, consider breaking the group into subteams.[41]

Member Preferences   Not every employee is a team player. Given the option, many employees will select themselves *out* of team participation. When people who prefer to work alone are required to team up, there is a direct threat to the team's morale and to individual member satisfaction.[42] This suggests that, when selecting team members, managers should consider individual preferences along with abilities, personalities, and skills. High-performing teams are likely to be composed of people who prefer working as part of a group.

Team Processes

The final category related to team effectiveness includes process variables such as member commitment to a common purpose, establishment of specific team goals, team efficacy, mental models, a managed level of conflict, and minimized social loafing. These will be especially important in larger teams and in teams that are highly interdependent.[43]

Why are processes important to team effectiveness? Teams should create outputs greater than the sum of their inputs, as when a diverse group develops creative alternatives. Exhibit 10-4 illustrates how group processes can have an impact on a group's actual effectiveness.[44] Teams are often used in research laboratories because they can draw on the diverse skills of various individuals to produce more meaningful research than researchers working independently—that is, they produce positive synergy, and their process gains exceed their process losses.

Effective teams maintain a common plan and purpose to their actions that concentrate their energies.

Common Plan and Purpose   Effective teams begin by analyzing the team's mission, developing goals to achieve that mission, and creating strategies for achieving the goals. Teams that consistently perform better have established a clear sense of what needs to be done and how.[45] This sounds obvious, but it is surprising how many teams ignore this fundamental process.

EXHIBIT 10-4 Effects of Group Processes

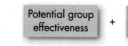

Potential group effectiveness + Process gains − Process losses = Actual group effectiveness

Members of successful teams put a tremendous amount of time and effort into discussing, shaping, and agreeing on a purpose that belongs to them both collectively and individually. This common purpose, when accepted by the team, becomes what GPS is to a self-driving car: It provides direction and guidance under any conditions. Like a car following the wrong road, teams that don't have good planning skills are doomed, executing the wrong plan.[46] Teams should agree on whether their goal is to learn about and master a task or simply to perform the task; evidence suggests that different perspectives on learning versus performance goals lead to lower levels of team performance overall.[47] It appears that these differences in goal orientation produce their effects by reducing the sharing of information. In sum, having all employees on a team strive for the same *type* of goal is important.

Effective teams show **reflexivity**, meaning they reflect on and adjust their master plan when necessary. A team has to have a good plan, but it also has to be willing and able to adapt when conditions call for it.[48] Interestingly, some evidence suggests that teams high in reflexivity are better able to adapt to conflicting plans and goals among team members.[49]

Specific Goals   Successful teams translate their common purpose into specific, measurable, and realistic performance goals. Specific goals facilitate clear communication. They help teams maintain their focus on getting results.

Consistently with the research on individual goals, team goals should be challenging. Difficult but achievable goals raise team performance on those criteria at which they're aiming. So, for instance, goals for quantity tend to raise quantity, goals for accuracy raise accuracy, and so on.[50]

Team Efficacy   Effective teams have confidence in themselves; they believe they can succeed. We call this *team efficacy*.[51] Teams that have been successful raise their beliefs about future success, which, in turn, motivates them to work harder. In addition, teams that have a shared knowledge of individual capabilities can strengthen the link between team members' self-efficacy and their individual creativity because members can more effectively solicit opinions from their teammates.[52] What can management do to increase team efficacy? Two options are helping the team achieve small successes that build confidence and providing training to improve members' technical and interpersonal skills. The greater the abilities of team members, the more likely the team will develop confidence and the ability to deliver on that confidence.

Mental Models   Effective teams share accurate **mental models**—organized mental representations of the key elements within a team's environment that team members share.[53] (If team mission and goals pertain to *what* a team needs to do to be effective, mental models pertain to *how* a team does its work.) If team members have the wrong mental models, which is particularly likely in teams under acute stress, their performance suffers.[54] The similarity of team members' mental models matters, too. If team members have different ideas about how to do things, the team will fight over methods rather than focus on what needs to be done.[55] One review of 65 independent studies of team cognition found that teams with shared mental models engaged in more frequent interactions with one another, were more motivated, had more positive attitudes toward their work, and had higher levels of objectively rated performance.[56]

Conflict Levels   Conflict on a team isn't necessarily bad. Conflict has a complex relationship with team performance. *Relationship conflicts*—those based on interpersonal incompatibility, tension, and animosity toward others—are almost always dysfunctional. However, when teams are performing non-routine activities, disagreements about task content—called *task conflicts*—stimulate discussion, promote critical assessment of problems and options, and can lead to better team decisions. The timing of conflict matters, too. A study conducted in China found that moderate levels of task conflict during the initial phases of team performance were positively related to team creativity, but both very low and very high levels of task conflict were negatively related to team performance.[57] In other words, both too much and too little disagreement about how a team should initially perform a creative task can inhibit performance.

The way conflicts are resolved can make the difference between effective and ineffective teams. A study of ongoing comments made by 37 autonomous work groups showed that effective teams resolved conflicts by explicitly discussing the issues, whereas ineffective teams experienced conflicts focused more on personalities and the way things were said.[58]

Social Loafing   As we noted earlier, individuals can engage in social loafing and coast on the group's effort when their particular contributions can't be identified. Effective teams undermine this tendency by making members individually and jointly accountable for the team's purpose, goals, and approach.[59] Therefore, members should be clear on what they are individually responsible for and what they are jointly responsible for on the team.

TURNING INDIVIDUALS INTO TEAM PLAYERS

We've made a case for the value and growing popularity of teams. But many people are not inherently team players, and many organizations have historically nurtured individual accomplishments. Teams fit well in countries that score high on collectivism, but what if an organization wants to introduce teams into a work population of individuals born and raised in an individualistic society? A veteran employee of a large company, who had done well working in an individualistic company in an individualist country, described the experience of joining a team: "I'm learning my lesson. I just had my first negative performance appraisal in 20 years."[60]

So what can organizations do to enhance team effectiveness—to turn individual contributors into team members? It is a difficult question, as details about the context and personalities involved make a big difference, so there isn't one right answer. Discussed below are options for managers trying to turn individuals into team players.

Selecting: Hiring Team Players

Some people already possess the interpersonal skills to be effective team players. When hiring team members, be sure candidates can fulfill their team roles as well as technical requirements.[61]

Creating teams often means resisting the urge to hire top talent no matter what since their ability to be part of a team is distinct from their other skills. For example, New York Knicks professional basketball player Carmelo Anthony scores a lot of points for his team, but statistics show he scores many of them by taking more shots than other highly paid players in the league, which means fewer shots for his teammates.[62]

As a final consideration, personal traits appear to make some people better candidates for working in diverse teams. People who are open to new experiences, comfortable with ambiguity, empathetic, socially oriented, and engage in high levels of self-monitoring tend to be more effective at cross-cultural communication. Teams of members who like to work through difficult mental puzzles also seem more effective and able to capitalize on the multiple points of view that arise from diversity in age and education.[63]

Training: Creating Team Players

Training specialists conduct exercises that allow employees to experience the satisfaction teamwork can provide. Workshops help employees improve their problem-solving, communication, negotiation, conflict-management, and coaching skills.

Rewarding: Providing Incentives to Be a Good Team Player

An organization's reward system must be reworked to encourage cooperative efforts rather than competitive ones.[64] Hallmark Cards Inc. added to its basic individual-incentive system an annual bonus based on achievement of team goals. Whole Foods directs most of its performance-based rewards toward team performance. As a result, teams select new members carefully so they will contribute to team effectiveness (and thus team bonuses).[65] It is usually best to strike a cooperative tone as soon as possible in the life of a team. Teams that switch from a competitive to a cooperative system do not immediately share information, and they still tend to make rushed, poor-quality decisions.[66] Apparently, the low trust typical of the competitive group will not be readily replaced by high trust with a quick change in reward systems.

Promotions, pay raises, and other forms of recognition should be given to individuals who work effectively as team members by training new colleagues, sharing information, helping resolve team conflicts, and mastering needed skills. This doesn't mean individual contributions should be ignored; rather, they should be balanced with the contributions to the team. As always, it is important to examine rewards carefully to make sure they don't accidently encourage behaviours that undermine the team. For example, some manufacturing teams in the auto industry have historically been given a team incentive for attendance, meaning that if no members of the team were absent for a month the entire group received a bonus. This reward structure socially penalized workers who were already vulnerable, most notably those dealing with serious medical conditions or single parents without backup childcare. Both these groups are more likely to be absent. Over time this created resentment among their team members that undermined trust and led to ostracism and poor peer reviews for some workers. Since their disadvantage was based on things like disability and family status, it might be construed as systematic adverse impact.

Finally, don't forget the intrinsic rewards, such as camaraderie, that employees can receive from teamwork. It's exciting to be part of a successful team. The opportunity for development of self and teammates can be a very satisfying and rewarding experience.

BEWARE! TEAMS AREN'T ALWAYS THE ANSWER

Teamwork takes more time and often more resources than individual work. Teams have increased communication demands, conflicts to manage, and meetings to run. So the benefits of using teams have to exceed the costs, and that's not always possible.[67] Before you rush to implement teams, carefully assess whether the work will benefit from a collective effort.

How do you know whether the work of your group would be done better in teams? You can apply three tests.[68] First, can the work be done better by more than one person? A good indicator is the complexity of the work and the need for different perspectives. Simple tasks that don't require diverse input are probably better left to individuals. Second, does the work create a common purpose or set of goals for the people in the group that is more than the aggregate of individual goals? Many service departments of new-vehicle dealers have introduced teams that link customer service people, mechanics, parts specialists, and sales representatives. Such teams can better manage collective responsibility for ensuring that customer needs are properly met.

The final test is to determine whether the members of the group are interdependent. Using teams makes sense when there is interdependence among tasks—the success of the whole depends on the success of each one, *and* the success of each one depends on the success of the others. Soccer, for instance, is an obvious *team* sport. Success requires a great deal of coordination between interdependent players. Conversely, except possibly for relays, swim teams are not really teams. They're groups of individuals performing individually, whose total performance is merely the aggregate summation of their individual performances.

SUMMARY

- Few trends have influenced jobs as much as the massive movement to introduce teams into the workplace.

- Several different types of teams are commonly used in industry; these include problem-solving teams, self-managed teams, virtual teams, and cross-functional teams.

- The shift from working alone to working on teams requires employees to cooperate with others, share information, confront differences, and sublimate personal interests for the greater good of the team.

- Teams can be rendered more effective by ensuring they are an appropriate size and composition for the tasks at hand and having them use a formal process for information sharing and goal setting.

- Selection, training, and rewards systems can all support and reinforce team-friendly behaviours.

IMPLICATIONS FOR MANAGERS

- Effective teams have common characteristics. They have adequate resources, effective leadership, a climate of trust, and a performance evaluation and reward system that reflects team contributions. These teams have individuals with technical expertise as well as problem-solving, decision-making, and interpersonal skills, as well as the right traits, especially conscientiousness and openness.

- Effective teams tend to be small—fewer than 10 people, preferably of diverse backgrounds. They have members who fill role demands and who prefer to be part of a group. The work that these members do provides freedom and autonomy, the opportunity to use different skills and talents, the ability to complete a whole and identifiable task or product, and work that has a substantial impact on others.

- Effective teams have members who believe in the team's capabilities and are committed to a common plan and purpose, have an accurate shared mental model of what is to be accomplished, share specific team goals, maintain a manageable level of conflict, and show minimal social loafing.

- Because individualistic organizations and societies attract and reward individual accomplishments, it can be difficult to create team players in these environments. To make the conversion, try to select individuals who have the interpersonal skills to be effective team players, provide training to develop teamwork skills, and reward individuals for cooperative efforts.

BREAKOUT QUESTION FOR GROUP DISCUSSION

Imagine you are designing a peer evaluation system for use in a university or college business course that has a substantive group work component. The evaluation is intended to drive positive group behaviours. What types of things should you evaluate and what rewards or consequences should be associated with the evaluations to maximize both performance and fairness?

PIA PERSONAL INVENTORY ASSESSMENT

In the Personal Inventory Assessment found in MyManagementLab, take the assessment: Team Development Behaviours.

SELF-REFLECTION ACTIVITY

Are you a productive and effective team member? Does your presence make a team more or less likely to function well? Take the Personal Inventory Assessment found in MyManagementLab "Team Development Behaviours" to help you to determine the answer. Most people, when working in teams, spend much more time assessing and critiquing the behaviours of others than they spend assessing and critiquing themselves. This is a bad habit, because there is only one person whose behaviour you can fully control—you yourself! We cannot always select our coworkers but we can choose how we respond to group situations. Think carefully about any former group project that went badly. What do you think was the primary reason? Which team behaviours and communication techniques might have improved the outcome? Think also about any that went well. What was different about those teams? What specifically made the members work well together?

For concrete tips on becoming a more effective team member, see the extensive suggestions provided at the end of the quiz.

MINI CASE | LIFELONG LEARNING AND TEAMWORK

Oladele just couldn't take it anymore. She got up from her cubicle and put on her coat. "Where are you off to?" asked her coworker Wei. "I just need to get away from here for a few minutes," replied Oladele, "I'm going for a walk and I'll be back in 20 minutes."

As she walked around the downtown core of St. John's, she wondered how to fix the problems her strategy team was having realizing their goals. Three months previously she and four others had been taken away from some of their regular duties at the headquarters of LifeLong Learners Inc. to form a special project team. The company offered customized courses to mid-sized businesses. Their instructors travelled to the company site to teach anything from occupational health and safety to leadership development. Recent developments in online education, however, were starting to make their services redundant. Many of their clients could now buy similar courses online and have their employees complete them any time they liked. Many employees at LifeLong Learners thought in-class instruction was more effective, but the market didn't seem to agree. A special strategy team was formed to determine whether the company should begin to offer online courses and, if they did, how best to implement the change. The strategy team was to report to the CEO and the chairman of the board of LifeLong Learners.

When the team first met, they spoke with the CEO and the chairman of the board in separate meetings. The CEO told them she had serious concerns about online education. She was concerned they were moving too fast in an uncertain direction. "If we do go into online education," she stated, "it will be important to have all the details sorted out and a good quality control process before we begin. We'll only get one chance to get it right; otherwise, our reputation will suffer." The chairman of the board had a different perspective. "I am very excited about this initiative," he said, "and I think we should plunge in, find out what works, and correct as we go along. The most important thing is to have a product out the door as quickly as possible to begin to claim the online market."

Three months later, the team seemed mired in inertia. Three of the members had devised an online development course contract, and wanted to invite employees to submit proposals and begin development right away.

The three supporting the initiative were Oladele, Katie, and William. Oladele had emigrated from Jamaica four years ago and seen many successful online learning initiatives that reached out to students in remote areas in her home country. She thought LifeLong Learners was ridiculous for waiting so long to get started, something she explained to her colleagues at every opportunity. Katie and William had both been born and raised in St. John's and they also couldn't understand the slow pace. "Results, results, results," William was fond of saying. Well, after three months they had no results to speak of. In fact, they couldn't even get the entire team to agree to move forward and try something.

The other two team members were very concerned that no formal process had been undertaken to fully assess the market. There hadn't been any professional legal consultation around creating the online course development contract either.

"We can't just make something up," complained Wei. "This will set a precedent that will impact us all moving forward. I'm not sure online education is right for us, but if it is we should have a detailed plan formalized before we move ahead. We can't just figure this out as we go. Resources have to be in place first, not to mention training." Wei had emigrated from China two years ago, and he struggled to understand the careless attitude displayed by Oladele, Katie, and William. He secretly worried about their commitment to the project's success because they wanted to move forward so hastily.

The final member of the team, Ranj, had moved to St. John's from the Philippines seven years ago. He agreed with Wei's assessment, but was very concerned about saying so and contradicting the chairman of the board; nor did he want to contradict the CEO. So when the team had discussions, he would often abstain from commenting much.

This afternoon's meeting had been the final straw for Oladele. Not only would Wei and Ranj not agree to support their new contract, they were threatening to complain to the chairman that she was being difficult and disrespectful—all just because she had forcefully reminded them of the importance of *doing* something soon. Oladele knew the team was disintegrating. After a long walk to clear her head she decided to …

Discussion Questions

1. Is there anything this team might have done at the beginning to avoid the difficulties they are facing? If so, what is it?

2. Outline some of the underlying reasons why the individuals in this particular work team may have difficulty communicating with each other. What might they do about it?

3. What strategies might Oladele use now that would move the team forward in a productive direction?

MINI CASE TEAM INCENTIVES AND UNINTENDED CONSEQUENCES

Pittiulak looked over the latest accident report and sighed to himself. One of his most junior workers, a house painter, had slipped off a ladder and broken his arm. Pittiulak felt terrible for him and his family, and was also worried about his ability to staff upcoming jobs. The injured worker would be away for weeks, if not months. This was the third significant accident in four months and it was simply unacceptable. Something was going very wrong with his painting and renovation work teams. He would need to fix it before more people got hurt, but how?

Pittiulak owned and managed a small renovation, drywalling, and painting firm in Yellowknife. He had 12 full-time workers, each with different areas of expertise. Some were skilled tradespeople (he employed a carpenter, a plumber, and an electrician), while others were drywall experts, framers, painters, and general labourers. When he received a new job, Pittiulak would select the employees with the right skills for the job and then create a self-managed project team. The team would work together until the project was complete and then move on to the next. Some employees, most notably the tradespeople, would be on several teams simultaneously since they weren't necessarily needed at the job site every day.

Four months ago Pittiulak had noticed that many of the projects were taking longer than expected. This created scheduling problems as jobs got backlogged. Customers got upset, in particular those whose renovations involved breaching walls of their home. Such repairs needed to happen during the brief summer months, and with their harsh climate there was not a lot of room for error.

Pittiulak decided to create a new team incentive. He would provide each project team with a target completion date (as usual), but now if they met that deadline the entire team would get a cash bonus. The bonus depended on the project but ranged from $35 to $85 per person.

The bonus was well received and seemed to accomplish its goals. The percentage of projects completed on time increased from 68 percent to 83 percent over the four-month period. Pittiulak could understand why. Last time he had visited a job site, he had noticed the carpenter and drywall installers hurrying the painters up to make sure the job got done in time for them all to get a bonus. The painters had looked tired and harried but they had gotten it done! Unfortunately, they'd had to replace a few tiles because in their haste they hadn't moved a drop sheet over and paint had gotten on the floor. But still, it was done on time.

Initially Pittiulak had been thrilled with the success of his team incentive. He couldn't help but notice, however, that in the same four-month period three workers had been injured. One had fallen off a ladder trying to get a tool that was just out of reach, one had lost two fingers after failing to install the safety guard on a cutting tool, and the third had slipped on spilled coffee that nobody had cleaned up, hitting his head and getting a mild concussion. It was strange, since in the three previous years they had only had one significant accident.

Pittiulak wondered whether there might be any connection between his incentive program and their poor safety record. After consideration he realized that he needed to ...

Discussion Questions

1. Do you think the new incentive plan is impacting the safety of this workplace? Explain your reasoning.

2. What types of team incentives would maximize both efficiency and safety while maintaining a respectful workplace? Explain why your strategy would be effective.

3. What are the benefits and drawbacks of Pittiulak's self-directed project team structure? Is it a good choice for his business? Explain your answer.

PERSONAL INVENTORY ASSESSMENT

MyManagementLab

Study, practise, and explore real management situations with these helpful resources:
- **Interactive Lesson Presentations:** Work through interactive presentations and assessments to test your knowledge of management concepts.
- **PIA (Personal Inventory Assessments):** Enhance your ability to connect with key concepts through these engaging self-reflection assessments.
- **Study Plan:** Check your understanding of chapter concepts with self-study quizzes.
- **Simulations:** Practise decision making in simulated management environments.

Chapter 11

Communication

Pearson Educati

LEARNING OBJECTIVES

After studying this chapter, you should be able to:

1 Describe the communication process and formal and informal communication.

2 Contrast downward, upward, and lateral communication.

3 Compare and contrast formal small-group networks and the grapevine.

4 Discuss the strengths and weaknesses of oral, written (including electronic), and nonverbal communication.

5 Explain how channel richness underlies the choice o communication channel.

6 Differentiate between automatic and controlled processing of persuasive messages.

7 Identify common barriers to effective communicatior and recommend mitigation strategies.

8 Assess how to overcome the potential problems in cross-cultural communication.

One of the many challenges in organizations is communication. In this chapter, we'll analyze communication and ways in which we can make it more effective. Communication is powerful: no group or organization can exist without sharing meaning among its members.

Communication must include both the *transfer* and the *understanding* of meaning. Communicating is more than merely imparting meaning; that meaning must also be understood. It is only thus that we can convey information and ideas. In perfect communication, if it existed, a thought would be transmitted so the receiver understood the same mental picture the sender intended. Though it sounds elementary, perfect communication is never achieved in practice, for reasons we shall see later.

First let's describe the communication process.

THE COMMUNICATION PROCESS

For communication to take place, a message needs to be conveyed between a sender and a receiver. The sender encodes the message (converts it to a symbolic form) and passes it through a medium (channel) to the receiver, who decodes it. The result is the transfer of meaning from one person to another.[1]

Exhibit 11-1 depicts the **communication process**. The key parts of this model are (1) the sender, (2) encoding, (3) the message, (4) the channel, (5) decoding, (6) the receiver, (7) noise/barriers, and (8) feedback.

The *sender* initiates a message by encoding a thought. The *message* is the actual physical product of the sender's *encoding*. When we speak, the speech is the message. When we write, the writing is the message. When we gesture, our movements and expressions are the message. The *channel* is the medium through which the message travels. The sender selects it, determining whether to use a formal or informal channel. **Formal channels** are established by the organization and transmit messages related to the professional activities of members. They traditionally follow the authority chain within the organization. Other forms of messages, such as personal or social messages, follow **informal channels**, which are spontaneous and determined by individual choice.[2] The *receiver* is the person(s) to whom the message is directed, who must first translate the symbols into understandable form. This step is the *decoding* of the message. *Noise* represents communication barriers that distort the clarity of the message, such as perceptual problems, information overload, semantic difficulties, or cultural differences. The final link in the communication process is a feedback loop. *Feedback* is the check on how successful we have been in transferring our messages as originally intended. Feedback determines whether understanding has been achieved.

Downward, upward, and lateral directions of communication have their own challenges; it is important that all employees and their leaders understand and manage these unique challenges.

DIRECTION OF COMMUNICATION

Communication can flow vertically or laterally. We subdivide the vertical dimension into downward and upward directions.[3]

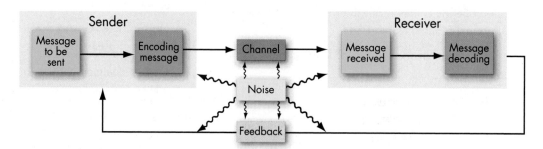

EXHIBIT 11-1 The Communication Process

Downward Communication

Communication that flows from one level of a group or organization to a lower level is *downward communication*. Group leaders and managers use it to assign goals, provide job instructions, explain policies and procedures, point out problems that need attention, and offer feedback.

In downward communication, managers must explain the reasons *why* a decision was made. One study found employees were twice as likely to be committed to changes when the reasons behind them were fully explained. Although this may seem like common sense, many managers feel they are too busy to explain things or that explanations will raise too many questions. Evidence clearly indicates, though, that explanations increase employee commitment and support of decisions.[4] Managers might think that sending a message one time is enough to get through to lower-level employees, but research suggests managerial communications must be repeated several times and through a variety of different media to be truly effective.[5]

Another problem in downward communication is its one-way nature; generally, managers inform employees but rarely solicit their advice or opinions. A study revealed that nearly two-thirds of employees say their boss rarely or never asks their advice. The study noted, "Organizations are always striving for higher employee engagement, but evidence indicates they unnecessarily create fundamental mistakes. People need to be respected and listened to." Companies like cellphone maker Nokia actively listen to employee suggestions, a practice the company thinks is especially important to innovation.[6] Research indicates the way advice is solicited also matters. Employees will not provide input, even when conditions are favourable, if doing so seems against their best interests.[7]

The best communicators explain the reasons behind their downward communications but also solicit communication from the employees they supervise. That leads us to the next direction: upward communication.

Upward Communication

Upward communication flows to a higher level in the group or organization. It's used to provide feedback to higher-ups, inform them of progress toward goals, and relay current problems. Upward communication keeps managers aware of how employees feel about their jobs, coworkers, and the organization in general. It also helps relay important feedback from customers since those customers usually have contact with lower-level employees not senior executives. Managers rely on upward communication for ideas on how working conditions and product offerings can be improved.

Given that most managers' job responsibilities have expanded, upward communication is increasingly difficult because managers are overwhelmed and easily distracted. To engage in effective upward communication, try to communicate in headlines not paragraphs (short summaries rather than long explanations), support your headlines with actionable items, and prepare an agenda to make sure you use your boss's attention well.[8] Although the "headline" approach is best, you should also be prepared to provide more detailed information should it be requested. Having supplementary information readily available helps minimize delays and ensured everyone's time is well spent.

Lateral Communication

When communication occurs between members of a work group, members at the same level in separate work groups, or any other horizontally equivalent workers, we describe it as *lateral communication*.

Lateral communication saves time and facilitates coordination. Many lateral relationships are formally sanctioned and are part of the official hierarchy. These sorts of relationships encourage effective functioning since they foster proactive collaboration and any problems can be addressed quickly and efficiently at lower levels in the organization. For example a marketing representative may be told by his manager to speak directly with a sales person about a specialized advertising campaign targeting their accounts and then the sales person may be told to speak directly with logistics to ensure they provide their customer with accurate shipping dates. Other times, lateral relationships are informally created to short-circuit an inefficient vertical hierarchy and expedite action. For example, two departments may share information on their cost structures before formal budgets are announced by the company's executives because they want to plan a shared program and they need to know what resources they have before making a proposal.

From management's viewpoint, lateral communication can be good or bad. Because strictly adhering to the formal vertical structure can be inefficient, lateral communication with management's support can be beneficial. But dysfunctional conflict can result when formal vertical channels are breached, when members go above or around their superiors, or when bosses find decisions were made without their knowledge.

ORGANIZATIONAL COMMUNICATION

Jan manages four fast-food pizza franchises in Regina. Each store sells exactly the same products and uses exactly the same processes. Lately Jan has been trying to find out what customers are happy with at each store and what could be improved. She asked her store managers to collect feedback from frontline employees, but discovered she is getting very little useful information back from three out of the four stores. She isn't sure why, and so wonders if an organizational communication assessment will help.

Organizational communication (also termed *managerial communication*) examines how information flows through an organization and how that in turns impacts human behaviour. It includes an assessment of formal communication channels, but also considers the role of group structure and informal networks such as the grapevine. For example, an organizational communication assessment specialist may come into a company experiencing issues and assess the impact of their group structure on data flow to identify problem areas and recommend solutions.

Formal Small-Group Networks

Formal organizational networks can be complicated, including hundreds of people and a half-dozen or more hierarchical levels. To simplify, we've condensed these networks into three common small groups of five people each (see Exhibit 11-2): chain, wheel, and all-channel.

The *chain* rigidly follows the formal chain of command; this network approximates the communication channels you might find in a rigid three-level organization. The *wheel* relies on a central figure to act as the conduit for all group communication; it simulates the communication network you would find on a team with a strong leader. The *all-channel*

EXHIBIT 11-2 Three Common Small-Group Networks

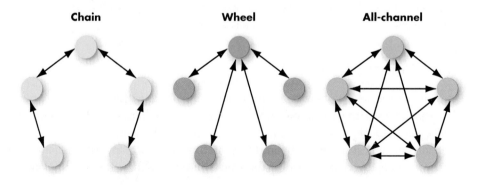

| Chain | Wheel | All-channel |

Criterion	Chain	Wheel	All-Channel
Speed	Moderate	Fast	Fast
Accuracy	High	High	Moderate
Emergence of a leader	Moderate	High	None
Member satisfaction	Moderate	Low	High

EXHIBIT 11-3 Small-Group Networks and Effective Criteria

network permits group members to actively communicate with each other; it's most often characterized in practice by self-managed teams, in which group members are free to contribute and no one person takes a leadership role.

As Exhibit 11-3 demonstrates, the effectiveness of each network depends on the dependent variable that concerns you. The structure of the wheel facilitates the emergence of a leader, the all-channel network is best if you desire high member satisfaction, and the chain is best if accuracy is most important. Exhibit 11-3 leads us to the conclusion that no single network will be best for all occasions.

The Grapevine

The informal communication network in a group or organization is called the **grapevine**.[9] Although rumours and gossip transmitted through the grapevine may be informal, it's still an important source of information for employees. Grapevine or word-of-mouth information about a company also has an impact on whether job applicants join an organization.[10]

Rumours emerge as a response to situations that are *important* to us, when there is *ambiguity*, and under conditions that arouse *anxiety*.[11] The fact that work situations frequently contain these three elements explains why rumours flourish in organizations. The secrecy and competition that typically prevail—around the appointment of new bosses, the relocation of offices, downsizing decisions, or the realignment of work assignments—encourage and sustain rumours on the grapevine. A rumour will persist until either the wants and expectations creating the uncertainty are fulfilled or the anxiety has been reduced.

The grapevine is an important part of any group or organization communication network. It gives managers a feel for the morale of their organizations, identifies issues employees consider important, and helps tap into employee anxieties. The grapevine also serves employees' needs: Small talk creates a sense of closeness and friendship among those who share information, although research suggests it often does so at the expense of the "out" group.[12] Evidence also indicates that gossip is driven largely by employee social networks that managers can study to learn more about how positive and negative information is flowing through the organization.[13] Thus, while the grapevine may not be sanctioned or controlled by the organization, it can be beneficial.

In Jan's case, she went to all four of the franchises to determine why three were not sharing customer feedback. She discovered a rumour had begun in those stores that managers were using feedback about customer interactions to assess the job performance of individual employees rather than to improve customer service. This silenced employees, who became concerned about their jobs. The manager of the fourth store had explicitly explained the reasons they were collecting feedback; as a result, those employees were more willing to participate. The problem was solved by better explaining the program to staff at the other stores and providing reassurance about the usage of the data collected.

Can managers entirely eliminate rumours? No, nor should they want to; they serve some purposes, as we have seen. Research also indicates that some forms of gossip provide prosocial motivation.[14] What managers should do is minimize the negative consequences by limiting rumours' range and impact. Exhibit 11-4 offers a few practical suggestions.

1. *Provide* information—in the long run, the best defence against rumours is a good offence (in other words, rumours tend to thrive in the absence of formal communication).
2. *Explain* actions and decisions that may appear inconsistent, unfair, or secretive.
3. *Refrain* from shooting the messenger—rumours are a natural fact of organizational life, so respond to them calmly, rationally, and respectfully.
4. *Maintain* open communication channels—constantly encourage employees to come to you with concerns, suggestions, and ideas.

EXHIBIT 11-4 Suggestions for Reducing the Negative Consequences of Rumours

Source: Based on L. Hirschhorn, "Managing Rumors," in L. Hirschhorn (ed.), *Cutting Back* (San Francisco: Jossey-Bass, 1983), pp. 54–56.

MODES OF COMMUNICATION

Oral, written, and nonverbal communication forms or mediums of communication have their unique purposes and specific limitations; utilize each medium when optimal, and try to avoid their limitations.

How do group members transfer meaning among each other? They rely on oral, written, and nonverbal communication.

Oral Communication

A primary means of conveying messages is oral communication. Speeches, formal one-on-one and group discussions, and the informal rumour mill or grapevine are popular forms of oral communication.

The advantages of oral communication are speed and feedback. We can convey a verbal message and receive a response in minimal time. If the receiver is unsure of the message, rapid feedback allows the sender to quickly detect and correct it. Oral communication also has the benefit of "tone," or emotional expression. The manner in which something is said can determine whether the speaker is joking or serious, thrilled or saddened, angry or calm. One major disadvantage of oral communication surfaces whenever a message has to pass through a number of people: the more people, the greater the potential distortion. Each person interprets the message in her own way. The message's content, when it reaches its destination, is often very different from the original. A related disadvantage is the lack of a paper trail, or evidence of what was said. This can be a problem if a dispute arises as a result of poor communication.

Written Communication: Traditional Print and Electronic Forms

Written communication includes any method that conveys written words or symbols. Thus, the earliest forms of written communication date back thousands of years, and since we have samples from these earliest writings, written communication is the longest-lasting form. Written business communication today is usually conducted via letters, e-mail, instant messaging, text messaging, social media, and blogs.

A significant limitation of written communication is lack of "tone" or emotional expression, which can lead to misunderstandings. The increased use of emoticons helps; however, such use is often considered unprofessional in work contexts, creating a dilemma for those who seek clearer written communication. Generational differences also interfere with the effectiveness of written communication. "Textspeak"—use of abbreviations such as BTW (by the way)—is widely understood by millennials and younger generations, but less so by older generations. Textspeak is therefore likely to hinder written communication effectiveness in diverse organizations and is therefore also considered unprofessional. For more tips on communicating clearly when using various forms of technology, see Exhibit 11-5.

Technology Type	Do:	Do Not:
Social media	• Post positive messages about your company and brand (check with management before doing this for the first time to see if there is a company policy). • Try to make ad campaigns go viral by encouraging employees and colleagues to click on links and get things started. • Personalize the user experience as much as possible. • Publicly apologize for customer service errors (management permission and legal review may be needed first in cases where liability is possible). • Reread content before posting to seek out and correct ambiguous phrases subject to misinterpretation.	• Post negative information about your employer, immediate supervisor, or coworkers (even on your personal, private pages). • Tag pictures of anyone without their express permission. • Scrape images from the web for use in online marketing campaigns. • Post images of yourself (even on your own personal pages) that include drinking to excess, illegal activities, bullying and/or humiliating others, advanced states of undress, or participating in protests and rallies that undermine the interests of your employer.
E-mail	• Use full words rather than "textspeak." • Use subject lines that clearly indicate the topic of the message. • Alert people if you are absent and not checking messages. Provide an alternative contact name and number. • Overtly explain the intended emotional tone of the message (especially relevant when discussing a conflict since even innocuous statements can seem harsh in an e-mail). • Mimic the level of formality of the other party. For example if they sign off using their first name only you may use their first name in later communications. • Keep messages short and concise.	• Use "Reply all" unless everyone actually needs to see your reply. • Use the blind copy (BCC) feature without an extremely compelling reason (it creates trust issues). • Use informal greetings (including first names) on initial communications. • Send repeated inquiries without waiting a reasonable amount of time for a response (usually at least one day at a minimum). • Use to discuss extremely emotional issues. When people are emotional, tone and body language are important sources of information.
Text messaging and Twitter	• Reread content before posting to seek out and correct ambiguous phrases subject to misinterpretation. • Read earlier posts in a chain before responding to ensure your point hasn't already been stated elsewhere. • Use full words rather than "textspeak" (for professional communications only). • Clarify when you are joking with an emoticon or comment that clearly indicates a jest.	• Respond in haste while emotional. • Include people on your distribution list without permission. • Send out excessive numbers of messages in a short period of time. • Expect instantaneous responses.
Cellphones	• Leave the room if people are working quietly and you need to take a call. • Alert people in your voicemail message if you are absent and not checking messages. Provide an alternative contact. • Give an indication of average expected callback times in your voicemail message.	• Use ringtones unsuitable for an work environment (for example, songs with sexually charged or violent lyrics). • Use your cell phone during business meetings, business lunches or dinners, or while serving a client. If it is unavoidable, use the vibrate rather than the ring feature. • Let your voicemail fill up to the point that messages can no longer be left.
Videoconferencing	• Put your speakers on mute when not actually speaking to the other party. This avoids the magnification of distracting noises such as rustling papers, etc. • Check the background and eliminate potential distractions. (For example, will people be likely to walk around behind you during the call?) • Dress in appropriate work attire even if participating from home.	• Engage in excessive movement and big gestures, since they can look odd on the video feed and be distracting for others, especially if there are bandwidth limitations. • Forget that you are on video and people can see your facial expressions! • Try to show people something written on a small paper (like a table or chart). Send PowerPoint slides instead.

EXHIBIT 11-5 Technology-Mediated Professional Communication Guidelines

Nonverbal Communication

Every time we deliver a verbal message, we also deliver a nonverbal one.[15] No discussion of communication would thus be complete without consideration of *nonverbal communication*— which includes body movements, the intonations or emphasis we give to words, facial expressions, and the physical distance between the sender and receiver. Nonverbal body language can either enhance the sender's verbal message (when the body language concurs with the message) or detract from the message (when the nonverbal cues tell a different story than the message). Sometimes nonverbal communication may stand alone without a verbal message.

We might argue that every *body movement* has meaning, and no movement is accidental (though some are unconscious). We act out our state of being with nonverbal body language. We can smile to project trustworthiness, uncross our arms to appear approachable, and stand to signal authority.[16]

Body language can convey status, level of engagement, and emotional state.[17] Body language adds to, and often complicates, verbal communication. A body position or movement can communicate something of the emotion behind a message, but when it is linked with spoken language, it gives fuller meaning to a sender's message. Studies indicate that people read much more about another's attitude and emotions from their nonverbal cues than their words. If the nonverbal cues conflict with the speaker's verbal message, the nonverbal cues are more likely to be believed by the listener since they are usually considered harder (although not impossible) to manipulate or fake.[18]

Occasionally nonverbal cues can create problems when communicating across cultures since they can lead to misunderstandings. Basic facial expressions tend to be relatively consistent across cultures, so that expressions of happiness, sadness, or anger look similar. Other aspects of nonverbal communication, however, vary enormously from one culture to another. In Canada and most European countries, direct eye contact with an authority figure indicates honesty and openness, while in many Western African nations it indicates disrespect and is perceived as a challenge. Similarly, workers from France would think nothing of kissing each other's cheeks as a standard greeting, while those same behaviours would be wildly unacceptable in Arab nations that discourage physical contact between the genders. Even something as simple as the amount of time spent reading a business card varies by culture—Chinese workers expecting to have their cards studied intently for several moments as a gesture of respect and American workers being more likely to stuff it into a pocket to look at later.

Physical distance also has meaning. What is considered proper spacing between people largely depends on cultural norms. A businesslike distance in some European countries feels too close and intimate in many parts of North America. If someone from the same culture

Sometimes nonverbal communication is all that is needed. Most people would recognize that this child's pose means a defiant "no," even without any verbal or written cues.

Wavebreak Media Ltd/123RF

stands closer to you than you, a North American, think appropriate, you might perceive aggressiveness or sexual interest; if he or she stands farther away, you might perceive disinterest or displeasure.

CHOICE OF COMMUNICATION CHANNEL

Why do people choose one channel of communication over another? A model of media richness helps explain channel selection among managers.[19]

Channel Richness

Channels differ in their capacity to convey information. Some are *rich* in that they can (1) handle multiple cues simultaneously, (2) facilitate rapid feedback, and (3) be very personal. Others are *lean* in that they score low on these factors. As Exhibit 11-6 illustrates, face-to-face conversation scores highest in **channel richness**, because it transmits the most information per communication episode—multiple information cues (words, postures, facial expressions, gestures, intonations), immediate feedback (both verbal and nonverbal), and the personal touch of being physically present. Impersonal written media such as formal reports and bulletins rate lowest in richness. Some communication forms that are inherently low in richness can be improved with effort, lessening potential for misunderstandings. Text messages, for instance, may be more or less rich depending on the use of emoticons, which provide emotional context for written statements.

Choosing Communication Methods

The choice of channel depends on several factors. The first is whether communication needs to be synchronous (meaning everyone participates at once) or can be asynchronous (meaning people contribute at different times). Discussion boards are asynchronous, whereas telephone discussions are synchronous. Synchrony is more efficient when there is complex information and potential for numerous questions and clarifications; however, asynchrony can be more efficient when information is routine and schedules are poorly aligned.[20]

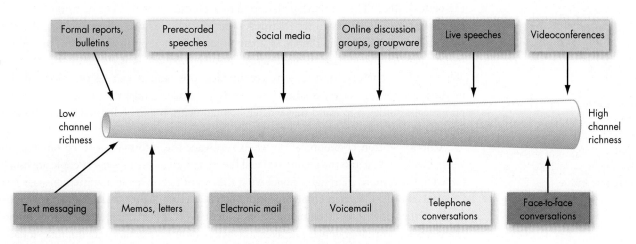

EXHIBIT 11-6 Information Richness and Communication Channels

Sources: Based on R. H. Lengel and R. L. Daft, "The Selection of Communication Media as an Executive Skill," *Academy of Management Executive* (August 1988), pp. 225–232; and R. L. Daft and R. H. Lengel, "Organizational Information Requirements, Media Richness, and Structural Design," *Managerial Science* (May 1996), pp. 554–572. Reproduced from R. L. Daft and R. A. Noe, *Organizational Behaviour* (Fort Worth, TX: Harcourt, 2001), p. 311.

The second important factor to consider is whether the message is routine. Routine messages tend to be straightforward and have minimal ambiguity, so channels low in richness can carry them efficiently. Non-routine communications, especially those outlining change initiatives, are likely to be complicated and have the potential for misunderstanding. Managers can communicate them effectively only by selecting rich channels.

Managers and workers should also consider the nature of the situation. High levels of emotion can interfere with information processing, so rich channels should be selected for emotional discussions even if the information being shared is relatively straightforward. This is especially important if negative emotions are involved. Most people, for example, would not be upset to learn about a promotion by text message, even though that may be a highly emotional experience. Being fired by text message, however, would be considered disrespectful, even cowardly. Social norms also need to be considered when selecting a communication form. Most people, for instance, consider Facebook a forum for quick communications. Lengthy, in-depth discussions are not the norm there and would be better conducted using alternate collaboration tools.

Often, a variety of modes of communication work best to convey important ideas. For example, when tough times hit Manpower Business Solutions during the recent economic recession, the company elected to communicate with employees daily using a variety of media to ensure that everyone remained informed.[21] Employees were given updates about the company's plans for dealing with economic problems, including advance warning before layoffs. The company believes its strategy of using rich communication channels for non-routine information has paid off by reducing employee anxiety and increasing employee engagement with the organization.

Channel richness is a helpful framework for choosing your mode of communication. It is not always easy to know when to choose oral rather than written communication, for instance. Experts say oral communication or "face time" with coworkers, clients, and upper management is key to success. However, if you seek out the CEO just to say hello, you may be remembered as an annoyance rather than a star, and signing up for every meeting on the calendar to increase your face time is counterproductive to getting the work of the organization done. Your communication choice is worth a moment's thought: Is the message you need to communicate better suited to a discussion or a diagram?

Whenever you need to gauge the receiver's receptivity, *oral communication* is usually the better choice. The marketing plan for a new product may need to be worked out with clients in person, so you can see their reactions to each idea you are proposing. Also consider the receiver's preferred mode of communication; some individuals focus on content better over the phone than in meetings. *Written communication* is generally the most reliable mode for complex and lengthy communications, and it can be the most efficient method for short messages, as when a two-sentence text can take the place of a 10-minute phone call. But keep in mind that written communication can be limited in its emotional expression.

Choose written communication when you want the information to be tangible and verifiable. Both you and the receiver(s) will have a record of the message. People are usually forced to think more thoroughly about what they want to convey in a written message than in a spoken one, so written communications can be well thought out, logical, and clear. But be aware that, as with oral communication, your delivery is just as important as the content. Managers report that grammar mistakes and lack of business formality are unprofessional ... and unacceptable. Finally, in choosing a communication channel it's important to be alert to *nonverbal* aspects of communication and consider your body language cues as well as the literal meaning of your words. You should particularly be aware of contradictions between the verbal and nonverbal messages, as a sender and as a receiver. Someone who frequently glances at her smartphone is giving the message that she would prefer to terminate the conversation no matter what she actually says, for instance. We misinform others when we express one message verbally, such as trust, but nonverbally communicate the contradictory one of "I don't have confidence in you."

Information Security

Security is a huge concern for nearly all organizations with private or proprietary information about clients, customers, and employees. Organizations worry about the security of the electronic information they seek to protect, such as hospital patient data; the physical information they still keep in file cabinets, which is decreasing but still important; and the security of the information they entrust their employees with knowing, such as Apple's project groups that are given information only on a need-to-know basis.

The recent adoption of cloud-based electronic data storage has brought a new level of worry; 51 percent of managers in a recent survey were considering cloud-based human resources software. Early research indicates that fears about cloud computing seem unwarranted, so its business use will likely increase.[22] An organization can lessen employee and shareholder concerns by engaging them in the creation of information-security policies and having written disaster recovery plans.[23]

PERSUASIVE COMMUNICATION

We've discussed a number of methods for communication up to this point. Now we turn our attention to one of the functions of communication and the features that might make messages more or less persuasive to an audience.

Automatic and Controlled Processing

To understand the process of communication, it is useful to consider two different ways that we process information.[24] Consider the last time you bought a can of pop. Did you carefully research brands, or did you choose the can that had the most appealing advertising images? If we're honest, we'll admit glitzy ads and catchy slogans do indeed influence our choices as consumers. We often rely on **automatic processing**, a relatively superficial consideration of evidence and information making use of heuristics. Automatic processing takes little time and minimal effort, so it makes sense to use it for processing persuasive messages related to topics you don't care much about. The disadvantage is that it lets us be easily fooled by a variety of tricks, like a cute jingle or a glamorous photo.

Now consider the last time you chose a place to live. You probably researched the area, gathered information about prices from a variety of sources, and considered the costs and benefits of renting versus buying. Here, you're relying on more effortful **controlled processing**, a detailed consideration of evidence and information relying on facts, figures, and logic. Controlled processing requires effort and energy, but it's harder to fool someone who has taken the time and effort to engage in it. So what makes someone engage in either automatic or controlled processing? There are a few rules of thumb for determining what types of processing an audience will use.

Interest Level

One of the best predictors of whether people will use an automatic or a controlled process for reacting to a persuasive message is their level of interest in the outcome.[25] Interest levels reflect the impact a decision is going to have on your life. When people are very interested in the outcome of a decision, they're more likely to process information carefully. That's probably why people look for so much more information when deciding about something important (like where to live) than something relatively unimportant (like which pop to drink).

Prior Knowledge

People who are very well informed about a subject area are more likely to use controlled processing strategies. They have already thought through various arguments for or against a specific course of action, and therefore they won't readily change their position unless very good, thoughtful reasons are provided. On the other hand, people who are poorly informed about a topic can change their minds more readily, even in the face of fairly superficial arguments presented without a great deal of evidence. Overall, then, a better-informed audience is likely to be much harder to persuade.

Personality

Do you always read at least five reviews of a movie before deciding whether to see it? Perhaps you even research recent films by the same stars and director. If so, you are probably high in *need for cognition*, a personality trait of individuals who are most likely to be persuaded by evidence and facts.[26] Those who are lower in need for cognition are more likely to use automatic processing strategies, relying on intuition and emotion to guide their evaluation of persuasive messages.

Message Characteristics

Another factor that influences whether people use an automatic or a controlled processing strategy is the characteristics of the message itself. Messages provided through relatively lean communication channels, with little opportunity for users to interact with the content of the message, encourage automatic processing. Conversely, messages provided through richer communication channels tend to encourage more deliberative processing.

The most important implication is to match your persuasive message to the type of processing your audience is likely to use. When the audience is not interested in a persuasive message topic, when they are poorly informed, when they are low in need for cognition, and when information is transmitted through relatively lean channels, they'll be more likely to use automatic processing. In these cases, use messages that are more emotionally laden and associate positive images with your preferred outcome. On the other hand, when the audience is interested in a topic, when they are high in need for cognition, or when the information is transmitted through rich channels, then it is a better idea to focus on rational arguments and evidence to make your case.

BARRIERS TO EFFECTIVE COMMUNICATION

A number of barriers can slow or distort effective communication. In this section, we highlight the most important.

Filtering

Filtering refers to a sender's purposely manipulating information so the receiver will see it more favourably. A manager who tells his boss what he feels the boss wants to hear is filtering information.

The more vertical levels in the organization's hierarchy, the more opportunities there are for filtering. But some filtering will occur wherever there are status differences. Factors such as fear of conveying bad news and the desire to please the boss often lead employees to tell their superiors what they think they want to hear, thus distorting upward communications.

Pearson Education

Filtering often leads to a failure to identify problems. This can compromise productivity and worker safety.

Selective Perception

Selective perception, discussed in Chapter 6, is important because the receivers in the communication process do see and hear selectively, on the basis of their needs, motivations, experience, background, and other personal characteristics. Receivers also project their interests and expectations into communications as they decode them. An employment interviewer who expects a female job applicant to put her family ahead of her career is likely to see that in all female applicants, regardless of whether they actually feel that way. As receivers, we don't see reality; we interpret what we see and call it reality.

Information Overload

Individuals have a finite capacity for processing data. When the information we have to work with exceeds our processing capacity, the result is information overload. We've seen that dealing with copious amounts of information has become a huge challenge for individuals and for organizations.

What happens when individuals have more information than they can sort and use? They tend to select, ignore, pass over, or forget. Or they may put off further processing until the overload situation ends. In any case, this results in lost information and less effective communication, making it all the more important to deal well with overload.

Emotions

You may interpret the same message differently when you're angry or distraught than when you're happy. For example, individuals in positive moods are more confident about their opinions after reading a persuasive message, so well-designed arguments have stronger impacts on their opinions.[27] People in negative moods are more likely to scrutinize messages in greater detail, whereas those in positive moods tend to accept communications at face value.[28] Extreme emotions such as jubilation or depression are most likely to hinder effective communication. In such instances, we are most prone to abandon our rational and objective thinking processes and substitute emotional judgments.

Language

Even when we're communicating in the same language, words mean different things to different people. Age, context, and culture are three of the biggest factors that influence such differences.

Age, context, and cultural factors are often at play when people from different generations and backgrounds interact. Those new to corporate lingo may find acronyms such as

ARA (accountability, responsibility, and authority), words such as *deliverables* (verifiable outcomes of a project), and phrases such as *get the low-hanging fruit* (deal with the easiest parts first) bewildering, in the same way parents might be mystified by teen slang.[29]

Another aspect of language—spoken accents—can combine with selective perception to create further communication barriers. While accents themselves can interfere with language intelligibility, this effect usually goes away quite quickly. Put another way, if you listen to an accent different from your own for a short while (minutes up to a couple of hours) it becomes much easier to understand. The subconscious discounting, stereotyping, and prejudice associated with some accents, however, is more difficult to mitigate and frequently influences job outcomes unfairly.[30] Poor job outcomes also occur because some people avoid communicating with colleagues who have accents different from their own, because they fear social embarrassment if they cannot understand the speaker. This avoidance deprives the individual of the opportunity to grow accustomed to the accent and understand it better. It is an immensely counterproductive strategy that contributes to poor productivity and a less inclusive society. Instead of avoidance, simple strategies such as politely asking people to repeat themselves or paraphrasing (repeating what someone said in your own words) can help insure smoother communication when accents pose a barrier. Note that many people subconsciously raise their voices when talking with people who are having problems understanding another language. This does not foster better communication, can easily be mistaken for anger, and should be avoided.

Our use of language is far from uniform even when we think we are speaking plainly. If we knew how each of us defines and interprets words we select, we could minimize communication difficulties, but we usually don't know. Senders tend to incorrectly assume the words and terms they use mean the same to the receiver as to them.

Silence

It's easy to ignore silence or lack of communication, because it is defined by the absence of information. This is often a mistake—silence itself can be the message, used to communicate non-interest, inability to deal with a topic, or political barriers to self-expression. Silence can also be a simple outcome of information overload, or a delaying period for considering a response. For whatever reasons, research suggests using silence and withholding communication are common and problematic.[31] One survey found that more than 85 percent of managers reported remaining silent about at least one issue of significant concern.[32] The impact of silence can be organizationally detrimental. Employee silence can mean managers lack information about ongoing operational problems. Silence regarding discrimination, harassment, corruption, and misconduct can mean top management will not take action to eliminate problematic behaviour.

Silence is less likely to occur where minority opinions are treated with respect, workgroup identification is high, and high procedural justice prevails.[33] Practically, this means managers must make sure they behave in a supportive manner when employees voice divergent opinions or concerns, and they must take these under advisement. One act of ignoring an employee for expressing concerns may well lead the employee to withhold important future communication.

Communication Apprehension

An estimated 5 to 20 percent of the population suffers debilitating **communication apprehension**, or social anxiety.[34] These people experience undue tension and anxiety in oral communication, written communication, or both.[35] They may find it very difficult to talk with others face to face, or may get very anxious when they have to use the phone, relying on memos or e-mails when a phone call would be faster and more appropriate.

Oral-communication apprehensives avoid situations, such as giving presentations, for which oral communication is a dominant requirement.[36] But almost all jobs require *some* oral communication. Of greater concern is evidence that high oral-communication apprehensives distort the communication demands of their jobs in order to minimize the need for communication. This means they severely limit their oral communication and tell themselves communicating isn't necessary for them to do their jobs properly. Those employees may need guidance, support, and training to correct these ineffective habits. Employers should also be aware that disciplining an employee for oral communication apprehension is inappropriate, as social anxiety is a mental health disability requiring reasonable accommodation. If support and training do not improve the situation, employers may need to simply accept written forms of communication from that individual.

Lying

The final barrier to effective communication is outright misrepresentation of information, or lying. People differ in their definition of a lie. For example, is deliberately withholding information about a mistake a lie, or do you have to actively deny your role in the mistake to pass the threshold? While the definition of a lie befuddles ethicists and social scientists, there is no denying the prevalence of lying. In one diary study, the average person reported telling one to two lies per day, with some individuals telling considerably more.[37] Compounded across a large organization, this is an enormous amount of deception happening every single day. Evidence shows that people are more comfortable lying over the phone than face to face and more comfortable lying in e-mails than when they have to write with pen and paper.[38] They are also more comfortable when the lie is intended to have a positive impact, such as telling a friend her haircut is flattering when it is not or telling someone you enjoy his poor cooking just to spare his feelings.

Can you detect liars? The literature suggests most people are not very good at detecting deception in others.[39] The problem is there are no nonverbal or verbal cues unique to lying—averting your gaze, pausing, and shifting your posture can also be signals of nervousness, shyness, or doubt. Most people who lie take steps to guard against being detected, so they might look a person in the eye when lying because they know that direct eye contact is (incorrectly) assumed to be a sign of truthfulness. Finally, many lies are embedded in truths; liars usually give a somewhat true account with just enough details changed to avoid detection.

In sum, the frequency of lying and the difficulty of detecting liars makes this an especially strong barrier to effective communication.

GLOBAL IMPLICATIONS

Effective communication is difficult under the best of conditions. Cross-cultural factors clearly create the potential for increased communication problems. A gesture that is well understood and acceptable—either oral, written, or nonverbal—in one culture can be meaningless or lewd in another. Only 18 percent of companies have documented strategies for communicating with employees across cultures, and only 31 percent require that corporate messages be customized for consumption in other cultures. Procter & Gamble seems to be an exception; more than half the company's employees don't speak English as their first language, so the company focuses on simple messages to make sure everyone knows what's important.[40]

A number of barriers—such as culture—often retard or distort effective communication; understand these barriers as a means of overcoming them.

Cultural Barriers

Researchers have identified a number of problems related to language difficulties in cross-cultural communications.[41]

First are *barriers caused by semantics*. Words mean different things to different people, particularly people from different national cultures. Some words simply don't translate between cultures. For instance, the new capitalists in Russia may have difficulty communicating with British or Canadian counterparts because English terms such as *efficiency*, *free market*, and *regulation* have no direct Russian equivalents.

Second are *barriers caused by word connotations*. Words imply different things in different languages. Negotiations between U.S. and Japanese executives can be difficult because the Japanese word *hai* translates as "yes," but its connotation is "Yes, I'm listening" rather than "Yes, I agree." Similarly, when we ask workers "How satisfied are you with your job?" people from individualistic cultures tend to rank themselves on their satisfaction with work tasks and compensation, while those from collectivist cultures more often rank on their relationships with their peers or their job security. The two groups are, for all practical purposes, answering different questions, although each question technically uses the same words. These types of communication barriers are quite subtle and can be difficult to identify, so explicitly defining your terms is helpful.

Third are *barriers caused by tone differences*. In some cultures, language is formal; in others, it's informal. The tone can also change depending on the context: People speak differently at home, in social situations, and at work. Using a personal, informal style when a more formal style is expected can be inappropriate.

Fourth are *differences in tolerance for conflict and methods for resolving conflicts*. People from individualist cultures tend to be more comfortable with direct conflicts and will make the source of their disagreements overt. Collectivists are more likely to acknowledge conflict only implicitly and avoid emotionally charged disputes. They may attribute conflicts to the situation more than to the individuals and therefore may not require explicit apologies to repair relationships, whereas individualists prefer explicit statements accepting responsibility for conflicts and public apologies to restore relationships.

Cultural Context

Cultures tend to differ in the degree to which context influences the meaning individuals take from communication.[42] In **high-context cultures** such as China, Korea, Japan, and Vietnam, people rely heavily on nonverbal and subtle situational cues in communicating with others, and a person's official status, place in society, and reputation carry considerable weight. What is *not* said may be more significant than what *is* said. In contrast, people from Europe and North America reflect their **low-context cultures**. They rely essentially on spoken and written words to convey meaning; body language and formal titles are secondary.

Contextual differences mean quite a lot in terms of communication. Communication in high-context cultures implies considerably more trust by both parties. What may appear to be casual and insignificant conversation in fact reflects the desire to build a relationship and create trust. Oral agreements imply strong commitments in high-context cultures. And who you are—your age, seniority, rank in the organization—is highly valued and heavily influences your credibility. But in low-context cultures, enforceable contracts tend to be in writing, precisely worded, and highly legalistic. Similarly, low-context cultures value directness. Managers are expected to be explicit and precise in conveying intended meaning. It's quite different in high-context cultures, in which managers tend to "make suggestions" rather than give orders.

A Cultural Guide

Much can be gained from business intercultural communications. It is safe to assume every single one of us has a different viewpoint that is culturally shaped. Because we do have differences, we have an opportunity to reach the most creative solutions possible with the help of others if we communicate effectively.

According to Fred Casmir, a leading expert in intercultural communication research, we often do not communicate well with people outside of our culture because we tend to generalize from only knowing their cultural origin. Also, attempts to be culturally sensitive to another person are often based on stereotypes propagated by media. These stereotypes usually do not have a correct or current relevance.

Casmir noted that because there are far too many cultures for anyone to understand completely, and individuals interpret their own cultures differently, intercultural communication should be based on sensitivity and pursuit of common goals. He found the ideal condition is an ad hoc "third culture" a group can form when seeking to incorporate aspects of each member's cultural communication preferences. The norms this subculture establishes through appreciating individual differences create a common ground for effective communication. Intercultural groups that communicate effectively can be highly productive and innovative.

When communicating with people from a different culture, what can you do to reduce misinterpretation? Casmir and other experts offer the following suggestions:

1. *Know yourself.* Recognizing your own cultural identity and biases is critical to understanding the unique viewpoint of others.
2. *Foster a climate of mutual respect, fairness, and democracy.* Clearly establish an environment of equality and mutual concern. This will be your "third culture" context for effective intercultural communication that transcends each person's cultural norms.
3. *Learn the cultural context of each person.* You may find more similarities or differences to your own frame of reference than you might expect. Be careful not to categorize them, however.
4. *When in doubt, listen.* If you speak your opinions too early, you may be more likely to offend the other person. You will also want to listen first to better understand the other person's intercultural language fluency and familiarity with your culture.
5. *State facts, not your interpretation.* Interpreting or evaluating what someone has said or done draws more on your own culture and background than on the observed situation. If you state only facts, you will have the opportunity to benefit from the other person's interpretation. Delay judgment until you've had sufficient time to observe and interpret the situation from the differing perspectives of all concerned.
6. *Consider the other person's viewpoint.* Before sending a message, put yourself in the recipient's shoes. What are his values, experiences, and frames of reference? What do you know about his education, upbringing, and background that can give you added insight? Try to see the people in the group as they really are first, and take a collaborative problem-solving approach whenever potential conflicts arise.
7. *Proactively maintain the identity of the group.* Like any culture, the establishment of a common-ground "third culture" for effective intercultural communication takes time and nurturing. Remind members of the group of your common goals, mutual respect, and need to adapt to individual communication preferences.[43]

SUMMARY

- There is a link between communication and employee satisfaction: the less communication uncertainty, the greater the satisfaction.

- It is important to foster three distinct types of communication, each for different reasons. They include downward, upward, and lateral communication.

- Distortions, ambiguities, and incongruities between oral, written, and nonverbal messages all increase uncertainty and reduce satisfaction.

- Channel richness and context-specific factors should be considered when making choices about how to best communicate.

- Cultural sensitivity is an important organizational component for establishing communications understanding.

IMPLICATIONS FOR MANAGERS

- Remember that your communication mode will partly determine your communication effectiveness.

- Obtain feedback from your employees to make certain your messages—however they are communicated—are understood.

- Remember that written communication creates more misunderstandings than oral communication; communicate with employees through in-person meetings when possible.

- Make sure you use communication strategies appropriate to your audience and the type of message you're sending.

- Keep in mind communication barriers such as gender and culture.

BREAKOUT QUESTION FOR GROUP DISCUSSION

It is not unusual for the grapevine to create some negative emotions in an organization, since people who work together tend to gossip about each other. In some workplaces this behaviour becomes excessive to the point where it diminishes productivity and job satisfaction. How might you address problematic gossip in the workplace? What might you do as a manager or supervisor to minimize hurtful gossip? What might you do as a regular employee?

PERSONAL INVENTORY ASSESSMENT

In the Personal Inventory Assessment found in MyManagementLab, take the assessment: Communication Styles. This will help you learn more about your personal communication style and the impact it may have on your communication effectiveness.

SELF-REFLECTION ACTIVITY

The Personal Inventory Assessment found in MyManagementLab associated with this chapter will help you learn more about your personal communication style and the impact it may have on perceived supportiveness and communication effectiveness. After you complete the quiz, there is an extensive debriefing that explains the different communication styles and their associated strengths and weaknesses. Reflect on the communication tactics you use most often. Are those tactics helping or hurting you? Changing our communication style requires mindfulness and careful effort. What specifically might you do that would help you remember to use communication styles associated with perceived supportiveness more frequently? How would you know you are becoming more effective? Who could you trust to provide open, honest feedback? The answers to these questions can help you develop a plan for adjusting your communication style.

Phedre was working her first shift at the Hyacinth Burger Bar. She had gone through some training with the owner Melisande the previous day. She had found Melisande intimidating, despite her politeness and calm demeanor. She felt her bored gaze throughout the training and registered her stiff and unwelcoming body language and slightly condescending tone.

Melisande had also warned her several times to pay attention, saying she wasn't prepared to waste her time explaining things twice. Phedre felt as though she might already be disappointing her new employer, and she hadn't even done anything yet!

Despite her social discomfort, Phedre had listened carefully to everything, in particular the instructions for cleanup at closing time. The most difficult part of cleanup was scraping the burger grill and emptying the grease trap. The collected grease from a day's worth of burgers and bacon was, once cool enough, put into garbage bags and disposed in a special container kept outside the restaurant in the back.

Melisande had been very specific the previous day. She had told her, "Put three scoops of grease in each bag and then throw them away." The supervisor on shift today, whose name was Joscelin, had told her something quite different though. "Make sure you double up on the bags," was his first comment, followed by "and make sure you only put two scoops in per bag and no more. If you put three the bags tend to break. A few weeks ago one guy had it break just as he threw it into the container and dirty grease spilled all over him. He was vomiting for a few minutes and then had to go home right away. We don't want that to happen again. Don't worry about Melisande seeing you not following instructions. She does get upset about that type of thing but she is hardly ever here. Your training session was the first time I've seen her in a month."

"Wow," thought Phedre. "Thank goodness Joscelin told me about that or something very nasty could have happened. I wonder why Melisande doesn't know about this—after all, she is the owner! If I had followed her instructions it could have made me sick."

Discussion Questions

1. Why do you think the grease trap cleaning issue has not been drawn to Melisande's attention? Be as specific as possible.

2. What might Melisande do differently to encourage more upward communication? Be specific.

3. Using this case as an example, discuss how the informal communication network can impact the effectiveness of orientation and training. Remember to consider both potential positive and potential negative impacts.

Rodrigo took a moment to swallow some of his irritation and annoyance before responding to his boss and company CEO, John. He looked around the meeting table and saw nothing but downcast eyes and uncomfortable fidgeting, so he knew he was on his own. "What do you expect people to say," he asked John wearily. "After a display like that do you really think anyone will talk?"

John had called a meeting with all of his supervisors, managers, and his executive team, including Rodrigo. They all worked for a firm that made a high-end line of gourmet salsas. The salsas were sold in specialty shops and small, privately owned grocery shops. The company had started off well eight years ago, seeing slow but steady growth for the first five years. The past three years had been characterized by new competitors and diminished profits.

During those difficult years each and every employee had made concessions to help the struggling company. For example, the production staff (responsible for turning fresh vegetables into canned salsas) hadn't had any raise at all, even a cost-of-living increase, for three years. Given that they were unionized and had the power to initiate a strike over wages, this had been a significant concession on the union's part. The executive team had also gone without raises and bonuses.

Now, however, things were looking up. Six months ago their signature salsa had been featured on the Food Network as a key ingredient in a well-known cooking competition. That had led to a deal with a major grocery chain to carry their line of products. Sales had skyrocketed, profits were up, and it was time to share the wealth. That's why they were all meeting, to discuss the best way to distribute the benefits of their newfound success.

At the beginning of the meeting, John had presented financial figures and asked his team what they thought should be done for the employees. He mentioned that he had his own ideas but wanted to hear what others thought. Few spoke up, so John proposed a 3 percent raise for everyone across the board. "Wait a minute," said Rodrigo. "Remember that these people haven't had cost-of-living increases in three years. Every one of them sacrificed to help this company during lean times. They all know that we've done very well lately and that this new contract is a game changer. I think that, under the circumstances, offering only 3 percent might be considered condescending or insulting. In a way this is really four years' worth of raises we are talking about. Frankly, 3 percent just sucks."

There was silence for a few seconds. Then the outburst began. "What do you mean it *sucks*?" bellowed John. "You should all be on board with this suggestion since it came from management. Aren't you a team player? I don't like your attitude." The rant continued for about two-and-a-half minutes, after which John asked, "Does anyone else feel the same as Rodrigo"? It was this request for additional feedback that had led to Rodrigo to say, "What do you expect people to say? After a display like that do you really think anyone will talk?"

Discussion Questions

1. List and explain all the communication errors you can in this scenario.

2. What communication barriers and/or perceptual biases may have contributing to John's overreaction to Rodrigo's comments? How might these have been avoided? Remember to consider what Rodrigo might have done differently and what John might have done differently.

3. What might John do now, after this event, to create an environment conducive to effective upward communication?

MyManagementLab

Study, practise, and explore real management situations with these helpful resources:
- **Interactive Lesson Presentations:** Work through interactive presentations and assessments to test your knowledge of management concepts.
- **PIA (Personal Inventory Assessments):** Enhance your ability to connect with key concepts through these engaging self-reflection assessments.
- **Study Plan:** Check your understanding of chapter concepts with self-study quizzes.
- **Simulations:** Practise decision making in simulated management environments.

PIA
PERSONAL INVENTORY ASSESSMENT

Chapter 12
Leadership

LEARNING OBJECTIVES

After studying this chapter, you should be able to:

1 Contrast leadership and management.

2 Summarize the conclusions of trait theories of leadership.

3 Identify the central tenets and main limitations of behavioural theories of leadership.

4 Assess contingency theories of leadership.

5 Contrast *charismatic* and *transformational leadership*.

6 Describe the roles of ethics and trust in *authentic leadership*.

7 Identify main differentiators between servant leadership and other forms of leadership.

8 Demonstrate the role mentoring plays in our understanding of leadership.

9 Address challenges to the effectiveness of leadership.

10 Describe how organizations can find or create effective leaders.

In this chapter, we look at what differentiates leaders from nonleaders. First, we'll present several theories of leadership and review the varied forms that it can take. Then, we'll discuss challenges to the meaning and importance of leadership. But before we review these approaches, let's clarify what we mean by the term *leadership*.

WHAT IS LEADERSHIP?

We define **leadership** as the ability to influence a group toward the achievement of a vision or set of goals. The source of influence may be formal, such as that provided by managerial rank in an organization. But not all managers are leaders, nor are all leaders managers. Just because an organization provides its managers with certain formal rights is no assurance they will lead effectively. Leaders can emerge from within a group as well as by formal appointment. Nonsanctioned leadership—the ability to influence that arises outside the formal structure of the organization—is often as important as or more important than formal positions of influence.

Organizations need strong leadership *and* strong management for optimal effectiveness. We need leaders to challenge the status quo, create visions of the future, and inspire organizational members to achieve these visions. We need managers to formulate detailed plans, create efficient organizational structures, and oversee day-to-day operations.

TRAIT THEORIES

Bruce believes strongly that some people are born leaders. These "naturals" will always perform better in leadership roles than people who don't have the innate qualities necessary. This belief means Bruce subscribes to trait-based theories of leadership.

Throughout history, strong leaders have usually been described by their traits. Therefore, leadership research has long sought to identify the personality, social, physical, or intellectual attributes that differentiate leaders from non-leaders. In recent research, the **trait theories of leadership** focus on personal qualities and characteristics, some of which have been shown to be particularly predictive of leadership ability.

The most common trait-based approach uses the Big Five personality framework to develop insight into the relationship between personality traits and leadership. A comprehensive review of the leadership literature organized around the Big Five personality framework (see Chapter 5) has found extraversion to be the most predictive trait of leadership.[1] However, extraversion relates more to the way leaders emerge than to their effectiveness. Sociable and dominant people are more likely to assert themselves in group situations, which can help extraverts be identified as leaders, but effective leaders are not domineering. One study found leaders who scored very high on assertiveness were actually less effective than those who scored moderately high.[2] Conscientiousness and openness to experience also predict leader effectiveness. In general, leaders who like being around people and are able to assert themselves (extraverted), who are disciplined and able to keep commitments they make (conscientious), and who are creative and flexible (open) do have an apparent advantage when it comes to leadership.

Based on the latest findings, we offer two conclusions. First, we can say that traits can predict leadership. Second, traits do a better job predicting the emergence of leaders than predicting actual performance as an established leader.[3] The fact that an individual exhibits the right traits and that others consider him a leader does not necessarily mean that he will be effective or successful at motivating the group to achieve its goals.

Trait theories help us predict who will become a leader, but they don't help us explain leadership effectiveness. What do successful leaders *do*? Are there different types of leader behaviours that are equally effective? Behavioural theories, discussed next, help us define the parameters of leadership.

BEHAVIOURAL THEORIES

Brittany believes strongly that leadership is an acquired skill. Leaders are made, not born. They are created by teaching people a particular set of behaviours that have been proven effective. These beliefs mean that Brittany subscribes to behavioural theories of leadership.

Behavioural theories of leadership imply that we can determine leadership effectiveness by leader behaviour, and perhaps train people to be leaders. The most comprehensive behavioural theories in use today resulted from the Ohio State Studies,[4] which sought to identify independent dimensions of leader behaviour. Beginning with more than a thousand behaviours, the studies narrowed the list to two dimensions that substantially accounted for most of the effective leadership behaviour described by employees: *initiating structure* and *consideration*.

Initiating structure is the extent to which a leader is likely to define and construct her role and those of employees in the search for goal attainment. It includes behaviour that attempts to organize work, work relationships, and goals. A leader high in initiating structure is someone task-oriented who "assigns group members to particular tasks," "expects workers to maintain definite standards of performance," and "emphasizes the meeting of deadlines."

Consideration is the extent to which a person's job relationships are characterized by mutual trust, respect for employees' ideas, and regard for their feelings. A leader high in consideration helps employees with personal problems, is friendly and approachable, treats all employees as equals, and expresses appreciation and support (people-oriented). Most of us want to work for considerate leaders—although the degree to which that is true can vary by culture, as we will see shortly.[5]

Leadership studies at the University of Michigan's Survey Research Center had objectives similar to those of the Ohio State Studies: to locate behavioural characteristics of leaders that related to performance effectiveness. The Michigan group identified two behavioural types: the **employee-oriented leader** emphasized interpersonal relationships by taking a personal interest in employees' needs and accepting individual differences, and the **production-oriented leader** emphasized technical or task aspects of jobs, focusing on accomplishing the group's tasks. These dimensions are closely related to the Ohio State dimensions. Employee-oriented leadership is similar to consideration, and production-oriented leadership is similar to initiating structure. In fact, most researchers use the terms synonymously.[6]

The results of behavioural theory studies have been mixed. However, a review of 160 studies found the followers of leaders high in consideration were more satisfied with their jobs, were more motivated, and had more respect for their leaders. Initiating structure, by contrast, was strongly related to higher levels of group and organization productivity and more positive performance evaluations.

The reason for some of the mixed results from behavioural theory tests may partly lie in follower preferences, particularly cultural preferences. Research from the GLOBE program—a study of 18,000 leaders from 825 organizations in 62 countries discussed in Chapter 5—suggested there are international differences in the preference for initiating structure and consideration.[7] The study found that leaders high in consideration succeeded best in countries where the cultural values did not favour unilateral decision making, such as Brazil. As one Brazilian manager noted, "We do not prefer leaders who take self-governing decisions and act alone without engaging the group. That's part of who we are." A U.S. manager leading a team in Brazil would therefore need to be high in consideration—team-oriented, participative, and humane—to be effective. In contrast, the French have a more bureaucratic view of leaders and are less likely to expect them to be humane and considerate. A leader high in initiating structure (relatively task-oriented) will do best and can make decisions in a relatively autocratic manner in this culture. On the other hand, a manager who scores high on consideration (people-oriented) may find his style backfires in France. In other cultures, both may be important—Chinese culture emphasizes being polite, considerate, and unselfish, but it has a high performance orientation. Thus, consideration and initiating structure may both be important for a manager to be effective in China.

Moving beyond initiating structure and consideration, the GLOBE studies also found that a country's history impacts behavioural preferences for leaders. Germans, for example, are particularly hostile to highly charismatic leaders, a legacy of collective trauma resulting from the leadership style of Adoph Hilter. Similarly, many Eastern European businesses operate in an uncertain developing market economy within the context of a highly masculine culture. In this environment some consideration behaviours may be perceived as a sign of weakness and actually undermine leadership effectiveness.

Summary of Trait Theories and Behavioural Theories

In general, research indicates there is validity for both the trait and behavioural theories. Parts of each theory can help explain facets of leadership emergence and effectiveness. The first difficulty is in correctly identifying whether a trait or a behaviour predicts a certain outcome. The second difficulty is in exploring which combinations of traits and behaviours yield certain outcomes. We've discussed some of these complex determinations as they are currently understood. Leaders who have certain traits desirable to their positions and who display culturally appropriate initiating structure and consideration behaviours do appear to be more effective. Some of the other determinations are less clear. For example, perhaps you're wondering whether conscientious leaders (trait) are more likely to be structuring (behaviour), and extraverted leaders (trait) to be considerate (behaviour). Unfortunately, we are not sure there is a connection. Future research is needed to determine the exact nature of these relationships.

As important as traits and behaviours are in identifying effective or ineffective leaders, they do not guarantee success. Some leaders may have the right traits or display the right behaviours and still fail. As we've mentioned, context matters, too, which has given rise to the contingency theories we discuss next.

CONTINGENCY THEORIES

Jamie believes that the best leadership style to use depends on the situation. Ideally leaders should adjust their behaviour to fit the situation or, if they are unable to do so, the person leading should be replaced to ensure a match between context and leadership style. These beliefs mean that Jamie subscribes to contingency theories of leadership.

Some tough-minded leaders seem to gain a lot of admirers when they take over struggling companies and lead them out of crises. However, predicting leadership success is more complex than finding a few hero examples. Also, the leadership style that works in very bad times doesn't necessarily translate into long-term success. When researchers looked at situational influences, it appeared that under condition a, leadership style x would be appropriate, whereas style y was more suitable for condition b, and style z for condition c. But what *were* conditions a, b, and c? We next consider the Fiedler model, one approach to isolating situational variables.

The Fiedler Model

Fred Fiedler developed the first comprehensive contingency model for leadership—it is still in use today.[8] The **Fiedler contingency model** proposes that effective group performance depends on the proper match between the leader's style and the degree to which the situation gives the leader control.

Identifying Leadership Style With the Fiedler model, a key factor in leadership success is the individual's leadership style, which is assumed to be stable and consistent across all situations. The model's **least preferred co-worker (LPC) questionnaire** identifies leadership style by measuring whether a person is *task-oriented* or *relationship-oriented*. The LPC questionnaire asks respondents to think of all the coworkers they have ever had and describe the one they *least enjoyed* working with, on a scale of 1 to 8, for 16 sets of contrasting adjectives (such as pleasant–unpleasant, efficient–inefficient, open–guarded, supportive–hostile). If you describe the person you are least able to work with in favorable terms (a high LPC score), you are relationship-oriented. If you rate your least-preferred coworker in unfavorable terms (a low LPC score), you are primarily interested in productivity and are task-oriented. About 16 percent of respondents score in the middle range[9] and thus fall outside the theory's predictions. Our discussion thus pertains to the 84 percent who score in the high or low range of the LPC questionnaire.

Defining the Situation With the Fiedler model, a fit must be found between the organizational situation and the leader's style for there to be leadership effectiveness. If a situation requires a task-oriented leader and the person in the leadership position is relationship oriented, either the situation has to be modified or the leader has to be replaced to achieve optimal effectiveness. We can assess the situation in terms of three contingency or situational dimensions:

1. **Leader–member relations** is the degree of confidence, trust, and respect members have in their leader.
2. **Task structure** is the degree to which the job assignments are procedurized (that is, structured or unstructured).
3. **Position power** is the degree of influence a leader has over power variables such as hiring, firing, discipline, promotions, and salary increases.

According to Fiedler's model, the higher the task structure becomes, the more procedures are added; and the stronger the position power, the more control the leader has. A very favorable situation (in which the leader has a great deal of control) might include a payroll manager who has the respect and confidence of his employees (good leader–member relations); activities that are clear and specific—such as wage computation, cheque writing, and report filing (high task structure); and considerable freedom to reward and punish employees (strong position power). The favorable situations are on the left-hand side of the model in Exhibit 12-1. An unfavorable situation, to the right in the model, might be that of the disliked chairperson of a volunteer United Way fundraising team (low leader–member relations, low task structure, low position power). In this job, the leader has very little control.

Matching Leaders and Situations Combining the three contingency dimensions yields eight possible categories of leadership situations. The Fiedler model proposes matching an individual's LPC score and these eight situations to achieve maximum leadership

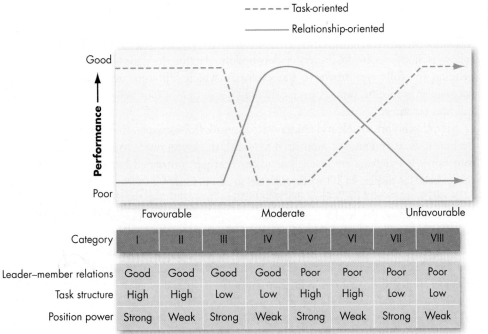

EXHIBIT 12-1 Findings from the Fiedler Model

Category	I	II	III	IV	V	VI	VII	VIII
Leader–member relations	Good	Good	Good	Good	Poor	Poor	Poor	Poor
Task structure	High	High	Low	Low	High	High	Low	Low
Position power	Strong	Weak	Strong	Weak	Strong	Weak	Strong	Weak

effectiveness.[10] Let's walk through an example. By the model, task-oriented leaders (represented by the dotted line) perform better in situations that are either very favorable to them and or are very unfavorable, but not as well in moderately favorable situations. So, when faced with a category I, II, III, VII, or VIII situation, task-oriented leaders perform better. Relationship-oriented leaders (represented by the solid line), however, perform better in moderately favorable situations—categories IV and V especially.

Note that each of the categories shows us what creates a favorable or unfavorable situation for each leadership style. Fiedler later condensed these eight situations down to three, with the same general findings:[11] Task-oriented leaders perform best in situations of high and low control, while relationship-oriented leaders perform best in moderate control situations.

How would you apply Fiedler's findings? You would match leaders—in terms of their LPC scores—with situations—in terms of leader–member relationships, task structure, and position power. But remember that the model considers an individual's leadership style as fixed. Therefore, there are only two ways to improve leader effectiveness.

First, you can change the leader to fit the situation—in the same way a baseball manager puts a right- or left-handed pitcher into the game depending on whether the hitter is right- or left-handed. If a group situation rates as highly unfavourable but is currently led by a relationship-oriented manager, for example, the group's performance might be improved under a manager who is task-oriented. The second alternative is to change the situation to fit the leader by restructuring tasks, or increasing or decreasing the leader's power to control factors such as salary increases, promotions, and disciplinary actions.

Evaluation Studies testing the overall validity of the Fiedler model find considerable evidence to support substantial parts of it.[12] If we use Fiedler's later three situation categories rather than the original eight, ample evidence supports his conclusions.[13] But the logic underlying the LPC questionnaire is not well understood, and respondents' scores are not stable.[14] The contingency variables are also complex and difficult for practitioners to assess.[15] Therefore, while the Fiedler model is widely known and referenced, and its concepts should be understood in organizations, its practical application is sometimes problematic.

Other Contingency Theories

Although the Fiedler model is the most researched contingency theory, two others deserve discussion: situational leadership theory and path–goal theory.

Situational Leadership Theory Situational leadership theory (SLT) focuses on the followers. It says successful leadership depends on selecting the right leadership style contingent on the followers' *readiness*, the extent to which followers are willing and able to accomplish a specific task. A leader should choose one of four behaviours depending on follower readiness.

If followers are *unable* and *unwilling* to do a task (for example, they are not well trained on how to do it and are not motivated to learn), the leader needs to give clear and specific directions. If followers are *unable* but *willing* (perhaps untrained but eager to learn), the leader needs to display high task orientation to compensate for followers' lack of ability, and high relationship orientation to get them to buy into the leader's desires. If followers are *able* but *unwilling*, the leader needs to use a supportive and participative style; if they are both *able* and *willing*, the leader doesn't need to do much.

SLT has intuitive appeal. It acknowledges the importance of followers and builds on the logic that leaders can compensate for followers' limited ability and motivation. Yet research efforts to test and support the theory have generally been disappointing.[16] Why? Possible explanations include internal ambiguities and inconsistencies in the model itself as well as problems with research methodology. So, despite its intuitive appeal and wide popularity, any endorsement must be cautious for now.

Path–Goal Theory   Developed by Robert House, **path–goal theory** extracts elements from the Ohio State leadership research on initiating structure and consideration, and the expectancy theory of motivation.[17] Path–goal theory suggests it's the leader's job to provide followers with information, support, or other resources necessary to achieve goals. (The term *path–goal* implies that effective leaders clarify followers' paths to their work goals and make the journey easier by reducing roadblocks.) The theory predicts:

- Directive leadership yields greater satisfaction when tasks are ambiguous or stressful than when they are highly structured and well laid out.

- Supportive leadership results in high performance and satisfaction when employees are performing structured tasks.

- Directive leadership is likely to be perceived as redundant by employees with high ability or considerable experience.

Of course, this is a simplification. The match between leadership style and situation can be individualistic. Some tasks may be both stressful and highly structured, and employees may have high ability or experience in some tasks and not others. Studies indicate that leaders who set goals enable conscientious followers to achieve higher performance but may cause stress for workers who are low in conscientiousness.

Altogether, the foundation of path–goal theory has merit. Directive or supportive leadership does matter to followers' performance, and leaders need to be aware of their important facilitating role. Additionally, the theory, like SLT and other contingency theories, reminds us that the effectiveness of leaders depends to a large degree on their followers and on the situation they find themselves in.

One contingency theory of leadership takes this concept further, highlighting that individual followers may not all have the same relationship with a given leader. This theory is called leader–member exchange, or LMX. The theory reminds us that leaders form a deep, trusting bond with some employees and not others, partly due to time constraints and resource limitations and partly due to personality dynamics and in-group effects. The nature of this dyadic relationship influences leadership outcomes, as the same leader will have varied outcomes depending on their individual relationship with specific followers. LMX theory has been well supported by research, indicating that a "high-quality exchange" relationship (meaning relationships with the leader that are characterized by high trust and perceived supportiveness), are associated with higher job satisfaction, reduced turnover, increased organizational citizenship, and better performance. "Low-quality exchanges," by contrast, are characterized by a lack of trust and little or no perceived supportiveness. They are associated with lowered job satisfaction, concerns about fairness, increased absenteeism, turnover, and reduced performance.[18]

CHARISMATIC LEADERSHIP AND TRANSFORMATIONAL LEADERSHIP

What makes the truly great leaders extraordinary? Two contemporary leadership theories—charismatic leadership and transformational leadership—attempt to explain how individuals go about becoming inspiring leaders.

Charismatic Leadership

Politician Justin Trudeau, human rights activist Malala, Apple co-founder Steven Jobs, hockey star Wayne Gretzky, and cosmetics tycoon Mary Kay Ash are all frequently cited as charismatic leaders. What do they have in common?

Nobel Peace Prize winner Malala Yousafzai has charmed, engaged, and inspired large audiences and individual politicians all over the world.

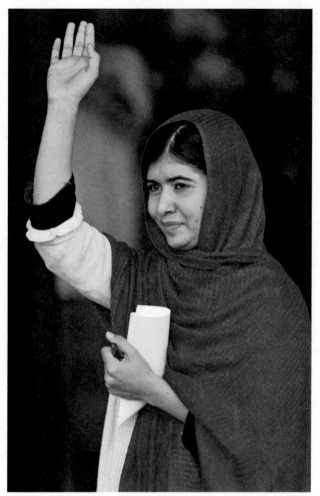

Daily Mail/Rex/Alamy Stock Photo

What is Charismatic Leadership? Sociologist Max Weber defined *charisma* (from the Greek for "gift") more than a century ago as "a certain quality of an individual personality, by virtue of which he or she is set apart from ordinary people and treated as endowed with supernatural, superhuman, or at least specifically exceptional powers or qualities. These are not accessible to the ordinary person and are regarded as of divine origin or as exemplary, and on the basis of them the individual concerned is treated as a leader."[19]

The first researcher to consider OB in terms of charismatic leadership was Robert House. According to House's **charismatic leadership theory**, followers attribute heroic or extraordinary leadership abilities when they observe certain behaviours and tend to give these leaders power.[20] A number of studies have attempted to identify the characteristics of charismatic leaders: They have a vision, are willing to take personal risks to achieve that vision, are sensitive to follower needs, and exhibit extraordinary behaviours[21] (see Exhibit 12-2).

EXHIBIT 12-2 Key Characteristics of a Charismatic Leader

Source: Based on J. A. Conger and R. N. Kanungo, *Charismatic Leadership in Organizations* (Thousand Oaks, CA: Sage, 1998), p. 94.

1. **Vision and articulation.** Has a vision—expressed as an idealized goal—that proposes a future better than the status quo and is able to clarify the importance of the vision in terms that are understandable to others.
2. **Personal risk.** Willing to take on high personal risk, incur high costs, and engage in self-sacrifice to achieve the vision.
3. **Sensitivity to follower needs.** Perceptive of others' abilities and responsive to their needs and feelings.
4. **Unconventional behaviour.** Engages in behaviours that are perceived as novel and counter to norms.

Are Charismatic Leaders Born or Made? Are charismatic leaders born with their qualities? Or can people actually learn to be charismatic leaders? Yes and yes.

Individuals *are* born with traits that make them charismatic. In fact, studies of identical twins found that twins scored similarly on charismatic leadership measures, even if they were raised in different households and never met. Personality is also relevant, as charismatic leaders are likely to be extraverted, self-confident, and achievement-oriented.[22] Recent research indicates that all of us can develop, within our own limitations, a more charismatic leadership style. If you stay active and central in your leadership roles, you will naturally communicate your vision for achieving goals to your followers, which increases the likelihood that you will be seen as charismatic.[23] To further develop an aura of charisma, use your passion as a catalyst for generating enthusiasm. Speak in an animated voice, reinforce your message with eye contact and facial expression, and gesture for emphasis. Bring out the potential in followers by tapping into their emotions, and create a bond that inspires them. Remember, enthusiasm is contagious!

How Charismatic Leaders Influence Followers How do charismatic leaders actually influence followers? By articulating an appealing **vision**, a long-term strategy for attaining a goal by linking the present with a better future for the organization. Desirable visions fit the times and circumstances and reflect the uniqueness of the organization. Followers are not inspired only by how passionately the leader communicates—there must also be an underlying vision that appeals to followers.

A vision needs an accompanying **vision statement**, a formal articulation of an organization's vision or mission. Charismatic leaders may use vision statements to imprint on followers an overarching goal and purpose. These leaders also set a tone of cooperation and mutual support. They build followers' self-esteem and confidence with high performance expectations and the belief that followers can attain them. Through words and actions, the leader conveys values and sets an example for followers to imitate. Finally, the charismatic leader engages in emotion-inducing and often unconventional behaviour to demonstrate courage and conviction about the vision.

Research indicates that charismatic leadership strategies work because followers "catch" the emotions and values their leader is conveying.[24] A study of 115 U.S. government employees found they had a stronger sense of personal belonging at work when they had charismatic leaders, increasing their willingness to engage in helping and compliance-oriented behaviour.[25] When followers mirror the desirable behaviours, the effectiveness of these leaders is heightened. One study of Israeli bank employees also showed charismatic leaders were more effective because their employees personally identified with them.

Does Effective Charismatic Leadership Depend on the Person and the Situation? Charismatic leadership has positive effects across many contexts. There are, however, characteristics of followers, and of the situation, that enhance or somewhat limit its effects.

One factor that enhances charismatic leadership is stress. People are especially receptive to charismatic leadership when they sense a crisis, when they are under stress, or when they fear for their lives. We may be more receptive to charismatic leadership under crises because we think bold leadership is needed. Some of it, however, may be more primal. When people are psychologically aroused, even in laboratory studies, they are more likely to respond to charismatic leaders.[26] This might explain why, when charismatic leaders surface, it's likely to be in politics or religion, during wartime, or when a business is in its infancy or facing a life-threatening crisis. Charismatic leaders are able to reduce stress for their followers, perhaps because they help make work seem more meaningful and interesting.[27]

Some personalities are especially susceptible to charismatic leadership.[28] For instance, an individual who lacks self-esteem and questions his self-worth is more likely to absorb a leader's direction rather than establish his own way of leading or thinking. For these people, the situation may matter much less than the charismatic qualities of the leader.

The Dark Side of Charismatic Leadership Unfortunately, charismatic leaders who are larger than life don't necessarily act in the best interests of their organizations.[29] Research has shown that individuals who are narcissistic are also higher in some behaviours associated with charismatic leadership.[30] Many charismatic—but corrupt—leaders have allowed their personal goals to override the goals of the organization. Leaders at Enron, Tyco, WorldCom, and HealthSouth recklessly used organizational resources for their personal benefit and violated laws and ethics to inflate stock prices, and then cashed in millions of dollars in personal stock options. Some charismatic leaders—Hitler, for example—are all too successful at convincing their followers to pursue a vision that can be disastrous. If charisma is power, then that power can be used for either good or ill.

It's not that charismatic leadership isn't effective; overall, it is. But a charismatic leader isn't always the answer. Success depends, to some extent, on the situation, on the leader's vision, and on the organizational checks and balances in place to monitor the outcomes.

Transformational Leadership

Charismatic leadership relies on leaders' ability to inspire followers to believe in them. **Transactional leaders**, by contrast, guide their followers toward established goals by clarifying role and task requirements. They create structure and they make sure needed resources are available. Transactional leaders are frequently contrasted with **transformational leaders**,[31] who focus more on emotion than structure and inspire followers to transcend their self-interests for the good of the organization. Transformational leaders can have an extraordinary effect on their followers and as a result they are often confused with charismatic leaders. There are some subtle differences between the two. Charismatic leaders inspire though the power of personality, while transformational leaders inspire by creating a common vision and sense of shared power and ability to implement change. Recent research suggests that transformational leaders are most effective when their followers are able to see the positive impact of their work through direct interaction with customers or other beneficiaries.[32] Exhibit 12-3 briefly identifies and defines characteristics that differentiate transactional from transformational leaders.

Transactional and transformational leadership complement each other; they aren't opposing approaches to leadership effectiveness.[33] The best leaders are transactional *and* transformational. Transformational leadership *builds on* transactional leadership and produces levels of follower effort and performance beyond what transactional leadership

EXHIBIT 12-3 Characteristics of Transactional and Transformational Leaders

Sources: Based on A. H. Eagly, M. C. Johannesen-Schmidt, and M. L. Van Engen, "Transformational, Transactional, and Laissez-faire Leadership Styles: A Meta-Analysis Comparing Women and Men," *Psychological Bulletin* 129, no. 4 (2003), pp. 569–591; and T. A. Judge and J. E. Bono, "Five Factor Model of Personality and Transformational Leadership," *Journal of Applied Psychology* 85, no. 5 (2000), pp. 751–765.

TRANSACTIONAL LEADER

Contingent reward. Contracts exchange of rewards for effort, promises rewards for good performance, recognizes accomplishments.
Management by exception (active). Watches and searches for deviations from rules and standards, takes correct action.
Management by exception (passive). Intervenes only if standards are not met.
Laissez-faire. Abdicates responsibilities, avoids making decisions.

TRANSFORMATIONAL LEADER

Idealized influence. Provides vision and sense of mission, instills pride, gains respect and trust.
Inspirational motivation. Communicates high expectations, uses symbols to focus efforts, expresses important purposes in simple ways.
Intellectual stimulation. Promotes intelligence, rationality, and careful problem solving.
Individualized consideration. Gives personal attention, treats each employee individually, coaches, advises.

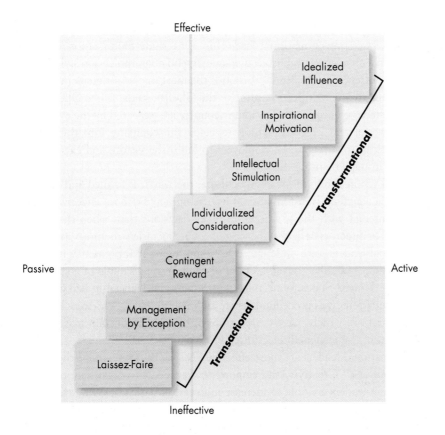

EXHIBIT 12-4 Full Range of Leadership Model

Effective

Idealized Influence

Inspirational Motivation

Intellectual Stimulation

Individualized Consideration

Contingent Reward

Management by Exception

Laissez-Faire

Transformational

Transactional

Passive

Active

Ineffective

alone can do. But the reverse isn't true. If you are a good transactional leader but do not have transformational qualities, you'll likely be only a mediocre leader. A model of leader behaviours indicates increasing effectiveness as a leader moves from passive, transactional behaviours to active, transformational behaviours (see Exhibit 12-4).

Full Range of Leadership Model Exhibit 12-4 shows the full range of leadership model. Laissez-faire, which literally means "to let be" (that is, to do nothing), is the most passive and therefore least effective of leader behaviours.[34] Management by exception, in which leaders primarily "put out fires" when there are crisis exceptions to normal operating procedures, often results in actions that are too late to be effective. Contingent reward leadership, in which predetermined rewards are given for employee efforts, can be an effective style of leadership but will not get employees to go above and beyond the call of duty.

Only with the four remaining styles—all aspects of transformational leadership—are leaders able to motivate followers to perform above expectations and transcend their self-interest for the sake of the organization. Individualized consideration, intellectual stimulation, inspirational motivation, and idealized influence (known as the "four I's") all result in extra effort from workers, higher productivity, higher morale and satisfaction, higher organizational effectiveness, lower turnover, lower absenteeism, and greater organizational adaptability. Based on this model, leaders are generally most effective when they regularly use the four I's.

Evaluation of Transformational Leadership The merit of transformational leadership has been supported at diverse job levels and occupations (school principals, teachers, marine commanders, ministers, presidents of MBA associations, military cadets, union shop stewards, sales reps). In general, organizations perform better when they have transformational leaders. Companies with transformational leaders show greater agreement among top managers about the organization's goals, which yields superior organizational performance.[35] The effect of transformational leadership on performance can vary by the situation. In general, transformational leadership has a greater impact on the bottom line in smaller, privately held firms than in more complex organizations.[36]

Just as vision helps explain how charismatic leadership works, it also explains part of the effectiveness of transformational leadership. One study found vision was even more important than a charismatic (effusive, dynamic, lively) communication style in explaining the success of entrepreneurial firms.[37] Vision is the most important element of transformational leadership in any culture, according to the GLOBE study.[38] The GLOBE team concluded that "effective business leaders in any country are expected by their subordinates to provide a powerful and proactive vision to guide the company into the future, strong motivational skills to stimulate all employees to fulfill the vision, and excellent planning skills to assist in implementing the vision."[39]

Although vision is important in any culture, the way it is formed and communicated may need to be adapted. Transformational leadership may be more effective when leaders can directly interact with the workforce to make decisions than when they report to an external board of directors or deal with a complex bureaucratic structure. One study showed transformational leaders were more effective in improving group potency in teams higher in power distance and collectivism.[40] Other research using a sample of employees both in China and the United States found that transformational leadership had a more positive relationship with perceived procedural justice among individuals who were lower in power-distance orientation, which suggests that transformational leadership may work in many cultures as long as the leaders interact directly with followers.[41]

Transformational leaders are more effective because they encourage those who follow them to be creative.[42] Creativity and empowerment are key to organizational success, and transformational leaders are able to increase follower self-efficacy, giving the group a "can do" spirit.[43] Empowered followers are more likely to pursue ambitious goals, agree on the strategic objectives of the organization, and believe the goals they are pursuing are personally important.[44]

Like charisma, transformational leadership can be learned. One study of Canadian bank managers found branches managed by those who underwent transformational leadership training performed significantly better than branches whose managers did not receive training.

Transformational Leadership and Charismatic Leadership In considering transformational and charismatic leadership, you will have noticed some commonalities. And indeed there are. Yet there are differences, too. Charismatic leadership places somewhat more emphasis on *how* leaders communicate (are they passionate and dynamic) while transformational leadership focuses more on *what* is communicated (especially a compelling vision); the theories are more alike than different. At their heart, both theories focus on the ability of leaders to inspire followers, and some of the ways they do this are the same in both theories. Because of this, some researchers believe the concepts are interchangeable.

One of the reasons transformational leadership works is that it empowers followers to use their own judgement to help reach a collective goal.

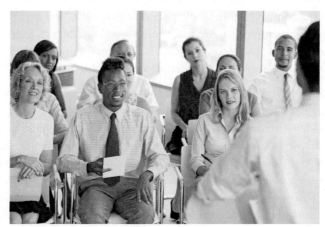

Cathy Yeulet/123RF

AUTHENTIC LEADERSHIP: ETHICS AND TRUST

Although theories have increased our understanding of effective leadership, they do not explicitly deal with the role of ethics and trust, which are essential to complete the picture. Here, we consider these two concepts under the rubric of authentic leadership.[45]

If we're looking for the best possible leader, it is not enough to be charismatic or visionary—one must also be ethical and authentic.

What Is Authentic Leadership?

Authentic leadership focuses on the moral aspects of being a leader. **Authentic leaders** know who they are, know what they believe in, and act on those values and beliefs openly and candidly. Their followers consider them ethical people. The primary quality produced by authentic leadership is trust. Authentic leaders share information, encourage open communication, and stick to their ideals. The result: People have faith in them.

There has been limited research on authentic leadership. However, recent research indicated that authentic leadership, especially when shared among top management team members, created a positive energizing effect that heightened firm performance.[46]

Ethical Leadership

For better or worse, leadership is not value-free. In assessing leadership effectiveness, we need to address the *means* a leader uses to achieve goals as well as the content of those goals. The role of the leader in creating the ethical expectations for all members is crucial.[47] Therefore, although every member of an organization is responsible for ethical behaviour, many initiatives aimed at increasing organizational ethical behaviour are focused on the leaders. A recent study of 2,572 soldiers underscored that ethical leadership among the top brass influences not only their direct followers, but all the way down the command structure as well, because top leaders create an ethical culture and expect lower-level leaders to behave along ethical guidelines.[48]

Ethics and authentic leadership intersect at a number of junctures. Leaders who treat their followers with fairness, especially by providing honest, frequent, and accurate information, are seen as more effective.[49] Related to this is the concept of humbleness, another characteristic ethical leaders often exhibit as part of being authentic. Research indicates that leaders who model humility help followers to understand the growth process for their own development.[50] Leaders rated as highly ethical also tend to have followers who engage in more organizational citizenship behaviours and who are more willing to bring problems to the leaders' attention.[51] Recent research also found that ethical leadership reduced interpersonal conflicts.[52]

Leaders can build on a foundation of trust to show their character, enhance a sense of unity, and create buy-in from followers. Research findings suggest that organizations should invest in ethical leadership training programs, especially in industries with few regulations.[53]

Servant Leadership

Scholars have recently considered ethical leadership from a new angle by examining **servant leadership**.[54] Servant leaders go beyond their self-interest and focus on opportunities to help followers grow and develop. They don't use power to achieve ends; they emphasize persuasion. Characteristic behaviours include listening, empathizing, persuading, accepting stewardship, and actively developing followers' potential. Because servant leadership emphasizes serving the needs of others, research has focused on its outcomes for the well-being of followers. Perhaps not surprisingly, a recent study of 126 CEOs found that servant leadership is negatively correlated with the trait of narcissism.[55]

What are the effects of servant leadership? One study of 123 supervisors found servant leadership resulted in higher levels of commitment to the supervisor, self-efficacy, and perceptions of justice, which all were related to organizational citizenship behaviour (OCB).[56] This relationship between servant leadership and follower OCB appears to be stronger when followers are focused on being dutiful and responsible.[57] Also, servant leadership increases team potency (a belief that one's team has above-average skills and abilities), which in turn leads to higher levels of group performance.[58] Third, a study with a nationally representative sample found a higher level of OCB was associated with a focus on growth and advancement, which in turn was associated with a higher level of creative performance.[59]

Servant leadership may be more prevalent and more effective in certain cultures.[60] When asked to draw images of leaders, for example, U.S. subjects tended to draw them in front of the group, giving orders to followers. Singaporeans tended to draw leaders at the back of the group, acting more to gather a group's opinions together and then unify them from the rear. This suggests the East Asian prototype is more like a servant leader, which might mean servant leadership is more effective in these cultures.

Trust and Leadership

Trust is a psychological state that exists when you agree to make yourself vulnerable to another person because you have positive expectations about how things are going to turn out.[61] Although you aren't completely in control of the situation, you are willing to take a chance that the other person will come through for you. Trust is a primary attribute associated with leadership; breaking it can have serious adverse effects on a group's performance.[62]

Trust is made up of three distinct component or beliefs. In order to fully trust someone you must believe that they are competent (they are able to do what they say they will do), benevolent (they have good intentions), and that they have integrity (they keep their promises). Having only two of the traits is insufficient.[63] Imagine being invited to dinner at a friend's house. That friend may have your best interests at heart and might always keep promises, but if you know he or she is a terrible cook (incompetent), you will not trust that it will be a good meal. Or he or she may be a great cook and be benevolent but have a track record of not being home when invited guests arrive (lack of integrity). In a worst case scenario you may fear that your friend is angry with you and seeks to poison you (lack of benevolence). In all three cases you wouldn't trust him or her to provide a decent meal; you would just have different reasons. Trust is a three-legged stool; remove a leg and the whole thing falls down. Leaders must exhibit competence, benevolence, and integrity to gain trust.

Followers who trust a leader are confident their rights and interests will not be abused.[64] Transformational leaders create support for their ideas in part by arguing that their direction will be in everyone's best interests. People are unlikely to look up to or follow someone they perceive as dishonest or may take advantage of them. Thus, as you might expect, transformational leaders generate higher levels of trust from their followers, which relate to higher levels of team confidence and, ultimately, higher levels of team performance.[65]

In a simple contractual exchange of goods and services, your employer is legally bound to pay you for fulfilling your job description. But today's rapid reorganizations, diffusion of responsibility, and collaborative team-based work style mean employment relationships are not stable long-term contracts with explicit terms. Rather, they are based more on trusting relationships than ever before. You have to trust that if you show your supervisor a creative project you've been working on, she won't steal the credit behind your back. You have to trust that the extra work you've been doing will be recognized in your performance appraisal. In contemporary organizations, where work is less closely documented and specified, voluntary employee contribution based on trust is absolutely necessary. Only a trusted leader will be able to encourage employees to reach beyond themselves to a transformational goal.

What Are the Consequences of Trust?

Trust between supervisors and employees has a number of advantages. Here are just a few that research has shown:

- *Trust encourages taking risks.* Whenever employees decide to deviate from the usual way of doing things, or to take their supervisors' word on a new direction, they are taking a risk. In both cases, a trusting relationship can facilitate that leap.

- *Trust facilitates information sharing.* One big reason employees fail to express concerns at work is that they don't feel psychologically safe revealing their views. When managers demonstrate they will give employees' ideas a fair hearing and actively make changes, employees are more willing to speak out.[66]

- *Trusting groups are more effective.* When a leader sets a trusting tone in a group, members are more willing to help each other and exert extra effort, which increases trust. Members of mistrusting groups tend to be suspicious of each other, constantly guard against exploitation, and restrict communication with others in the group. These actions tend to undermine and eventually destroy the group.

- *Trust enhances productivity.* The bottom-line interest of companies appears to be positively influenced by trust. Employees who trust their supervisors tend to receive higher performance ratings.[67] People respond to mistrust by concealing information and secretly pursuing their own interests.

One potentially significant opportunity for building trust within an organization is to encourage positive relationships between leaders and would-be leaders. Mentoring programs, discussed next, allow individuals from different organizational levels to get to know one another and create bonds of trust.

LEADING FOR THE FUTURE: MENTORING

Leaders often take responsibility for developing future leaders. Let's consider what makes mentoring valuable as well as its potential pitfalls.

Mentoring

A **mentor** is a senior employee who sponsors and supports a less experienced employee, a protégé. Successful mentors are good teachers. They present ideas clearly, listen well, and empathize with protégés' problems. Mentoring relationships, whether formal or informal, serve career functions and psychosocial functions.[68]

In formal mentoring relationships, protégé candidates are identified according to assessments of leadership potential and then matched with leaders in corresponding organizational functions. Informal mentoring relationships happen much the same way, but organically: first, a less experienced, lower-level employee who appears to have potential for future development is identified.[69] The protégé is often then tested with a particularly challenging assignment. If performance is acceptable, the leader will develop the mentoring relationship. In both formal and informal mentoring, the goal is to show the protégé how the organization *really* works outside its formal structures and procedures.

Are all employees in an organization likely to participate in a mentoring relationship? Unfortunately, no.[70] However, research indicates that employers should establish mentoring programs because they benefit both mentors and protégés. A recent study in Korea, for instance, found that mentors achieved higher levels of transformational leadership abilities as a result of the process, while organizational commitment and well-being increased for both mentors and protégés.[71] Mentoring has also proven effective for improving the outcomes of historically disadvantaged workers. In Canada, for example, government employers such as Manitoba Hydro have found formal mentoring particularly effective for improving job retention and promotion rates among First Nations people.[72]

Although begun with the best intentions, formal mentoring relationships are not as effective as informal ones,[73] perhaps due to poor planning, design, and communication. Mentors must see the relationship as beneficial to themselves and the protégé, and the protégé must feel he has input into the relationship.[74] Formal mentoring programs are also most likely to succeed if they appropriately match the work style, needs, and skills of protégé and mentor, and if resources and supports are provided to the mentors themselves.[75]

You might assume mentoring is valuable for objective outcomes like compensation and job performance, and sometimes that does indeed happen. More often, however, research suggests the gains are primarily psychological. Research further indicates that while mentoring can have an impact on career success, it is not as much of a contributing factor as ability and personality. It may *feel* nice to have a mentor, but it doesn't appear that having a good mentor, or any mentor, is critical to your career. Mentors may be effective not because of the functions they provide, but because of the resources they can obtain; a mentor connected to a powerful network can build relationships that will help the protégé advance. Network ties, whether built through a mentor or not, are a significant predictor of career success.[76] If a mentor is not well connected or not a very strong performer, the best mentoring advice in the world will not be very beneficial.

CHALLENGES TO THE LEADERSHIP CONSTRUCT

"In the 1500s, people ascribed all events they didn't understand to God. Why did the crops fail? God. Why did someone die? God. Now our all-purpose explanation is leadership."[77] This may be an astute observation from management consulting, but of course much of an organization's success or failure is due to factors outside the influence of leadership. Sometimes it's a matter of being in the right or wrong place at a given time. In this section, we present challenges to the accepted beliefs about the value of leadership.

Leadership as an Attribution

As you may remember from Chapter 6, attribution theory examines how people try to make sense of cause-and-effect relationships. The **attribution theory of leadership** says leadership is merely an attribution people make about other individuals.[78] That may help explain why people who are not stereotypically considered leaders, such as females, struggle to obtain equality in leadership representation. We attribute the following to leaders: intelligence, outgoing personality, strong verbal skills, aggressiveness, understanding, and industriousness.[79] At the organizational level, we tend, rightly or wrongly, to see leaders as responsible for both extremely negative and extremely positive performance.[80]

One study of 128 major U.S. corporations found that whereas perceptions of CEO charisma did not lead to objectively better company performance, company performance did lead to perceptions of charisma.[81] Attribution theory suggests it is important to project the *appearance* of being a leader rather than focusing on *actual accomplishments*. Leader-wannabes who can shape the perception that they're smart, personable, verbally adept, aggressive, hardworking, and consistent in their style can increase the probability that their bosses, colleagues, and employees will view them as effective leaders.

Substitutes for and Neutralizers of Leadership

One theory of leadership suggests that in many situations, leaders' actions are irrelevant.[82] Experience and training are among the **substitutes** that can replace the need for a leader's support or ability to create structure. Recently, companies such as video game producer Valve Corporation, Gore-Tex maker W. L. Gore, and collaboration-software firm GitHub have experimented with eliminating leaders and management. Governance in the "bossless" work environment is achieved through accountability to coworkers, who determine team composition and even sometimes pay.[83] Organizational characteristics such as explicit formalized goals, rigid rules and procedures, and cohesive work groups can replace formal leadership, while indifference to organizational rewards can neutralize its effects. **Neutralizers** make it impossible for leader behaviour to make any difference to follower outcomes (see Exhibit 12-5).

Sometimes the difference between substitutes and neutralizers is fuzzy. If I'm working on a task that's intrinsically enjoyable, theory predicts leadership will be less important because the task provides motivation. But does that mean intrinsically enjoyable tasks neutralize leadership effects, or substitute for them, or both? Another problem with the theory is that while substitutes for leadership (such as employee characteristics, the nature of the task, etc.) matter to performance, we can't infer that leadership doesn't matter.[84]

Defining Characteristics	Relationship-Oriented Leadership	Task-Oriented Leadership
Individual		
Experience/training	No effect on	Substitutes for
Professionalism	Substitutes for	Substitutes for
Indifference to rewards	Neutralizes	Neutralizes
Job		
Highly structured task	No effect on	Substitutes for
Provides its own feedback	No effect on	Substitutes for
Intrinsically satisfying	Substitutes for	No effect on
Organization		
Explicit formalized goals	No effect on	Substitutes for
Rigid rules and procedures	No effect on	Substitutes for
Cohesive work groups	Substitutes for	Substitutes for

EXHIBIT 12-5 Substitutes for and Neutralizers of Leadership

Source: Based on S. Kerr and J. M. Jermier, "Substitutes for Leadership: Their Meaning and Measurement," *Organizational Behaviour and Human Performance* (December 1978), p. 378.

FINDING AND CREATING EFFECTIVE LEADERS

Given all this complexity and all the different perspectives, how can organizations find or create effective leaders? Let's try to answer that question.

Selecting Leaders

The process organizations go through to fill management positions is an exercise in the identification of effective leaders. You might begin by reviewing the knowledge, skills, and abilities needed to do the job effectively. Personality tests can identify traits associated with leadership—extraversion, conscientiousness, and openness to experience. High self-monitors are better at reading situations and adjusting their behaviour accordingly. Candidates with high emotional intelligence should have an advantage, especially in situations requiring transformational leadership.[85] Experience is a poor predictor of leader effectiveness, but situation-specific experience is relevant.

Training Leaders

Organizations spend billions of dollars on leadership training and development.[86] These take many forms, from expensive executive leadership programs offered by universities such as University of Toronto to canoeing and wilderness camping experiences offered by the Outward Bound program. Business schools and companies are putting renewed emphasis on leadership development.

How can managers get the most from their leadership-training budgets? First, leadership training is likely to be more successful with high self-monitors. Such individuals have the flexibility to change their behaviour. Second, organizations can teach implementation skills. Third, we can teach skills such as trust building and mentoring. Leaders can be taught situational-analysis skills. They can learn how to evaluate situations, modify them to better fit their style, and assess which leader behaviours might be most effective in given situations.

Fourth, behavioural training through modelling exercises can increase an individual's ability to exhibit charismatic leadership qualities. Fifth, leaders should engage in regularly reviewing their leadership after key organizational events. These after-event reviews are especially effective for leaders who are high in conscientiousness and openness to experience, and who are emotionally stable (low in neuroticism).[87] Finally, leaders can be trained in transformational leadership skills that have bottom-line results.

SUMMARY

- Leadership plays a central part in understanding group behaviour, because it's the leader who usually directs us toward our goals.

- Knowing what makes a good leader should be valuable in improving group performance.

- The early search for a set of universal leadership traits failed. However, recent efforts using the Big Five personality framework show strong and consistent relationships between leadership and extraversion, conscientiousness, and openness to experience.

- The behavioural approach's major contribution was narrowing leadership into task-oriented (initiating structure) and people-oriented (consideration) styles.

- By considering the situation in which the leader operates, contingency theories improve on the behavioural approach.

- Research on charismatic and transformational leadership has made major contributions to our understanding of leadership effectiveness.
- The concept of authentic leadership encompasses the dimensions of ethics and trust that characterize the best leadership practices, although the need for leadership to increase performance is not always certain.
- Servant leadership involves helping others grow and develop.
- Regardless of the type of leadership style used, trust is key for leadership effectiveness.

IMPLICATIONS FOR MANAGERS

- For maximum leadership effectiveness, ensure that your preferences on the initiating structure and consideration dimensions are a match for your work dynamics and culture.
- Hire candidates who exhibit transformational leadership qualities and who have demonstrated success in working through others to meet a long-term vision. Personality tests can reveal candidates higher in extraversion, conscientiousness, and openness, which may indicate leadership readiness.
- For management roles, hire candidates whom you believe are ethical and trustworthy, and train current managers in your organization's ethical standards to increase leadership effectiveness.
- Seek to develop trusting relationships with followers because, as organizations have become less stable and predictable, strong bonds of trust are replacing bureaucratic rules in defining expectations and relationships.
- Consider investing in leadership training such as formal courses, workshops, rotating job responsibilities, coaching, and mentoring.

BREAKOUT QUESTION FOR GROUP DISCUSSION

Can a leader who has lost the trust of their followers ever recover it? If so, what strategies might be effective? Remember to consider all three dimensions of trust (competence, benevolence, and integrity) when answering.

PERSONAL INVENTORY ASSESSMENT

In the Personal Inventory Assessment found in MyManagementLab, take the assessment: Ethical Leadership Assessment.

SELF-REFLECTION ACTIVITY

Do you have the skills, abilities, and attitudes needed to engage in ethical leadership? Ethical leadership helps foster healthy, fair, and productive workplaces, but it is not always clear what behaviours constitute ethical leadership. Take the Personal Inventory Assessment found in MyManagementLab to see where you rank. After reading the debriefing at the end of the quiz, reflect on your score. Do you think it is accurate? Why or why not? Would your coworkers and/or direct reports agree with your self-assessment? Do you get different answers if you take the quiz twice, thinking about a different context each time (for example, work behaviour versus behaviour while acting as a volunteer coach). If there is a difference in your score based on context, what does that suggest for the practice of ethics in leadership roles?

MINI CASE · A STUDY OF LEADERSHIP STYLE

Although he is still young, 24-year-old Bryce Williams knows a great deal about leadership. He is the elected Chief of the Tsawwassen First Nation (TFN). The TFN treaty went into effect in April 2009, making the TFN the first urban self-governed nation in British Columbia. While this opened up enormous opportunities for economic development, it also raised concerns about cultural maintenance. Bryce William's commitment to balance led to his election as Chief in 2012. Asked about his surprise win against older and more experienced candidates, Williams replied, "I think my people-first mentality is a big part of getting elected—and being involved with the community quite often and having that want and need to strengthen the culture."

Bryce Williams has the credibility that comes from being directly involved in cultural maintenance himself. As an elected leader, he strives to foster the creation of "culture-bearers" by supporting traditional arts such as weaving, dancing, singing, and carving. Williams himself is a talented carver who teaches Coast Salish art to children in his community. This contact makes him accessible to local children and youth. Peggy McCleod, who facilitates the classes, says "having that time the way they do every week, with one of the leaders, I think really goes a long way to speak to how valued they [the children] are." As for Williams, his perspective is very straightforward. "Part of being a Haida artist or a Coast Salish artist is being willing to pass on those traditions. It uplifts me to be able to pass along some of that knowledge."

Williams's cultural support is carried out in a way that also leads to economic opportunity. For example, in January 2014 the TFN broke ground on two new destination shopping malls on Tsawwassen land. These mega malls will not only generate profits for the band, they also help provide a forum for the display and sale of traditional arts products. "Obviously it's good to keep the culture alive, but you can't host programs and services when you don't have money to move those things forward, so they're both very important," observes Williams.

When asked about what traits a chief should have, Bryce Williams says that a leader is someone who can be the "voice of the people." He doesn't mean being loud or opinionated. In fact, during his nation's legislative assembly he is often silent, even in tense debates. He is listening, carefully absorbing everyone's viewpoint and perspective. Some recall that prior chiefs had a different style, getting more involved and advocating strongly for one side of a debate. Steven Stark, a member of legislature, observed: "Bryce is conservative. He watches. He is quiet but he uses his words wisely. He has that open ear." Listening carefully helps Williams find mutually beneficial solutions to problems. For example, when discussing a dispute with a local municipality over sewer lines he said that "there has to be relationship building there and we just have to find a way to work together so that we can find ways to benefit all of our communities."

Sources: P. Holdsworth and E. Riva-Guerra, "Young B.C. Chief Balances Major Development with Tradition," *CBC News*, April 23, 2014, http://www.cbc.ca/news/aboriginal/young-b-c-chief-balances-major-development-with-tradition-1.2618187; Staff reporter, "Construction of Tsawwassen First Nation Mega Mall Begins," *CBC News*, January 24, 2014, http://www.cbc.ca/news/canada/british-columbia/construction-of-tsawwassen-first-nation-mega-malls-begins-1.2510438; K. Hilderman, "Chief Bryce Williams, Tsawwassen First Nation," *BC Business*, July 2, 2013, http://www.bcbusiness.ca/people/chief-bryce-williams-tsawwassen-first-nation.

Discussion Questions

1. How would you characterize Bryce Williams's leadership style or styles? Justify your answer. Remember that he may be combining styles or exhibiting varied styles at different times or in different contexts.

2. Is Bryce's leadership style or styles suitable for the context that he is working in? Justify your answer.

3. Describe two jobs/scenarios in which Bryce's current primary leadership style would likely be ineffective. Explain your answer.

MINI CASE SITUATIONAL LEADERSHIP COMES CLEAN

Martha couldn't help but notice the various grimaces on her employee's faces as she gave out instructions that morning. She carefully explained in which order the windows should be cleaned and which safety harnesses they should use. She decided to improve their attitude with a promise. "Hey," she told her six-person crew, "if you do a good job, tomorrow's coffee is on me." She had expected a cheer or at least a few smiles but all she got was bored looks and rolled eyes. Martha decided to just let it go and get on with the workday.

She couldn't believe how different her work experiences were last summer and this summer. She had worked for exactly the same company this year doing the same job, so she had no idea why things were turning out so differently.

Martha was a site supervisor for a window washing company that operated in the summer months, employing significant numbers of students. It was her job to direct and train new hires, plan the day's work, assign tasks, and make sure everyone complied with safety regulations. She also helped with the actual work. Martha had been given the supervisory role after her first year of college, after having worked there for three summers while in high school.

Her first summer as a site supervisor had been great! She had had a team of six high school students aged 15 and 16, four female and two male, for most of whom this was their first real job. Many of them were unfamiliar with basic safety gear and were happy to listen to her advice about the best way to complete a job.

This first crew were generally a good bunch, but they tended to get distracted and goof off. Martha had found it easy to minimize this by checking on them regularly (sometimes using what she called her "mom voice" to remind them to get back to work), and offering small rewards like free pop and coffee.

Her second summer she had been assigned to a level 2 crew. Such crews took on the more difficult assignments. For example, they would wash windows at multi-storey, sheer office towers, whereas other teams focused on suburban homes. Her level 2 crew consisted of college and university students who had worked there a minimum of two summers previously and had also taken a specialized ropes and harnesses course to learn about safety while cleaning skyscrapers. The average age was 21 and her crew included four males and two females.

Pleased by her success the previous year, Martha had done all the same things. She gave full and complete directions each morning, she used her "mom voice" when she felt someone wasn't performing, and she offered small rewards. Yet her team wasn't responding the same way at all, and they didn't seem to like or respect her much. Martha though about it for a long time and decided that she needed to …

Discussion Questions

1. Why is the same leadership style leading to such different results year over year? Explain your answer in detail.

2. How should Martha adjust her leadership style for her new team? Justify your answer using a contingency-based theory of leadership.

3. Does gender have anything to do with her team's response to Martha? Explain and justify why gender might matter, and why it might not. If her team is indeed responding to her gender, what might Martha do about it?

PERSONAL INVENTORY ASSESSMENT

MyManagementLab

Study, practise, and explore real management situations with these helpful resources:

- **Interactive Lesson Presentations:** Work through interactive presentations and assessments to test your knowledge of management concepts.
- **PIA (Personal Inventory Assessments):** Enhance your ability to connect with key concepts through these engaging self-reflection assessments.
- **Study Plan:** Check your understanding of chapter concepts with self-study quizzes.
- **Simulations:** Practise decision making in simulated management environments.

Chapter 13
Power and Politics

Justin Tang/CP Images, Jeff McIntosh/CP Images, Geoff Robins/CP Images, Fernando Morales/The Globe and Mail/CP Images

LEARNING OBJECTIVES

After studying this chapter, you should be able to:

1 Define *power*.

2 Contrast leadership and power.

3 Describe the five bases of power.

4 Identify nine power or influence tactics and their contingencies.

5 Explain how power affects people.

6 Define *organizational politics* and evaluate the role of politics in organizations.

7 Identify the causes and consequences of political behaviour.

8 Assess whether a political action is ethical.

9 Describe the political mapping process and its advantages.

In both research and practice, *power* and *politics* have been described as dirty words. It is easier for most of us to talk about sex or money than about power or political behaviour. People who have power deny it, people who want it try not to look like they're seeking it, and those who are good at getting it are generally secretive about how they do so.[1]

In this chapter, we show that power determines what goals a group will pursue and how the group's resources will be distributed among its members. Further, we show how group members with good political skills use their power to influence the distribution of resources in their favour.

A DEFINITION OF POWER

Power refers to a capacity that A has to influence the behaviour of B so B acts in accordance with A's wishes.[2] Someone can thus have power but not use it; it is a capacity or potential. Probably the most important aspect of power is that it is a function of **dependence**. The greater B's dependence on A, the greater A's power in the relationship. Dependence, in turn, is based on alternatives that B perceives and the importance B puts on the alternative(s) that A controls. A person can have power over you only if he controls something you desire. If you want a college degree and have to pass a certain course to get it, and your current instructor is the only faculty member in the college who teaches that course, she has power over you. Your alternatives are highly limited, and you place a high degree of importance on the outcome. Similarly, if you're attending college on funds provided by your parents, you probably recognize the power they hold over you. You're dependent on them for financial support. But once you're out of school, have a job, and are making a good income, your parents' power is reduced significantly. Who among us has not known or heard of a rich relative who is able to control a large number of family members merely through the implicit or explicit threat of "writing them out of the will"?

In a disturbing example of the power of dependence, Wall Street portfolio manager Ping Jiang allegedly was able to coerce analyst Andrew Tong into taking female hormones and wearing lipstick and makeup. Why such power? Jiang controlled Tong's access to day trading. That's how much power dependencies can bring.[3]

Money is often a dependence factor in power and politics, but it is not the only means by which one person or group creates dependence from another. Before we examine the ways power is gained and exercised, let's be certain we understand the important differences between leadership and power.

CONTRASTING LEADERSHIP AND POWER

A careful comparison of our description of power with our description of leadership in Chapter 12 reveals that the concepts are closely intertwined. Official leaders have formal power, and they use it as a means of attaining group goals. (Official leaders may also have informal types of power which complement and supplement their formal power.) Other people may have strong influence within an organization, but without the formal authority associated with a leadership role they rely on alternative sources of power.

To get more specific, how are the two terms different? Power does not require goal compatibility, merely dependence. Leadership, on the other hand, requires some congruence between the goals of the leader and those being led. A second difference relates to the direction of influence. Leadership research focuses on the downward influence on followers. It minimizes the importance of lateral and upward influence patterns. Power research takes all factors into consideration. For a third difference, leadership research often emphasizes style. It seeks answers to questions such as: How supportive should a leader be? How much decision making should be shared with followers? In contrast, the research on power focuses on tactics for gaining compliance. Lastly, leadership concentrates on the individual leader's influence, while the study of power acknowledges that groups as well as individuals can use power to control other individuals or groups.

You may have noted that for a power situation to exist, one person or group needs to have control over resources the other person or group values. This is usually the case in established leadership situations. However, it is important to remember that power relationships exist potentially in all areas of life and power can be obtained in many ways. Let's explore the various sources of power next.

BASES OF POWER

Where does power come from? What gives an individual or a group influence over others? We answer by dividing the bases or sources of power into two general groupings—formal and personal—and then breaking each of these down into more specific categories.[4]

Formal Power

Formal power is based on an individual's position in an organization. It can come from the ability to coerce, the ability to reward, or formal authority (also termed *legitimate power*). Each of these three types of formal power will now be explored further.

Coercive Power   Khalad is a temporary foreign worker who needs to be employed in order to stay in Canada. His boss uses that vulnerability to get him to work overtime without pay, since Khalad has no other local job prospects and needs to support a family back home. His boss is using coercive power. The **coercive power** base depends on fear of the negative results from failing to comply. On the physical level, coercive power rests on the application, or the threat of application, of bodily distress through the infliction of pain, the restriction of movement, or the withholding of basic physiological or safety needs.

At the organizational level, A has coercive power over B if A can dismiss, suspend, or demote B, assuming B values his job. If A can assign B work activities B finds unpleasant, or treat B in a manner B finds embarrassing, A possesses coercive power over B. Coercive power can also come from withholding key information. People in an organization who have knowledge others need can make others dependent on them.

Reward Power   Elza is responsible for logistics and scheduling at her courier firm. People that treat her nicely and make their deliveries on time tend to get assigned the easiest and quickest routes whereas those who annoy her or are responsible for customer complaints get assigned the difficult, traffic-laden routes. Elza has reward power. The opposite of coercive power is **reward power**, with which people comply because it produces positive benefits; someone who can distribute rewards others view as valuable will have power over them. These rewards can be either financial—such as controlling pay rates, raises, and bonuses—or nonfinancial, including recognition, promotions, interesting work assignments, friendly colleagues, and preferred work shifts or sales territories.[5]

Legitimate Power   Bryce owns a company. When he makes a request people comply simply because he is the boss. He has legitimate power. In formal groups and organizations, probably the most common access to one or more of the power bases is through **legitimate power**. It represents the formal authority to control and use organizational resources based on structural position in the organization.

Legitimate power is broader than the power to coerce and reward. Specifically, it includes members' acceptance of the authority of a position. We associate power so closely with the concept of hierarchy that just drawing longer lines in an organization chart leads people to infer the leaders are especially powerful.[6] When school principals, bank presidents, or army captains speak, teachers, tellers, and first lieutenants listen and usually comply.

Personal Power

Many of the most competent and productive chip designers at Intel have power, but they aren't managers and have no formal power. What they have is *personal power*, which comes from an individual's unique characteristics. There are two bases of personal power: expertise, and the respect and admiration of others, which is also termed referent power.

Expert Power   Susan has developed a custom database for her company's customer records. She is the only one who knows enough about the database structure to administer and maintain it and the information kept inside is critical to the company's success. Susan has expert power. **Expert power** is influence wielded as a result of expertise, special skills, or knowledge. As jobs become more specialized, we become increasingly dependent on experts to achieve goals. It is generally acknowledged that physicians have expertise and hence expert

sundatoon/Fotolia

Coercive power is often only useful when directly supervising employees continuously. Otherwise people tend to resent the use of such tactics and stop performing well once they are no longer observed. As a result, coercive tactics can actually lessen overall performance.

power: Most of us follow our doctor's advice. Computer specialists, tax accountants, economists, industrial psychologists, and other specialists wield power as a result of their expertise.

Referent Power   Joey is the best amateur junior hockey player in his city, which makes him popular among his peers. He also attends high school. Joey finds it easy to get his way with his colleagues. For example, if they disagree about what movie to see or which videogame to play, Joey's choice always wins out. In his social group he has referent power. **Referent power** is based on identification with a person who has desirable resources or personal traits. If I like, respect, and admire you, you can exercise power over me because I want to please you.

Referent power develops out of admiration of another and a desire to be like that person. It helps explain, for instance, why celebrities are paid millions of dollars to endorse products in commercials. With a little practice, you and I could probably deliver as smooth a sales pitch as these celebrities, but the buying public doesn't identify with you and me. Some people who are not in formal leadership positions nonetheless have referent power and exert influence over others because of their charismatic dynamism, likability, and emotional effects on us.

Which Bases of Power Are Most Effective?

Formal power can come either from the ability to coerce or reward or from formal authority. However, evidence suggests that informal expert and referent power are the most important to acquire.

Of the three bases of formal power (coercive, reward, legitimate) and two bases of personal power (expert, referent), which is most important to have? Research suggests pretty clearly that the personal sources of power are most effective. Both expert and referent power are positively related to employees' satisfaction with supervision, their organizational commitment, and their performance, whereas reward and legitimate power seem to be unrelated to these outcomes. One source of formal power—coercive power—is negatively related to employee satisfaction and commitment.[7] Unfortunately, inexperienced managers and managers with poor emotional intelligence are more likely to use coercive power, especially when under stress and forced to make a decision quickly. It is important that they be made aware of the limitations of this form of power and taught how to uses other forms to ensure maximal effectiveness.

No matter which base of power is planned, it will be effective only if the power tactics are effective. Let's explore the concept of power tactics more fully.

POWER TACTICS

Political behaviours are one important means of gaining power and influence. The most effective influence behaviours—consultation and inspirational appeal—tend to be the least widely used. You should make these influence tactics part of your repertoire.

What **power tactics** do people use to translate power bases into specific action? What options do they have for influencing their bosses, coworkers, and employees? Following are some popular tactical options and the conditions that may make one option more effective than another. Research has identified nine distinct influence tactics:[8]

1. **Legitimacy.** Relying on your authority position, or saying that a request accords with organizational policies or rules.
2. **Rational persuasion.** Presenting logical arguments and factual evidence to demonstrate that a request is reasonable.
3. **Inspirational appeals.** Developing emotional commitment by appealing to a target's values, needs, hopes, and aspirations.
4. **Consultation.** Increasing support by involving the target in deciding how you will accomplish your plan.
5. **Exchange.** Rewarding the target with benefits or favours in exchange for following a request.
6. **Personal appeals.** Asking for compliance based on friendship or loyalty.
7. **Ingratiation.** Using flattery, praise, or friendly behaviour prior to making a request.
8. **Pressure.** Using warnings, repeated demands, and threats.
9. **Coalitions.** Enlisting the aid or support of others to persuade the target to agree.

Some tactics are more effective than others. Rational persuasion, inspirational appeals, and consultation tend to be the most effective, especially when the audience is highly invested in the outcomes of a decision process. These tactics are also the most likely to be formally permitted, encouraged, and ethical. The pressure tactic tends to backfire and is typically the least effective of the nine tactics.[9] It is less likely to be overtly approved and sanctioned by organizational leaders and may be unethical depending on the context. You can increase your chance of success by using two or more tactics together or sequentially, as long as your choices are compatible.[10] For example, using both ingratiation and legitimacy can lessen negative reactions, but only when the audience does not really care about the outcome of a decision process or the policy is routine.[11]

Let's consider the most effective way of getting a raise. You can start with a rational approach—figure out how your pay compares with that of your organizational peers, land a competing job offer, gather data that testify to your performance, or use salary calculators like Salary.com to compare your pay with that of others in your occupation—and share your results with your manager. Kitty Dunning, a vice-president at Don Jagoda Associates, landed a 16 percent raise when she e-mailed her boss numbers showing she had increased sales.[12]

While rational persuasion might work for you, the effectiveness of some influence tactics depends on the direction of influence.[13] As Exhibit 13-1 shows, rational persuasion is the only tactic effective across organizational levels. Inspirational appeals work best as a downward-influencing tactic with subordinates. When pressure works, it's generally downward only. Personal appeals and coalitions are most effective as lateral influence, although well-organized coalitions such as unions may exercise upward influence that would be otherwise unattainable for individual workers. Other factors that impact the effectiveness of influence include the sequencing of tactics, a person's skill in using the tactic, and the organizational culture.

You're more likely to be effective if you begin with "softer" tactics that rely on personal power, such as personal and inspirational appeals, rational persuasion, and consultation. If these fail, you can move on to "harder" tactics, such as exchange, coalitions, and pressure, which emphasize formal power and incur greater costs and risks.[14] Interestingly, a single soft tactic is more effective than a single hard tactic, and combining two soft tactics or a soft tactic and rational persuasion is more effective than any single tactic or combination of hard tactics.[15] The effectiveness of tactics depends on the audience.[16] People especially likely to comply with soft power tactics tend to be more reflective and intrinsically motivated; they have high self-esteem and a greater desire for control. Those likely to comply with hard power tactics are more action-oriented and extrinsically motivated, and are more focused on getting along with others than on getting their own way.

There are some gender role congruency effects when it comes to the use of influence tactics. Men and women who use the exact same tactic in the same situation may be

EXHIBIT 13-1

Preferred Power Tactics
by Influence Direction

Upward Influence	Downward Influence	Lateral Influence
Rational persuasion	Rational persuasion	Rational persuasion
Coalitions	Inspirational appeals	Consultation
	Pressure	Ingratiation
	Consultation	Exchange
	Ingratiation	Legitimacy
	Exchange	Personal appeals
	Legitimacy	Coalitions

perceived differently. Females are often penalized for using tactics perceived as more aggressive, including confrontation. They are rewarded for using tactics that emphasize creation of harmony and consensus. Men, by contrast, may be perceived as "weak" when using softer, consensus-based tactics. These differences are readily observable. It is common, for example, for women to complain about being called domineering, controlling, or even bitchy whereas men engaging in the same behaviours are seen as "taking charge" and "getting it done." Men complain about being called "wimpy" and "uncertain" when women engaging in the same behaviours are termed "team builders" and "emotionally aware." Both these responses are a product of non-conscious stereotyping.[17] Mental vigilance and introspection can help lessen such stereotyping, creating more options for influence for both genders.

People in different countries prefer different power tactics.[18] Those from individualistic countries tend to see power in personalized terms and as a legitimate means of advancing their personal ends, whereas those in collectivistic countries see power in social terms and as a legitimate means of helping others.[19] A study comparing managers in the United States and China found that U.S. managers preferred rational persuasion, whereas Chinese managers preferred coalition tactics.[20] These differences tend to be consistent with the values in these two countries. Reason-based tactics are consistent with the U.S. preference for direct confrontation and rational persuasion to influence others and resolve differences, while coalition tactics align with the Chinese preference for meeting difficult or controversial requests with indirect approaches. A similar study conducted with Malaysian and Canadian managers found that "while ingratiation was equally effective in both countries, all other influence tactics were significantly more effective in Malaysia, which has high power distance and a high collectivism culture, as compared to Canada. Our results ... suggest that managers have less need for influence tactics in countries with high power distance, as employees will comply with requests simply out of respect for the manager's authority."[21] Finally, Canadian Native peoples, whose varied cultures tend to be collectivistic and emphasize "power with" rather than "power over," generally respond better to softer tactics that help develop consensus and shared understanding. This is especially true since they have historically been victimized by aggressively excessive expressions of government power, such as the forced removal of large numbers of children from their homes and their subsequent placement into residential schools.

People differ in their **political skill**, or their ability to influence others to enhance their own objectives. The politically skilled are more effective users of all the influence tactics. Political skill is also more effective when the stakes are high, such as when the individual is accountable for important organizational outcomes. Finally, the politically skilled are able to exert their influence without others detecting it, a key element in being effective (it's damaging to be labeled as political).[22] However, these individuals are most able to use their political skills in environments marked by low levels of procedural and distributive justice. When an organization is run with open and fairly applied rules, free of favouritism or biases, political skill is actually negatively related to job performance ratings.[23]

Lastly, we know cultures within organizations differ markedly—some are warm, relaxed, and supportive; others are formal and conservative. Some encourage participation and consultation, some encourage reason, and still others rely on pressure. People who fit the culture of the organization tend to obtain more influence.[24] Specifically, extraverts tend to be more influential in team-oriented organizations, and highly conscientious people are more influential in organizations that value working alone on technical tasks. People who fit the culture are influential because they can perform especially well in the domains deemed most important for success. In other words, they are influential because they are competent. Thus, the organization itself will influence which subset of power tactics is viewed as acceptable for use.

HOW POWER AFFECTS PEOPLE

To this point, we've discussed what power is and how it is acquired. But we've not yet answered one important question: Does power corrupt?

There is certainly evidence that there are corrupting aspects of power. Research suggests that power leads people to place their own interests ahead of others. Why does this happen? Interestingly, research suggests that power not only leads people to focus on their self-interests because they can, but it also liberates people to focus inward and thus come to place greater weight on their goals and interests. Power also appears to lead individuals to "objectify" others (to see them as tools to obtain their instrumental goals) and to see relationships as more peripheral.[25]

That's not all. Powerful people react—especially negatively—to any threats to their competence. They're more willing to denigrate others. People given power are more likely to make self-interested decisions when faced with a moral hazard (such as when hedge fund managers take more risks with other people's money because they're rewarded for gains but less often punished for losses). Power also leads to overconfident decision making.[26]

Frank Lloyd Wright, a well-known architect, is a good example of power's corrupting effects. Early in his career, Wright worked for and was mentored by renowned architect Louis Sullivan (sometimes known as "the father of the skyscraper"). Before Wright achieved greatness, he was copious in his praise for Sullivan. Later in his career, that praise faded, and Wright even took credit for one of Sullivan's noted designs. Wright was never a benevolent man, but as his power accumulated, so did his potential to behave in a "monstrous" way toward others.[27]

So, yes, power does appear to have some important disturbing effects on us. But that is hardly the whole story—it's more complicated than that. Power doesn't affect everyone in the same way, and there are even positive effects of power. Let's consider each of these in turn.

First, the toxic effects of power depend on one's personality. Research suggests that if we have an anxious personality, power does not corrupt us because we are less likely to think that using power benefits us.[28] Those that score high on the dark triad, by contrast, are more likely to be corrupted by power due to their narcissism, low levels of empathy, and Machiavellian tendencies. Second, the corrosive effect of power can be contained by organizational systems. One study found, for example, that while power made people behave in a self-serving manner, when accountability of this behaviour was initiated the self-serving behaviour stopped. Third—and forgive the pun—we have the power to blunt the negative effects of power. One study showed that simply expressing gratitude toward powerful others made them less likely to aggress against us. Finally, remember the saying that those with little power grab and abuse what little they have? There appears to be some truth to this, in that those most likely to abuse power are low-status people who gain power. Why? It appears that having low status is threatening, and this fear comes out in negative ways if power is given.[29]

As you can see, some factors can ameliorate the negative effects of power. But there also appear to be general positive effects. Power energizes and leads to approach motivation (that is, more motivation to achieve goals). It also can enhance people's motivation to help others, at least for certain people. One study found, for example, that values toward helping others translated into actual work behaviour only when people felt a sense of power.[30]

This study points up an important insight about power. It is not so much that power corrupts as it *reveals*. Supporting this line of reasoning, another study revealed that power led to self-interested behaviour only for those with a weak moral identity (the degree to which morals are core to one's identity). For those with a strong moral identity, power actually enhanced their moral awareness.[31]

POLITICS: POWER IN ACTION

When people get together in groups, power will be exerted. People want to carve out a niche from which to exert influence, earn rewards, and advance their careers. When employees in organizations convert their power into action, we describe them as being engaged in *politics*. Those with good political skills have the ability to use their bases of power effectively.[32]

Definition of Organizational Politics

There is no shortage of definitions of *organizational politics*. Essentially, this type of politics focuses on the use of power to affect decision making in an organization, or on self-serving and organizationally unsanctioned behaviours.[33] For our purposes, **political behaviour** in organizations consists of activities that are not required as part of an individual's formal role but that influence, or attempt to influence, the distribution of advantages and disadvantages within the organization.[34]

This definition encompasses what most people mean when they talk about organizational politics. Political behaviour is outside specified job requirements. It requires some attempt to use power bases. It includes efforts to influence the goals, criteria, or processes used for decision making. Our definition is broad enough to include varied political behaviours such as withholding key information from decision makers, joining a coalition, whistle-blowing, spreading rumours, leaking confidential information to the media, exchanging favours with others in the organization for mutual benefit, and lobbying on behalf of or against a particular individual or decision alternative.

The Reality of Politics

Interviews with experienced managers show that most of them believe political behaviour is a major part of organizational life.[35] Many managers report that some use of political behaviour is both ethical and necessary, as long as it doesn't directly harm anyone else. They describe politics as a necessary evil and believe someone who *never* uses political behaviour will have a hard time getting things done. Most also indicate they have never been trained to use political behaviour effectively. But why, you may wonder, must politics exist? Isn't it possible for an organization to be politics-free? It's *possible*—but unlikely.

Organizations are made up of individuals and groups with different values, goals, and interests.[36] This sets up the potential for conflict over the allocation of limited resources such as departmental budgets, space, project responsibilities, and salary adjustments.[37] If resources were abundant, then all constituencies within the organization could satisfy their goals. But because they are limited, not everyone's interests can be satisfied. Furthermore, gains by one individual or group are often *perceived* as coming at the expense of others within the organization (whether they are or not). These forces create real competition among members for the organization's limited resources.

Maybe the most important factor leading to politics within organizations is the realization that most of the "facts" used to allocate the limited resources are open to interpretation. What, for instance, is *good* performance? One person's "selfless effort to benefit the organization" is seen by another as a "blatant attempt to further one's interest."[38] It is in this large and ambiguous middle ground of organizational life—where the facts *don't* speak for themselves—that politics flourish.

Finally, because most decisions have to be made in a climate of ambiguity—where facts are rarely fully objective and thus are open to interpretation—people within organizations will use whatever influence they can to taint facts to support their goals and interests. That, of course, creates the activities we call *politicking*.

Therefore, to answer the question of whether it is possible for an organization to be politics-free, we can say yes—if all members of that organization hold the same goals and interests, if organizational resources are not scarce, and if performance outcomes are completely clear and objective. But that doesn't describe the organizational world in which most of us live.

CAUSES AND CONSEQUENCES OF POLITICAL BEHAVIOUR

Factors Contributing to Political Behaviour

Not all groups or organizations are equally political. In some organizations, for instance, politicking is overt and rampant, while in others, politics play a small role in influencing outcomes. Why this variation? Recent research and observation have identified a number of factors that appear to encourage political behaviour. Some are individual characteristics, others are a result of the organization's culture or internal environment. Both individual and organizational factors can increase political behaviour and provide favourable outcomes (increased rewards and averted punishments) for individuals and groups in the organization.

Individual Factors At the individual level, researchers have identified certain personality traits, needs, and other factors likely to be related to political behaviour. In terms of traits, we find that employees who are high self-monitors, possess an internal locus of control, and have a high need for power are more likely to engage in political behaviour.[39] The high self-monitor is more sensitive to social cues, exhibits higher levels of social conformity, and is more likely to be skilled in political behaviour than the low self-monitor. Because they believe they can control their environment, individuals with an internal locus of control are more prone to take a proactive stance and attempt to manipulate situations in their favour. Not surprisingly, the Machiavellian personality—characterized by the will to manipulate and the desire for power—is comfortable using politics as a means to further personal interests.

In addition, an individual's investment in the organization, perceived alternatives, and expectations of success influence the degree to which she will pursue illegitimate means of political action.[40] The more a person expects increased future benefits from the organization, and the more that person has to lose if forced out, the less likely that individual is to use illegitimate means. Conversely, the more alternative job opportunities an individual has—due to a favourable job market, the possession of scarce skills or knowledge, a prominent reputation, or influential contacts outside the organization—the more likely he is to risk illegitimate political actions. Finally, an individual with low expectations of success from illegitimate means is unlikely to use them. High expectations of success from such measures are most likely to be the province of experienced and powerful individuals with polished political skills, as well as inexperienced and naïve employees who misjudge their chances.

Organizational Factors Although we acknowledge the role individual differences can play, the evidence more strongly suggests that certain situations and cultures promote politics. Specifically, when an organization's resources are declining, when the existing pattern of resources is changing, and when there is opportunity for promotions, politicking is more likely to surface.[41] When organizations downsize to improve efficiency, resources must be reduced, and people may engage in political actions to safeguard what they have. But *any* changes, especially those that imply a significant reallocation of resources within the organization, are likely to stimulate conflict and increase politicking. The opportunity for promotion or advancement has consistently been found to encourage competition for a limited resource as people try to positively influence the decision outcome.

Cultures characterized by low trust, role ambiguity, unclear performance evaluation systems, zero-sum (win–lose) reward allocation practices, democratic decision making, high pressure for performance, and self-serving senior managers will create breeding grounds for politicking.[42] The less trust within the organization, the higher the level of political behaviour and the more likely it will be of the illegitimate kind. Consequently, high trust should suppress political behaviour in general and inhibit illegitimate actions in particular.

Role ambiguity means the prescribed employee behaviours are unclear. There are, therefore, fewer limits to the scope and functions of the employee's political actions. Because political activities are defined as those not required as part of the employee's formal role, the greater the role ambiguity, the more employees can engage in unnoticed political activity.

Performance evaluation is far from a perfect science. The more organizations use subjective criteria in the appraisal, emphasize a single outcome measure, or allow significant time to pass between the time of an action and its appraisal, the greater the likelihood that an employee can get away with politicking. Subjective performance criteria create ambiguity. The use of a single outcome measure encourages individuals to do whatever is necessary to "look good" on that measure, but often at the cost of good performance on other important parts of the job that are not being appraised.

The more an organization's culture emphasizes the zero-sum or win–lose approach to reward allocation, the more employees will be motivated to engage in politicking. The **zero-sum approach** treats the reward "pie" as fixed, so any gain one person or group achieves has to come at the expense of another person or group. If $15,000 in annual raises is to be distributed among five employees, any employee who gets more than $3,000 takes money away from one or more of the others. Such a practice encourages making others look bad and increasing the visibility of what you do.

Tone from the top is very important when establishing a culture that encourages or discourages politicking.

Pearson Education

Finally, when employees see the people on top engaging in political behaviour, especially doing so successfully and being rewarded for it, a climate is created that supports politicking. Politicking by top management in a sense gives those lower in the organization permission to play politics by implying that such behaviour is acceptable.

How Do People Respond to Organizational Politics?

Trish loves her job as a writer on a weekly television comedy series, but hates the internal politics. "A couple of the writers here spend more time kissing up to the executive producer than doing any work. And our head writer clearly has his favourites. While they pay me a lot and I get to really use my creativity, I'm sick of having to be on alert for backstabbers and constantly having to self-promote my contributions. I'm tired of doing most of the work and getting little of the credit." Are Trish's comments typical of people who work in highly politicized workplaces? We all know friends or relatives who regularly complain about the politics at their jobs. But how do people in general react to organizational politics? Let's look at the evidence.

In our earlier discussion in this chapter of factors that contribute to political behaviour, we focused on the favourable outcomes. But for most people—who have modest political skills or are unwilling to play the politics game—outcomes tend to be predominantly negative. Exhibit 13-2 summarizes the extensive research (mostly conducted in the United States) on the relationship between organizational politics and individual outcomes.[43] Very strong evidence indicates, for instance, that perceptions of organizational politics are negatively related to job satisfaction.[44] The perception of politics also tends to increase job anxiety and stress, possibly because people believe they may be losing ground to others who are active politickers or, conversely, because they feel additional pressures from entering into and competing in the political arena.[45] Politics may lead to self-reported declines in employee performance, perhaps because employees perceive political environments to be unfair, which demotivates them.[46] Not surprisingly, when politicking becomes too much to handle, it can lead employees to quit.[47]

Researchers have noted several interesting qualifiers. First, the politics–performance relationship appears to be moderated by an individual's understanding of the hows and whys of organizational politics. "An individual who has a clear understanding of who is responsible for making decisions and why they were selected to be the decision makers would have a better understanding of how and why things happen the way they do than someone who does not understand the decision-making process in the organization."[48] When both politics

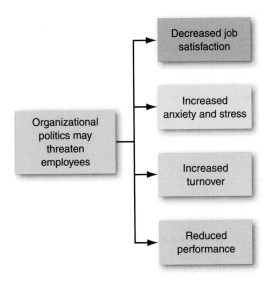

EXHIBIT 13-2

Employee Responses to Organizational Politics

Avoiding Action

Overconforming. Strictly interpreting your responsibility by saying things like "The rules clearly state ... " or "This is the way we've always done it."

Buck passing. Transferring responsibility for the execution of a task or decision to someone else.

Playing dumb. Avoiding an unwanted task by falsely pleading ignorance or inability.

Stretching. Prolonging a task so that one person appears to be occupied—for example, turning a two week task into a four month job.

Stalling. Appearing to be more or less supportive publicly while doing little or nothing privately.

Avoiding Blame

Buffing. This is a nice way to refer to "covering your rear." It describes the practice of rigorously documenting activity to project an image of competence and thoroughness.

Playing safe. Evading situations that may reflect unfavourably. It includes taking on only projects with a high probability of success, having risky decisions approved by superiors, qualifying expressions of judgment, and taking neutral positions in conflicts.

Justifying. Developing explanations that lessen one's responsibility for a negative outcome and/or apologizing to demonstrate remorse, or both.

Scapegoating. Placing the blame for a negative outcome on external factors that are not entirely blameworthy.

Misrepresenting. Manipulation of information by distortion, embellishment, deception, selective presentation, or obfuscation.

Avoiding Change

Prevention. Trying to prevent a threatening change from occurring.

Self-protection. Acting in ways to protect one's self-interest during change by guarding information or other resources.

EXHIBIT 13-3

Defensive Behaviours

and understanding are high, performance is likely to increase because the individual will see political actions as an opportunity. This is consistent with what you might expect among individuals with well-honed political skills. But when understanding is low, individuals are more likely to see politics as a threat, which can have a negative effect on job performance.[49]

Second, political behaviour at work moderates the effects of ethical leadership.[50] One study found that male employees were more responsive to ethical leadership and showed the most citizenship behaviour when levels of both politics and ethical leadership were high. Women, on the other hand, appeared most likely to engage in citizenship behaviour when the environment was consistently ethical and *apolitical*.

Third, when employees see politics as a threat, they often respond with **defensive behaviours**—reactive and protective behaviours to avoid action, blame, or change.[51] (Exhibit 13-3 provides examples of these behaviours.) Defensive behaviours are often associated with negative feelings toward the job and work environment.[52] In the short run, employees may find that defensiveness protects their self-interest, but in the long run it wears them down. People who consistently rely on defensiveness find that, eventually, it is the only way they know how to behave. At that point, they lose the trust and support of their peers, bosses, employees, and clients.

Impression Management

We know people have an ongoing interest in how others perceive and evaluate them. For example, Canadians spend millions of dollars on diets, health club memberships, cosmetics, and plastic surgery—all intended to make them more attractive to others. Being perceived positively by others should have benefits for people in organizations. It might, for instance, help them initially to get the jobs they want in an organization and, once hired, to get

Impression management is a specific suite of political behaviours designed to alter others, immediate perceptions of us. Some examples include conformity flattery, self-promotion, and even doing favours and making excuses. Evidence suggests that the effectiveness of impression management techniques depends on the setting (for example, self-promotion works better in interviews than in performance evaluations).

favourable evaluations, superior salary increases, and more rapid promotions. In a political context, it might help sway the distribution of advantages in their favour. The process by which individuals attempt to control the impression others form of them is called **impression management (IM)**.[53]

Who might we predict will engage in IM? No surprise here. It's the high self-monitor.[54] Low self-monitors tend to present images of themselves that are consistent with their personalities, regardless of the beneficial or detrimental effects for them. In contrast, high self-monitors are good at reading situations and moulding their appearance and behaviour to fit each situation. If you want to control the impression others form of you, what IM techniques might you use? Exhibit 13-4 summarizes some of the most popular and provides an example of each.

Keep in mind that when people engage in IM, they are sending a false message that might be true under other circumstances.[55] Excuses, for instance, may be offered with sincerity. Referring to the example in Exhibit 13-4, you can *actually* believe that ads contribute little to sales in your region. But misrepresentation can have a high cost. If you "cry wolf" once too

---

Conformity

Agreeing with someone else's opinion to gain his approval is a *form of ingratiation*.

Example: A manager tells his boss, "You're absolutely right on your reorganization plan for the western regional office. I couldn't agree with you more."

Favours

Doing something nice for someone to gain that person's approval is a *form of ingratiation*.

Example: A salesperson says to a prospective client, "I've got two tickets to the theater tonight that I can't use. Take them. Consider it a thank-you for taking the time to talk with me."

Excuses

Explanations of a predicament-creating event aimed at minimizing the apparent severity of the predicament is a *defensive IM technique*.

Example: A sales manager says to her boss, "We failed to get the ad in the paper on time, but no one responds to those ads anyway."

Apologies

Admitting responsibility for an undesirable event and simultaneously seeking to get a pardon for the action is a *defensive IM technique*.

Example: An employee says to his boss, "I'm sorry I made a mistake on the report. Please forgive me."

Self-Promotion

Highlighting one's best qualities, downplaying one's deficits, and calling attention to one's achievements is a *self-focused IM technique*.

Example: A salesperson tells her boss, "Matt worked unsuccessfully for three years to try to get that account. I sewed it up in six weeks. I'm the best closer this company has."

Enhancement

Claiming that something you did is more valuable than most other members of the organizations would think is a *self-focused IM technique*.

Example: A journalist tells his editor, "My work on this celebrity divorce story was really a major boost to our sales" (even though the story only made it to page 3 in the entertainment section).

EXHIBIT 13-4

Impression Management (IM) Techniques

(*Continued*)

Flattery

Complimenting others about their virtues in an effort to make oneself appear perceptive and likeable is an *assertive IM technique.*

Example: A new sales trainee says to her peer, "You handled that client's complaint so tactfully! I could never have handled that as well as you did."

Exemplification

Doing more than you need to in an effort to show how dedicated and hardworking you are is an *assertive IM technique.*

Example: An employee sends e-mails from his work computer when he works late so that his supervisor will know how long he's been working.

EXHIBIT 13-4 Impression Management (IM) Techniques (*Continued*)

Sources: Based on B. R. Schlenker, *Impression Management* (Monterey, CA: Brooks/Cole, 1980); M. C. Bolino, K. M. Kacmar, W. H. Turnley, and J. B. Gilstrap, "A Multi-Level Review of Impression Management Motives and Behaviours," *Journal of Management* 34, no. 6 (2008), pp. 1080–1109; and R. B. Cialdini, "Indirect Tactics of Image Management Beyond Basking," in R. A. Giacalone and P. Rosenfeld (eds.), *Impression Management in the Organization* (Hillsdale, NJ: Lawrence Erlbaum, 1989), pp. 45–71.

often, no one is likely to believe you when the wolf really comes. So the impression manager must be cautious not to be perceived as insincere or manipulative.[56] Consider the effect of implausible name-dropping as an example of this principle. Participants in a study in Switzerland disliked an experimental confederate who claimed to be a personal friend of the well-liked Swiss tennis star Roger Federer, but they generally liked confederates who just said they were fans.[57] Another study found that when managers attributed an employee's citizenship behaviours to impression management, they actually felt angry (probably because they felt manipulated) and gave the subordinate lower performance ratings. When managers attributed the same behaviours to prosocial values and concern about the organization, they felt happy and gave higher performance ratings.[58] In sum, people don't like to feel others are manipulating them through impression management, so such tactics should be employed with caution.

Most of the studies undertaken to test the effectiveness of IM techniques have related it to two criteria: interview success and performance evaluation. Let's consider each of these.

The evidence indicates most job applicants use IM techniques in interviews and that it works.[59] In one study, for instance, interviewers felt applicants for a position as a customer service representative who used IM techniques performed better in the interview, and the interviewers seemed somewhat more inclined to hire these people.[60] Moreover, when the researchers considered applicants' credentials, they concluded it was the IM techniques alone that influenced the interviewers—that is, it didn't seem to matter whether applicants were well or poorly qualified. If they used IM techniques, they did better in the interviews.

Some IM techniques work better in interviews than others. Researchers have compared applicants whose IM techniques focused on promoting their accomplishments (*self-promotion*) to those who focused on complimenting the interviewer and finding areas of agreement (such as flattery, conformity, or favours). In general, applicants appear to use self-promotion more than ingratiatory tactics such as flattery.[61] What's more, self-promotion may be more important to interviewing success. Applicants who work to create an appearance of competence by enhancing their accomplishments, taking credit for successes, and explaining away failures do better in interviews. These effects reach beyond the interview: Applicants who use more self-promotion also seem to get more follow-up job-site visits, even after adjusting for grade-point average, gender, and job type. Ingratiation also works well in interviews; applicants who compliment the interviewer, agree with his opinions, and emphasize areas of fit do better than those who don't.[62]

In terms of performance ratings, the picture is quite different. Ingratiation is positively related to performance ratings, meaning those who ingratiate themselves with their supervisors get higher performance evaluations. However, self-promotion appears to backfire: Those who self-promote actually seem to receive *lower* performance evaluations.[63] There is an important qualifier to this general result. It appears that individuals high in political skill are able to translate IM into higher performance appraisals, whereas those lower in political skill are more likely to be hurt by their IM attempts.[64] Self-promotion may also work better for males than females. Women who use it are sometimes inappropriately labelled a "braggart" or "pushy" due to gender role stereotypes that favour modesty for females. That does not mean that women should not engage in self-promotion; in fact, failing to do so in appropriate contexts may disadvantage their careers.[65] It does mean, however, that managers and coworkers should be aware of these stereotypes and make an effort to avoid them.

What explains the results unrelated to gender? If you think about them, they make sense. Ingratiating always works because everyone—both interviewers and supervisors—likes to be treated nicely. However, self-promotion may work only in interviews and backfire on the job, because, whereas the interviewer has little idea whether you're blowing smoke about your accomplishments, the supervisor knows because it's her job to observe you. Thus, if you're going to self-promote, remember that what works in an interview won't always work once you're on the job, and stick to the truth.

Are our conclusions about responses to politics globally valid? Should we expect employees in Israel, for instance, to respond the same way to workplace politics that employees in Canada do? Almost all our conclusions on employee reactions to organizational politics are based on studies conducted in North America. The few studies that have included other countries suggest some minor modifications.[66] One study of managers in U.S. culture and three Chinese cultures (People's Republic of China, Hong Kong, and Taiwan) found U.S. managers evaluated "gentle persuasion" tactics such as consultation and inspirational appeals as more effective than did their Chinese counterparts.[67] Other research suggests that effective North American leaders achieve influence by focusing on personal goals of group members and the tasks at hand (an analytical approach), whereas influential East Asian leaders focus on relationships among group members and meeting the demands of the people around them (a holistic approach).[68]

As another example, Israelis and the British seem to generally respond as North Americans do—their perception of organizational politics relates to decreased job satisfaction and increased turnover.[69] In countries that are more politically unstable, employees seem to demonstrate greater tolerance of intense political processes in the workplace, perhaps because they are used to power struggles and have more experience in coping with them.[70] This suggests that people from politically turbulent countries in the Middle East or Latin America might be more accepting of organizational politics, and more willing to use aggressive political tactics in the workplace, than people from countries such as Great Britain or Switzerland.

THE ETHICS OF BEHAVING POLITICALLY

Although there are no clear-cut ways to differentiate ethical from unethical politicking, there are some questions you should consider. For example, what is the utility of engaging in politicking? Sometimes we do it for little good reason. Outright lies are a rather extreme example of impression management, but many of us have at least distorted information to make a favourable impression. One thing to keep in mind is whether it's really worth the risk. Another question to ask is this: How does this impact others? Complimenting a supervisor on his appearance in order to curry favour is probably much less harmful than grabbing credit for a project that others deserve.

Finally, does the political activity conform to standards of equity and justice? Sometimes it is difficult to weigh the costs and benefits of a political action, but its ethicality is clear. The department head who inflates the performance evaluation of a favoured employee and deflates the evaluation of a disfavoured employee—and then uses these evaluations to justify giving the former a big raise and nothing to the latter—has treated the disfavoured employee unfairly.

Unfortunately, powerful people can become very good at rationalizing and explaining self-serving behaviours in terms of the organization's best interests. They can persuasively argue that unfair actions are really fair and just. Our point is that immoral people can justify almost any behaviour. Those who are powerful, articulate, and persuasive are most vulnerable to ethical lapses because they are likely to be able to get away with unethical practices successfully. When faced with an ethical dilemma regarding organizational politics, try to consider whether playing politics is worth the risk and whether others might be harmed in the process. If you have a strong power base, recognize the ability of power to corrupt. Remember that it's a lot easier for the powerless to act ethically, if for no other reason than that they typically have very little political discretion to exploit.

MAPPING YOUR POLITICAL CAREER

As we have seen, politics are not just for politicians. You can use the concepts presented in this chapter in some very tangible ways we have outlined. However, there is another application: you.

One of the most useful ways to think about power and politics is in terms of your own career. Think about your career in your organization of choice. What are your ambitions? Who has the power to help you get there? What is your relationship with these people? The best way to answer these questions is with a political map, which can help you sketch out your relationships with the people upon whom your career depends. Exhibit 13-5 shows such a map.[71] Let's walk through it.

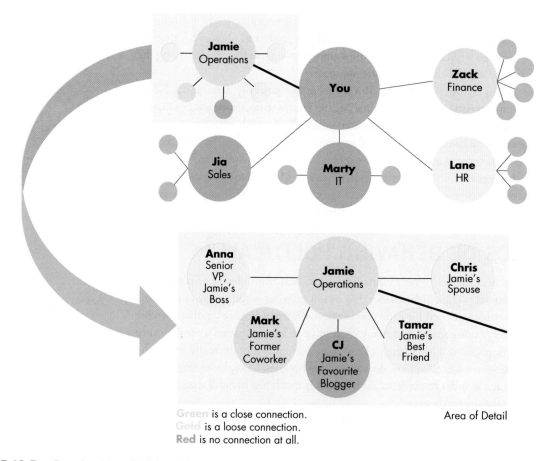

Green is a close connection.
Gold is a loose connection.
Red is no connection at all.

Area of Detail

EXHIBIT 13-5 Drawing Your Political Map

Source: Based on D. Clark, "A Campaign Strategy for Your Career," *Harvard Business Review* (November 2012), pp. 131–134.

Assume that your future promotion depends on five people, including Jamie, your immediate supervisor. As you can see in the exhibit, you have a close relationship with Jamie (you would be in real trouble otherwise). You also have a close relationship with Zack in finance. However, for the others, you have either a loose relationship (Lane) or none at all (Jia, Marty). One obvious implication of this is to formulate a plan for more influence over, and a closer relationship with, these people. How might you do that?

The map also provides for a useful way to think about the power network. Assume that the five individuals have their own networks. In this case, though, assume these aren't so much power networks, but influence networks representing your knowledge of the people who influence the individuals in power positions.

One of the best ways to influence people is indirectly. What if you played in a tennis league with Mark, Jamie's former coworker who you know remains friends with Jamie? To influence Mark, in many cases, may also be to influence Jamie. Why not post an entry on CJ's blog? This same analysis can then be completed with the other four decision makers.

Of course, this map doesn't show you everything you need to know—no map does. For example, rarely would all five people have the same amount of power. Moreover, maps are harder to construct in the era of large social networks. Try to keep this basic, to the people who *really* matter to your career.

All of this may seem a bit Machiavellian to you. However, remember, only one person gets the promotion, and your competition may have a map of his own. As we noted in the early part of the chapter, power and politics are a part of organizational life. To decide not to play is deciding not to be effective. Better to be explicit about it with a political map than to proceed as if power and politics didn't matter.

SUMMARY

- An effective manager accepts the political nature of organizations.

- Some people are significantly more politically astute than others, meaning that they are aware of the underlying politics and can manage impressions.

- Those who are good at playing politics can be expected to get higher performance evaluations and, hence, larger salary increases and more promotions than the politically naïve or inept. The politically astute are also likely to exhibit higher job satisfaction and be better able to neutralize job stressors.

- People respond differently to the various power bases. Expert and referent power are derived from an individual's personal qualities. In contrast, coercion, reward, and legitimate power are essentially organizationally derived.

- Cultural differences impact the types and forms of power tactics and impression management tactics considered appropriate for the workplace.

- Gender stereotypes influence the effectiveness of certain influence and impression management tactics, however these stereotypes are counterproductive and efforts should be made to avoid them when assessing others. Organizations influence the degree of politicking that take place within them via their policies, organizational culture, reward systems, and tone from the top.

- Political mapping is a useful tool to help understand and manage politics in your organization.

IMPLICATIONS FOR MANAGERS

If you want to get things done in a group or an organization, it helps to have power. Here are several suggestions for how to deal with power in your own work life:

- As a manager who wants to maximize your power, you will want to increase others' dependence on you. You can, for instance, increase your power in relation to your boss by developing knowledge or a skill she needs and for which she perceives no ready substitute.

- You will not be alone in attempting to build your power bases. Others, particularly employees and peers, will be seeking to increase your dependence on them, while you are trying to minimize it and increase their dependence on you. The result is a continual battle.

- Avoid putting others in a position where they feel they have no power.

- By assessing behaviour in a political framework, you can better predict the actions of others and use that information to formulate political strategies that will gain advantages for you and your work unit.

- Consider that employees who have poor political skills or are unwilling to play the politics game generally relate perceived organizational politics to lower job satisfaction and self-reported performance, increased anxiety, and higher turnover. Therefore, if you are adept at organizational politics, help others understand the importance of becoming politically savvy.

BREAKOUT QUESTION FOR GROUP DISCUSSION

Based on what you've learned here, what influence tactics do you think would be most effective when attempting to get a professor or instructor to reevaluate an assigned grade on a research paper? What individual attributes of the instructor/professor need to be considered when selecting a tactic?

PERSONAL INVENTORY ASSESSMENT

In the Personal Inventory Assessment found in MyManagementLab, take the assessment: Gaining Power and Influence.

SELF-REFLECTION ACTIVITY

Do you use power in positive and productive ways? Do you know how to influence people, even without formal power? Can you resist being influenced by others when appropriate? Gaining Power and Influence the Personal Inventory Assessment, found in MyManagementLab can help you answer these questions. Once you have completed the assessment, read the debrief information provided to get more insight into specific influence behaviours that you use effectively and areas where there is room for improvement. It is important to note that power and influence can be used in positive or destructive ways. It is well known that power tends to corrupt people. As you improve your ability to wield power and influence, how will you make sure that you are using those skills for the right reason? What could you do to create checks and balances for yourself that will help you identify when you begin to use power inappropriately? What might you do to create similar checks and balances for employees/direct reports?

A popular up-and-coming social media company shocked its employees and the public with the announcement that the company was severing ties with one of its senior managers. The manager was a social media mogul, well known and respected by the public. The company's decision was made in response to emerging media reports indicating that the manager had abused, sexually assaulted, and harassed several women in both private and work contexts. It wasn't long before further details emerged, with more than a dozen women making allegations of violent sexual acts, and several more individuals complaining of workplace sexual harassment. The allegations dated back several years. The accused manager, once a powerhouse, became isolated, having lost many of his supporters in both the public and private spheres. Eventually, he was formally charged with multiple counts of sexual and physical assault.

Why was this manager able to engage in such inappropriate behaviours at work for so long before being disciplined? As a well-known spokesperson for the social media company, the accused manager enjoyed celebrity status in public, and therefore had a great deal of formal and informal power within the company. Sandra, a former employee who worked in the accused manager's department, explained how he would harass and intimidate her with impunity. She reported that he had made violent, sexualized comments, and would inappropriately grab and touch her at work. When she complained to her immediate supervisor, Sandra was told that this behaviour was normal for the manager and that she would need to learn to ignore it. Sandra believed that the company allowed a two-tiered workplace to emerge, one in which the most powerful employees didn't have to comply with the law or workplace norms as long as they were keeping the company profitable and popular in the public eye. Regular workers only had job security if they accepted these abuses of authority. Sandra further observed that no other managers who were complicit in creating or maintaining this toxic environment were disciplined. Genevieve, another complainant who had made sexual harassment allegations about the manager several years earlier, reported that the company's human resources department met with her and tried to make the workplace less toxic, but they realized that even they were fairly powerless as long as the perpetrator maintained his celebrity status with the public. Genevieve's union was ineffective at addressing her complaints for similar reasons. Both Genevieve and Sandra eventually took their complaints to the media.

The social media company remains in damage-control mode. Senior executives have denied any awareness of sexual harassment allegations, and the company has retained an employment lawyer to lead an independent investigation. The company has committed to preventing similar occurrences in the future by revisiting their policies and procedures related to sexual harassment.

But were policies and procedures really the problem in the first place? Can policy overcome the types of power politics seen in this situation?

1. The media firm involved is re-examining their sexual harassment policies and procedures. Were the policies and procedures really the problem in the first place? Explain your answer.

2. What type(s) of power did the media celebrity described in this scenario have and why was he able to wield it so effectively?

3. When people in formal authority failed to respond, what sources of power were left to victims to help them address and cope with this situation? What form of power would be most useful to them and why?

In 2013, the Canadian academic community was shocked to learn that five established professors in McMaster's DeGroote School of Business were sanctioned for harassment and for creating a hostile working environment. The sanctions imposed included lengthy multiyear suspensions that essentially ended the academic careers of some of the perpetrators. The dispute arose because the professors involved sought to deny their dean, Paul Bates, a second term. Even when he was first appointed, Bates was a controversial choice. He was selected to revive an underperforming undergraduate and graduate business program. His prior career had been in business and his academic experience was limited. Some professors felt this made him ill suited to lead a teaching and research-focused faculty, while others considered his industry experience a strength. As it happened, several of the individuals who were against the appointment were later angered by decisions Bates made about related programs and affiliated institutes. For example, one of the ringleaders of the group of five, Dr. Bart, was removed from his executive role at the Director's College of Canada, a McMaster-affiliated governance school that educated industry professionals. Another, Dr. Taylor, had his Health Leadership Institute shut down due to extremely poor financial performance. These decisions, while financially and strategically sound for the university as a whole, solidified their resistance to Bates.

Professors have a right to share opinions about the appropriateness of academic appointments in their department; however, the tactics used by the five were inappropriate. All five were tenured, meaning that they had a remarkable level of job security. They were also well-respected, valued senior experts in their fields. They tried to interfere with the promotions of a total of nine junior faculty members, including those who did not yet have tenure, if those junior faculty members did not share their perspective on Bates. Since promotion decisions in academic departments are made by committees that would have included some of these five as members, these threats were credible. The five also unfairly undermined the research efforts of Bates supporters through excessive, harsh, ongoing criticism that went well beyond the normal peer review processes, and through denial of contracts for extra teaching activities beyond the normal workload. Victims reported extreme stress and anxiety as a result of this harassment, up to and including the development of depression and sleep disorders requiring medical intervention. Support staff were also impacted, one administrator going so far as to ask for a panic button in her office lest violence break out as a result of the tense workplace atmosphere.

Interestingly enough, the panel that decided upon the suspensions noted that they would have recommended firings rather than mere suspensions, except that the university failed to respond to the situation appropriately as it developed. This heightened the problem to the point where "manageable issues and differences among faculty became insidious and destructive." But the university's problems did not end there. In 2014, over 15,000 pages of documentation were submitted to the Ontario Divisional Court as part of an application for judicial review of the suspensions. The review was requested due to concerns about the process used to suspend the five professors. The harassment itself is not disputed, but the fairness of the disciplinary process is under consideration.

Originally, two investigations had been conducted: one by McMaster's Human Rights and Equity Services office and another by a panel of professors from other departments. Both found substantive breaches of the institution's antiharassment policy. University spokesperson Gord Arbeau said, upon hearing about the judicial review, that "the university is confident that its processes and policies are fair and balanced and looks forward to the start of the review." The faculty involved disagree. They argue that the process was unfair because no informal resolution or mediation was attempted, the deadlines they were given to submit information were unfair, and group complaints were consolidated. There was also secrecy surrounding the process. Sessions were closed and people providing affidavits were told to keep the process secret. The university did not release details about the complaints to the public and did not name accusers or accused, or even all the details of the sanctions taken. This deficit of information and attendant silencing creating an environment that made a fair hearing difficult.

This case will likely remain open for some time as details are further examined. In the meantime many uses of power can be observed, some of them inappropriate.

Sources: S. Arnold, "McMaster University Business Professors Win Important Victory," *The Hamilton Spectator*, July 15, 2015, http://www.thespec.com/news-story/5735940-mcmaster-university-business-professors-win-important-victory; S. Arnold, "Appeal Shatters Secrecy Around Suspension," *Hamilton Spectator*, August 23, 2015, http://www.thespec.com/news-story/4775265-special-report-appeal-shatters-secrecy-around-suspension-of-mac-faculty; and S. Arnold, "Macs Class Wars," *Hamilton Spectator*, August 22, 2015, http://thespec-reports.com/2014/08/22/nasty-business-the-main-story/#more-230.

Discussion Questions

1. Using power as your lens, explain why Dr. Bart and Dr. Taylor may have felt they could get away with intimidation and harassment in this context.

2. How do the universities policies and processes contribute to an individual's ability to use power in this situation? Explain your answer.

3. Assume five years have passed and the suspended professors have *not* retired, but have decided to return to their jobs. How might you manage their return to work to avoid destructive power issues reemerging on either side?

MyManagementLab

Study, practise, and explore real management situations with these helpful resources:
- **Interactive Lesson Presentations:** Work through interactive presentations and assessments to test your knowledge of management concepts.
- **PIA (Personal Inventory Assessments):** Enhance your ability to connect with key concepts through these engaging self-reflection assessments.
- **Study Plan:** Check your understanding of chapter concepts with self-study quizzes.
- **Simulations:** Practise decision making in simulated management environments.

PERSONAL INVENTORY ASSESSMENT

Chapter 14
Conflict and Negotiation

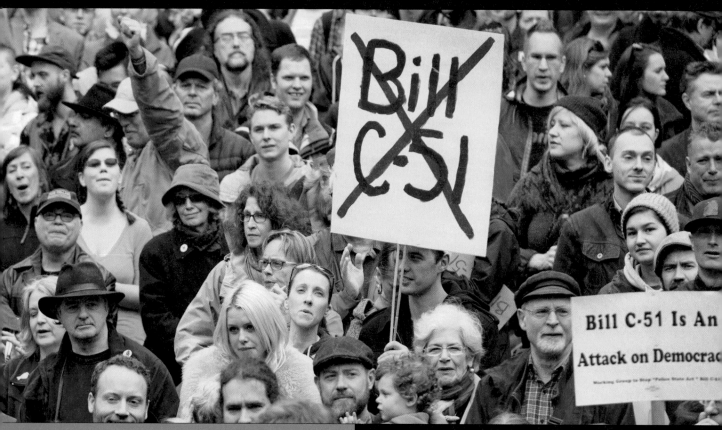

Jonathan Hayward/The Canadian Press/AP Images

LEARNING OBJECTIVES

After studying this chapter, you should be able to:

1 Differentiate between the traditional and interactionist views of conflict.

2 Describe the three types of conflict and the three loci of conflict.

3 Outline the conflict process.

4 Contrast distributive and integrative bargaining.

5 Apply the five steps of the negotiation process.

6 Show how individual differences influence negotiations.

Conflict and negotiation are often complex—and controversial—interpersonal processes. While we generally see conflict as a negative topic and negotiation as a positive one, what we deem positive or negative depends on our perspective.

Conflict can often turn personal. It can create chaotic conditions that make it nearly impossible for employees to work as a team. However, conflict also has a less well-known positive side. We'll explain the difference between negative and positive conflicts in this chapter and provide a guide to help you understand how conflicts develop. We'll also present a topic closely akin to conflict: negotiation.

A DEFINITION OF CONFLICT

There has been no shortage of definitions of *conflict*,[1] but common to most is the idea that conflict is a perception. If no one is aware of a conflict, then it is generally agreed no conflict exists. Also needed to begin the conflict process are opposition or incompatibility, and interaction.

We define **conflict** broadly as a process that begins when one party perceives another party has negatively affected or is about to negatively affect something the first party cares about.[2] Conflict describes the point in ongoing activity when interaction becomes interparty disagreement. People experience a wide range of conflicts in organizations: incompatibility of goals, differences over interpretations of facts, disagreements based on behavioural expectations, and the like. Our definition covers the full range of conflict levels from overt and violent acts to subtle forms of disagreement.

Ironically, there has been disagreement over the role of conflict in groups and organizations. One school of thought argues that conflict must be avoided—that conflict indicates a malfunction within the group. We call this the *traditional* view. Another perspective proposes not only that conflict can be a positive force in a group but that some conflict is absolutely necessary for a group to perform effectively. We label this the *interactionist* view. Let's take a closer look at each.

The Traditional View of Conflict

The **traditional view of conflict** was consistent with attitudes about group behaviour that prevailed in the 1930s and 1940s. Conflict was seen as a dysfunctional outcome resulting from poor communication, a lack of openness and trust between people, and the failure of managers to be responsive to the needs and aspirations of their employees. Conflict was discussed with the terms *violence*, *destruction*, and *irrationality*.

While the idea that all conflict is bad and should be avoided certainly offers a simple approach to looking at the behaviour of people who create disagreements, researchers realized that some level of conflict was inevitable. We need merely study the causes of conflict and correct the malfunctions to improve group and organizational performance.

The Interactionist View of Conflict

The **interactionist view of conflict** encourages conflict on the grounds that a harmonious, peaceful, tranquil, and cooperative group is prone to becoming static, apathetic, and unresponsive to needs for change and innovation.[3] This relates to the concept of "groupthink" discussed in earlier chapters. The major contribution of this view is recognizing that a minimal level of conflict can help keep a group viable, self-critical, and creative.

The interactionist view does not propose that all conflicts are good. In fact, **functional conflict** supports the goals of the group and improves its performance, and is thus constructive. Conflict that hinders group performance—**dysfunctional conflict**—is destructive. What differentiates the two? To a large degree, this depends on the *type* of conflict and the *locus* of conflict. We will review each of these in turn.

Conflict is an inherent part of organizational life. Indeed, some level of conflict is probably necessary for optimal organizational functioning.

TYPES AND LOCI OF CONFLICT

Types of Conflict

Task conflict is more constructive than process or, especially, relationship conflict.

Moirin, Bao, and Jehanne all work for the same pharmaceutical company and they have all experienced conflict recently. Each experienced a completely different type of conflict, though.

Moirin, a biochemist working in the product development department, believes their main task is finding new medicines to help ease suffering. Many of her colleagues, however, think their main task is finding new products that will be highly profitable. As a result, Moirin wants to focus resources on different projects than the rest of the team.

Bao, a security expert, is more concerned with safety than efficiency. He proposed a thorough security clearance process for site visitors and temporary employees to prevent theft of key research. He is having a conflict with the public relations department, who want to accommodate visitors with more ease and think his process goes too far.

Jehanne works in field sales, and although she is charming and charismatic with clients she can be petty and mean to her fellow sales representatives. In fact, she made several of them cry over the last month by criticizing everything from their sales skills to their wardrobe choices.

One means of understanding conflict is to identify the *type* of disagreement, or what the conflict is about. Is it a disagreement about goals? Is it about people who just rub one another the wrong way? Or is it about the best way to get things done? Although each conflict is unique, researchers have classified conflicts into three categories: task, relationship, and process.

In the above example, Moirin experienced **task conflict**, which relates to the content and goals of the work. **Relationship conflict** focuses on interpersonal relationships, which is the type of conflict that Jehanne created in the example above. Finally, Bao experienced **process conflict**, which is about how the work gets done.

Studies demonstrate that relationship conflicts, at least in work settings, are almost always dysfunctional.[4] Why? It appears that the friction and interpersonal hostilities inherent in relationship conflicts increase personality clashes and decrease mutual understanding, which hinders the completion of organizational tasks. Of the three types, relationship conflicts also appear to be the most psychologically exhausting to individuals.[5] Because they tend to revolve around personalities, you can see how relationship conflicts can become destructive. After all, we can't expect to change our coworkers' personalities, and we would generally take offense at criticisms directed at who we *are* as opposed to how we behave. (A useful thing to remember when providing feedback to others!)

While scholars agree that relationship conflict is dysfunctional, there is considerably less agreement on whether task and process conflicts are functional. Early research suggested that task conflict within groups was associated with higher group performance, but a recent review of 116 studies found that task conflict was essentially unrelated to group performance. However, there were factors that could create a relationship between conflict and performance.[6]

One such factor was whether the conflict included top management or occurred lower in the organization. Task conflict among top management teams was positively associated with their performance, whereas conflict lower in the organization was negatively associated with group performance. This review also found that it mattered whether other types of conflict were occurring at the same time. If task and relationship conflict occurred together, task conflict was more likely negative, whereas if task conflict occurred by itself, it was more likely positive. Finally, some scholars have argued that the strength of the conflict is important—if task conflict is very low, people aren't really engaged or addressing the important issues. If task conflict is too high, however, infighting will quickly degenerate into relationship conflict. According to this view, moderate levels of task conflict are optimal. Supporting this argument, one study in China found that moderate levels of task conflict in the early development stage increased creativity in groups, but high levels decreased team performance.[7]

Finally, the personalities of the teams appear to matter. A recent study demonstrated that teams made up of individuals who are, on average, high in openness and emotional stability are better able to turn task conflict into increased group performance.[8] The reason may be that open and emotionally stable teams can put task conflict in perspective and focus on how the variance in ideas can help solve the problem, rather than letting it degenerate into relationship conflict.

What about process conflict? Researchers found that process conflict revolves around delegation and roles. Conflicts over delegation often revolve around shirking, and conflicts over roles can leave some group members feeling marginalized. Thus, process conflict often becomes highly personalized and quickly devolves into relationship conflict. It's also true, of course, that arguing about how to do something takes time away from actually doing it. We've all been part of groups in which the arguments and debates about roles and responsibilities seem to go nowhere.

Loci of Conflict

Another way to understand conflict is to consider its *locus*, or where the conflict occurs. Here, too, there are three basic types. **Dyadic conflict** is conflict between two people. **Intragroup conflict** occurs *within* a group or team. **Intergroup conflict** is conflict *between* groups or teams.

Nearly all the literature on task, relationship, and process conflict considers intragroup conflict (within the group). That makes sense given that groups and teams often exist only to perform a particular task. However, it doesn't necessarily tell us about the other loci of conflict. For example, research has found that for intragroup task conflict to influence performance within the team, it is important that the teams have a supportive climate in which mistakes aren't penalized and every team member "[has] the other's back."[9] But is this concept useful for understanding the effects of intergroup conflict for the organization? Think about, say, NHL hockey. For a team to adapt and improve, perhaps a certain amount of task conflict is good for team performance, especially when the team members support one another. But would we care whether members from one team supported members from another team? Probably not. In fact, if groups are competing with one another so that only one team can "win," intergroup conflict seems almost inevitable. When is that helpful, and when is it a concern?

One study that focused on intergroup conflict found an interplay between an individual's position within a group and the way that individual managed conflict between groups. Group members who were relatively peripheral in their own group were better at resolving conflicts between their group and another one. But this happened only when those peripheral members were still accountable to their group.[10] Thus, being at the core of your work group does not necessarily make you the best person to manage conflict with other groups.

Another intriguing question about loci is whether conflicts interact or buffer one another. Assume, for example, that Dana and Scott are on the same team. What happens if they don't get along interpersonally (dyadic conflict) *and* their team also has high personality conflict? What happens to their team if two other team members, Shawna and Justin, do get along well? It's also possible to ask this question at the

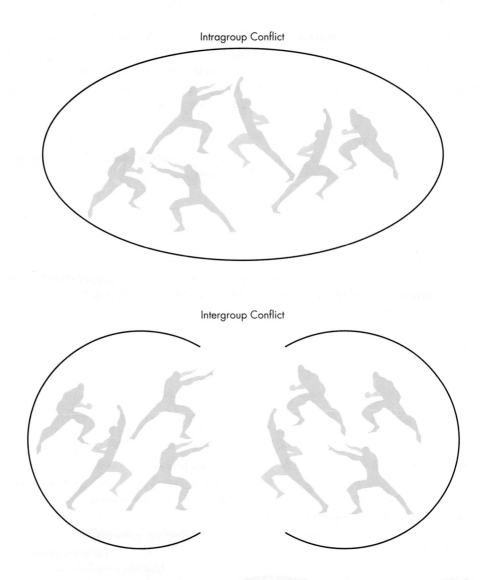

Intragroup Conflict

Intergroup Conflict

intragroup and intergroup level. Intense intergroup conflict can be quite stressful to group members and might well affect the way they interact. One study found, for example, that high levels of conflict between teams caused individuals to focus on complying with norms within their teams.[11]

Thus, understanding functional and dysfunctional conflict requires not only that we identify the type of conflict; we also need to know where it occurs. It's possible that while the concepts of task, relationship, and process conflict are useful in understanding intragroup or even dyadic conflict, they are less useful in explaining the effects of intergroup conflict.

In sum, the traditional view that all conflict should be eliminated is short-sighted. The interactionist view that conflict can stimulate active discussion without spilling over into negative, disruptive emotions is incomplete. Thinking about conflict in terms of type and locus helps us realize that conflict is probably inevitable in most organizations. When conflict does occur, we can seek to manage the variables of the conflict process, discussed next, to make the resolution as productive as possible.

THE CONFLICT PROCESS

The **conflict process** has five stages: potential opposition or incompatibility, cognition and personalization, intentions, behaviour, and outcomes (see Exhibit 14-1).

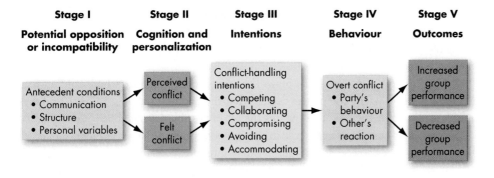

EXHIBIT 14-1 The Conflict Process

Stage I	Stage II	Stage III	Stage IV	Stage V
Potential opposition or incompatibility	Cognition and personalization	Intentions	Behaviour	Outcomes

Stage I: Potential Opposition or Incompatibility

The first stage of conflict is the appearance of conditions—causes or sources—that create opportunities for it to arise. These conditions *need not* lead directly to conflict, but one of them is necessary if it is to surface. We group the conditions into three general categories: communication, structure, and personal variables.

Communication   Communication can be a source of conflict[12] arising from semantic difficulties, misunderstandings, and "noise" in the communication channel (Chapter 11). These factors, along with jargon and insufficient information, can be barriers to communication and therefore create conflict. The potential for conflict has also been found to increase with too little or *too much* communication. Communication is functional up to a point, after which it is possible to over communicate, increasing the potential for conflict.

Structure   The term *structure* in this context includes variables such as size of group, degree of specialization in tasks assigned to group members, jurisdictional clarity (meaning whether or not it is clear who is in charge of what), member–goal compatibility, leadership styles, reward systems, and degree of dependence between groups. The larger the group and the more specialized its activities, the greater the likelihood for conflict. Tenure and conflict are inversely related; potential for conflict is greatest when group members are younger and when turnover is high. The greater the ambiguity about where responsibility for actions lies, the greater the potential for conflict. Jurisdictional ambiguities increase fighting for control of resources and territory. Diversity of goals among groups is also a major source of conflict. Reward systems, too, create conflict when one member's gain comes at another's expense. Finally, if a group is dependent on another group (in contrast to the two being mutually independent), or if interdependence allows one group to gain at another's expense, opposing forces are stimulated.

Personal Variables   Our last category of potential sources of conflict is personal variables, which include personality, emotions, and values. People high in the personality traits of disagreeableness, neuroticism, or self-monitoring are prone to tangle with other people more often—and to react poorly when conflicts occur.[13] Emotions can also cause conflict even when they are not directed at others. An employee who shows up to work irate from her hectic morning commute may carry that anger into her workday and create a tension-filled meeting.[14] People are furthermore more likely to cause conflict when their values are opposed.

Stage II: Cognition and Personalization

If the conditions cited in Stage I negatively affect something one party cares about, then the potential for opposition or incompatibility becomes realized in the second stage.

As we noted in our definition of conflict, one or more of the parties must be aware that antecedent conditions exist. However, because a disagreement is a **perceived conflict** does not mean it is personalized. In other words, "A may be aware that B and A are in serious disagreement . . . but it may not make A tense or anxious, and it may have no effect whatsoever on A's affection toward B."[15] For example, you may disagree strenuously with another person's political orientation and voting intentions but still be their close friend. It is at the **felt conflict** level, when individuals become emotionally involved, that they experience anxiety, tension, frustration, or hostility.

Keep in mind two points. First, Stage II is important because it's where conflict issues tend to be defined, where the parties decide what the conflict is about.[16] The definition of conflict is important because it delineates the set of possible settlements.

Second, emotions play a major role in shaping perceptions.[17] Negative emotions allow us to oversimplify issues, lose trust, and put negative interpretations on the other party's behaviour.[18] In contrast, positive feelings increase our tendency to see potential relationships among elements of a problem, take a broader view of the situation, and develop innovative solutions.[19]

Stage III: Intentions

Intentions intervene between people's perceptions and emotions, and their overt behaviour. They are decisions to act in a given way.[20]

Intentions are a distinct stage because we have to infer the other's intent to know how to respond to this behaviour. Many conflicts escalate simply because one party attributes the wrong intentions to the other. For example, if a team member is late, the others may believe that they don't care about the project and are disrespecting the group when in fact their car simply wouldn't start that morning, or they missed their bus. There is slippage between intentions and behaviour, so behaviour does not always accurately reflect a person's intentions.

Using two dimensions—*cooperativeness* (the degree to which one party attempts to satisfy the other party's concerns) and *assertiveness* (the degree to which one party attempts to satisfy her own concerns)—we can identify five conflict-handling intentions: *competing* (assertive and uncooperative), *collaborating* (assertive and cooperative), *avoiding* (unassertive and uncooperative), *accommodating* (unassertive and cooperative), and *compromising* (midrange on both assertiveness and cooperativeness).[21]

1. *Competing.* When one person seeks to satisfy his own interests regardless of the impact on the other parties to the conflict, that person is **competing**. You compete when you place a bet that only one person can win, for example.
2. *Collaborating.* When parties in conflict each desire to fully satisfy the concerns of all parties, there is cooperation and a search for a mutually beneficial outcome. In **collaborating**,

erhui1979/DigitalVision Vectors/ Getty Images

erhui1979/DigitalVision Vectors/ Getty Images

erhui1979/DigitalVision Vectors/ Getty Images

erhui1979/DigitalVision Vectors/ Getty Images

erhui1979/DigitalVision Vectors/ Getty Images

parties intend to solve a problem by clarifying differences rather than by accommodating various points of view. If you attempt to find a win–win solution that allows both parties' goals to be completely achieved, that's collaborating.

3. *Avoiding.* A person may recognize a conflict exists and want to withdraw from or suppress it. Examples of **avoiding** are trying to ignore a conflict and avoiding others with whom you disagree.

4. *Accommodating.* A party who seeks to appease an opponent may be willing to place the opponent's interests above his own, sacrificing to maintain the relationship. We refer to this intention as **accommodating**. Supporting someone else's opinion despite your reservations about it, for example, is accommodating.

5. *Compromising.* In **compromising**, there is no winner or loser. Rather, there is a willingness to ration the object of the conflict and accept a solution with incomplete satisfaction of both parties' concerns. The distinguishing characteristic of compromising, therefore, is that each party intends to give up something.

Intentions are not always fixed. During the course of a conflict, intentions might change if the parties are able to see the other's point of view or to respond emotionally to the other's behaviour. (How many times during an argument have you thought to yourself, "Well, I would have done what you wanted if you had said *that*"?) People generally have preferences among the five conflict-handling intentions. We can predict a person's intentions rather well from a combination of intellectual and personality characteristics. Gender also plays a role, with females more strongly associated with cooperative and collaborative conflict resolution styles and males more strongly associated with competitive styles.[22] That said, it can be difficult to separate out actual gender differences from attribution errors of the type described in Chapter 6. For example, two people might both say, "I'm not leaving until we resolve this," but that statement might be perceived as competitive and combative coming from a male but collaborative and supportive coming from a female. The degree to which gender-based differences in conflict handling are due to perceptual error, inherent biological differences, or learning and socialization remains highly controversial. In the meantime, people of both genders might benefit from assessing their own style and attempting to expand their repertoire, using alternative styles in appropriate situations.

Stage IV: Behaviour

When most people think of conflict, they tend to focus on Stage IV, because this is where conflicts become visible. The behaviour stage includes statements, actions, and reactions made by conflicting parties, usually as overt attempts to implement their own intentions. As a result of miscalculations or unskilled enactments, overt behaviours sometimes deviate from original intentions.[23] For example, someone who intends to passionately explain their point of view, sharing information in the process, may come across as aggressive and out of control if that information is delivered in a highly emotional tone.

Stage IV is a dynamic process of interaction. For example, you make a demand on me, I respond by arguing, you threaten me, I threaten you back, and so on. Exhibit 14-2 provides a way of visualizing conflict behaviour. All conflicts exist somewhere along this continuum. At the lower end are conflicts characterized by subtle, indirect, and highly controlled forms of tension, such as a student questioning in class a point the instructor has just made. Conflict intensities escalate as they move upward along the continuum until they become highly destructive. Strikes, riots, and wars clearly fall in this upper range. Conflicts that reach the upper ranges of the continuum are almost always dysfunctional. Functional conflicts are typically confined to the lower range of the continuum.

If a conflict is dysfunctional, what can the parties do to deescalate it? Or, conversely, what options exist if conflict is too low and needs to be increased? This brings us to

Annihilatory conflict — Overt efforts to destroy the other party

Aggressive physical attacks

Threats and ultimatums

Assertive verbal attacks

Overt questioning or challenging of others

Minor disagreements or misunderstandings

No conflict

EXHIBIT 14-2   Conflict-Intensity Continuum

Sources: Based on S. P. Robbins, *Managing Organizational Conflict: A Nontraditional Approach* (Upper Saddle River, NJ: Prentice Hall, 1974), pp. 93–97; and F. Glasi, "The Process of Conflict Escalation and the Roles of Third Parties," in G. B. J. Bomers and R. Peterson (eds.), *Conflict Management and Industrial Relations* (Boston: Kluwer-Nijhoff, 1982), pp. 119–140.

techniques of **conflict management**. We have already described several techniques as part of conflict-handling intentions. Under ideal conditions, a person's intentions should translate into comparable behaviours.

Stage V: Outcomes

The action–reaction interplay of conflicting parties creates consequences. As our model demonstrates (see Exhibit 14-1), these outcomes may be functional, if the conflict improves the group's performance, or dysfunctional, if it hinders performance.

Functional Outcomes   How might conflict act as a force to increase group performance? It is hard to visualize a situation in which open or violent aggression could be functional. But it's possible to see how low or moderate levels of conflict could improve group effectiveness. Note that all our examples focus on task and process conflicts and exclude the relationship variety.

Conflict is constructive when it improves the quality of decisions, stimulates creativity and innovation, encourages interest and curiosity among group members, provides the medium for problems to be aired and tensions released, and fosters self-evaluation and change.

Conflict is an antidote for groupthink (see Chapter 9). Conflict doesn't allow the group to passively rubber-stamp decisions that may be based on weak assumptions, inadequate consideration of relevant alternatives, or other debilities. Conflict challenges the status quo and furthers the creation of new ideas, promotes reassessment of group goals and activities, and increases the probability that the group will respond to change. An open discussion focused on higher-order goals can make functional outcomes more likely. Groups that are extremely polarized do not manage their underlying disagreements effectively and tend to accept suboptimal solutions, or they avoid making decisions altogether rather than work out the conflict.[24] Research studies in diverse settings confirm the functionality of active discussion. Team members with greater differences in work styles and experience tend to share more information with one another.[25]

Dysfunctional Outcomes   The destructive consequences of conflict on the performance of a group or an organization are generally well known: Uncontrolled opposition breeds discontent, which acts to dissolve common ties and eventually leads to the destruction of the group. And, of course, a substantial body of literature documents how dysfunctional conflicts can reduce group effectiveness.[26] Among the undesirable consequences are poor communication, reductions in group cohesiveness, and subordination of group goals to the primacy of infighting among members. All forms of conflict—even the functional varieties—appear to reduce group member satisfaction and trust.[27] When active discussions turn into open conflicts between members, information sharing between members decreases significantly.[28] At the extreme, conflict can bring group functioning to a halt and threaten the group's survival.

Managing Functional Conflict   If managers recognize that in some situations conflict can be beneficial, what can they do to manage conflict effectively in their organizations? Let's look at some approaches organizations are using to encourage their people to challenge the system and develop fresh ideas.

One of the keys to minimizing counterproductive conflict is recognizing when there really is a disagreement. Many apparent conflicts are due to people using a different language to discuss the same general course of action. For example, someone in marketing might focus on "distribution problems," while someone from operations will talk about "supply chain management" to describe essentially the same issue. Successful conflict management recognizes these different approaches and attempts to resolve them by encouraging open, frank discussion focused on interests rather than issues (we'll have more to say about this when we contrast distributive and integrative bargaining styles later in this chapter). Another approach is to have opposing groups pick the issues that are most important to them and then focus on how each side can get its top needs satisfied. Neither side may get exactly what it wants, but each side will get the most important parts of its agenda.[29]

Groups that resolve conflicts successfully discuss differences of opinion openly, share information, and are prepared to manage conflict when it arises.[30] The most disruptive conflicts are those that are never addressed directly. An open discussion makes it much easier to develop a shared perception of the problems at hand; it also allows groups to work toward a mutually acceptable solution. Managers need to emphasize shared interests in resolving conflicts, so groups that disagree with one another don't become too entrenched in their points of view and start to take the conflicts personally. Groups with cooperative conflict styles and a strong underlying identification to the overall group goals are more effective than groups with a competitive style.[31]

Differences across countries in conflict resolution strategies may be based on collectivistic tendencies and motives.[32] Collectivist cultures see people as deeply embedded in social situations, whereas individualist cultures see them as autonomous. As a result, collectivists are more likely to seek to preserve relationships and promote the good of the group as a whole. They will avoid the direct expression of conflicts, preferring indirect methods for resolving differences of opinion. Collectivists may also be more interested in demonstrations of concern and working through third parties to resolve disputes, whereas individualists will be more likely to confront differences of opinion directly and openly. Power distance and masculinity (see Chapter 5) will also impact which conflict resolution styles are socially acceptable. People low in the hierarchy in high-power-distance countries would be unlikely to use competing strategies with higher-ups and would most likely avoid conflict with them altogether. Masculine cultures, by contrast, would encourage competitive behaviours and see avoidance as weakness.

Some research supports this theory. Compared to collectivist Japanese negotiators, their more individualist U.S. counterparts are more likely to see offers from their counterparts as unfair and to reject them. Another study revealed that whereas North American managers were more likely to use competing tactics in the face of conflict, compromise and avoidance are the most preferred methods of conflict management in China.[33] Interview data, however, suggest that top management teams in Chinese high-technology firms prefer collaboration even more than compromising and avoiding.[34]

Having considered conflict—its nature, causes, and consequences—we now turn to negotiation, which often resolves conflict.

NEGOTIATION

Negotiation permeates the interactions of almost everyone in groups and organizations. There's the obvious: Labour bargains with management. There's the not-so-obvious: Managers negotiate with employees, peers, and bosses; salespeople negotiate with customers; purchasing agents negotiate with suppliers. And there's the even-more-subtle: An

The most effective negotiators utilize different tactics for distributive and integrative bargaining; this chapter provides clear ways for you to improve each type of bargaining.

employee agrees to cover for a colleague for a few minutes in exchange for future benefit. In today's loosely structured organizations, in which members work with colleagues over whom they have no direct authority and with whom they may not even share a common boss, negotiation skills are critical.

We can define **negotiation** as a process that occurs when two or more parties decide how to allocate scarce resources.[35] Although we commonly think of the outcomes of negotiation in one-shot economic terms, like negotiating over the price of a car, every negotiation in organizations also affects the relationship between negotiators and the way negotiators feel about themselves.[36] Depending on how much the parties are going to interact with one another, sometimes maintaining the social relationship and behaving ethically will be just as important as achieving an immediate outcome of bargaining. That is why, for example, most people would give a friend who was buying their used car a better price then they would offer a stranger. They would also be more likely to tell the friend about any potential minor problems with the vehicle because they value the friendship, not just the profit they can earn today.

Note that throughout this chapter we use the terms *negotiation* and *bargaining* interchangeably. Next, we contrast two bargaining strategies, provide a model of the negotiation process, and ascertain the role of individual differences in negotiation effectiveness.

Bargaining Strategies

There are two general approaches to negotiation—*distributive bargaining* and *integrative bargaining*.[37] As Exhibit 14-3 shows, the approaches differ in their goal and motivation, focus, interests, information sharing, and duration of relationship. Let's define each and illustrate the differences.

Distributive Bargaining You see a used car advertised for sale online that looks great. You go see the car. It's perfect, and you want it. The owner tells you the asking price. You don't want to pay that much. The two of you negotiate. The negotiating strategy you're engaging in is called **distributive bargaining**. Its identifying feature is that it operates under zero-sum conditions—that is, any gain I make is at your expense, and vice versa. Every dollar you can get the seller to cut from the car's price is a dollar you save, and every dollar the seller can get from you comes at your expense. The essence of distributive bargaining is negotiating over who gets what share of a fixed pie. By **fixed pie**, we mean a set amount of

EXHIBIT 14-3

Distributive Versus Integrative Bargaining

Bargaining Characteristic	Distributive Bargaining	Integrative Bargaining
Goal	Get as much of the pie as possible	Expand the pie so that both parties are satisfied
Motivation	Win–lose	Win–win
Focus	Positions ("I can't go beyond this point on this issue")	Interests ("Can you explain why this issue is so important to you?")
Interests	Opposed	Congruent
Information sharing	Low (sharing information will only allow other party to take advantage)	High (sharing information will allow each party to find ways to satisfy interests of each party)
Duration of relationship	Short term	Long term

goods or services to be divvied up. When the pie is fixed, or the parties believe it is, they tend to bargain distributively.

The most widely cited example of distributive bargaining may be labour–management negotiations over wages. Typically, labour's representatives come to the bargaining table determined to get as much money as possible from management. Because every cent labour negotiates increases management's costs, each party bargains aggressively and treats the other as an opponent to defeat.

The essence of distributive bargaining is depicted in Exhibit 14-4. Parties A and B represent two negotiators. Each has a *target point* that defines what she would like to achieve. Each also has a *resistance point*, which marks the lowest acceptable outcome—the point below which the party would break off negotiations rather than accept a less favourable settlement. The area between these two points makes up each party's aspiration range. As long as there is some overlap between A's and B's aspiration range, there exists a settlement range in which each one's aspirations can be met.

When engaged in distributive bargaining, one of the best things you can do is make the first offer, and an aggressive one. This approach shows power; individuals in power are much more likely to make initial offers, speak first at meetings, and thereby gain the advantage. Another reason it is a good strategy is the anchoring bias, mentioned in Chapter 6. People tend to fixate on initial information. Once that anchoring point is set, people fail to adequately adjust it in view of subsequent information. A savvy negotiator sets an anchor with the initial offer, and scores of negotiation studies show that such anchors greatly favour the person who sets them.[38]

Integrative Bargaining   Jake was a luxury clothing boutique owned by Jim Wetzel and Lance Lawson. In the early days of the business, Wetzel and Lawson moved millions of dollars of merchandise from many up-and-coming designers. They developed such a good rapport that many designers would send allotments to Jake without requiring advance payment. When the economy soured in 2008, Jake had trouble selling inventory, and designers were not being paid for what they had shipped to the store. Many designers, however, were quite willing to work with the store on a delayed payment plan; one, Doo-Ri Chung, said, "you kind of feel this familiarity with people who supported you for so long. When they have cash-flow issues, you want to make sure you are there for them as well."[39]

Chung's attitude shows the promise of **integrative bargaining**. In contrast to distributive bargaining, integrative bargaining assumes that one or more of the possible settlements can create a win–win solution. Of course, as we'll highlight later, both parties must be engaged for integrative bargaining to work.

In terms of intraorganizational behaviour, integrative bargaining is preferable to distributive bargaining, because the former builds long-term relationships. Integrative bargaining bonds negotiators and allows them to leave the bargaining table feeling that they have achieved a victory. Distributive bargaining, however, leaves one party a loser. It tends to build animosity and deepen divisions when people have to work together on an ongoing basis. Research shows that over repeated bargaining episodes, a losing party who feels positive about the negotiation outcome is much more likely to bargain cooperatively in subsequent negotiations. This highlights an important advantage of integrative negotiations:

EXHIBIT 14-4   Staking Out the Bargaining Zone

Even when you win, you want your opponent to feel good about the negotiation, especially if another negotiation might be coming along in the future.[40]

Why, then, don't we see more integrative bargaining in organizations? The answer lies in the conditions necessary for it to succeed. These include opposing parties who are trusting, open with information, candid about concerns, sensitive to the other's needs, and able to maintain flexibility.[41] Because these conditions seldom exist in organizations, negotiations often take on a win-at-any-cost dynamic. Historical emphasis on distributive bargaining in business has also created cultural expectations favouring it—these beliefs and practices change slowly, as is typical of cultural change on such a large scale.

Individuals who bargain in teams reach more integrative agreements than those who bargain individually, because more ideas are generated when more people are at the bargaining table.[42] Another way to achieve higher joint-gain settlements is to put more issues on the table. The more negotiable issues introduced into a negotiation, the more opportunity for "logrolling," in which issues are traded off according to individual preferences. This creates better outcomes for each side than if they negotiated each issue individually.[43] It is also good to focus on the underlying interests of both sides rather than on issues. In other words, it is better to concentrate on *why* an employee wants a raise rather than to focus just on the raise amount—some unseen potential for integrative outcomes may arise if both sides concentrate on what they really want rather than on specific items they're bargaining over. Typically, it's easier to concentrate on underlying interests when parties stay focused on broad, overall goals rather than on immediate outcomes of a specific decision.[44] Negotiations when both parties are focused on learning and understanding the other side tend to yield higher joint outcomes than those in which parties are more interested in their individual bottom-line outcomes.[45]

Compromise may be your worst enemy in negotiating a win–win agreement, as it reduces the pressure to bargain integratively. After all, if you or your opponent cave in easily, no one needs to be creative to reach a settlement. People then settle for less than they might have obtained if they had been forced to consider the other party's interests, trade off issues, and be creative.[46] Consider a classic example in which two sisters are arguing over who gets an orange. Unknown to them, one sister wants the orange to drink the juice, whereas the other wants the orange peel to bake a cake. If one sister capitulates and gives the other sister the orange, they will not be forced to explore their reasons for wanting the orange, and thus they will never find the win–win solution: They could *both* have the orange because they want different parts!

THE NEGOTIATION PROCESS

Exhibit 14-5 provides a simplified model of the negotiation process. It views negotiation as made up of five steps: (1) preparation and planning, (2) definition of ground rules, (3) clarification and justification, (4) bargaining and problem solving, and (5) closure and implementation.[47]

Steps in the Negotiation Process

Preparation and Planning Before you start negotiating, do your homework. What's the nature of the conflict? What's the history leading up to this negotiation? Who's involved and what are their perceptions of the conflict? What do you want from the negotiation? What are *your* goals? If you're a supply manager at Dell Computer, for instance, and your goal is to get a significant cost reduction from your supplier of keyboards, make sure this goal stays paramount in discussions and doesn't get overshadowed by other issues. It helps to put your goals in writing and develop a range of outcomes—from "most hopeful" to "minimally acceptable"—to keep your attention focused.

EXHIBIT 14-5
The Negotiation Process

You should assess what you think are the other party's goals. What are they likely to ask? How entrenched is their position likely to be? What intangible or hidden interests may be important to them? On what might they be willing to settle? When you can anticipate your opponent's position, you are better equipped to counter arguments with facts and figures that support your position.

Relationships change as a result of negotiation, so take that into consideration. If you could "win" a negotiation but push the other side into resentment or animosity, it might be wiser to pursue a more compromising style. If preserving the relationship will make you seem easily exploited, you may consider a more aggressive style. As an example of how the tone of a relationship set in negotiations matters, people who feel good about the *process* of a job offer negotiation are more satisfied with their jobs and less likely to turn over a year later regardless of their actual *outcomes* from these negotiations.[48]

Once you've gathered your information, develop a strategy. For example, expert chess players know how they will respond to any given situation. You should determine your and the other side's **b**est **a**lternative **t**o a **n**egotiated **a**greement, or **BATNA**.[49] Your BATNA determines the lowest value acceptable to you for a negotiated agreement. Any offer you receive that is higher than your BATNA is better than an impasse. Conversely, you shouldn't expect success in your negotiation effort unless you're able to make the other side an offer it finds more attractive than its BATNA. If you go into your negotiation having a good idea of what the other party's BATNA is, you might be able to elicit a change even if you're not able to meet it. Think carefully about what the other side is willing to give up. People who underestimate their opponent's willingness to give on key issues before the negotiation even starts end up with lower outcomes from a negotiation.[50]

Definition of Ground Rules   Once you've done your planning and developed a strategy, you're ready to begin defining with the other party the ground rules and procedures of the negotiation itself. Who will do the negotiating? Where will it take place? What time constraints, if any, will apply? To what issues will negotiation be limited? Will you follow a specific procedure if an impasse is reached? During this phase, the parties will also exchange their initial proposals or demands.

Clarification and Justification   When you have exchanged initial positions, you and the other party will explain, amplify, clarify, bolster, and justify your original demands. This step needn't be confrontational. Rather, it's an opportunity for educating each other on the issues, why they are important, and how you arrived at your initial demands. Provide the other party with any documentation that supports your position.

Bargaining and Problem Solving The essence of the negotiation process is the actual give-and-take in trying to hash out an agreement. This is where both parties need to make concessions.

Closure and Implementation The final step in the negotiation process is formalizing your agreement and developing procedures necessary for implementing and monitoring it. For major negotiations—from labour–management negotiations to bargaining over lease terms—this requires hammering out the specifics in a formal contract. For other cases, closure of the negotiation process is nothing more formal than a handshake.

INDIVIDUAL DIFFERENCES IN NEGOTIATION EFFECTIVENESS

In negotiations, individual differences do matter. Differences in personalities, moods and emotions, culture, and gender influence our negotiation effectiveness.

Are some people better negotiators than others? The answer is complex. Four factors influence how effectively individuals negotiate: personality, moods/emotions, culture, and gender.

Personality Traits in Negotiation

Can you predict an opponent's negotiating tactics if you know something about his personality? Because personality and negotiation outcomes are related only weakly, the answer is, at best, "sort of." Most research has focused on the Big Five trait of agreeableness, for obvious reasons—agreeable individuals are cooperative, compliant, kind, and conflict-averse. We might think such characteristics make agreeable individuals easy prey in negotiations, especially distributive ones. The evidence suggests, however, that overall agreeableness is weakly related to negotiation outcomes. Why is this?

It appears that the degree to which agreeableness, and personality more generally, affects negotiation outcomes depends on the situation. The importance of being extraverted in negotiations, for example, will depend very much on how the other party reacts to someone who is assertive and enthusiastic. One complicating factor for agreeableness is that it has two facets: The tendency to be cooperative and compliant is one, but so is the tendency to be warm and empathetic.[51] It may be that while the former is a hindrance to negotiating favourable outcomes, the latter helps. Empathy, after all, is the ability to take the perspective of another person and to gain insight/understanding of them. We know so-called perspective-taking benefits integrative negotiations, so perhaps the null effect for agreeableness is due to the two tendencies pulling against one another.

Moods/Emotions in Negotiation

Do moods and emotions influence negotiation? They do, but the way they work depends on the emotion as well as the context. A negotiator who shows anger generally induces concessions, for instance, because the other negotiator believes no further concessions from the angry party are possible. One factor that governs this outcome, however, is power—you should show anger in negotiations only if you have at least as much power as your counterpart. If you have less, showing anger actually seems to provoke hardball reactions from the other side.[52] Another factor is how genuine your anger is. "Faked" anger, or anger produced from so-called *surface acting* (see Chapter 4), is not effective, but showing anger that is genuine (so-called *deep acting*) does.[53] It also appears that having a history of showing anger, rather than sowing the seeds of revenge, actually induces more concessions, because the other party perceives the negotiator as tough.[54] Finally, culture seems to matter. For instance, one study found that when East Asian participants showed anger, it induced more concessions than when the negotiator expressing anger was from the United States or Europe, perhaps because of the stereotype of East Asians as refusing to show anger.[55]

Another relevant emotion is disappointment. Generally, a negotiator who perceives disappointment from her counterpart concedes more because disappointment makes many negotiators feel guilty. In one study, Dutch students were given 100 chips to bargain over. Negotiators who expressed disappointment were offered 14 more chips than those who didn't. In a second study, showing disappointment yielded an average concession of 12 chips. Unlike a show of anger, the relative power of the negotiators made no difference in either study.[56]

Anxiety also appears to have an impact on negotiation. For example, one study found that individuals who experienced more anxiety about a negotiation used more deceptions in dealing with others.[57] Another study found that anxious negotiators expect lower outcomes, respond to offers more quickly, and exit the bargaining process more quickly, leading them to obtain worse outcomes.[58]

As you can see, emotions—especially negative ones—matter in negotiation. Even emotional unpredictability affects outcomes; researchers have found that negotiators who express positive and negative emotions in an unpredictable way extract more concessions because it makes the other party feel less in control.[59] As one negotiator put it, "Out of the blue, you may have to react to something you have been working on in one way, and then something entirely new is introduced, and you have to veer off and refocus."[60]

Culture in Negotiations

Do people from different cultures negotiate differently? The simple answer is the obvious one: Yes, they do. However, there are many nuances in the way this works. Success in negotiations depends on the context.

So, what can we say about culture and negotiations? First, it appears that people generally negotiate more effectively within cultures than between them. For example, a Colombian is apt to do better negotiating with a Colombian than with a Sri Lankan. Second, it appears that in cross-cultural negotiations, it is especially important that the negotiators be high in openness. This suggests choosing cross-cultural negotiators who are high on openness to experience, but also avoiding factors—such as time pressure—that tend to inhibit learning to understand the other party.[61]

It is also important to understand the differences in negotiation strategy between *high-context* and *low-context* cultures (see Chapter 11 for a definition of each culture type). The two types gain information about priorities and preferences differently—either indirectly through the pattern of proposals and counterproposals (high context) or directly through questions (low context). Low-context negotiators are therefore likely to see an offer as a "deal-closing" tool. They make fewer offers and present them later in the process. High-context negotiators use offers as information gathering tools, so they present them early and often. When members of a high-context culture negotiate with members of a low-context culture, both groups tend to get frustrated, as they do not have a shared understanding of the purpose of a proposal. The former may believe the latter are wasting their time with too many counteroffers representing only marginal changes, and the latter believe the former are withholding information, are pushy and overly rushed, creating distrust.[62]

Finally, because emotions are culturally sensitive and influenced by shared memories of historical events, negotiators need to be especially aware of the emotional dynamics in cross-cultural negotiation. One study, for example, explicitly compared how U.S. and Chinese negotiators reacted to an angry counterpart. Chinese negotiators increased their use of distributive negotiating tactics, whereas U.S. negotiators decreased their use of these tactics. That is, Chinese negotiators began to drive a harder bargain once they saw that their negotiation partner was becoming angry, whereas U.S. negotiators actually capitulated somewhat in the face of angry demands. Why the difference? It may be that individuals from East Asian cultures feel that using anger to get their way in a negotiation is not a legitimate tactic, so they respond by refusing to cooperate when their opponents become upset.[63] Even cultures that seem to have similarities, such as Canada and the United States, can have very different negotiating cultures. Canadians, for instance, tend to focus on collaborative problem solving and respond poorly to the "hard sell" tactics that are often quite successful in the United States.[64] First Nations cultures also tend to emphasize cooperation and collaboration when negotiating within and between bands. Historically, however, they have been mistreated by colonial governments and their treaties have been violated and/or ignored, so the tone of contemporary negotiations with government agencies will be influenced by that history of confrontation and associated emotion. This may make their tactics more assertive and competition focused than they would be otherwise.

Gender Differences in Negotiations

There are many areas of organizational behaviour in which men and women are not that different. Negotiation is not one of them. It seems fairly clear that men and women negotiate differently, and these differences affect outcomes.

A popular stereotype is that women are more cooperative and pleasant in negotiations than men. Though this is controversial, there is some merit to it. Men tend to put a higher value on status, power, and recognition, whereas women tend to put a higher value on compassion and altruism. Moreover, women tend to value relationship outcomes more, and men tend to value economic outcomes more.[65]

These differences affect both negotiation behaviour and negotiation outcomes. Compared to men, women tend to behave in a less assertive, less self-interested, and more accommodating manner. As one review concluded, women "are more reluctant to initiate negotiations, and when they do initiate negotiations, they ask for less, are more willing to accept [the] offer, and make more generous offers to their negotiation partners than men do."[66] A study of MBA students at Carnegie-Mellon University found that male MBA students took the step of negotiating their first offer 57 percent of the time, compared to 4 percent for female MBA students. The net result? A $4,000 difference in starting salaries.[67]

Evidence suggests women's own attitudes and behaviours hurt them in negotiations. Managerial women demonstrate less confidence than men in anticipation of negotiating and are less satisfied with their performance afterward, even when their performance and the outcomes they achieve are similar to those for men.[68] Women are also less likely than men to see an ambiguous situation as an opportunity for negotiation. Women may unduly penalize themselves by failing to engage in negotiations that would be in their best interests. Some research suggests that women are less aggressive in negotiations because they are worried about backlash from others. There is an interesting qualifier to this result: Women are more likely to engage in assertive negotiations when they are bargaining on behalf of someone else than when they are bargaining on their own behalf.[69]

SUMMARY

- While many people assume conflict lowers group and organizational performance, this assumption is frequently incorrect. Conflict can be either constructive or destructive to the functioning of a group or unit.

- An optimal level of conflict is one that prevents stagnation, stimulates creativity, allows tensions to be released, and initiates the seeds of change without being disruptive or preventing coordination of activities.

- Negotiation can focus on win–lose (distributive) or win–win (integrative). While historically distributive tactics have dominated Western business practice, integrative negotiation is becoming increasingly important.

- Negotiation often resolves conflict, particularly if the negotiators seek integrative solutions and constructively work through the negotiation process.

- Negotiations can be further improved when the parties take their individual differences into account, particularly cultural and gender-based differences.

IMPLICATIONS FOR MANAGERS

- Choose an authoritarian management style in emergencies, when unpopular actions need to be implemented (such as cost cutting, enforcement of unpopular rules, or discipline) and when the issue is vital to the organization's welfare. Be certain to communicate your logic to ensure that employees remain engaged and productive.

- Seek integrative solutions when your objective is to learn, when you want to merge insights from people with different perspectives, when you need to gain commitment by incorporating concerns into a consensus, and when you need to work through feelings that have interfered with a relationship.

- You can build trust by accommodating others when you find you're wrong, when you need to demonstrate reasonableness, when other positions need to be heard, when issues are more important to others than to yourself, when you want to satisfy others and maintain cooperation, when you can build social credit for later issues, to minimize loss when you are outmatched and losing, and when employees should learn from their own mistakes.

- Consider compromising when goals are important but not worth potential disruption, when opponents with equal power are committed to mutually exclusive goals, and when you need temporary settlements to complex issues.

- Make sure you set aggressive negotiating goals and try to find creative ways to achieve the objectives of both parties, especially when you value the long-term relationship with the other party. That doesn't mean sacrificing your self-interest; rather, it means trying to find creative solutions that give both parties what they really want.

BREAKOUT QUESTION FOR GROUP DISCUSSION

In theory, the federal and provincial governments should always be involved in integrative negotiations, since they have a shared responsibility to citizens. In the summer of 2015, however, a public spat between Ontario Premier Kathleen Wynne and Prime Minister Stephen Harper broke out. The public negotiations were anything but integrative. Harper flatly rejected the whole idea of an Ontario Pension Plan, a campaign promise made by Wynne that she was in the process of implementing.

Consider the Canadian political landscape in the summer of 2015. What conflict conditions existed that helped ensure this would be a distributive rather than integrative negotiation process?

In the Personal Inventory Assessment found in MyManagementLab, take the assessment: Strategies for Handling Conflict.

SELF-REFLECTION ACTIVITY

There are many different ways of addressing conflict: compromise, collaboration, avoidance, accommodation, and forcing of one's point of view on others. While everyone uses each of these strategies at some point in time, we tend to have a "go-to" strategy or style—one we use most frequently. Take the Personal Inventory Assessment found in MyManagementLab, "Strategies for Handling Conflict," will help you assess your own go-to strategy. When completing the assessment, remember to think about work contexts. You may find that your responses (and scores) change on the basis of context, since many people deal with professional and personal conflict in slightly different ways.

Reflect carefully on the usage of your go-to strategy over time. Has it helped or hindered your ability to resolve conflicts in a productive, respectful manner? When you have used the other strategies, have your outcomes been better or worse? It might also be helpful to think back to times when coworkers may have used these strategies on you. How did you respond to each? What does that suggest to you when it comes to wielding influence yourself?

MINI CASE | WIN–LOSE NEGOTIATION TACTICS LEAD TO CORPORATE HUMILIATION

Conflict that takes place within an organization can quickly make its way outside the organization, leading to public embarrassment and brand diminishment. This reality hit home for Premier Tech (PT) and its controlling shareholder Gestion Bernard Belanger (GBB) in July 2015 when the Quebec Court of Appeal dismissed their appeal and supported an earlier court decision related to their former executive Christian Dollo. Christian had engaged in a lengthy and ultimately successful legal battle to win back $2,000,000 worth of stock options. The options had been lost when he was terminated, a termination deemed unjust and problematic by the courts.

The situation developed in early 2001. Christian Dollo was a senior executive in a PT subsidiary and his compensation package included significant stock options. Between 2001 and 2010 he was granted and he vested over 200,000 options. In 2007, the company reverted from a publicly traded to a private corporation; however, this did not impact his options. In fact, it seemed like a wise decision.

The company succeeded as a private entity. The stock tripled in value in the three years (between 2007–2010), such that Christian's shares were worth almost $2,000,000 by 2010. He expected the trend to continue and intended to hold onto his options for the long term, seeing them as contributing to his eventual retirement.

Christian's financial future was top of mind for him in 2010; he was going through a divorce and focused on division of assets. As part of that process he reviewed his stock option plan, and was surprised and chagrined to find a clause stipulating that termination for any reason would result in a loss of all stock options even if the termination was not for cause. Concerned, Christian contacted PT's CEO and CFO, to whom he reported. Both provided assurances they would never fire him without also permitting him to keep his options. But the fact that the written regulations stated something different continued to make Christian very uncomfortable. Weeks later, he made a formal request to have the written clause changed. Once again, his concerns were dismissed. The regulations remained unchanged. Christian left for a brief vacation still very worried.

On his return he was called into another meeting with the PT CEO at which he was fired and offered a severance package. When he asked about stock options, the CEO would not answer him. He later discovered that his options had been rescinded. He wrote to the board of directors to make a formal complaint and request that the options be reinstated. They flatly refused without making a counteroffer or engaging in negotiations.

However, this decision represented a clear conflict of interest: it had been made on the basis of legal advice provided by the law firm representing GBB, the majority shareholder in PT. Paying out the options would have significant financial repercussions for GBB.

Upset by what he perceived as unfair treatment, Christian launched a suit before the Superior Court. He argued that he was terminated without cause, that the provision withdrawing options upon termination was abusive, and furthermore that he had been intentionally misled about its applicability to his situation. Christian also argued that the board members had acted in bad faith in relying on a legal opinion that they should have known was biased.

Justice Clement Samson agreed, on all counts. His employer was required to allow Christian to sell his stock options and take his profits. He was also awarded interest on the sales price, since the court proceedings had delayed the sale. Both GBB and PT filed appeals, neither successful. In fact, all the appeals did was highlight the many procedural errors they had made along the way, most notably at the board-of-directors level.

It is too early to fully assess the costs of this fiasco for GBB and PT. There are direct costs associated with providing the stock options and paying court costs, but there are also indirect costs. The company has gotten a reputation for being abusive and untrustworthy. This reputation will impact everything from consumer perceptions to the calibre of candidates they can attract for future executive roles. They have also acquired a reputation as manipulative and unwilling to negotiate in good faith. The ramifications of that image in the public eye remain to be seen.

Source: Miller Thompson law firm staff report, 2015, http://www.millerthomson.com/en/publications/communiques-and-updates/labour-and-employment-communique/august-6-2015?utm_source=Mondaq&utm_medium=syndication&utm_campaign=View-Original.

Discussion Questions

1. Why do you think PT/GBB failed to attempt a mutually beneficial integrative negotiating strategy when addressing Christian's concerns? (Remember to consider content from this chapter *and* Chapter 13 on power and politics.)

2. At what point(s) in this scenario were there opportunities for integrative style negotiating? Who could have started the process and how?

3. Moving forward, how could PT help prevent conflicts over stock options in the future?

MINI CASE COMING BACK FROM CONFLICT

Brittany sat in her office with her stomach churning. How had she misjudged a situation so badly? She knew she had just made an enemy, but it had been an accident. Now she wanted nothing more than to explain, fix it, and smooth things over. But Oscar wouldn't even look at her, never mind talk to her. So now what?

Brittany worked for a unionized food processing facility. In addition to her HR responsibilities, she was the chairperson of an important executive committee that met regularly to discuss employee performance, rewards, and compensation. The committee did not do individual performance appraisals, but they were responsible for establishing, monitoring, evaluating, and modifying both the performance appraisal process and the process for distributing associated rewards such as bonuses. They used hiring, performance, employee satisfaction, and turnover data from the previous year to find weak spots and assess the effectiveness of their compensation strategies. As a result of this process, the appraisal rules were revisited every year and minor changes were made.

Last year, the company had introduced a new waste reduction program. During the town hall meeting to explain the program, one employee, Oscar, had raised his hand and asked the CEO if helping with waste reduction would be part of the bonus system the following year. It was a good question. Since bonuses were often tied to achieving very specific objectives, it was important to know what was being measured in any given year—especially since everyone had too much to do and needed to prioritize effectively to maximize performance. The CEO had confidently assured everyone that waste reduction would be considered when bonus time came around.

Eleven weeks later the committee met to review bonus criteria. Of the six members on the committee, not one had been present for the CEO's announcement, so the committee developed bonus criteria that did not include waste reduction activities. The CEO signed off on them without noting the discrepancy and they became official.

Oscar contacted Brittany to complain. "The CEO promised that waste reduction would count for bonuses," he said, "and now that isn't what has happened." He explained that he had already begun working hard on waste reduction targets. "Had I known," he said, "I would have focused my efforts on something else. As a result, this has really impacted my performance and that isn't fair. I'm not a troublemaker and I don't want people to think I am, but I plan to file a grievance with the union. This isn't the first time I've been given the wrong information about bonuses, and I've had enough! I just wanted to give you a personal heads-up out of respect for your role as Committee chair. I didn't want to blindside you with this."

Brittany was understandably concerned about the potential for a union grievance. She called in the other committee members for a quick meeting. "We're in trouble," she told the committee. "Oscar is planning to file a grievance against us!" She shared the details of his work performance and the associated complaint. They agreed to think on it overnight and discuss it again in the morning.

Someone on the committee must have met up with Oscar in the hallway afterwards, because the next thing she knew Oscar was in her office literally shaking with anger. "How could you do that?" he demanded. "I warned you ahead of time that I would file a grievance out of courtesy, since you are Committee chair, but I didn't expect you to advertise it to everyone. It was supposed to be confidential! I report to two different people on that committee. How will I ever be evaluated fairly now that they see me as a troublemaker? I am *never* telling you anything again." With that he stormed out.

Brittany was stunned and chagrined. She had misunderstood Oscar's intent. She had honestly thought he wanted her to alert committee members that a grievance was coming. She tried to contact him and apologize, but he wanted nothing to do with her. The miscommunication had made her seem to be deliberately undermining him.

She knew how to resolve the dispute about the bonus itself—formal processes were in place to address that issue. But how could she fix things with Oscar and return to a trusting and satisfactory working relationship? Especially when he seemed convinced that she had intentionally betrayed him?

Discussion Questions

1. Identify the types of conflict being described in this scenario. What aspect of the conflict is most likely to turn highly toxic and why?

2. Discuss the linkages between poor communication and conflict that you observe in this scenario. In addition to poor communication, what else makes conflict more likely in this setting?

3. What (if anything) should Brittany do now to mend her relationship with Oscar?

MyManagementLab

Study, practise, and explore real management situations with these helpful resources:
- **Interactive Lesson Presentations:** Work through interactive presentations and assessments to test your knowledge of management concepts.
- **PIA (Personal Inventory Assessments):** Enhance your ability to connect with key concepts through these engaging self-reflection assessments.
- **Study Plan:** Check your understanding of chapter concepts with self-study quizzes.
- **Simulations:** Practise decision making in simulated management environments.

PERSONAL INVENTORY ASSESSMENT

Chapter 15
Foundations of Organization Structure

dotshock/123RF

Even for a start-up company with only a few employees, organizational structure is far more than simply deciding who's the boss and how many employees will be needed. The organization's structure will determine what relationships form, the formality of those relationships, and many work outcomes. The structure may also change as organizations grow and shrink, as management trends dictate, and as research uncovers better ways of maximizing productivity. In this chapter, we'll explore how structure impacts employee behaviour and the organization as a whole.[1]

WHAT IS ORGANIZATIONAL STRUCTURE?

An **organizational structure** defines how job tasks are formally divided, grouped, and coordinated. Managers need to address six key elements when they design their organization's structure: work specialization, departmentalization, chain of command, span of control, centralization and decentralization, and formalization.[2] Exhibit 15-1 presents each of these elements as an answer to an important structural question, and the following sections describe them.

Work Specialization

Henry Ford, one of the founders of modern assembly line manufacturing processes, is famous for demonstrating that work can be performed more efficiently if employees are allowed to specialize. Today, we use the term **work specialization**, or *division of labour*, to describe the degree to which activities in the organization are divided into separate jobs. The essence of work specialization is to divide a job into a number of steps, each completed by a separate individual. Individuals specialize in doing part of an activity rather than the entirety.

By the late 1940s, most manufacturing jobs in industrialized countries featured high work specialization. Because not all employees in an organization have the same skills, management saw specialization as a means of making the most efficient use of its employees' skills and successfully improving them through repetition. Less time is spent in changing tasks, putting away tools and equipment from a prior step, and getting ready for another. Equally importantly, it's easier and less costly to find and train workers to do specific and repetitive tasks, especially in highly sophisticated and complex operations. Could Cessna produce one Citation jet a year if one person had to build the entire plane alone? Not likely! Finally, work specialization increases efficiency and productivity by encouraging the creation of customized inventions and machinery.

Thus, for much of the first half of the 20th century, managers viewed work specialization as an unending source of increased productivity. And they were probably right. When specialization was not widely practised, its introduction almost always generated higher productivity. But by the 1960s, it increasingly seemed a good thing could be carried too far. Workers who were faced with the same repetitive tasks each day reported challenges including boredom, fatigue, stress, low productivity, poor quality, increased absenteeism, and high turnover. These problems offset the economic advantages of extreme specialization

The Key Question	The Answer Is Provided By:
1. To what degree are activities subdivided into separate jobs?	Work specialization
2. On what basis will jobs be grouped together?	Departmentalization
3. To whom do individuals and groups report?	Chain of command
4. How many individuals can a manager efficiently and effectively direct?	Span of control
5. Where does decision-making authority lie?	Centralization and decentralization
6. To what degree will there be rules and regulations to direct employees and managers?	Formalization

EXHIBIT 15-1 Key Design Questions and Answers for Designing the Proper Organizational Structure

EXHIBIT 15-2 Economies and Diseconomies of Work Specialization

(see Exhibit 15-2). Managers soon discovered that they could increase productivity by enlarging, rather than narrowing, the scope of job activities. This practice improves employee motivation and also allows for greater insight and creativity since employees are able to personally observe linkages between work activities that they could not observe when highly specialized. As we saw in Chapter 7, giving employees a variety of activities to do, allowing them to do a whole and complete job, and putting them into teams with interchangeable skills often achieved significantly higher output, with increased employee satisfaction.

One of the decisions managers must make today is how much specialization is best for the particular tasks they need to complete based on the characteristics of their workers. This requires careful thought since managers need to balance process efficiency with effective motivational strategies. There still may be advantages to be had in specialization, particularly for offices where job sharing and part-time work are prevalent.[3] This needs to be balanced, however, with an awareness of the mental health needs of employees.

Departmentalization

Once jobs have been divided through work specialization, they must be grouped so common tasks can be coordinated. The basis by which jobs are grouped is called **departmentalization**.

One of the most popular ways to group activities is by the *functions* performed. A manufacturing manager might organize a plant into engineering, accounting, manufacturing, personnel, and supply specialists departments. A hospital might have departments devoted to research, surgery, intensive care, accounting, and so forth. A professional hockey franchise might have departments for personnel, ticket sales, and travel and accommodations. The major advantage of this type of functional departmentalization is the efficiency gained from putting like specialists together.

We can also departmentalize jobs by the type of *product* or *service* the organization produces. Canadian Tire stores, for example, have sales staff who are permanently assigned to individual departments such automotive parts or sporting goods. The major advantage is that sales staff can be highly trained in one area, making them better able to help customers who are seeking technical advice or detailed product specifications. Ultimately this improves the customer experience, enhancing sales and brand loyalty.

When a firm is departmentalized on the basis of *geography*, or territory, the sales function, for instance, might have western, Prairie, eastern, and Maritime regions, each in effect a department organized around geography. This form of departmentalization is valuable when an organization's customers are scattered over a large geographic area and have special needs based on their location. Insurance companies such as Equitable, Great-West, and Sun Life often use this basis, as needs vary significantly by region. The insurance requirements of farmers in Saskatchewan, for example, will be quite different from those of urban dwellers in Montreal. Insurers use their local presence as a selling point, highlighting the strategic value of using this basis of departmentalization in their industry. The widely used marketing slogan "Like a good neighbor, State Farm is there" is an excellent example.[4]

Process departmentalization occurs when departments are organized around a particular business process. This is different from functional departmentalization because individuals with different skills and roles may all be involved in the same process and therefore be on the same team. For example, Energizer has separate factories for manufacturing their batteries and for packaging them. Each factory has a plant manager and full range of employees in HR, accounting, quality control, and production. Each group also includes relevant specialists. For example the manufacturing plant would employ chemists, whereas the packaging plant would employ marketing experts. By focusing on one process, each team is able to focus on and better excel in their key area.

A final category of departmentalization uses the particular *type* of customer the organization seeks to reach. Microsoft, for example, is organized around four customer markets: consumers, large corporations, software developers, and small businesses. Customers from each market have a common set of problems and needs best met by having specialists for each. Banks such as the Royal Bank and CIBC also use this basis of departmentalization, with different employees specializing in managing the needs of business accounts, high-income investors, etc.

Chain of Command

While "chain of command" was once a cornerstone of the design of organizations, it has far less importance today. A **chain of command** is an unbroken line of authority that extends from the top of the organization to the lowest echelon and clarifies who reports to whom.

We can't discuss the chain of command without also discussing *authority* and *unity of command*. **Authority** refers to the rights inherent in a managerial position to give orders and expect them to be obeyed. The principle of **unity of command** helps preserve the concept of an unbroken line of authority. It says a person should have one and only one superior to whom she reports and she should not attempt to go to higher levels in the hierarchy with requests or problems, nor should people at those higher levels approach her directly without going through her manager first. If the unity of command is broken, an employee might have to cope with conflicting demands or priorities from several superiors, as is often the case in the weaker "dotted-line" reporting relationships in some organizations.

Times change, and so do the basic tenets of organizational design. A low-level employee today can access information in seconds that was available only to top managers a generation ago, and many employees are empowered to make decisions previously reserved for management. Add the popularity of self-managed and cross-functional teams, and the creation of new structural designs that include multiple bosses, and you can see why authority and unity of command might appear to hold less relevance. Some organizations do still find they can be most productive by enforcing the chain of command, so the culture of the company is a relevant factor influencing the degree to which formal reported relationships are respected.

Span of Control

How many employees can a manager efficiently and effectively direct? This question of **span of control** is important, because it largely determines the number of levels and managers an organization creates. All things being equal, the wider or larger the span, the more efficient the organization.

EXHIBIT 15-3 Contrasting Spans of Control

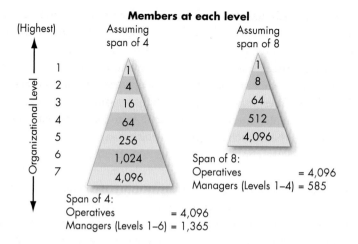

Members at each level

(Highest)

Organizational level

1
2
3
4
5
6
7

Assuming span of 4

1
4
16
64
256
1,024
4,096

Assuming span of 8

1
8
64
512
4,096

Span of 8:
Operatives = 4,096
Managers (Levels 1–4) = 585

Span of 4:
Operatives = 4,096
Managers (Levels 1–6) = 1,365

Assume two organizations each have about 4,100 operative-level employees. One has a uniform span of four and the other a span of eight. As Exhibit 15-3 illustrates, the wider span will have two fewer levels and approximately 800 fewer managers. If the average manager makes $50,000 a year, the wider span will save $40 million a year in management salaries! Obviously, wider spans are more efficient in terms of cost. However, at some point when supervisors no longer have time to provide the necessary leadership and support, they reduce effectiveness and employee performance suffers.

Narrow or small spans have their advocates. By keeping the span of control to five or six employees, a manager can maintain close control and have a high level of awareness about each individual worker and their needs.[5] But narrow spans have three major drawbacks. First, they're expensive because they add levels of management. Second, they make vertical communication in the organization more complex. The added levels of hierarchy slow down decision making and tend to isolate upper management. Third, narrow spans encourage overly tight supervision and discourage employee autonomy.

The trend in recent years has been to ward wider spans of control, as they are consistent with firms' efforts to reduce costs, cut overhead, speed decision making, increase flexibility, get closer to customers, and empower employees. However, to ensure performance doesn't suffer, organizations have been investing heavily in employee training. Managers recognize that they can handle a wider span best when employees know their jobs inside and out or can turn to coworkers when they have questions.

Centralization and Decentralization

Centralization refers to the degree to which decision making is concentrated at a single point in the organization. In *centralized* organizations, top managers make all the decisions, and lower-level managers merely carry out their directives. In organizations at the other extreme, *decentralized* decision making is pushed down to the managers closest to the action or even to work groups.

An organization characterized by centralization is inherently different structurally from one that's decentralized. A decentralized organization can act more quickly to solve problems, more people provide input into decisions, and employees are less likely to feel alienated from those who make decisions that affect their work lives. Recent research indicates that the effects of centralization and decentralization can be predicted: Centralized organizations are better for avoiding errors of commission (bad choices), while decentralized organizations are better for avoiding errors of omission (lost opportunities).[6]

Management efforts to make organizations more flexible and responsive have produced a recent trend toward decentralized decision making by lower-level managers, who are closer to the action and typically have more detailed knowledge about problems and customer needs than top managers. When Procter & Gamble empowered small groups of employees to make decisions about new-product development independently of the usual hierarchy, it was able to rapidly increase the proportion of new products ready for market.[7] Research investigating a large number of Finnish organizations demonstrated that companies with decentralized research and development offices in multiple locations were better at producing innovation than companies that centralized all research and development in a single office.[8]

Formalization

Formalization refers to the degree to which jobs within the organization are standardized. If a job is highly formalized, the incumbent has minimal discretion in what to do and when and how to do it. Employees can be expected always to handle the same input in exactly the same way, resulting in a consistent and uniform output. There are explicit job descriptions, lots of organizational rules, and clearly defined procedures covering work processes with high formalization. Where formalization is low, job behaviours are relatively unprogrammed, and employees have a great deal of freedom to exercise discretion in their work. Formalization not only eliminates the possibility of employees engaging in alternative behaviours, but even removes the need for employees to consider alternatives.

The degree of formalization can vary widely between and within organizations. In general, research from 94 high-technology Chinese firms showed that formalization is detrimental to team flexibility in decentralized organization structures, suggesting it does not work as well when duties are inherently interactive, or when there is a need to be flexible and innovative.[9] For example, publishing representatives who call on college and university professors to inform them of their company's new publications have a great deal of freedom in their jobs. They have only a general sales pitch, which they tailor as needed, and rules and procedures governing their behaviour may be little more than the requirement to submit a weekly sales report and suggestions on what to emphasize about forthcoming titles. At the other extreme, clerical and editorial employees in the same publishing houses may need to be at their desks by 8:00 A.M. and follow a set of precise procedures dictated by management.

To review, we have discussed in detail each of the six key elements of organizational structure that managers must address for their organizations: work specialization, departmentalization, chain of command, span of control, centralization and decentralization, and formalization. You probably have personal experience with at least some of the issues and opportunities that arise from the decisions leaders have made in your school or workplace on these factors, but it might not always be easy to discern their intentions. The organizational design, which can be depicted by a drawing of an organizational chart, can help you clarify leadership intentions. We discuss the common organizational designs in the next section.

COMMON ORGANIZATIONAL DESIGNS

We now turn to three of the more common organizational designs: the *simple structure*, the *bureaucracy*, and the *matrix structure*.

The Simple Structure

What do a small retail store, an electronics firm run by a hard-driving entrepreneur, and an airline's "war room" in the midst of a pilot's strike have in common? They probably all use the **simple structure**.

We can think of the simple structure in terms of what it is *not* rather than what it is. The simple structure is not elaborate. It has a low degree of departmentalization, wide spans of

The simple structure has a low degree of departmentalization, wide spans of control, authority centralized in a single person, and little formalization.

control, authority centralized in a single person, and little formalization. It is a "flat" organization; it usually has only two or three vertical levels, a loose body of employees, and one individual in whom decision-making authority is centralized. For this reason, the simple structure allows for the fastest possible decision making, which is why this organizational design is appropriate for "war room"–type situations.

Most companies start as a simple structure, and many innovative technology-based firms with short expected lifespans like cellphone app development firms remain compact by design.[10] The simple structure is most widely adopted in small businesses in which the manager and owner are one and the same. Consider a retail men's store owned and managed by Jack Gold. He employs five full-time salespeople, a cashier, and extra workers for weekends and holidays, but it is he who runs the show. Though this arrangement is typical of small businesses, large companies in times of crisis often simplify their structures as a means of focusing their resources.

The strength of the simple structure lies in its simplicity. It's fast, flexible, and inexpensive to operate, and accountability is clear. One major weakness is that it becomes increasingly inadequate as an organization grows, because low formalization and high centralization tend to create information overload at the top. As size increases, decision making typically becomes slower and can eventually come to a standstill as the single executive tries to continue making all the decisions. This proves the undoing of many small businesses. If the structure isn't changed and made more elaborate, the firm often loses momentum and can eventually fail. The simple structure's other weakness is that it's risky—everything depends on one person. One illness can literally destroy the organization's information and decision-making centre.

The Bureaucracy

Standardization! That's the key concept that underlies all bureaucracies. Consider the bank where you keep your checking account; the department store where you buy clothes; or the government offices that collect your taxes, enforce health regulations, or provide local fire protection. They all rely on standardized work processes for coordination and control.

The **bureaucracy** is characterized by highly routine operating tasks achieved through specialization, strictly formalized rules and regulations, tasks grouped into functional departments, centralized authority, narrow spans of control, and decision making that follows the chain of command. *Bureaucracy* is a dirty word in many people's minds. However, it does have advantages. Its primary strength is its ability to achieve standardized activities in a highly efficient manner. Putting like specialties together in functional departments results in economies of scale, minimum duplication of people and equipment, and employees who can "speak the same language" among their peers. Bureaucracies can get by with

Simple structures are very common in start-up companies, which makes them common in fast-paced industries such as software and bioscience.

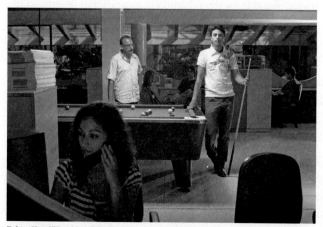
Zubin Shroff/Stockbyte/Getty Images

less talented—and hence less costly—middle- and lower-level managers, because rules and regulations substitute for managerial discretion. Standardized operations and high formalization allow decision making to be centralized. There is little need for innovative and experienced decision makers below the level of senior executives.

Bureaucratic specialization can create conflicts in which functional-unit goals override the overall goals of the organization. The other major weakness of a bureaucracy is something we've all witnessed: obsessive concern with following the rules. When cases don't precisely fit the rules, there is no room for modification. The bureaucracy is efficient only as long as employees confront familiar problems with programmed decision rules.

The Matrix Structure

You'll find the **matrix structure** in advertising agencies, aerospace firms, research and development laboratories, construction companies, hospitals, government agencies, universities, management consulting firms, and entertainment companies.[11] It combines two forms of departmentalization: functional and product. Companies that use matrix-like structures include ABB, Boeing, BMW, IBM, Energizer, and Procter & Gamble. Energizer was used as an example of process-based departmentalization earlier since they have separate facilities for manufacturing batteries and for packaging them. Within the packaging plants, however, there is also geographic departmentalization. For example, there is a Canadian packaging plant in Walkerton, Ontario responsible for all Canadian packaging and advertising, while a different group in St. Louis handles American packaging and advertising. This matrix structure is more efficient due to unique packaging needs in each market. In Canada, for instance, warning labels have to appear in both English and French, whereas in the U.S. English-and-Spanish labelling is more common.

The strength of functional departmentalization is putting like specialists together, which minimizes the number necessary while allowing the pooling and sharing of specialized resources across products. Its major disadvantage is the difficulty of coordinating the tasks of diverse functional specialists on time and within budget. Product departmentalization has exactly the opposite benefits and disadvantages. It facilitates coordination among specialties to achieve on-time completion and meet budget targets. It provides clear responsibility for all activities related to a product, but with duplication of activities and costs. The matrix attempts to gain the strengths of each while avoiding their weaknesses.

Exhibit 15-4 shows the matrix form in a university's department of business administration. The academic departments of accounting, decision and information systems, marketing, and so forth are functional units. Overlaid on them are specific programs (that is, products). Thus, members in a matrix structure have a dual chain of command: to their functional department and to their product group. A professor of accounting teaching an

Programs / Academic Departments	Undergraduate	Master's	PhD	Research	Executive Development	Community Service
Accounting						
Finance						
Decision and Information Systems						
Management						
Marketing						

EXHIBIT 15-4 Matrix Structure for a University Department of Business Administration

undergraduate course may report to the director of undergraduate programs as well as to the chairperson of the accounting department.

The strength of the matrix is its ability to facilitate coordination when the organization has a number of complex and interdependent activities. Direct and frequent contact between different specialties can let information permeate the organization and more quickly reach the people who need it. The matrix reduces "bureaupathologies"—the dual lines of authority reduce people's tendency to become so busy protecting their little worlds that the organization's goals become secondary.[12] A matrix also achieves economies of scale and facilitates the allocation of specialists by providing both the best resources and an effective way of ensuring their efficient deployment.

The major disadvantages of the matrix lie in the confusion it creates, its tendency to foster power struggles, and the stress it puts on individuals.[13] Without the unity-of-command concept, ambiguity about who reports to whom is significantly increased and often leads to conflict. It's not unusual for product managers to fight over getting the best specialists assigned to their products. Bureaucracy reduces the risk of power grabs by defining the rules of the game. When those rules are "up for grabs" in a matrix, power struggles between functional and product managers result. For individuals who desire security and absence of ambiguity, this work climate can be stressful. Reporting to more than one boss introduces role conflict, and unclear expectations introduce role ambiguity. The comfort of bureaucracy's predictability is replaced by insecurity and stress.

Did you recognize any of your organizations as having a simple, bureaucracy, or matrix structure? It wouldn't be surprising if you said no. Increasingly, leaders have been exploring new design options for their organizations, which we will discuss next.

NEW DESIGN OPTIONS

Senior managers in a number of organizations have been developing new structural options with fewer layers of hierarchy and more emphasis on opening the boundaries of the organization.[14] In this section, we describe two such designs: the *virtual organization* and the *boundaryless organization*. We'll also discuss how efforts to reduce bureaucracy and increase strategic focus have made downsizing routine.

The Virtual Organization

Why own when you can rent? This question captures the essence of the **virtual organization** (also sometimes called the *network*, or *modular*, *organization*), typically a small, core organization that outsources its major business functions.[15] In structural terms, the virtual organization is highly centralized, with little or no departmentalization.

The prototype of the virtual structure is today's movie-making organization. In Hollywood's golden era, movies were made by huge, vertically integrated corporations. Studios such as MGM, Warner Brothers, and 20th Century Fox owned large movie lots and employed thousands of full-time specialists—set designers, camera people, film editors, directors, and even actors. Today, most movies are made by a collection of individuals and small companies who come together and make films project by project.[16] This structural form allows each project to be staffed with the talent best suited to its demands, rather than just with the people employed by the studio. It minimizes bureaucratic overhead because there is no lasting organization to maintain. And it lessens long-term risks and their costs because there *is* no long term—a team is assembled for a finite period and then disbanded. Finally, this approach gives movie companies more geographic flexibility because they are no longer tied to large, expensive studios. This has helped encourage the blossoming of film industry communities in places such as Vancouver, further increasing flexibility.

EXHIBIT 15-5   A Virtual Organization

Philip Rosedale co-founded a virtual company called LoveMachine (now called SendLove) that lets employees send brief electronic messages to one another acknowledging a job well done; the messages can then be used to facilitate company bonuses. The company has no full-time software development staff—instead, the company outsources assignments to freelancers who submit bids for projects like debugging software or designing new features. Programmers work from around the world, including Russia, India, Canada, Australia, and the United States.[17] Similarly, Newman's Own, the food products company founded by actor Paul Newman, sells hundreds of millions of dollars in food every year, yet employs only 32 people.[18] This is possible because it outsources almost everything: manufacturing, procurement, shipping, and quality control.

Exhibit 15-5 shows a virtual organization in which management outsources all the primary functions of the business. The core of the organization is a small group of executives whose job is to oversee directly any activities done in-house and to coordinate relationships with the other organizations that manufacture, distribute, and perform crucial functions for the virtual organization. The dotted lines represent the relationships typically maintained under contracts. In essence, managers in virtual structures spend most of their time coordinating and controlling external relations, typically by way of computer network links.

The major advantage of the virtual organization is its flexibility, which allows individuals with an innovative idea and little money to successfully compete against larger, more established organizations. Virtual organizations also save a great deal of money by eliminating permanent offices and hierarchical roles.[19]

Virtual organizations' drawbacks have become increasingly clear as their popularity has grown.[20] They are in a state of perpetual flux and reorganization, which means roles, goals, and responsibilities are unclear, setting the stage for political behaviour. Cultural alignment and shared goals can be lost because of the low degree of interaction among members. Team members who are geographically dispersed and communicate infrequently find it difficult to share information and knowledge, which can limit innovation and slow response time. Ironically, some virtual organizations are less adaptable and innovative than those with well-established communication and collaboration networks. A leadership presence that reinforces the organization's purpose and facilitates communication is thus especially valuable.

The Boundaryless Organization

General Electric's former chairperson, Jack Welch, coined the term **boundaryless organization** to describe what he wanted GE to become: a "family grocery store."[21] That is, in spite of GE's monstrous size (2013 revenues were $142.5 billion),[22] Welch wanted to eliminate *vertical* and *horizontal* boundaries within the company and break down *external* barriers between the company and its customers and suppliers. The boundaryless organization seeks to eliminate the chain of command, have limitless spans of control, and replace departments with empowered teams.

Although GE has not yet achieved this ideal state—and probably never will—it has made significant progress. So have other large multinational companies, such as Hewlett-Packard, AT&T, Motorola, and 3M. Let's see what a boundaryless organization looks like and what some firms are doing to make it a reality.

By removing vertical boundaries, management flattens the hierarchy and minimizes status and rank. Cross-hierarchical teams (which include top executives, middle managers, supervisors, and operative employees), participative decision-making practices, and the use of 360-degree performance appraisals (in which peers and others above and below the employee evaluate performance) are examples of what GE does to break down vertical boundaries.

Functional departments create horizontal boundaries that stifle interaction among functions, product lines, and units. The way to reduce those boundaries is to replace functional departments with cross-functional teams and organize activities around processes. Some AT&T units prepare annual budgets based not on functions or departments but on processes, such as the maintenance of a worldwide telecommunications network. Another way to lower horizontal barriers is to rotate people through different functional areas using lateral transfers. This approach turns specialists into generalists.

When fully operational, the boundaryless organization breaks down geographic barriers. Today, most large Canadian companies see themselves as global corporations; many, like Farrows and Research in Motion, do as much business overseas as in Canada, and others are working to incorporate new geographic regions into their structure.

The boundaryless organization approach is sometimes need-based. Such is the case for Chinese companies, which have made 93 acquisitions in the oil and gas industry since 2008 to meet the forecasted demand their resources in China cannot meet.[23] The boundaryless organization provides one solution because it considers geography more of a tactical, logistical issue than a structural one. In short, the goal is to break down cultural barriers.

One way to do so is through strategic alliances.[24] Firms such as NEC Corporation, Boeing, and Apple have strategic alliances or joint partnerships with dozens of companies. These alliances blur the distinction between one organization and another as employees work on joint projects. Research from 119 international joint ventures (IJVs) in China indicated that the partnerships allowed firms to learn from each other and obtain higher new product performance, especially where a strong learning culture existed.[25] Other companies allow customers to perform functions previously done by management. Some AT&T units receive bonuses based on customer evaluations of the teams that serve them. Finally, telecommuting is blurring organizational boundaries. The security analyst with Merrill Lynch who does her job from her ranch in Alberta, or the software designer in Yellowknife who works for an American firm located in New York, are just two of the millions of workers operating outside the physical boundaries of their employers' premises.

The Leaner Organization: Downsizing

The goal of the new organizational forms we've described is to improve agility by creating a lean, focused, and flexible organization. "Lean" does not always imply that people will lose their jobs. Lean organizations maximize process efficiencies wherever they can, so "lean" initiatives might include reducing waste, finding less expensive service delivery modes (providing eBooks rather than printed user manuals, for example), or even minimizing the need for warehouse space through careful inventory management. One common way to do more with less is by adjusting job tasks, processes, and product offerings so that fewer people are needed to complete the work. This is why lean organizations are often associated with downsizing. *Downsizing* is a systematic effort to make an organization leaner by closing locations, reducing staff, or selling off business units that don't add value.

The radical shrinking of Target Corporation in late 2014 and early 2015 was a case of downsizing to survive after a significant strategic failure. Target made an unsuccessful bid to launch their brand in Canada. Their eventual retreat from the Canadian marketplace resulted in 17,600 layoffs, a number large enough to impact federal employment figures for the quarter in which most dismissals took place.[26]

Other firms downsize to direct all their efforts toward their core competencies or because of changes in technology or market conditions. Both of the latter have occurred in Canada's energy sector. Technological advances have made some jobs redundant, while depressed oil and gas prices have forced companies to lower production rates. Between September 2014 and May 2015, over 13,000 energy-related jobs disappeared in Alberta alone. For example, Husky Energy was forced to lay off 1,000 workers, Penn West Petroleum parted with 400, the Canadian Association of Oilwell Drilling Contractors let 3,400 go, and Cenovus Energy shed 1,200 jobs.[27] Some companies focus on lean management techniques as part of downsizing efforts to reduce bureaucracy and speed decision making. Starbucks adopted lean initiatives in 2009, which encompassed all levels of management and also focused on faster barista techniques and manufacturing processes. Customers have generally applauded the shortened wait times and product consistency at this well-run corporation, while the company has capitalized on strategic downsizing opportunities. Starbucks continues to reap returns from its lean initiatives, posting notable revenue gains each quarter.[28]

Despite the advantages of being a lean organization, the impact of downsizing on organizational performance has been a source of controversy.[29] Reducing the size of the workforce has an immediately positive outcome in the form of lower wage costs. Companies downsizing to improve strategic focus often see positive effects on stock prices after the announcement. A recent example of this is Russia's Gorky Automobile Factory (GAZ), which realized a profit for the first time in many years after President Bo Andersson fired 50,000 workers, half the workforce.[30] On the other hand, among companies that only cut employees but don't restructure, profits and stock prices usually decline. Part of the problem is the effect of downsizing on employee attitudes. Employees who remain often feel worried about future layoffs and may be less committed to the organization.[31] Stress reactions can lead to increased sickness absences, lower concentration on the job, and lower creativity. In companies that don't invest much in their employees, downsizing can lead to more voluntary turnover, so vital human capital is lost. The result is a company that is more anemic than lean.

Companies can reduce negative impacts by preparing in advance, thus alleviating some employee stress and strengthening support for the new direction.[32] Listed below are some

IRC/Shutterstock

The oil and gas sector experienced significant layoffs in 2015 as economic conditions and associated price fluctuations forced many companies to reduce production and downsize their workforce.

effective strategies for downsizing, most closely linked to the principles for organizational justice we've discussed:

- **Investment.** Companies that downsize to focus on core competencies are more effective when they invest in high-involvement work practices afterward.

- **Communication.** When employers make efforts to discuss downsizing with employees early, employees are less worried about the outcomes and feel the company is taking their perspective into account.

- **Participation.** Employees worry less if they can participate in the process in some way. Voluntary early-retirement programs or severance packages can help achieve leanness without layoffs.

- **Assistance.** Severance pay and packages, extended healthcare benefits, and job search assistance demonstrate that a company cares about its employees and honours their contributions.

In short, companies that make themselves lean can be more agile, efficient, and productive—but only if they make cuts carefully and help employees through the process.

No doubt you are well aware by now that there is considerable variation in the structures an organization may choose. Let's take a moment to next consider why structures differ and what organizational strategies may be most conducive to certain structures.

WHY DO STRUCTURES DIFFER?

We've described organizational designs ranging from the highly structured bureaucracy to the amorphous boundaryless organization. The other designs we discussed exist somewhere in between.

Exhibit 15-6 recaps our discussions by presenting two extreme models of organizational design. One we'll call the **mechanistic model**. It's generally synonymous with bureaucracy in that it has highly standardized processes for work, high formalization, and more managerial hierarchy. The other extreme, the **organic model**, looks a lot like the boundaryless organization. It's flat, has fewer formal procedures for making decisions, has multiple decision makers, and favors flexible practices.[33]

EXHIBIT 15-6 Mechanistic Versus Organic Models

The Mechanistic Model

- High specialization
- Rigid departmentalization
- Clear chain of command
- Narrow spans of control
- Centralization
- High formalization

The Organic Model

- Cross-functional teams
- Cross-hierarchical teams
- Free flow of information
- Wide spans of control
- Decentralization
- Low formalization

With these two models in mind, let's ask a few questions: Why are some organizations structured along more mechanistic lines, whereas others follow organic characteristics? What forces influence the choice of design? In this section, we present the major causes or determinants of an organization's structure.[34]

Organizational Strategies

Because structure is a means to achieve objectives, and objectives derive from the organization's overall strategy, it's only logical that structure should follow strategy. If management significantly changes the organization's strategy, the structure must change to accommodate.[35] Most current strategy frameworks focus on three strategy dimensions—innovation, cost minimization, and imitation—and the structural design that works best with each.[36]

To what degree does an organization introduce major new products or services? An **innovation strategy** strives to achieve meaningful and unique innovations. Obviously, not all firms pursue innovation. The magazine *Canadian Business* names Canada's most innovative companies every March. In 2015, companies such as online education platform creators D2L, eco-lighting company Lumenpulse, grocer Loblaws, and the medical marijuana firm Tweed all made the list.[37] Innovative firms will use competitive pay and benefits to attract top candidates and motivate employees to take risks. Some degree of mechanistic structure can actually benefit innovation. Well-developed communication channels, policies for enhancing long-term commitment, and clear channels of authority all may make it easier for rapid changes to occur smoothly.

An organization pursuing a **cost-minimization strategy** tightly controls costs, refrains from incurring unnecessary expenses, and cuts prices in selling a basic product. This describes the strategy pursued by Walmart and the makers of generic or store-label grocery products. Cost-minimizing organizations pursue fewer policies meant to develop commitment among their workforce.

Organizations following an **imitation strategy** try to both minimize risk and maximize opportunity for profit, moving new products or entering new markets only after innovators have proven their viability. Mass-market fashion manufacturers that copy designer styles follow this strategy, as do firms such as Hewlett-Packard and Caterpillar. They follow smaller and more innovative competitors with their products, but only after competitors have demonstrated that the market is there.

Organization Size

An organization's size significantly affects its structure. Organizations that employ 2,000 or more people tend to have more specialization, more departmentalization, more vertical levels, and more rules and regulations than small organizations. However, size becomes less important as an organization expands. Why? At around 2,000 employees, an organization is already fairly mechanistic; 500 more employees won't have much impact. But adding 500 employees to an organization of only 300 is likely to significantly shift it toward a more mechanistic structure.

Technology

Technology describes the way an organization transfers inputs into outputs. Every organization has at least one technology for converting financial, human, and physical resources into products or services. Ford Motor Company uses an assembly line process to make its products. Colleges and universities might use a number of instructional technologies—the ever-popular lecture method, case analyses, experiential exercises, programmed learning, online instruction, and distance learning. Nevertheless, organizational structures adapt to their technology.

Numerous studies have examined the technology–structure relationship.[38] What differentiates technologies is their *degree of routineness*. Routine activities are characterized by automated and standardized operations. Examples are injection-mould production of plastic knobs, automated processing of sales transactions, and the printing and binding of books. Non-routine activities are customized and require frequent revision and updating: furniture restoring, custom shoemaking, genetic research, and the writing and editing of books. In general, organizations engaged in non-routine activities prefer organic structures, whereas those performing routine activities prefer mechanistic structures.

Environment

An organization's **environment** includes outside institutions or forces that can affect its performance, such as suppliers, customers, competitors, government regulatory agencies, and public pressure groups. Dynamic environments create significantly more uncertainty for managers than static ones. To minimize uncertainty in key market arenas, managers may broaden their structure to sense and respond to threats. For example, most companies, including Pepsi and WestJet, have added social networking departments to counter negative information posted on blogs. Or companies may form strategic alliances with other companies.

Any organization's environment has three dimensions: capacity, volatility, and complexity.[39] *Capacity* refers to the degree to which the environment can support growth. Rich and growing environments generate excess resources, which can buffer the organization in times of relative scarcity.

Volatility describes the degree of instability in the environment. A dynamic environment with a high degree of unpredictable change makes it difficult for management to make accurate predictions. Because information technology changes at such a rapid pace, for instance, more organizations' environments are becoming volatile.

Finally, *complexity* reflects the number of competitors in an industry, the degree of difference in product offerings and production methods between competitors, and how the various environmental elements are managed and controlled. Simple environments—such as the tobacco industry, in which the methods of production, competition, regulatory pressures, and the like haven't changed in quite some time— are highly concentrated. Complex environments characterized by multifaceted differences between competitors and dispersion—such as the broadband industry—are diverse.

Given this three-dimensional definition of *environment*, we can offer some general conclusions about environmental uncertainty and structural arrangements. The more scarce, dynamic, and complex the environment, the more organic a structure should be. The more abundant, stable, and simple the environment, the more the mechanistic structure will be preferred.

While factors such as the organization's environment can provide clues as to which type of structure may be most effective, the best structure for any organization is one that fits the organization's strategy . . . and its people. To conclude our exploration on the foundations of organization structure, we will focus on the effects of structure on behaviour.

ORGANIZATIONAL DESIGNS AND EMPLOYEE BEHAVIOUR

We opened this chapter by implying that an organization's structure can have significant effects on its members. What might those effects be?

A review of the evidence leads to a pretty clear conclusion: You can't generalize! Not everyone prefers the freedom and flexibility of organic structures. Different factors stand out in different structures. In highly formalized, heavily structured, mechanistic organizations, the level of fairness in formal policies and procedures is a very important predictor of satisfaction. In more personal, individually adaptive organic organizations, employees value

Kurhan/Fotolia

interpersonal justice more.[40] Some people are most productive and satisfied when work tasks are standardized and ambiguity minimized—that is, in mechanistic structures. So, any discussion of the effect of organizational design on employee behaviour has to address individual differences. To do so, let's consider employee preferences for work specialization, span of control, and centralization.[41]

The evidence generally indicates that *work specialization* contributes to higher employee productivity—but at the price of reduced job satisfaction. However, work specialization is not an unending source of higher productivity. Problems start to surface, and productivity begins to suffer, when the human diseconomies of doing repetitive and narrow tasks overtake the economies of specialization. As the workforce has become more highly educated and desirous of jobs that are intrinsically rewarding, we seem to reach the point at which productivity begins to decline as a function of specialization more quickly than in the past. While decreased productivity often prompts companies to add oversight and inspection roles, the better answer may be to reorganize work functions and accountability.[42]

A segment of the workforce still prefers the routine and repetitiveness of highly specialized jobs. Some individuals want work that makes minimal intellectual demands and provides the security of routine; for them, high work specialization is a source of job satisfaction. The question, of course, is whether they represent 2 percent of the workforce or 52 percent. Research suggests the "real" answer is closer to 2 percent than 52 percent. Given that some self-selection operates in the choice of careers, we might conclude that negative behavioural outcomes from high specialization are most likely to surface in professional jobs occupied by individuals with a high need for personal growth and diversity.

It is probably safe to say no evidence supports a relationship between *span of control* and employee satisfaction or performance. Although it is intuitive that large spans might lead to higher employee performance because they provide more distant supervision and more opportunity for personal initiative, the research fails to support this notion. Some people like to be left alone; others prefer the security of a boss who is quickly available at all times. Consistently with several of the contingency theories of leadership discussed in Chapter 12, we would expect factors such as employees' experiences and abilities and the degree of structure in their tasks to explain when wide or narrow spans of control are likely to contribute to their performance and job satisfaction. However, some evidence indicates that a *manager's* job satisfaction increases as the number of employees supervised increases.

We find fairly strong evidence linking *centralization* and job satisfaction. In general, less centralized organizations have a greater amount of autonomy. And autonomy appears positively related to job satisfaction. But, again, while one employee may value freedom, another may find autonomous environments frustratingly ambiguous.

Our conclusion: To maximize employee performance and satisfaction, managers must take individual differences, such as experience, personality, and the work task, into account. Culture should factor in, too. National culture impacts organizational culture norms, which in turns impact worker expectations and preferences for certain types of organizational structures. For example, people from cultures that score high on uncertainty avoidance and power distance often prefer the more rigid, formalized structure inherent in mechanistic models. Collectivistic cultures, including many First Nations cultures, tend to prefer structures that enable consensus-based decision making, pushing them toward organic models. Power distance and uncertainty avoidance will also influence the span of control and degree of centralization considered preferable.[43] We will explore these relationships in more detail in Chapter 16 when we discuss the influence of national culture on organizational culture.

Meanwhile we can draw one obvious insight: All things being equal, people don't select employers randomly. They are attracted to, are selected by, and stay with organizations that suit their personal preferences and characteristics.[44] Job candidates who prefer predictability are likely to seek out and take employment in mechanistic structures, and those who want autonomy are more likely to end up in an organic structure. Thus, the effect of structure on employee behaviour is undoubtedly reduced when the selection process facilitates proper matching of individual characteristics with organizational characteristics. Furthermore, companies should strive to establish, promote, and maintain the unique identities of their structures since skilled employees may quit as a result of dramatic changes.[45]

SUMMARY

- An organization's internal structure contributes to explaining and predicting behaviour. That is, in addition to individual and group factors, the structural relationships in which people work have a bearing on employee attitudes and behaviour.

- Key aspects of structure to consider include work specialization, basis of departmentalization, chain of command, span of control, and degree of centralization and formality.

- Organizational structures can be put into broad categories, each with their own unique characteristics. Mechanistic and organic structures are two of the key categories.

- Other types of structures seen more and more often in today's workplace include matrix, virtual, and boundaryless organizations.

- Alignment between individual preferences and structure can contribute to maximizing productivity, fit, and satisfaction.

IMPLICATIONS FOR MANAGERS

- Specialization can make operations more efficient, but remember that excessive specialization can create dissatisfaction and reduce motivation.

- Avoid designing rigid hierarchies that overly limit employees' empowerment and autonomy.

- Balance the advantages of virtual and boundaryless organizations against the potential pitfalls before adding flexible workplace options.

- Downsize your organization to realize major cost savings, and focus the company around core competencies—but only if necessary, because downsizing can have a significant negative impact on employee affect.

- Consider the scarcity, dynamism, and complexity of the environment, and balance the organic and mechanistic elements when designing an organizational structure.

As a newly hired employee, what benefit is there to studying the organizational chart for your company? What type of insight might this practice give you to help you navigate the political landscape? What can't the organizational chart tell you or help you with? Explain your answer.

In the Personal Inventory Assessment found in MyManagementLab, take the assessment: Organizational Structure.

SELF-REFLECTION ACTIVITY

What sort of organizational structure would be the best fit for you? The answer depends on things like your personality and fundamental values. In the Personal Inventory Assessment found in MyManagementLab, take the Organizational Structure Assessment to determine which type of organizational structure would be the best fit for you. This process can help to direct your attention to organizations and industries with the characteristics most likely to match your personality and work preferences, ultimately leading to higher job satisfaction and stronger performance.

Unfortunately, we don't always have the luxury of choosing our work environment, especially when labour market conditions are poor. If you find yourself in an organizational structure poorly suited to your personality (for example, one that is highly regulated and bureaucratic when you prefer open, organic structures with few formal rules), what is the best way to cope? What strategies might managers use to lessen some of the weaknesses or frustrations associated with highly bureaucratic structures? What strategies might they use to lessen some of the weaknesses and frustrations associated with flexible organic structures?

The not-for-profit organization Revitalisation St. Pierre is tasked with a dual mission of poverty reduction and facilitating the revitalization of the St. Pierre neighbourhood, a socioeconomically disadvantaged area within Montreal. Revitalisation is run by and for local residents. David Marshall, its executive director, is committed to keeping control of the agency in the hands of neighbourhood citizens.

How did they go about embedding community participation into their organizational structure? For starters, they took inspiration from practices that have emerged from the cooperative business model. Cooperatives are a unique form of business ownership characterized by three things: their express purpose is to meet the needs of members (not maximize profits), each member gets a voice (usually in the form of voting rights), and profits are returned back to the members.

In the case of Revitalisation St. Pierre, all strategic and most tactical decisions are made by committee. These committees have 6 to 20 members, at least 50 percent of whom must be local citizens. One such committee was formed to identify the agency's priorities when they were first established in 2003. This resulted in the identification of four priorities: the revitalization of the main street, increased access to outdoor sports facilities, the creation of a community festival, and the creation of a general store that would stock low-cost fruits and vegetables. Each of these projects has since been realized and expanded upon, in part because community involvement has helped ensure the ongoing engagement and commitment of local volunteers. Their organizational structure therefore encourages strong focus on individual projects (each one gets its own committee) and helps to avoid the "volunteer fatigue" common within other service agencies.

David Marshall says that the small size of the organization helps keep formalization to a minimum, allowing for a responsive organic structure that evolves comparatively easily as the agency expands and broadens its mandate. "Having fewer staff and letting the people who actually use our services decide where to focus our attention helps keep us relevant," he explains. "It also fosters creativity and innovation." For example, in 2003 knowledge about how to prepare the most affordable forms of fresh food was identified as an issue, resulting in the creation of a community kitchen and learning space. This added a whole new branch to their structure and resulted in some reshuffling of reporting relationships, but the change was readily accommodated and communication was relatively simple considering the magnitude of the change.

The organization's success has been based in part on their organic consensus-driven model and their ability to respond with rapid structural changes as needed. Now Revitalisation is continuing to expand. They have purchased a truck to allow them to open mobile food markets in other impoverished areas of the city, gotten involved in community gardens, and expanded their sport and recreational programs.

It remains to be seen whether their existing structure can handle the growth. What will happen when staff levels increase to the point where more specialization is needed? How will communication flow then? How can they maintain community input on priorities if there start being 40 project committees instead of five or six? How can Revitalisation St. Pierre maintain their positive momentum?

Discussion Questions

1. What organizational structure–related problems do you anticipate emerging as Revitalisation continues to expand and grow?

2. Should they change their organizational structure in response to growth? If so, how? What will the likely impact on their mandate and mission be?

3. Do for-profit companies experience similar "growing pains"? How might their issues differ from those of not-for-profit and charitable organizations? How might they be the same?

MINI CASE STRUCTURING FOR MULTIPLE PURPOSES—FINDING THE RIGHT BALANCE

Jamel stared at the organization chart in front of him one more time and sighed. He still wasn't sure about the right thing to do. Jamel owned a chain of specialty gastropubs. His pubs were located in 10 diverse areas across Southern Ontario, each with a very different consumer profile. His Scarborough restaurant, for example, was in a neighbourhood dominated by young immigrant families from Southeast Asia, his Oshawa pub was near several factories at the outskirts of the city and attracted large numbers of farmers and older line workers, his Mississauga pub was frequented by middle-aged office workers from a wide range of backgrounds, and his Georgetown pub attracted a retired European crowd.

Early on, Jamal had decided that the best way to manage restaurants in such disparate neighbourhoods was to decentralize decision making. He therefore departmentalized several key functions by geography, including food purchasing, menu planning, hiring, and advertising. Each store had its own general manager, head chef, assistant head chef, administrator (for food purchasing, advertising and marketing contract administration, hiring, etc.), part-time assistant administrative clerk (for staff scheduling and payroll), and head waiter. There were also line cooks, dishwashers, servers, bartenders, and bussers.

Exhibit 15-7 outlines the reporting relationships within each individual restaurant. The general manager reported directed to Jamal. The administrator reported to the general manager. The head chef, who was responsible for menu planning, experimentation, kitchen staff culinary training, and cooking for special VIP events, also reported to the general manager. The assistant head chef reported to the head chef and managed the line cooks and dishwashers. The assistant head chef was the primary supervisor day to day in the kitchen, did a lot of cooking personally, and was responsible for expediting order (ensuring quality control). The assistant administrative clerk, head waiter, and bartenders reported to the administrator. Bussers and servers reported to the head waiter.

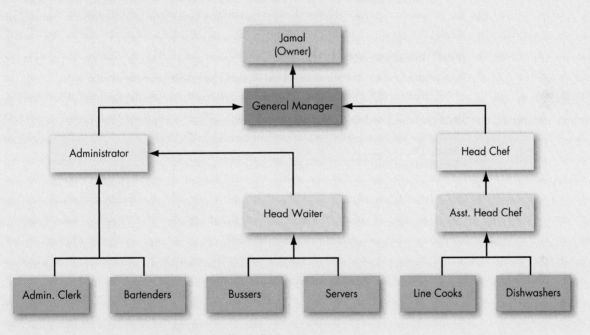

EXHIBIT 15-7 Reporting Structure in Each Restaurant

The staff members of each individual restaurant were trained separately and knew the menus and processes used in their own establishment. The processes were established by the general managers and were not necessarily consistent between facilities. This being so, it was difficult for a server or bartender in one restaurant to cover a shift in another. This was inconvenient, as unexpected turnover was not uncommon in the industry and special events like a local festival might drastically (but temporarily) increase demand at one location. In addition, each restaurant had separate contracts with food suppliers and local advertisers such as radio shows and newspapers. These contracts were negotiated by the administrators, who send out bids and made plans in isolation.

Three years after initially deciding upon decentralization and geographic departmentalization, Jamal is now wondering if he made the right choice. Each pub has high customer satisfaction ratings and high numbers of repeat customers. Each pub fits well into its community and has become a social hub for the neighbourhood. His payroll costs, however, represent anywhere from 42 to 47 percent of gross sales. He has reviewed industry benchmarks published by expert Baker Tilly, and has noticed that comparable full-service restaurants have average staffing costs that are only 30 to 35 percent of their gross sales. His pubs simply aren't profitable enough.

Jamal has tried controlling food costs and has invested in staff training and process efficiencies, but his cost structure remains high due to the excessive staffing costs. The head chef roles in particular require comparatively high salaries in order to attract competent talent who will generate excitement and contribute to the gastropub brand.

Jamal is afraid that any changes or standardization will make him lose his market focus and competitive edge. Layoffs might be the answer, but then customer service will be impacted and he will have even fewer people available to call on when sporadic staffing shortages occur. After careful consideration he decided on a structure that would look like this . . .

Discussion Questions

1. What type of organizational structure would you recommend for Jamal? Why?

2. What are the risks of your proposed structure? How might you counter those risks?

PERSONAL INVENTORY ASSESSMENT

MyManagementLab

Study, practise, and explore real management situations with these helpful resources:

• **Interactive Lesson Presentations:** Work through interactive presentations and assessments to test your knowledge of management concepts.

• **PIA (Personal Inventory Assessments):** Enhance your ability to connect with key concepts through these engaging self-reflection assessments.

• **Study Plan:** Check your understanding of chapter concepts with self-study quizzes.

• **Simulations:** Practise decision making in simulated management environments.

Chapter 16
Organizational Culture

LEARNING OBJECTIVES

After studying this chapter, you should be able to:

1 Describe the common characteristics of organizational culture.

2 Compare the functional and dysfunctional effects of organizational culture on people and the organization.

3 Identify the factors that create and sustain an organization's culture.

6 Explain how culture is transmitted to employees.

7 Demonstrate how an ethical culture can be encouraged and fostered.

8 Describe a positive organizational culture.

9 Assess how national culture can affect the way organizational culture is interpreted.

A strong organizational culture provides stability to an organization. For some organizations, culture can be a major barrier to change. In this chapter, we show that every organization has a culture that, depending on its strength, can have a significant influence on the attitudes and behaviours of organization members.

The culture of any organization, although it may be hard to measure precisely, nevertheless exists and is generally recognized by its employees. We call this variable *organizational culture*. Just as national cultures have norms and taboos that dictate how each member should act toward fellow members and outsiders, organizations have cultures that govern how members behave. In this chapter, we'll discuss just what organizational culture is, how it affects employee attitudes and behaviour, where it comes from, and whether it can be changed.

WHAT IS ORGANIZATIONAL CULTURE?

An executive once was asked what he thought *organizational culture* meant. He gave essentially the same answer U.S. Supreme Court Justice Potter Stewart gave in defining pornography: "I can't define it, but I know it when I see it." In this section, we propose one definition of organizational culture and review several related ideas.

A Definition of Organizational Culture

An organization's culture develops over many years and is rooted in deeply held values to which employees are strongly committed.

Organizational culture refers to a system of shared meaning held by members that distinguishes the organization from other organizations.[1] Seven primary characteristics seem to capture the essence of an organization's culture:[2]

1. *Innovation and risk taking.* The degree to which employees are encouraged to be innovative and take risks.
2. *Attention to detail.* The degree to which employees are expected to exhibit precision, analysis, and attention to detail.
3. *Outcome orientation.* The degree to which management focuses on results or outcomes rather than on the techniques and processes used to achieve them.
4. *People orientation.* The degree to which management decisions take into consideration the effect of outcomes on people within the organization.
5. *Team orientation.* The degree to which work activities are organized around teams rather than individuals.
6. *Aggressiveness.* The degree to which people are aggressive and competitive rather than easygoing.
7. *Stability.* The degree to which organizational activities emphasize maintaining the status quo in contrast to growth.

Each of these characteristics exists on a continuum from low to high. Appraising the organization on these seven dimensions, then, gives a composite picture of its culture and a basis for the shared understanding members have about the organization, how things are done in it, and the way they are supposed to behave.

Culture Is a Descriptive Term

Organizational culture shows how employees perceive the characteristics of an organization, not whether they like them—that is, it's a descriptive term. Research on organizational culture has sought to measure how employees see the organization: Does it encourage teamwork? Does it reward innovation? Does it stifle initiative? In contrast, job satisfaction seeks to measure how employees feel about the organization's expectations, reward practices, and the like. Although the two terms have overlapping characteristics, keep in mind that *organizational culture* is descriptive, whereas *job satisfaction* is evaluative.

Do Organizations Have Uniform Cultures?

Organizational culture represents a perception the organization's members hold in common. We should therefore expect individuals with different backgrounds or at different levels in the organization to describe its culture in similar terms.[3]

That doesn't mean, however, that there are no subcultures. Most large organizations have a dominant culture and numerous subcultures.[4] A **dominant culture** expresses the **core values** a majority of members share and that give the organization its distinct personality.[5] **Subcultures** tend to develop in large organizations to reflect common problems or experiences members face in the same department or location. The purchasing department can have a subculture that includes the core values of the dominant culture plus additional values unique to members of that department.

If organizations were composed only of numerous subcultures, organizational culture as an independent variable would be significantly less powerful. It is the "shared meaning" aspect of culture that makes it such a potent device for guiding and shaping behaviour. That's what allows us to say, for example, that WestJet's culture values customer care and service more than rigid compliance with formal policies, and to use that information to better understand the behaviour of WestJet's executives and employees.[6]

Strong Versus Weak Cultures

It's possible to differentiate between strong and weak cultures.[7] The terms strong and weak should not be confused with positive or negative. Strength refers to the degree to which a culture has been widely accepted and solidified, not the nature of the culture itself. If most employees (responding to management surveys) have the same opinions about the organization's mission and values, the culture is strong; if opinions vary widely, the culture is weak.

In a **strong culture**, the organization's core values are both intensely held and widely shared.[8] The more members who accept the core values and the greater their commitment, the stronger the culture and the greater its influence on member behaviour. This is because the high degree of shared values and intensity create a climate of high behavioural control. Employees know in no uncertain terms what is expected of them and these expectations go a long way in shaping their behaviour. Many small, remote Inuit communities have services and stores that operate based on a cooperative business model in which all adult members have decision-making influence and voting rights. The relative homogeneity among community members combined with familiarity and shared values makes many of these organizations an excellent example of strong organizational cultures.

A strong culture, when that culture is positive, should reduce employee turnover, because it demonstrates high agreement about what the organization represents. Such unanimity of purpose builds cohesiveness, loyalty, and organizational commitment. These qualities, in turn, lessen employees' propensity to leave.[9] One study found that the more employees agreed on customer orientation in a service organization, the higher the profitability of the business unit.[10] Another study found that when team managers and team members disagreed about perceptions of organizational support, there were more negative moods among team members, and the performance of teams was lower.[11] These negative effects are especially strong when managers believe the organization provides more support than employees think it does.

Culture Versus Formalization

We've seen that high formalization creates predictability, orderliness, and consistency. A strong culture achieves the same end without the need for written documentation.[12] Therefore, we should view formalization and culture as two different roads to a common destination. The stronger an organization's culture, the less management needs to be concerned with developing formal rules and regulations to guide employee behaviour. Those guides will be internalized in employees when they accept the organization's culture.

WHAT DO CULTURES DO?

Let's review the role culture performs and when it can be a liability for an organization.

The Functions of Culture

First, culture has a boundary-defining role: It creates distinctions between organizations. Second, it conveys a sense of identity for organization members. Third, culture facilitates commitment to something larger than individual self-interest. Fourth, it enhances the stability of the social system. Culture is the social glue that helps hold the organization together by providing standards for what employees should say and do. Finally, it is a sense-making and control mechanism that guides and shapes employees' attitudes and behaviour. This last function is of particular interest to us.[13] Culture defines the rules of the game.

Today's trend toward decentralized organizations makes culture more important than ever, but ironically it also makes establishing a strong culture more difficult. When formal authority and control systems are reduced, culture's *shared meaning* can point everyone in the same direction. However, employees organized in teams may show greater allegiance to their team and its values than to the organization as a whole. In virtual organizations, the lack of frequent face-to-face contact makes establishing a common set of norms very difficult. Strong leadership that communicates frequently about common goals and priorities is especially important in innovative organizations.[14]

Individual–organization "fit"—that is, whether the applicant's or employee's attitudes and behaviour are compatible with the culture—strongly influences who gets a job offer, a favourable performance review, or a promotion. It's no coincidence that Disney theme park employees and people working for the luxury Fairmont Hotel chain appear almost universally attractive, clean, and wholesome with bright smiles. The company selects employees who will maintain that image. On the job, a strong culture supported by formal rules and regulations ensures employees will act in a relatively uniform and predictable way.

Culture Creates Climate

If you've worked with someone whose positive attitude inspired you to do your best, or with a lacklustre team that drained your motivation, you've experienced the effects of climate. **Organizational climate** refers to the shared perceptions organizational members have about their organization and work environment.[15] This aspect of culture is like team spirit at the organizational level. When everyone has the same general feelings about what's important or how well things are working, the effect of these attitudes will be more than the sum of the individual parts. One meta-analysis found that across dozens of different samples, psychological climate was strongly related to individuals' level of job satisfaction, involvement, commitment, and motivation.[16] A positive overall workplace climate has been linked to higher customer satisfaction and financial performance as well.[17]

Positive workplace cultures can help employees be happier, more productive, and even safer. They create a shared understanding about how people will interact and do their jobs.

Kadmy/Fotolia

Dozens of dimensions of climate have been studied, including innovation, creativity, communication, warmth and support, involvement, safety, justice, diversity, and customer service.[18] A person who encounters a positive climate for performance will think about doing a good job more often and will believe others support her success. Someone who encounters a positive climate for diversity will feel more comfortable collaborating with coworkers regardless of their demographic background. Climates can interact with one another to produce behaviour. For example, a positive climate for worker empowerment can lead to higher levels of performance in organizations that also have a climate for personal accountability.[19] Climate also influences habits. If the climate for safety is positive, everyone wears safety gear and follows safety procedures even if individually they wouldn't normally think very often about being safe—indeed, many studies have shown that a positive safety climate decreases the number of documented injuries on the job.[20]

Culture as a Liability

Culture can enhance organizational commitment and increase the consistency of employee behaviour, which clearly benefits an organization. Culture is valuable to employees too, because it spells out how things are done and what's important. But we shouldn't ignore the potentially dysfunctional aspects of culture, especially a strong culture, on an organization's effectiveness. The Canadian military, for example, has openly acknowledged that their traditional hyper-masculine culture has contributed to shockingly high rates of sexual and gender-based harassment, sexual assault, and bullying of female soldiers and support workers.[21] This has in turn lead to issues with morale, occupational safety, skill utilization, and turnover.

Institutionalization   When an organization undergoes **institutionalization** and becomes *institutionalized*—that is, it is valued for itself and not for the goods or services it produces—it takes on a life of its own, apart from its founders or members.[22] Institutionalized organizations often don't go out of business even if the original goals are no longer relevant. Acceptable modes of behaviour become largely self-evident to members, and although this isn't entirely negative, it does mean behaviours and habits go unquestioned, which can stifle innovation and make maintaining the organization's culture an end in itself.

Barriers to Change   Culture is a liability when the shared values don't agree with those that further the organization's effectiveness. This is most likely when an organization's environment is undergoing rapid change, and its entrenched culture may no longer be appropriate.[23] Consistency of behaviour, an asset in a stable environment, may then burden the organization and make it difficult to respond to changes.

Barriers to Diversity   Hiring new employees who differ from the majority in race, age, gender, disability, or other characteristics creates a paradox:[24] Management wants to demonstrate support for the differences these employees bring to the workplace, but newcomers who wish to fit in must accept the organization's core culture. Second, because diverse behaviours and unique strengths are likely to diminish as people assimilate, strong cultures can become liabilities when they eliminate the advantages of diversity. Third, a strong culture that condones prejudice, supports bias, or becomes insensitive to differences can undermine formal diversity policies.

Barriers to Acquisitions and Mergers   Historically, when management looked at acquisition or merger decisions, the key factors were financial advantage and product synergy. In recent years, cultural compatibility has become the primary concern.[25] All things being equal, whether the acquisition actually works seems to have much to do with how well the two organizations' cultures match up.

A survey by consulting firm A. T. Kearney revealed that 58 percent of mergers failed to reach their financial goals.[26] As one expert commented, "Mergers have an unusually high failure rate, and it's always because of people issues"—in other words, because of conflicting organizational cultures. The $183 billion merger between America Online (AOL) and Time Warner in 2001 was the largest in U.S. corporate history. It was also a disaster. Only two years later, the stock had fallen an astounding 90 percent, and the new company reported what was then the largest financial loss in U.S. history. Culture clash is commonly argued to be one of the causes of AOL Time Warner's problems.

CREATING AND SUSTAINING CULTURE

An organization's culture doesn't pop out of thin air, and once established it rarely fades away. What influences the creation of a culture? What reinforces and sustains it once it is in place?

How a Culture Begins

An organization's current customs, traditions, and general way of doing things are largely due to what it has done before and how successful it was in doing it. This leads us to the ultimate source of an organization's culture: the founders.[27] Free of previous customs or ideologies, founders have a vision of what the organization should be, and the firm's small size makes it easy to impose that vision on all members.

Culture creation occurs in three ways.[28] First, founders hire and keep only employees who think and feel the same way they do. Second, they indoctrinate and socialize employees to their way of thinking and feeling. And finally, the founders' own behaviour encourages employees to identify with them and internalize their beliefs, values, and assumptions. When the organization succeeds, the founders' personality becomes embedded in the culture.

The fierce, competitive style and disciplined, authoritarian nature of Hyundai, the giant Korean conglomerate, exhibits the same characteristics often used to describe founder Chung Ju-Yung. Other founders with immeasurable impact on their organization's culture are Bill Gates at Microsoft, Ingvar Kamprad at IKEA, Herb Kelleher at Southwest Airlines, and Canadian Craig Kielburger at Free the Children.

Keeping a Culture Alive

Once a culture is in place, practices within the organization maintain it by giving employees a set of similar experiences.[29] The selection process, performance evaluation criteria, training and development activities, and promotion procedures (1) ensure those hired fit in with the culture, (2) reward those who support it, and (3) penalize (or even expel) those who challenge it. Three forces play a particularly important part in sustaining a culture: selection practices, actions of top management, and socialization methods. Let's look at each.

Selection Practices   The explicit goal of the selection process is to identify and hire individuals with the knowledge, skills, and abilities to perform successfully. The final decision, because it is significantly influenced by the decision maker's judgment of how well the candidates will fit into the organization, identifies people whose values are essentially consistent with at least a good portion of the organization's.[30] Selection also provides information to applicants. Individuals who perceive a conflict between their values and those of the organization can remove themselves from the applicant pool. Selection thus becomes a two-way street, allowing employer or applicant to avoid a mismatch and sustaining an organization's culture by removing those who might attack or undermine its core values.

W. L. Gore & Associates, the maker of Gore-Tex fabric used in outerwear, prides itself on its democratic culture and teamwork. There are no job titles, bosses, or chains of command. All work is done in teams. In Gore's selection process, teams put job applicants through extensive interviews to ensure they can deal with the level of uncertainty, flexibility, and teamwork that's normal in Gore plants. Not surprisingly, W. L. Gore appears regularly on *Fortune*'s list of 100 Best Companies to Work For (number 21 in 2013).[31]

Top Management Actions   The actions of top management also have a major impact on the organization's culture.[32] Through words and behaviour, senior executives establish norms that filter through the organization about, for instance, whether risk taking is desirable, how much freedom managers give employees, what is appropriate dress, and what actions earn pay raises, promotions, and other rewards.

The culture at the Aboriginal Peoples Television Network, headquartered in Winnipeg, Manitoba, is reinforced by senior managers through their own personal behaviour and through their strategic decisions. The organizational culture is focused on respect, creating a space for Aboriginal people to voice freely, and sharing stories. Individual senior executives personify these goals. Executive Director of Programming Monika Ille, for example, is herself a member of the Abenaki First Nation of Odanak. Her prior work includes projects focused on enabling voicing. She developed a training program for budding First Nations filmmakers and she has worked closely with the Assembly of First Nations and Quebec Native Women in Montreal.[33] This voice-focused culture is also supported in strategic decision making. The organization directly supports the development of Aboriginal programming by providing a vehicle to exhibit it, by providing funding and training opportunities, and by sponsoring branding and awards events. Half of their programming consists of shows that cannot be seen anywhere else, and 28 percent of them are broadcast in an indigenous language. All of this reinforces a broader culture in which employees feel comfortable bringing up issues and sharing their own stories and perspectives.[34]

Socialization Methods   No matter how good a job the organization does in recruiting and selection, new employees need help adapting to the prevailing culture. That help is **socialization**.[35] The degree to which organizations are attentive to their formal socialization process varies enormously, with some throwing employees into their tasks with minimal support or preparation and others taking great pains to formally induct people into their culture. For example, the consulting firm Booz Allen Hamilton begins its process of bringing new employees on board even before they start their first day of work. New recruits go to an internal web portal to learn about the company and engage in some activities that help them understand the culture of the organization. After they start work, they continue to learn about the organization through an ongoing social networking application that links new workers with more established members of the firm and helps ensure that culture

Francis Vachon/Alamy Stock Photo

EXHIBIT 16-1 A Socialization Model

Socialization process   Outcomes

Prearrival → Encounter → Metamorphosis → Productivity / Commitment / Turnover

is transmitted over time.[36] Clear Channel Communications, Facebook, Google, WestJet, and other companies are adopting fresh "onboarding" (new-hire) procedures, including assigning "peer coaches," holding socializing events, personalizing orientation programs, and giving out immediate work assignments. "When we can stress the personal identity of people, and let them bring more of themselves to work, they are more satisfied with their job and have better results," researcher Francesca Gino of Harvard said.[37]

We can think of socialization as a process with three stages: prearrival, encounter, and metamorphosis.[38] This process, charted in Exhibit 16-1, has an impact on the new employee's work productivity, commitment to the organization's objectives, and eventual decision to stay with the organization.

The **prearrival stage** recognizes that each individual arrives with a set of values, attitudes, and expectations about both the work and the organization. One major purpose of a business school, for example, is to socialize business students to the attitudes and behaviours business firms want. Newcomers to high-profile organizations with a strong market position will make their own assumptions about what it must be like to work there.[39] Most new recruits will expect technology firms such as Research in Motion or D2L to be dynamic and exciting, while prestigious law firms are expected to be high in pressure and rewards, and the Canadian Special Forces is expected to require both discipline and courage. No matter how well managers think they can socialize newcomers, however, the most important predictor of future behaviour is past behaviour. What people know before they join the organization, and how proactive their personality is, are critical predictors of how well they adjust to a new culture.[40]

One way to capitalize on pre-hire characteristics in socialization is to use the selection process to inform prospective employees about the organization as a whole. We've also seen how the selection process ensures inclusion of the "right type"—those who will fit in.

On entry into the organization, the new member enters the **encounter stage** and confronts the possibility that expectations—about the job, coworkers, the boss, and the organization in general—may differ from reality. If expectations were fairly accurate, this stage merely cements earlier perceptions. However, this is often not the case. At the extreme, a new member may become disillusioned enough to resign. For example a francophone employee hired in Montreal who expected to interact with colleagues exclusively in French might be distressed to discover that some of their colleagues expect to interact in English. This turn of events might or might not lead them to reconsider working there. Proper expectation setting during recruiting and selection should significantly reduce that outcome, along with encouraging friendship ties in the organization—newcomers are more committed when friends and coworkers help them learn the ropes.[41]

Finally, to work out any problems discovered during the encounter stage, the new member changes or goes through the **metamorphosis stage**. The options presented in Exhibit 16-2 are alternatives designed to bring about the desired metamorphosis. Most research suggests there are two major "bundles" of socialization practices. The more management relies on formal, collective, sequential, fixed, and serial socialization programs and emphasizes divestiture, the more likely newcomers' differences will be stripped away and replaced by standardized predictable behaviours. These *institutional* practices are common in police departments, fire departments, and other organizations that value rule following

EXHIBIT 16-2 Entry Socialization Options

Formal vs. informal The more a new employee is segregated from the ongoing work setting and differentiated in some way to make explicit his newcomer's role, the more socialization is formal. Specific orientation and training programs are examples. Informal socialization puts the new employee directly into the job, with little or no special attention.

Individual vs. collective New members can be socialized individually. This describes how it's done in many professional offices. They can also be grouped and processed through an identical set of experiences, as in military boot camp.

Fixed vs. variable This refers to the time schedule in which newcomers make the transition from outsider to insider. A fixed schedule establishes standardized stages of transition. This characterizes rotational training programs. It also includes probationary periods, such as the four-to-six-year "assistant professor" status used by universities before deciding on whether a candidate deserves tenure. Variable schedules, by contrast, give no advance notice of their transition timetable. Variable schedules describe the typical promotion system, in which one is not advanced to the next stage until one is "ready."

Serial vs. random Serial socialization is characterized by the use of role models who train and encourage the newcomer. Apprenticeship and mentoring programs are examples. In random socialization, role models are deliberately withheld. New employees are left on their own to figure things out.

Investiture vs. divestiture Investiture socialization assumes that the newcomer's qualities and qualifications are the necessary ingredients for job success, so these qualities and qualifications are confirmed and supported. Divestiture socialization tries to strip away certain characteristics of the recruit. Fraternity and sorority "pledges" go through divestiture socialization to shape them into the proper role.

and order. Programs that are informal, individual, random, variable, and disjunctive and that emphasize investiture are more likely to give newcomers an innovative sense of their roles and methods of working. Creative fields, such as research and development, advertising, and filmmaking, rely on these *individual* practices. Most research suggests that high levels of institutional practices encourage person–organization fit and high levels of commitment, whereas individual practices produce more role innovation.[42]

The three-part entry socialization process is complete when new members have internalized and accepted the norms of the organization and their work group, are confident in their competence, and feel trusted and valued by their peers. They understand the system—not only their own tasks but the rules, procedures, and informally accepted practices as well. Finally, they know what is expected of them and what criteria will be used to measure and evaluate their work. As Exhibit 16-2 showed, successful metamorphosis should have a positive impact on new employees' productivity and their commitment to the organization, and reduce their propensity to leave the organization.

Researchers have begun to examine how employees change during socialization by measuring attitudes at several points over the first few months. One study has documented patterns of "honeymoons" and "hangovers" for new workers, showing that the period of initial adjustment is often marked by decreases in job satisfaction as idealized hopes come into contact with the reality of organizational life.[43] Other research suggests that role conflict and role overload for newcomers rise over time, and workers with the largest increases in these role problems experience the largest decreases in commitment and satisfaction.[44] It may be that the initial adjustment period for newcomers presents increasing demands and difficulties, at least in the short term.

Summary: How Cultures Form

Exhibit 16-3 summarizes how an organization's culture is established and sustained. The original culture derives from the founders' philosophy and strongly influences hiring criteria as the firm grows. Top managers' actions set the general climate, including what is acceptable behaviour and what is not. The way employees are socialized will depend both on the

EXHIBIT 16-3 How Organization Cultures Form

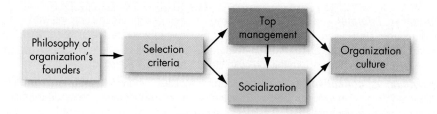

degree of success achieved in matching new employees' values to those of the organization in the selection process, and on top management's preference for socialization methods.

HOW EMPLOYEES LEARN CULTURE

Culture is transmitted to employees in a number of forms, the most potent being stories, rituals, material symbols, and language.

Stories

When Henry Ford II was chairman of Ford Motor Company, you would have been hard pressed to find a manager who hadn't heard how he reminded his executives, when they got too arrogant, "It's my name that's on the building." The message was clear: Henry Ford II ran the company.

A number of senior Nike executives spend much of their time serving as corporate storytellers.[45] When they tell how co-founder (and Oregon track coach) Bill Bowerman went to his workshop and poured rubber into a waffle iron to create a better running shoe, they're talking about Nike's spirit of innovation. When new hires hear tales of Oregon running star Steve Prefontaine's battles to make running a professional sport and attain better performance equipment, they learn of Nike's commitment to helping athletes.

Stories such as these circulate through many organizations, anchoring the present in the past and legitimating current practices. They typically include narratives about the organization's founders, rule breaking, rags-to-riches successes, reductions in the workforce, relocation of employees, reactions to past mistakes, and organizational coping.[46] Employees also create their own narratives about how they came to either fit or not fit with the organization during the process of socialization, including first days on the job, early interactions with others, and first impressions of organizational life.[47]

Rituals

Rituals are repetitive sequences of activities that express and reinforce the key values of the organization—what goals are most important, which people are important, and which are expendable.[48] One of the best known rituals is Walmart's company chant. Begun by the company's founder, the late Sam Walton, as a way to motivate his workforce, "Gimme a W, gimme an A, gimme an L, gimme a squiggle, give me an M, A, R, T!" became a ritual to bond workers together and reinforce Walton's belief that employees made the company successful. Other companies have non-traditional rituals to help support the values of their cultures. WestJet flight attendants, for instance, are actively encouraged to make jokes during their pre-flight safety demonstrations, as this helps to maintain their fun-loving, relaxed, customer-oriented culture.

Symbols

The layout of corporate headquarters, the types of automobiles top executives are given, and the presence or absence of corporate aircraft are a few examples of **material symbols**. Others include the size of offices, and the elegance of furnishings, perks, and attire.[49] These convey to employees who is important, the degree of egalitarianism top management desires, and the kinds of behaviour that are appropriate, such as risk-taking, conservative, authoritarian, participative, individualistic, or social.

One example is the Kitchener-Waterloo online learning platform provider Desire2Learn (also known as D2L). In the early years when management sought to solidify a culture of creativity and collaboration the office space was dominated by a (largely non-alcoholic) tiki bar. The bar permitted coworkers to assemble in a casual atmosphere conducive to thinking differently. Elaborate weekly theme parties further encouraged social engagement and new ideas.[50] In another example, Dynegy's headquarters doesn't look like your typical head-office operation. There are few individual offices, even for senior executives. The space is essentially made up of cubicles, common areas, and meeting rooms. This informality conveys to employees that Dynegy values openness, equality, creativity, and flexibility.

Language

Many organizations and subunits within them use language to help members identify with the culture, attest to their acceptance of it, and help preserve it. Unique terms describe equipment, officers, key individuals, suppliers, customers, or products that relate to the business. New employees may at first be overwhelmed by acronyms and jargon that, once assimilated, act as a common denominator to unite members of a given culture or subculture.

Since culture is key to the essence of an organization and is perceived both inside and outside the organization, it is important to establish a culture that reflects the values of its founders and top management. Let's next explore the ways an ethical, positive culture can be created and transmitted around the world.

CREATING AN ETHICAL ORGANIZATIONAL CULTURE

The organizational culture most likely to shape high ethical standards among its members is high in risk tolerance, low to moderate in aggressiveness, and focused on means as well as outcomes.[51] This type of culture takes a long-term perspective and balances the rights of multiple stakeholders, including employees, stockholders, and the community. Managers are supported for taking risks and innovating, discouraged from engaging in unbridled competition, and guided to heed not just *what* goals are achieved but also *how*.

If the culture is strong and supports high ethical standards, it should have a very powerful and positive influence on employee behaviour. Examples of organizations that have failed to establish proper codes of ethical conduct can be found in the media nearly every day. Some actively deceive customers or clients. Others produce products that harm consumers or the environment, or they harass or discriminate against certain groups of employees. Others are more subtle and cover up or fail to report wrongdoing. The negative consequences of a systematic culture of unethical behaviour can be severe and include customer boycotts, fines, lawsuits, and government regulation of an organization's practices.

What can managers do to create a more ethical culture? They can adhere to the following principles:[52]

- **Be a visible role model.** Employees will look to the actions of top management as a benchmark for appropriate behaviour. Send a positive message.
- **Communicate ethical expectations.** Minimize ethical ambiguities by sharing an organizational code of ethics that states the organization's primary values and ethical rules employees must follow.

- **Provide ethical training.** Set up seminars, workshops, and training programs to reinforce the organization's standards of conduct, clarify what practices are permissible (or impermissible), and address potential ethical dilemmas.

- **Visibly reward ethical acts and punish unethical ones.** Appraise managers on how their decisions measure up against the organization's code of ethics. Review the means as well as the ends. Visibly reward those who act ethically and conspicuously punish those who don't.

- **Provide protective mechanisms.** Provide formal mechanisms so employees can discuss ethical dilemmas and report unethical behaviour without fear of reprimand. These might include ethical counselors, ombudspeople, or ethical officers.

The work of setting a positive ethical climate has to start at the top of the organization.[53] A study of 195 managers demonstrated that when top management emphasizes strong ethical values, supervisors are more likely to practice ethical leadership. Positive attitudes transfer down to line employees, who show lower levels of deviant behaviour and higher levels of cooperation and assistance. A study involving auditors found perceived pressure from organizational leaders to behave unethically was associated with increased intentions to engage in unethical practices.[54] Clearly the wrong type of organizational culture can negatively influence employee ethical behaviour. Finally, employees whose ethical values are similar to those of their department are more likely to be promoted, so we can think of ethical culture as flowing from the bottom up as well.[55]

CREATING A POSITIVE ORGANIZATIONAL CULTURE

It is possible to form ethical cultures and positive organizational cultures, but the means by which such cultures are attained are quite different.

At first blush, creating a positive culture may sound hopelessly naïve or like a Dilbert-style conspiracy. The one thing that makes us believe this trend is here to stay, however, are signs that management practice and OB research are converging.

A **positive organizational culture** emphasizes building on employee strengths, rewards more than it punishes, and emphasizes individual vitality and growth.[56] Let's consider each of these areas.

Building on Employee Strengths

Although a positive organizational culture does not ignore problems, it does emphasize showing workers how they can capitalize on their strengths. As management guru Peter Drucker has said, "Most workers do not know what their strengths are. When you ask them, they look at you with a blank stare, or they respond in terms of subject knowledge, which is the wrong answer." Wouldn't it be better to be in an organizational culture that helped you discover your strengths and learn how to make the most of them?

As CEO of Auglaize Provico, an agribusiness based in Ohio, Larry Hammond used this approach when you'd least expect it: during his firm's darkest days. In the midst of the firm's worst financial struggles, when it had to lay off one-quarter of its workforce, Hammond tried a different approach. Rather than dwell on what was wrong, he took advantage of what was right. "If you really want to [excel], you have to know yourself—you have to know what you're good at, and you have to know what you're not so good at," said Hammond. With the help of Gallup consultant Barry Conchie, Hammond focused on discovering and using employee strengths, and helped the company turn itself around. "You ask Larry [Hammond] what the difference is, and he'll say that it's individuals using their natural talents," said Conchie.[57]

Rewarding More Than Punishing, and the Value of the "Small" Stuff

Although most organizations are sufficiently focused on major rewards such as pay and promotions, they often forget about the power of smaller (and cheaper) rewards such as praise, respect, and even token incentives. Many common disciplinary issues, such as tardiness or the occasional failure to wear safety equipment, are more effectively addressed through these small rewards rather than punishments. For example when conducting random safety audits it might be better to openly praise employees wearing their safety equipment and give them a gift card than to just yell at noncompliant workers. Part of creating a positive organizational culture is "catching employees doing something right." Many managers withhold praise because they're afraid employees will coast or because they think praise is not valued. Employees generally don't ask for praise, and managers usually don't realize the costs of failing to give it.

Consider Elżbieta Górska-Kolodziejczyk, a plant manager for International Paper's facility in Kwidzyn, Poland. Employees worked in a bleak windowless basement. Staffing became roughly one-third its prior level, while production tripled. These challenges had done in the previous three managers. So when Górska-Kolodziejczyk took over, although she had many ideas about transforming the organization, at the top were recognition and praise. She initially found it difficult to give praise to those who weren't used to it, especially men. "They were like cement at the beginning," she said. "Like cement." Over time, however, she found they valued and even reciprocated praise. One day a department supervisor pulled her over to tell her she was doing a good job. "This I do remember, yes," she said.[58]

Emphasizing Vitality and Growth

No organization will get the best from employees who see themselves as mere cogs in the machine. A positive culture recognizes the difference between a job and a career. It supports not only what the employee contributes to organizational effectiveness but also how the organization can make the employee more effective—personally and professionally. Top companies recognize the value of helping people grow. 1-800-GOT-JUNK founder and CEO Brian Scudamore attributes much of his company's success to the organization's emphasis on personal development. He encourages managers to support staff growth in many ways. "Sometimes that means spending money," he reports, and "sometimes it means hooking someone up with a mentor. Often we'll get people to go to other businesses that we've become friends with and say 'go learn from this company.'"[59]

Although it may take more creativity to encourage employee growth in other industries, consider the food industry. At MasterFoods in Belgium, Philippe Lescornez led a team of employees including Didier Brynaert, who worked in Luxembourg, nearly 150 miles away. Brynaert was considered a good sales promoter who was meeting expectations when Lescornez decided Brynaert's job could be made more important if he were seen less as just another sales promoter and more as an expert on the unique features of the Luxembourg market. So Lescornez asked Brynaert for information he could share with the home office. He hoped that by raising Brynaert's profile, he could create in him a greater sense of ownership for his remote sales territory. "I started to communicate much more what he did to other people [within the company], because there's quite some distance between the Brussels office and the section he's working in. So I started to communicate, communicate, communicate. The more I communicated, the more he started to provide material," said Lescornez. As a result, "Now he's recognized as the specialist for Luxembourg—the guy who is able to build a strong relationship with the Luxembourg clients," says Lescornez. What's good for Brynaert was, of course, also good for Lescornez, who got credit for helping Brynaert grow and develop.[60]

Limits of Positive Culture

Is a positive culture a cure-all? Though many companies have embraced aspects of a positive organizational culture, it is a new enough idea for us to be uncertain about how and when it works best.

Not all national cultures value being positive as much as Canadian culture does, and even within Canadian culture there surely are limits to how far companies should go. The limits may need to be dictated by the culture and the industry. For example, Admiral, a British insurance company, has established a Ministry of Fun in its call centres to organize poem writing, foosball, conkers (a British game involving chestnuts), and fancy-dress days, while other companies in the insurance industry have maintained more serious cultures. When does the pursuit of a positive culture start to seem coercive or even Orwellian? As one critic notes, "Promoting a social orthodoxy of positiveness focuses on a particular constellation of desirable states and traits but, in so doing, can stigmatize those who fail to fit the template."[61] There may be benefits to establishing a positive culture, but an organization also needs to be objective and not pursue it past the point of effectiveness.

GLOBAL IMPLICATIONS

Organizational culture and national culture are not the same thing, though to some degree an organization's culture reflects the dominant values of its host country.

We considered global cultural values (collectivism–individualism, power distance, and so on) in Chapter 5. Here our focus is a bit narrower: How is organizational culture affected by a global context? Organizational culture is so powerful it often transcends national boundaries. But that doesn't mean organizations should, or could, ignore local cultures.

Organizational cultures often reflect national culture. Trompenaars, a former managing director at the United Nations, studied the relationship between the two and discovered interesting patterns. The elements of national culture that seemed to influence organizational culture the most included whether the culture emphasizes equity or hierarchy (power distance) and whether it generally prioritized people or tasks (this is related to Hofstede's concept of masculinity/femininity). As we can see in Exhibit 16-4, Trompenaars identified the four types of organizational cultures most likely to emerge on the basis of these two dimensions.[62] *Incubator* cultures, common in places like India, Israel, and Silicon Valley, emphasize fulfillment; *guided missile* cultures, common in places like Canada and Ireland, emphasize project completion; *family* cultures emphasize power relationships and are common in places like Pakistan and China; and *Eiffel tower* cultures emphasize rules, roles, and formal procedure and are common in

EXHIBIT 16-4
Trompenaars's Four Types of Organizational Cultures

places like France and Germany. Each type fosters different expectations for communication style, motivation techniques, promotion paths, and other important workplace behaviours.

In addition to the patterns identified by Trompenaars, there are many other connections between national culture and organizational culture. The culture at AirAsia, a Malaysia-based airline, emphasizes openness and friendships. The carrier has lots of parties, participative management, and no private offices, reflecting Malaysia's relatively collectivistic culture. The culture of the largest Canadian airline, Air Canada, does not reflect the same degree of informality; however, WestJet's culture does. If either of these Canadian airlines was to merge with AirAsia, it would need to take these cultural differences into account; and we might expect Air Canada to have more difficulty than WestJet due to the greater disparity in existing cultures.

Organizational culture differences are not always due to international culture differences, though. One of the chief challenges of the merger between US Airways and American Airlines was the integration of US Airway's "open collar" culture with American's "button-down" culture.[63]

One of the primary things Canadian managers can do is be culturally sensitive. Some ways in which managers can be culturally sensitive include speaking slowly if English is not the other party's first language, listening more, paraphrasing comments back to ensure understanding, asking clarifying questions when unsure about someone's point of view (rather than making assumptions), and avoiding discussions of religion and politics.

The management of ethical behaviour is one area where national culture can rub up against corporate culture.[64] Canadian managers endorse the supremacy of anonymous market forces and implicitly or explicitly view profit maximization as a moral obligation for business organizations. This worldview sees bribery, nepotism, and favouring personal contacts as highly unethical. Any action that deviates from profit maximization may indicate that inappropriate or corrupt behaviour may be occurring. In contrast, managers in developing economies are more likely to see ethical decisions as embedded in a social environment. That means that doing special favours for family and friends is not only appropriate but possibly even an ethical responsibility. Managers in many nations also view capitalism skeptically and believe the interests of workers should be put on a par with the interests of shareholders.

SUMMARY

- Employees form an overall subjective perception of the organization based on factors such as degree of risk tolerance, team emphasis, and support of individuals.

- This overall perception becomes, in effect, the organization's culture or personality and affects employee performance and satisfaction, with stronger cultures having greater impact.

- Cultures are sustained and transmitted through both formal and informal socialization. The role of informal socialization is such that subcultures can develop within organizations.

- It is possible to foster ethical, positive, and safety-minded cultures if those cultures are properly modelled and reinforced.

- National culture will influence organizational culture preferences and expectations. This can be a source of confusion in a globalized work setting.

IMPLICATIONS FOR MANAGERS

- Realize that an organization's culture is relatively fixed in the short term. To effect change, involve top management and strategize a long-term plan.

- Hire individuals whose values align with those of the organization; these employees will tend to remain committed and satisfied. Not surprisingly, "misfits" have considerably higher turnover rates.

- Understand that employees' performance and socialization depend to a considerable degree on their knowing what and what not to do. Train your employees well and keep them informed of changes to their job roles.

- As a manager, you can shape the culture of your work environment, sometimes as much as it shapes you. All managers can do their part to create an ethical culture.

- Be aware that your company's organizational culture may not be "transportable" to other countries. Understand the cultural relevance of your organization's norms before introducing new plans or initiatives overseas.

BREAKOUT QUESTION FOR GROUP DISCUSSION

Mergers and acquisitions often fail as a result of culture clashes. Identify two companies that have recently proposed a merger. Review their websites and glean whatever information you can about their corporate culture. Do you foresee any problems combining these two cultures? Why or why not? How might that impact the success of the proposed merger?

PERSONAL INVENTORY ASSESSMENT

In the Personal Inventory Assessment found in MyManagementLab, take the assessment: Comfort with Change Scale.

SELF-REFLECTION ACTIVITY

Some people are very comfortable with change, while others prefer to avoid it. Where do you fall on that continuum? In the Personal Inventory Assessment found in MyManagementLab, take the assessment Comfort with Change Scale to gain insight into your own attitudes about change and your degree of knowledge about fostering change effectively. This information can help guide career decisions, as some occupations and industries are known to be high-change environments (software development and cellphone manufacturing being good examples), while others are comparatively stable (such as, forestry, government services, and childcare).

Sometimes change is unavoidable. Think back to times when you experienced significant changes at work or school. Do you notice any patterns related to when those changes went well and when they went poorly? Think about things like communication flow and clarity, the motivations of the people involved in the change, and how the change was initiated, supported, and evaluated when considering your answer.

MINI CASE   DEVELOPING AND MAINTAINING A SAFETY CULTURE

Sanjay and Sophia looked out over the factory floor in dismay. They both worked in human resources management, and just a week ago they had delivered some safety training in an attempt to reduce their higher-than-average rate of workplace injuries. They had lectured all the employees about safety for three hours and then given them a written test. Although all employees had passed, nothing had actually changed. Sanjay and Sophia were chagrined and wondered what else they needed to do to change the culture.

As they looked out over the factory floor from the second-storey lunchroom, they began to share their observations.

"Look," said Sanjay, "there is the CEO rushing out to talk to someone wearing only his dress shoes again. I keep telling him he needs safety shoes and safety glasses on the manufacturing floor, but he just keeps telling me he's only out there for a minute so it is too much of a pain to change shoes and find glasses."

While Sophia found that distressing, she was more concerned with the newly hired junior employees, whom she saw joking and pushing each other around the forklift loading area. "You know," she told Sanjay, "I mentioned that the new hires are goofing off around the loading area, and their supervisor just said that they work hard and need to blow off a little steam now and then. He said I should leave them alone. The other day I even saw him get involved in one of their little pranks, making a guy jump out of his skin by blaring the forklift horn. When I asked him about it, he said pranks help the workers relax when they are stressed about manufacturing quotas."

"Well, I'm not surprised they're stressed," said Sanjay. "After all, the entire team's bonus is based on productivity targets, and nobody wants to be the one who lets everyone else down. If they miss their target because of one worker, the poor guy will never hear the end of it."

"I know," replied Sophia. "Just last week, someone came in with active pneumonia because he didn't want his team to miss their target. I know other workers covered for him a bit, but he kept at it no matter what. I even caught him trying to take the handguard off his machine so he could work it faster. He said he was behind from coughing and needed to catch up!"

"It's so strange," observed Sanjay. "All these workers passed the safety test with flying colours but nobody actually *does* any of the stuff we talked about. What's happening?"

"I don't know," said Sophia. "Maybe if we put some safety posters up to remind people about risks, that will help."

Discussion Questions

1. Why have Sanjay and Sophia failed to foster a safety culture in their workplace? What specifically acts to undermine that change?

2. Will their new strategy (putting up posters) work? If yes, why? If no, why not?

3. What would they have to do to institute meaningful change in the safety culture at this organization?

MINI CASE   CULTURE CHANGE AT THE RCMP

Changing a deeply entrenched organizational culture can be very difficult, as the Canadian Royal Mounted Police have discovered. The widespread prevalence of sexual harassment of female officers in the service resulted in the launch of a class action lawsuit in 2012. Efforts to address this problem have focused on enforcement of antiharassment policies and on changing the patriarchal, macho culture associated with the RCMP.

Stories that have emerged as a result of the lawsuit have highlighted the extent of the problem. Female officers have reported incidents ranging from inappropriate joking to having pornography and sex toys left in their workspaces. Others have reported unwanted physical contact, up to and including being raped by fellow officers. Official responses to complaints were generally inadequate, with many women reporting that they, as complainants, were put on leave while their harassers received extremely light sanctions, if any. In one case a female officer was still away on administrative leave a year later "pending investigation" while the officer she had accused of rape was promoted.

Part of the reason the RCMP has had such difficulty addressing these issues is that they are not "change ready," according to Dr. Linda Duxbury, who wrote an independent report assessing their culture. She reported that the general culture was "exploitative, paramilitary, respectful of the position rather than the person, low trust, risk adverse, and defensive." The culture has also been characterized as patriarchal and "macho." Dr. Duxbury further characterized their culture as "a victim of the success spiral, which occurs when an organization holds on too long to a culture in the belief that what has worked in the past will continue to confer a competitive advantage in the future. The RCMP has failed to realign its organizational culture to take into account new environmental realities. This has resulted in key elements of RCMP culture being liabilities as the organization moves forward with reforms."

Bob Paulson, the RCMP Commissioner appointed in 2012 to fix the mess, has openly admitted to a culture of bullying and associated inadequate harassment investigations. He stated that his "mandate was to clear-cut problems that have taken root so deeply in the police culture that some Mounties are now embarrassed to tell neighbours where they work." The numbers are telling—in the four years before Paulson's appointment, the number of female cadets at the RCMP dropped by 52 percent. Currently only 20 percent of the 19,000-member force are women. Change will not be easy, though. Paulson has committed to new policies, enforcement of existing policies, and ongoing monitoring of results, but he recognizes that it is a difficult road given the strength of the existing culture.

Discussion Questions

1. Why do you think the culture within the RCMP is so strong and deeply rooted? Does the nature of the job itself impact the strength of the culture? Why or why not?

2. What specific steps and policies might help encourage a more ethical and equitable organizational culture?

3. Discuss the role a leader plays in organizational culture maintenance and change. Was the change in leadership necessary in this situation? Why or why not?

Sources: L. Payton, "RCMP Culture Needs to Change to Fight Harassment," *CBC News*, November 20, 2012, http://www.cbc.ca/news/politics/rcmp-culture-needs-to-change-to-fight-harassment-mps-told-1.1199701; L. Duxbury, "The RCMP Yesterday, Today, and Tomorrow," 2007, http://www.rcmp-grc.gc.ca/pubs/duxbury-eng.htm; and Staff editorial, "RCMP Commissioner Paulson the Right Man to Lead Change," *Globe and Mail*, November 25, 2012, http://www.theglobeandmail.com/globe-debate/editorials/rcmp-commissioner-paulson-the-right-man-to-lead-change/article5613053.

MyManagementLab

Study, practise, and explore real management situations with these helpful resources:
- **Interactive Lesson Presentations:** Work through interactive presentations and assessments to test your knowledge of management concepts.
- **PIA (Personal Inventory Assessments):** Enhance your ability to connect with key concepts through these engaging self-reflection assessments.
- **Study Plan:** Check your understanding of chapter concepts with self-study quizzes.
- **Simulations:** Practise decision making in simulated management environments.

P I A

PERSONAL INVENTORY ASSESSMENT

Chapter 17

Organizational Change and Stress Management

Executive Meeting

At last our new change initiative is ready. After our long months of planning, I'm sure our employees will be just as excited about this as we are.

So what do they want us to do?

Change Initiative

Pearson Education

LEARNING OBJECTIVES

After studying this chapter, you should be able to:

1 Identify forces that act as stimulants to change.

2 Describe the sources of resistance to change.

3 Compare the four main approaches to managing organizational change.

4 Explain two ways of creating a culture for change.

5 Identify the potential sources and consequences of stress.

6 Describe techniques for managing stress and assess the suitability of those techniques based on relevant situational factors.

This chapter is about change and stress. We describe environmental forces that require firms to change, why people and organizations often resist change, and how this resistance can be overcome. We review processes for managing organizational change.

With change often comes stress. Stress is an important topic for organizations to address in strengthening and retaining talented individuals. We will discuss the topic of stress and its consequences. In closing, we will explore what individuals and organizations can do to better manage stress levels.

FORCES FOR CHANGE

No company today is in a particularly stable environment. Even those with dominant market share must change, sometimes radically. In the 20 years between 1997 and 2017, there were fundamental transformations in many industries ranging from security to agriculture, telecommunications to healthcare. For example, during that time period consumers saw a

Pictures/Shutterstock

drastic rise in wireless-based communications and mobile apps while also witnessing the near-elimination of the traditional household land-based telephone line. Affordable drones now perform some front-line military functions previously carried out by humans, fundamentally changing military defence tactics and the power dynamics between nations. Political pressure to reduce greenhouse gas emissions eventually led to viable alternative-fuel vehicles being mass-produced for the first time. At the same time, new automotive manufacturing competitors that were focused on no-frills, affordable vehicles emerged from developing economies such as India. New genetically modified crops were introduced that could transform food production, yet political pressures and social concerns may lessen the usefulness of the technology. Poultry farming is changing in response to immense consumer pressure to improve the living conditions of farm animals. Customized cancer therapies based on individual genetic profiles have begun to transform oncological care, while regulatory differences between nations have led to a rise in "health tourism" as people seek treatments unavailable in their home countries. The list of changes seems endless and very few industries have escaped.

"Change or die!" is the rallying cry among today's managers worldwide. In a number of places in this text, we've discussed the *changing nature of the workforce*. Almost every organization must adjust to a multicultural environment, demographic changes, immigration, and outsourcing. *Technology* is continually changing jobs and organizations. Technological change is so frequent that a specific change management process called the *software development lifecycle* is commonly used to manage new implementations of everything from ERP systems and data warehouses to mobile applications. It is not hard to imagine the very idea of the traditional office with immobile workstations becoming an antiquated concept in the near future.

Competition is changing. Competitors are as likely to come from across the ocean as from across town. Successful organizations will be fast on their feet, capable of developing new products rapidly and getting them to market quickly. They will be flexible and will require an equally flexible and responsive workforce. Sometimes, government regulations affect organizational behaviour decisions. For instance, increasingly in Canada and Europe, the government regulates business practices, including executive pay.

Social trends don't remain static. Consumers who are otherwise strangers now meet and share product information in chat rooms and blogs. Companies must continually adjust product and marketing strategies to be sensitive to changing social trends, as Liz Claiborne did when it sold off fashion brands such as Ellen Tracy, deemphasized large vendors such as Macy's, streamlined operations, and cut staff. Consumers, employees, and organizational leaders are increasingly sensitive to environmental concerns. "Green" practices are quickly becoming expected rather than optional.

Not even globalization's strongest proponents could have imagined how *world politics* would change in recent years. We've seen a major set of financial crises that have rocked global markets, a dramatic rise in the power and influence of China, and intense shakeups in governments in the Middle East. In Canada, political changes have been less drastic, but still significant. The recent election of Justin Trudeau with a Liberal majority may ultimately create business opportunities in areas previously unavailable in the economy. The anticipated legalization of marijuana and the development of associated growing and distribution firms is one example. Throughout the industrialized world, businesses—particularly in the financial, transportation, and energy sectors—have come under new scrutiny and been impacted by policy changes at national government levels.

RESISTANCE TO CHANGE

Our egos are fragile, and we often see change as threatening. One study showed that even when employees are shown data that suggest they need to change, they latch onto whatever data they can find that suggest they are okay and don't need to change.[1] Employees who have negative feelings about a change cope by not thinking about it, increasing their use of sick time, or quitting. These reactions can sap the organization of vital energy when it is most needed.[2]

> One of the most well-documented findings from studies of individual and organizational behaviour is that organizations and their members resist change.

Resistance to change can be positive if it leads to open discussion and debate.[3] Open-dialogue responses are usually preferable to apathy or silence and can indicate that members of the organization are engaged in the process, which then provides change agents with an opportunity to explain the change effort. Change agents are individuals who are fully committed to a change. They help to motivate and encourage others either formally or informally. They do this in a range of ways: for example, modelling the change themselves, providing coaching to others, openly discussing the benefits of the change, and providing ongoing feedback. Change agents can also use points of resistance they hear about to modify the change to fit the preferences of members of the organization.

Resistance doesn't necessarily surface in standardized ways. It can be overt, implicit, immediate, or deferred. Management can most easily deal with overt and immediate resistance, such as complaints, a work slowdown, or a strike threat. The greater challenge is managing resistance that is implicit or deferred. These responses—loss of loyalty or motivation, increased errors or absenteeism—are more subtle and more difficult to recognize for what they are. Deferred actions may surface weeks, months, or even years later and thus cloud the link between the change and the reaction to it. A single change of little inherent impact may be the straw that breaks the camel's back because resistance to earlier changes has been deferred and stockpiled.

Exhibit 17-1 summarizes major forces for resistance to change, categorized by their sources. Individual sources reside in human characteristics such as perceptions, personalities, and needs. Organizational sources reside in the structural makeup of organizations themselves.

It's worth noting that not all change is good. Speed can lead to bad decisions, and sometimes those initiating change fail to realize the full magnitude of the effects or their true costs. Sometimes they are influenced by trends and are implementing change for the wrong reasons or without sufficient forethought and preparation. Rapid, transformational change is risky, and some organizations have collapsed for this reason.[4] Clothing retailer JCPenney, under a new CEO, decided to radically change its pricing strategy (eliminate "permanent" sales that cut into margins). After its sales and stock price dropped roughly one-third, it reversed course, but has not yet recovered to its pre-change levels. The lesson? Change *can* be good, but change agents need to carefully think through the implications.

Overcoming Resistance to Change

Eight tactics can help change agents deal with resistance to change.[5] Let's review them briefly.

EXHIBIT 17-1 Sources of
Resistance to Change

INDIVIDUAL SOURCES

Habit. To cope with life's complexities, we rely on habits or programmed responses. But when confronted with change, this tendency to respond in our accustomed ways becomes a source of resistance.

Security. People with a high need for security are likely to resist change because it threatens feelings of safety.

Economic factors. Changes in job tasks or established work routines can arouse economic fears if people are concerned that they won't be able to perform the new tasks or routines to their previous standards, especially when pay is closely tied to productivity.

Fear of the unknown. Change substitutes ambiguity and uncertainty for the unknown.

Selective information processing. Individuals are guilty of selectively processing information in order to keep their perceptions intact. They hear what they want to hear, and they ignore information that challenges the world they've created.

ORGANIZATIONAL SOURCES

Structural inertia. Organizations have built-in mechanisms—like their selection processes and formalized regulations—to produce stability. When an organization is confronted with change, this structural inertia acts as a counterbalance to sustain stability.

Limited focus of change. Organizations are made up of a number of interdependent subsystems. One can't be changed without affecting the others. So limited changes in subsystems tend to be nullified by the larger system.

Group inertia. Even if individuals want to change their behaviour, group norms may act as a constraint.

Threat to expertise. Changes in organizational patterns may threaten the expertise of specialized groups.

Threat to established power relationships. Any redistribution of decision-making authority can threaten long-established power relationships within the organization.

Education and Communication   Communicating the logic of a change can reduce employee resistance on two levels. First, it fights the effects of misinformation and poor communication: If employees receive the full facts and clear up misunderstandings, resistance should subside. One study of an organization in the Philippines found that formal change information sessions decreased employees' anxiety about the change, while providing high-quality information about the change increased their commitment to it.[6] Second, communication can help "sell" the need for change by packaging it properly.[7] For example, a study of German companies revealed that changes are most effective when a company communicates a rationale balancing the interests of various stakeholders (shareholders, employees, community, and customers) rather than considering the viewpoint of shareholders only.[8]

Participation   It's difficult to resist a change decision in which we've participated. Assuming participants have the expertise to make a meaningful contribution, their involvement can reduce resistance, obtain commitment, and increase the quality of the change decision. However, against these advantages are the negatives: potential for a poor solution and great consumption of time.

Building Support and Commitment   When employees' fear and anxiety are high, counselling and therapy, new-skills training, or a short paid leave of absence may facilitate adjustment. When managers or employees have low emotional commitment to change, they favor the status quo and resist it.[9] Employees are also more accepting of changes when they are committed to the organization as a whole.[10] So, firing up employees and emphasizing their commitment to the organization overall can help them emotionally commit to the change rather than embrace the status quo.

Monkey Business Images/Shutterstock

Develop Positive Relationships People are more willing to accept changes if they trust the managers implementing them.[11] One study surveyed 235 employees from a large housing corporation in the Netherlands that was experiencing a merger. Those who had a more positive relationship with their supervisors, and who felt that the work environment supported development, were much more positive about the change process.[12] Another set of studies found that individuals who were dispositionally resistant to change felt more positive about the change if they trusted the change agent.[13] This research suggests that if managers are able to facilitate positive relationships, they may be able to overcome resistance to change even among those who ordinarily don't like changes.

Implementing Changes Fairly One way organizations can minimize negative impact is to make sure change is implemented fairly. As we saw in Chapter 7, procedural fairness is especially important when employees perceive an outcome as negative, so it's crucial that employees see the reason for the change and perceive its implementation as consistent and fair.[14]

Manipulation and Cooptation *Manipulation* refers to covert influence attempts. Twisting facts to make them more attractive, withholding information, and creating false rumours to get employees to accept change are all examples of manipulation. If management threatens to close a manufacturing plant whose employees are resisting an across-the-board pay cut, and if the threat is actually untrue, management is using manipulation. *Cooptation*, on the other hand, combines manipulation and participation. It seeks to "buy off" the leaders of a resistance group by giving them a key role, seeking their advice not to find a better solution but to get their endorsement. Both manipulation and cooptation are relatively inexpensive ways to gain the support of adversaries, but they can backfire if the targets become aware they are being tricked or used. Once discovered, the change agent's credibility may drop to zero.

Selecting People Who Accept Change One study of managers in the United States, Europe, and Asia found those with a positive self-concept and high risk tolerance coped better with organizational change. Research suggests that the ability to easily accept and adapt to change is related to personality—some people simply have more positive attitudes about change than others.[15] Such individuals are open to experience, are willing to take risks, and are flexible in their behaviour. A study of 258 police officers found those who were higher in growth-needs, internal locus of control, and internal work motivation had more positive attitudes about organizational change efforts.[16] Individuals higher in general mental ability are also better able to learn and adapt to changes in the workplace.[17] In sum, an impressive body of evidence shows organizations can facilitate change by selecting people predisposed to accept it.

Besides selecting individuals who are willing to accept changes, it is also possible to select teams that are more adaptable. Studies have shown that teams that are strongly motivated by learning about and mastering tasks are better able to adapt to changing environments.[18] This research suggests it may be necessary to consider not just individual motivation, but also group motivation when trying to implement changes. Fostering a learning organization can help with this process. A learning organization facilitates continuous transformation by encouraging the development of a shared vision while simultaneously supporting systematic questioning of the status quo and standard modes of operating (mental models). Individuals are encouraged to develop personal mastery in their areas of expertise. Ongoing dialogue and discussion transform that individual mastery into team learning.

Coercion Last on the list of tactics is *coercion*, the application of direct threats or force on the dissenters. If management really is determined to close a manufacturing plant whose employees don't acquiesce to a pay cut, the company is using coercion. Other examples of coercion tools are forced transfers, loss of promotions, negative performance evaluations, and a poor letter of recommendation. The advantages and drawbacks of coercion are approximately the same as for manipulation and cooptation.

APPROACHES TO MANAGING ORGANIZATIONAL CHANGE

Now we turn to several approaches to managing change: Lewin's classic three-step model of the change process, Kotter's eight-step plan, and organizational development.

Lewin's Three-Step Model

Kurt Lewin argued that successful change in organizations should follow three steps: **unfreezing** the status quo, **movement** to a desired end state, and **refreezing** the new change to make it permanent[19] (see Exhibit 17-2).

The status quo is an equilibrium state. To move from equilibrium—to overcome the pressures of both individual resistance and group conformity—unfreezing must happen in one of three ways (see Exhibit 17-3). The **driving forces**, which direct behaviour away from the status quo, can be increased. The **restraining forces**, which hinder movement away from equilibrium, can be decreased. A third alternative is to combine the first two approaches. Companies that have been successful in the past are likely to encounter restraining forces because people question the need for change.[20] Similarly, research shows that companies with strong cultures excel at incremental change but are overcome by restraining forces against radical change.[21]

Research on organizational change has shown that, to be effective, the actual change has to happen quickly.[22] Organizations that build up to change do less well than those that get to and through the movement stage quickly.

Once change has been implemented, to be successful the new situation must be refrozen so it can be sustained over time. Without this last step, change will likely be short-lived, and employees will attempt to revert to the previous equilibrium state. The objective of refreezing, then, is to stabilize the new situation by balancing the driving and restraining forces.

EXHIBIT 17-2 Lewin's Three-Step Change Model

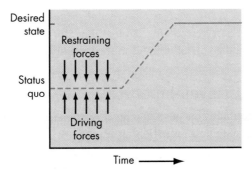

EXHIBIT 17-3   Unfreezing the Status Quo

Kotter's Eight-Step Plan for Implementing Change

John Kotter of Harvard Business School built on Lewin's three-step model to create a more detailed approach for implementing change.[23] Kotter began by listing common mistakes managers make when trying to initiate change. They may fail to create a sense of urgency about the need for change, to create a coalition for managing the change process, to have a vision for change and effectively communicate it, to remove obstacles that could impede the vision's achievement, to provide short-term and achievable goals, and/or to anchor the changes into the organization's culture. They may also declare victory too soon.

Kotter then established eight sequential steps to overcome these problems. They're listed in Exhibit 17-4 along with an example for each stage. Notice how Kotter's first four steps essentially describe Lewin's "unfreezing" stage. Steps 5, 6, and 7 represent "movement," and the final step works on "refreezing." So Kotter's contribution lies in providing

EXHIBIT 17-4   Kotter's Eight-Step Plan for Implementing Change

Source: Based on M. du Plessis, "Re-implementing an Individual Performance Management System as a Change Intervention at Higher Education Institutions—Overcoming Staff Resistance," *Proceedings of the 7th European Conference on Management Leadership and Governance* (2011), pp. 105–115.

1. ***Establish a sense of urgency by creating a compelling reason for why change is needed.*** A manager may point out that the company is underperforming and has lost market share to new competitors, so they need to change in order to win back their market share and stay in business.
2. ***Form a coalition with enough power to lead the change.*** That manager would then create a team to help make a plan. That team may include a marketing manager, sales manager, research and development expert, the CEO, etc.
3. ***Create a new vision to direct the change and strategies for achieving the vision.*** The team will develop a plan for regaining market share—perhaps new product features or an innovative ad campaign or a loyalty program.
4. ***Communicate the vision throughout the organization.*** The team will communicate the new strategy.
5. ***Empower others to act on the vision by removing barriers to change and encouraging risk taking and creative problem solving.*** Managers in each department will make sure their teams have what they need to do their part (develop the new feature, design the new ad campaign, etc.). This should include tie-ins to the employees' individual performance assessments and compensation/rewards.
6. ***Plan for, create, and reward short-term "wins" that move the organization toward the new vision.*** The managers will reward progress such as the first prototype of a new feature or the storyboarding of an innovative ad campaign. Rewards could include cash bonuses, recognition, praise, and other forms of incentive.
7. ***Consolidate improvements, reassess changes, and make necessary adjustments in the new programs.*** As the changes roll out, managers evaluate and assess, changing the plan as needed.
8. ***Reinforce the changes by demonstrating the relationship between new behaviours and organizational success.*** Managers would then highlight exactly how the new feature or the new ad campaign or loyalty program contributed to market share and profitability.

managers and change agents with a more detailed guide for successfully implementing change. Rather than just referencing "unfreezing," for example, Kotter tells managers exactly how they would go about doing it in their workplace.

Organizational Development

Organizational development (OD) is a collection of change methods that try to improve organizational effectiveness and employee well-being.[24]

OD methods value human and organizational growth, collaborative and participative processes, and a spirit of inquiry.[25] Contemporary OD borrows heavily from postmodern philosophy in putting heavy emphasis on the subjective ways in which people see their environment. The focus is on how individuals make sense of their work environment. The change agent may take the lead in OD, but there is a strong emphasis on collaboration. These are the underlying values in most OD efforts:

1. *Respect for people.* Individuals are perceived as responsible, conscientious, and caring. They should be treated with dignity and respect.
2. *Trust and support.* An effective and healthy organization is characterized by trust, authenticity, openness, and a supportive climate.
3. *Power equalization.* Effective organizations deemphasize hierarchical authority and control.
4. *Confrontation.* Problems should be openly confronted, not swept under the rug.
5. *Participation.* The more engaged in the decisions they are, the more people affected by a change will be committed to implementing it.

What are some OD techniques or interventions for bringing about change? Here are five.

1. *Survey feedback.* One tool for assessing attitudes held by organizational members, identifying discrepancies among member perceptions, and solving these differences is the **survey feedback** approach.[26] Everyone in an organization can participate in survey feedback, but of key importance is the organizational "family"—the manager of any given unit and the employees who report directly to her. All usually complete a questionnaire about their perceptions and attitudes on a range of topics, including decision-making practices; communication effectiveness; coordination among units; and satisfaction with the organization, job, peers, and immediate supervisor.

    Data from this questionnaire are tabulated with data pertaining to an individual's specific "family" and to the entire organization. They become the springboard for identifying problems and clarifying issues that may be creating difficulties for people. Particular attention is given to encouraging discussion and ensuring that it focuses on issues and ideas, and not on attacking individuals. For instance, are people listening? Are new ideas being generated? Can decision making, interpersonal relations, or job assignments be improved? Answers should lead the group to commit to various remedies for the problems identified.

2. *Process consultation.* Managers often sense their unit's performance can be improved but are unable to identify what to improve and how. The purpose of **process consultation (PC)** is for an outside consultant to assist a client, usually a manager, "to perceive, understand, and act upon process events" with which the manager must deal.[27]

    PC is similar to sensitivity training in assuming that we can improve organizational effectiveness by dealing with interpersonal problems and by emphasizing involvement.

But PC is more task-directed, and consultants are there to "give the client 'insight' into what is going on around him, within him, and between him and other people."[28] The consultants do not solve the organization's problems, but rather guide or coach the client to solve the problems alone after *jointly* diagnosing what needs improvement. The client develops the skill to analyze processes within the organizational unit to solve current and future problems.

3. *Team building.* We've noted throughout this text that organizations increasingly rely on teams to accomplish work tasks. **Team building** uses high-interaction group activities to increase trust and openness among team members, improve coordinative efforts, and increase team performance.[29] Team building typically includes goal setting, development of interpersonal relations among team members, role analysis to clarify each member's role and responsibilities, and team process analysis. It may emphasize or exclude certain activities, depending on the purpose of the development effort and the specific problems with which the team is confronted.

4. *Intergroup development.* A major area of concern in OD is dysfunctional conflict among groups. **Intergroup development** seeks to change groups' attitudes, stereotypes, and perceptions about each other. Here, training sessions closely resemble diversity training (in fact, diversity training largely evolved from intergroup development in OD), except that, rather than focusing on demographic differences, they focus on differences among occupations, departments, or divisions within an organization.

   Among several approaches for improving intergroup relations, a popular one emphasizes problem solving.[30] Each group meets independently to list its perceptions of itself and of the other group and how it believes the other group perceives it. The groups share their lists, discuss similarities and differences, and look for the causes of disparities. Once they have identified the causes of the difficulty, the groups move to the integration phase—developing solutions to improve relations between them. Subgroups can be formed of members from each of the conflicting groups to conduct further diagnoses and formulate alternative solutions.

5. *Appreciative inquiry.* Most OD approaches are problem-centred. They identify a problem or set of problems, then look for a solution. **Appreciative inquiry (AI)** instead accentuates the positive.[31] Rather than looking for problems to fix, it seeks to identify the unique qualities and special strengths of an organization, which members can build on to improve performance. That is, AI focuses on an organization's successes rather than its problems. The AI process consists of four steps—discovery, dreaming, design, and destiny—often played out in a large-group meeting over a two-or-three-day time period and overseen by a trained change agent. *Discovery* sets out to identify what people think are the organization's strengths. Employees recount times they felt the organization worked best or when they specifically felt most satisfied with their jobs. In *dreaming*, employees use information from the discovery phase to speculate on possible futures, such as what the organization will be like in five years. In *design*, participants find a common vision of how the organization will look in the future and agree on its unique qualities. For the fourth step, participants seek to define the organization's *destiny* or how to fulfill their dream, and they typically write action plans and develop implementation strategies.

CREATING A CULTURE FOR CHANGE

We've considered how organizations can *adapt* to change. But recently, some OB scholars have focused on a more proactive approach—how organizations can *embrace* change by transforming their cultures.

Various approaches can be used to manage organizational change and for developing a culture for change; it is unlikely one approach is always best in every situation.

Stimulating a Culture of Innovation

How can an organization become more innovative? An excellent model is W. L. Gore, the $2.6-billion-per-year company best known as the maker of Gore-Tex fabric.[32] Gore has established a reputation as an innovative company by developing a stream of diverse products—including guitar strings, dental floss, medical devices, and fuel cells.

What's the secret of Gore's success? What can other organizations do to duplicate its track record for innovation? Although there is no guaranteed formula, certain characteristics surface repeatedly when researchers study innovative organizations. We consider the characteristics as structural, cultural, and human resources. Change agents should consider introducing these characteristics into their organization to create an innovative climate. Let's start by clarifying what we mean by innovation.

Definition of Innovation   We have said change refers to making things different. **Innovation**, a more specialized kind of change, is a new idea applied to initiating or improving a product, process, or service.[33] So all innovations imply change, but not all changes necessarily introduce new ideas or lead to significant improvements. Innovations can range from small incremental improvements, such as tablets, to radical breakthroughs, such as Soylent, a liquid food product that is cheaper and more environmentally sustainable than nearly every other food source.[34]

Sources of Innovation   *Structural variables* have been the most studied potential source of innovation.[35] A comprehensive review of the structure–innovation relationship leads to the following conclusions:[36]

1. Organic structures positively influence innovation. Because they're lower in vertical differentiation, formalization, and centralization, organic organizations facilitate the flexibility, adaptation, and cross-fertilization that make the adoption of innovations easier.
2. Long tenure in management is associated with innovation. Managerial tenure apparently provides legitimacy and knowledge of how to accomplish tasks and obtain desired outcomes.
3. Innovation is nurtured when there are slack resources. Having an abundance of resources allows an organization to afford to purchase innovations, bear the cost of instituting them, and absorb failures.
4. Interunit communication is high in innovative organizations.[37] These organizations are high users of committees, task forces, cross-functional teams, and other mechanisms that facilitate interaction across departmental lines.

Innovative organizations tend to have similar *cultures*. They encourage experimentation. They reward both successes and failures. They celebrate mistakes. Unfortunately, in too many organizations, people are rewarded for the absence of failures rather than for the presence of successes. Such cultures extinguish risk taking and innovation. People will suggest and try new ideas only when they feel such behaviours exact no penalties. Managers in innovative organizations recognize that failures are a natural by-product of venturing into the unknown.

Within the *human resources* category, innovative organizations actively promote the training and development of their members so they keep current, offer high job security so employees don't fear getting fired for making mistakes, and encourage individuals to become champions of change. Once a new idea is developed, **idea champions** actively and enthusiastically promote it, build support, overcome resistance, and ensure it is implemented.[38] Champions have common personality characteristics: extremely high self-confidence, persistence, energy, and a tendency to take risks. They also display characteristics associated with transformational leadership—they inspire and energize others with their vision of an innovation's potential and their strong personal conviction about their mission. Idea champions are good at gaining the commitment of others, and their jobs provide considerable decision-making discretion; this autonomy helps them introduce and implement innovations.[39]

Do successful idea champions do things differently in different cultures? Yes.[40] People in collectivist cultures prefer appeals for cross-functional support for innovation efforts; people in high-power-distance cultures prefer champions to work closely with those in authority to approve innovative activities before work is begun; and the higher the uncertainty avoidance of a society, the more champions should work within the organization's rules and procedures to develop the innovation. These findings suggest that effective managers will alter their organization's championing strategies to reflect cultural values. So, for instance, although idea champions in Russia might succeed by ignoring budgetary limitations and working around confining procedures, champions in Austria, Denmark, Germany, or other cultures high in uncertainty avoidance will be more effective by closely following budgets and procedures.

WORK STRESS AND ITS MANAGEMENT

Friends say they're stressed from greater workloads and longer hours because of downsizing at their companies. Parents worry about the lack of job stability and reminisce about a time when a job with a large company implied lifetime security. We read surveys in which employees complain about the stress of trying to balance work and family responsibilities.[41] Harris, Rothenberg International, a leading provider of employee assistance programs (EAPs), finds that employees are having mental breakdowns and needing professional help at higher rates than ever.[42] Indeed, work is, for most people, the most significant source of stress in their life. What are the consequences of stress, and what can individuals and organizations do to reduce it?

Change is often stressful to individuals, making the topics of change and stress management inextricably interlinked. That said, researchers are beginning to accept that not all stress is harmful. Excessive stress, whether in the context of change or not, is detrimental. Some level of stress can be functional, though, as we will see shortly.

What Is Stress?

Stress is a dynamic condition in which an individual is confronted with an opportunity, demand, or resource related to what the individual desires and for which the outcome is perceived to be both uncertain and important.[43] This is a complicated definition. Let's look at its components more closely.

Although stress is typically discussed in a negative context, it is not necessarily bad in and of itself; it also has a positive value.[44] In response to stress, your nervous system, hypothalamus, pituitary, and adrenal glands supply you with stress hormones to cope. Your heartbeat

mariesacha/Fotolia

Many people find the challenge of balancing work, family, and their personal life to be highly stressful.

and breathing accelerate to increase oxygen, while your muscles tense for action.[45] This is an opportunity when it offers potential gain. Consider, for example, the superior performance an athlete, stage performer, or field sales person gives in a "clutch" situation. These individuals often use stress positively to energize themselves, help them rise to the occasion, and perform at their maximum. Similarly, many professionals see the pressures of heavy workloads and deadlines as positive challenges that enhance the quality of their work and the satisfaction they get from their job. However, when the situation is negative, stress is harmful and may hinder your progress by elevating your blood pressure uncomfortably and creating an erratic heart rhythm as you struggle to speak and think logically.[46]

Researchers have argued that **challenge stressors**—stressors associated with workload, pressure to complete tasks, and time urgency—operate quite differently from **hindrance stressors**—stressors that keep you from reaching your goals (for example, red tape, office politics, confusion over job responsibilities). Evidence suggests that challenge stressors produce less strain than hindrance stressors.[47]

Researchers have sought to clarify the conditions under which each type of stress exists. It appears that employees who have stronger commitment to their organizations can transfer psychological stress into greater focus and higher sales performance, whereas employees with low levels of commitment perform worse under stress.[48] And when challenge stress increases, those with high levels of organizational support have higher role-based performance, but those with low levels of organizational support do not.[49]

More typically, stress is associated with **demands** and **resources**. Demands are responsibilities, pressures, obligations, and uncertainties individuals face in the workplace. Resources are things within an individual's control that he can use to resolve the demands. Let's discuss what this demands–resources model means.[50]

When you take a test at school or undergo your annual performance review at work, you feel stress because you confront opportunities and performance pressures. A good performance review may lead to a promotion, greater responsibilities, and a higher salary. A poor review may prevent you from getting a promotion. An extremely poor review might even result in your being fired. To the extent you can apply resources to the demands on you—such as being prepared, placing the exam or review in perspective, or obtaining social support—you will feel less stress.

Research suggests that adequate resources help reduce the stressful nature of demands if demands and resources match. If emotional demands are stressing you, having emotional resources in the form of social support is especially important. If the demands are cognitive—say, information overload—then job resources in the form of computer support or information are more important. Thus, under the demands–resources perspective, coping resources are just as important in offsetting stress as demands are in increasing stress.[51]

Consequences of Stress

Stress shows itself in a number of ways, such as high blood pressure, ulcers, irritability, difficulty making routine decisions, loss of appetite, accident-proneness, and the like. These symptoms fit under three general categories: physiological, psychological, and behavioural.

Physiological Symptoms   Most early concern with stress was directed at physiological symptoms because most researchers were specialists in the health and medical sciences. Their work led to the conclusion that stress could create changes in metabolism, increase heart and breathing rates and blood pressure, bring on headaches, and induce heart attacks.

Evidence clearly suggests that stress may have harmful physiological effects. One study linked stressful job demands to increased susceptibility to upper-respiratory illnesses and poor immune system functioning, especially for individuals with low self-efficacy.[52] A long-term study conducted in the United Kingdom found that job strain was associated with higher levels of coronary heart disease.[53] Still another study conducted with Danish human services workers found that higher levels of psychological burnout at the work-unit level were related to significantly higher levels of sickness absence.[54] Many other studies have shown similar results linking work stress to a variety of indicators of poor health.

Psychological Symptoms Job dissatisfaction is an obvious cause of stress. But stress shows itself in other psychological states including tension, anxiety, irritability, boredom, and procrastination. For example, a study that tracked responses of employees over time found that stress due to high workloads was related to lower emotional well-being.[55]

Jobs that make multiple and conflicting demands or that lack clarity about the incumbent's duties, authority, and responsibilities increase both stress and dissatisfaction.[56] Similarly, the less control people have over the pace of their work, the greater their stress and dissatisfaction. Jobs that provide a low level of variety, significance, autonomy, feedback, and identity appear to create stress and reduce satisfaction and involvement in the job.[57] Not everyone reacts to autonomy in the same way, however. For those with an external locus of control, increased job control increases the tendency to experience stress and exhaustion.[58]

Behavioural Symptoms Research on behaviour and stress has been conducted across several countries and over time, and the relationships appear relatively consistent. Behaviour-related stress symptoms include reductions in productivity, absence, and turnover, as well as changes in eating habits, increased smoking or consumption of alcohol, rapid speech, fidgeting, and sleep disorders.[59]

Managing Stress

Because low to moderate levels of stress can be functional and lead to higher performance, management may not be concerned when employees experience them. Employees, however, are likely to perceive even low levels of stress as undesirable. It's not unlikely, therefore, for employees and management to have different notions of what constitutes an acceptable level of stress on the job. What management may consider to be "a positive stimulus that keeps the adrenaline running" is very likely to be seen as "excessive pressure" by the employee. Keep this in mind as we discuss individual and organizational approaches to managing stress.[60]

Individual Approaches An employee can take personal responsibility for reducing stress levels. People who have a high score on emotional intelligence tests are often better able to recognize when their stress level is becoming excessive, so proactively selecting people with this trait when hiring for high-stress jobs and/or providing emotional intelligence training may improve resilience. Individual stress mitigation strategies that have proven effective include time-management techniques, increased physical exercise, relaxation training, and expanded social support networks.

Many people manage their time poorly. The well-organized employee, like the well-organized student, can often accomplish twice as much as the person who is poorly organized. So an understanding and utilization of basic time-management principles can help individuals better cope with tensions created by job demands.[61] A few of the best-known time-management principles are: (1) making daily lists of activities to be accomplished, (2) prioritizing activities by importance and urgency, (3) scheduling activities according to the priorities set, (4) knowing your daily cycle and handling the most demanding parts of your job when you are most alert and productive, and (5) avoiding electronic distractions like frequently checking e-mail, which can limit attention and reduce efficiency.[62] Such skills can help minimize procrastination by focusing efforts on immediate goals and boosting motivation even in the face of tasks that are less desirable.[63]

Exercise and a healthy lifestyle are among the most effective ways to combat day-to-day stress.

AntonioDiaz/Fotolia

Physicians have recommended noncompetitive *physical exercise*, such as aerobics, walking, jogging, swimming, and riding a bicycle, as a way to deal with excessive stress levels. These activities increase lung capacity, lower the resting heart rate, and provide a mental diversion from work pressures, effectively reducing work-related levels of stress.[64]

Individuals can also teach themselves to reduce tension through *relaxation techniques* such as meditation, hypnosis, and deep breathing. The objective is to reach a state of deep physical relaxation in which you focus all your energy on release of muscle tension.[65] Deep relaxation for 15 or 20 minutes a day releases strain and provides a pronounced sense of peacefulness, as well as significant changes in heart rate, blood pressure, and other physiological factors. A growing body of research shows that simply taking breaks from work at routine intervals can facilitate psychological recovery, and reduce stress significantly, and may improve job performance; these effects are even greater if relaxation techniques are employed.[66]

As we have noted, friends, family, or work colleagues can provide an outlet when stress levels become excessive. Expanding your *social support network* provides someone to hear your problems and offers a more objective perspective on a stressful situation than your own.

Organizational Approaches   Several organizational factors that cause stress—particularly task and role demands—are controlled by management and thus can be modified or changed. Strategies to consider include improved employee selection and job placement, training, realistic goal setting, redesign of jobs, increased employee involvement, improved organizational communication, employee sabbaticals, and corporate wellness programs.

Certain jobs are more stressful than others but, as we've seen, individuals differ in their response to stressful situations. We know that individuals with little experience or an external locus of control tend to be more prone to stress. *Selection and placement* decisions should take these facts into consideration. Obviously, management shouldn't restrict hiring to only experienced individuals with an internal locus, but such individuals may adapt better to high-stress jobs and perform those jobs more effectively. Similarly, *training* can increase an individual's self-efficacy and thus lessen job strain.

We discussed *goal setting* in Chapter 7. Individuals perform better when they have specific and challenging goals and receive feedback on their progress toward these goals. Goal setting can reduce stress as well as provide motivation.[67] Employees who are highly committed to their goals and see purpose in their jobs experience less stress, partly because they are more likely to perceive stressors as challenges rather than hindrances. Specific goals perceived as attainable clarify performance expectations. In addition, goal feedback reduces uncertainties about actual job performance. The result is less employee frustration, role ambiguity, and stress.

Redesigning jobs to give employees more responsibility, more meaningful work, more autonomy, and increased feedback can reduce stress because these factors give employees greater control over work activities and lessen their dependence on others. But as we noted in our discussion of work design, not all employees want enriched jobs. The right redesign for employees with a low need for growth might be less responsibility and increased specialization. If individuals prefer structure and routine, reducing skill variety should also reduce uncertainties and stress levels.

Role stress is detrimental to a large extent because employees feel uncertain about goals, expectations, how they'll be evaluated, and the like. By giving employees a voice in the decisions that directly affect their job performance, management can increase employee control and reduce role stress. Thus, managers should consider *increasing employee involvement* in decision making because evidence clearly shows that increases in employee empowerment reduce psychological strain.[68]

Increasing formal *organizational communication* with employees reduces uncertainty by lessening role ambiguity and role conflict. Given the importance that perceptions play in moderating the stress–response relationship, management can also use effective communications as a means to shape employee perceptions. Remember that what employees categorize as demands, threats, or opportunities at work is an interpretation and that interpretation can be affected by the symbols and actions communicated by management.

Our final suggestion is to create organizationally supported **wellness programs**. These typically provide workshops to help people quit smoking, control alcohol use, lose weight, eat better, and develop a regular exercise program; they focus on the employee's total physical and mental condition.[69] Some help employees improve their psychological health as well. A meta-analysis of 36 programs designed to reduce stress (including wellness programs) showed that interventions to help employees reframe stressful situations and use active coping strategies appreciably reduced stress levels.[70] Most wellness programs assume employees need to take personal responsibility for their physical and mental health and that the organization provides a means to that end.

SUMMARY

- The real world is turbulent, requiring organizations and their members to undergo dynamic change if they are to perform at competitive levels.

- Resistance to change is common and should be anticipated.

- Formal change management strategies and tactics such as those outlined in the Kotter model can help lessen resistance and increase the probability of launching successful change initiatives.

- Organizations can select employees and structure themselves in ways that encourage acceptance of change and innovation.

- Stress is a natural by-product of work life affecting organizational behaviour.

- Successful organizations recognize the factors that cause undue stress and take an active role in helping employees perform optimally.

IMPLICATIONS FOR MANAGERS

- Consider that, as a manager, you are a change agent in your organization. The decisions you make and your role-modelling behaviours will help shape the organization's change culture.

- Your management policies and practices will determine the degree to which the organization learns and adapts to changing environmental factors.

- Some stress is good. Low to moderate amounts of stress enable many people to perform their jobs better by increasing their work intensity, alertness, and ability to react. This is especially true if stress arises due to challenges on the job rather than hindrances that prevent employees from doing their jobs effectively.

- You can help alleviate harmful workplace stress for you and any employees you supervise by accurately matching workloads to employees, providing employees with stress-coping resources, and responding to their concerns.

- You can identify extreme stress when performance declines, turnover increases, health-related absenteeism increases, and engagement declines. However, by the time these symptoms are visible, it may be too late to be helpful, so stay alert for early indicators and be proactive.

BREAKOUT QUESTION FOR GROUP DISCUSSION

What personal strategies have you found most effective when trying to manage day-to-day work-related stress? Do different strategies prove more effective depending on the specific source of the stress? If so, why do you think that is?

PERSONAL INVENTORY ASSESSMENT

In the Personal Inventory Assessment found in MyManagementLab, take the assessment: Tolerance of Ambiguity Scale.

SELF-REFLECTION ACTIVITY

How comfortable are you with uncertainty? In the Personal Inventory Assessment found in MyManagementLab, take the assessment Tolerance of Ambiguity Scale which can help you to answer that question. Ambiguity tends to be much higher in certain occupations so this information can help direct career decisions. It can also help you understand why you may have a different response to change than others around you. If you have an unusually high tolerance for ambiguity, for instance, you may find it difficult to understand why others hesitate to embrace changes that you yourself are comfortable with.

Most people have some level of discomfort with ambiguity so it can be useful to think about how to minimize ambiguity for coworkers and direct reports. One of the most difficult ambiguous situations that managers deal with is layoffs—employees often know they are coming but do not know who will be impacted, which is very stressful. Given that the names of laid off workers cannot be leaked prior to the actual layoffs, how might a manager help employees deal with this particular form of uncertainty and associated stress?

MINI CASE STRESSED IN SOFTWARE

Kaitlyn was in a difficult situation and didn't know what to do. Should she continue along her current career path or make a change? She didn't know the best way to balance her life and she felt so overwhelmed that it was hard to even think about the issue clearly. Kaitlyn looked back to how she had ended up in such a difficult place.

Kaitlyn had graduated six years earlier at the height of a recession. Unable to find work in her field (psychology), she had taken the only job offered: answering phones in the call centre of a large software company. Over time, she had worked her way up from customer service agent to telemarketer, then to inside sales. She received considerable support and training from her employer throughout her career ascent. Two years ago she had received her most recent promotion to field sales representative. In that role Kaitlyn sold ERP database solutions to large companies.

She focused on new accounts within government. Deals generally took well over a year to close, but when they did her commission might easily exceed $10,000 for each individual deal. Her salary only barely kept her above the poverty line; but Kaitlyn was very good at her job, and her commissions were such that at the age of 27 she was earning $106,000 per year.

At first Kaitlyn loved the field sales role. She enjoyed the work itself; in fact she found field sales to be a lot like applied psychology, which fascinated her. She thought it glamorous to fly all over Canada and the United States to see clients. She often had the chance to indulge in tourist activities while on business trips. In just the past six weeks she had visited Mount St. Helens and the Calgary Stampede, and gone whale watching near Victoria.

She also really enjoyed her income, which she knew would be difficult to replace in any other job. Of course, that income was never guaranteed; and if she had a few slow months even making the rent was a challenge. She worried about that often, but somehow she always managed to get by, even if she had to temporarily ring up credit card debts to do it.

After just over two years, however, Kaitlyn's perspective began to change. She had four slow months in a row. Her boss now looked at her differently; she felt like he was watching her every move rather than trusting her to do her job. Her overall performance was good enough that she survived a major layoff in the department, but knowing future layoffs could be in the works was a source of ongoing anxiety.

Her three weeks of travel every month now seemed exhausting, not glamorous. She was tired of always eating out alone, and harassment from males also travelling solo was common in hotel restaurants so that she seldom felt safe exploring cities on her own after dark; so she ate a lot of fast food alone in her room.

It was hard to stick to an exercise regime with all the travel, and she had gained an unhealthy amount of weight. She never felt 100 percent well. She had recurring bouts of acid indigestion and sometimes fell into what she described as a "black funk" for several days, calling in sick and staying in bed watching reruns of 70s TV shows.

Even worse, since she was away so frequently her friends and family had stopped inviting her to events. They always assumed she would be unavailable. Her frequent absences also made it challenging to date. Her time at home was spent going by herself to spas, yoga classes, and any other stress-relieving events she could find. Despite these efforts she often felt slightly anxious and had trouble sleeping.

When Kaitlyn was actually with a customer and was "on" she still felt great. She still enjoyed applying psychological principles to make sales. She felt exhilarated whenever a deal closed, and proud that she could hold her own in a room full of C-suite executives and high-level decision makers. But everything seemed harder now. Before, being "on" came naturally; now it was work. Kaitlyn didn't know why, but it became harder and harder to relate to her client's problems and needs, a critical competency in field sales.

Kaitlyn liked her job much of the time and really, really loved her five-figure commission cheques, both for the money itself and because of what they said about her independence and ability to provide for herself. That said, she was tired of travel, tired of always being in "sales mode," tired of quotas and pressure. She wondered if there was a way she could better manage stress to make this job easier. Perhaps her employer might make some adjustments? Or should she just look at starting a new career elsewhere?

Discussion Questions

1. What contributes to Kaitlyn's stress? Of those contributing factors, which can she control and which does her employer control?

2. If she stays with this company, what might Kaitlyn do herself to better manage stress? What could her employer do?

3. What do you think would happen if Kaitlyn continued on her current course, unchanged? Explain your answer.

4. If you were Kaitlyn, what would you do next and why?

MINI CASE   MAKE WAY FOR INNOVATION

Michael looked over the new ideas his workers had submitted, feeling increasingly frustrated. As head of the research and development department, he knew innovation was the only thing that would save the company.

He and his team worked for an independent online dating service that tailored its sites to specific lifestyle groups such as adventure travellers, swingers, homesteaders, and even Trekkies. Unfortunately, there had been an explosion of competitive offerings recently, and their websites were getting less and less popular. Other dating sites had much more sophisticated features, including mobile apps, the ability to locate people nearby at the moment, and complex personality matching algorithms based on answers that clients provide to various psychological indexes. Their traditional "list stuff on your webpage and message each other" approach just couldn't compete.

Michael knew they needed some innovative suggestions—he had just been hired six months earlier to lead that exact process—but everything his team brought him had already been done before. There weren't any truly new ideas. Michael was surprised. He had done several things to motivate innovation. He had made sure everyone knew the hierarchy and that the final decision about new products was ultimately his, so they had better be prepared to impress him. He had then set up a performance incentive. The individual with the best idea in the first year would get a $10,000 bonus. There was no prize for second place, so people were encouraged to keep their projects to themselves to prevent idea theft. Some of his employees had asked if they could go for training on mobile device application development to help them wrap their head around these capabilities. Michael saw this as a distraction from their main task, so he refused to release funds for it. "Once you have proven you can give us a competitive edge, then we'll invest in training," he explained.

Yet despite his best efforts he wasn't getting the performance he needed from his team. What now?

Discussion Questions

1. Does Michael's strategy represent best practices in fostering innovation? Why or why not?

2. Propose an alternative structure and incentive system that might help foster innovation at this company. What form would it take? Be as specific as possible.

3. If Michael were to change his tactics, how should he introduce that change with his team to maximize buy-in and acceptance? Explain your answer.

MyManagementLab

Study, practise, and explore real management situations with these helpful resources:

- **Interactive Lesson Presentations:** Work through interactive presentations and assessments to test your knowledge of management concepts.
- **PIA (Personal Inventory Assessments):** Enhance your ability to connect with key concepts through these engaging self-reflection assessments.
- **Study Plan:** Check your understanding of chapter concepts with self-study quizzes.
- **Simulations:** Practise decision making in simulated management environments.

PERSONAL INVENTORY ASSESSMENT

The end of a book typically has the same meaning to an author that it has to the reader: It generates feelings of both accomplishment and relief. As all of us rejoice at having completed our tour of the essential concepts in organizational behaviour, this is a good time to examine where we've been and what it all means.

The underlying theme of this book has been that the behaviour of people at work is not a random phenomenon. Employees are complex entities, but their attitudes and behaviour can nevertheless be explained and predicted with a reasonable degree of accuracy. Our approach has been to look at organizational behaviour at three levels: the individual, the group, and the organization system.

We started with the individual and reviewed the major psychological contributions to understanding why individuals act as they do. We found that people's perceptions vary by age, gender, personality, and culture, and that those perceptions can be flawed due to non-conscious biases. We learned how to better identify and mitigate those biases. We also discovered that people seek out fairness, equity, recognition, respect, opportunity, and the ability to live a life they find fulfilling. Evidence-based generalizations can be made about the best way for organizations to fulfill those needs, thereby maximizing productivity and efficiency. For example, we know that individuals with a conventional type of personality are better matched to certain jobs in corporate management than are people with investigative personalities. So placing people into jobs that are compatible with their personality types should result in higher-performing and more satisfied employees.

Next, our analysis moved to the group level. We argued that the understanding of group behaviour is more complex than merely multiplying what we know about individuals by the number of members in the group, because people act differently in a group than when they are alone. We demonstrated how roles, norms, leadership styles, power relationships, and other, similar group factors affect the behaviour of employees.

Finally, we overlaid system-wide variables on our knowledge of individual and group behaviour to further improve our understanding of organizational behaviour. Major emphasis was given to showing how an organization's structure, design, and culture affect both the attitudes and the behaviour of employees.

It might be tempting to criticize the stress this book has put on theoretical concepts, but as noted psychologist Kurt Lewin is purported to have said, "There is nothing so practical as a good theory." Of course, it's also true that there is nothing so impractical as a good theory that leads nowhere. To avoid presenting theories that lead nowhere, this book has included a wealth of examples and illustrations. And we have regularly stopped to inquire about the implications of theory for the practice of management. The result has been the presentation of numerous concepts that not only offer insights into behaviour individually, but also, when taken together, provide a complex system to help us explain, predict, and control organizational behaviour.

Chapter 1

1. S. Albert, quoted with permission from private e-mail correspondence with University of Winnipeg faculty member Dr. Katherine Breward, March 28, 2015.
2. Canada's Top Employers website, accessed March 15, 2015 at http://www.canadastop100.com/national.
3. S. E. Humphrey, J. D. Nahrgang, and F. P. Morgeson, "Integrating Motivational, Social, and Contextual Work Design Features: A Meta-analytic Summary and Theoretical Extension of the Work Design Literature," *Journal of Applied Psychology* 92, no. 5 (2007), pp. 1332–1356.
4. E. R. Burris, "The Risks and Rewards of Speaking Up: Managerial Responses to Employee Voice," *Academy of Management Journal* 55, no. 4 (2012), pp. 851–875.
5. T. L. Miller, C. L. Wesley II, and D. E. Williams, "Educating the Minds of Caring Hearts: Comparing the Views of Practitioners and Educators on the Importance of Social Entrepreneurship Competencies," *Academy of Management Learning & Education* 2, no. 3 (2012), pp. 349–370.
6. H. Aguinis and A. Glavas, "What We Don't Know About Corporate Social Responsibility: A Review and Research Agenda," *Journal of Management* (July 2012), pp. 932–968.
7. See, for instance, C. Heath, and S. B. Sitkin, "Big-B Versus Big-O: What Is Organizational About Organizational Behavior?" *Journal of Organizational Behavior* (February 2001), pp. 43–58. For a review of what one researcher believes should be included in organizational behavior, based on survey data, see J. B. Miner, "The Rated Importance, Scientific Validity, and Practical Usefulness of Organizational Behavior Theories: A Quantitative Review," *Academy of Management Learning & Education* (September 2003), pp. 250–268.
8. D. M. Rousseau and S. McCarthy, "Educating Managers from an Evidence-Based Perspective," *Academy of Management Learning & Education* 6, no. 1 (2007), pp. 84–101; and S. L. Rynes, T. L. Giluk, and K. G. Brown, "The Very Separate Worlds of Academic and Practitioner Periodicals in Human Resource Management: Implications for Evidence-Based Management," *Academy of Management Journal* 50, no. 5 (2007), pp. 987–1008.
9. M. J. Mauboussin, "Most Companies Use the Wrong Metrics. Don't Be One of Them," *Harvard Business Review* (October 2012), pp. 46–56.
10. A. Stanton, *Neuroeconomics and the Firm* (Cheltenham, UK: Edward Elgar, 2010).
11. E. Mayo, *The Human Problems of an Industrial Civilization* (New York: Macmillan, 1933); and F. J. Roethlisberger and W. J. Dickson, *Management and the Worker* (Cambridge, MA: Harvard University Press, 1939).
12. Clem Tisdell, *Bounded Rationality and Economic Evolution: A Contribution to Decision Making, Economics, and Management* (Cheltenham, UK: Brookfield, 1996).
13. G. Hofstede, G. Hofstede, and M. Minkov, *Cultures and Organizations: Software of the Mind* (New York: McGraw Hill, 2010).
14. V. Talotta, "TD Bank Cuts Forecast for Canadian Economy," *Toronto Star*, January 26, 2015, http://www.thestar.com/business/2015/01/26/td-bank-cuts-forecast-for-canadian-economy.html.
15. See, for instance, M. Workman and W. Bommer, "Redesigning Computer Call Center Work: A Longitudinal Field Experiment," *Journal of Organizational Behavior* (May 2004), pp. 317–337.
16. S. Shellenbarger, "Single and off the Fast Track," *The Wall Street Journal* (May 23, 2012), pp. D1, D3.
17. F. Luthans and C. M. Youssef, "Emerging Positive Organizational Behavior," *Journal of Management* (June 2007), pp. 321–349; C. M. Youssef and F. Luthans, "Positive Organizational Behavior in the Workplace: The Impact of Hope, Optimism, and Resilience," *Journal of Management* 33, no. 5 (2007), pp. 774–800; and J. E. Dutton and S. Sonenshein, "Positive Organizational Scholarship," in C. Cooper and J. Barling (eds.), *Encyclopedia of Positive Psychology* (Thousand Oaks, CA: Sage, 2007).
18. L. M. Roberts, G. Spreitzer, J. Dutton, R. Quinn, E. Heaphy, and B. Barker, "How to Play to Your Strengths," *Harvard Business Review* (January 2005), pp. 1–6; and L. M. Roberts, J. E. Dutton, G. M. Spreitzer, E. D. Heaphy, and R. E. Quinn, "Composing the Reflected Best-Self Portrait: Becoming Extraordinary in Work Organizations," *Academy of Management Review* 30, no. 4 (2005), pp. 712–736.
19. W. Bailey and A. Spicer, "When Does National Identity Matter? Convergence and Divergence in International Business Ethics," *Academy of Management Journal* 50, no. 6 (2007), pp. 1462–1480; and A. B. Oumlil and J. L. Balloun, "Ethical Decision-Making Differences Between American and Moroccan Managers," *Journal of Business Ethics* 84, no. 4 (2009), pp. 457–478.
20. J. Merritt, "For MBAs, Soul-Searching 101," *Business Week* (September 16, 2002), pp. 64–66; and S. Greenhouse, "The Mood at Work: Anger and Anxiety," *The New York Times* (October 29, 2002), p. E1.
21. D. M. Mayer, M. Kuenzi, R. Greenbaum, M. Bardes, and R. Salvador, "How Low Does Ethical Leadership Flow? Test of a Trickle-Down Model," *Organizational Behavior and Human Decision Processes* 108, no. 1 (2009), pp. 1–13; and A. Ardichvili, J. A. Mitchell, and D. Jondle, "Characteristics of Ethical Business Cultures," *Journal of Business Ethics* 85, no. 4 (2009), pp. 445–451.

Chapter 2

1. Government of Canada, Justice Laws website, accessed on February 15, 2015 at http://laws-lois.justice.gc.ca/eng/acts/C-18.7/page-1.html#h-1.
2. Government of Canada, *Canadian Multiculturalism: An Inclusive Citizenship*, accessed February 15, 2015 at http://www.cic.gc.ca/english/multiculturalism/citizenship.asp.
3. Government of Canada, *Indicators of Well-Being in Canada: Work – Employment Rate*, accessed February 3, 2015 at http://www4.hrsdc.gc.ca/.3ndic.1t.4r@-eng.jsp?iid=13#M_2.
4. L. Colley, "Not Codgers in Cardigans! Female Workforce Participation and Ageing Public Services," *Gender Work and Organization* (May 2013), pp. 327–238; and M. DiNatale and S. Boraas, "The Labor Force Experience of Women from Generation X," *Monthly Labor Review* (March 2002), pp. 1–15.
5. Government of Canada, *Indicators of Well-Being in Canada: Work–Employment Rate*, accessed February 3, 2015 at http://www4.hrsdc.gc.ca/.3ndic.1t.4r@-eng.jsp?iid=13#M_4.

6. P. Kelly, S. Park, and L. Lepper, Economic Recession and Immigrant Labour Markets in Canada, *Toronto Immigrant Employment Data Initiative*, 2011, accessed February 5, 2015 at http://ceris.metropolis.net/wp-content/uploads/virtual_library/Kelly_et_al_2011b.pdf.

7. Government of Canada, *Indicators of Well-Being in Canada: Work–Employment Rate*, accessed February 3, 2015 at http://www4.hrsdc.gc.ca/.3ndic.1t.4r@-eng.jsp?iid=13#M_3.

8. HRPA Webinar Series, Managing the Dynamics of an Aging Workforce, accessed February 2, 2015 at http://www.hrpa.ca/ProfessionalDevelopment/Pages/On-Demand-Webinar-Age-Discrimination-Managing-the-Dynamics-of-an-Aging-Workforce.aspx.

9. P. Chattopadhyay, M. Tluchowska, and E. George, "Identifying the Ingroup: A Closer Look at the Influence of Demographic Dissimilarity on Employee Social Identity," *Academy of Management Review* 29, no. 2 (2004), pp. 180–202.

10. P. Chattopadhyay, "Beyond Direct and Symmetrical Effects: The Influence of Demographic Dissimilarity on Organizational Citizenship Behavior," *Academy of Management Journal* 42, no. 3 (1999), pp. 273–287.

11. D. A. Harrison, K. H. Price, J. H. Gavin, and A. T. Florey, "Time, Teams, and Task Performance: Changing Effects of Surface- and Deep-Level Diversity on Group Functioning," *Academy of Management Journal* 45, no. 5 (2002), pp. 1029–1045; and A. H. Eagly and J. L. Chin, "Are Memberships in Race, Ethnicity, and Gender Categories Merely Surface Characteristics?" *American Psychologist* 65 (2010), pp. 934–935.

12. T. Grant, "More Canadians to Consider Delaying Retirement Past 65: Poll," *Globe and Mail* (February 18, 2015), http://www.theglobeandmail.com/globe-investor/personal-finance/retirement-rrsps/more-canadians-considering-delaying-retirement-past-age-of-65-poll/article23038027.

13. K. A. Wrenn and T. J. Maurer, "Beliefs About Older Workers' Learning and Development Behavior in Relation to Beliefs About Malleability of Skills, Age-Related Decline, and Control," *Journal of Applied Social Psychology* 34, no. 2 (2004), pp. 223–242; and R. A. Posthuma and M. A. Campion, "Age Stereotypes in the Workplace: Common Stereotypes, Moderators, and Future Research Directions," *Journal of Management* 35 (2009), pp. 158–188.

14. T. W. H. Ng and D. C. Feldman, "Re-examining the Relationship Between Age and Voluntary Turnover," *Journal of Vocational Behavior* 74 (2009), pp. 283–294.

15. T. W. H. Ng and D. C. Feldman, "The Relationship of Age to Ten Dimensions of Job Performance," *Journal of Applied Psychology* 93 (2008), pp. 392–423.

16. T. W. H. Ng and D. C. Feldman, "Evaluating Six Common Stereotypes About Older Workers with Meta-analytical Data," *Personnel Psychology* 65 (2012), pp. 821–858.

17. See Ng and Feldman, "The Relationship of Age to Ten Dimensions of Job Performance."

18. T. W. H. Ng and D. C. Feldman, "The Relationship of Age with Job Attitudes: A Meta-analysis," *Personnel Psychology* 63 (2010), pp. 677–718.

19. F. Kunze, S. A. Boehm, and H. Bruch, "Age Diversity, Age Discrimination Climate and Performance Consequences—A Cross Organizational Study," *Journal of Organizational Behavior* 32 (2011), pp. 264–290.

20. P. L. Roth, K. L. Purvis, and P. Bobko, "A Meta-analysis of Gender Group Differences for Measures of Job Performance in Field Studies," *Journal of Management* (March 2012), pp. 719–739.

21. See E. M. Weiss, G. Kemmler, E. A. Deisenhammer, W. W. Fleischhacker, and M. Delazer, "Sex Differences in Cognitive Functions," *Personality and Individual Differences* (September 2003), pp. 863–875; and A. F. Jorm, K. J. Anstey, H. Christensen, and B. Rodgers, "Gender Differences in Cognitive Abilities: The Mediating Role of Health State and Health Habits," *Intelligence* (January 2004), pp. 7–23.

22. Pay Equity Commission, Government of Ontario, *Gender Wage Gap*, accessed February 17, 2015 at http://www.payequity.gov.on.ca/en/about/pubs/genderwage/wagegap.php.

23. Statistics Canada, "Education in Canada: Attainment, Field of Study and Location of Study," http://www12.statcan.gc.ca/nhs-enm/2011/as-sa/99-012-x/99-012-x2011001-eng.cfm#a2.

24. R. K. Chang, "Bias Persists for Women of Science, A Study Finds," *Science, The New York Times* (September 25, 2012), pp. 1, 6.

25. K. Peters, M. Ryan, S. A. Haslam, and H. Fernandes, "To Belong or Not to Belong: Evidence That Women's Occupational Disidentification Is Promoted by Lack of Fit with Masculine Occupational Prototypes," *Journal of Personnel Psychology* 2 (2012), pp. 148–158.

26. P. Kellet, D. Gregory, and J. Evans, "Patriarchal Paradox: Gender Performance and Men's Nursing Careers," *Gender in Management* 29(2) (2014), pp. 77–90; and E. Jeanes, D. Knights, and P. Martin, *Handbook of Gender, Work, and Organization* (West Sussex, UK: Wiley, 2011).

27. R. E. Silverman, "Study Suggests Fix for Gender Bias on the Job," *The Wall Street Journal* (January 9, 2013), p. D4.

28. E. B. King et al., "Benevolent Sexism at Work: Gender Differences in the Distribution of Challenging Developmental Experiences," *Journal of Management* (November 2012), pp. 1835–1866.

29. M. E. Heilman and T. G. Okimoto, "Why Are Women Penalized for Success at Male Tasks? The Implied Communality Deficit," *Journal of Applied Psychology* 92, no. 1 (2007), pp. 81–92.

30. See, for instance, J. Bussey, "How Women Can Get Ahead: Advice from Female CEOs," *The Wall Street Journal* (May 18, 2012), pp. B1–B2; T. Gara, "Sandberg Opens Up on Women and Work," *The Wall Street Journal* (February 6, 2013); and L. Petrecca, "High-Paying Careers Top More Young Women's Lists," *The Wall Street Journal* (April 20, 2012) pp. 1A–2A.

31. D. R. Avery, P. F. McKay, and D. C. Wilson, "What Are the Odds? How Demographic Similarity Affects the Prevalence of Perceived Employment Discrimination," *Journal of Applied Psychology* 93 (2008), pp. 235–249.

32. J. L. Raver and L. H. Nishii, "Once, Twice, or Three Times as Harmful? Ethnic Harassment, Gender Harassment, and Generalized Workplace Harassment," *Journal of Applied Psychology* 95 (2010), pp. 236–254.

33. J. I. Hancock, D. G. Allen, F. A. Bosco, K. R. McDaniel, and C. A. Pierce, "Meta-analytic Review of Employee Turnover as a Predictor of Firm Performance," *Journal of Management* (March 2013), pp. 573–603.

34. A. Tilcsik, "Pride and Prejudice: Employment Discrimination Against Openly Gay Men in the United States," *American Journal of Sociology* 117 (2011), pp. 586–626.

35. C. Burns, "The Costly Business of Discrimination," *Center for American Progress* (March 2012), p. 13, http://www.scribd.com/doc/81214767/The-Costly-Business-of-Discrimination.

36. J. M. McCarthy, C. H. Van Iddekinge, and M. A. Campion, "Are Highly Structured Job Interviews Resistant to Demographic Similarity Effects?" *Personnel Psychology* 63 (2010), pp. 325–359; and G. N. Powell and D. A. Butterfield, "Exploring the Influence of Decision Makers' Race and Gender on Actual Promotions to Top Management," *Personnel Psychology* 55, no. 2 (2002), pp. 397–428.

37. Avery, McKay, and Wilson, "What Are the Odds? How Demographic Similarity Affects the Prevalence of Perceived

Employment Discrimination"; and Raver and Nishii, "Once, Twice, or Three Times as Harmful? Ethnic Harassment, Gender Harassment, and Generalized Workplace Harassment."

38. Government of Canada, *Indicators of Well-Being in Canada: Work–Unemployment Rate*, accessed February 15, 2015 at http://www4.hrsdc.gc.ca/.3ndic.1t.4r@-eng.jsp?iid=16.

39. D. Wilson and D. McDonald, "The Income Gap Between Aboriginal Peoples and the Rest of Canada," Canadian Center for Policy Alternatives, 2010, accessed February 1, 2015 at http://ywcacanada.ca/data/research_docs/00000121.pdf.

40. "Should Canada Accept More Refugees?" Yahoo News, https://ca.news.yahoo.com/blogs/canada-politics/canada-accept-more-refugees-124712264.html.

41. United Nations, "Background Briefing on Intersectionality," Working Group on Women and Human Rights, 45th session of the UN CSW, 2001.

42. J. Gilmore, "The Canadian Immigrant Labour Market in 2007," 2007, *Statistics Canada*, ISBN 978-0-662-48773-9.

43. B. R. Ragins, J. A. Gonzalez, K. Ehrhardt, and R. Singh, "Crossing the Threshold: The Spillover of Community Racial Diversity and Diversity Climate to the Workplace," *Personnel Psychology* 65 (2012), pp. 755–787.

44. P. F. McKay, D. R. Avery, and M. A. Morris, "Mean Racial–Ethnic Differences in Employee Sales Performance: The Moderating Role of Diversity Climate," *Personnel Psychology* 61, no. 2 (2008), pp. 349–374.

45. D. R. Avery, J. A. Richeson, M. R. Hebl, and N. Ambady, "It Does Not Have to Be Uncomfortable: The Role of Behavioral Scripts in Black–White Interracial Interactions," *Journal of Applied Psychology* 94 (2009), pp. 1382–1393.

46. G. Hofstede, *Culture's Consequences 2nd Edition* (Thousand Oaks, CA: Sage Publications, 2001).

47. H. Kaye, "Stuck at the Bottom Rung: Occupational Characteristics of Workers with Disabilities," *Journal of Occupational Rehabilitation* 19, no. 2 (2009), pp. 115–28; and L. A. Schur, "Barriers or Opportunities? The Causes of Contingent and Part-Time Work Among People with Disabilities," *Industrial Relations* 42 (2003), pp. 589–622.

48. R. Barrett, "Best Disability Employment Practices: Creating and Implementing Changes in Recruiting and Hiring," presentation at the 68th Annual Meeting of the Academy of Management, August 8–13, 2008, Anaheim, CA.

49. M. Campolieti, Worker Adaptation and the Desire for Accommodation After the Onset of a Disability, *Industrial Relations* 48 (2009), pp. 329–349, 135; M. Campolieti, "The Correlates of Accommodations for Permanently Disabled Workers," *Industrial Relations* 43 (2004), pp. 546–572; Canadian Human Rights Commission, 2011, accessed February 12, 2015 at http://www.hrsdc.gc.ca/eng/disability_issues/labour_market_agreements/index.shtml; and J. A. Cook et al., "Effects of Co-occurring Disorders on Employment Outcomes in a Multisite Randomized Study of Supported Employment for People with Severe Mental Illness," *Journal of Rehabilitation Research & Development* 44(6) (2007), pp. 837–849.

50. M. Lynk, 2008, "Disability and Work: The Transformation of the Legal Status of Employees with Disabilities in Canada," working paper, at SSRN: http://ssrn.com/abstract=1068403 or http://dx.doi.org/10.2139/ssrn.1068403.

51. Court case from 1990 (2.S.C.R. 489), as described in Lynk, 2008, "Disability and Work: The Transformation of the Legal Status of Employees with Disabilities in Canada," working paper, at SSRN: http://ssrn.com/abstract=1068403 or http://dx.doi.org/10.2139/ssrn.1068403.

52. Annenberg Washington Program, "Communicating the Americans with Disabilities Act: Transcending Compliance—A Case Report on Sears Roebuck & Co.," white paper (Washington, DC: 1994).

53. B. S. Bell and K. J. Klein, "Effect of Disability, Gender, and Job Level on Ratings of Job Applicants," *Rehabilitation Psychology* 46, no. 3 (2001), pp. 229–246; and E. Louvet, "Social Judgment Toward Job Applicants with Disabilities: Perception of Personal Qualities and Competences," *Rehabilitation Psychology* 52, no. 3 (2007), pp. 297–303.

54. L. R. Ren, R. L. Paetzold, and A. Colella, "A Meta-analysis of Experimental Studies on the Effects of Disability on Human Resource Judgments," *Human Resource Management Review* 18, no. 3 (2008), pp. 191–203.

55. M. Lengnick, P. Gaunt, and M. Kulkarni, "Overlooked and Underutilized: People with Disabilities Are an Untapped Human Resource," *Human Resource Management* 47 (2008), 2, p. 255.

56. D. Helly, "Are Muslims Discriminated Against in Canada Since September 2001?" *Canadian Ethnic Studies Journal* 36 (2004), no. 1; and Ontario Human Rights Commission, "Discrimination Experienced by Muslims in Ontario," http://www.ohrc.on.ca/en/creed-freedom-religion-and-human-rights-special-issue-diversity-magazine-volume-93-summer-2012/discrimination-experienced-muslims-ontario.

57. Janice Arnold, "Muslims Real Target of Charter, Law Prof Says," *Canadian Jewish News*, http://www.cjnews.com/montreal/muslims-real-target-charter-law-prof-says.

58. P. A. Freund and N. Kasten, "How Smart Do You Think You Are? A Meta-analysis of the Validity of Self-Estimates of Cognitive Ability," *Psychological Bulletin* 138 (2012), pp. 296–321.

59. R. E. Nisbett et al., "Intelligence: New Findings and Theoretical Developments," *American Psychologist* (February–March 2012), pp. 130–159.

60. M. D. Dunnette, "Aptitudes, Abilities, and Skills," in M. D. Dunnette (ed.), *Handbook of Industrial and Organizational Psychology* (Chicago: Rand McNally, 1976), pp. 478–483.

61. J. W. B. Lang, M. Kersting, U. R. Hülscheger, and J. Lang, "General Mental Ability, Narrower Cognitive Abilities, and Job Performance: The Perspective of the Nested-Factors Model of Cognitive Abilities," *Personnel Psychology* 63 (2010), pp. 595–640.

62. J. F. Salgado, N. Anderson, S. Moscoso, C. Bertua, F. de Fruyt, and J. P. Rolland, "A Meta-analytic Study of General Mental Ability Validity for Different Occupations in the European Community," *Journal of Applied Psychology* (December 2003), pp. 1068–1081; and F. L. Schmidt and J. E. Hunter, "Select on Intelligence," in E. A. Locke (ed.), *Handbook of Principles of Organizational Behavior* (Malden, MA: Blackwell, 2004).

63. M. E. Beier and F. L. Oswald, "Is Cognitive Ability a Liability? A Critique and Future Research Agenda on Skilled Performance," *Journal of Experimental Psychology: Applied* 18 (2012), pp. 331–345.

64. Y. Ganzach, "Intelligence and Job Satisfaction," *Academy of Management Journal* 41, no. 5 (1998), pp. 526–539; and Y. Ganzach, "Intelligence, Education, and Facets of Job Satisfaction," *Work and Occupations* 30, no. 1 (2003), pp. 97–122.

65. J. J. Caughron, M. D. Mumford, and E. A. Fleishman, "The Fleishman Job Analysis Survey: Development, Validation, and Applications," in M. A. Wilson, W. Bennett Jr., S. G. Gibson, and G. M. Alliger (eds.), *The Handbook of Work Analysis: Methods, Systems, Applications and Science of Work Measurement in Organizations* (New York: Routledge/Taylor & Francis Group, 2012); P. D. Converse, F. L. Oswald, M. A. Gillespie, K. A. Field, and E. B. Bizot, "Matching Individuals to Occupations Using Abilities and the O*Net: Issues and an Application in

Career Guidance," *Personnel Psychology* (Summer 2004), pp. 451–487; and E. A. Fleishman, "Evaluating Physical Abilities Required by Jobs," *Personnel Administrator* (June 1979), pp. 82–92.

66. L. M. Cortina, "Unseen Injustice: Incivility as Modern Discrimination in Organizations," *Academy of Management Review* 33, no. 1 (2008), pp. 55–75.

67. P. Devine, "Stereotypes and Prejudice: Their Automatic and Controlled Components," *Journal of Personality and Social Psychology* 56 (1989), pp. 5–18.

68. G. Bodenhausen and C. Macrae, "The Self-Regulation of Intergroup Perception: Mechanisms and Consequences of Stereotype Suppression," in C. Macrae, C. Stangor, and M. Hewstone (eds.), *Stereotypes and Stereotyping* (Guilford Press, NY, 1996), pp. 227–253.

69. D. R. Avery, "Reactions to Diversity in Recruitment Advertising: Are the Differences Black and White?" *Journal of Applied Psychology* 88, no. 4 (2003), pp. 672–679; P. F. McKay and D. R. Avery, "What Has Race Got to Do with It? Unraveling the Role of Racioethnicity in Job Seekers' Reactions to Site Visits," *Personnel Psychology* 59, no. 2 (2006), pp. 395–429; and D. R. Avery and P. F. McKay, "Target Practice: An Organizational Impression Management Approach to Attracting Minority and Female Job Applicants," *Personnel Psychology* 59, no. 1 (2006), pp. 157–187.

70. C. C. Miller, "Google Search and Replace," *The New York Times* (August 23, 2012), pp. B1, B5.

71. A. Overholt, "More Women Coders," *Fortune* (February 25, 2013), p. 14.

72. M. R. Buckley, K. A. Jackson, M. C. Bolino, J. G. Veres, and H. S. Field, "The Influence of Relational Demography on Panel Interview Ratings: A Field Experiment," *Personnel Psychology* 60 (2007), pp. 627–646; J. M. Sacco, C. R. Scheu, A. M. Ryan, and N. Schmitt, "An Investigation of Race and Sex Similarity Effects in Interviews: A Multilevel Approach to Relational Demography," *Journal of Applied Psychology* 88 (2003), pp. 852–865; and J. C. Ziegert and P. J. Hanges, "Employment Discrimination: The Role of Implicit Attitudes, Motivation, and a Climate for Racial Bias," *Journal of Applied Psychology* 90 (2005), pp. 553–562.

73. K. Bezrukova, K. A. Jehn, and C. S. Spell, "Reviewing Diversity Training: Where We Have Been and Where We Should Go," *Academy of Management Learning & Education* 2 (2012), pp. 207–227.

74. S. T. Bell, "Deep-Level Composition Variables as Predictors of Team Performance: A Meta-analysis," *Journal of Applied Psychology* 92, no. 3 (2007), pp. 595–615; S. K. Horwitz and I. B. Horwitz, "The Effects of Team Diversity on Team Outcomes: A Meta-analytic Review of Team Demography," *Journal of Management* 33, no. 6 (2007), pp. 987–1015; G. L. Stewart, "A Meta-analytic Review of Relationships Between Team Design Features and Team Performance," *Journal of Management* 32, no. 1 (2006), pp. 29–54; and A. Joshi and H. Roh, "The Role of Context in Work Team Diversity Research: A Meta-analytic Review," *Academy of Management Journal* 52, no. 3 (2009), pp. 599–627.

75. A. C. Homan, J. R. Hollenbeck, S. E. Humphrey, D. Van Knippenberg, D. R. Ilgen, and G. A. Van Kleef, "Facing Differences with an Open Mind: Openness to Experience, Salience of Intragroup Differences, and Performance of Diverse Work Groups," *Academy of Management Journal* 51, no. 6 (2008), pp. 1204–1222.

76. E. Kearney and D. Gebert, "Managing Diversity and Enhancing Team Outcomes: The Promise of Transformational Leadership," *Journal of Applied Psychology* 94, no. 1 (2009), pp. 77–89.

77. C. L. Holladay and M. A. Quiñones, "The Influence of Training Focus and Trainer Characteristics on Diversity Training

Effectiveness," *Academy of Management Learning and Education* 7, no. 3 (2008), pp. 343–354; and R. Anand and M. Winters, "A Retrospective View of Corporate Diversity Training from 1964 to the Present," *Academy of Management Learning and Education* 7, no. 3 (2008), pp. 356–372.

78. M. Ozbilgin, *Equality, Diversity, and Inclusion at Work: A Research Companion* (Northampton, MA: Edward Elgar, 2009).

79. A. Kalev, F. Dobbin, and E. Kelly, "Best Practices or Best Guesses? Assessing the Efficacy of Corporate Affirmative Action and Diversity Policies," *American Sociological Review* 71, no. 4 (2006), pp. 589–617.

80. R. J. Crisp and R. N. Turner, "Cognitive Adaptation to the Experience of Social and Cultural Diversity," *Psychological Bulletin* 137 (2011), pp. 242–266.

81. A. Sippola and A. Smale, "The Global Integration of Diversity Management: A Longitudinal Case Study," *International Journal of Human Resource Management* 18, no. 11 (2007), pp. 1895–1916.

Chapter 3

1. A. Barsky, S. A. Kaplan, and D. J. Beal, "Just Feelings? The Role of Affect in the Formation of Organizational Fairness Judgments," *Journal of Management* (January 2011), pp. 248–279; S. J. Breckler, "Empirical Validation of Affect, Behavior, and Cognition as Distinct Components of Attitude," *Journal of Personality and Social Psychology* (May 1984), pp. 1191–1205; J. A. Mikels, S. J. Maglio, A. E. Reed, and L. J. Kaplowitz, "Should I Go with My Gut? Investigating the Benefits of Emotion-Focused Decision Making," *Emotion* (August 2011), pp. 743–753; and A. J. Rojas Tejada, O. M. Lozano Rojas, M. Navas Luque, and P. J. Pérez Moreno, "Prejudiced Attitude Measurement Using the Rasch Scale Model," *Psychological Reports* (October 2011), pp. 553–572.

2. A. W. Wicker, "Attitude Versus Action: The Relationship of Verbal and Overt Behavioral Responses to Attitude Objects," *Journal of Social Issues* (Autumn 1969), pp. 41–78.

3. See I. Ajzen, "Nature and Operation of Attitudes," in S. T. Fiske, D. L. Schacter, and C. Zahn-Waxler (eds.), *Annual Review of Psychology* 52 (Palo Alto, CA: Annual Reviews Inc., 2001), pp. 27–58; L. R. Glasman and D. Albarracín, "Forming Attitudes That Predict Future Behavior: A Meta-analysis of the Attitude–Behavior Relation," *Psychological Bulletin* (September 2006), pp. 778–822; and M. Riketta, "The Causal Relation Between Job Attitudes and Performance: A Meta-analysis of Panel Studies," *Journal of Applied Psychology* 93, no. 2 (2008), pp. 472–481.

4. L. Festinger, *A Theory of Cognitive Dissonance* (Stanford, CA: Stanford University Press, 1957).

5. See, for instance, L. R. Fabrigar, R. E. Petty, S. M. Smith, and S. L. Crites, "Understanding Knowledge Effects on Attitude–Behavior Consistency: The Role of Relevance, Complexity, and Amount of Knowledge," *Journal of Personality and Social Psychology* 90, no. 4 (2006), pp. 556–577; and D. J. Schleicher, J. D. Watt, and G. J. Greguras, "Reexamining the Job Satisfaction–Performance Relationship: The Complexity of Attitudes," *Journal of Applied Psychology* 89, no. 1 (2004), pp. 165–177.

6. See L. R. Glasman and D. Albarracin, "Forming Attitudes That Predict Future Behavior: A Meta-analysis of the Attitude–Behavior Relation," *Psychological Bulletin* (September 2006), pp. 778–822; I. Azjen, "Nature and Operation of Attitudes," in S. T. Fiske, D. L. Schacter, and C. Zahn-Waxler (eds.), *Annual Review of Psychology* 52 (Palo Alto, CA: Annual Reviews, 2001), pp. 27–58; and M. Riketta, "The Causal Relation Between Job Attitudes and Performance: A Meta-analysis of

Panel Studies," *Journal of Applied Psychology* 93, no. 2 (2008), pp. 472–481.

7. D. A. Harrison, D. A. Newman, and P. L. Roth, "How Important Are Job Attitudes? Meta-analytic Comparisons of Integrative Behavioral Outcomes and Time Sequences," *Academy of Management Journal* 49, no. 2 (2006), pp. 305–325.

8. D. P. Moynihan and S. K. Pandey, "Finding Workable Levers over Work Motivation: Comparing Job Satisfaction, Job Involvement, and Organizational Commitment," *Administration & Society* 39, no. 7 (2007), pp. 803–832.

9. See, for example, J. M. Diefendorff, D. J. Brown, and A. M. Kamin, "Examining the Roles of Job Involvement and Work Centrality in Predicting Organizational Citizenship Behaviors and Job Performance," *Journal of Organizational Behavior* (February 2002), pp. 93–108.

10. Based on G. J. Blau and K. R. Boal, "Conceptualizing How Job Involvement and Organizational Commitment Affect Turnover and Absenteeism," *Academy of Management Review* (April 1987), p. 290.

11. G. Chen and R. J. Klimoski, "The Impact of Expectations on Newcomer Performance in Teams as Mediated by Work Characteristics, Social Exchanges, and Empowerment," *Academy of Management Journal* 46, no. 5 (2003), pp. 591–607; A. Ergeneli, G. Saglam, and S. Metin, "Psychological Empowerment and Its Relationship to Trust in Immediate Managers," *Journal of Business Research* (January 2007), pp. 41–49; and S. E. Seibert, S. R. Silver, and W. A. Randolph, "Taking Empowerment to the Next Level: A Multiple-Level Model of Empowerment, Performance, and Satisfaction," *Academy of Management Journal* 47, no. 3 (2004), pp. 332–349.

12. B. J. Avolio, W. Zhu, W. Koh, and P. Bhatia, "Transformational Leadership and Organizational Commitment: Mediating Role of Psychological Empowerment and Moderating Role of Structural Distance," *Journal of Organizational Behavior* 25, no. 8 (2004), pp. 951–968.

13. M. Singh and A. Sarkar, "The Relationship Between Psychological Empowerment and Innovative Behavior," *Journal of Personnel Psychology* 2 (2012), pp. 127–137.

14. J. M. Diefendorff, D. J. Brown, A. M. Kamin, and R. G. Lord, "Examining the Roles of Job Involvement and Work Centrality in Predicting Organizational Citizenship Behaviors and Job Performance," *Journal of Organizational Behavior* (February 2002), pp. 93–108.

15. O. N. Solinger, W. van Olffen, and R. A. Roe, "Beyond the Three-Component Model of Organizational Commitment," *Journal of Applied Psychology* 93 (2008), pp. 70–83.

16. B. J. Hoffman, C. A. Blair, J. P. Meriac, and D. J. Woehr, "Expanding the Criterion Domain? A Quantitative Review of the OCB Literature," *Journal of Applied Psychology* 92, no. 2 (2007), pp. 555–566.

17. T. A. Wright and D. G. Bonett, "The Moderating Effects of Employee Tenure on the Relation Between Organizational Commitment and Job Performance: A Meta-analysis," *Journal of Applied Psychology* (December 2002), pp. 1183–1190.

18. T. W. H. Ng, D. C. Feldman, and S. S. K. Lam, "Psychological Contract Breaches, Organizational Commitment, and Innovation-Related Behaviors: A Latent Growth Modeling Approach," *Journal of Applied Psychology* 95 (2010), pp. 744–751.

19. See, for instance, K. Bentein, C. Vandenberghe, R. Vandenberg, and F. Stinglhamber, "The Role of Change in the Relationship Between Commitment and Turnover: A Latent Growth Modeling Approach," *Journal of Applied Psychology* 90 (2005), pp. 468–482; and J. D. Kammeyer-Mueller, C. R. Wanberg, T. M. Glomb, and D. Ahlburg, "The Role of Temporal Shifts in Turnover Processes: It's About Time," *Journal of Applied Psychology* 90 (2005), pp. 644–658.

20. J. P. Hausknecht, N. J. Hiller, and R. J. Vance, "Work-Unit Absenteeism: Effects of Satisfaction, Commitment, Labor Market Conditions, and Time," *Academy of Management Journal* 51 (2008), pp. 1223–1245.

21. D. A. Kaplan, "Salesforce's Happy Workforce," *Fortune* (February 6, 2012), pp. 101–112.

22. L. Rhoades, R. Eisenberger, and S. Armeli, "Affective Commitment to the Organization: The Contribution of Perceived Organizational Support," *Journal of Applied Psychology* 86, no. 5 (2001), pp. 825–836.

23. P. Eder and R. Eisenberger, "Perceived Organizational Support: Reducing the Negative Influence of Coworker Withdrawal Behavior," *Journal of Management* 34, no. 1 (2008), pp. 55–68; and C. Vandenberghe, K. Bentein, R. Michon, J. Chebat, M. Tremblay, and J. Fils, "An Examination of the Role of Perceived Support and Employee Commitment in Employee–Customer Encounters," *Journal of Applied Psychology* 92, no. 4 (2007), pp. 1177–1187.

24. J. Farh, R. D. Hackett, and J. Liang, "Individual-Level Cultural Values as Moderators of Perceived Organizational Support–Employee Outcome Relationships in China: Comparing the Effects of Power Distance and Traditionality," *Academy of Management Journal* 50, no. 3 (2007), pp. 715–729.

25. B. L. Rich, J. A. Lepine, and E. R. Crawford, "Job Engagement: Antecedents and Effects on Job Performance," *Academy of Management Journal* 53 (2010), pp. 617–635.

26. J. K. Harter, F. L. Schmidt, and T. L. Hayes, "Business-Unit-Level Relationship Between Employee Satisfaction, Employee Engagement, and Business Outcomes: A Meta-analysis," *Journal of Applied Psychology* 87, no. 2 (2002), pp. 268–279.

27. N. R. Lockwood, *Leveraging Employee Engagement for Competitive Advantage* (Alexandria, VA: Society for Human Resource Management, 2007); and R. J. Vance, *Employee Engagement and Commitment* (Alexandria, VA: Society for Human Resource Management, 2006).

28. "Employee Engagement," *Workforce Management* (February 2013), p. 19; and "The Cornerstone OnDemand 2013 U.S. Employee Report," *Cornerstone OnDemand* (2013), http://www.cornerstoneondemand.com/resources/research/survey-2013.

29. W. H. Macey and B. Schneider, "The Meaning of Employee Engagement," *Industrial and Organizational Psychology* 1 (2008), pp. 3–30; and A. Saks, "The Meaning and Bleeding of Employee Engagement: How Muddy Is the Water?" *Industrial and Organizational Psychology* 1 (2008), pp. 40–43.

30. Y. Brunetto, S. T. T. Teo, K. Shacklock, and R. Farr-Wharton, "Emotional Intelligence, Job Satisfaction, Well-being and Engagement: Explaining Organisational Commitment and Turnover Intentions in Policing," *Human Resource Management Journal* (2012), pp. 428–441.

31. P. Petrou, E. Demerouti, M. C. W. Peeters, W. B. Schaufeli, and Jørn Hetland, "Crafting a Job on a Daily Basis: Contextual Correlates and the Link to Work Engagement," *Journal of Organizational Behavior* (November 2012), pp. 1120–1141.

32. P. W. Hom, T. R. Mitchell, T. W. Lee, and R. W. Griffeth, "Reviewing Employee Turnover: Focusing on Proximal Withdrawal States and an Expanded Criterion," *Psychological Bulletin* 138, no. 5 (2012), pp. 831–858.

33. The Wyatt Company's 1989 national Work America study identified 12 dimensions of satisfaction: Work organization, working conditions, communications, job performance and performance review, coworkers, supervision, company management, pay, benefits, career development and training, job content and satisfaction, and company image and change.

34. See E. Spector, *Job Satisfaction: Application, Assessment, Causes, and Consequences* (Thousand Oaks, CA: Sage, 1997), p. 3.

35. C. L. Dolbier, J. A. Webster, K. T. McCalister, M. W. Mallon, and M. A. Steinhardt, "Reliability and Validity of a Single-Item

Measure of Job Satisfaction," *American Journal of Health Promotion* (January–February 2005), pp. 194–198; and J. Wanous, A. E. Reichers, and M. J. Hudy, "Overall Job Satisfaction: How Good Are Single-Item Measures?" *Journal of Applied Psychology* (April 1997), pp. 247–252.

36. Staff researcher, "Canadian Workers Most Satisfied with Jobs, says International Monster GfK Survey," *PR NewsWire*, 2013, accessed March 25, 2015 at http://www.prnewswire.com/news-releases/canadian-workers-most-satisfied-with-jobs-says-international-monster-gfk-survey-232319951.html.

37. J. Chowdan, "Who Has More Job Satisfaction, Immigrant or Canadian Born Employees?" McMaster University Degroote School of Business Faculty Blog, 2015, accessed March 27, 2015 at http://www.degroote.mcmaster.ca/articles/job-satisfaction-immigrants-canadian-born-employees.

38. Staff researcher, "Canadian Workers Most Satisfied with Jobs, says International Monster GfK Survey," *PR NewsWire*, 2013, accessed March 25, 2015 at http://www.prnewswire.com/news-releases/canadian-workers-most-satisfied-with-jobs-says-international-monster-gfk-survey-232319951.html; and Staff researcher, "Youth Unemployment in Canada: Challenging Conventional Thinking," *Certified General Accounting Association of Canada*, 2012, ISBN 978-1-55219-663-2, accessed March 25, 2015 at http://www.cga-canada.org/en-ca/ResearchReports/ca_rep_2012-10_youthunemployment.pdf.

39. W. K. Balzer, J. A. Kihm, P. C. Smith, J. L. Irwin, P. D. Bachiochi, C. Robie, E. F. Sinar, and L. F. Parra, *Users' Manual for the Job Descriptive Index (JDI; 1997 Revision) and the Job in General Scales* (Bowling Green, OH: Bowling Green State University, 1997).

40. M. J. Gelfand, M. Erez, and Z. Aycan, "Cross-Cultural Organizational Behavior," *Annual Review of Psychology* 58 (2007), pp. 479–514; and A. S. Tsui, S. S. Nifadkar, and A. Y. Ou, "Cross-National, Cross-Cultural Organizational Behavior Research: Advances, Gaps, and Recommendations," *Journal of Management* (June 2007), pp. 426–478.

41. World Business Culture, "Doing Business in South Korea," http://www.worldbusinessculture.com/Business-in-South-Korea.html, accessed June 24, 2013; and J. K. Andreassi, L. Lawter, M. Brockerhoff, and P. Rutigliano, "Job Satisfaction Determinants: A Study Across 48 Nations," http://digitalcommons.sacredheart.edu/cgi/viewcontent.cgi?article=1239&context=wcob_fac.

42. J. Barling, E. K. Kelloway, and R. D. Iverson, "High-Quality Work, Job Satisfaction, and Occupational Injuries," *Journal of Applied Psychology* 88, no. 2 (2003), pp. 276–283; and F. W. Bond and D. Bunce, "The Role of Acceptance and Job Control in Mental Health, Job Satisfaction, and Work Performance," *Journal of Applied Psychology* 88, no. 6 (2003), pp. 1057–1067.

43. D. S. Chiaburu and D. A. Harrison, "Do Peers Make the Place? Conceptual Synthesis and Meta-analysis of Coworker Effect on Perceptions, Attitudes, OCBs, and Performance," *Journal of Applied Psychology* 93, no. 5 (2008), pp. 1082–1103; and S. E. Humphrey, J. D. Nahrgang, and F. P. Morgeson, "Integrating Motivational, Social, and Contextual Work Design Features: A Meta-analytic Summary and Theoretical Extension of the Work Design Literature," *Journal of Applied Psychology* 92, no. 5 (2007), pp. 1332–1356.

44. T. A. Judge, R. F. Piccolo, N. P. Podsakoff, J. C. Shaw, and B. L. Rich, "The Relationship Between Pay and Job Satisfaction: A Meta-analysis of the Literature," *Journal of Vocational Behavior* 77 (2010), pp. 157–167.

45. E. C. Bianchi, "The Bright Side of Bad Times: The Affective Advantages of Entering the Workforce in a Recession," *Administrative Science Quarterly* (December 2013), pp. 587–623.

46. R. E. Silverman, "Work as Labor or Love?" *The Wall Street Journal* (October 18, 2012), p. D3.

47. S. Masterson, K. Lewis, B. Goldman, and S. Taylor, "Integrating Justice and Social Exchange: The Differing Effects of Fair Procedures and Treatment on Work Relationships," *Academy of Management Journal* 43, no. 4 (August 1, 2000), pp. 738–748.

48. Steven W. Schmidt, "The Relationship Between Satisfaction with Workplace Training and Overall Job Satisfaction," http://www.researchgate.net/profile/Steven_Schmidt5/publication/227657996_The_relationship_between_satisfaction_with_workplace_training_and_overall_job_satisfaction/links/54ad66e70cf2828b29fc7ede.pdf.

49. See A. Davis-Blake, J. P. Broschak, and E. George, "Happy Together? How Using Nonstandard Workers Affects Exit, Voice, and Loyalty Among Standard Employees," *Academy of Management Journal* 46, no. 4 (2003), pp. 475–485; D. Farrell, "Exit, Voice, Loyalty, and Neglect as Responses to Job Dissatisfaction: A Multidimensional Scaling Study," *Academy of Management Journal* (December 1983), pp. 596–606; J. B. Olson-Buchanan and W. R. Boswell, "The Role of Employee Loyalty and Formality in Voicing Discontent," *Journal of Applied Psychology* (December 2002), pp. 1167–1174; C. E. Rusbult, D. Farrell, G. Rogers, and A. G. Mainous III, "Impact of Exchange Variables on Exit, Voice, Loyalty, and Neglect: An Integrative Model of Responses to Declining Job Satisfaction," *Academy of Management Journal* (September 1988), pp. 599–627; M. J. Withey and W. H. Cooper, "Predicting Exit, Voice, Loyalty, and Neglect," *Administrative Science Quarterly* (December 1989), pp. 521–539; and J. Zhou and J. M. George, "When Job Dissatisfaction Leads to Creativity: Encouraging the Expression of Voice," *Academy of Management Journal* (August 2001), pp. 682–696.

50. A. J. Nyberg and R. E. Ployhart, "Context-Emergent Turnover (CET) Theory: A Theory of Collective Turnover," *Academy of Management Review* 38 (2013), pp. 109–131.

51. T. A. Judge, C. J. Thoresen, J. E. Bono, and G. K. Patton, "The Job Satisfaction–Job Performance Relationship: A Qualitative and Quantitative Review," *Psychological Bulletin* (May 2001), pp. 376–407.

52. J. K. Harter, F. L. Schmidt, and T. L. Hayes, "Business-Unit Level Relationship Between Employee Satisfaction, Employee Engagement, and Business Outcomes: A Meta-analysis," *Journal of Applied Psychology* (April 2002), pp. 268–279; C. Ostroff, "The Relationship Between Satisfaction, Attitudes, and Performance: An Organizational Level Analysis," *Journal of Applied Psychology* (December 1992), pp. 963–974; and A. M. Ryan, M. J. Schmit, and R. Johnson, "Attitudes and Effectiveness: Examining Relations at an Organizational Level," *Personnel Psychology* (Winter 1996), pp. 853–882.

53. See P. M. Podsakoff, S. B. MacKenzie, J. B. Paine, and D. G. Bachrach, "Organizational Citizenship Behaviors: A Critical Review of the Theoretical and Empirical Literature and Suggestions for Future Research," *Journal of Management* 26, no. 3 (2000), pp. 513–563.

54. B. J. Hoffman, C. A. Blair, J. P. Maeriac, and D. J. Woehr, "Expanding the Criterion Domain? A Quantitative Review of the OCB Literature," *Journal of Applied Psychology* 92, no. 2 (2007), pp. 555–566.

55. S. L. Blader and T. R. Tyler, "Testing and Extending the Group Engagement Model: Linkages Between Social Identity, Procedural Justice, Economic Outcomes, and Extrarole Behavior," *Journal of Applied Psychology* 94, no. 2 (2009), pp. 445–464.

56. D. S. Chiaburu and D. A. Harrison, "Do Peers Make the Place? Conceptual Synthesis and Meta-analysis of Coworker Effect on Perceptions, Attitudes, OCBs, and Performance," *Journal of Applied Psychology* 93, no. 5 (2008), pp. 1082–1103.

57. R. Ilies, I. S. Fulmer, M. Spitzmuller, and M. D. Johnson, "Personality and Citizenship Behavior: The Mediating Role of Job Satisfaction," *Journal of Applied Psychology* 94 (2009), pp. 945–959.

58. R. Ilies, B. A. Scott, and T. A. Judge, "The Interactive Effects of Personal Traits and Experienced States on Intraindividual Patterns of Citizenship Behavior," *Academy of Management Journal* 49 (2006), pp. 561–575.

59. See, for instance, D. J. Koys, "The Effects of Employee Satisfaction, Organizational Citizenship Behavior, and Turnover on Organizational Effectiveness: A Unit-Level, Longitudinal Study," *Personnel Psychology* (Spring 2001), pp. 101–114; M. Schulte, C. Ostroff, S. Shmulyian, and A. Kinicki, "Organizational Climate Configurations: Relationships to Collective Attitudes, Customer Satisfaction, and Financial Performance," *Journal of Applied Psychology* 94 (2009), pp. 618–634; and C. Vandenberghe, K. Bentein, R. Michon, J. Chebat, M. Tremblay, and J. Fils, "An Examination of the Role of Perceived Support and Employee Commitment in Employee-Customer Encounters," *Journal of Applied Psychology* 92, no. 4 (2007), pp. 1177–1187.

60. J. M. O'Brien, "Zappos Knows How to Kick It," *Fortune* (February 2, 2009), pp. 55–60.

61. K. D. Scott and G. S. Taylor, "An Examination of Conflicting Findings on the Relationship Between Job Satisfaction and Absenteeism: A Meta-analysis," *Academy of Management Journal* (September 1985), pp. 599–612; R. P. Steel and J. R. Rentsch, "Influence of Cumulation Strategies on the Long-Range Prediction of Absenteeism," *Academy of Management Journal* (December 1995), pp. 1616–1634; and J. F. Ybema, P. G. W. Smulders, and P. M. Bongers, "Antecedents and Consequences of Employee Absenteeism: A Longitudinal Perspective on the Role of Job Satisfaction and Burnout," *European Journal of Work and Organizational Psychology* 19 (2010), pp. 102–124.

62. J. P. Hausknecht, N. J. Hiller, and R. J. Vance, "Work-Unit Absenteeism: Effects of Satisfaction, Commitment, Labor Market Conditions, and Time," *Academy of Management Journal* 51, no. 6 (2008), pp. 1123–1245.

63. G. Chen, R. E. Ployhart, H. C. Thomas, N. Anderson, and P. D. Bliese, "The Power of Momentum: A New Model of Dynamic Relationships Between Job Satisfaction Change and Turnover Intentions," *Academy of Management Journal* (February 2011), pp. 159–181; R. W. Griffeth, P. W. Hom, and S. Gaertner, "A Meta-analysis of Antecedents and Correlates of Employee Turnover: Update, Moderator Tests, and Research Implications for the Next Millennium," *Journal of Management* 26, no. 3 (2000), p. 479; and W. Hom and R. W. Griffeth, *Employee Turnover* (Cincinnati, OH: South-Western Publishing, 1995).

64. D. Liu, T. R. Mitchell, T. W. Lee, B. C. Holtom, and T. R. Hinkin, "When Employees Are Out of Step with Coworkers: How Job Satisfaction Trajectory and Dispersion Influence Individual- and Unit-Level Voluntary Turnover," *Academy of Management Journal* 55, no. 6 (2012), pp. 1360–1380.

65. T. H. Lee, B. Gerhart, I. Weller, and C. O. Trevor, "Understanding Voluntary Turnover: Path-Specific Job Satisfaction Effects and the Importance of Unsolicited Job Offers," *Academy of Management Journal* 51, no. 4 (2008), pp. 651–671.

66. K. Jiang, D. Liu, P. F. McKay, T. W. Lee, and T. R. Mitchell, "When and How Is Job Embeddedness Predictive of Turnover? A Meta-analytic Investigation," *Journal of Applied Psychology* 97 (2012), pp. 1077–1096.

67. Sandra L. Robinson and Rebecca J. Bennett, "A Typology of Deviant Workplace Behaviors: A Multidimensional Scaling Study," *The Academy of Management Journal* 38, no. 2 (April 1995), pp. 555–572.

68. D. S. Chiaburu and D. A. Harrison, "Do Peers Make the Place? Conceptual Synthesis and Meta-analysis of Coworker Effect on Perceptions, Attitudes, OCBs, and Performance," *Journal of Applied Psychology* 93, no. 5 (2008), pp. 1082–1103; and P. E. Spector, S. Fox, L. M. Penney, K. Bruursema, A. Goh, and S. Kessler, "The Dimensionality of Counterproductivity: Are All Counterproductive Behaviors Created Equal?" *Journal of Vocational Behavior* 68, no. 3 (2006), pp. 446–460.

69. K. Holland, "Inside the Minds of Your Employees," *The New York Times* (January 28, 2007), p. B1; "Study Sees Link Between Morale and Stock Price," *Workforce Management* (February 27, 2006), p. 15; and "The Workplace as a Solar System," *The New York Times* (October 28, 2006), p. B5.

70. E. White, "How Surveying Workers Can Pay Off," *The Wall Street Journal* (June 18, 2007), p. B3.

Chapter 4

1. See, for instance, C. D. Fisher and N. M. Ashkanasy, "The Emerging Role of Emotions in Work Life: An Introduction," *Journal of Organizational Behavior*, Special Issue 2000, pp. 123–129; N. M. Ashkanasy, C. E. J. Hartel, and W. J. Zerbe (eds.), *Emotions in the Workplace: Research, Theory, and Practice* (Westport, CT: Quorum Books, 2000); N. M. Ashkanasy and C. S. Daus, "Emotion in the Workplace: The New Challenge for Managers," *Academy of Management Executive* (February 2002), pp. 76–86; and N. M. Ashkanasy, C. E. J. Hartel, and C. S. Daus, "Diversity and Emotion: The New Frontiers in Organizational Behavior Research," *Journal of Management* 28, no. 3 (2002), pp. 307–338.

2. S. G. Barsade and D. E. Gibson, "Why Does Affect Matter in Organizations?" *Academy of Management Perspectives* (February 2007), pp. 36–59.

3. See N. H. Frijda, "Moods, Emotion Episodes and Emotions," in M. Lewis and J. M. Haviland (eds.), *Handbook of Emotions* (New York: Guilford Press, 1993), pp. 381–403.

4. H. M. Weiss and R. Cropanzano, "Affective Events Theory: A Theoretical Discussion of the Structure, Causes and Consequences of Affective Experiences at Work," in B. M. Staw and L. L. Cummings (eds.), *Research in Organizational Behavior* 18 (Greenwich, CT: JAI Press, 1996), pp. 17–19.

5. See P. Ekman and R. J. Davidson (eds.), *The Nature of Emotions: Fundamental Questions* (Oxford, UK: Oxford University Press, 1994).

6. See, for example, P. Ekman, "An Argument for Basic Emotions," *Cognition and Emotion* (May/July 1992), pp. 169–200; C. E. Izard, "Basic Emotions, Relations Among Emotions, and Emotion–Cognition Relations," *Psychological Bulletin* (November 1992), pp. 561–565; and J. L. Tracy and R. W. Robins, "Emerging Insights into the Nature and Function of Pride," *Current Directions in Psychological Science* 16, no. 3 (2007), pp. 147–150.

7. R. C. Solomon, "Back to Basics: On the Very Idea of 'Basic Emotions,'" *Journal for the Theory of Social Behaviour* 32, no. 2 (June 2002), pp. 115–144.

8. P. Ekman, *Emotions Revealed: Recognizing Faces and Feelings to Improve Communication and Emotional Life* (New York: Times Books/Henry Holt and Co., 2003).

9. Weiss and Cropanzano, "Affective Events Theory," pp. 20–22.

10. Cited in R. D. Woodworth, *Experimental Psychology* (New York: Holt, 1938).

11. D. Watson, L. A. Clark, and A. Tellegen, "Development and Validation of Brief Measures of Positive and Negative Affect: The PANAS Scales," *Journal of Personality and Social Psychology* (1988), pp. 1063–1070.

12. A. Ben-Ze'ev, *The Subtlety of Emotions* (Cambridge, MA: MIT Press, 2000), p. 94.

13. J. T. Cacioppo and W. L. Gardner, "Emotion," in *Annual Review of Psychology* 50 (Palo Alto, CA: Annual Reviews, 1999), pp. 191–214.

14. D. Holman, "Call Centres," in D. Holman, T. D. Wall, C. Clegg, P. Sparrow, and A. Howard (eds.), *The Essentials of the New Work Place: A Guide to the Human Impact of Modern Working Practices* (Chichester, UK: Wiley, 2005), pp. 111–132.

15. A. Ben-Ze'ev, *The Subtlety of Emotions* (Cambridge, MA: MIT Press, 2000), p. 99.

16. M. Eid and E. Diener, "Norms for Experiencing Emotions in Different Cultures: Inter- and International Differences," *Journal of Personality & Social Psychology* 81, no. 5 (2001), pp. 869–885.

17. O. Burkeman, "The Power of Negative Thinking," *The New York Times* (August 5, 2012), p. 9.

18. E. Jaffe, "Positively Negative," *Association for Psychological Science* (November 2012), pp. 13–17.

19. L. M. Poverny and S. Picascia, "There Is No Crying in Business," Womensmedia.com, October 20, 2009, http://www.womensmedia.com/new/Crying-at-Work.shtml.

20. M.-A. Reinhard and N. Schwartz, "The Influence of Affective States on the Process of Lie Detection," *Journal of Experimental Psychology* 18 (2012), pp. 377–389.

21. J. Haidt, "The New Synthesis in Moral Psychology," *Science* 316 (May 18, 2007), pp. 998, 1002; I. E. de Hooge, R. M. A. Nelissen, S. M. Breugelmans, and M. Zeelenberg, "What Is Moral About Guilt? Acting 'Prosocially' at the Disadvantage of Others," *Journal of Personality and Social Psychology* 100 (2011), pp. 462–473; and C. A. Hutcherson and J. J. Gross, "The Moral Emotions: A Social-Functionalist Account of Anger, Disgust, and Contempt," *Journal of Personality and Social Psychology* 100 (2011), pp. 719–737.

22. D. C. Rubin, R. M. Hoyle, and M. R. Leary, "Differential Predictability of Four Dimensions of Affect Intensity," *Cognition and Emotion* 26 (2012), pp. 25–41.

23. L. L. Carstensen, M. Pasupathi, M. Ulrich, and J. R. Nesselroade, "Emotional Experience in Everyday Life Across the Adult Life Span," *Journal of Personality and Social Psychology* 79, no. 4 (2000), pp. 644–655.

24. M. LaFrance and M. Banaji, "Toward a Reconsideration of the Gender–Emotion Relationship," in M. Clark (ed.), *Review of Personality and Social Psychology* 14 (Newbury Park, CA: Sage, 1992), pp. 178–197; and A. M. Kring and A. H. Gordon, "Sex Differences in Emotion: Expression, Experience, and Physiology," *Journal of Personality and Social Psychology* (March 1998), pp. 686–703.

25. M. G. Gard and A. M. Kring, "Sex Differences in the Time Course of Emotion," *Emotion* 7, no. 2 (2007), pp. 429–437; M. Jakupcak, K. Salters, K. L. Gratz, and L. Roemer, "Masculinity and Emotionality: An Investigation of Men's Primary and Secondary Emotional Responding," *Sex Roles* 49 (2003), pp. 111–120; and M. Grossman and W. Wood, "Sex Differences in Intensity of Emotional Experience: A Social Role Interpretation," *Journal of Personality and Social Psychology* (November 1992), pp. 1010–1022.

26. S. A. Golder and M. W. Macy, "Diurnal and Seasonal Mood Vary with Work, Sleep, and Daylength Across Diverse Cultures," *Science* 333 (2011), pp. 1878–1881.

27. Golder and Macy, "Diurnal and Seasonal Mood Vary."

28. J. J. A. Denissen, L. Butalid, L. Penke, and M. A. G. van Aken, "The Effects of Weather on Daily Mood: A Multilevel Approach," *Emotion* 8, no. 5 (2008), pp. 662–667; M. C. Keller, B. L. Fredrickson, O. Ybarra, S. Côté, K. Johnson, J. Mikels, A. Conway, and T. Wagner, "A Warm Heart and a Clear Head: The Contingent Effects of Weather on Mood and Cognition," *Psychological Science* 16 (2005) pp. 724–731; and Watson, *Mood and Temperament*.

29. Staff Member, "Seasonal Affect Disorder", *Mayo Clinic*, accessed April 3, 2015 at http://www.mayoclinic.org/diseases-conditions/seasonal-affective-disorder/basics/definition/con-20021047.

30. D. Watson, *Mood and Temperament* (New York: Guilford Press, 2000).

31. S. Dembling, "The Introverts Way: Living a Quiet Life in a Noisy World," *Perigee Books* (2012), ISBN 978-0399537691.

32. D. Meinert, "Sleepless in Seattle . . . and Cincinnati and Syracuse," *HR Magazine* (October 2012), pp. 55–57.

33. B. A. Scott and T. A. Judge, "Insomnia, Emotions, and Job Satisfaction: A Multilevel Study," *Journal of Management* 32, no. 5 (2006), pp. 622–645.

34. Statistics Canada, (2005), "Who Gets Any Sleep These Days?" accessed April 4, 2015 at http://www.mayoclinic.org/diseases-conditions/seasonal-affective-disorder/basics/definition/con-20021047.

35. P. R. Giacobbi, H. A. Hausenblas, and N. Frye, "A Naturalistic Assessment of the Relationship Between Personality, Daily Life Events, Leisure-Time Exercise, and Mood," *Psychology of Sport & Exercise* 6, no. 1 (January 2005), pp. 67–81.

36. S. Gordon, 2012) "Diabetes Can Take a Toll of Your Emotion," *HealthDay*, accessed April 4, 2012 at http://consumer.healthday.com/mental-health-information-25/anxiety-news-33/diabetes-can-take-a-toll-on-your-emotions-664847.html.

37. A. R. Hochschild, "Emotion Work, Feeling Rules, and Social Structure," *American Journal of Sociology* (November 1979), pp. 551–575; W.-C. Tsai, "Determinants and Consequences of Employee Displayed Positive Emotions," *Journal of Management* 27, no. 4 (2001), pp. 497–512; M. W. Kramer and J. A. Hess, "Communication Rules for the Display of Emotions in Organizational Settings," *Management Communication Quarterly* (August 2002), pp. 66–80; and J. M. Diefendorff and E. M. Richard, "Antecedents and Consequences of Emotional Display Rule Perceptions," *Journal of Applied Psychology* (April 2003), pp. 284–294.

38. J. M. Diefendorff and G. J. Greguras, "Contextualizing Emotional Display Rules: Examining the Roles of Targets and Discrete Emotions in Shaping Display Rule Perceptions," *Journal of Management* 35 (2009), pp. 880–898.

39. A. A. Grandey, "When 'The Show Must Go On,'" *Academy of Management Journal* 46 (2003), pp. 86–96.

40. U. R. Hulsheger, H. J. E. M. Alberts, A. Feinholdt, and J. W. B. Lang, "Benefits of Mindfulness at Work: The Role of Mindfulness in Emotion Regulation, Emotional Exhaustion, and Job Satisfaction," *Journal of Applied Psychology* (March 2013), pp. 310–325.

41. J. P. Trougakos, D. J. Beal, S. G. Green, and H. M. Weiss, "Making the Break Count: An Episodic Examination of Recovery Activities, Emotional Experiences, and Positive Affective Displays," *Academy of Management Journal* 51 (2008), pp. 131–146.

42. H. M. Weiss and R. Cropanzano, "An Affective Events Approach to Job Satisfaction," *Research in Organizational Behavior* 18 (1996), pp. 1–74.

43. J. Basch and C. D. Fisher, "Affective Events–Emotions Matrix: A Classification of Work Events and Associated Emotions," in N. M. Ashkanasy, C. E. J. Hartel, and W. J. Zerbe (eds.), *Emotions in the Workplace* (Westport, CT: Quorum Books, 2000), pp. 36–48.

44. N. M. Ashkanasy, C. E. J. Hartel, and C. S. Daus, "Diversity and Emotion: The New Frontiers in Organizational Behavior Research," *Journal of Management* 28, no. 3 (2002), p. 324.

45. This section is based on Daniel Goleman, *Emotional Intelligence* (New York: Bantam, 1995); P. Salovey and D. Grewal, "The Science of Emotional Intelligence," *Current Directions in Psychological Science* 14, no. 6 (2005), pp. 281–285; M. Davies, L. Stankov, and R. D. Roberts, "Emotional Intelligence: In Search

of an Elusive Construct," *Journal of Personality and Social Psychology* (October 1998), pp. 989–1015; and D. Geddes and R. R. Callister, "Crossing the Line(s): A Dual Threshold Model of Anger in Organizations," *Academy of Management Review* 32, no. 3 (2007), pp. 721–746.

46. P. A. Vernon, K. V. Petrides, D. Bratko, and J. A. Schermer, "A Behavioral Genetic Study of Trait Emotional Intelligence," *Emotion* 8, no. 5 (2008), pp. 635–642.

47. E. A. Locke, "Why Emotional Intelligence Is an Invalid Concept," *Journal of Organizational Behavior* 26, no. 4 (June 2005), pp. 425–431.

48. J. M. Conte, "A Review and Critique of Emotional Intelligence Measures," *Journal of Organizational Behavior* 26, no. 4 (June 2005), pp. 433–440; and M. Davies, L. Stankov, and R. D. Roberts, "Emotional Intelligence," pp. 989–1015.

49. D. L. Joseph and D. A. Newman, "Emotional Intelligence: An Integrative Meta-analysis and Cascading Model," *Journal of Applied Psychology* 95 (2010), pp. 54–78.

50. S. L. Koole, "The Psychology of Emotion Regulation: An Integrative Review," *Cognition and Emotion* 23 (2009), pp. 4–41; and H. A. Wadlinger and D. M. Isaacowitz, "Fixing Our Focus: Training Attention to Regulate Emotion," *Personality and Social Psychology Review* 15 (2011), pp. 75–102.

51. D. H. Kluemper, T. DeGroot, and S. Choi, "Emotion Management Ability: Predicting Task Performance, Citizenship, and Deviance," *Journal of Management* (May 2013), pp. 878–905.

52. T. L. Webb, E. Miles, and P. Sheeran, "Dealing with Feeling: A Meta-analysis of the Effectiveness of Strategies Derived from the Process Model of Emotion Regulation," *Psychological Bulletin* 138, no. 4 (2012), pp. 775–808; S. Srivastava, M. Tamir, K. M. McGonigal, O. P. John, and J. J. Gross, "The Social Costs of Emotional Suppression: A Prospective Study of the Transition to College," *Journal of Personality and Social Psychology* 96 (2009), pp. 883–897; Y. Liu, L. M. Prati, P. L. Perrewé, and R. A. Brymer, "Individual Differences in Emotion Regulation, Emotional Experiences at Work, and Work-Related Outcomes: A Two-Study Investigation," *Journal of Applied Social Psychology* 40 (2010), pp. 1515–1538; and H. A. Wadlinger and D. M. Isaacowitz, "Fixing Our Focus: Training Attention to Regulate Emotion," *Personality and Social Psychology Review* 15 (2011), pp. 75–102.

53. J. V. Wood, S. A. Heimpel, L. A. Manwell, and E. J. Whittington, "This Mood Is Familiar and I Don't Deserve to Feel Better Anyway: Mechanisms Underlying Self-Esteem Differences in Motivation to Repair Sad Moods," *Journal of Personality and Social Psychology* 96 (2009), pp. 363–380.

54. S.-C. S. Chi and S.-G. Liang, "When Do Subordinates' Emotion-Regulation Strategies Matter? Abusive Supervision, Subordinates' Emotional Exhaustion, and Work Withdrawal," *Leadership Quarterly* (February 2013), pp. 125–137.

55. R. H. Humphrey, "How Do Leaders Use Emotional Labor?" *Journal of Organizational Behavior* (July 2012), pp. 740–744.

56. P. Totterdell, "Catching Moods and Hitting Runs: Mood Linkage and Subjective Performance in Professional Sports Teams," *Journal of Applied Psychology* 85, no. 6 (2000), pp. 848–859.

57. See A. M. Isen, "Positive Affect and Decision Making," in M. Lewis and J. M. Haviland-Jones (eds.), *Handbook of Emotions*, 2nd ed. (New York: Guilford, 2000), pp. 261–277.

58. L. B. Alloy and L. Y. Abramson, "Judgment of Contingency in Depressed and Nondepressed Students: Sadder but Wiser?" *Journal of Experimental Psychology: General* 108 (1979), pp. 441–485.

59. N. Ambady and H. M. Gray, "On Being Sad and Mistaken: Mood Effects on the Accuracy of Thin-Slice Judgments," *Journal of Personality and Social Psychology* 83, no. 4 (2002), pp. 947–961.

60. S. Lyubomirsky, L. King, and E. Diener, "The Benefits of Frequent Positive Affect: Does Happiness Lead to Success?" *Psychological Bulletin* 131, no. 6 (2005), pp. 803–855; and M. Baas, C. K. W. De Dreu, and B. A. Nijstad, "A Meta-analysis of 25 Years of Mood-Creativity Research: Hedonic Tone, Activation, or Regulatory Focus," *Psychological Bulletin* 134 (2008), pp. 779–806.

61. M. J. Grawitch, D. C. Munz, and E. K. Elliott, "Promoting Creativity in Temporary Problem-Solving Groups: The Effects of Positive Mood and Autonomy in Problem Definition on Idea-Generating Performance," *Group Dynamics* 7, no. 3 (September 2003), pp. 200–213.

62. S. Lyubomirsky, L. King, and E. Diener, "The Benefits of Frequent Positive Affect: Does Happiness Lead to Success?" *Psychological Bulletin* 131, no. 6 (2005), pp. 803–855.

63. N. Madjar, G. R. Oldham, and M. G. Pratt, "There's No Place Like Home? The Contributions of Work and Nonwork Creativity Support to Employees' Creative Performance," *Academy of Management Journal* 45, no. 4 (2002), pp. 757–767.

64. J. M. George and J. Zhou, "Understanding When Bad Moods Foster Creativity and Good Ones Don't: The Role of Context and Clarity of Feelings," *Journal of Applied Psychology* 87, no. 4 (August 2002), pp. 687–697; and J. P. Forgas and J. M. George, "Affective Influences on Judgments and Behavior in Organizations: An Information Processing Perspective," *Organizational Behavior and Human Decision Processes* 86, no. 1 (2001), pp. 3–34.

65. C. K. W. De Dreu, M. Baas, and B. A. Nijstad, "Hedonic Tone and Activation Level in the Mood–Creativity Link: Toward a Dual Pathway to Creativity Model," *Journal of Personality and Social Psychology* 94, no. 5 (2008), pp. 739–756; J. M. George and J. Zhou, "Dual Tuning in a Supportive Context: Joint Contributions of Positive Mood, Negative Mood, and Supervisory Behaviors to Employee Creativity," *Academy of Management Journal* 50, no. 3 (2007), pp. 605–622.

66. A. Erez and A. M. Isen, "The Influence of Positive Affect on the Components of Expectancy Motivation," *Journal of Applied Psychology* 87, no. 6 (2002), pp. 1055–1067.

67. R. Ilies and T. A. Judge, "Goal Regulation Across Time: The Effect of Feedback and Affect," *Journal of Applied Psychology* 90, no. 3 (May 2005), pp. 453–467.

68. J. E. Bono, H. J. Foldes, G. Vinson, and J. P. Muros, "Workplace Emotions: The Role of Supervision and Leadership," *Journal of Applied Psychology* 92, no. 5 (2007), pp. 1357–1367.

69. S. G. Liang and S.-C. S. Chi, "Transformational Leadership and Follower Task Performance: The Role of Susceptibility to Positive Emotions and Follower Positive Emotions," *Journal of Business and Psychology* (March 2013), pp. 17–19.

70. T. Sy, S. Côté, and R. Saavedra, "The Contagious Leader: Impact of the Leader's Mood on the Mood of Group Members, Group Affective Tone, and Group Processes," *Journal of Applied Psychology* 90, no. 2 (2005), pp. 295–305.

71. V. A. Visser, D. van Knippenberg, G. van Kleef, and B. Wisse, "How Leader Displays of Happiness and Sadness Influence Follower Performance: Emotional Contagion and Creative versus Analytical Performance," *Leadership Quarterly* (February 2013), pp. 172–188.

72. B. E. Ashforth and R. H. Humphrey, "Emotion in the Workplace: A Reappraisal," *Human Relations* (February 1995), pp. 97–125.

73. G. A. Van Kleef, C. K. W. De Dreu, and A. S. R. Manstead, "The Interpersonal Effects of Emotions in Negotiations: A Motivated Information Processing Approach," *Journal of Personality and Social Psychology* 87, no. 4 (2004), pp. 510–528; and G. A. Van Kleef, C. K. W. De Dreu, and A. S. R. Manstead, "The Interpersonal Effects of Anger and Happiness in

Negotiations," *Journal of Personality and Social Psychology* 86, no. 1 (2004), pp. 57–76.

74. E. van Dijk, G. A. Van Kleef, W. Steinel, and I. van Beest, "A Social Functional Approach to Emotions in Bargaining: When Communicating Anger Pays and When It Backfires," *Journal of Personality and Social Psychology* 94, no. 4 (2008), pp. 600–614.

75. K. M. O'Connor and J. A. Arnold, "Distributive Spirals: Negotiation Impasses and the Moderating Role of Disputant Self-Efficacy," *Organizational Behavior and Human Decision Processes* 84, no. 1 (2001), pp. 148–176.

76. B. Shiv, G. Loewenstein, A. Bechara, H. Damasio, and A. R. Damasio, "Investment Behavior and the Negative Side of Emotion," *Psychological Science* 16, no. 6 (2005), pp. 435–439.

77. W.-C. Tsai and Y.-M. Huang, "Mechanisms Linking Employee Affective Delivery and Customer Behavioral Intentions," *Journal of Applied Psychology* (October 2002), pp. 1001–1008.

78. See P. B. Barker and A. A. Grandey, "Service with a Smile and Encounter Satisfaction: Emotional Contagion and Appraisal Mechanisms," *Academy of Management Journal* 49, no. 6 (2006), pp. 1229–1238; and S. D. Pugh, "Service with a Smile: Emotional Contagion in the Service Encounter," *Academy of Management Journal* (October 2001), pp. 1018–1027.

79. D. E. Rupp and S. Spencer, "When Customers Lash Out: The Effects of Customer Interactional Injustice on Emotional Labor and the Mediating Role of Emotions, *Journal of Applied Psychology* 91, no. 4 (2006), pp. 971–978; and Tsai and Huang, "Mechanisms Linking Employee Affective Delivery and Customer Behavioral Intentions."

80. R. Ilies and T. A. Judge, "Understanding the Dynamic Relationships Among Personality, Mood, and Job Satisfaction: A Field Experience Sampling Study," *Organizational Behavior and Human Decision Processes* 89 (2002), pp. 1119–1139.

81. T. A. Judge and R. Ilies, "Affect and Job Satisfaction: A Study of Their Relationship at Work and at Home," *Journal of Applied Psychology* 89 (2004), pp. 661–673.

82. Z. Song, M. Foo, and M. A. Uy, "Mood Spillover and Crossover Among Dual-Earner Couples: A Cell Phone Event Sampling Study," *Journal of Applied Psychology* 93, no. 2 (2008), pp. 443–452.

83. See R. J. Bennett and S. L. Robinson, "Development of a Measure of Workplace Deviance," *Journal of Applied Psychology*, June 2000, pp. 349–360; see also P. R. Sackett and C. J. DeVore, "Counterproductive Behaviors at Work," in N. Anderson, D. S. Ones, H. K. Sinangil, and C. Viswesvaran (eds.), *Handbook of Industrial, Work & Organizational Psychology* 1 (Thousand Oaks, CA: Sage, 2001), pp. 145–164.

84. K. Lee and N. J. Allen, "Organizational Citizenship Behavior and Workplace Deviance: The Role of Affect and Cognition," *Journal of Applied Psychology* 87, no. 1 (2002), pp. 131–142; T. A. Judge, B. A. Scott, and R. Ilies, "Hostility, Job Attitudes, and Workplace Deviance: Test of a Multilevel Model," *Journal of Applied Psychology* 91, no. 1 (2006), 126–138; and S. Kaplan, J. C. Bradley, J. N. Luchman, and D. Haynes, "On the Role of Positive and Negative Affectivity in Job Performance: A Meta-analytic Investigation," *Journal of Applied Psychology* 94, no. 1 (2009), pp. 162–176.

85. A. K. Khan, S. Ouratulain, and J. R. Cranshaw, "The Mediating Role of Discrete Emotions in the Relationship Between Injustice and Counterproductive Work Behaviors: A Study in Pakistan," *Journal of Business and Psychology* (March 2013), pp. 49–61.

86. R. D. Iverson and P. J. Erwin, "Predicting Occupational Injury: The Role of Affectivity," *Journal of Occupational and Organizational Psychology* 70, no. 2 (1997), pp. 113–128; Kaplan, Bradley, Luchman, and Haynes, "On the Role of Positive and Negative Affectivity in Job Performance: A Meta-analytic Investigation;" and J. Maiti, "Design for Worksystem Safety Using Employees' Perception About Safety," *Work—A Journal of Prevention Assessment & Rehabilitation* 41 (2012), pp. 3117–3122.

Chapter 5

1. G. W. Allport, *Personality: A Psychological Interpretation* (New York: Holt, Rinehart & Winston, 1937), p. 48. For a brief critique of current views on the meaning of personality, see R. T. Hogan and B. W. Roberts, "Introduction: Personality and Industrial and Organizational Psychology," in B. W. Roberts and R. Hogan (eds.), *Personality Psychology in the Workplace* (Washington, DC: American Psychological Association, 2001), pp. 11–12.

2. K. I. van der Zee, J. N. Zaal, and J. Piekstra, "Validation of the Multicultural Personality Questionnaire in the Context of Personnel Selection," *European Journal of Personality* 17, Supl. 1 (2003), pp. S77–S100.

3. S. A. Birkeland, T. M. Manson, J. L. Kisamore, M. T. Brannick, and M. A. Smith, "A Meta-analytic Investigation of Job Applicant Faking on Personality Measures," *International Journal of Selection and Assessment* 14, no. 14 (2006), pp. 317–335.

4. See R. Illies, R. D. Arvey, and T. J. Bouchard, "Darwinism, Behavioral Genetics, and Organizational Behavior: A Review and Agenda for Future Research," *Journal of Organizational Behavior* 27, no. 2 (2006), pp. 121–141; and W. Johnson, E. Turkheimer, I. I. Gottesman, and T. J. Bouchard, Jr., "Beyond Heritability: Twin Studies in Behavioral Research," *Current Directions in Psychological Science* 18, no. 4 (2009), pp. 217–220.

5. S. Srivastava, O. P. John, and S. D. Gosling, "Development of Personality in Early and Middle Adulthood: Set Like Plaster or Persistent Change?" *Journal of Personality and Social Psychology* 84, no. 5 (2003), pp. 1041–1053; and B. W. Roberts, K. E. Walton, and W. Viechtbauer, "Patterns of Mean-Level Change in Personality Traits Across the Life Course: A Meta-analysis of Longitudinal Studies," *Psychological Bulletin* 132, no. 1 (2006), pp. 1–25.

6. S. E. Hampson and L. R. Goldberg, "A First Large Cohort Study of Personality Trait Stability over the 40 Years Between Elementary School and Midlife," *Journal of Personality and Social Psychology* 91, no. 4 (2006), pp. 763–779.

7. See A. H. Buss, "Personality as Traits," *American Psychologist* 44, no. 11 (1989), pp. 1378–1388; R. R. McCrae, "Trait Psychology and the Revival of Personality and Culture Studies," *American Behavioral Scientist* 44, no. 1 (2000), pp. 10–31; and L. R. James and M. D. Mazerolle, *Personality in Work Organizations* (Thousand Oaks, CA: Sage, 2002).

8. See, for instance, G. W. Allport and H. S. Odbert, "Trait Names, A Psycholexical Study," *Psychological Monographs* no. 47 (1936); and R. B. Cattell, "Personality Pinned Down," *Psychology Today* (July 1973), pp. 40–46.

9. R. B. Kennedy and D. A. Kennedy, "Using the Myers-Briggs Type Indicator in Career Counseling," *Journal of Employment Counseling* 41, no. 1 (2004), pp. 38–44.

10. Research Staff Member, "Myers Briggs Type Indicator Instrument in French and English Canada," *Psychometrics*, accessed April 3, 2015 at https://www.psychometrics.com/docs/mbti-in-canada.pdf.

11. Research Staff Member. "MBTI and Strong Assessments Help Aboriginal Student Success at University of Saskatchewan," *Psychometrics*, accessed April 4, 2015 at https://www.psychometrics.com/docs/university-saskatchewancs.pdf.

12. A. Grant, "Goodbye to MBTI, the Fad That Won't Die," *Huffington Post* (September 18, 2013), http://www.

huffingtonpost.com/adam-grant/goodbye-to-mbti-the-fad-t_b_3947014.html.

13. See, for instance, D. J. Pittenger, "Cautionary Comments Regarding the Myers-Briggs Type Indicator," *Consulting Psychology Journal: Practice and Research* 57, no. 3 (2005), pp. 10–221; L. Bess and R. J. Harvey, "Bimodal Score Distributions and the Myers-Briggs Type Indicator: Fact or Artifact?" *Journal of Personality Assessment* 78, no. 1 (2002), pp. 176–186; R. M. Capraro and M. M. Capraro, "Myers-Briggs Type Indicator Score Reliability Across Studies: A Meta-analytic Reliability Generalization Study," *Educational & Psychological Measurement* 62, no. 4 (2002), pp. 590–602; and R. C. Arnau, B. A. Green, D. H. Rosen, D. H. Gleaves, and J. G. Melancon, "Are Jungian Preferences Really Categorical? An Empirical Investigation Using Taxometric Analysis," *Personality & Individual Differences* 34, no. 2 (2003), pp. 233–251.

14. See, for example, I. S. Oh, G. Wang, and M. K. Mount, "Validity of Observer Ratings of the Five-Factor Model of Personality Traits: A Meta-analysis"; and M. R. Barrick and M. K. Mount, "Yes, Personality Matters: Moving On to More Important Matters," *Human Performance* 18, no. 4 (2005), pp. 359–372.

15. W. Fleeson and P. Gallagher, "The Implications of Big Five Standing for the Distribution of Trait Manifestation in Behavior: Fifteen Experience-Sampling Studies and a Meta-analysis," *Journal of Personality and Social Psychology* 97, no. 6 (2009), pp. 1097–1114.

16. See, for instance, I. Oh and C. M. Berry, "The Five-Factor Model of Personality and Managerial Performance: Validity Gains Through the Use of 360 Degree Performance Ratings," *Journal of Applied Psychology* 94, no. 6 (2009), pp. 1498–1513; G. M. Hurtz and J. J. Donovan, "Personality and Job Performance: The Big Five Revisited," *Journal of Applied Psychology* 85, no. 6 (2000), pp. 869–879; J. Hogan and B. Holland, "Using Theory to Evaluate Personality and Job-Performance Relations: A Socioanalytic Perspective," *Journal of Applied Psychology* 88, no. 1 (2003), pp. 100–112; and M. R. Barrick and M. K. Mount, "Select on Conscientiousness and Emotional Stability," in E. A. Locke (ed.), *Handbook of Principles of Organizational Behavior* (Malden, MA: Blackwell, 2004), pp. 15–28.

17. M. K. Mount, M. R. Barrick, and J. P. Strauss, "Validity of Observer Ratings of the Big Five Personality Factors," *Journal of Applied Psychology* 79, no. 2 (1994), p. 272. Additionally confirmed by Hurtz and Donovan, "Personality and Job Performance: The Big Five Revisited"; and Oh and Berry, "The Five-Factor Model of Personality and Managerial Performance."

18. A. E. Poropat, "A Meta-analysis of the Five-Factor Model of Personality and Academic Performance," *Psychological Bulletin* 135, no. 2 (2009), pp. 322–338.

19. H. Le, I. Oh, S. B. Robbins, R. Ilies, E. Holland, and P. Westrick, "Too Much of a Good Thing: Curvilinear Relationships Between Personality Traits and Job Performance," *Journal of Applied Psychology* 96, no. 1 (2011), pp. 113–133.

20. T. Bogg and B. W. Roberts, "Conscientiousness and Health-Related Behaviors: A Meta-analysis of the Leading Behavioral Contributors to Mortality," *Psychological Bulletin* 130, no. 6 (2004), pp. 887–919.

21. G. J. Feist, "A Meta-analysis of Personality in Scientific and Artistic Creativity," *Personality and Social Psychology Review* 2, no. 4 (1998), pp. 290–309; C. Robert and Y. H. Cheung, "An Examination of the Relationship Between Conscientiousness and Group Performance on a Creative Task," *Journal of Research in Personality* 44, no. 2 (2010), pp. 222–231; and M. Batey, T. Chamorro-Premuzic, and A. Furnham, "Individual Differences in Ideational Behavior: Can the Big Five and Psychometric

Intelligence Predict Creativity Scores?" *Creativity Research Journal* 22, no. 1 (2010), pp. 90–97.

22. R. J. Foti and M. A. Hauenstein, "Pattern and Variable Approaches in Leadership Emergence and Effectiveness," *Journal of Applied Psychology* 92, no. 2 (2007), pp. 347–355.

23. L. I. Spirling and R. Persaud, "Extraversion as a Risk Factor," *Journal of the American Academy of Child & Adolescent Psychiatry* 42, no. 2 (2003), p. 130.

24. B. Weiss, and R. S. Feldman, "Looking Good and Lying to Do It: Deception as an Impression Management Strategy in Job Interviews," *Journal of Applied Social Psychology* 36, no. 4 (2006), pp. 1070–1086.

25. J. A. LePine, J. A. Colquitt, and A. Erez, "Adaptability to Changing Task Contexts: Effects of General Cognitive Ability, Conscientiousness, and Openness to Experience," *Personnel Psychology* 53, no. 3 (2000), pp. 563–595; S. Clarke and I. Robertson, "An Examination of the Role of Personality in Accidents Using Meta-analysis," *Applied Psychology: An International Review* 57, no. 1 (2008), pp. 94–108; and M. Baer, "The Strength-of-Weak-Ties Perspective on Creativity: A Comprehensive Examination and Extension," *Journal of Applied Psychology* 95, no. 3 (2010), pp. 592–601.

26. R. Ilies, I. S. Fulmer, M. Spitzmuller, and M. D. Johnson, "Personality and Citizenship Behavior: The Mediating Role of Job Satisfaction," *Journal of Applied Psychology* 94, no. 4 (2009), pp. 945–959.

27. See, for instance, S. Yamagata, A. Suzuki, J. Ando, Y. Ono, K. Yutaka, N. Kijima, et al., "Is the Genetic Structure of Human Personality Universal? A Cross-Cultural Twin Study from North America, Europe, and Asia," *Journal of Personality and Social Psychology* 90, no. 6 (2006), pp. 987–998; H. C. Triandis and E. M. Suh, "Cultural Influences on Personality," *Annual Review of Psychology* 53, no. 1 (2002), pp. 133–160; and R. R. McCrae, P. T. Costa Jr., T. A. Martin, V. E. Oryol, A. A. Rukavishnikov, I. G. Senin, et al., "Consensual Validation of Personality Traits Across Cultures," *Journal of Research in Personality* 38, no. 2 (2004), pp. 179–201.

28. J. F. Rauthmann, "The Dark Triad and Interpersonal Perception: Similarities and Differences in the Social Consequences of Narcissism, Machiavellianism, and Psychopathy," *Social Psychological and Personality Science* 3 (2012), pp. 487–496.

29. P. K. Jonason, S. Slomski, and J. Partyka, "The Dark Triad at Work: How Toxic Employees Get Their Way," *Personality and Individual Differences* 52 (2012), pp. 449–453.

30. E. H. O'Boyle, D. R. Forsyth, G. C. Banks, and M. A. McDaniel, "A Meta-analysis of the Dark Triad and Work Behavior: A Social Exchange Perspective," *Journal of Applied Psychology* 97 (2012), pp. 557–579.

31. L. Zhang, and M. A. Gowan, "Corporate Social Responsibility, Applicants' Individual Traits, and Organizational Attraction: A Person–Organization Fit Perspective," *Journal of Business and Psychology* 27 (2012), pp. 345–362.

32. D. N. Hartog and F. D. Belschak, "Work Engagement and Machiavellianism in the Ethical Leadership Process," *Journal of Business Ethics* 107 (2012), pp. 35–47.

33. J. J. Sosik, J. U. Chun, and W. Zhu, "Hang On to Your Ego: The Moderating Role of Leader Narcissism on Relationships Between Leader Charisma and Follower Psychological Empowerment and Moral Identity," *Journal of Business Ethics* (February 12, 2013); and B. M. Galvin, D. A. Waldman, and P. Balthazard, "Visionary Communication Qualities as Mediators of the Relationship Between Narcissism and Attributions of Leader Charisma," *Personnel Psychology* 63, no. 3 (2010), pp. 509–537.

34. K. A. Byrne and D. A. Worthy, "Do Narcissists Make Better Decisions? An Investigation of Narcissism and Dynamic

Decision-Making Performance," *Personality and Individual Differences* (July 2013), pp. 112–117.

35. C. Andreassen, H. Ursin, H. Eriksen, S. Pallesen, "The Relationship of Narcissism with Workaholism, Work Engagement, and Professional Position," *Social Behavior and Personality* 40, no. 6 (2012), pp. 881–890.

36. B. J. Hoffman, S. E. Strang, K. W. Kuhnert, W. K. Campbell, C. L. Kennedy, et al., "Leader Narcissism and Ethical Context: Effects on Ethical Leadership and Leader Effectiveness," *Journal of Leadership & Organizational Studies* 20 (2013), pp. 25–37.

37. L. L. Meier and N. K. Semmer, "Lack of Reciprocity and Strain: Narcissism as a Moderator of the Association Between Feeling Under-benefited and Irritation," *Work & Stress* 26 (2012), pp. 56–67.

38. M. Maccoby, "Narcissistic Leaders: The Incredible Pros, the Inevitable Cons," *The Harvard Business Review* (January–February 2000), pp. 69–77, http://www.maccoby.com/Articles/NarLeaders.shtml.

39. A. Chatterjee and D. C. Hambrick, "Executive Personality, Capability Cues, and Risk Taking: How Narcissistic CEOs React to Their Successes and Stumbles," *Administrative Science Quarterly* 56 (2011), pp. 202–237.

40. C. J. Resick, D. S. Whitman, S. M. Weingarden, and N. J. Hiller, "The Bright-Side and Dark-Side of CEO Personality: Examining Core Self-Evaluations, Narcissism, Transformational Leadership, and Strategic Influence," *Journal of Applied Psychology* 94, no. 6 (2009), pp. 1365–1381.

41. C. Carpenter, "Narcissism on Facebook: Self-Promotional and Anti-social Behavior," *Personality and Individual Differences* 52 (2012), pp. 482–486.

42. O'Boyle, Forsyth, Banks, and McDaniel, "A Meta-analysis of the Dark Triad and Work Behavior: A Social Exchange Perspective," p. 558.

43. B. Wille, F. De Fruyt, and B. De Clercq, "Expanding and Reconceptualizing Aberrant Personality at Work: Validity of Five-Factor Model Aberrant Personality Tendencies to Predict Career Outcomes," *Personnel Psychology* 66 (2013), pp. 173–223.

44. P. K. Jonason, S. Slomski, and J. Partyka, "The Dark Triad at Work: How Toxic Employees Get Their Way," *Personality and Individual Differences* 52 (2012), pp. 449–453; and H. M. Baughman, S. Dearing, E. Giammarco, and P. A. Vernon, "Relationships Between Bullying Behaviours and the Dark Triad: A Study with Adults," *Personality and Individual Differences* 52 (2012), pp. 571–575.

45. M. Lynk, "Disability and Work: The Transformation of the Legal Status of Employees with Disabilities in Canada," 2008, working paper, available online at http://ssrn.com/abstract=1068403 or http://dx.doi.org/10.2139/ssrn.1068403.

46. D. L. Ferris, R. E. Johnson, C. C. Rosen, E. Djurdjevic, C.-H. Chang, et al., "When Is Success Not Satisfying? Integrating Regulatory Focus and Approach/Avoidance Motivation Theories to Explain the Relation Between Core Self-Evaluation and Job Satisfaction," *Journal of Applied Psychology* 98 (2013), pp. 342–353.

47. K. Murayama and A. J. Elliot, "The Competition–Performance Relation: A Meta-analytic Review and Test of the Opposing Processes Model of Competition and Performance," *Psychological Bulletin* 138 (2012), pp. 1035–1070.

48. S. Nifadkar, A. S. Tsui, and B. E. Ashforth, "The Way You Make Me Feel and Behave: Supervisor-Triggered Newcomer Affect and Approach-Avoidance Behavior," *Academy of Management Journal* 55 (2012), pp. 1146–1168.

49. T. A. Judge and J. E. Bono, "A Rose by Any Other Name . . .: Are Self-Esteem, Generalized Self-Efficacy, Neuroticism, and Locus of Control Indicators of a Common Construct?" in B. W. Roberts and R. Hogan (eds.), *Personality Psychology in the*

Workplace (Washington, DC: American Psychological Association, 2001), pp. 93–118.

50. A. Erez and T. A. Judge, "Relationship of Core Self-Evaluations to Goal Setting, Motivation, and Performance," *Journal of Applied Psychology* 86, no. 6 (2001), pp. 1270–1279.

51. A. N. Salvaggio, B. Schneider, L. H. Nishi, D. M. Mayer, A. Ramesh, and J. S. Lyon, "Manager Personality, Manager Service Quality Orientation, and Service Climate: Test of a Model," *Journal of Applied Psychology* 92, no. 6 (2007), pp. 1741–1750; B. A. Scott and T. A. Judge, "The Popularity Contest at Work: Who Wins, Why, and What Do They Receive?" *Journal of Applied Psychology* 94, no. 1 (2009), pp. 20–33; and T. A. Judge and C. Hurst, "How the Rich (and Happy) Get Richer (and Happier): Relationship of Core Self-Evaluations to Trajectories in Attaining Work Success," *Journal of Applied Psychology* 93, no. 4 (2008), pp. 849–863.

52. A. M. Grant and A. Wrzesniewksi, "I Won't Let You Down . . . or Will I? Core Self-Evaluations, Other-Orientation, Anticipated Guilt and Gratitude, and Job Performance," *Journal of Applied Psychology* 95, no. 1 (2010), pp. 108–121.

53. U. Malmendier and G. Tate, "CEO Overconfidence and Corporate Investment," *Journal of Finance* 60, no. 6 (2005), pp. 2661–2700.

54. See M. Snyder, *Public Appearances/Private Realities: The Psychology of Self-Monitoring* (New York: W. H. Freeman, 1987); and S. W. Gangestad and M. Snyder, "Self-Monitoring: Appraisal and Reappraisal," *Psychological Bulletin* 126, no. 4 (2000), pp. 530–555.

55. F. J. Flynn and D. R. Ames, "What's Good for the Goose May Not Be as Good for the Gander: The Benefits of Self-Monitoring for Men and Women in Task Groups and Dyadic Conflicts," *Journal of Applied Psychology* 91, no. 2 (2006), pp. 272–281; and Snyder, *Public Appearances/Private Realities*.

56. D. V. Day, D. J. Shleicher, A. L. Unckless, and N. J. Hiller, "Self-Monitoring Personality at Work: A Meta-analytic Investigation of Construct Validity," *Journal of Applied Psychology* 87, no. 2 (2002), pp. 390–401.

57. H. Oh and M. Kilduff, "The Ripple Effect of Personality on Social Structure: Self-Monitoring Origins of Network Brokerage," *Journal of Applied Psychology* 93, no. 5 (2008), pp. 1155–1164; and A. Mehra, M. Kilduff, and D. J. Brass, "The Social Networks of High and Low Self-Monitors: Implications for Workplace Performance," *Administrative Science Quarterly* 46, no. 1 (2001), pp. 121–146.

58. J. M. Crant, "Proactive Behavior in Organizations," *Journal of Management* 26, no. 3 (2000), p. 436.

59. P. D. Converse, Patrick J. Pathak, A. M. DePaul-Haddock, T. Gotlib, and M. Merbedone, "Controlling Your Environment and Yourself: Implications for Career Success," *Journal of Vocational Behavior* 80 (2012), pp. 148–159.

60. G. Chen, J. Farh, E. M. Campbell-Bush, Z. Wu, and X. Wu, "Teams as Innovative Systems: Multilevel Motivational Antecedents of Innovation in R&D Teams," *Journal of Applied Psychology* (2013).

61. Z. Zhang, M. Wang, J. Shi, Junqi, "Leader-Follower Congruence in Proactive Personality and Work Outcomes: The Mediating Role of Leader–Member Exchange," *Academy of Management Journal* 55 (2012), pp. 111–130.

62. G. Van Hoye and H. Lootens, "Coping with Unemployment: Personality, Role Demands, and Time Structure," *Journal of Vocational Behavior* 82 (2013), pp. 85–95.

63. R. D. Meyer, R. S. Dalal, and R. Hermida, "A Review and Synthesis of Situational Strength in the Organizational Sciences," *Journal of Management* 36 (2010), pp. 121–140.

64. A. M. Grant and N. P. Rothbard, "When in Doubt, Seize the Day? Security Values, Prosocial Values, and Proactivity Under Ambiguity," *Journal of Applied Psychology* (2013).

65. Y. Kim, L. Van Dyne, D. Kamdar, and R. E. Johnson, "Why and When Do Motives Matter? An Integrative Model of Motives, Role Cognitions, and Social Support as Predictors of OCB," *Organizational Behavior and Human Decision Processes* (2013).

66. M. Rokeach, *The Nature of Human Values* (New York: The Free Press, 1973), p. 5.

67. M. Rokeach and S. J. Ball-Rokeach, "Stability and Change in American Value Priorities, 1968–1981," *American Psychologist* 44, no. 5 (1989), pp. 775–784; and A. Bardi, J. A. Lee, N. Hofmann-Towfigh, and G. Soutar, "The Structure of Intraindividual Value Change," *Journal of Personality and Social Psychology* 97, no. 5 (2009), pp. 913–929.

68. S. Roccas, L. Sagiv, S. H. Schwartz, and A. Knafo, "The Big Five Personality Factors and Personal Values," *Personality and Social Psychology Bulletin* 28, no. 6 (2002), pp. 789–801.

69. B. C. Holtz and C. M. Harold, "Interpersonal Justice and Deviance: The Moderating Effects of Interpersonal Justice Values and Justice Orientation," *Journal of Management* (February 2013), pp. 339–365.

70. J. L. Holland, *Making Vocational Choices: A Theory of Vocational Personalities and Work Environments* (Odessa, FL: Psychological Assessment Resources, 1997).

71. D. A. McKay and D. M. Tokar, "The HEXACO and Five-Factor Models of Personality in Relation to RIASEC Vocational Interests," *Journal of Vocational Behavior* (October 2012), pp. 138–149.

72. See B. Schneider, H. W. Goldstein, and D. B. Smith, "The ASA Framework: An Update," *Personnel Psychology* 48, no. 4 (1995), pp. 747–773; B. Schneider, D. B. Smith, S. Taylor, and J. Fleenor, "Personality and Organizations: A Test of the Homogeneity of Personality Hypothesis," *Journal of Applied Psychology* 83, no. 3 (1998), pp. 462–470; W. Arthur Jr., S. T. Bell, A. J. Villado, and D. Doverspike, "The Use of Person–Organization Fit in Employment Decision-Making: An Assessment of Its Criterion-Related Validity," *Journal of Applied Psychology* 91, no. 4 (2006), pp. 786–801; and J. R. Edwards, D. M. Cable, I. O. Williamson, L. S. Lambert, and A. J. Shipp, "The Phenomenology of Fit: Linking the Person and Environment to the Subjective Experience of Person–Environment Fit," *Journal of Applied Psychology* 91, no. 4 (2006), pp. 802–827.

73. T. A. Judge and D. M. Cable, "Applicant Personality, Organizational Culture, and Organization Attraction," *Personnel Psychology* 50, no. 2 (1997), pp. 359–394; and A. Leung and S. Chaturvedi, "Linking the Fits, Fitting the Links: Connecting Different Types of PO Fit to Attitudinal Outcomes," *Journal of Vocational Behavior* (October 2011), pp. 391–402.

74. M. L. Verquer, T. A. Beehr, and S. E. Wagner, "A Meta-analysis of Relations Between Person–Organization Fit and Work Attitudes," *Journal of Vocational Behavior* 63, no. 3 (2003), pp. 473–489; and J. C. Carr, A. W. Pearson, M. J. Vest, and S. L. Boyar, "Prior Occupational Experience, Anticipatory Socialization, and Employee Retention, *Journal of Management* 32, no. 32 (2006), pp. 343–359.

75. A. Ramesh and M. J. Gelfand, "Will They Stay or Will They Go? The Role of Job Embeddedness in Predicting Turnover in Individualistic and Collectivistic Cultures," *Journal of Applied Psychology* 95, no. 5 (2010), pp. 807–823.

76. G. Hofstede, *Cultures and Organizations: Software of the Mind* (London: McGraw-Hill, 1991); G. Hofstede, "Cultural Constraints in Management Theories," *Academy of Management Executive* 7, no. 1 (1993), pp. 81–94; G. Hofstede and M. F. Peterson, "National Values and Organizational Practices," in N. M. Ashkanasy, C. M. Wilderom, and M. F. Peterson (eds.), *Handbook of Organizational Culture and Climate* (Thousand Oaks, CA: Sage, 2000), pp. 401–416; and G. Hofstede, *Culture's Consequences: Comparing Values, Behaviors, Institutions, and Organizations Across Nations*, 2nd ed. (Thousand Oaks, CA: Sage, 2001). For criticism of this research, see B. McSweeney, "Hofstede's Model of National Cultural Differences and Their Consequences: A Triumph of Faith—A Failure of Analysis," *Human Relations* 55, no. 1 (2002), pp. 89–118.

77. V. Taras, B. L. Kirkman, and P. Steel, "Examining the Impact of Culture's Consequences: A Three-Decade, Multilevel, Meta-analytic Review of Hofstede's Cultural Value Dimensions," *Journal of Applied Psychology* 95, no. 5 (2010), pp. 405–439.

78. M. Javidan and R. J. House, "Cultural Acumen for the Global Manager: Lessons from Project GLOBE," *Organizational Dynamics* 29, no. 4 (2001), pp. 289–305; and R. J. House, P. J. Hanges, M. Javidan, and P. W. Dorfman (eds.), *Leadership, Culture, and Organizations: The GLOBE Study of 62 Societies* (Thousand Oaks, CA: Sage, 2004).

79. J. P. Meyer, D. J. Stanley, T. A. Jackson, K. J. McInnis, E. R. Maltin, et al., "Affective, Normative, and Continuance Commitment Levels Across Cultures: A Meta-analysis," *Journal of Vocational Behavior* 80 (2012), pp. 225–245.

80. Michael Adams, "Fire and Ice Revisited: American and Canadian Social Values in the Age of Obama and Harper," slide presentation, March 14, 2014 (Toronto: Environics Institute for Survey Research).

81. Province of Alberta, "Our Words, Our Ways," *Alberta Department of Education*, accessed April 2, 2015 at http://www.education.alberta.ca/media/307113/o02.pdf.

82. G. Hofstede, *Cultures and Organizations: Software of the Mind* (London, ON: McGraw-Hill, 1991).

83. Berry, J. W. (1997). Immigration, acculturation and adaptation. *Applied Psychology: An International Review* 46, no. 1, pp. 5–68.

84. L. Ekstrand, Ethnic Minorities and Immigrants in a Cross-cultural Perspective, selected papers from the Regional IACCP Conference, Ethnic Minority and Immigrant Research, held in Malmö, Sweden, June 25–28, 1986.

85. R. Bourhis, G. Barrette, S. E-Geledi, and R. Schmidster, "Acculturation Orientations and Social Relations Between Immigrant and Host Community Members in California," *Journal of Cross-Cultural Psychology* 40, no. 3 (2009), pp. 443–467; and R. Bourhis, "Towards an Interactive Acculturation Model: A Social Psychological Approach," *International Journal of Psychology* 32, no. 6 (1997), pp. 369–3.

Chapter 6

1. H. H. Kelley, "Attribution in Social Interaction," in E. Jones et al. (eds.), *Attribution: Perceiving the Causes of Behavior* (Morristown, NJ: General Learning Press, 1972); and M. J. Martinko, P. Harvey, and M. T. Dasborough, "Attribution Theory in the Organizational Sciences: A Case of Unrealized Potential," *Journal of Organizational Behavior* 32, no. 1 (2011), pp. 144–149.

2. See P. W. Andrews, "The Psychology of Social Chess and the Evolution of Attribution Mechanisms: Explaining the Fundamental Attribution Error," *Evolution and Human Behavior* (January 2001), pp. 11–29; and L. Ross, "The Intuitive Psychologist and His Shortcomings," in L. Berkowitz (ed.), *Advances in Experimental Social Psychology* 10 (Orlando, FL: Academic Press, 1977), pp. 174–220.

3. T. S. Duval and P. J. Silvia, "Self-Awareness, Probability of Improvement, and the Self-Serving bias," *Journal of Personality and Social Psychology* (January 2002), pp. 49–61; M. Goerke, J. Moller, S. Schulz-Hardt, U. Napiersky, and D. Frey, "'It's Not My Fault—But Only I Can Change It': Counterfactual

and Prefactual Thoughts of Managers," *Journal of Applied Psychology* 89, no. 2 (2004), pp. 279–292; and E. G. Hepper, R. H. Gramzow, and C. Sedikides, "Individual Differences in Self-Enhancement and Self-Protection Strategies: An Integrative Analysis," *Journal of Personality* 78, no. 2 (2010), pp. 781–814.

4. See, for instance, A. H. Mezulis, L. Y. Abramson, J. S. Hyde, and B. L. Hankin, "Is There a Universal Positivity Bias in Attributions: A Meta-analytic Review of Individual, Developmental, and Cultural Differences in the Self-Serving Attributional Bias," *Psychological Bulletin* 130, no. 5 (2004), pp. 711–747; C. F. Falk, S. J. Heine, M. Yuki, and K. Takemura, "Why Do Westerners Self-Enhance More Than East Asians?" *European Journal of Personality* 23, no. 3 (2009), pp. 183–203; and F. F. T. Chiang and T. A. Birtch, "Examining the Perceived Causes of Successful Employee Performance: An East–West Comparison," *International Journal of Human Resource Management* 18, no. 2 (2007), pp. 232–248.

5. S. Nam, "Cultural and Managerial Attributions for Group Performance," unpublished doctoral dissertation, University of Oregon. Cited in R. M. Steers, S. J. Bischoff, and L. H. Higgins, "Cross-cultural Management Research," *Journal of Management Inquiry* (December 1992), pp. 325–326.

6. T. Menon, M. W. Morris, C. Chiu, and Y. Y. Hong, "Culture and the Construal of Agency: Attribution to Individual Versus Group Dispositions," *Journal of Personality and Social Psychology* 76, no. 5 (1999), pp. 701–717; and R. Friedman, W. Liu, C. C. Chen, and S.-C. S. Chi, "Causal Attribution for Interfirm Contract Violation: A Comparative Study of Chinese and American Commercial Arbitrators," *Journal of Applied Psychology* 92, no. 3 (2007), pp. 856–864.

7. J. Spencer-Rodgers, M. J. Williams, D. L. Hamilton, K. Peng, and L. Wang, "Culture and Group Perception: Dispositional and Stereotypic Inferences About Novel and National Groups," *Journal of Personality and Social Psychology* 93, no. 4 (2007), pp. 525–543.

8. J. D. Brown, "Across the (Not So) Great Divide: Cultural Similarities in Self-Evaluative Processes," *Social and Personality Psychology Compass* 4, no. 5 (2010), pp. 318–330.

9. A. Zhang, C. Reyna, Z. Qian, and G. Yu, "Interpersonal Attributions of Responsibility in the Chinese Workplace: A Test of Western Models in a Collectivistic Context," *Journal of Applied Social Psychology* 38, no. 9 (2008), pp. 2361–2377; and A. Zhang, F. Xia, and C. Li, "The Antecedents of Help Giving in Chinese Culture: Attribution, Judgment of Responsibility, Expectation Change and the Reaction of Affect," *Social Behavior and Personality* 35, no. 1 (2007), pp. 135–142.

10. See P. Rosenzweig, *The Halo Effect* (New York: The Free Press, 2007); I. Dennis, "Halo Effects in Grading Student Projects," *Journal of Applied Psychology* 92, no. 4 (2007), pp. 1169–1176; C. E. Naquin and R. O. Tynan, "The Team Halo Effect: Why Teams Are Not Blamed for Their Failures," *Journal of Applied Psychology* 88, no. 2 (2003), pp. 332–340; and T. M. Bechger, G. Maris, and Y. P. Hsiao, "Detecting Halo Effects in Performance-Based Evaluations," *Applied Psychological Measurement* 34, no. 8 (2010), pp. 607–619.

11. S. E. Asch, "Forming Impressions of Personality," *Journal of Abnormal and Social Psychology* 41, no. 3 (1946), pp. 258–290.

12. H. Tajfel, *Social Identity and Inter Group Behaviour* (Cambridge, MA: Cambridge University Press, 1982).

13. H. Tajfel and J. C. Turner, The Social Identity Theory of Inter-group Behavior, in S. Worchel and L. W. Austin (eds.), *Psychology of Intergroup Relations* (Chicago: Nelson-Hall, 1986).

14. J. L. Hilton and W. von Hippel, "Stereotypes," *Annual Review of Psychology* 47 (1996), pp. 237–271; and L. Jia, C. L. Dickter, J. Luo, X. Xiao, Q. Yang, et al., "Different Brain Mechanisms Between Stereotype Activation and Application: Evidence from an ERP Study," *International Journal of Psychology* 47, no. 1 (2012), pp. 58–66.

15. See, for example, C. Ostroff and L. E. Atwater, "Does Whom You Work with Matter? Effects of Referent Group Gender and Age Composition on Managers' Compensation," *Journal of Applied Psychology* 88, no. 4 (2003), pp. 725–740; M. E. Heilman, A. S. Wallen, D. Fuchs, and M. M. Tamkins, "Penalties for Success: Reactions to Women Who Succeed at Male Gender-Typed Tasks," *Journal of Applied Psychology* 89, no. 3 (2004), pp. 416–427; V. K. Gupta, D. B. Turban, and N. M. Bhawe, "The Effect of Gender Stereotype Activation on Entrepreneurial Intentions," *Journal of Applied Psychology* 93, no. 5 (2008), pp. 1053–1061; and R. A. Posthuma and M. A. Campion, "Age Stereotypes in the Workplace: Common Stereotypes, Moderators, and Future Research Directions," *Journal of Management* 35, no. 1 (2009), pp. 158–188.

16. See, for example, N. Dasgupta, D. DeSteno, L. A. Williams, and M. Hunsinger, "Fanning the Flames of Prejudice: The Influence of Specific Incidental Emotions on Implicit Prejudice," *Emotion* 9, no. 4 (2009), pp. 585–591; and J. C. Ziegert and P. C. Hanges, "Strong Rebuttal for Weak Criticisms: Reply to Blanton et al. (2009)," *Journal of Applied Psychology* 94, no. 3 (2009), pp. 590–597.

17. The Provincial Court of Manitoba, *Fatality Inquiry Report*, 2014, http://www.manitobacourts.mb.ca/site/assets/files/1051/brian_sinclair_inquest_-_dec_14.pdf.

18. A. S. Rosette, G. J. Leonardelli, and K. W. Phillips, "The White Standard: Racial Bias in Leader Categorization," *Journal of Applied Psychology* 93, no. 4 (2008), pp. 758–777.

19. R. Sanders, *The Executive Decisionmaking Process: Identifying Problems and Assessing Outcomes* (Westport, CT: Quorum, 1999); and K. Tasa and G. Whyte, "Collective Efficacy and Vigilant Problem Solving in Group Decision Making: A Non-linear Model," *Organizational Behavior and Human Decision Processes* (March 2005), pp. 119–129.

20. See H. A. Simon, "Rationality in Psychology and Economics," *Journal of Business* (October 1986), pp. 209–224; and E. Shafir and R. A. LeBoeuf, "Rationality," *Annual Review of Psychology* 53 (2002), pp. 491–517.

21. For a review of the rational decision-making model, see M. H. Bazerman and D. A. Moore, *Judgment in Managerial Decision Making*, 7th ed. (Hoboken, New Jersey: Wiley, 2008).

22. J. G. March, *A Primer on Decision Making* (New York: The Free Press, 2009); and D. Hardman and C. Harries, "How Rational Are We?" *Psychologist* (February 2002), pp. 76–79.

23. Bazerman and Moore, *Judgment in Managerial Decision Making*.

24. J. E. Russo, K. A. Carlson, and M. G. Meloy, "Choosing an Inferior Alternative," *Psychological Science* 17, no. 10 (2006), pp. 899–904.

25. D. Kahneman, "Maps of Bounded Rationality: Psychology for Behavioral Economics," *The American Economic Review* 93, no. 5 (2003), pp. 1449–1475; and J. Zhang, C. K. Hsee, and Z. Xiao, "The Majority Rule in Individual Decision Making," *Organizational Behavior and Human Decision Processes* 99 (2006), pp. 102–111.

26. See H. A. Simon, *Administrative Behavior*, 4th ed. (New York: The Free Press, 1997); and M. Augier, "Simon Says: Bounded Rationality Matters," *Journal of Management Inquiry* (September 2001), pp. 268–275.

27. G. Gigerenzer, "Why Heuristics Work," *Perspectives on Psychological Science* 3, no. 1 (2008), pp. 20–29; and A. K. Shah

and D. M. Oppenheimer, "Heuristics Made Easy: An Effort-Reduction Framework," *Psychological Bulletin* 134, no. 2 (2008), pp. 207–222.

28. See A. W. Kruglanski and G. Gigerenzer, "Intuitive and Deliberate Judgments Are Based on Common Principles," *Psychological Review* 118 (2011), pp. 97–109.

29. E. Dane and M. G. Pratt, "Exploring Intuition and Its Role in Managerial Decision Making," *Academy of Management Review* 32, no. 1 (2007), pp. 33–54; and J. A. Hicks, D. C. Cicero, J. Trent, C. M. Burton, and L. A. King, "Positive Affect, Intuition, and Feelings of Meaning," *Journal of Personality and Social Psychology* 98 (2010), pp. 967–979.

30. C. Akinci and E. Sadler-Smith, "Intuition in Management Research: A Historical Review," *International Journal of Management Reviews* 14 (2012), pp. 104–122.

31. S. P. Robbins, *Decide & Conquer: Making Winning Decisions and Taking Control of Your Life* (Upper Saddle River, NJ: Financial Times/Prentice Hall, 2004), p. 13.

32. S. Ludwig and J. Nafziger, "Beliefs About Overconfidence," *Theory and Decision* (April 2011), pp. 475–500.

33. S. Plous, *The Psychology of Judgment and Decision Making* (New York: McGraw-Hill, 1993), p. 217.

34. C. R. M. McKenzie, M. J. Liersch, and I. Yaniv, "Overconfidence in Interval Estimates: What Does Expertise Buy You?" *Organizational Behavior and Human Decision Processes* 107 (2008), pp. 179–191.

35. J. Kruger and D. Dunning, "Unskilled and Unaware of It: How Difficulties in Recognizing One's Own Incompetence Lead to Inflated Self-Assessments," *Journal of Personality and Social Psychology* (November 1999), pp. 1121–1134; and R. P. Larrick, K. A. Burson, and J. B. Soll, "Social Comparison and Confidence: When Thinking You're Better Than Average Predicts Overconfidence (and When It Does Not)" *Organizational Behavior and Human Decision Processes* 102 (2007), pp. 76–94.

36. K. M. Hmieleski and R. A. Baron, "Entrepreneurs' Optimism and New Venture Performance: A Social Cognitive Perspective," *Academy of Management Journal* 52, no. 3 (2009), pp. 473–488.

37. See, for instance, J. P. Simmons, R. A. LeBoeuf, and L. D. Nelson, "The Effect of Accuracy Motivation on Anchoring and Adjustment: Do People Adjust from Their Provided Anchors?" *Journal of Personality and Social Psychology* 99 (2010), pp. 917–932.

38. C. Janiszewski and D. Uy, "Precision of the Anchor Influences the Amount of Adjustment," *Psychological Science* 19, no. 2 (2008), pp. 121–127.

39. See E. Jonas, S. Schultz-Hardt, D. Frey, and N. Thelen, "Confirmation Bias in Sequential Information Search after Preliminary Decisions," *Journal of Personality and Social Psychology* (April 2001), pp. 557–571; and W. Hart, D. Albarracín, A. H. Eagly, I. Brechan, M. Lindberg, and L. Merrill, "Feeling Validated Versus Being Correct: A Meta-analysis of Selective Exposure to Information," *Psychological Bulletin* 135 (2009), pp. 555–588.

40. T. Pachur, R. Hertwig, and F. Steinmann, "How Do People Judge Risks: Availability Heuristic, Affect Heuristic, or Both?" *Journal of Experimental Psychology: Applied* 18 (2012), pp. 314–330; and A. Tversky and D. Kahneman, "Availability: A Heuristic for Judging Frequency and Probability," in D. Kahneman, P. Slovic, and A. Tversky (eds.), *Judgment Under Uncertainty: Heuristics and Biases* (Cambridge, UK: Cambridge University Press, 1982), pp. 163–178.

41. K. Moser, H.-G. Wolff, and A. Kraft, "The De-escalation of Commitment: Predecisional Accountability and Cognitive Processes," *Journal of Applied Social Psychology* (February 2013), pp. 363–376; and B. M. Staw, "The Escalation of Commitment

to a Course of Action," *Academy of Management Review* (October 1981), pp. 577–587.

42. T. Schultze, F. Pfeiffer, and S. Schulz-Hardt, "Biased Information Processing in the Escalation Paradigm: Information Search and Information Evaluation as Potential Mediators of Escalating Commitment," *Journal of Applied Psychology* 97 (2012), pp. 16–32.

43. See, for example, D. J. Keys and B. Schwartz, "Leaky Rationality: How Research on Behavioral Decision Making Challenges Normative Standards of Rationality," *Psychological Science* 2, no. 2 (2007), pp. 162–180; and U. Simonsohn, "Direct Risk Aversion: Evidence from Risky Prospects Valued Below Their Worst Outcome," *Psychological Science* 20, no. 6 (2009), pp. 686–692.

44. J. K. Maner, M. T. Gailliot, D. A. Butz, and B. M. Peruche, "Power, Risk, and the Status Quo: Does Power Promote Riskier or More Conservative Decision Making?" *Personality and Social Psychology Bulletin* 33, no. 4 (2007), pp. 451–462.

45. A. Chakraborty, S. Sheikh, and N. Subramanian, "Termination Risk and Managerial Risk Taking," *Journal of Corporate Finance* 13 (2007), pp. 170–188.

46. R. L. Guilbault, F. B. Bryant, J. H. Brockway, and E. J. Posavac, "A Meta-analysis of Research on Hindsight Bias," *Basic and Applied Social Psychology* (September 2004), pp. 103–117; and L. Werth, F. Strack, and J. Foerster, "Certainty and Uncertainty: The Two Faces of the Hindsight Bias," *Organizational Behavior and Human Decision Processes* (March 2002), pp. 323–341.

47. J. Bell, "The Final Cut?" *Oregon Business* 33, no. 5 (2010), p. 27.

48. E. Dash and J. Creswell, "Citigroup Pays for a Rush to Risk," *The New York Times* (November 20, 2008), pp. 1, 28; S. Pulliam, S. Ng, and R. Smith, "Merrill Upped Ante as Boom in Mortgage Bonds Fizzled," *The Wall Street Journal* (April 16, 2008), pp. A1, A14; and M. Gladwell, "Connecting the Dots," *The New Yorker* (March 10, 2003).

49. G. Christie, *Aboriginal Nationhood and the Inherent Right to Self-Government*, http://fngovernance.org/ncfng_research/gordon_christie.pdf.

50. G. F. Cavanagh, D. J. Moberg, and M. Valasquez, "The Ethics of Organizational Politics," *Academy of Management Journal* (June 1981), pp. 363–374; and G. N. Gotsis and Z. Kortezi, "Ethical Considerations in Organizational Politics: Expanding the Perspective," *Journal of Business Ethics* 93, no. 4 (2010), pp. 497–517.

51. "Is Your Art Killing You?" Investorideas.com (May 13, 2013), accessed May 14, 2013 at http://www.investorideas.com/news/2013/renewable-energy/05134.asp.

52. G. Anderson, "Three Tips to Foster Creativity at Your Startup," *ArcticStartup* (May 8, 2013), accessed May 14, 2013 at http://www.arcticstartup.com.

53. T. Burgman, "Operation Blue Sky Crowdsourcing Ideas for Aboriginal Healthcare," accessed May 21 2015 from http://www.theglobeandmail.com/life/health-and-fitness/health/operation-blue-sky-crowdsourcing-ideas-for-aboriginal-health-care/article23711206.

54. Z. Harper, "Mark Cuban Wants You to Design the New Dallas Mavericks Uniforms," CBSSports.com (May 13, 2013), accessed May 14, 2013 at http://www.cbssports.com/nba.

55. C. K. W. De Dreu, B. A. Nijstad, M. Baas, I. Wolsink, and M. Roskes, "Working Memory Benefits Creative Insight, Musical Improvisation, and Original Ideation Through Maintained Task-Focused Attention," *Personality and Social Psychology Bulletin* 38 (2012), pp. 656–669.

56. S. M. Wechsler, C. Vendramini, and T. Oakland, "Thinking and Creative Styles: A Validity Study," *Creativity Research Journal* 24 (April 2012), pp. 235–242.

57. Y. Gong, S. Cheung, M. Wang, and J. Huang, "Unfolding the Proactive Processes for Creativity: Integration of the Employee Proactivity, Information Exchange, and Psychological Safety Perspectives," *Journal of Management* 38 (2012), pp. 1611–1633.
58. S. N. de Jesus, C. L. Rus, W. Lens, and S. Imaginário, "Intrinsic Motivation and Creativity Related to Product: A Meta-analysis of the Studies Published Between 1990–2010," *Creativity Research Journal* 25 (2013), pp. 80–84.
59. L. Sun, Z. Zhang, J. Qi, and Z. X. Chen, "Empowerment and Creativity: A Cross-Level Investigation," *Leadership Quarterly* 23 (2012), pp. 55–65.
60. J. S. Mueller, S. Melwani, and J. A. Goncalo, "The Bias Against Creativity: Why People Desire but Reject Creative Ideas," *Psychological Science* 23 (2012), pp. 13–17.
61. T. Montag, C. P. Maertz, and M. Baer, "A Critical Analysis of the Workplace Creativity Criterion Space," *Journal of Management* 38 (2012), pp. 1362–1386.

Chapter 7

1. See, for example, G. P. Latham and C. C. Pinder, "Work Motivation Theory and Research at the Dawn of the Twenty-First Century," *Annual Review of Psychology* 56 (2005), pp. 485–516; and C. C. Pinder, *Work Motivation in Organizational Behavior*, 2nd ed. (London, UK: Psychology Press, 2008).
2. R. Wagner and J. K. Harter, *12: The Elements of Great Managing* (Washington, DC: Gallup Press, 2006).
3. "The 2013 Wasting Time at Work Survey: Everything You've Always Wanted to Know About Wasting Time in the Office," Salary.com, 2013, http://www.salary.com.
4. See, for instance, Pinder, *Work Motivation in Organizational Behavior*.
5. A. Maslow, *Motivation and Personality* (New York: Harper & Row, 1954).
6. See, for example, E. E. Lawler III and J. L. Suttle, "A Causal Correlation Test of the Need Hierarchy Concept," *Organizational Behavior and Human Performance* 7, no. 2 (1972), pp. 265–287; D. Lester, "Measuring Maslow's Hierarchy of Needs," *Psychological Reports* (August 2013), pp. 15–17; and J. Rauschenberger, N. Schmitt, and J. E. Hunter, "A Test of the Need Hierarchy Concept by a Markov Model of Change in Need Strength," *Administrative Science Quarterly* 25, no. 4 (1980), pp. 654–670.
7. D. T. Kenrick, V. Griskevicius, S. L. Neuberg, and M. Schaller, "Renovating the Pyramid of Needs: Contemporary Extensions Built on Ancient Foundations," *Perspectives on Psychological Science* 5, no. 3 (2010), pp. 292–314.
8. D. McGregor, *The Human Side of Enterprise* (New York: McGraw-Hill, 1960). For an updated analysis of Theory X and Theory Y constructs, see R. E. Kopelman, D. J. Prottas, and D. W. Falk, "Construct Validation of a Theory X/Y Behavior Scale," *Leadership and Organization Development Journal* 31, no. 2 (2010), pp. 120–135.
9. F. Herzberg, B. Mausner, and B. Snyderman, *The Motivation to Work* (New York: Wiley, 1959).
10. R. J. House and L. A. Wigdor, "Herzberg's Dual-Factor Theory of Job Satisfaction and Motivations: A Review of the Evidence and Criticism," *Personnel Psychology* 20, no. 4 (1967), pp. 369–389; T. A. Judge, C. J. Thoresen, J. E. Bono, & G. K. Patton, "The Job Satisfaction–Job Performance Relationship: A Qualitative and Quantitative Review," *Psychological Bulletin* (May 2001), pp. 376–407; D. P. Schwab and L. L. Cummings, "Theories of Performance and Satisfaction: A Review," *Industrial Relations* 9, no. 4 (1970), pp. 403–430; and J. Phillipchuk and J. Whittaker, "An Inquiry into the Continuing Relevance of Herzberg's Motivation Theory," *Engineering Management Journal* 8 (1996), pp. 15–20.
11. D. C. McClelland, *The Achieving Society* (New York: Van Nostrand Reinhold, 1961); J. W. Atkinson and J. O. Raynor, *Motivation and Achievement* (Washington, DC: Winston, 1974); D. C. McClelland, *Power: The Inner Experience* (New York: Irvington, 1975); and M. J. Stahl, *Managerial and Technical Motivation: Assessing Needs for Achievement, Power, and Affiliation* (New York: Praeger, 1986).
12. D. C. McClelland and D. G. Winter, *Motivating Economic Achievement* (New York: The Free Press, 1969); J. B. Miner, N. R. Smith, and J. S. Bracker, "Role of Entrepreneurial Task Motivation in the Growth of Technologically Innovative Firms: Interpretations from Follow-up Data," *Journal of Applied Psychology* 79, no. 4 (1994), pp. 627–630; and J. Schueler, V. Brandstaetter, and K. M. Sheldon, "Do Implicit Motives and Basic Psychological Needs Interact to Predict Well-Being and Flow? Testing a Universal Hypothesis and a Matching Hypothesis," *Motivation and Emotion* (September 2013), pp. 480–495.
13. McClelland, *Power*; D. C. McClelland and D. H. Burnham, "Power Is the Great Motivator," *Harvard Business Review* (March–April 1976), pp. 100–110; and R. E. Boyatzis, "The Need for Close Relationships and the Manager's Job," in D. A. Kolb, I. M. Rubin, and J. M. McIntyre, *Organizational Psychology: Readings on Human Behavior in Organizations*, 4th ed. (Upper Saddle River, NJ: Prentice Hall, 1984), pp. 81–86.
14. D. G. Winter, "The Motivational Dimensions of Leadership: Power, Achievement, and Affiliation," in R. E. Riggio, S. E. Murphy, and F. J. Pirozzolo (eds.), *Multiple Intelligences and Leadership* (Mahwah, NJ: Lawrence Erlbaum, 2002), pp. 119–138.
15. J. B. Miner, *Studies in Management Education* (New York: Springer, 1965).
16. Ibid.
17. E. Deci and R. Ryan (eds.), *Handbook of Self-Determination Research* (Rochester, NY: University of Rochester Press, 2002); R. Ryan and E. Deci, "Self-Determination Theory and the Facilitation of Intrinsic Motivation, Social Development, and Well-Being," *American Psychologist* 55, no. 1 (2000), pp. 68–78; and M. Gagné and E. L. Deci, "Self-Determination Theory and Work Motivation," *Journal of Organizational Behavior* 26, no. 4 (2005), pp. 331–362.
18. See, for example, E. L. Deci, R. Koestner, and R. M. Ryan, "A Meta-analytic Review of Experiments Examining the Effects of Extrinsic Rewards on Intrinsic Motivation," *Psychological Bulletin* 125, no. 6 (1999), pp. 627–668; G. J. Greguras and J. M. Diefendorff, "Different Fits Satisfy Different Needs: Linking Person–Environment Fit to Employee Commitment and Performance Using Self-Determination Theory," *Journal of Applied Psychology* 94, no. 2 (2009), pp. 465–477; and D. Liu, X. Chen, and X. Yao, "From Autonomy to Creativity: A Multilevel Investigation of the Mediating Role of Harmonious Passion," *Journal of Applied Psychology* 96, no. 2 (2011), pp. 294–309.
19. R. Eisenberger and L. Rhoades, "Incremental Effects of Reward on Creativity," *Journal of Personality and Social Psychology* 81, no. 4 (2001), 728–741; and R. Eisenberger, W. D. Pierce, and J. Cameron, "Effects of Reward on Intrinsic Motivation—Negative, Neutral, and Positive: Comment on Deci, Koestner, and Ryan (1999)," *Psychological Bulletin* 125, no. 6 (1999), pp. 677–691.
20. M. Burgess, M. E. Enzle, and R. Schmaltz, "Defeating the Potentially Deleterious Effects of Externally Imposed Deadlines: Practitioners' Rules-of-Thumb," *Personality and Social Psychology Bulletin* 30, no. 7 (2004), pp. 868–877.

21. K. M. Sheldon, A. J. Elliot, and R. M. Ryan, "Self- Concordance and Subjective Well-Being in Four Cultures," *Journal of Cross-Cultural Psychology* 35, no. 2 (2004), pp. 209–223.

22. J. E. Bono and T. A. Judge, "Self-Concordance at Work: Toward Understanding the Motivational Effects of Transformational Leaders," *Academy of Management Journal* 46, no. 5 (2003), pp. 554–571.

23. L. M. Graves, M. N. Ruderman, P. J. Ohlott, and Todd J. Webber, "Driven to Work and Enjoyment of Work: Effects on Managers' Outcomes," *Journal of Management* 38, no. 5 (2012), pp. 1655–1680.

24. J. P. Meyer, T. E. Becker, and C. Vandenberghe, "Employee Commitment and Motivation: A Conceptual Analysis and Integrative Model," *Journal of Applied Psychology* 89, no. 6 (2004), pp. 991–1007.

25. E. A. Locke, "Toward a Theory of Task Motivation and Incentives," *Organizational Behavior and Human Performance* 3, no. 2 (1968), pp. 157–189.

26. P. C. Earley, P. Wojnaroski, and W. Prest, "Task Planning and Energy Expended: Exploration of How Goals Influence Performance," *Journal of Applied Psychology* 72, no. 1 (1987), pp. 107–114.

27. See M. E. Tubbs, "Goal Setting: A Meta-analytic Examination of the Empirical Evidence," *Journal of Applied Psychology* 71, no. 3 (1986), pp. 474–483; and E. A. Locke and G. P. Latham, "New Directions in Goal-Setting Theory," *Current Directions in Psychological Science* 15, no. 5 (2006), pp. 265–268.

28. E. A. Locke and G. P. Latham, "Building a Practically Useful Theory of Goal Setting and Task Motivation," *American Psychologist* 57, no. 2 (2002), pp. 705–717.

29. C. Gabelica, P. Van den Bossche, M. Segers, and W. Gijselaersa, "Feedback, a Powerful Lever in Teams: A Review," *Educational Research Review* (June 2012), pp. 123–144.

30. K. Dewettinck and H. van Dijk, "Linking Belgian Employee Performance Management System Characteristics with Performance Management System Effectiveness: Exploring the Mediating Role of Fairness," *International Journal of Human Resource Management* (February 1, 2013), pp. 806–825; and M. Erez, P. C. Earley, and C. L. Hulin, "The Impact of Participation on Goal Acceptance and Performance: A Two-Step Model," *Academy of Management Journal* 28, no. 1 (1985), pp. 50–66.

31. T. S. Bateman and B. Bruce, "Masters of the Long Haul: Pursuing Long-Term Work Goals," *Journal of Organizational Behavior* (October 2012), pp. 984–1006; and E. A. Locke, "The Motivation to Work: What We Know," *Advances in Motivation and Achievement* 10 (1997), pp. 375–412.

32. Ibid.

33. J. E. Bono and A. E. Colbert, "Understanding Responses to Multi-source Feedback: The Role of Core Self-Evaluations," *Personnel Psychology* 58, no. 1 (2005), pp. 171–203; and S. A. Jeffrey, A. Schulz, and A. Webb, "The Performance Effects of an Ability-Based Approach to Goal Assignment," *Journal of Organizational Behavior Management* 32 (2012), pp. 221–241.

34. A. M. O'Leary-Kelly, J. J. Martocchio, and D. D. Frink, "A Review of the Influence of Group Goals on Group Performance," *Academy of Management Journal* 37, no. 5 (1994), pp. 1285–1301; and T. Tammemagi, D. O'Hora, and K. A. Maglieri, "The Effects of a Goal Setting Intervention on Productivity and Persistence in an Analogue Work Task," *Journal of Organizational Behavior Management* (March 1, 2013), pp. 31–54.

35. D. F. Crown, "The Use of Group and Groupcentric Individual Goals for Culturally Heterogeneous and Homogeneous Task Groups: An Assessment of European Work Teams," *Small Group Research* 38, no. 4 (2007), pp. 489–508; J. Kurman, "Self-Regulation Strategies in Achievement Settings: Culture and Gender Differences," *Journal of Cross-cultural Psychology* 32, no. 4 (2001), pp. 491–503; and M. Erez and P. C. Earley, "Comparative Analysis of Goal-Setting Strategies Across Cultures," *Journal of Applied Psychology* 72, no. 4 (1987), pp. 658–665.

36. C. Sue-Chan and M. Ong, "Goal Assignment and Performance: Assessing the Mediating Roles of Goal Commitment and Self-Efficacy and the Moderating Role of Power Distance," *Organizational Behavior and Human Decision Processes* 89, no. 2 (2002), pp. 1140–1161.

37. G. P. Latham and E. A. Locke, "Enhancing the Benefits and Overcoming the Pitfalls of Goal Setting," *Organizational Dynamics* 35, no. 6, pp. 332–340; L. D. Ordóñez, M. E. Schweitzer, A. D. Galinsky, and M. H. Bazerman, "Goals Gone Wild: The Systematic Side Effects of Overprescribing Goal Setting," *Academy of Management Perspectives* 23, no. 1 (2009), pp. 6–16; and E. A. Locke and G. P. Latham, "Has Goal Setting Gone Wild, or Have Its Attackers Abandoned Good Scholarship?" *Academy of Management Perspectives* 23, no. 1 (2009), pp. 17–23.

38. S. J. Perry, L. A. Witt, L. M. Penney, and L. Atwater, "The Downside of Goal-Focused Leadership: The Role of Personality in Subordinate Exhaustion," *Journal of Applied Psychology* 95, no. 6 (2010), pp. 1145–1153.

39. K. Lanaj, C. D. Chang, and R. E. Johnson, "Regulatory Focus and Work-Related Outcomes: A Review and Meta-analysis," *Psychological Bulletin* 138, no. 5 (2012), pp. 998–1034.

40. "KeyGroup Survey Finds Nearly Half of All Employees Have No Set Performance Goals," *IPMA-HR Bulletin* (March 10, 2006), p. 1; S. Hamm, "SAP Dangles a Big, Fat Carrot," *Businessweek* (May 22, 2006), pp. 67–68; and "P&G CEO Wields High Expectations but No Whip," *USA Today* (February 19, 2007), p. 3B.

41. See, for instance, C. Antoni, "Management by Objectives—An Effective Tool for Teamwork?" *International Journal of Human Resource Management* (February 2005), pp. 174–184; S. J. Carroll and H. L. Tosi, *Management by Objectives: Applications and Research* (New York: Macmillan, 1973); and R. Rodgers and J. E. Hunter, "Impact of Management by Objectives on Organizational Productivity," *Journal of Applied Psychology* 76, no. 2 (1991), pp. 322–336.

42. A. Bandura, *Self-Efficacy: The Exercise of Control* (New York: Freeman, 1997).

43. A. D. Stajkovic and F. Luthans, "Self-Efficacy and Work-Related Performance: A Meta-analysis," *Psychological Bulletin* 124, no. 2 (1998), pp. 240–261; and A. Bandura, "Cultivate Self-Efficacy for Personal and Organizational Effectiveness," in E. Locke (ed.), *Handbook of Principles of Organizational Behavior* (Malden, MA: Blackwell, 2004), pp. 120–136.

44. M. Salanova, S. Llorens, and W. B. Schaufeli, "Yes I Can, I Feel Good, and I Just Do It! On Gain Cycles and Spirals of Efficacy Beliefs, Affect, and Engagement," *Applied Psychology* 60, no. 2 (2011), pp. 255–285.

45. P. Tierney and S. M. Farmer, "Creative Self-Efficacy Development and Creative Performance over Time," *Journal of Applied Psychology* 96, no. 2 (2011), pp. 277–293.

46. A. Bandura and D. Cervone, "Differential Engagement in Self-Reactive Influences in Cognitively-Based Motivation," *Organizational Behavior and Human Decision Processes* 38, no. 1 (1986), pp. 92–113; and A. P. Tolli and A. M. Schmidt, "The Role of Feedback, Causal Attributions, and Self-Efficacy in Goal Revision," *Journal of Applied Psychology* (May 2008), pp. 692–701.

47. Bandura, *Self-Efficacy*.

48. R. C. Rist, "Student Social Class and Teacher Expectations: The Self-Fulfilling Prophecy in Ghetto Education," *Harvard Educational Review* 70, no. 3 (2000), pp. 266–301.

49. D. Eden, "Self-Fulfilling Prophecies in Organizations," in J. Greenberg (ed.), *Organizational Behavior: The State of the*

Science, 2nd ed. (Mahwah, NJ: Lawrence Erlbaum, 2003), pp. 91–122.

50. Ibid.

51. C. L. Holladay and M. A. Quiñones, "Practice Variability and Transfer of Training: The Role of Self-Efficacy Generality," *Journal of Applied Psychology* 88, no. 6 (2003), pp. 1094–1103.

52. E. C. Dierdorff, E. A. Surface, and K. G. Brown, "Frame-of-Reference Training Effectiveness: Effects of Goal Orientation and Self-Efficacy on Affective, Cognitive, Skill-Based, and Transfer Outcomes," *Journal of Applied Psychology* 95, no. 6 (2010), pp. 1181–1191; and R. Grossman, and E. Salas, "The Transfer of Training: What Really Matters," *International Journal of Training and Development* 15, no. 2 (2011), pp. 103–120.

53. T. A. Judge, C. L. Jackson, J. C. Shaw, B. Scott, and B. L. Rich, "Self-Efficacy and Work-Related Performance: The Integral Role of Individual Differences," *Journal of Applied Psychology* 92, no. 1 (2007), pp. 107–127.

54. Ibid.

55. D. Richardson, "Pay, Performance, and Competitive Behaviours in the National Hockey League, *Eastern Economic Journal* 26, no. 4, pp. 393–417; C. O. Trevor, G. Reilly, and B. Gerhart, "Reconsidering Pay Dispersion's Effect on the Performance of Interdependent Work: Reconciling Sorting and Pay Inequality," *Academy of Management Journal* (June 2012), pp. 585–610.

56. See, for example, R. Cropanzano, J. H. Stein, and T. Nadisic, *Social Justice and the Experience of Emotion* (New York: Routledge/Taylor and Francis Group, 2011).

57. P. S. Goodman and A. Friedman, "An Examination of Adams' Theory of Inequity," *Administrative Science Quarterly* 16, no. 3 (1971), pp. 271–288; R. P. Vecchio, "An Individual-Differences Interpretation of the Conflicting Predictions Generated by Equity Theory and Expectancy Theory," *Journal of Applied Psychology* 66, no. 4 (1981), pp. 470–481; R. T. Mowday, "Equity Theory Predictions of Behavior in Organizations," in R. Steers, L. W. Porter, and G. Bigley (eds.), *Motivation and Work Behavior,* 6th ed. (New York: McGraw-Hill, 1996), pp. 111–131; R. W. Griffeth and S. Gaertner, "A Role for Equity Theory in the Turnover Process: An Empirical Test," *Journal of Applied Social Psychology* 31, no. 5 (2001), pp. 1017–1037; and L. K. Scheer, N. Kumar, and J.-B. E. M. Steenkamp, "Reactions to Perceived Inequity in U.S. and Dutch Interorganizational Relationships," *Academy of Management* 46, no. 3 (2003), pp. 303–316.

58. See, for instance, J. A. Colquitt, D. E. Conlon, M. J. Wesson, C. O. L. H. Porter, and K.-Y. Ng, "Justice at the Millennium: A Meta-analytic Review of the 25 Years of Organizational Justice Research," *Journal of Applied Psychology* 86, no. 3 (2001), pp. 425–445; T. Simons and Q. Roberson, "Why Managers Should Care About Fairness: The Effects of Aggregate Justice Perceptions on Organizational Outcomes," *Journal of Applied Psychology* 88, no. 3 (2003), pp. 432–443; and B. C. Holtz and C. M. Harold, "Fair Today, Fair Tomorrow? A Longitudinal Investigation of Overall Justice Perceptions," *Journal of Applied Psychology* 94, no. 5 (2009), pp. 1185–1199.

59. J. Brockner and B. M. Wiesenfeld, "An Integrative Framework for Examining Reactions to Decisions: Interactive Effects of Outcomes and Procedures," *Psychological Bulletin* 120 (1996), pp. 189–208; and J. Brockner, B. M. Wiesenfeld, and K. A. Diekmann, "Towards a 'Fairer' Conception of Process Fairness: Why, When, and How More May Not Always Be Better Than Less," *Academy of Management Annals* 3 (2009), pp. 183–216.

60. R. Folger and D. P. Skarlicki, "Fairness as a Dependent Variable: Why Tough Times Can Lead to Bad Management," in R. Cropanzano (ed.), *Justice in the Workplace: From Theory to Practice* (Mahway, NJ: Erlbaum, 2001), pp. 97–118.

61. C. R. Wanberg, L. W. Bunce, and M. B. Gavin, "Perceived Fairness of Layoffs Among Individuals Who Have Been Laid Off," *Personnel Psychology* 52 (1999), pp. 59–84; B. M. Wiesenfeld, J. Brockner, and V. Thibault, "Procedural Fairness, Managers' Self-Esteem, and Managerial Behaviors Following a Layoff," *Organizational Behavior and Human Decision Processes* (September 2000), pp. 1–32; and J. C. Shaw, E. Wild, and J. A. Colquitt, "To Justify or Excuse? A Meta-analytic Review of the Effects of Explanations," *Journal of Applied Psychology* 88, no. 3 (2003), pp. 444–458.

62. R. Loi, J. Yang, and J. M. Diefendorff, "Four Factor Justice and Daily Job Satisfaction: A Multilevel Investigation," *Journal of Applied Psychology* 94, no. 3 (2009), pp. 770–781.

63. Callister Gibson, "Anger in Organizations: Review and Integration," *Journal of Management* 36, no. 1 (2010), pp. 66–93.

64. D. McIntyre and V. Calio, "Nine CEOs with the Worst Reputations," Yahoo Finance, 2014, http://finance.yahoo.com/news/nine-ceos-worst-reputations-191237027.html.

65. J. M. Robbins, M. T. Ford, and L. E. Tetrick, "Perceived Unfairness and Employee Health: A Meta-analytic Integration," *Journal of Applied Psychology* 97, no. 2 (2012), pp. 235–272.

66. J. A. Colquitt, B. A. Scott, J. B. Rodell, D. M. Long, C. P. Zapata, D. E. Conlon, and M. J. Wesson, "Justice at the Millennium, A Decade Later: A Meta-analytic Test of Social Exchange and Affect-Based Perspectives," *Journal of Applied Psychology* 98, no. 2 (2013), pp. 199–236.

67. R. J. Bies, "Are Procedural and Interactional Justice Conceptually Distinct?" in J. Greenberg and J. A. Colquitt (eds.), *Handbook of Organizational Justice* (Mahwah, NJ: Erlbaum, 2005), pp. 85–112; and B. A. Scott, J. A. Colquitt, and E. L. Paddock, "An Actor-Focused Model of Justice Rule Adherence and Violation: The Role of Managerial Motives and Discretion," *Journal of Applied Psychology* 94, no. 3 (2009), pp. 756–769.

68. G. A. Van Kleef, A. C. Homan, B. Beersma, D. V. Knippenberg, B. V. Knippenberg, and F. Damen, "Searing Sentiment or Cold Calculation? The Effects of Leader Emotional Displays on Team Performance Depend on Follower Epistemic Motivation," *Academy of Management Journal* 52, no. 3 (2009), pp. 562–580.

69. R. Fischer and P. B. Smith, "Reward Allocation and Culture: A Meta-analysis," *Journal of Cross-cultural Psychology* 34, no. 3 (2003), pp. 251–268.

70. F. F. T. Chiang and T. Birtch, "The Transferability of Management Practices: Examining Cross-national Differences in Reward Preferences," *Human Relations* 60, no. 9 (2007), pp. 1293–1330; A. E. Lind, T. R. Tyler, and Y. J. Huo, "Procedural Context and Culture: Variation in the Antecedents of Procedural Justice Judgments," *Journal of Personality and Social Psychology* 73, no. 4 (1997), pp. 767–780; and M. J. Gelfand, M. Erez, and Z. Aycan, "Cross-cultural Organizational Behavior," *Annual Review of Psychology* 58 (2007), pp. 479–514.

71. J. K. Giacobbe-Miller, D. J. Miller, and V. I. Victorov, "A Comparison of Russian and U.S. Pay Allocation Decisions, Distributive Justice Judgments, and Productivity Under Different Payment Conditions," *Personnel Psychology* 51, no. 1 (1998), pp. 137–163; and J. K. Giacobbe-Miller, D. J. Miller, W. Zhang, and V. I. Victorov, "Country and Organizational-Level Adaptation to Foreign Workplace Ideologies: A Comparative Study of Distributive Justice Values in China, Russia, and the United States," *Journal of International Business Studies* 23 (2003), pp. 289–406.

72. M. C. Bolino and W. H. Turnley, "Old Faces, New Places: Equity Theory in Cross-Cultural Contexts," *Journal of Organizational Behavior* 29, no. 1 (2008), pp. 29–50.

73. K. Leung, K. Tong, and S. S. Ho, "Effects of Interactional Justice on Egocentric Bias in Resource Allocation Decisions," *Journal of*

Applied Psychology 89, no. 3 (2004), pp. 405–415; L. Francis-Gladney, N. R. Manger, and R. B. Welker, "Does Outcome Favorability Affect Procedural Fairness as a Result of Self-Serving Attributions?" *Journal of Applied Social Psychology* 40, no. 1 (2010), pp. 182–194; and L. J. Barlcay and D. P. Skarlicki, "Healing the Wounds of Organizational Injustice: Examining the Benefits of Expressive Writing," *Journal of Applied Psychology* 94, no. 2 (2009), pp. 511–523.

74. V. H. Vroom, *Work and Motivation* (New York: Wiley, 1964).

75. L. W. Porter and E. E. Lawler III, *Managerial Attitudes and Performance* (Homewood, IL: Irwin, 1968); and J. J. Donovan, "Work Motivation," in N. Anderson et al. (eds.), *Handbook of Industrial, Work & Organizational Psychology* 2 (Thousand Oaks, CA: Sage, 2001), pp. 56–59.

76. W. Van Eerde and H. Thierry, "Vroom's Expectancy Models and Work-Related Criteria: A Meta-analysis," *Journal of Applied Psychology* 81, no. 5 (1996), pp. 575–586.

77. H. G. Heneman III and D. P. Schwab, "Evaluation of Research on Expectancy Theory Prediction of Employee Performance," *Psychological Bulletin* 78, no. 1 (1972), pp. 1–9; T. R. Mitchell, "Expectancy Models of Job Satisfaction, Occupational Preference and Effort: A Theoretical, Methodological and Empirical Appraisal," *Psychological Bulletin* 81, no. 12 (1974), pp. 1053–1077; J. House, H. J. Shapiro, and M. A. Wahba, "Expectancy Theory as a Predictor of Work Behavior and Attitudes: A Reevaluation of Empirical Evidence," *Decision Sciences* 5, no. 3 (1974), pp. 481–506; and Y. Hao and G. Jianping, "Research on Employee Motivation Mechanism in Modern Enterprises Based on Victor H. Vroom's Expectancy Theory," *Proceedings of the 9th International Conference on Innovation and Management* (2012), pp. 988–991.

78. W. A. Kahn, "Psychological Conditions of Personal Engagement and Disengagement at Work," *Academy of Management Journal* 33, no. 4 (1990), pp. 692–724.

79. http://www.gallup.com/consulting/52/Employee-Engagement.aspx.

80. J. K. Harter, F. L. Schmidt, and T. L. Hayes, "Business-Unit-Level Relationship Between Employee Satisfaction, Employee Engagement, and Business Outcomes: A Meta-analysis," *Journal of Applied Psychology* 87, no. 2 (2002), pp. 268–279.

81. M. S. Christian, A. S. Garza, and J. E. Slaughter, "Work Engagement: A Quantitative Review and Test of Its Relations with Task and Contextual Performance," *Personnel Psychology* 64, no. 1 (2011), pp. 89–136.

82. W. B. Schaufeli, A. B. Bakker, and W. van Rhenen, "How Changes in Job Demands and Resources Predict Burnout, Work Engagement, and Sickness Absenteeism," *Journal of Organizational Behavior* 30, no. 7 (2009), pp. 893–917; E. R. Crawford, J. A. LePine, and B. L. Rich, "Linking Job Demands and Resources to Employee Engagement and Burnout: A Theoretical Extension and Meta-analytic Test," *Journal of Applied Psychology* 95, no. 5 (2010), pp. 834–848; and D. Xanthopoulou, A. B. Bakker, E. Demerouti, and W. B. Schaufeli, "Reciprocal Relationships Between Job Resources, Personal Resources, and Work Engagement," *Journal of Vocational Behavior* 74, no 3 (2010), pp. 617–635.

83. B. L. Rich, J. A. LePine, and E. R. Crawford, "Job Engagement: Antecedents and Effects on Job Performance," *Academy of Management Journal* 53, no. 3 (2010), pp. 617–635.

84. M. Tims, A. B. Bakker, and D. Xanthopoulou, "Do Transformational Leaders Enhance Their Followers' Daily Work Engagement?" *Leadership Quarterly* 22, no. 1 (2011), pp. 121–131.

85. D. A. Newman and D. A. Harrison, "Been There, Bottled That: Are State and Behavioral Work Engagement New and Useful Construct 'Wines?'" *Industrial and Organizational Psychology* 1, no. 1 (2008), pp. 31–55; and A. J. Wefald and R. G. Downey, "Job Engagement in Organizations: Fad, Fashion, or Folderol," *Journal of Organizational Behavior* 30, no. 1 (2009), pp. 141–145.

86. J. M. George, "The Wider Context, Costs, and Benefits of Work Engagement," *European Journal of Work and Organizational Psychology* 20, no. 1 (2011), pp. 53–59; and J. R. B. Halbesleben, J. Harvey, and M. C. Bolino, "Too Engaged? A Conservation of Resources View of the Relationship Between Work Engagement and Work Interfere with Family," *Journal of Applied Psychology* 94, no. 6 (2009), pp. 1452–1465.

Chapter 8

1. J. R. Hackman and G. R. Oldham, "Motivation Through the Design of Work: Test of a Theory," *Organizational Behavior and Human Performance* 16, no. 2 (1976), pp. 250–279; and J. R. Hackman and G. R. Oldham, *Work Redesign* (Reading, MA: Addison-Wesley, 1980).

2. J. R. Hackman, "Work Design," in J. R. Hackman and J. L. Suttle (eds.), *Improving Life at Work* (Santa Monica, CA: Goodyear, 1977), p. 129.

3. B. M. Meglino and A. M. Korsgaard, "The Role of Other Orientation in Reactions to Job Characteristics," *Journal of Management* 33, no. 1 (2007), pp. 57–83.

4. M. F. Peterson and S. A. Ruiz-Quintanilla, "Cultural Socialization as a Source of Intrinsic Work Motivation," *Group & Organization Management* 28, no. 2 (2003), pp. 188–216.

5. A. Christini and D. Pozzoli, "Workplace Practices and Firm Performance in Manufacturing: A Comparative Study of Italy and Britain," *International Journal of Manpower* 31, no. 7 (2010), pp. 818–842; and K. Kaymaz, "The Effects of Job Rotation Practices on Motivation: A Research on Managers in the Automotive Organizations," *Business and Economics Research Journal* 1, no. 3 (2010), pp. 69–86.

6. T. Silver, "Rotate Your Way to Higher Value," *Baseline* (March/April 2010), p. 12; and J. J. Salopek, "Coca-Cola Division Refreshes Its Talent with Diversity Push on Campus," *Workforce Management Online* (March 2011), http://www.workforce.com.

7. Skytrax website review of Singapore Airlines, accessed May 31, 2013 at http://www.airlinequality.com/Airlines/SQ.htm.

8. Hackman and Oldham, *Work Redesign*.

9. A. M. Grant, J. E. Dutton, and B. D. Rosso, "Giving Commitment: Employee Support Programs and the Prosocial Sensemaking Process," *Academy of Management Journal* 51, no. 5 (2008), pp. 898–918.

10. See, for example, R. W. Griffin, "Effects of Work Redesign on Employee Perceptions, Attitudes, and Behaviors: A Long-Term Investigation," *Academy of Management Journal* 34, no. 2 (1991), pp. 425–435; and M. Subramony, "A Meta-analytic Investigation of the Relationship Between HRM Bundles and Firm Performance," *Human Resource Management* 48, no. 5 (2009), pp. 745–768.

11. R. D. Pritchard, M. M. Harrell, D. DiazGrandos, and M. J. Guzman, "The Productivity Measurement and Enhancement System: A Meta-analysis," *Journal of Applied Psychology* 93, no. 3 (2008), pp. 540–567.

12. F. W. Bond, P. E. Flaxman, and D. Bunce, "The Influence of Psychological Flexibility on Work Redesign: Mediated Moderation of a Work Reorganization Intervention," *Journal of Applied Psychology* 93, no. 3 (2008), pp. 645–654.

13. A. M. Grant, "Leading with Meaning: Beneficiary Contact, Prosocial Impact, and the Performance Effects of Transformational Leadership," *Academy of Management Journal* 55 (2012), pp. 458–476; and A. M. Grant and S. K. Parker, "Redesigning Work Design Theories: The Rise of Relational and

Proactive Perspectives," *Annals of the Academy of Management* 3, no. 1 (2009), pp. 317–375.

14. Y. N. Turner, I. Hadas-Halperin, and D. Raveh, "Patient Photos Spur Radiologist Empathy and Eye for Detail," paper presented at the annual meeting of the Radiological Society of North America (November 2008).

15. A. M. Grant, E. M. Campbell, G. Chen, K. Cottone, D. Lapedis, and K. Lee, "Impact and the Art of Motivation Maintenance: The Effects of Contact with Beneficiaries on Persistence Behavior," *Organizational Behavior and Human Decision Processes* 103, no. 1 (2007), pp. 53–67.

16. Society for Human Resource Management, *2012 Employee Benefits* (Alexandria, VA: Author, 2012).

17. T. McMahon, "The War on Work–Life Balance," *Maclean's* (November 7, 2013), accessed June 27, 2015 at http://www.macleans.ca/economy/business/out-of-office-out-of-luck.

18. R. Waring, "Sunday Dialogue: Flexible Work Hours," *The New York Times* (January 19, 2013), http://www.nytimes.com.

19. S. Westcott, "Beyond Flextime: Trashing the Workweek," *Inc.* (August 2008), p. 30.

20. See, for example, D. A. Ralston and M. F. Flanagan, "The Effect of Flextime on Absenteeism and Turnover for Male and Female Employees," *Journal of Vocational Behavior* 26, no. 2 (1985), pp. 206–217; B. B. Baltes, T. E. Briggs, J. W. Huff, J. A. Wright, and G. A. Neuman, "Flexible and Compressed Workweek Schedules: A Meta-analysis of Their Effects on Work-Related Criteria," *Journal of Applied Psychology* 84, no. 4 (1999), pp. 496–513; K. M. Shockley, and T. D. Allen, "When Flexibility Helps: Another Look at the Availability of Flexible Work Arrangements and Work–Family Conflict," *Journal of Vocational Behavior* 71, no. 3 (2007), pp. 479–493; J. G. Grzywacz, D. S. Carlson, and S. Shulkin, "Schedule Flexibility and Stress: Linking Formal Flexible Arrangements and Perceived Flexibility to Employee Health," *Community, Work, and Family* 11, no. 2 (2008), pp. 199–214; and L. A. McNall, A. D. Masuda, and J. M. Nicklin, "Flexible Work Arrangements, Job Satisfaction, and Turnover Intentions: The Mediating Role of Work-to-Family Enrichment," *Journal of Psychology* 144, no. 1 (2010), pp. 61–81.

21. K. M. Shockley and T. D. Allen, "Investigating the Missing Link in Flexible Work Arrangement Utilization: An Individual Difference Perspective," *Journal of Vocational Behavior* 76, no. 1 (2010), pp. 131–142.

22. J. LaReau, "Ford's 2 Julies Share Devotion—and Job," *Automotive News* (October 25, 2010), p. 4.

23. Society for Human Resource Management, 2012 Employee Benefits.

24. S. Chase and O. Moore, "Canadian Workers Cozy Up to Job Sharing," *Globe and Mail* (August 23, 2012), accessed June 27, 2015 at http://www.theglobeandmail.com/news/politics/canadian-workers-cozy-up-to-job-sharing/article4307864.

25. L. Woellert, "U.S. Work Share Program Helps Employers Avoid Layoffs," *Bloomberg Businessweek* (January 24, 2013), http://www.businessweek.com/articles/2013-01-24/u-dot-s-dot-work-share-program-helps-employers-avoid-layoffs.

26. P. R. Gregory, "Why Obama Cannot Match Germany's Jobs Miracle," *Forbes* (May 5, 2013), http://www.forbes.com/sites/paulroderickgregory/2013/05/05/why-obama-cannot-match-germanys-jobs-miracle.

27. See, for example, E. J. Hill, M. Ferris, and V. Martinson, "Does It Matter Where You Work? A Comparison of How Three Work Venues (Traditional Office, Virtual Office, and Home Office) Influence Aspects of Work and Personal/Family Life," *Journal of Vocational Behavior* 63, no. 2 (2003), pp. 220–241; B. Williamson, "Managing Virtual Workers," *Bloomberg Businessweek* (July 16, 2009), http://www.businessweek.com; and

B. A. Lautsch; and E. E. Kossek, "Managing a Blended Workforce: Telecommuters and Non-telecommuters," *Organizational Dynamics* 40, no. 1 (2010), pp. 10–17.

28. B. Belton, "Best Buy Copies Yahoo, Reins in Telecommuting," *USA Today* (March 6, 2013), http://www.usatoday.com.

29. C. Tkaczyk, "Marissa Mayer Breaks Her Silence on Yahoo's Telecommuting Policy," CNNMoney.com (April 19, 2013), accessed April 8, 2014 at http://tech.fortune.cnn.com/2013/04/19/marissa-mayer-telecommuting.

30. Statistics Canada, "Working from Home: An Update," accessed June 28, 2015 at http://www.statcan.gc.ca/pub/11-008-x/2011001/article/11366-eng.htm#a3.

31. Society for Human Resource Management, *2012 Employee Benefits.*

32. N. Bogart, "Telecommuting Offers Benefits for Employee and Employer," Global News Canada (March 23, 2013), accessed June 28, 2015 at http://globalnews.ca/news/427470/telecommuting-offers-benefits-for-employee-and-employer-contrary-to-popular-belief.

33. M. Conlin, "The Easiest Commute of All," http://www.bloomberg.com/news/articles/2005-12-11/the-easiest-commute-of-all.

34. E. E. Kossek, B. A. Lautsch, S. C. Eaton, "Telecommuting, Control, and Boundary Management: Correlates of Policy Use and Practice, Job Control, and Work-Family Effectiveness," *Journal of Vocational Behavior* 68, no. 2 (2006), pp. 347–367.

35. J. Kotkin, "Marissa Mayer's Misstep and the Unstoppable Rise of Telecommuting," *Forbes* (March 26, 2013).

36. J. M. Stanton and J. L. Barnes-Farrell, "Effects of Electronic Performance Monitoring on Personal Control, Task Satisfaction, and Task Performance," *Journal of Applied Psychology* 81, no. 6 (1996), pp. 738–745; and L. Taskin and F. Bridoux, "Telework: A Challenge to Knowledge Transfer in Organizations," *International Journal of Human Resource Management* 21, no. 13 (2010), pp. 2503–2520.

37. J. Welch and S. Welch, "The Importance of Being There," *Businessweek* (April 16, 2007), p. 92; and Z. I. Barsness, K. A. Diekmann, and M. L. Seidel, "Motivation and Opportunity: The Role of Remote Work, Demographic Dissimilarity, and Social Network Centrality in Impression Management," *Academy of Management Journal* 48, no. 3 (2005), pp. 401–419.

38. See, for example, the increasing body of literature on empowerment, such as D. P. Ashmos, D. Duchon, R. R. McDaniel Jr., and J. W. Huonker, "What a Mess! Participation as a Simple Managerial Rule to 'Complexify' Organizations," *Journal of Management Studies* 39, no. 2 (2002), pp. 189–206; S. E. Seibert, S. R. Silver, and W. A. Randolph, "Taking Empowerment to the Next Level: A Multiple-Level Model of Empowerment, Performance, and Satisfaction," *Academy of Management Journal* 47, no. 3 (2004), pp. 332–349; M. M. Butts, R. J. Vandenberg, D. M. DeJoy, B. S. Schaffer, and M. G. Wilson, "Individual Reactions to High Involvement Work Processes: Investigating the Role of Empowerment and Perceived Organizational Support," *Journal of Occupational Health Psychology* 14, no. 2 (2009), pp. 122–136; R. Park, E. Applebaum, and D. Kruse, "Employee Involvement and Group Incentives in Manufacturing Companies: A Multi-level Analysis," *Human Resource Management Journal* 20, no. 3 (2010), pp. 227–243; D. C. Jones, P. Kalmi, and A. Kauhanen, "How Does Employee Involvement Stack Up? The Effects of Human Resource Management Policies in a Retail Firm," *Industrial Relations* 49, no. 1 (2010), pp. 1–21; and M. T. Maynard, L. L. Gilson, and J. E. Mathieu, "Empowerment—Fad or Fab? A Multilevel Review of the Past Two Decades of Research," *Journal of Management* 38, no. 4 (2012), pp. 1231–1281.

39. See, for instance, A. Sagie and Z. Aycan, "A Cross-cultural Analysis of Participative Decision-Making in Organizations,"

Human Relations 56, no. 4 (2003), pp. 453–473; and J. Brockner, "Unpacking Country Effects: On the Need to Operationalize the Psychological Determinants of Cross-national Differences," in R. M. Kramer and B. M. Staw (eds.), *Research in Organizational Behavior* 25 (Oxford, UK: Elsevier, 2003), pp. 336–340.

40. C. Robert, T. M. Probst, J. J. Martocchio, R. Drasgow, and J. J. Lawler, "Empowerment and Continuous Improvement in the United States, Mexico, Poland, and India: Predicting Fit on the Basis of the Dimensions of Power Distance and Individualism," *Journal of Applied Psychology* 85, no. 5 (2000), pp. 643–658.

41. Z. X. Chen and S. Aryee, "Delegation and Employee Work Outcomes: An Examination of the Cultural Context of Mediating Processes in China," *Academy of Management Journal* 50, no. 1 (2007), pp. 226–238.

42. G. Huang, X. Niu, C. Lee, and S. J. Ashford, "Differentiating Cognitive and Affective Job Insecurity: Antecedents and Outcomes," *Journal of Organizational Behavior* 33, no. 6 (2012), pp. 752–769.

43. J. J. Caughron and M. D. Mumford, "Embedded Leadership: How Do a Leader's Superiors Impact Middle-Management Performance?" *Leadership Quarterly* (June 2012), pp. 342–353.

44. See, for instance, K. L. Miller and P. R. Monge, "Participation, Satisfaction, and Productivity: A Meta-analytic Review," *Academy of Management Journal* (December 1986), pp. 727–753; J. A. Wagner III, "Participation's Effects on Performance and Satisfaction: A Reconsideration of Research Evidence," *Academy of Management Review* 19, no. 2 (1994), pp. 312–330; C. Doucouliagos, "Worker Participation and Productivity in Labor-Managed and Participatory Capitalist Firms: A Meta-analysis," *Industrial and Labor Relations Review* 49, no. 1 (1995), pp. 58–77; J. A. Wagner III, C. R. Leana, E. A. Locke, and D. M. Schweiger, "Cognitive and Motivational Frameworks in U.S. Research on Participation: A Meta-analysis of Primary Effects," *Journal of Organizational Behavior* 18, no. 1 (1997), pp. 49–65; and A. Pendleton and A. Robinson, "Employee Stock Ownership, Involvement, and Productivity: An Interaction-Based Approach," *Industrial and Labor Relations Review* 64, no. 1 (2010), pp. 3–29.

45. D. K. Datta, J. P. Guthrie, and P. M. Wright, "Human Resource Management and Labor Productivity: Does Industry Matter?" *Academy of Management Journal* 48, no. 1 (2005), pp. 135–145; C. M. Riordan, R. J. Vandenberg, and H. A. Richardson, "Employee Involvement Climate and Organizational Effectiveness." *Human Resource Management* 44, no. 4 (2005), pp. 471–488; and J. Kim, J. P. MacDuffie, and F. K. Pil, "Employee Voice and Organizational Performance: Team Versus Representative Influence," *Human Relations* 63, no. 3 (2010), pp. 371–394.

46. J. L. Cotton, *Employee Involvement* (Thousand Oaks, CA: Sage Publications, 1993), p. 114.

47. See, for example, M. Gilman and P. Marginson, "Negotiating European Works Council: Contours of Constrained Choice," *Industrial Relations Journal* 33, no. 1 (2002), pp. 36–51; J. T. Addison and C. R. Belfield, "What Do We Know About the New European Works Council? Some Preliminary Evidence from Britain," *Scottish Journal of Political Economy* 49, no. 4 (2002), pp. 418–444; and B. Keller, "The European Company Statute: Employee Involvement—and Beyond," *Industrial Relations Journal* 33, no. 5 (2002), pp. 424–445.

48. Cotton, *Employee Involvement*, pp. 129–130, 139–140.

49. Ibid., p. 140.

50. E. White, "Opportunity Knocks, and It Pays a Lot Better," *The Wall Street Journal* (November 13, 2006), p. B3.

51. D. A. McIntyre and S. Weigley, "8 Companies That Most Owe Workers a Raise," *USA Today* (May 13, 2013), http://www.usatoday.com/story/money/business/2013/05/12/8-companies-that-most-owe-workers-a-raise/2144013.

52. M. Sabramony, N. Krause, J. Norton, and G. N. Burns "The Relationship Between Human Resource Investments and Organizational Performance: A Firm-Level Examination of Equilibrium Theory," *Journal of Applied Psychology* 93, no. 4 (2008), pp. 778–788.

53. Alphonso, C. (Jan 23, 2014), Teachers Pay Should be Based on Performance not Years Worked, *Globe and Mail*, accessed June 28, 2015 at http://www.theglobeandmail.com/news/national/education/teachers-pay-should-be-based-on-performance-not-years-worked-report/article16471184.

54. Based on J. R. Schuster and P. K. Zingheim, "The New Variable Pay: Key Design Issues," *Compensation & Benefits Review* (March–April 1993), p. 28; K. S. Abosch, "Variable Pay: Do We Have the Basics in Place?" *Compensation & Benefits Review* (July–August 1998), pp. 12–22; and K. M. Kuhn and M. D. Yockey, "Variable Pay as a Risky Choice: Determinants of the Relative Attractiveness of Incentive Plans," *Organizational Behavior and Human Decision Processes* 90, no. 2 (2003), pp. 323–341.

55. Hay Group, "Hay Group Research Finds Increased Use of Variable Pay for Employees," *Investment Weekly News* (July 24, 2010), p. 269.

56. S. Miller, "Companies Worldwide Rewarding Performance with Variable Pay," *Society for Human Resource Management* (March 1, 2010), http://www.shrm.org.

57. S. Miller, "Asian Firms Offer More Variable Pay Than Western Firms," *Society for Human Resource Management* (March 28, 2012), http://www.shrm.org.

58. H. Kim, K. L. Sutton, and Y. Gong, "Group-Based Pay-for-Performance Plans and Firm Performance: The Moderating Role of Empowerment Practices," *Asia Pacific Journal of Management* (March 2013), pp. 31–52.

59. G. D. Jenkins Jr., N. Gupta, A. Mitra, and J. D. Shaw, "Are Financial Incentives Related to Performance? A Meta-analytic Review of Empirical Research," *Journal of Applied Psychology* 83, no. 5 (1998), pp. 777–787; and S. L. Rynes, B. Gerhart, and L. Parks, "Personnel Psychology: Performance Evaluation and Pay for Performance," *Annual Review of Psychology* 56, no. 1 (2005), pp. 571–600.

60. C. M. Barnes, J. Reb, and D. Ang, "More Than Just the Mean: Moving to a Dynamic View of Performance-Based Compensation," *Journal of Applied Psychology* 97, no. 3 (2012), pp. 711–718.

61. Atkins, E. (March 25, 2015),"CN Rail Caps CEO Bonus, " *Globe and Mail*, accessed June 26, 2015 at http://www.theglobeandmail.com/report-on-business/careers/management/executive-compensation/cn-rail-caps-ceos-bonus-due-to-rise-in-train-derailments-employee-injuries/article23621375.

62. D. Alexander, "Bonus Falls at Canada's Big Banks Rise Least Since 2010," *Financial Post* (December 10, 2013), accessed June 26, 2015 at http://business.financialpost.com/news/fp-street/bonus-pools-at-canadas-big-banks-rise-least-since-2010.

63. S. S. Wiltermuth and F. Gino, "'I'll Have One of Each': How Separating Rewards into (Meaningless) Categories Increases Motivation," *Journal of Personality and Social Psychology* (January 2013), pp. 1–13.

64. G. E. Ledford Jr., "Paying for the Skills, Knowledge, and Competencies of Knowledge Workers," *Compensation & Benefits Review* (July–August 1995), pp. 55–62; B. Murray and B. Gerhart, "An Empirical Analysis of a Skill-Based Pay Program and Plant Performance Outcomes," *Academy of Management Journal* 41, no. 1 (1998), pp. 68–78; J. R. Thompson and C. W. LeHew, "Skill-Based Pay as an Organizational Innovation,"

Review of Public Personnel Administration 20, no. 1 (2000), pp. 20–40; and J. D. Shaw, N. Gupta, A. Mitra, and G. E. Ledford, Jr., "Success and Survival of Skill-Based Pay Plans," *Journal of Management* 31, no. 1 (2005), pp. 28–49.

65. A. Mitra, N. Gupta, and J. D. Shaw, "A Comparative Examination of Traditional and Skill-Based Pay Plans," *Journal of Managerial Psychology* 26, no. 4 (2011), pp. 278–296.

66. E. C. Dierdorff and E. A. Surface, "If You Pay for Skills, Will They Learn? Skill Change and Maintenance Under a Skill-Based Pay System," *Journal of Management* 34, no. 4 (2008), pp. 721–743.

67. F. Giancola, "Skill-Based Pay—Issues for Consideration," *Benefits and Compensation Digest* 44, no. 5 (2007), pp. 1–15.

68. Research in Motion annual reports, 2001 through 2009.

69. "Mark Zuckerberg Reaped $2.3 Billion on Facebook Stock Options," *Huffington Post* (April 26, 2013), http://www.huffingtonpost.com.

70. N. Chi and T. Han, "Exploring the Linkages Between Formal Ownership and Psychological Ownership for the Organization: The Mediating Role of Organizational Justice," *Journal of Occupational and Organizational Psychology* 81, no. 4 (2008), pp. 691–711.

71. See, for instance, D. O. Kim, "Determinants of the Survival of Gainsharing Programs," *Industrial & Labor Relations Review* 53, no. 1 (1999), pp. 21–42; "Why Gainsharing Works Even Better Today Than in the Past," *HR Focus* (April 2000), pp. 3–5; L. R. Gomez-Mejia, T. M. Welbourne, and R. M. Wiseman, "The Role of Risk Sharing and Risk Taking Under Gainsharing," *Academy of Management Review* 25, no. 3 (2000), pp. 492–507; M. Reynolds, "A Cost-Reduction Strategy That May Be Back," *Healthcare Financial Management* (January 2002), pp. 58–64; M. R. Dixon, L. J. Hayes, and J. Stack, "Changing Conceptions of Employee Compensation," *Journal of Organizational Behavior Management* 23, no. 2–3 (2003), pp. 95–116; and I. M. Leitman, R. Levin, M. J. Lipp, L. Sivaprasad, C. J. Karalakulasingam, D. S. Bernard, P. Friedmann, and D. J. Shulkin, "Quality and Financial Outcomes from Gainsharing for Inpatient Admissions: A Three-Year Experience," *Journal of Hospital Medicine* 5, no. 9 (2010), pp. 501–517.

72. T. M. Welbourne and C. J. Ferrante, "To Monitor or Not to Monitor: A Study of Individual Outcomes from Monitoring One's Peers Under Gainsharing and Merit Pay," *Group & Organization Management* 33, no. 2 (2008), pp. 139–162.

73. A. A. Buchko, "The Effects of Employee Ownership on Employee Attitudes: A Test of Three Theoretical Perspectives," *Work and Occupations* 19, no. 1 (1992), 59–78; and R. P. Garrett, "Does Employee Ownership Increase Innovation?" *New England Journal of Entrepreneurship* 13, no. 2, (2010), pp. 37–46.

74. D. McCarthy, E. Reeves, and T. Turner, "Can Employee Share-Ownership Improve Employee Attitudes and Behaviour?" *Employee Relations* 32, no. 4 (2010), pp. 382–395.

75. A. Pendleton and A. Robinson, "Employee Stock Ownership, Involvement, and Productivity: An Interaction-Based Approach," *Industrial and Labor Relations Review* 64, no. 1 (2010), pp. 3–29.

76. X. Zhang, K. M. Bartol, K. G. Smith, M. D. Pfarrer, and D. M. Khanin, "CEOs on the Edge: Earnings Manipulation and Stock-Based Incentive Misalignment," *Academy of Management Journal* 51, no. 2 (2008), pp. 241–258.

77. D. D'Art and T. Turner, "Profit Sharing, Firm Performance, and Union Influence in Selected European Countries," *Personnel Review* 33, no. 3 (2004), pp. 335–350; and D. Kruse, R. Freeman, and J. Blasi, *Shared Capitalism at Work: Employee Ownership, Profit and Gain Sharing, and Broad-Based Stock Options* (Chicago: University of Chicago Press, 2010).

78. A. Bayo-Moriones and M. Larraza-Kintana, "Profit-Sharing Plans and Affective Commitment: Does the Context Matter?" *Human Resource Management* 48, no. 2 (2009), pp. 207–226.

79. C. B. Cadsby, F. Song, and F. Tapon, "Sorting and Incentive Effects of Pay for Performance: An Experimental Investigation," *Academy of Management Journal* 50, no. 2 (2007), pp. 387–405.

80. S. C. L. Fong and M. A. Shaffer, "The Dimensionality and Determinants of Pay Satisfaction: A Cross-cultural Investigation of a Group Incentive Plan," *International Journal of Human Resource Management* 14, no. 4 (2003), pp. 559–580.

81. See, for instance, M. W. Barringer and G. T. Milkovich, "A Theoretical Exploration of the Adoption and Design of Flexible Benefit Plans: A Case of Human Resource Innovation," *Academy of Management Review* 23, no. 2 (1998), pp. 305–324; D. Brown, "Everybody Loves Flex," *Canadian HR Reporter* (November 18, 2002), p. 1; J. Taggart, "Putting Flex Benefits Through Their Paces," *Canadian HR Reporter* (December 2, 2002), p. G3; and N. D. Cole and D. H. Flint, "Perceptions of Distributive and Procedural Justice in Employee Benefits: Flexible Versus Traditional Benefit Plans," *Journal of Managerial Psychology* 19, no. 1 (2004), pp. 19–40.

82. D. Lovewell, "Flexible Benefits: Benefits on Offer," *Employee Benefits* (March 2010), p. S15.

83. Ibid.

84. Go2HR, accessed June 26, 2015 at https://www.go2hr.ca/articles/fairmont-stands-out-employee-recognition-programs.

85. L. Shepherd, "On Recognition, Multinationals Think Globally," *Workforce Management* (September 2010), p. 26.

86. R. J. Long and J. L. Shields, "From Pay to Praise? Non-Case Employee Recognition in Canadian and Australian Firms," *International Journal of Human Resource Management* 21, no. 8 (2010), pp. 1145–1172.

87. S. E. Markham, K. D. Scott, and G. H. McKee, "Recognizing Good Attendance: A Longitudinal, Quasi-Experimental Field Study," *Personnel Psychology* 55, no. 3 (2002), p. 641; and S. J. Peterson and F. Luthans, "The Impact of Financial and Nonfinancial Incentives on Business Unit Outcomes over Time," *Journal of Applied Psychology* 91, no. 1 (2006), pp. 156–165.

88. A. D. Stajkovic and F. Luthans, "Differential Effects of Incentive Motivators on Work Performance," *Academy of Management Journal* 4, no. 3 (2001), p. 587. See also F. Luthans and A. D. Stajkovic, "Provide Recognition for Performance Improvement," in E. A. Locke (ed.), *Handbook of Principles of Organizational Behavior* (Malden, MA: Blackwell, 2004), pp. 166–180.

Chapter 9

1. B. W. Tuckman, "Developmental Sequences in Small Groups," *Psychological Bulletin*, June 1965, pp. 384–399; B. W. Tuckman and M. C. Jensen, "Stages of Small-Group Development Revisited," *Group and Organizational Studies*, December 1977, pp. 419–427; M. F. Maples, "Group Development: Extending Tuckman's Theory," *Journal for Specialists in Group Work* (Fall 1988), pp. 17–23; and K. Vroman and J. Kovacich, "Computer-Mediated Interdisciplinary Teams: Theory and Reality," *Journal of Interprofessional Care* 16, no. 2 (2002), pp. 159–170.

2. J. E. Mathieu and T. L. Rapp, "Laying the Foundation for Successful Team Performance Trajectories: The Roles of Team Charters and Performance Strategies," *Journal of Applied Psychology* 94, no. 1 (2009), pp. 90–103; and E. C. Dierdorff, S. T. Bell, and J. A. Belohlav, "The Power of 'We': Effects of Psychological Collectivism on Team Performance Over Time," *Journal of Applied Psychology* 96, no. 2 (2011), pp. 247–262.

3. M. M. Kazmer, "Disengaging from a Distributed Research Project: Refining a Model of Group Departures," *Journal of the*

American Society for Information Science and Technology (April 2010), pp. 758–771.

4. C. J. G. Gersick, "Time and Transition in Work Teams: Toward a New Model of Group Development," *Academy of Management Journal* (March 1988), pp. 9–41; and C. J. G. Gersick, "Marking Time: Predictable Transitions in Task Groups," *Academy of Management Journal* (June 1989), pp. 274–309.

5. Gersick, "Time and Transition in Work Teams"; Gersick, "Marking Time"; M. J. Waller, J. M. Conte, C. B. Gibson, and M. A. Carpenter, "The Effect of Individual Perceptions of Deadlines on Team Performance," *Academy of Management Review* (October 2001), pp. 586–600; and A. Chang, P. Bordia, and J. Duck, "Punctuated Equilibrium and Linear Progression: Toward a New Understanding of Group Development," *Academy of Management Journal* (February 2003), pp. 106–117.

6. Gersick, "Time and Transition in Work Teams"; and Gersick, "Marking Time."

7. M. M. Kazmer, "Disengaging from a Distributed Research Project: Refining a Model of Group Departures," *Journal of the American Society for Information Science and Technology* (April 2010), pp. 758–771.

8. See M. F. Peterson et al., "Role Conflict, Ambiguity, and Overload: A 21-Nation Study," *Academy of Management Journal* (April 1995), pp. 429–452; and I. H. Settles, R. M. Sellers, and A. Damas Jr., "One Role or Two? The Function of Psychological Separation in Role Conflict," *Journal of Applied Psychology* (June 2002), pp. 574–582.

9. For a review of the research on group norms, see J. R. Hackman, "Group Influences on Individuals in Organizations," in M. D. Dunnette and L. M. Hough (eds.), *Handbook of Industrial & Organizational Psychology*, 2nd ed., vol. 3 (Palo Alto, CA: Consulting Psychologists Press, 1992), pp. 235–250. For a more recent discussion, see M. G. Ehrhart and S. E. Naumann, "Organizational Citizenship Behavior in Work Groups: A Group Norms Approach," *Journal of Applied Psychology* (December 2004), pp. 960–974.

10. Adapted from P. S. Goodman, E. Ravlin, and M. Schminke, "Understanding Groups in Organizations," in L. L. Cummings and B. M. Staw (eds.), *Research in Organizational Behavior* 9 (Greenwich, CT: JAI Press, 1987), p. 159; and L. Rosh, L. R. Offermann, and R. Van Diest, "Too Close for Comfort? Distinguishing Between Team Intimacy and Team Cohesion," *Human Resource Management Review* (June 2012), pp. 116–127.

11. E. Mayo, *The Human Problems of an Industrial Civilization* (New York: Macmillan, 1933); and F. J. Roethlisberger and W. J. Dickson, *Management and the Worker* (Cambridge, MA: Harvard University Press, 1939).

12. C. A. Kiesler and S. B. Kiesler, *Conformity* (Reading, MA: Addison-Wesley, 1969); and R. B. Cialdini and N. J. Goldstein, "Social Influence: Compliance and Conformity," *Annual Review of Psychology* 55 (2004), pp. 591–621.

13. S. E. Asch, "Effects of Group Pressure upon the Modification and Distortion of Judgments," in H. Guetzkow (ed.), *Groups, Leadership and Men* (Pittsburgh: Carnegie Press, 1951), pp. 177–190; and S. E. Asch, "Studies of Independence and Conformity: A Minority of One Against a Unanimous Majority," *Psychological Monographs: General and Applied* 70, no. 9 (1956), pp. 1–70.

14. B. Hamper, *Rivethead: Tales from the Assembly Line* (New York: Grand Central Publishing, 1992).

15. R. Bond and P. B. Smith, "Culture and Conformity: A Meta-analysis of Studies Using Asch's (1952, 1956) Line Judgment Task," *Psychological Bulletin* (January 1996), pp. 111–137.

16. See S. L. Robinson and A. M. O'Leary-Kelly, "Monkey See, Monkey Do: The Influence of Work Groups on the Antisocial Behavior of Employees," *Academy of Management Journal* (December 1998), pp. 658–672; R. J. Bennett and S. L. Robinson, "The Past, Present, and Future of Workplace Deviance," in J. Greenberg (ed.), *Organizational Behavior: The State of the Science*, 2nd ed. (Mahwah, NJ: Erlbaum, 2003), pp. 237–271; and C. M. Berry, D. S. Ones, and P. R. Sackett, "Interpersonal Deviance, Organizational Deviance, and Their Common Correlates: A Review and Meta-analysis," *Journal of Applied Psychology* 92, no. 2 (2007), pp. 410–424.

17. C. M. Pearson, L. M. Andersson, and C. L. Porath, "Assessing and Attacking Workplace Civility," *Organizational Dynamics* 29, no. 2 (2000), p. 130; see also C. Pearson, L. M. Andersson, and C. L. Porath, "Workplace Incivility," in S. Fox and P. E. Spector (eds.), *Counterproductive Work Behavior: Investigations of Actors and Targets* (Washington, DC: American Psychological Association, 2005), pp. 177–200.

18. S. Lim, L. M. Cortina, V. J. Magley, "Personal and Workgroup Incivility: Impact on Work and Health Outcomes," *Journal of Applied Psychology* 93, no. 1 (2008), pp. 95–107.

19. M. S. Christian and A. P. J. Ellis, "Examining the Effects of Sleep Deprivation on Workplace Deviance: A Self-Regulatory Perspective," *Academy of Management Journal* 54, no. 5 (2011), pp. 913–934.

20. Robinson and O'Leary-Kelly, "Monkey See, Monkey Do"; and T. M. Glomb and H. Liao, "Interpersonal Aggression in Workgroups: Social Influence, Reciprocal, and Individual Effects," *Academy of Management Journal* 46 (2003), pp. 486–496.

21. P. Bamberger and M. Biron, "Group Norms and Excessive Absenteeism: The Role of Peer Referent Others," *Organizational Behavior and Human Decision Processes* 103, no. 2 (2007), pp. 179–196; and A. Väänänen, N. Tordera, M. Kivimäki, A. Kouvonen, J. Pentti, A. Linna, and J. Vahtera, "The Role of Work Group in Individual Sickness Absence Behavior," *Journal of Health & Human Behavior* 49, no. 4 (2008), pp. 452–467.

22. M. S. Cole, F. Walter, and H. Bruch, "Affective Mechanisms Linking Dysfunctional Behavior to Performance in Work Teams: A Moderated Mediation Study," *Journal of Applied Psychology* 93, no. 5 (2008), pp. 945–958.

23. See J. Berger, M. H. Fisek, R. Z. Norman, and M. Zelditch, *Status Characteristics and Social Interaction: An Expected States Approach* (New York: Elsevier, 1977).

24. Cited in Hackman, "Group Influences on Individuals in Organizations," p. 236.

25. R. R. Callister and J. A. Wall Jr., "Conflict Across Organizational Boundaries: Managed Care Organizations Versus Health Care Providers," *Journal of Applied Psychology* 86, no. 4 (2001), pp. 754–763; and P. Chattopadhyay, W. H. Glick, and G. P. Huber, "Organizational Actions in Response to Threats and Opportunities," *Academy of Management Journal* 44, no. 5 (2001), pp. 937–955.

26. P. F. Hewlin, "Wearing the Cloak: Antecedents and Consequences of Creating Facades of Conformity," *Journal of Applied Psychology* 94, no. 3 (2009), pp. 727–741.

27. B. Groysberg, J. T. Polzer, and H. A. Elfenbein, "Too Many Cooks Spoil the Broth: How High-Status Individuals Decrease Group Effectiveness," *Organization Science* (May–June 2011), pp. 722–737.

28. See J. M. Levine and R. L. Moreland, "Progress in Small Group Research," in J. T. Spence, J. M. Darley, and D. J. Foss (eds.), *Annual Review of Psychology* 41 (Palo Alto, CA: Annual Reviews, 1990), pp. 585–634; S. D. Silver, B. P. Cohen, and J. H. Crutchfield, "Status Differentiation and Information Exchange in Face-to-Face and Computer-Mediated Idea Generation," *Social Psychology Quarterly* (1994), pp. 108–123; and J. M. Twenge, "Changes in Women's Assertiveness in

Response to Status and Roles: A Cross-temporal Meta-analysis, 1931–1993," *Journal of Personality and Social Psychology* (July 2001), pp. 133–145.

29. A. M. Christie and J. Barling, "Beyond Status: Relating Status Inequality to Performance and Health in Teams," *Journal of Applied Psychology* 95, no. 5 (2010), pp. 920–934; and L. H. Nishii and D. M. Mayer, "Do Inclusive Leaders Help to Reduce Turnover in Diverse Groups? The Moderating Role of Leader–Member Exchange in the Diversity to Turnover Relationship," *Journal of Applied Psychology* 94, no. 6 (2009), pp. 1412–1426.

30. See, for instance, D. R. Comer, "A Model of Social Loafing in Real Work Groups," *Human Relations* (June 1995), pp. 647–667; S. M. Murphy, S. J. Wayne, R. C. Liden, and B. Erdogan, "Understanding Social Loafing: The Role of Justice Perceptions and Exchange Relationships," *Human Relations* (January 2003), pp. 61–84; and R. C. Liden, S. J. Wayne, R. A. Jaworski, and N. Bennett, "Social Loafing: A Field Investigation," *Journal of Management* (April 2004), pp. 285–304.

31. W. Moede, "Die Richtlinien der Leistungs-Psychologie," *Industrielle Psychotechnik* 4 (1927), pp. 193–207. See also D. A. Kravitz and B. Martin, "Ringelmann Rediscovered: The Original Article," *Journal of Personality and Social Psychology* (May 1986), pp. 936–941.

32. See, for example, J. A. Shepperd, "Productivity Loss in Performance Groups: A Motivation Analysis," *Psychological Bulletin* (January 1993), pp. 67–81; and S. J. Karau and K. D. Williams, "Social Loafing: A Meta-analytic Review and Theoretical Integration," *Journal of Personality and Social Psychology* (October 1993), pp. 681–706.

33. A. W. Delton, L. Cosmides, M. Guemo, T. E. Robertson, and J. Tooby, "The Psychosemantics of Free Riding: Dissecting the Architecture of a Moral Concept," *Journal of Personality and Social Psychology* 102, no. 6 (2012), pp. 1252–1270.

34. S. G. Harkins and K. Szymanski, "Social Loafing and Group Evaluation," *Journal of Personality and Social Psychology* (December 1989), pp. 934–941.

35. D. L. Smrt and S. J. Karau, "Protestant Work Ethic Moderates Social Loafing," *Group Dynamics: Theory Research and Practice* (September 2011), pp. 267–274.

36. A. Gunnthorsdottir and A. Rapoport, "Embedding Social Dilemmas in Intergroup Competition Reduces Free-Riding," *Organizational Behavior and Human Decision Processes* 101 (2006), pp. 184–199; and E. M. Stark, J. D. Shaw, and M. K. Duffy, "Preference for Group Work, Winning Orientation, and Social Loafing Behavior in Groups," *Group and Organization Management* 32, no. 6 (2007), pp. 699–723.

37. Ibid.

38. Based on J. L. Gibson, J. M. Ivancevich, and J. H. Donnelly Jr., *Organizations*, 8th ed. (Burr Ridge, IL: Irwin, 1994), p. 323; and L. L. Greer, "Group Cohesion: Then and Now," *Small Group Research* (December 2012), pp. 655–661.

39. D. S. Staples and L. Zhao, "The Effects of Cultural Diversity in Virtual Teams Versus Face-to-Face Teams," *Group Decision and Negotiation* (July 2006), pp. 389–406.

40. N. Chi, Y. Huang, and S. Lin, "A Double-Edged Sword? Exploring the Curvilinear Relationship Between Organizational Tenure Diversity and Team Innovation: The Moderating Role of Team-Oriented HR Practices," *Group and Organization Management* 34, no. 6 (2009), pp. 698–726.

41. K. J. Klein, A. P. Knight, J. C. Ziegert, B. C. Lim, and J. L. Saltz, "When Team Members' Values Differ: The Moderating Role of Team Leadership," *Organizational Behavior and Human Decision Processes* 114, no. 1 (2011), pp. 25–36; and G. Park and R. P. DeShon, "A Multilevel Model of Minority Opinion Expression and Team Decision-Making Effectiveness," *Journal of Applied Psychology* 95, no. 5 (2010), pp. 824–833.

42. M. Rigoglioso, "Diverse Backgrounds and Personalities Can Strengthen Groups," Stanford Knowledgebase (August 15, 2006), http://www.stanford.edu/group/knowledgebase.

43. K. W. Phillips and D. L. Loyd, "When Surface and Deep-Level Diversity Collide: The Effects on Dissenting Group Members," *Organizational Behavior and Human Decision Processes* 99 (2006), pp. 143–160; and S. R. Sommers, "On Racial Diversity and Group Decision Making: Identifying Multiple Effects of Racial Composition on Jury Deliberations," *Journal of Personality and Social Psychology* (April 2006), pp. 597–612.

44. E. Mannix and M. A. Neale, "What Differences Make a Difference? The Promise and Reality of Diverse Teams in Organizations," *Psychological Science in the Public Interest* (October 2005), pp. 31–55.

45. See M. B. Thatcher and P. C. Patel, "Group Faultlines: A Review, Integration, and Guide to Future Research," *Journal of Management* 38, no. 4 (2012), pp. 969–1009.

46. K. Bezrukova, S. M. B. Thatcher, K. A. Jehn, and C. S. Spell, "The Effects of Alignments: Examining Group Faultlines, Organizational Cultures, and Performance," *Journal of Applied Psychology* 97, no. 1 (2012), pp. 77–92.

47. R. Rico, M. Sanchez-Manzanares, M. Antino, and D. Lau, "Bridging Team Faultlines by Combining Task Role Assignment and Goal Structure Strategies," *Journal of Applied Psychology* 97, no. 2 (2012), pp. 407–420.

48. See N. R. F. Maier, "Assets and Liabilities in Group Problem Solving: The Need for an Integrative Function," *Psychological Review* (April 1967), pp. 239–249; G. W. Hill, "Group Versus Individual Performance: Are N + 1 Heads Better Than One?" *Psychological Bulletin* (May 1982), pp. 517–539; M. D. Johnson and J. R. Hollenbeck, "Collective Wisdom as an Oxymoron: Team-Based Structures as Impediments to Learning," in J. Langan-Fox, C. L. Cooper, and R. J. Klimoski (eds), *Research Companion to the Dysfunctional Workplace: Management Challenges and Symptoms* (Northampton, MA: Edward Elgar Publishing, 2007), pp. 319–331; and R. F. Martell and M. R. Borg, "A Comparison of the Behavioral Rating Accuracy of Groups and Individuals," *Journal of Applied Psychology* (February 1993), pp. 43–50.

49. D. Gigone and R. Hastie, "Proper Analysis of the Accuracy of Group Judgments," *Psychological Bulletin* (January 1997), pp. 149–167; and B. L. Bonner, S. D. Sillito, and M. R. Baumann, "Collective Estimation: Accuracy, Expertise, and Extroversion as Sources of Intra-group Influence," *Organizational Behavior and Human Decision Processes* 103 (2007), pp. 121–133.

50. See, for example, W. C. Swap and Associates, *Group Decision Making* (Newbury Park, CA: Sage, 1984).

51. I. L. Janis, *Groupthink* (Boston: Houghton Mifflin, 1982); W.-W. Park, "A Review of Research on Groupthink," *Journal of Behavioral Decision Making* (July 1990), pp. 229–245; J. N. Choi and M. U. Kim, "The Organizational Application of Groupthink and Its Limits in Organizations," *Journal of Applied Psychology* (April 1999), pp. 297–306; and W.-W. Park, "A Comprehensive Empirical Investigation of the Relationships Among Variables of the Groupthink Model," *Journal of Organizational Behavior* (December 2000), pp. 873–887.

52. Janis, *Groupthink*.

53. G. Park and R. P. DeShon, "A Multilevel Model of Minority Opinion Expression and Team Decision-Making Effectiveness," *Journal of Applied Psychology* 95, no. 5 (2010), pp. 824–833.

54. R. Benabou, "Groupthink: Collective Delusions in Organizations and Markets," *Review of Economic Studies* (April 2013), pp. 429–462; and M. E. Turner and A. R. Pratkanis, "Mitigating Groupthink by Stimulating Constructive Conflict," in C. K. W. De Dreu and E. Van de Vliert (eds.), *Using Conflict in Organizations* (London, UK: Sage, 1997), pp. 53–71.

55. J. A. Goncalo, E. Polman, and C. Maslach, "Can Confidence Come Too Soon? Collective Efficacy, Conflict, and Group

Performance Over Time," *Organizational Behavior and Human Decision Processes* 113, no. 1 (2010), pp. 13–24.

56. See N. R. F. Maier, *Principles of Human Relations* (New York: Wiley, 1952); I. L. Janis, *Groupthink: Psychological Studies of Policy Decisions and Fiascoes*, 2nd ed. (Boston: Houghton Mifflin, 1982); N. Richardson Ahlfinger and J. K. Esser, "Testing the Groupthink Model: Effects of Promotional Leadership and Conformity Predisposition," *Social Behavior & Personality* 29, no. 1 (2001), pp. 31–41; and S. Schultz-Hardt, F. C. Brodbeck, A. Mojzisch, R. Kerschreiter, and D. Frey, "Group Decision Making in Hidden Profile Situations: Dissent as a Facilitator for Decision Quality," *Journal of Personality and Social Psychology* 91, no. 6 (2006), pp. 1080–1093.

57. See P. W. Paese, M. Bieser, and M. E. Tubbs, "Framing Effects and Choice Shifts in Group Decision Making," *Organizational Behavior and Human Decision Processes* (October 1993), pp. 149–165; and I. Yaniv, "Group Diversity and Decision Quality: Amplification and Attenuation of the Framing Effect," *International Journal of Forecasting* (January–March 2011), pp. 41–49.

58. R. D. Clark III, "Group-Induced Shift Toward Risk: A Critical Appraisal," *Psychological Bulletin* (October 1971), pp. 251–270; M. Brauer and C. M. Judd, "Group Polarization and Repeated Attitude Expression: A New Take on an Old Topic," *European Review of Social Psychology* 7, (1996), pp. 173–207; and M. P. Brady and S. Y. Wu, "The Aggregation of Preferences in Groups: Identity, Responsibility, and Polarization," *Journal of Economic Psychology* 31, no. 6 (2010), pp. 950–963.

59. Z. Krizan and R. S. Baron, "Group Polarization and Choice-Dilemmas: How Important Is Self-Categorization?" *European Journal of Social Psychology* 37, no. 1 (2007), pp. 191–201.

60. A. F. Osborn, *Applied Imagination: Principles and Procedures of Creative Thinking*, 3rd ed. (New York: Scribner, 1963). See also R. P. McGlynn, D. McGurk, V. S. Effland, N. L. Johll, and D. J. Harding, "Brainstorming and Task Performance in Groups Constrained by Evidence," *Organizational Behavior and Human Decision Processes* (January 2004), pp. 75–87; and R. C. Litchfield, "Brainstorming Reconsidered: A Goal-Based View," *Academy of Management Review* 33, no. 3 (2008), pp. 649–668.

61. N. L. Kerr and R. S. Tindale, "Group Performance and Decision-Making," *Annual Review of Psychology* 55 (2004), pp. 623–655.

62. See A. L. Delbecq, A. H. Van deVen, and D. H. Gustafson, *Group Techniques for Program Planning: A Guide to Nominal and Delphi Processes* (Glenview, IL: Scott Foresman, 1975); and P. B. Paulus and H.-C. Yang, "Idea Generation in Groups: A Basis for Creativity in Organizations," *Organizational Behavior and Human Decision Processing* (May 2000), pp. 76–87.

63. C. Faure, "Beyond Brainstorming: Effects of Different Group Procedures on Selection of Ideas and Satisfaction with the Process," *Journal of Creative Behavior* 38 (2004), pp. 13–34.

64. A. G. Bedeian and A. A. Armenakis, "A Path-Analytic Study of the Consequences of Role Conflict and Ambiguity," *Academy of Management Journal* (June 1981), pp. 417–424; and P. L. Perrewe, K. L. Zellars, G. R. Ferris, A. M. Rossi, C. J. Kacmar, and D. A. Ralston, "Neutralizing Job Stressors: Political Skill as an Antidote to the Dysfunctional Consequences of Role Conflict," *Academy of Management Journal* (February 2004), pp. 141–152.

65. M. E. Shaw, *Group Dynamics: The Psychology of Small Group Behavior*, 3rd ed. (New York: McGraw-Hill, 1981).

Chapter 10

1. This section is based on J. R. Katzenbach and D. K. Smith, *The Wisdom of Teams* (Cambridge, MA: Harvard University Press, 1993), pp. 21, 45, 85; and D. C. Kinlaw, *Developing Superior Work Teams* (Lexington, MA: Lexington Books, 1991), pp. 3–21.

2. J. Mathieu, M. T. Maynard, T. Rapp, and L. Gilson, "Team Effectiveness 1997–2007: A Review of Recent Advancements and a Glimpse into the Future," *Journal of Management* 34, no. 3 (2008), pp. 410–476.

3. J. H. Shonk, *Team-Based Organizations* (Homewood, IL: Business One Irwin, 1992); and M. A. Verespej, "When Workers Get New Roles," *IndustryWeek* (February 3, 1992), p. 11.

4. G. Bodinson and R. Bunch, "AQP's National Team Excellence Award: Its Purpose, Value and Process," *The Journal for Quality and Participation* (Spring 2003), pp. 37–42.

5. Staff reporter, "New Chief of Defense Staff Issues First Order to Canadian Forces: Sexual Harassment Stops Now," *National Post*, July 23, 2015, accessed July 25, 2015 at http://news.nationalpost.com/news/canada/new-chief-of-defence-staff-issues-first-order-to-canadian-forces-sexual-harassment-stops-now.

6. See, for example, A. Erez, J. A. LePine, and H. Elms, "Effects of Rotated Leadership and Peer Evaluation on the Functioning and Effectiveness of Self-Managed Teams: A Quasi-experiment," *Personnel Psychology* (Winter 2002), pp. 929–948.

7. See, for instance, C. W. Langfred, "Too Much of a Good Thing? Negative Effects of High Trust and Individual Autonomy in Self-Managing Teams," *Academy of Management Journal* (June 2004), pp. 385–399.

8. G. L. Stewart, S. H. Courtright, and M. R. Barrick, "Peer-Based Control in Self-Managing Teams: Linking Rational and Normative Influence with Individual and Group Performance," *Journal of Applied Psychology* 97, no. 2 (2012), pp. 435–447.

9. C. W. Langfred, "The Downside of Self-Management: A Longitudinal Study of the Effects of Conflict on Trust, Autonomy, and Task Interdependence in Self-Managing Teams," *Academy of Management Journal* 50, no. 4 (2007), pp. 885–900.

10. B. H. Bradley, B. E. Postlethwaite, A. C. Klotz, M. R. Hamdani, and K. G. Brown, "Reaping the Benefits of Task Conflict in Teams: The Critical Role of Team Psychological Safety Climate," *Journal of Applied Psychology*, 97, no. 1 (2012), pp. 151–158.

11. J. Devaro, "The Effects of Self-Managed and Closely Managed Teams on Labor Productivity and Product Quality: An Empirical Analysis of a Cross-Section of Establishments," *Industrial Relations* 47, no. 4 (2008), pp. 659–698.

12. R. Kulweic, "Self-Managed Work Teams Reality or Fad?" *Material Handling and Logistics*, April 1, 2001, accessed at http://mhlnews.com/labor-management/self-managed-work-teams-reality-or-fad.

13. A. Shah, "Starbucks Strives for Instant Gratification with Via Launch," *PRWeek* (December 2009), p. 15.

14. B. Freyer and T. A. Stewart, "Cisco Sees the Future," *Harvard Business Review* (November 2008), pp. 73–79.

15. See, for example, L. L. Martins, L. L. Gilson, and M. T. Maynard, "Virtual Teams: What Do We Know and Where Do We Go from Here?" *Journal of Management* (November 2004), pp. 805–835; and B. Leonard, "Managing Virtual Teams," *HR Magazine* (June 2011), pp. 39–42.

16. A. Malhotra, A. Majchrzak, and B. Rosen, "Leading Virtual Teams," *Academy of Management Perspectives* (February 2007), pp. 60–70; and J. M. Wilson, S. S. Straus, and B. McEvily, "All in Due Time: The Development of Trust in Computer-Mediated and Face-to-Face Teams," *Organizational Behavior and Human Decision Processes* 19 (2006), pp. 16–33.

17. R. S. Gajendran and A. Joshi, "Innovation in Globally Distributed Teams: The Role of LMX, Communication Frequency, and Member Influence on Team Decisions, *Journal of Applied Psychology* 97, no. 6 (2012), pp. 1252–1261.

18. J. R. Mesmer-Magnus, L. A. DeChurch, M. Jimenez-Rodriguez, J. Wildman, and M. Shuffler, "A Meta-analytic Investigation of Virtuality and Information Sharing in Teams," *Organizational Behavior and Human Decision Processes* 115, no. 2 (2011), pp. 214–225.

19. P. Balkundi and D. A. Harrison, "Ties, Leaders, and Time in Teams: Strong Inference About Network Structure's Effects on Team Viability and Performance," *Academy of Management Journal* 49, no. 1 (2006), pp. 49–68; G. Chen, B. L. Kirkman, R. Kanfer, D. Allen, and B. Rosen, "A Multilevel Study of Leadership, Empowerment, and Performance in Teams," *Journal of Applied Psychology* 92, no. 2 (2007), pp. 331–346; L. A. DeChurch and M. A. Marks, "Leadership in Multiteam Systems," *Journal of Applied Psychology* 91, no. 2 (2006), pp. 311–329; A. Srivastava, K. M. Bartol, and E. A. Locke, "Empowering Leadership in Management Teams: Effects on Knowledge Sharing, Efficacy, and Performance," *Academy of Management Journal* 49, no. 6 (2006), pp. 1239–1251; and J. E. Mathieu, K. K. Gilson, and T. M. Ruddy, "Empowerment and Team Effectiveness: An Empirical Test of an Integrated Model," *Journal of Applied Psychology* 91, no. 1 (2006), pp. 97–108.

20. R. B. Davison, J. R. Hollenbeck, C. M. Barnes, D. J. Sleesman, and D. R. Ilgen, "Coordinated Action in Multiteam Systems," *Journal of Applied Psychology* 97, no. 4 (2012), pp. 808–824.

21. This model is based on M. A. Campion, E. M. Papper, and G. J. Medsker, "Relations Between Work Team Characteristics and Effectiveness: A Replication and Extension," *Personnel Psychology* (Summer 1996), pp. 429–452; D. E. Hyatt and T. M. Ruddy, "An Examination of the Relationship Between Work Group Characteristics and Performance," *Personnel Psychology* 50, no. 3, pp. 553–585; S. G. Cohen and D. E. Bailey, "What Makes Teams Work: Group Effectiveness Research from the Shop Floor to the Executive Suite," *Journal of Management* 23, no. 3 (1997), pp. 239–290; L. Thompson, *Making the Team* (Upper Saddle River, NJ: Prentice Hall, 2000), pp. 18–33; and J. R. Hackman, *Leading Teams: Setting the Stage for Great Performance* (Boston: Harvard Business School Press, 2002).

22. See G. L. Stewart and M. R. Barrick, "Team Structure and Performance: Assessing the Mediating Role of Intrateam Process and the Moderating Role of Task Type," *Academy of Management Journal* (April 2000), pp. 135–148.

23. J. R. Hackman and R. Wageman, "A Theory of Team Coaching." *Academy of Management Review* 30, no. 2 (April 1, 2005), pp. 269–287, DOI:10.5465/AMR.2005.16387885.

24. Hyatt and Ruddy, "An Examination of the Relationship Between Work Group Characteristics and Performance," p. 577.

25. P. Balkundi and D. A. Harrison, "Ties, Leaders, and Time in Teams: Strong Inference About Network Structure's Effects on Team Viability and Performance," *Academy of Management Journal* 49, no. 1 (2006), pp. 49–68; G. Chen, B. L. Kirkman, R. Kanfer, D. Allen, and B. Rosen, "A Multilevel Study of Leadership, Empowerment, and Performance in Teams," *Journal of Applied Psychology* 92, no. 2 (2007), pp. 331–346; L. A. DeChurch and M. A. Marks, "Leadership in Multiteam Systems," *Journal of Applied Psychology* 91, no. 2 (2006), pp. 311–329; A. Srivastava, K. M. Bartol, and E. A. Locke, "Empowering Leadership in Management Teams: Effects on Knowledge Sharing, Efficacy, and Performance," *Academy of Management Journal* 49, no. 6 (2006), pp. 1239–1251; and J. E. Mathieu, K. K. Gilson, and T. M. Ruddy, "Empowerment and Team Effectiveness: An Empirical Test of an Integrated Model," *Journal of Applied Psychology* 91, no. 1 (2006), pp. 97–108.

26. J. B. Carson, P. E. Tesluk, and J. A. Marrone, "Shared Leadership in Teams: An Investigation of Antecedent Conditions and Performance," *Academy of Management Journal* 50, no. 5 (2007), pp. 1217–1234.

27. K. T. Dirks, "Trust in Leadership and Team Performance: Evidence from NCAA Basketball," *Journal of Applied Psychology* (December 2000), pp. 1004–1012; M. Williams, "In Whom We Trust: Group Membership as an Affective Context for Trust Development," *Academy of Management Review* (July 2001), pp. 377–396; and J. Schaubroeck, S. S. K. Lam, and A. C. Peng, "Cognition-Based and Affect-Based Trust as Mediators of Leader Behavior Influences on Team Performance," *Journal of Applied Psychology*, Online First Publication (February 7, 2011), DOI:10.1037/a0022625.

28. B. A. De Jong, and K. T. Dirks, "Beyond Shared Perceptions of Trust and Monitoring in Teams: Implications of Asymmetry and Dissensus," *Journal of Applied Psychology* 97, no. 2 (2012), pp. 391–406.

29. See F. Aime, C. J. Meyer, and S. E. Humphrey, "Legitimacy of Team Rewards: Analyzing Legitimacy as a Condition for the Effectiveness of Team Incentive Designs," *Journal of Business Research* 63, no. 1 (2010), pp. 60–66; P. A. Bamberger and R. Levi, "Team-Based Reward Allocation Structures and the Helping Behaviors of Outcome-Interdependent Team Members," *Journal of Managerial Psychology* 24, no. 4 (2009), pp. 300–327; and M. J. Pearsall, M. S. Christian, and A. P. J. Ellis, "Motivating Interdependent Teams: Individual Rewards, Shared Rewards, or Something in Between?" *Journal of Applied Psychology* 95, no. 1 (2010), pp. 183–191.

30. R. R. Hirschfeld, M. H. Jordan, H. S. Feild, W. F. Giles, and A. A. Armenakis, "Becoming Team Players: Team Members' Mastery of Teamwork Knowledge as a Predictor of Team Task Proficiency and Observed Teamwork Effectiveness," *Journal of Applied Psychology* 91, no. 2 (2006), pp. 467–474; and K. R. Randall, C. J. Resick, and L. A. DeChurch, "Building Team Adaptive Capacity: The Roles of Sensegiving and Team Composition," *Journal of Applied Psychology* 96, no. 3 (2011), pp. 525–540.

31. H. Moon, J. R. Hollenbeck, and S. E. Humphrey, "Asymmetric Adaptability: Dynamic Team Structures as One-Way Streets," *Academy of Management Journal* 47, no. 5 (October 2004), pp. 681–695; A. P. J. Ellis, J. R. Hollenbeck, and D. R. Ilgen, "Team Learning: Collectively Connecting the Dots," *Journal of Applied Psychology* 88, no. 5 (October 2003), pp. 821–835; C. L. Jackson and J. A. LePine, "Peer Responses to a Team's Weakest Link: A Test and Extension of LePine and Van Dyne's Model," *Journal of Applied Psychology* 88, no. 3 (June 2003), pp. 459–475; and J. A. LePine, "Team Adaptation and Postchange Performance: Effects of Team Composition in Terms of Members' Cognitive Ability and Personality," *Journal of Applied Psychology* 88, no. 1 (February 2003), pp. 27–39.

32. S. T. Bell, "Deep-Level Composition Variables as Predictors of Team Performance: A Meta-analysis," *Journal of Applied Psychology* 92, no. 3 (2007), pp. 595–615; and M. R. Barrick, G. L. Stewart, M. J. Neubert, and M. K. Mount, "Relating Member Ability and Personality to Work-Team Processes and Team Effectiveness," *Journal of Applied Psychology* (June 1998), pp. 377–391.

33. T. A. O'Neill and N. J. Allen, "Personality and the Prediction of Team Performance," *European Journal of Personality* 25, no. 1 (2011), pp. 31–42.

34. Ellis, Hollenbeck, and Ilgen, "Team Learning"; C. O. L. H. Porter, J. R. Hollenbeck, and D. R. Ilgen, "Backing Up Behaviors in Teams: The Role of Personality and Legitimacy of Need," *Journal of Applied Psychology* 88, no. 3 (June 2003), pp. 391–403; J. A. Colquitt, J. R. Hollenbeck, and D. R. Ilgen, "Computer-Assisted Communication and Team Decision-Making Performance: The Moderating Effect of Openness to Experience," *Journal of Applied Psychology* 87, no. 2 (April 2002), pp. 402–410; J. A. LePine, J. R. Hollenbeck, D. R. Ilgen, and J. Hedlund, "The Effects of Individual Differences on the Performance of Hierarchical Decision Making Teams: Much More Than G," *Journal of Applied Psychology* 82 (1997), pp. 803–811; Jackson and LePine, "Peer Responses to a Team's

Weakest Link"; and LePine, "Team Adaptation and Postchange Performance."

35. Barrick, Stewart, Neubert, and Mount, "Relating Member Ability and Personality to Work-Team Processes and Team Effectiveness," p. 388; and S. E. Humphrey, J. R. Hollenbeck, C. J. Meyer, and D. R. Ilgen, "Trait Configurations in Self-Managed Teams: A Conceptual Examination of the Use of Seeding for Maximizing and Minimizing Trait Variance in Teams," *Journal of Applied Psychology* 92, no. 3 (2007), pp. 885–892.

36. S. E. Humphrey, F. P. Morgeson, and M. J. Mannor, "Developing a Theory of the Strategic Core of Teams: A Role Composition Model of Team Performance," *Journal of Applied Psychology* 94, no. 1 (2009), pp. 48–61.

37. K. Y. Williams and C. A. O'Reilly III, "Demography and Diversity in Organizations: A Review of 40 Years of Research," in B. M. Staw and L. L. Cummings (eds.), *Research in Organizational Behavior* 20 (Stamford, CT: Jai Press, 1998) pp. 77–140; and A. Joshi, "The Influence of Organizational Demography on the External Networking Behavior of Teams," *Academy of Management Review* (July 2006), pp. 583–595.

38. W. E. Watson, K. Kumar, and L. K. Michaelsen, "Cultural Diversity's Impact on Interaction Process and Performance: Comparing Homogeneous and Diverse Task Groups," *Academy of Management Journal* (June 1993), pp. 590–602; P. C. Earley and E. Mosakowski, "Creating Hybrid Team Cultures: An Empirical Test of Transnational Team Functioning," *Academy of Management Journal* (February 2000), pp. 26–49; and S. Mohammed and L. C. Angell, "Surface- and Deep-Level Diversity in Workgroups: Examining the Moderating Effects of Team Orientation and Team Process on Relationship Conflict," *Journal of Organizational Behavior* (December 2004), pp. 1015–1039.

39. Watson, Kumar, and Michaelsen, "Cultural Diversity's Impact on Interaction Process and Performance."

40. D. Coutu, "Why Teams Don't Work" *Harvard Business Review* (May 2009), pp. 99–105. The evidence in this section is described in Thompson, *Making the Team*, pp. 65–67. See also L. A. Curral, R. H. Forrester, and J. F. Dawson, "It's What You Do and the Way That You Do It: Team Task, Team Size, and Innovation-Related Group Processes," *European Journal of Work & Organizational Psychology* 10, no. 2 (June 2001), pp. 187–204; R. C. Liden, S. J. Wayne, and R. A. Jaworski, "Social Loafing: A Field Investigation," *Journal of Management* 30, no. 2 (2004), pp. 285–304; and J. A. Wagner, "Studies of Individualism–Collectivism: Effects on Cooperation in Groups," *Academy of Management Journal* 38, no. 1 (February 1995), pp. 152–172.

41. "Is Your Team Too Big? Too Small? What's the Right Number? *Knowledge@Wharton* (June 14, 2006), pp. 1–5; see also A. M. Carton and J. N. Cummings, "A Theory of Subgroups in Work Teams," *Academy of Management Review* 37, no. 3 (2012), pp. 441–470.

42. Hyatt and Ruddy, "An Examination of the Relationship Between Work Group Characteristics and Performance"; J. D. Shaw, M. K. Duffy, and E. M. Stark, "Interdependence and Preference for Group Work: Main and Congruence Effects on the Satisfaction and Performance of Group Members," *Journal of Management* 26, no. 2 (2000), pp. 259–279; and S. A. Kiffin-Peterson and J. L. Cordery, "Trust, Individualism, and Job Characteristics of Employee Preference for Teamwork," *International Journal of Human Resource Management* (February 2003), pp. 93–116.

43. J. A. LePine, R. F. Piccolo, C. L. Jackson, J. E. Mathieu, and J. R. Saul, "A Meta-analysis of Teamwork Processes: Tests of a Multidimensional Model and Relationships with Team Effectiveness Criteria," *Personnel Psychology* 61 (2008), pp. 273–307.

44. I. D. Steiner, *Group Processes and Productivity* (New York: Academic Press, 1972).

45. J. A. LePine, R. F. Piccolo, C. L. Jackson, J. E. Mathieu, and J. R. Saul, "A Meta-analysis of Teamwork Processes: Tests of a Multidimensional Model and Relationships with Team Effectiveness Criteria"; and J. E. Mathieu and T. L. Rapp, "Laying the Foundation for Successful Team Performance Trajectories: The Roles of Team Charters and Performance Strategies," *Journal of Applied Psychology* 94, no. 1 (2009), pp. 90–103.

46. J. E. Mathieu and W. Schulze, "The Influence of Team Knowledge and Formal Plans on Episodic Team Process–Performance Relationships," *Academy of Management Journal* 49, no. 3 (2006), pp. 605–619.

47. A. N. Pieterse, D. van Knippenberg, and W. P. van Ginkel, "Diversity in Goal Orientation, Team Reflexivity, and Team Performance," *Organizational Behavior and Human Decision Processes* 114, no. 2 (2011), pp. 153–164.

48. A. Gurtner, F. Tschan, N. K. Semmer, and C. Nagele, "Getting Groups to Develop Good Strategies: Effects of Reflexivity Interventions on Team Process, Team Performance, and Shared Mental Models," *Organizational Behavior and Human Decision Processes* 102 (2007), pp. 127–142; M. C. Schippers, D. N. Den Hartog, and P. L. Koopman, "Reflexivity in Teams: A Measure and Correlates," *Applied Psychology: An International Review* 56, no. 2 (2007), pp. 189–211; and C. S. Burke, K. C. Stagl, E. Salas, L. Pierce, and D. Kendall, "Understanding Team Adaptation: A Conceptual Analysis and Model," *Journal of Applied Psychology* 91, no. 6 (2006), pp. 1189–1207.

49. A. N. Pieterse, D. van Knippenberg, and W. P. van Ginkel, "Diversity in Goal Orientation, Team Reflexivity, and Team Performance," *Organizational Behavior and Human Decision Processes* 114, no. 2 (2011), pp. 153–164.

50. E. Weldon and L. R. Weingart, "Group Goals and Group Performance," *British Journal of Social Psychology* (Spring 1993), pp. 307–334. See also R. P. DeShon, S. W. J. Kozlowski, A. M. Schmidt, K. R. Milner, and D. Wiechmann, "A Multiple-Goal, Multilevel Model of Feedback Effects on the Regulation of Individual and Team Performance," *Journal of Applied Psychology* (December 2004), pp. 1035–1056.

51. K. Tasa, S. Taggar, and G. H. Seijts, "The Development of Collective Efficacy in Teams: A Multilevel and Longitudinal Perspective," *Journal of Applied Psychology* 92, no. 1 (2007), pp. 17–27; D. I. Jung and J. J. Sosik, "Group Potency and Collective Efficacy: Examining Their Predictive Validity, Level of Analysis, and Effects of Performance Feedback on Future Group Performance," *Group & Organization Management* (September 2003), pp. 366–391; and R. R. Hirschfeld and J. B. Bernerth, "Mental Efficacy and Physical Efficacy at the Team Level: Inputs and Outcomes Among Newly Formed Action Teams," *Journal of Applied Psychology* 93, no. 6 (2008), pp. 1429–1437.

52. A. W. Richter, G. Hirst, D. van Knippenberg, and M. Baer, "Creative Self-Efficacy and Individual Creativity in Team Contexts: Cross-level Interactions with Team Informational Resources," *Journal of Applied Psychology* 97, no. 6 (2012), pp. 1282–1290.

53. S. Mohammed, L. Ferzandi, and K. Hamilton, "Metaphor No More: A 15-Year Review of the Team Mental Model Construct," *Journal of Management* 36, no. 4 (2010), pp. 876–910.

54. A. P. J. Ellis, "System Breakdown: The Role of Mental Models and Transactive Memory on the Relationships Between Acute Stress and Team Performance," *Academy of Management Journal* 49, no. 3 (2006), pp. 576–589.

55. S. W. J. Kozlowski and D. R. Ilgen, "Enhancing the Effectiveness of Work Groups and Teams," *Psychological Science in the Public Interest*

(December 2006), pp. 77–124; and B. D. Edwards, E. A. Day, W. Arthur Jr., and S. T. Bell, "Relationships Among Team Ability Composition, Team Mental Models, and Team Performance," *Journal of Applied Psychology* 91, no. 3 (2006), pp. 727–736.

56. L. A. DeChurch and J. R. Mesmer-Magnus, "The Cognitive Underpinnings of Effective Teamwork: A Meta-analysis," *Journal of Applied Psychology* 95, no. 1 (2010), pp. 32–53.

57. J. Farh, C. Lee, and C. I. C. Farh, "Task Conflict and Team Creativity: A Question of How Much and When," *Journal of Applied Psychology* 95, no. 6 (2010), pp. 1173–1180.

58. K. J. Behfar, R. S. Peterson, E. A. Mannix, and W. M. K. Trochim, "The Critical Role of Conflict Resolution in Teams: A Close Look at the Links Between Conflict Type, Conflict Management Strategies, and Team Outcomes," *Journal of Applied Psychology* 93, no. 1 (2008), pp. 170–188.

59. K. H. Price, D. A. Harrison, and J. H. Gavin, "Withholding Inputs in Team Contexts: Member Composition, Interaction Processes, Evaluation Structure, and Social Loafing," *Journal of Applied Psychology* 91, no. 6 (2006), pp. 1375–1384.

60. See, for instance, B. L. Kirkman and D. L. Shapiro, "The Impact of Cultural Values on Employee Resistance to Teams: Toward a Model of Globalized Self-Managing Work Team Effectiveness," *Academy of Management Review*, July 1997, pp. 730–757; and B. L. Kirkman, C. B. Gibson, and D. L. Shapiro, "'Exporting' Teams: Enhancing the Implementation and Effectiveness of Work Teams in Global Affiliates," *Organizational Dynamics* 30, no. 1 (2001), pp. 12–29.

61. G. Hertel, U. Konradt, and K. Voss, "Competencies for Virtual Teamwork: Development and Validation of a Web-Based Selection Tool for Members of Distributed Teams," *European Journal of Work and Organizational Psychology* 15, no. 4 (2006), pp. 477–504.

62. T. V. Riper, "The NBA's Most Overpaid Players," *Forbes* (April 5, 2013), accessed June 10, 2013 at http://www.forbes.com.

63. E. Kearney, D. Gebert, and S. C. Voelpel, "When and How Diversity Benefits Teams: The Importance of Team Members' Need for Cognition," *Academy of Management Journal* 52, no. 3 (2009), pp. 581–598.

64. C.-H. Chuang, S. Chen, and C.-W. Chuang, "Human Resource Management Practices and Organizational Social Capital: The Role of Industrial Characteristics," *Journal of Business Research* (May 2013), pp. 678–687; and L. Prusak and D. Cohen, "How to Invest in Social Capital," *Harvard Business Review* (June 2001), pp. 86–93.

65. T. Erickson and L. Gratton, "What It Means to Work Here," *Businessweek* (January 10, 2008), http://www.businessweek.com.

66. M. D. Johnson, J. R. Hollenbeck, S. E. Humphrey, D. R. Ilgen, D. Jundt, and C. J. Meyer, "Cutthroat Cooperation: Asymmetrical Adaptation to Changes in Team Reward Structures," *Academy of Management Journal* 49, no. 1 (2006), pp. 103–119.

67. C. E. Naquin and R. O. Tynan, "The Team Halo Effect: Why Teams Are Not Blamed for Their Failures," *Journal of Applied Psychology*, April 2003, pp. 332–340.

68. E. R. Crawford and J. A. Lepine, "A Configural Theory of Team Processes: Accounting for the Structure of Taskwork and Teamwork," *Academy of Management Review* (January 2013), pp. 32–48; and A. B. Drexler and R. Forrester, "Teamwork—Not Necessarily the Answer," *HR Magazine* (January 1998), pp. 55–58.

Chapter 11

1. D. K. Berlo, *The Process of Communication* (New York: Holt, Rinehart & Winston, 1960), pp. 30–32; see also K. Byron, "Carrying Too Heavy a Load? The Communication and Miscommunication of Emotion by Email," *Academy of Management Review* 33, no. 2 (2008), pp. 309–327.

2. J. Langan-Fox, "Communication in Organizations: Speed, Diversity, Networks, and Influence on Organizational Effectiveness, Human Health, and Relationships," in N. Anderson, D. S. Ones, H. K. Sinangil, and C. Viswesvaran (eds.), *Handbook of Industrial, Work and Organizational Psychology* 2 (Thousand Oaks, CA: Sage, 2001), p. 190.

3. R. L. Simpson, "Vertical and Horizontal Communication in Formal Organizations," *Administrative Science Quarterly* (September 1959), pp. 188–196; A. G. Walker and J. W. Smither, "A Five-Year Study of Upward Feedback: What Managers Do with Their Results Matter," *Personnel Psychology* (Summer 1999), pp. 393–424; and J. W. Smither and A. G. Walker, "Are the Characteristics of Narrative Comments Related to Improvement in Multirater Feedback Ratings over Time?" *Journal of Applied Psychology* 89, no. 3 (June 2004), pp. 575–581.

4. P. Dvorak, "How Understanding the 'Why' of Decisions Matters," *The Wall Street Journal* (March 19, 2007), p. B3.

5. T. Neeley and P. Leonardi, "Effective Managers Say the Same Thing Twice (or More)," *Harvard Business Review* (May 2011), pp. 38–39.

6. J. Ewing, "Nokia: Bring on the Employee Rants," *BusinessWeek* (June 22, 2009), p. 50.

7. H. A. Richardson and S. G. Taylor, "Understanding Input Events: A Model of Employees' Responses to Requests for Their Input," *Academy of Management Review* 37 (2012), pp. 471–491.

8. E. Nichols, "Hyper-Speed Managers," *HR Magazine* (April 2007), pp. 107–110.

9. See, for example, N. B. Kurland and L. H. Pelled, "Passing the Word: Toward a Model of Gossip and Power in the Workplace," *Academy of Management Review* (April 2000), pp. 428–438; and G. Michelson, A. van Iterson, and K. Waddington, "Gossip in Organizations: Contexts, Consequences, and Controversies," *Group and Organization Management* 35, no. 4 (2010), pp. 371–390.

10. G. Van Hoye and F. Lievens, "Tapping the Grapevine: A Closer Look at Word-of-Mouth as a Recruitment Source," *Journal of Applied Psychology* 94, no. 2 (2009), pp. 341–352.

11. R. L. Rosnow and G. A. Fine, *Rumor and Gossip: The Social Psychology of Hearsay* (New York: Elsevier, 1976).

12. J. K. Bosson, A. B. Johnson, K. Niederhoffer, and W. B. Swann Jr., "Interpersonal Chemistry Through Negativity: Bonding by Sharing Negative Attitudes About Others," *Personal Relationships* 13 (2006), pp. 135–150.

13. T. J. Grosser, V. Lopez-Kidwell, and G. Labianca, "A Social Network Analysis of Positive and Negative Gossip in Organizational Life," *Group and Organization Management* 35, no. 2 (2010), pp. 177–212.

14. M. Feinberg, R. Willer, J. Stellar, and D. Keltner, "The Virtues of Gossip: Reputational Information Sharing as Prosocial Behavior," *Journal of Personality and Social Psychology* 102 (2012), pp. 1015–1030.

15. L. S. Rashotte, "What Does That Smile Mean? The Meaning of Nonverbal Behaviors in Social Interaction," *Social Psychology Quarterly* (March 2002), pp. 92–102.

16. C. K. Goman, "5 Body Language Tips to Increase Your Curb Appeal," *Forbes* (March 4, 2013), http://www.forbes.com/sites/carolkinseygoman/2013/03/14/5-body-language-tips-to-increase-your-curb-appeal.

17. A. Metallinou, A. Katsamanis, and S. Narayanan, "Tracking Continuous Emotional Trends of Participants During Affective Dyadic Interactions Using Body Language and Speech Information," *Image and Vision Computing* (February 2013), pp. 137–152.

18. J. Smith, "10 Nonverbal Cues That Convey Confidence at Work," *Forbes* (March 11, 2013), http://www.forbes.com/sites/

jacquelynsmith/2013/03/11/10-nonverbal-cues-that-convey-confidence-at-work.

19. See R. L. Daft and R. H. Lengel, "Information Richness: A New Approach to Managerial Behavior and Organization Design," in B. M. Staw and L. L. Cummings (eds.), *Research in Organizational Behavior* 6 (Greenwich, CT: JAI Press, 1984), pp. 191–233; R. L. Daft and R. H. Lengel, "Organizational Information Requirements, Media Richness, and Structural Design," *Managerial Science* (May 1986), pp. 554–572; R. E. Rice, "Task Analyzability, Use of New Media, and Effectiveness," *Organization Science* (November 1992), pp. 475–500; S. G. Straus and J. E. McGrath, "Does the Medium Matter? The Interaction of Task Type and Technology on Group Performance and Member Reaction," *Journal of Applied Psychology* (February 1994), pp. 87–97; L. K. Trevino, J. Webster, and E. W. Stein, "Making Connections: Complementary Influences on Communication Media Choices, Attitudes, and Use," *Organization Science* (March–April 2000), pp. 163–182; and N. Kock, "The Psychobiological Model: Towards a New Theory of Computer-Mediated Communication Based on Darwinian Evolution," *Organization Science* 15, no. 3 (May–June 2004), pp. 327–348.

20. Ashley, J. (2003) "Synchronous and Asynchronous Communication Tools", *Executive Update Online*, http://www.asaecenter.org/Resources/articledetail.cfm?itemnumber=13572.

21. E. Frauenheim, "Communicating for Engagement During Tough Times," *Workforce Management Online* (April 2010), http://www.workforce.com.

22. M. V. Rafter, "Falling from a Cloud," *Workforce Management* (February 2013), pp. 22–23.

23. "At Many Companies, Hunt for Leakers Expands Arsenal of Monitoring Tactics," *The Wall Street Journal* (September 11, 2006), pp. B1, B3; and B. J. Alge, G. A. Ballinger, S. Tangirala, and J. L. Oakley, "Information Privacy in Organizations: Empowering Creative and Extrarole Performance," *Journal of Applied Psychology* 91, No. 1 (2006), pp. 221–232.

24. R. E. Petty and P. Briñol, "Persuasion: From Single to Multiple to Metacognitive Processes," *Perspectives on Psychological Science* 3, no. 2 (2008), pp. 137–147; and F. A. White, M. A. Charles, and J. K. Nelson, "The Role of Persuasive Arguments in Changing Affirmative Action Attitudes and Expressed Behavior in Higher Education," *Journal of Applied Psychology* 93, no. 6 (2008), pp. 1271–1286.

25. B. T. Johnson, and A. H. Eagly, "Effects of Involvement on Persuasion: A Meta-analysis," *Psychological Bulletin* 106, no. 2 (1989), pp. 290–314; and K. L. Blankenship and D. T. Wegener, "Opening the Mind to Close It: Considering a Message in Light of Important Values Increases Message Processing and Later Resistance to Change," *Journal of Personality and Social Psychology* 94, no. 2 (2008), pp. 196–213.

26. See R. E. Petty and L. R. Fabrigar, "Affective and Cognitive Meta-bases of Attitudes: Unique Effects of Information Interest and Persuasion," *Journal of Personality and Social Psychology* 94, no. 6 (2008), pp. 938–955; M. S. Key, J. E. Edlund, B. J. Sagarin, and G. Y. Bizer, "Individual Differences in Susceptibility to Mindlessness," *Personality and Individual Differences* 46, no. 3 (2009), pp. 261–264; and M. Reinhard and M. Messner, "The Effects of Source Likeability and Need for Cognition on Advertising Effectiveness Under Explicit Persuasion," *Journal of Consumer Behavior* 8, no. 4 (2009), pp. 179–191.

27. P. Briñol, R. E. Petty, and J. Barden, "Happiness Versus Sadness as a Determinant of Thought Confidence in Persuasion: A Self-Validation Analysis," *Journal of Personality and Social Psychology* 93, no. 5 (2007), pp. 711–727.

28. R. C. Sinclair, S. E. Moore, M. M. Mark, A. S. Soldat, and C. A. Lavis, "Incidental Moods, Source Likeability, and Persuasion: Liking Motivates Message Elaboration in Happy People," *Cognition*

and Emotion 24, no. 6 (2010), pp. 940–961; and V. Griskevicius, M. N. Shiota, and S. L. Neufeld, "Influence of Different Positive Emotions on Persuasion Processing: A Functional Evolutionary Approach," *Emotion* 10, no. 2 (2010), pp. 190–206.

29. J. Sandberg, "The Jargon Jumble: Kids Have 'Skeds,' Colleagues, 'Needs,'" *The Wall Street Journal* (October 24, 2006), http://online.wsj.com/article/SB116165746415401680.html.

30. G. Creese and E. Kambere, "What Colour Is Your English?" *CRSA/RCSA* 40, no. 5 (2003), pp. 565–573; B. Nguyen, "Accent Discrimination and the Test of Spoken English: A Call for an Objective Assessment of the Comprehensibility of Non-native Speakers," *California Law Review*, 81 (1993), pp. 1325–1361; and M. Gill, "Accent and Stereotypes: Their Effect on Perception of Teachers and Lecture Comprehension," *Journal of Applied Communication Research* 22 (1994), pp. 348–361.

31. E. W. Morrison and F. J. Milliken, "Organizational Silence: A Barrier to Change and Development in a Pluralistic World," *Academy of Management Review* 25, no. 4 (2000), pp. 706–725; and B. E. Ashforth and V. Anand, "The Normalization of Corruption in Organizations," *Research in Organizational Behavior* 25 (2003), pp. 1–52.

32. F. J. Milliken, E. W. Morrison, and P. F. Hewlin, "An Exploratory Study of Employee Silence: Issues That Employees Don't Communicate Upward and Why," *Journal of Management Studies* 40, no. 6 (2003), pp. 1453–1476.

33. S. Tangirala and R. Ramunujam, "Employee Silence on Critical Work Issues: The Cross-level Effects of Procedural Justice Climate," *Personnel Psychology* 61, no. 1 (2008), pp. 37–68; and F. Bowen and K. Blackmon, "Spirals of Silence: The Dynamic Effects of Diversity on Organizational Voice," *Journal of Management Studies* 40, no. 6 (2003), pp. 1393–1417.

34. B. R. Schlenker and M. R. Leary, "Social Anxiety and Self-Presentation: A Conceptualization and Model," *Psychological Bulletin* 92 (1982), pp. 641–669; and L. A. Withers, and L. L. Vernon, "To Err Is Human: Embarrassment, Attachment, and Communication Apprehension," *Personality and Individual Differences* 40, no. 1 (2006), pp. 99–110.

35. See, for instance, S. K. Opt and D. A. Loffredo, "Rethinking Communication Apprehension: A Myers-Briggs Perspective," *Journal of Psychology* (September 2000), pp. 556–570; and B. D. Blume, G. F. Dreher, and T. T. Baldwin, "Examining the Effects of Communication Apprehension within Assessment Centres," *Journal of Occupational and Organizational Psychology* 83, no. 3 (2010), pp. 663–671.

36. See, for example, J. A. Daly and J. C. McCroskey, "Occupational Desirability and Choice as a Function of Communication Apprehension," *Journal of Counseling Psychology* 22, no. 4 (1975), pp. 309–313; and T. L. Rodebaugh, "I Might Look OK, but I'm Still Doubtful, Anxious, and Avoidant: The Mixed Effects of Enhanced Video Feedback on Social Anxiety Symptoms," *Behaviour Research & Therapy* 42, no. 12 (December 2004), pp. 1435–1451.

37. B. M. Depaulo, D. A. Kashy, S. E. Kirkendol, M. M. Wyer, and J. A. Epstein, "Lying in Everyday Life," *Journal of Personality and Social Psychology* 70, No. 5 (1996), pp. 979–995; and K. B. Serota, T. R. Levine, and F. J. Boster, "The Prevalence of Lying in America: Three Studies of Self-Reported Lies," *Human Communication Research* 36, no. 1. (2010), pp. 2–25.

38. DePaulo, Kashy, Kirkendol, Wyer, and Epstein, "Lying in Everyday Life"; and C. E. Naguin, T. R. Kurtzberg, and L. Y. Belkin, "The Finer Points of Lying Online: E-mail Versus Pen and Paper," *Journal of Applied Psychology* 95, no. 2 (2010), pp. 387–394.

39. A. Vrij, P. A. Granhag, and S. Porter, "Pitfalls and Opportunities in Nonverbal and Verbal Lie Detection," *Psychological Science in the Public Interest* 11, no. 3 (2010), pp. 89–121.

40. R. E. Axtell, *Gestures: The Do's and Taboos of Body Language Around the World* (New York: Wiley, 1991); Watson Wyatt Worldwide, "Effective Communication: A Leading Indicator of Financial Performance—2005/2006 Communication ROI Study," http://www.watsonwyatt.com/research/resrender. asp?id=w-868; and A. Markels, "Turning the Tide at P&G," *U.S. News & World Report* (October 30, 2006), p. 69.

41. See M. Munter, "Cross-cultural Communication for Managers," *Business Horizons* (May–June 1993), pp. 75–76; and H. Ren and B. Gray, "Repairing Relationship Conflict: How Violation Types and Culture Influence the Effectiveness of Restoration Rituals," *Academy of Management Review* 34, no. 1 (2009), pp. 105–126.

42. See E. T. Hall, *Beyond Culture* (Garden City, NY: Anchor Press/Doubleday, 1976); W. L. Adair, "Integrative Sequences and Negotiation Outcome in Same- and Mixed-Culture Negotiations," *International Journal of Conflict Management* 14, no. 3–4 (2003), pp. 1359–1392; W. L. Adair and J. M. Brett, "The Negotiation Dance: Time, Culture, and Behavioral Sequences in Negotiation," *Organization Science* 16, no. 1 (2005), pp. 33–51; E. Giebels and P. J. Taylor, "Interaction Patterns in Crisis Negotiations: Persuasive Arguments and Cultural Differences," *Journal of Applied Psychology* 94, no. 1 (2009), pp. 5–19; and M. G. Kittler, D. Rygl, and A. Mackinnon, "Beyond Culture or Beyond Control? Reviewing the Use of Hall's High-/Low-Context Concept," *International Journal of Cross-cultural Management* 11, no. 1 (2011), pp. 63–82.

43. M. C. Hopson, T. Hart, and G. C. Bell, "Meeting in the Middle: Fred L. Casmir's Contributions to the Field of Intercultural Communication," *International Journal of Intercultural Relations* (November 2012), pp. 789–797.

Chapter 12

1. See T. A. Judge, J. E. Bono, R. Ilies, and M. W. Gerhardt, "Personality and Leadership: A Qualitative and Quantitative Review," *Journal of Applied Psychology* (August 2002), pp. 765–780.

2. D. R. Ames and F. J. Flynn, "What Breaks a Leader: The Curvilinear Relation Between Assertiveness and Leadership," *Journal of Personality and Social Psychology* 92, no. 2 (2007), pp. 307–324.

3. N. Ensari, R. E. Riggio, J. Christian, and G. Carslaw, "Who Emerges as a Leader? Meta-analyses of Individual Differences as Predictors of Leadership Emergence," *Personality and Individual Differences* (September 2011), pp. 532–536.

4. R. M. Stogdill and A. E. Coons (eds.), *Leader Behavior: Its Description and Measurement*, Research Monograph no. 88 (Columbus: Ohio State University, Bureau of Business Research, 1951). This research is updated in C. A. Schriesheim, C. C. Cogliser, and L. L. Neider, "Is It 'Trustworthy'? A Multiple-Levels-of-Analysis Reexamination of an Ohio State Leadership Study, with Implications for Future Research," *Leadership Quarterly* (Summer 1995), pp. 111–145; and T. A. Judge, R. F. Piccolo, and R. Ilies, "The Forgotten Ones? The Validity of Consideration and Initiating Structure in Leadership Research," *Journal of Applied Psychology* (February 2004), pp. 36–51.

5. D. Akst, "The Rewards of Recognizing a Job Well Done," *The Wall Street Journal* (January 31, 2007), p. D9.

6. Judge, Piccolo, and Ilies, "The Forgotten Ones?"

7. M. Javidan, P. W. Dorfman, M. S. de Luque, and R. J. House, "In the Eye of the Beholder: Cross Cultural Lessons in Leadership from Project GLOBE," *Academy of Management Perspectives* (February 2006), pp. 67–90.

8. F. E. Fiedler, *A Theory of Leadership Effectiveness* (New York: McGraw-Hill, 1967).

9. S. Shiflett, "Is There a Problem with the LPC Score in LEADER MATCH?" *Personnel Psychology* (Winter 1981), pp. 765–769.

10. F. E. Fiedler, M. M. Chemers, and L. Mahar, *Improving Leadership Effectiveness: The Leader Match Concept* (New York: Wiley, 1977).

11. Cited in R. J. House and R. N. Aditya, "The Social Scientific Study of Leadership," *Journal of Management* 23, no. 3 (1997), p. 422.

12. L. H. Peters, D. D. Hartke, and J. T. Pohlmann, "Fiedler's Contingency Theory of Leadership: An Application of the Meta-analysis Procedures of Schmidt and Hunter," *Psychological Bulletin* (March 1985), pp. 274–285; C. A. Schriesheim, B. J. Tepper, and L. A. Tetrault, "Least Preferred Coworker Score, Situational Control, and Leadership Effectiveness: A Meta-analysis of Contingency Model Performance Predictions," *Journal of Applied Psychology* (August 1994), pp. 561–573; and R. Ayman, M. M. Chemers, and F. Fiedler, "The Contingency Model of Leadership Effectiveness: Its Levels of Analysis," *Leadership Quarterly* (Summer 1995), pp. 147–167.

13. House and Aditya, "The Social Scientific Study of Leadership."

14. See, for instance, R. W. Rice, "Psychometric Properties of the Esteem for the Least Preferred Coworker (LPC) Scale," *Academy of Management Review* (January 1978), pp. 106–118; C. A. Schriesheim, B. D. Bannister, and W. H. Money, "Psychometric Properties of the LPC Scale: An Extension of Rice's Review," *Academy of Management Review* (April 1979), pp. 287–290; and J. K. Kennedy, J. M. Houston, M. A. Korgaard, and D. D. Gallo, "Construct Space of the Least Preferred Coworker (LPC) Scale," *Educational & Psychological Measurement* (Fall 1987), pp. 807–814.

15. See E. H. Schein, *Organizational Psychology*, 3rd ed. (Upper Saddle River, NJ: Prentice Hall, 1980), pp. 116–117; and B. Kabanoff, "A Critique of Leader Match and Its Implications for Leadership Research," *Personnel Psychology* (Winter 1981), pp. 749–764.

16. See, for instance, Ibid., pp. 67–84; C. L. Graeff, "Evolution of Situational Leadership Theory: A Critical Review," *Leadership Quarterly* 8, no. 2 (1997), pp. 153–170; and R. P. Vecchio and K. J. Boatwright, "Preferences for Idealized Styles of Supervision," *Leadership Quarterly* (August 2002), pp. 327–342.

17. R. J. House, "A Path-Goal Theory of Leader Effectiveness," *Administrative Science Quarterly* (September 1971), pp. 321–338; R. J. House and T. R. Mitchell, "Path-Goal Theory of Leadership," *Journal of Contemporary Business* (Autumn 1974), pp. 81–97; and R. J. House, "Path-Goal Theory of Leadership: Lessons, Legacy, and a Reformulated Theory," *Leadership Quarterly* (Fall 1996), pp. 323–352.

18. G. B. Graen and M. Uhl-Bien, "The Relationship-Based Approach to Leadership: Development of LMX Theory of Leadership over 25 Years: Applying a Multi-level, Multi-domain Perspective," *Leadership Quarterly* 6, no. 2 (1995), pp. 219–247, DOI:10.1016/1048-9843(95)90036-5; Tayla Bauer and Berrin Ergoden, *The Oxford Handbook of Leader–Member Exchange* (New York: Oxford University Press, 2015); and Charlotte R. Gerstner and David V. Day, "Meta-analytic Review of Leader–Member Exchange Theory: Correlates and Construct Issues," *Journal of Applied Psychology* 82, no. 6 (1997), pp. 827–844.

19. M. Weber, *The Theory of Social and Economic Organization*, A. M. Henderson and T. Parsons (trans.) (New York: The Free Press, 1947).

20. J. A. Conger and R. N. Kanungo, "Behavioral Dimensions of Charismatic Leadership," in J. A. Conger, R. N. Kanungo, and Associates (eds.), *Charismatic Leadership* (San Francisco: Jossey-Bass, 1988), p. 79; and A.-K. Samnani and P. Singh, "When Leaders Victimize: The Role of Charismatic Leaders in Facilitating Group Pressures," *Leadership Quarterly* (pp. 189–202).

21. J. A. Conger and R. N. Kanungo, *Charismatic Leadership in Organizations* (Thousand Oaks, CA: Sage, 1998); and R. Awamleh and W. L. Gardner, "Perceptions of Leader Charisma and Effectiveness: The Effects of Vision Content, Delivery, and Organizational Performance," *Leadership Quarterly* (Fall 1999), pp. 345–373.

22. R. J. House and J. M. Howell, "Personality and Charismatic Leadership," *Leadership Quarterly* 3 (1992), pp. 81–108; D. N. Den Hartog and P. L. Koopman, "Leadership in Organizations," in N. Anderson and D. S. Ones (eds.), *Handbook of Industrial, Work and Organizational Psychology* 2 (Thousand Oaks, CA: Sage, 2002), pp. 166–187.

23. P. Balkundi, M. Kilduff, and D. A. Harrison, "Centrality and Charisma: Comparing How Leader Networks and Attributions Affect Team Performance," *Journal of Applied Psychology* 96 (2012), pp. 1209–1222.

24. A. Erez, V. F. Misangyi, D. E. Johnson, M. A. LePine, and K. C. Halverson, "Stirring the Hearts of Followers: Charismatic Leadership as the Transferal of Affect," *Journal of Applied Psychology* 93, no. 3 (2008), pp. 602–615. For reviews on the role of vision in leadership, see S. J. Zaccaro, "Visionary and Inspirational Models of Executive Leadership: Empirical Review and Evaluation," in S. J. Zaccaro (ed.), *The Nature of Executive Leadership: A Conceptual and Empirical Analysis of Success* (Washington, DC: American Psychological Association, 2001), pp. 259–278; and M. Hauser and R. J. House, "Lead Through Vision and Values," in E. A. Locke (ed.), *Handbook of Principles of Organizational Behavior* (Malden, MA: Blackwell, 2004), pp. 257–273.

25. D. N. Den Hartog, A. H. B. De Hoogh, and A. E. Keegan, "The Interactive Effects of Belongingness and Charisma on Helping and Compliance," *Journal of Applied Psychology* 92, no. 4 (2007), pp. 1131–1139.

26. J. C. Pastor, M. Mayo, and B. Shamir, "Adding Fuel to Fire: The Impact of Followers' Arousal on Ratings of Charisma," *Journal of Applied Psychology* 92, no. 6 (2007), pp. 1584–1596.

27. A. H. B. De Hoogh and D. N. Den Hartog, "Neuroticism and Locus of Control as Moderators of the Relationships of Charismatic and Autocratic Leadership with Burnout," *Journal of Applied Psychology* 94, no. 4 (2009), pp. 1058–1067.

28. F. Cohen, S. Solomon, M. Maxfield, T. Pyszczynski, and J. Greenberg, "Fatal Attraction: The Effects of Mortality Salience on Evaluations of Charismatic, Task-Oriented, and Relationship-Oriented Leaders," *Psychological Sciences* (December 2004), pp. 846–851; and M. G. Ehrhart and K. J. Klein, "Predicting Followers' Preferences for Charismatic Leadership: The Influence of Follower Values and Personality," *Leadership Quarterly* (Summer 2001), pp. 153–179.

29. See, for instance, R. Khurana, *Searching for a Corporate Savior: The Irrational Quest for Charismatic CEOs* (Princeton, NJ: Princeton University Press, 2002); and J. A. Raelin, "The Myth of Charismatic Leaders," *Training & Development* (March 2003), pp. 47–54.

30. B. M. Galvin, D. A. Waldman, and P. Balthazard, "Visionary Communication Qualities as Mediators of the Relationship between Narcissism and Attributions of Leader Charisma," *Personnel Psychology* 63, no. 3 (2010), pp. 509–537.

31. See, for instance, B. M. Bass, B. J. Avolio, D. I. Jung, and Y. Berson, "Predicting Unit Performance by Assessing Transformational and Transactional Leadership," *Journal of Applied Psychology* (April 2003), pp. 207–218; and T. A. Judge and R. F. Piccolo, "Transformational and Transactional Leadership: A Meta-analytic Test of Their Relative Validity," *Journal of Applied Psychology* (October 2004), pp. 755–768.

32. A. M. Grant, "Leading with Meaning: Beneficiary Contact, Prosocial Impact, and the Performance Effects of Transformational Leadership," *Academy of Management Journal* 55 (2012), pp. 458–476.

33. B. M. Bass, "Leadership: Good, Better, Best," *Organizational Dynamics* (Winter 1985), pp. 26–40; and J. Seltzer and B. M. Bass, "Transformational Leadership: Beyond Initiation and Consideration," *Journal of Management* (December 1990), pp. 693–703.

34. T. R. Hinkin and C. A. Schriescheim, "An Examination of 'Nonleadership': From Laissez-Faire Leadership to Leader Reward Omission and Punishment Omission," *Journal of Applied Psychology* 93, no. 6 (2008), pp. 1234–1248.

35. A. E. Colbert, A. E. Kristof-Brown, B. H. Bradley, and M. R. Barrick, "CEO Transformational Leadership: The Role of Goal Importance Congruence in Top Management Teams," *Academy of Management Journal* 51, no. 1 (2008), pp. 81–96.

36. Y. Ling, Z. Simsek, M. H. Lubatkin, and J. F. Veiga, "The Impact of Transformational CEOs on the Performance of Small- to Medium-Sized Firms: Does Organizational Context Matter?" *Journal of Applied Psychology* 93, no. 4 (2008), pp. 923–934.

37. J. R. Baum, E. A. Locke, and S. A. Kirkpatrick, "A Longitudinal Study of the Relation of Vision and Vision Communication to Venture Growth in Entrepreneurial Firms," *Journal of Applied Psychology* (February 2000), pp. 43–54.

38. R. J. House, M. Javidan, P. Hanges, and P. Dorfman, "Understanding Cultures and Implicit Leadership Theories Across the Globe: An Introduction to Project GLOBE," *Journal of World Business* (Spring 2002), pp. 3–10.

39. D. E. Carl and M. Javidan, "Universality of Charismatic Leadership: A Multi-nation Study," paper presented at the National Academy of Management Conference, Washington, DC, August 2001, p. 29.

40. J. Schaubroeck, S. S. K. Lam, and S. E. Cha, "Embracing Transformational Leadership: Team Values and the Impact of Leader Behavior on Team Performance," *Journal of Applied Psychology* 92, no. 4 (2007), pp. 1020–1030.

41. B. L. Kirkman, G. Chen, J. Farh, Z. X. Chen, and K. B. Lowe, "Individual Power Distance Orientation and Follower Reactions to Transformational Leaders: A Cross-level, Cross-cultural Examination," *Academy of Management Journal* 52, no. 4 (2009), pp. 744–764.

42. S. J. Shin and J. Zhou, "Transformational Leadership, Conservation, and Creativity: Evidence from Korea," *Academy of Management Journal* (December 2003), pp. 703–714; V. J. García-Morales, F. J. Lloréns-Montes, and A. J. Verdú-Jover, "The Effects of Transformational Leadership on Organizational Performance Through Knowledge and Innovation," *British Journal of Management* 19, no. 4 (2008), pp. 299–313; and S. A. Eisenbeiss, D. van Knippenberg, and S. Boerner, "Transformational Leadership and Team Innovation: Integrating Team Climate Principles," *Journal of Applied Psychology* 93, no. 6 (2008), pp. 1438–1446.

43. F. O. Walumbwa, B. J. Avolio, and W. Zhu, "How Transformational Leadership Weaves Its Influence on Individual Job Performance: The Role of Identification and Efficacy Beliefs," *Personnel Psychology* 61, no. 4 (2008), pp. 793–825.

44. J. E. Bono and T. A. Judge, "Self-Concordance at Work: Toward Understanding the Motivational Effects of Transformational Leaders," *Academy of Management Journal* (October 2003), pp. 554–571; Y. Berson and B. J. Avolio, "Transformational Leadership and the Dissemination of Organizational Goals: A Case Study of a Telecommunication Firm," *Leadership Quarterly* (October 2004), pp. 625–646; and Schaubroeck, Lam, and Cha, "Embracing Transformational Leadership: Team Values and the Impact of Leader Behavior on Team Performance."

45. See B. J. Avolio, W. L. Gardner, F. O. Walumbwa, F. Luthans, and D. R. May, "Unlocking the Mask: A Look at the Process by

Which Authentic Leaders Impact Follower Attitudes and Behaviors," *Leadership Quarterly* (December 2004), pp. 801–823; W. L. Gardner and J. R. Schermerhorn Jr., "Performance Gains Through Positive Organizational Behavior and Authentic Leadership," *Organizational Dynamics* (August 2004), pp. 270–281; and M. M. Novicevic, M. G. Harvey, M. R. Buckley, J. A. Brown-Radford, and R. Evans, "Authentic Leadership: A Historical Perspective," *Journal of Leadership and Organizational Behavior* 13, no. 1 (2006), pp. 64–76.

46. K. M. Hmieleski, M. S. Cole, and R. A. Baron, "Shared Authentic Leadership and New Venture Performance," *Journal of Management* (September 2012), pp. 1476–1499.

47. J. Stouten, M. van Dijke, and D. De Cremer, "Ethical Leadership: An Overview and Future Perspectives," *Journal of Personnel Psychology* 11 (2012), pp. 1–6.

48. J. M. Schaubroeck, S. T. Hannah, B. J. Avolio, S. W. J. Kozlowski, et al., "Embedding Ethical Leadership Within and Across Organization Levels," *Academy of Management Journal* 55 (2012), pp. 1053–1078.

49. D. van Knippenberg, D. De Cremer, and B. van Knippenberg, "Leadership and Fairness: The State of the Art," *European Journal of Work and Organizational Psychology* 16, no. 2 (2007), pp. 113–140.

50. B. P. Owens and D. R. Hekman, "Modeling How to Grow: An Inductive Examination of Humble Leader Behaviors, Contingencies, and Outcomes," *Academy of Management Journal* 55 (2012), pp. 787–818.

51. K. M. Kacmar, D. G. Bachrach, K. J. Harris, and S. Zivnuska, "Fostering Good Citizenship Through Ethical Leadership: Exploring the Moderating Role of Gender and Organizational Politics," *Journal of Applied Psychology* 96, no. 3 (May 2011), pp. 633–642; and F. O. Walumbwa and J. Schaubroeck, "Leader Personality Traits and Employee Voice Behavior: Mediating Roles of Ethical Leadership and Work Group Psychological Safety," *Journal of Applied Psychology* 94, no. 5 (2009), pp. 1275–1286.

52. D. M. Mayer, K. Aquino, R. L. Greenbaum, and M. Kuenzi, "Who Displays Ethical Leadership, and Why Does It Matter? An Examination of Antecedents and Consequences of Ethical Leadership," *Academy of Management Journal* 55 (2012), pp. 151–171.

53. S. A. Eisenbeiss and S. R. Giessner, "The Emergence and Maintenance of Ethical Leadership in Organizations," *Journal of Personnel Psychology* 11 (2012), pp. 7–19.

54. D. van Dierendonck, "Servant Leadership: A Review and Synthesis," *Journal of Management* 37, no. 4 (2011), pp. 1228–1261.

55. S. J. Peterson, F. M. Galvin, and D. Lange, "CEO Servant Leadership: Exploring Executive Characteristics and Firm Performance," *Personnel Psychology* 65 (2012), pp. 565–596.

56. F. Walumbwa, C. A. Hartnell, and A. Oke, "Servant Leadership, Procedural Justice Climate, Service Climate, Employee Attitudes, and Organizational Citizenship Behavior: A Cross-level Investigation," *Journal of Applied Psychology* 95, no. 3 (2010), pp. 517–529.

57. D. De Cremer, D. M. Mayer, M. van Dijke, B. C. Schouten, and M. Bardes, "When Does Self-Sacrificial Leadership Motivate Prosocial Behavior? It Depends on Followers' Prevention Focus," *Journal of Applied Psychology* 2009, no. 4 (2009), pp. 887–899.

58. J. Hu and R. C. Liden, "Antecedents of Team Potency and Team Effectiveness: An Examination of Goal and Process Clarity and Servant Leadership," *Journal of Applied Psychology* 96, no. 4 (July 2011), pp. 851–862.

59. M. J. Neubert, K. M. Kacmar, D. S. Carlson, L. B. Chonko, and J. A. Roberts, "Regulatory Focus as a Mediator of the Influence of Initiating Structure and Servant Leadership on Employee Behavior," *Journal of Applied Psychology* 93, no. 6 (2008), pp. 1220–1233.

60. T. Menon, J. Sim, J. Ho-Ying Fu, C. Chiu, and Y. Hong, "Blazing the Trail Versus Trailing the Group: Culture and Perceptions of the Leader's Position," *Organizational Behavior and Human Decision Processes* 113, no. 1 (2010), pp. 51–61.

61. D. M. Rousseau, S. B. Sitkin, R. S. Burt, and C. Camerer, "Not So Different After All: A Cross-discipline View of Trust," *Academy of Management Review* (July 1998), pp. 393–404; and J. A. Simpson, "Psychological Foundations of Trust," *Current Directions in Psychological Science* 16, no. 5 (2007), pp. 264–268.

62. See, for instance, K. T. Dirks and D. L. Ferrin, "Trust in Leadership: Meta-analytic Findings and Implications for Research and Practice," *Journal of Applied Psychology* 87, no. 4, (2002), pp. 611–628; D. I. Jung and B. J. Avolio, "Opening the Black Box: An Experimental Investigation of the Mediating Effects of Trust and Value Congruence on Transformational and Transactional Leadership," *Journal of Organizational Behavior* (December 2000), pp. 949–964; and A. Zacharatos, J. Barling, and R. D. Iverson, "High-Performance Work Systems and Occupational Safety," *Journal of Applied Psychology* (January 2005), pp. 77–93.

63. R. Mayer, J. Davies, and F. Schoorman, "An Integrative Model of Organizational Trust," *Academy of Management* 20, no. 3 (1995), pp. 709–734.

64. Based on L. T. Hosmer, "Trust: The Connecting Link Between Organizational Theory and Philosophical Ethics," *Academy of Management Review* (April 1995), p. 393; R. C. Mayer, J. H. Davis, and F. D. Schoorman, "An Integrative Model of Organizational Trust," *Academy of Management Review* (July 1995), pp. 709–734; and F. D. Schoorman, R. C. Mayer, and J. H. Davis, "An Integrative Model of Organizational Trust: Past, Present, and Future," *Academy of Management Review* 32, no. 2 (2007), pp. 344–354.

65. J. Schaubroeck, S. S. K. Lam, and A. C. Peng, "Cognition-Based and Affect-Based Trust as Mediators of Leader Behavior Influences on Team Performance." *Journal of Applied Psychology* 96, no. 4 (July 2011), pp. 863–871.

66. J. R. Detert and E. R. Burris, "Leadership Behavior and Employee Voice: Is the Door Really Open?" *Academy of Management Journal* 50, no. 4 (2007), pp. 869–884.

67. J. A. Colquitt, B. A. Scott, and J. A. LePine, "Trust, Trustworthiness, and Trust Propensity: A Meta-analytic Test of Their Unique Relationships with Risk Taking and Job Performance," *Journal of Applied Psychology* 92, no. 4 (2007), pp. 909–927.

68. See, for example, M. Murray, *Beyond the Myths and Magic of Mentoring: How to Facilitate an Effective Mentoring Process*, rev. ed. (New York: Wiley, 2001); K. E. Kram, "Phases of the Mentor Relationship," *Academy of Management Journal* (December 1983), pp. 608–625; R. A. Noe, "An Investigation of the Determinants of Successful Assigned Mentoring Relationships," *Personnel Psychology* (Fall 1988), pp. 559–580; and L. Eby, M. Buits, and A. Lockwood, "Protégés' Negative Mentoring Experiences: Construct Development and Nomological Validation," *Personnel Psychology* (Summer 2004), pp. 411–447.

69. B. R. Ragins and J. L. Cotton, "Easier Said Than Done: Gender Differences in Perceived Barriers to Gaining a Mentor," *Academy of Management Journal* 34, no. 4 (1993), pp. 939–951; C. R. Wanberg, E. T. Welsh, and S. A. Hezlett, "Mentoring Research: A Review and Dynamic Process Model," in G. R. Ferris and J. J. Martocchio (eds.), *Research in Personnel and Human Resources Management* 22 (Greenwich, CT: Elsevier Science, 2003), pp. 39–124; and T. D. Allen, "Protégé Selection by Mentors: Contributing Individual and Organizational Factors," *Journal of Vocational Behavior* 65, no. 3 (2004), pp. 469–483.

70. See, for example, K. E. Kram and D. T. Hall, "Mentoring in a Context of Diversity and Turbulence," in E. E. Kossek and S. A. Lobel (eds.), *Managing Diversity* (Cambridge, MA: Blackwell, 1996), pp. 108–136; B. R. Ragins and J. L. Cotton, "Mentor Functions and Outcomes: A Comparison of Men and Women in Formal and Informal Mentoring Relationships," *Journal of Applied Psychology* (August 1999), pp. 529–550; and D. B. Turban, T. W. Dougherty, and F. K. Lee, "Gender, Race, and Perceived Similarity Effects in Developmental Relationships: The Moderating Role of Relationship Duration," *Journal of Vocational Behavior* (October 2002), pp. 240–262.

71. J. U. Chun, J. J. Sosik, and N. Y. Yun, "A Longitudinal Study of Mentor and Protégé Outcomes in Formal Mentoring Relationships," *Journal of Organizational Behavior* (November 12, 2012), pp. 35–49.

72. Manitoba Hydro press release, November 19, 2013, accessed July 12, 2015 at https://www.hydro.mb.ca/corporate/news_media/in_the_news/higher_aboriginal_representation.shtml.

73. Ragins and Cotton, "Mentor Functions and Outcomes"; and C. M. Underhill, "The Effectiveness of Mentoring Programs in Corporate Settings: A Meta-analytical Review of the Literature," *Journal of Vocational Behavior* 68, no. 2 (2006), pp. 292–307.

74. T. D. Allen, E. T. Eby, and E. Lentz, "The Relationship Between Formal Mentoring Program Characteristics and Perceived Program Effectiveness," *Personnel Psychology* 59 (2006), pp. 125–153; T. D. Allen, L. T. Eby, and E. Lentz, "Mentorship Behaviors and Mentorship Quality Associated with Formal Mentoring Programs: Closing the Gap Between Research and Practice," *Journal of Applied Psychology* 91, no. 3 (2006), pp. 567–578; and M. R. Parise and M. L. Forret, "Formal Mentoring Programs: The Relationship of Program Design and Support to Mentors' Perceptions of Benefits and Costs," *Journal of Vocational Behavior* 72, no. 2 (2008), pp. 225–240.

75. L. T. Eby and A. Lockwood, "Protégés' and Mentors' Reactions to Participating in Formal Mentoring Programs: A Qualitative Investigation," *Journal of Vocational Behavior* 67, no. 3 (2005), pp. 441–458; G. T. Chao, "Formal Mentoring: Lessons Learned from Past Practice," *Professional Psychology: Research and Practice* 40, no. 3 (2009), pp. 314–320; and C. R. Wanberg, J. D. Kammeyer-Mueller, and M. Marchese, "Mentor and Protégé Predictors and Outcomes of Mentoring in a Formal Mentoring Program," *Journal of Vocational Behavior* 69 (2006), pp. 410–423.

76. M. K. Feeney and B. Bozeman, "Mentoring and Network Ties," *Human Relations* 61, no. 12 (2008), pp. 1651–1676; N. Bozionelos, "Intra-organizational Network Resources: How They Relate to Career Success and Organizational Commitment," *Personnel Review* 37, no. 3 (2008), pp. 249–263; and S. A. Hezlett and S. K. Gibson, "Linking Mentoring and Social Capital: Implications for Career and Organization Development," *Advances in Developing Human Resources* 9, no. 3 (2007), pp. 384–412.

77. Comment by Jim Collins, cited in J. Useem, "Conquering Vertical Limits," *Fortune* (February 19, 2001), p. 94.

78. See, for instance, J. R. Meindl, "The Romance of Leadership as a Follower-Centric Theory: A Social Constructionist Approach," *Leadership Quarterly* (Fall 1995), pp. 329–341; and B. Schyns, J. Felfe, and H. Blank, "Is Charisma Hyper-Romanticism? Empirical Evidence from New Data and a Meta-analysis," *Applied Psychology: An International Review* 56, no. 4 (2007), pp. 505–527.

79. M. J. Martinko, P. Harvey, D. Sikora, and S. C. Douglas, "Perceptions of Abusive Supervision: The Role of Subordinates' Attribution Styles," *Leadership Quarterly* (August 2011), pp. 751–764.

80. J. R. Meindl, S. B. Ehrlich, and J. M. Dukerich, "The Romance of Leadership," *Administrative Science Quarterly* (March 1985), pp. 78–102; and M. C. Bligh, J. C. Kohles, C. L. Pearce, J. E. Justin, and J. F. Stovall, "When the Romance Is Over: Follower Perspectives of Aversive Leadership," *Applied Psychology: An International Review* 56, no. 4 (2007), pp. 528–557.

81. B. R. Agle, N. J. Nagarajan, J. A. Sonnenfeld, and D. Srinivasan, "Does CEO Charisma Matter?" *Academy of Management Journal* 49, no. 1 (2006), pp. 161–174.

82. M. Van Vugt and B. R. Spisak, "Sex Differences in the Emergence of Leadership During Competitions Within and Between Groups," *Psychological Science* 19, no. 9 (2008), pp. 854–8.

83. R. E. Silverman, "Who's the Boss? There Isn't One," *The Wall Street Journal* (June 20, 2012), pp. B 1, B8.58.

84. S. D. Dionne, F. J. Yammarino, L. E. Atwater, and L. R. James, "Neutralizing Substitutes for Leadership Theory: Leadership Effects and Common-Source Bias," *Journal of Applied Psychology*, 87 (2002), pp. 454–464; and J. R. Villa, J. P. Howell, P. W. Dorfman, and D. L. Daniel, "Problems with Detecting Moderators in Leadership Research Using Moderated Multiple Regression," *Leadership Quarterly* 14 (2002), pp. 3–23.

85. B. M. Bass, "Cognitive, Social, and Emotional Intelligence of Transformational Leaders," in R. E. Riggio, S. E. Murphy, and F. J. Pirozzolo (eds.), *Multiple Intelligences and Leadership* (Mahwah, NJ: Lawrence Erlbaum, 2002), pp. 113–114.

86. See, for instance, P. Dvorak, "M.B.A. Programs Hone 'Soft Skills,'" *The Wall Street Journal* (February 12, 2007), p. B3.

87. D. S. DeRue, J. D. Nahrgang, J. R. Hollenbeck, and K. Workman, "A Quasi-experimental Study of After-Event Reviews and Leadership Development," *Journal of Applied Psychology* 97 (2012), pp. 997–1015.

Chapter 13

1. R. M. Kanter, "Power Failure in Management Circuits," *Harvard Business Review* (July–August 1979), p. 65.

2. Based on B. M. Bass, *Bass & Stogdill's Handbook of Leadership*, 3rd ed. (New York: The Free Press, 1990).

3. M. Gongloff, "Steve Cohen, Super-Rich and Secretive T rader, Faces Possible SEC Investigation," *Huffington Post* (November 28, 2012), accessed May 24, 2013 at http://www.huffingtonpost.com.

4. J. R. P. French Jr. and B. Raven, "The Bases of Social Power," in D. Cartwright (ed.), *Studies in Social Power* (Ann Arbor, MI: University of Michigan, Institute for Social Research, 1959), pp. 150–167; B. H. Raven, "The Bases of Power: Origins and Recent Developments," *Journal of Social Issues* (Winter 1993), pp. 227–251; and G. Yukl, "Use Power Effectively," in E. A. Locke (ed.), *Handbook of Principles of Organizational Behavior* (Malden, MA: Blackwell, 2004), pp. 242–247.

5. E. A. Ward, "Social Power Bases of Managers: Emergence of a New Factor," *Journal of Social Psychology* (February 2001), pp. 144–147.

6. S. R. Giessner and T. W. Schubert, "High in the Hierarchy: How Vertical Location and Judgments of Leaders' Power Are Interrelated," *Organizational Behavior and Human Decision Processes* 104, no. 1 (2007), pp. 30–44.

7. P. M. Podsakoff and C. A. Schriesheim, "Field Studies of French and Raven's Bases of Power: Critique, Reanalysis, and Suggestions for Future Research," *Psychological Bulletin* (May 1985), pp. 387–411; T. R. Hinkin and C. A. Schriesheim, "Development and Application of New Scales to Measure the French and Raven (1959) Bases of Social Power," *Journal of Applied Psychology* (August 1989), pp. 561–567; and P. P. Carson, K. D. Carson, and C. W. Roe, "Social Power Bases: A Meta-analytic Examination of Interrelationships and Outcomes,"

Journal of Applied Social Psychology 23, no. 14 (1993), pp. 1150–1169.

8. See, for example, D. Kipnis and S. M. Schmidt, "Upward-Influence Styles: Relationship with Performance Evaluations, Salary, and Stress," *Administrative Science Quarterly* (December 1988), pp. 528–542; G. Yukl and J. B. Tracey, "Consequences of Influence Tactics Used with Subordinates, Peers, and the Boss," *Journal of Applied Psychology* (August 1992), pp. 525–535; G. Blickle, "Influence Tactics Used by Subordinates: An Empirical Analysis of the Kipnis and Schmidt Subscales," *Psychological Reports* (February 2000), pp. 143–154; and G. Yukl, "Use Power Effectively," pp. 249–252.

9. G. Yukl, *Leadership in Organizations*, 5th ed. (Upper Saddle River, NJ: Prentice Hall, 2002), pp. 141–174; G. R. Ferris, W. A. Hochwarter, C. Douglas, F. R. Blass, R. W. Kolodinsky, and D. C. Treadway, "Social Influence Processes in Organizations and Human Resource Systems," in G. R. Ferris and J. J. Martocchio (eds.), *Research in Personnel and Human Resources Management* 21 (Oxford, UK: JAI Press/Elsevier, 2003), pp. 65–127; and C. A. Higgins, T. A. Judge, and G. R. Ferris, "Influence Tactics and Work Outcomes: A Meta-analysis," *Journal of Organizational Behavior* (March 2003), pp. 89–106.

10. C. M. Falbe and G. Yukl, "Consequences for Managers of Using Single Influence Tactics and Combinations of Tactics," *Academy of Management Journal* (July 1992), pp. 638–653.

11. R. E. Petty and P. Briñol, "Persuasion: From Single to Multiple to Metacognitive Processes," *Perspectives on Psychological Science* 3, no. 2 (2008), pp. 137–147.

12. J. Badal, "Getting a Raise from the Boss," *The Wall Street Journal* (July 8, 2006), pp. B1, B5.

13. Yukl, *Leadership in Organizations*.

14. Ibid.

15. Falbe and Yukl, "Consequences for Managers of Using Single Influence Tactics and Combinations of Tactics."

16. A. W. Kruglanski, A. Pierro, and E. T. Higgins, "Regulatory Mode and Preferred Leadership Styles: How Fit Increases Job Satisfaction," *Basic and Applied Social Psychology* 29, no. 2 (2007), pp. 137–149; and A. Pierro, L. Cicero, and B. H. Raven, "Motivated Compliance with Bases of Social Power," *Journal of Applied Social Psychology* 38, no. 7 (2008), pp. 1921–1944.

17. A. Smith, M. Watkins, M. Burke, and M. Christian, "A Gender Role Perspective on the Use and Effectiveness of Influence Tactics," *Journal of Management* 39, no. 5 (2013), pp. 1156–1183.

18. P. P. Fu and G. Yukl, "Perceived Effectiveness of Influence Tactics in the United States and China," *Leadership Quarterly* (Summer 2000), pp. 251–266; O. Branzei, "Cultural Explanations of Individual Preferences for Influence Tactics in Cross-cultural Encounters," *International Journal of Cross Cultural Management* (August 2002), pp. 203–218; G. Yukl, P. P. Fu, and R. McDonald, "Cross-Cultural Differences in Perceived Effectiveness of Influence Tactics for Initiating or Resisting Change," *Applied Psychology: An International Review* (January 2003), pp. 66–82; and P. P. Fu, T. K. Peng, J. C. Kennedy, and G. Yukl, "Examining the Preferences of Influence Tactics in Chinese Societies: A Comparison of Chinese Managers in Hong Kong, Taiwan, and Mainland China," *Organizational Dynamics* 33, no. 1 (2004), pp. 32–46.

19. C. J. Torelli and S. Shavitt, "Culture and Concepts of Power," *Journal of Personality and Social Psychology* 99, no. 4 (2010), pp. 703–723.

20. Fu and Yukl, "Perceived Effectiveness of Influence Tactics in the United States and China."

21. K. Hunter and M. Asari, "Social Influence Tactics and Influence Outcomes: The Role of Leader–Member Exchange and Culture," http://people.uleth.ca/~mahfooz.ansari/SIOP%2013-Influence-LMX.pdf.

22. G. R. Ferris, D. C. Treadway, P. L. Perrewé, R. L. Brouer, C. Douglas, and S. Lux, "Political Skill in Organizations," *Journal of Management* (June 2007), pp. 290–320; K. J. Harris, K. M. Kacmar, S. Zivnuska, and J. D. Shaw, "The Impact of Political Skill on Impression Management Effectiveness," *Journal of Applied Psychology* 92, no. 1 (2007), pp. 278–285; W. A. Hochwarter, G. R. Ferris, M. B. Gavin, P. L. Perrewé, A. T. Hall, and D. D. Frink, "Political Skill as Neutralizer of Felt Accountability–Job Tension Effects on Job Performance Ratings: A Longitudinal Investigation," *Organizational Behavior and Human Decision Processes* 102 (2007), pp. 226–239; and D. C. Treadway, G. R. Ferris, A. B. Duke, G. L. Adams, and J. B. Tatcher, "The Moderating Role of Subordinate Political Skill on Supervisors' Impressions of Subordinate Ingratiation and Ratings of Subordinate Interpersonal Facilitation," *Journal of Applied Psychology* 92, no. 3 (2007), pp. 848–855.

23. M. C. Andrews, K. M. Kacmar, and K. J. Harris, "Got Political Skill? The Impact of Justice on the Importance of Political Skills for Job Performance." *Journal of Applied Psychology* 94, no. 6 (2009), pp. 1427–1437.

24. C. Anderson, S. E. Spataro, and F. J. Flynn, "Personality and Organizational Culture as Determinants of Influence," *Journal of Applied Psychology* 93, no. 3 (2008), pp. 702–710.

25. Y. Cho and N. J. Fast, "Power, Defensive Denigration, and the Assuaging Effect of Gratitude Expression," *Journal of Experimental Social Psychology* 48, 2012, pp. 778–782.

26. M. Pitesa and S. Thau, "Masters of the Universe: How Power and Accountability Influence Self-Serving Decisions Under Moral Hazard," *Journal of Applied Psychology* 98 (2013), pp. 550–558; and N. J. Fast, N. Sivanathan, D. D. Mayer, and A. D. Galinsky, "Power and Overconfident Decision-Making," *Organizational Behavior and Human Decision Processes* 117, 2012, pp. 249–260.

27. A. Grant, "Yes, Power Corrupts, but Power Also Reveals," *Government Executive* (May 23, 2013), accessed May 23, 2013 at http://www.govexec.com.

28. J. K. Maner, M. T. Gaillot, A. J. Menzel, and J. W. Kunstman, "Dispositional Anxiety Blocks the Psychological Effects of Power," *Personality and Social Psychology Bulletin* 38 (2012), pp. 1383–1395.

29. N. J. Fast, N. Halevy, and A. D. Galinsky, "The Destructive Nature of Power Without Status," *Journal of Experimental Social Psychology* 48 (2012), pp. 391–394.

30. T. Seppälä, J. Lipponen, A. Bardi, and A. Pirttilä-Backman, "Change-Oriented Organizational Citizenship Behaviour: An Interactive Product of Openness to Change Values, Work Unit Identification, and Sense of Power," *Journal of Occupational and Organizational Psychology* 85 (2012), pp. 136–155.

31. K. A. DeCelles, D. S. DeRue, J. D. Margolis, and T. L. Ceranic, "Does Power Corrupt or Enable? When and Why Power Facilitates Self-Interested Behavior," *Journal of Applied Psychology* 97 (2012), pp. 681–689.

32. H. Mintzberg, *Power In and Around Organizations* (Upper Saddle River, NJ: Prentice Hall, 1983), p. 26. See also K. M. Kacmar and R. A. Baron, "Organizational Politics: The State of the Field, Links to Related Processes, and an Agenda for Future Research," in G. R. Ferris (ed.), *Research in Personnel and Human Resources Management* 17 (Greenwich, CT: JAI Press, 1999), pp. 1–39; and G. R. Ferris, D. C. Treadway, R. W. Kolokinsky, W. A. Hochwarter, C. J. Kacmar, and D. D. Frink, "Development and Validation of the Political Skill Inventory," *Journal of Management* (February 2005), pp. 126–152.

33. S. B. Bacharach and E. J. Lawler, "Political Alignments in Organizations," in R. M. Kramer and M. A. Neale (eds.), *Power and Influence in Organizations* (Thousand Oaks, CA: Sage, 1998), pp. 68–69.

34. A. Drory and T. Romm, "The Definition of Organizational Politics: A Review," *Human Relations* (November 1990), pp. 1133–1154; and R. S. Cropanzano, K. M. Kacmar, and D. P. Bozeman, "Organizational Politics, Justice, and Support: Their Differences and Similarities," in R. Cropanzano and K. M. Kacmar (eds.), *Organizational Politics, Justice and Support: Managing Social Climate at Work* (Westport, CT: Quorum Books, 1995), pp. 1–18; and G. R. Ferris and W. A. Hochwarter, "Organizational Politics," in S. Zedeck (ed.), *APA Handbook of Industrial and Organizational Psychology* 3 (Washington, DC: American Psychological Association, 2011), pp. 435–459.

35. D. A. Buchanan, "You Stab My Back, I'll Stab Yours: Management Experience and Perceptions of Organization Political Behavior," *British Journal of Management* 19, no. 1 (2008), pp. 49–64.

36. J. Pfeffer, *Power: Why Some People Have It—And Others Don't* (New York: Harper Collins, 2010).

37. Drory and Romm, "The Definition of Organizational Politics."

38. S. M. Rioux and L. A. Penner, "The Causes of Organizational Citizenship Behavior: A Motivational Analysis," *Journal of Applied Psychology* (December 2001), pp. 1306–1314; M. A. Finkelstein and L. A. Penner, "Predicting Organizational Citizenship Behavior: Integrating the Functional and Role Identity Approaches," *Social Behavior & Personality* 32, no. 4 (2004), pp. 383–398; and J. Schwarzwald, M. Koslowsky, and M. Allouf, "Group Membership, Status, and Social Power Preference," *Journal of Applied Social Psychology* 35, no. 3 (2005), pp. 644–665.

39. See, for example, G. R. Ferris, G. S. Russ, and P. M. Fandt, "Politics in Organizations," in R. A. Giacalone and P. Rosenfeld (eds.), *Impression Management in the Organization* (Hillsdale, NJ: Lawrence Erlbaum, 1989), pp. 155–156; and W. E. O'Connor and T. G. Morrison, "A Comparison of Situational and Dispositional Predictors of Perceptions of Organizational Politics," *Journal of Psychology* (May 2001), pp. 301–312.

40. D. Farrell and J. C. Petersen, "Patterns of Political Behavior in Organizations," *Academy of Management Review* 7, no. 3 (1982), pp. 403–412.

41. G. R. Ferris and K. M. Kacmar, "Perceptions of Organizational Politics," *Journal of Management* (March 1992), pp. 93–116.

42. See, for example, P. M. Fandt and G. R. Ferris, "The Management of Information and Impressions: When Employees Behave Opportunistically," *Organizational Behavior and Human Decision Processes* (February 1990), pp. 140–158; Ferris, Russ, and Fandt, "Politics in Organizations," p. 147; and J. M. L. Poon, "Situational Antecedents and Outcomes of Organizational Politics Perceptions," *Journal of Managerial Psychology* 18, no. 2 (2003), pp. 138–155.

43. Ferris and Hochwarter, "Organizational Politics."

44. W. A. Hochwarter, C. Kiewitz, S. L. Castro, P. L. Perrewe, and G. R. Ferris, "Positive Affectivity and Collective Efficacy as Moderators of the Relationship Between Perceived Politics and Job Satisfaction," *Journal of Applied Social Psychology* (May 2003), pp. 1009–1035; and C. C. Rosen, P. E. Levy, and R. J. Hall, "Placing Perceptions of Politics in the Context of Feedback Environment, Employee Attitudes, and Job Performance," *Journal of Applied Psychology* 91, no. 1 (2006), pp. 211–230.

45. G. R. Ferris, D. D. Frink, M. C. Galang, J. Zhou, K. M. Kacmar, and J. L. Howard, "Perceptions of Organizational Politics: Prediction, Stress-Related Implications, and Outcomes," *Human Relations* (February 1996), pp. 233–266; and E. Vigoda, "Stress-Related Aftermaths to Workplace Politics: The Relationships Among Politics, Job Distress, and Aggressive Behavior in Organizations," *Journal of Organizational Behavior* (August 2002), pp. 571–591.

46. S. Aryee, Z. Chen, and P. S. Budhwar, "Exchange Fairness and Employee Performance: An Examination of the Relationship Between Organizational Politics and Procedural Justice," *Organizational Behavior & Human Decision Processes* (May 2004), pp. 1–14; and K. M. Kacmar, D. P. Bozeman, D. S. Carlson, and W. P. Anthony, "An Examination of the Perceptions of Organizational Politics Model," *Human Relations* 52, no. 3 (1999), pp. 383–416.

47. C. Kiewitz, W. A. Hochwarter, G. R. Ferris, and S. L. Castro, "The Role of Psychological Climate in Neutralizing the Effects of Organizational Politics on Work Outcomes," *Journal of Applied Social Psychology* (June 2002), pp. 1189–1207; and M. C. Andrews, L. A. Witt, and K. M. Kacmar, "The Interactive Effects of Organizational Politics and Exchange Ideology on Manager Ratings of Retention," *Journal of Vocational Behavior* (April 2003), pp. 357–369.

48. Kacmar, Bozeman, Carlson, and Anthony, "An Examination of the Perceptions of Organizational Politics Model," p. 389.

49. Ibid., p. 409.

50. K. M. Kacmar, D. G. Bachrach, K. J. Harris, and S. Zivnuska, "Fostering Good Citizenship Through Ethical Leadership: Exploring the Moderating Role of Gender and Organizational Politics," *Journal of Applied Psychology* 96 (2011), pp. 633–642.

51. B. E. Ashforth and R. T. Lee, "Defensive Behavior in Organizations: A Preliminary Model," *Human Relations* (July 1990), pp. 621–648.

52. M. Valle and P. L. Perrewe, "Do Politics Perceptions Relate to Political Behaviors? Tests of an Implicit Assumption and Expanded Model," *Human Relations* (March 2000), pp. 359–386.

53. See, for instance, W. L. Gardner and M. J. Martinko, "Impression Management in Organizations," *Journal of Management* (June 1988), pp. 321–338; M. C. Bolino and W. H. Turnley, "More Than One Way to Make an Impression: Exploring Profiles of Impression Management," *Journal of Management* 29, no. 2 (2003), pp. 141–160; S. Zivnuska, K. M. Kacmar, L. A. Witt, D. S. Carlson, and V. K. Bratton, "Interactive Effects of Impression Management and Organizational Politics on Job Performance," *Journal of Organizational Behavior* (August 2004), pp. 627–640; and M. C. Bolino, K. M. Kacmar, W. H. Turnley, and J. B. Gilstrap, "A Multi-level Review of Impression Management Motives and Behaviors," *Journal of Management* 34, no. 6 (2008), pp. 1080–1109.

54. M. Snyder and J. Copeland, "Self-Monitoring Processes in Organizational Settings," in R. A. Giacalone and P. Rosenfeld (eds.), *Impression Management in the Organization* (Hillsdale, NJ: Lawrence Erlbaum, 1989), p. 11; Bolino and Turnley, "More Than One Way to Make an Impression"; and W. H. Turnley and M. C. Bolino, "Achieved Desired Images While Avoiding Undesired Images: Exploring the Role of Self-Monitoring in Impression Management," *Journal of Applied Psychology* (April 2001), pp. 351–360.

55. M. R. Leary and R. M. Kowalski, "Impression Management: A Literature Review and Two-Component Model." *Psychological Bulletin* (January 1990), pp. 34–47.

56. J. Ham and R. Vonk, "Impressions of Impression Management: Evidence of Spontaneous Suspicion of Ulterior Motivation," *Journal of Experimental Social Psychology* 47, no. 2 (2011), pp. 466–471; and W. M. Bowler, J. R. B. Halbesleben, and J. R. B. Paul, "If You're Close with the Leader, You Must Be a Brownnose: The Role of Leader–Member Relationships in Follower, Leader, and Coworker Attributions of Organizational Citizenship Behavior Motives," *Human Resource Management Review* 20, no. 4 (2010), pp. 309–316.

57. C. Lebherz, K. Jonas, and B. Tomljenovic, "Are We Known by the Company We Keep? Effects of Name Dropping on First Impressions," *Social Influence* 4, no. 1 (2009), pp. 62–79.

58. J. R. B. Halbesleben, W. M. Bowler, M. C. Bolino, and W. H Turnley, "Organizational Concern, Prosocial Values, or Impression Management? How Supervisors Attribute Motives to Organizational Citizenship Behavior," *Journal of Applied Social Psychology* 40, no. 6 (2010), pp. 1450–1489.

59. C. K. Stevens and A. L. Kristof, "Making the Right Impression: A Field Study of Applicant Impression Management During Job Interviews," *Journal of Applied Psychology* 80 (1995), pp. 587–606; L. A. McFarland, A. M. Ryan, and S. D. Kriska, "Impression Management Use and Effectiveness Across Assessment Methods," *Journal of Management* 29, no. 5 (2003), pp. 641–661; C. A. Higgins and T. A. Judge, "The Effect of Applicant Influence Tactics on Recruiter Perceptions of Fit and Hiring Recommendations: A Field Study," *Journal of Applied Psychology* 89, no. 4 (2004), pp. 622–632; and W. C. Tsai, C.-C. Chen, and S. F. Chiu, "Exploring Boundaries of the Effects of Applicant Impression Management Tactics in Job Interviews," *Journal of Management* (February 2005), pp. 108–125.

60. D. C. Gilmore and G. R. Ferris, "The Effects of Applicant Impression Management Tactics on Interviewer Judgments," *Journal of Management* 15, no. 4 (1989), pp. 557–564.

61. Stevens and Kristof, "Making the Right Impression."

62. C. A. Higgins, T. A. Judge, and G. R. Ferris, "Influence Tactics and Work Outcomes: A Meta-analysis," *Journal of Organizational Behavior* (March 2003), pp. 89–106.

63. Ibid.

64. K. J. Harris, K. M. Kacmar, S. Zivnuska, and J. D. Shaw, "The Impact of Political Skill on Impression Management Effectiveness," *Journal of Applied Psychology* 92, no. 1 (2007), pp. 278–285; and D. C. Treadway, G. R. Ferris, A. B. Duke, G. L. Adams, and J. B. Thatcher, "The Moderating Role of Subordinate Political Skill on Supervisors' Impressions of Subordinate Ingratiation and Ratings of Subordinate Interpersonal Facilitation," *Journal of Applied Psychology* 92, no. 3 (2007), pp. 848–855.

65. L. Rutman, "Self-Promotion as a Risk Factor for Women: The Costs and Benefits of Counterstereotypical Impression," *Management Journal of Personality and Social Psychology* 74, no. 3 (1998), pp. 629–645.

66. See T. Romm and A. Drory, "Political Behavior in Organizations: A Cross-cultural Comparison," *International Journal of Value Based Management* 1 (1988), pp. 97–113; and E. Vigoda, "Reactions to Organizational Politics: A Cross-cultural Examination in Israel and Britain," *Human Relations* (November 2001), pp. 1483–1518.

67. J. L. T. Leong, M. H. Bond, and P. P. Fu, "Perceived Effectiveness of Influence Strategies in the United States and Three Chinese Societies," *International Journal of Cross Cultural Management* (May 2006), pp. 101–120.

68. Y. Miyamoto and B. Wilken, "Culturally Contingent Situated Cognition: Influencing Other People Fosters Analytic Perception in the United States but Not in Japan," *Psychological Science* 21, no. 11 (2010), pp. 1616–1622.

69. Vigoda, "Reactions to Organizational Politics," p. 1512.

70. Ibid., p. 1510.

71. D. Clark, "A Campaign Strategy for Your Career," *Harvard Business Review* (November 2012), pp. 131–134.

Chapter 14

1. See, for instance, D. Tjosvold, "Defining Conflict and Making Choices About Its Management: Lighting the Dark Side of Organizational Life," *International Journal of Conflict Management* 17, no. 2 (2006), pp. 87–95; and M. A. Korsgaard, S. S. Jeong, D. M. Mahony, and A. H. Pitariu, "A Multilevel View of Intragroup Conflict," *Journal of Management* 34, no. 6 (2008), pp. 1222–1252.

2. K. W. Thomas, "Conflict and Negotiation Processes in Organizations," in M. D. Dunnette and L. M. Hough (eds.), *Handbook of Industrial and Organizational Psychology*, 2nd ed., vol. 3 (Palo Alto, CA: Consulting Psychologists Press, 1992), pp. 651–717.

3. For a comprehensive review of the interactionist approach, see C. K. W. De Dreu and E. Van de Vliert (eds.), *Using Conflict in Organizations* (London: Sage, 1997).

4. J. Yang and K. W. Mossholder, "Decoupling Task and Relationship Conflict: The Role of Intragroup Emotional Processing," *Journal of Organizational Behavior* 25, no. 5 (August 2004), pp. 589–605; and N. Gamero, V. González-Romá, and J. M. Peiró, "The Influence of Intra-team Conflict on Work Teams' Affective Climate: A Longitudinal Study," *Journal of Occupational and Organizational Psychology* 81, no. 1 (2008), pp. 47–69.

5. N. Halevy, E. Y. Chou, and A. D. Galinsky, "Exhausting or Exhilarating? Conflict as Threat to Interests, Relationships and Identities," *Journal of Experimental Social Psychology* 48 (2012), pp. 530–537.

6. F. R. C. de Wit, L. L. Greer, and K. A. Jehn, "The Paradox of Intragroup Conflict: A Meta-analysis," *Journal of Applied Psychology* 97 (2012), pp. 360–390.

7. J. Farh, C. Lee, and C. I. C. Farh, "Task Conflict and Team Creativity: A Question of How Much and When," *Journal of Applied Psychology* 95, no. 6 (2010), pp. 1173–1180.

8. B. H. Bradley, A. C. Klotz, B. F. Postlethwaite, and K. G. Brown, "Ready to Rumble: How Team Personality Composition and Task Conflict Interact to Improve Performance," *Journal of Applied Psychology* 98 (2013), pp. 385–392.

9. B. H. Bradley, B. F. Postlethwaite, A. C. Klotz, M. R. Hamdani, and K. G. Brown, "Reaping the Benefits of Task Conflict in Teams: The Critical Role of Team Psychological Safety Climate," *Journal of Applied Psychology* 97 (2012), pp. 151–158.

10. G. A. Van Kleef, W. Steinel, and A. C. Homan, "On Being Peripheral and Paying Attention: Prototypicality and Information Processing in Intergroup Conflict," *Journal of Applied Psychology* 98 (2013), pp. 63–79.

11. S. Benard, "Cohesion from Conflict: Does Intergroup Conflict Motivate Intragroup Norm Enforcement and Support for Centralized Leadership?" *Social Psychology Quarterly* 75 (2012), pp. 107–130.

12. R. S. Peterson and K. J. Behfar, "The Dynamic Relationship Between Performance Feedback, Trust, and Conflict in Groups: A Longitudinal Study," *Organizational Behavior & Human Decision Processes* (September–November 2003), pp. 102–112.

13. T. M. Glomb and H. Liao, "Interpersonal Aggression in Work Groups: Social Influence, Reciprocal, and Individual Effects," *Academy of Management Journal* 46, no. 4 (2003), pp. 486–496; and V. Venkataramani and R. S. Dalal, "Who Helps and Harms Whom? Relational Aspects of Interpersonal Helping and Harming in Organizations," *Journal of Applied Psychology* 92, no. 4 (2007), pp. 952–966.

14. R. Friedman, C. Anderson, J. Brett, M. Olekalns, N. Goates, and C. C. Lisco, "The Positive and Negative Effects of Anger on Dispute Resolution: Evidence from Electronically Mediated Disputes," *Journal of Applied Psychology* (April 2004), pp. 369–376.

15. L. R. Pondy, "Organizational Conflict: Concepts and Models," *Administrative Science Quarterly* (September 1967), p. 302.

16. See, for instance, J. R. Curhan, "What Do People Value When They Negotiate? Mapping the Domain of Subjective Value in Negotiation," *Journal of Personality and Social Psychology* (September 2006), pp. 117–126; R. L. Pinkley, "Dimensions of Conflict Frame: Disputant Interpretations of Conflict," *Journal of Applied Psychology* (April 1990), pp. 117–126; and R. L. Pinkley

and G. B. Northcraft, "Conflict Frames of Reference: Implications for Dispute Processes and Outcomes," *Academy of Management Journal* (February 1994), pp. 193–205.

17. A. M. Isen, A. A. Labroo, and P. Durlach, "An Influence of Product and Brand Name on Positive Affect: Implicit and Explicit Measures," *Motivation & Emotion* (March 2004), pp. 43–63.

18. Ibid.

19. P. J. D. Carnevale and A. M. Isen, "The Influence of Positive Affect and Visual Access on the Discovery of Integrative Solutions in Bilateral Negotiations," *Organizational Behavior and Human Decision Processes* (February 1986), pp. 1–13; and C. Montes, D. Rodriguez, and G. Serrano, "Affective Choice of Conflict Management Styles," *International Journal of Conflict Management* 23 (2012), pp. 6–18.

20. Thomas, "Conflict and Negotiation Processes in Organizations."

21. Ibid.

22. K. Thomas, G. Thomas, Conflict "Styles of Men and Women at Six Organizational Levels," *International Journal of Conflict Management* 14, no. 2 (2008), accessed August 9, 2015 at https://www.cpp.com/pdfs/TKI_Article_On_Conflict_Styles.pdf.

23. Thomas, "Conflict and Negotiation Processes in Organizations."

24. B. A. Nijstad and S. C. Kaps, "Taking the Easy Way Out: Preference Diversity, Decision Strategies, and Decision Refusal in Groups," *Journal of Personality and Social Psychology* 94, no. 5 (2008), pp. 860–870.

25. M. E. Zellmer-Bruhn, M. M. Maloney, A. D. Bhappu, and R. Salvador, "When and How Do Differences Matter? An Exploration of Perceived Similarity in Teams," *Organizational Behavior and Human Decision Processes* 107, no. 1 (2008), pp. 41–59.

26. For example, see J. A. Wall Jr. and R. R. Callister, "Conflict and Its Management," *Journal of Management* 21, no. 3 (1995), pp. 523–526 for evidence supporting the argument that conflict is almost uniformly dysfunctional. See also P. J. Hinds and D. E. Bailey, "Out of Sight, Out of Sync: Understanding Conflict in Distributed Teams," *Organization Science* (November–December 2003), pp. 615–632.

27. K. A. Jehn, L. Greer, S. Levine, and G. Szulanski, "The Effects of Conflict Types, Dimensions, and Emergent States on Group Outcomes," *Group Decision and Negotiation* 17, no. 6 (2005), pp. 777–796.

28. Zellmer-Bruhn, Maloney, Bhappu, and Salvador, "When and How Do Differences Matter?"

29. J. Fried, "I Know You Are, But What Am I?" *Inc.* (July/August 2010), pp. 39–40.

30. K. J. Behfar, R. S. Peterson, E. A. Mannix, and W. M. K. Trochim, "The Critical Role of Conflict Resolution in Teams: A Close Look at the Links Between Conflict Type, Conflict Management Strategies, and Team Outcomes," *Journal of Applied Psychology* 93, no. 1 (2008), pp. 170–188; A. G. Tekleab, N. R. Quigley, and P. E. Tesluk, "A Longitudinal Study of Team Conflict, Conflict Management, Cohesion, and Team Effectiveness," *Group and Organization Management* 34, no. 2 (2009), pp. 170–205; and E. Van de Vliert, M. C. Euwema, and S. E. Huismans, "Managing Conflict with a Subordinate or a Superior: Effectiveness of Conglomerated Behavior," *Journal of Applied Psychology* 80 (1995), pp. 271–281.

31. A. Somech, H. S. Desivilya, and H. Lidogoster, "Team Conflict Management and Team Effectiveness: The Effects of Task Interdependence and Team Identification," *Journal of Organizational Behavior* 30, no. 3 (2009), pp. 359–378.

32. H. R. Markus and S. Kitayama, "Culture and the Self: Implications for Cognition, Emotion, and Motivation," *Psychological Review* 98, no. 2 (1991), pp. 224–253; and H. Ren and B. Gray, "Repairing Relationship Conflict: How Violation Types and Culture Influence the Effectiveness of Restoration

Rituals," *Academy of Management Review* 34, no. 1 (2009), pp. 105–126.

33. M. J. Gelfand, M. Higgins, L. H. Nishii, J. L. Raver, A. Dominguez, F. Murakami, S. Yamaguchi, and M. Toyama, "Culture and Egocentric Perceptions of Fairness in Conflict and Negotiation," *Journal of Applied Psychology* (October 2002), pp. 833–845; and Z. Ma, "Chinese Conflict Management Styles and Negotiation Behaviours: An Empirical Test," *International Journal of Cross Cultural Management* (April 2007), pp. 101–119.

34. P. P. Fu, X. H. Yan, Y. Li, E. Wang, and S. Peng, "Examining Conflict-Handling Approaches by Chinese Top Management Teams in IT Firms," *International Journal of Conflict Management* 19, no. 3 (2008), pp. 188–209.

35. M. H. Bazerman, J. R. Curhan, D. A. Moore, and K. L. Valley, "Negotiation," *Annual Review of Psychology* 51 (2000), pp. 279–314.

36. See, for example, D. R. Ames, "Assertiveness Expectancies: How Hard People Push Depends on the Consequences They Predict," *Journal of Personality and Social Psychology* 95, no. 6 (2008), pp. 1541–1557; and J. R. Curhan, H. A. Elfenbein, and H. Xu, "What Do People Value When They Negotiate? Mapping the Domain of Subjective Value in Negotiation," *Journal of Personality and Social Psychology* 91, no. 3 (2006), pp. 493–512.

37. R. Lewicki, D. Saunders, and B. Barry, *Negotiation*, 6th ed. (New York: McGraw-Hill/Irwin, 2009).

38. J. C. Magee, A. D. Galinsky, and D. H. Gruenfeld, "Power, Propensity to Negotiate, and Moving First in Competitive Interactions," *Personality and Social Psychology Bulletin* (February 2007), pp. 200–212.

39. E. Wilson, "The Trouble with Jake," *The New York Times* (July 15, 2009), http://www.nytimes.com.

40. J. R. Curhan, H. A. Elfenbein, and H. Xu, "What Do People Value When They Negotiate? Mapping the Domain of Subjective Value in Negotiation," *Journal of Personality and Social Psychology* 91, no. 3 (2006), pp. 493–512.

41. Thomas, "Conflict and Negotiation Processes in Organizations."

42. P. M. Morgan and R. S. Tindale, "Group vs. Individual Performance in Mixed-Motive Situations: Exploring an Inconsistency," *Organizational Behavior & Human Decision Processes* (January 2002), pp. 44–65.

43. C. E. Naquin, "The Agony of Opportunity in Negotiation: Number of Negotiable Issues, Counterfactual Thinking, and Feelings of Satisfaction," *Organizational Behavior & Human Decision Processes* (May 2003), pp. 97–107.

44. M. Giacomantonio, C. K. W. De Dreu, and L. Mannetti, "Now You See It, Now You Don't: Interests, Issues, and Psychological Distance in Integrative Negotiation," *Journal of Personality and Social Psychology* 98, no. 5 (2010), pp. 761–774.

45. F. S. Ten Velden, B. Beersma, and C. K. W. De Dreu, "It Takes One to Tango: The Effect of Dyads' Epistemic Motivation Composition in Negotiation," *Personality and Social Psychology Bulletin* 36, no. 11 (2010), pp. 1454–1466.

46. C. K. W. De Dreu, L. R. Weingart, and S. Kwon, "Influence of Social Motives on Integrative Negotiation: A Meta-analytic Review and Test of Two Theories," *Journal of Personality & Social Psychology* (May 2000), pp. 889–905.

47. This model is based on R. J. Lewicki, "Bargaining and Negotiation," *Exchange: The Organizational Behavior Teaching Journal* 6, no. 2 (1981), pp. 39–40.

48. J. R. Curhan, H. A. Elfenbein, and G. J. Kilduff, "Getting Off on the Right Foot: Subjective Value Versus Economic Value in Predicting Longitudinal Job Outcomes from Job Offer Negotiations," *Journal of Applied Psychology* 94, no. 2 (2009), pp. 524–534.

49. M. H. Bazerman and M. A. Neale, *Negotiating Rationally* (New York: The Free Press, 1992), pp. 67–68.

50. R. P. Larrick and G. Wu, "Claiming a Large Slice of a Small Pie: Asymmetric Disconfirmation in Negotiation," *Journal of Personality and Social Psychology* 93, no. 2 (2007), pp. 212–233.

51. T. A. Judge, B. A. Livingston, and C. Hurst, "Do Nice Guys—and Gals—Really Finish Last? The Joint Effects of Sex and Agreeableness on Income," *Journal of Personality and Social Psychology* 102 (2012), pp. 390–407.

52. G. Lelieveld, E. Van Dijk, I. Van Beest, and G. A. Van Kleef, "Why Anger and Disappointment Affect Other's Bargaining Behavior Differently: The Moderating Role of Power and the Mediating Role of Reciprocal Complementary Emotions," *Personality and Social Psychology Bulletin* 38 (2012), pp. 1209–1221.

53. S. Côté, I. Hideg, and G. A. Van Kleef, "The Consequences of Faking Anger in Negotiations," *Journal of Experimental Social Psychology* 49 (2013), pp. 453–463.

54. G. A. Van Kleef and C. K. W. De Dreu, "Longer-Term Consequences of Anger Expression in Negotiation: Retaliation or Spillover?" *Journal of Experimental Social Psychology* 46, no. 5 (2010), pp. 753–760.

55. H. Adam and A. Shirako, "Not All Anger Is Created Equal: The Impact of the Expresser's Culture on the Social Effects of Anger in Negotiations," *Journal of Applied Psychology* (2013).

56. Lelieveld, Van Dijk, Van Beest, and Van Kleef, "Why Anger and Disappointment Affect Other's Bargaining Behavior Differently."

57. M. Olekalns and P. L Smith, "Mutually Dependent: Power, Trust, Affect, and the Use of Deception in Negotiation," *Journal of Business Ethics* 85, no. 3 (2009), pp. 347–365.

58. A. W. Brooks and M. E. Schweitzer, "Can Nervous Nellie Negotiate? How Anxiety Causes Negotiators to Make Low First Offers, Exit Early, and Earn Less Profit," *Organizational Behavior and Human Decision Processes* 115, no. 1 (2011), pp. 43–54.

59. M. Sinaceur, H. Adam, G. A. Van Kleef, and A. D. Galinsky, "The Advantages of Being Unpredictable: How Emotional Inconsistency Extracts Concessions in Negotiation," *Journal of Experimental Social Psychology* 49 (2013), pp. 498–508.

60. K. Leary, J. Pillemer, and M. Wheeler, "Negotiating with Emotion," *Harvard Business Review* (January–February 2013), pp. 96–103.

61. L. A. Liu, R. Friedman, B. Barry, M. J. Gelfand, and Z. Zhang, "The Dynamics of Consensus Building in Intracultural and Intercultural Negotiations," *Administrative Science Quarterly* 57 (2012), pp. 269–304.

62. G. H. Hofstede, G. J. Hofstede, and M. Minkov, *Cultures and Organizations: Software of the Mind*, 2nd ed. (New York: McGraw-Hill, 2010).

63. M. Liu, "The Intrapersonal and Interpersonal Effects of Anger on Negotiation Strategies: A Cross-Cultural Investigation," *Human Communication Research* 35, no. 1 (2009), pp. 148–169; and H. Adam, A. Shirako, and W. W. Maddux, "Cultural Variance in the Interpersonal Effects of Anger in Negotiations," *Psychological Science* 21, no. 6 (2010), pp. 882–889.

64. L. Katz, *Negotiating International Business: The Negotiator's Reference Guide to 50 Countries Around the World*, 2006, ISBN: 978-1419631900.

65. P. D. Trapnell and D. L. Paulhus, "Agentic and Communal Values: Their Scope and Measurement," *Journal of Personality Assessment* 94 (2012), pp. 39–52.

66. C. T. Kulik and M. Olekalns, "Negotiating the Gender Divide: Lessons from the Negotiation and Organizational Behavior Literatures," *Journal of Management* 38 (2012), pp. 1387–1415.

67. C. Suddath, "The Art of Haggling," *Bloomberg Businessweek* (November 26, 2012), p. 98.

68. D. A. Small, M. Gelfand, L. Babcock, and H. Gettman, "Who Goes to the Bargaining Table? The Influence of Gender and Framing on the Initiation of Negotiation," *Journal of Personality and Social Psychology* 93, no. 4 (2007), pp. 600–613.

69. E. T. Amanatullah and M. W. Morris, "Negotiating Gender Roles: Gender Differences in Assertive Negotiating Are Mediated by Women's Fear of Backlash and Attenuated When Negotiating on Behalf of Others," *Journal of Personality and Social Psychology* 98, no. 2 (2010), pp. 256–267.

Chapter 15

1. L. Garicano and Y. Wu, "Knowledge, Communication, and Organizational Capabilities," *Organization Science* (September–October 2012), pp. 1382–1397.

2. See, for instance, R. L. Daft, *Organization Theory and Design*, 10th ed. (Cincinnati, OH: South-Western Publishing, 2010).

3. J. G. Miller, "The Real Women's Issue: Time," *The Wall Street Journal* (March 9–10, 2013), p. C3.

4. State Farm Corporate website, accessed August, 2015 at https://www.statefarm.ca/about-us.

5. See, for instance, J. H. Gittell, "Supervisory Span, Relational Coordination, and Flight Departure Performance: A Reassessment of Postbureaucracy Theory," *Organization Science* (July–August 2001), pp. 468–483.

6. F. A. Csascar, "Organizational Structure as a Determinant of Performance: Evidence from Mutual Funds," *Strategic Management Journal* (June 2013), pp. 611–632.

7. B. Brown and S. D. Anthony, "How P&G Tripled Its Innovation Success Rate," *Harvard Business Review* (June 2011), pp. 64–72.

8. A. Leiponen and C. E. Helfat, "Location, Decentralization, and Knowledge Sources for Innovation," *Organization Science* 22, no. 3 (2011), pp. 641–658.

9. P. Hempel, Z.-X. Zhang, and Y. Han, "Team Empowerment and the Organizational Context: Decentralization and the Contrasting Effects of Formalization," *Journal of Management* (March 2012), pp. 475–501.

10. A. Murray, "Built Not to Last," *The Wall Street Journal* (March 18, 2013), p. A11.

11. L. R. Burns and D. R. Wholey, "Adoption and Abandonment of Matrix Management Programs: Effects of Organizational Characteristics and Interorganizational Networks," *Academy of Management Journal* (February 1993), pp. 106–138; J. R. Galbraith, *Designing Matrix Organizations That Actually Work: How IBM, Procter & Gamble, and Others Design for Success* (San Francisco: Jossey Bass, 2009); and E. Krell, "Managing the Matrix," *HR Magazine* (April 2011), pp. 69–71.

12. See, for instance, M. Bidwell, "Politics and Firm Boundaries: How Organizational Structure, Group Interests, and Resources Affect Outsourcing," *Organization Science* (November–December 2012), pp. 1622–1642.

13. See, for instance, T. Sy and L. S. D'Annunzio, "Challenges and Strategies of Matrix Organizations: Top-Level and Mid-Level Managers' Perspectives," *Human Resource Planning* 28, no. 1 (2005), pp. 39–48; and T. Sy and S. Cote, "Emotional Intelligence: A Key Ability to Succeed in the Matrix Organization," *Journal of Management Development* 23, no. 5 (2004), pp. 437–455.

14. N. Anand and R. L. Daft, "What Is the Right Organization Design?" *Organizational Dynamics* 36, no. 4 (2007), pp. 329–344.

15. See, for instance, R. E. Miles and C. C. Snow, "The New Network Firm: A Spherical Structure Built on Human Investment Philosophy," *Organizational Dynamics* (Spring 1995), pp. 5–18; D. Pescovitz, "The Company Where Everybody's a Temp," *New York Times Magazine* (June 11, 2000), pp. 94–96; B. Hedberg, G. Dahlgren, J. Hansson, and N. Olve, *Virtual Organizations and Beyond* (New York: Wiley, 2001); N. S. Contractor, S. Wasserman, and K. Faust, "Testing Multitheoretical, Multilevel Hypotheses About Organizational Networks: An Analytic Framework and Empirical Example," *Academy of Management Review* 31, no. 3 (2006) pp. 681–703; and

Y. Shin, "A Person–Environment Fit Model for Virtual Organizations," *Journal of Management* (October 2004), pp. 725–743.

16. J. Bates, "Making Movies and Moving On," *Los Angeles Times* (January 19, 1998), p. A1; and T. Hope, "38 Ways the Film Industry Is Failing Today," *Huffington Post The Blog* (May 10, 2010), accessed May 28, 2014 at http://www.huffingtonpost.com/ted-hope/38-ways-the-film-industry_b_569260.html.

17. D. Dahl, "Want a Job? Let the Bidding Begin," *Inc.* (March 2011), pp. 94–96.

18. M. Smerconish, "The Pulse: Local Help from Newman's Own," *The Inquirer/Daily News* (September 3, 2012), accessed May 28, 2014 at http://articles.philly.com/2012-09-03/news/33549630_1_paul-newman-newman-s-own-foundation-profits-and-royalties.

19. J. Schramm, "At Work in a Virtual World," *HR Magazine* (June 2010), p. 152.

20. C. B. Gibson and J. L. Gibbs, "Unpacking the Concept of Virtuality: The Effects of Geographic Dispersion, Electronic Dependence, Dynamic Structure, and National Diversity on Team Innovation," *Administrative Science Quarterly* 51, no. 3 (2006), pp. 451–495; H. M. Latapie and V. N. Tran, "Subculture Formation, Evolution, and Conflict Between Regional Teams in Virtual Organizations," *The Business Review* (Summer 2007), pp. 189–193; and S. Davenport and U. Daellenbach, "'Belonging' to a Virtual Research Center: Exploring the Influence of Social Capital Formation Processes on Member Identification in a Virtual Organization," *British Journal of Management* 22, no. 1 (2011), pp. 54–76.

21. "GE: Just Your Average Everyday $60 Billion Family Grocery Store," *IndustryWeek* (May 2, 1994), pp. 13–18.

22. General Electric Company annual financials, MarketWatch, *The Wall Street Journal*, accessed May 28, 2014 at http://www.market-watch.com/investing/stock/ge/financials.

23. J. Scheck, L. Moloney, and A. Flynn, "Eni, CNPC Link Up in Mozambique," *The Wall Street Journal* (March 15, 2013), p. B3.

24. See, for example, U. Wassmer, "Alliance Portfolios: A Review and Research Agenda," *Journal of Management* 36, no. 1 (2010), pp. 141–171; A. M. Hess and F. T. Rothaemel, "When Are Assets Complementary? Star Scientists, Strategic Alliances, and Innovation in the Pharmaceutical Industry," *Strategic Management Journal* 32, no. 8 (2011), pp. 895–909; and J. A. Adegbesan and M. J. Higgins, "The Intra-alliance Division of Value Created Through Collaboration," *Strategic Management Journal* 32, no. 2 (2011), pp. 187–211.

25. Z. Yao, Z. Yang, G. Fisher, C. Ma, and E. Fang, "Knowledge Complementarity, Knowledge Absorption Effectiveness, and New Product Performance: The Exploration of International Joint Ventures in China," *International Business Review* (February 2013), pp. 216–227.

26. S. Brearton, "Biggest Layoffs in Canadian History," *Canadian Business* (January 23, 2015), accessed September 2015 at http://www.canadianbusiness.com/lists-and-rankings/the-biggest-layoffs-in-canadian-history.

27. L. Geddes, "Tracking the Layoffs in Alberta's Oil Patch," *Global News* (May 11, 2015), accessed September 2015 at http://globalnews.ca/news/1889598/timeline-tracking-the-layoffs-in-albertas-oilpatch.

28. "Starbucks Reports 13% Rise in Profit," *The New York Times* (January 24, 2013), http://www.nytimes.com/2013/01/25/business/starbucks-earnings-increased-13-in-latest-quarter.html?_r=0.

29. See J. P. Guthrie and D. K. Datta, "Dumb and Dumber: The Impact of Downsizing on Firm Performance as Moderated by Industry Conditions," *Organization Science* 19, no. 1 (2008), pp. 108–123; and K. P. De Meuse, T. J. Bergmann, P. A. Vanderheiden, and C. E. Roraff, "New Evidence Regarding Organizational Downsizing and a Firm's Financial Performance:

A Long-Term Analysis," *Journal of Managerial Issues* 16, no. 2 (2004), pp. 155–177.

30. L. Alpert, "Can Imported CEO Fix Russian Cars?" *The Wall Street Journal* (March 20, 2013), p. B1.

31. See, for example, C. O. Trevor and A. J. Nyberg, "Keeping Your Headcount When All About You Are Losing Theirs: Downsizing, Voluntary Turnover Rates, and the Moderating Role of HR Practices," *Academy of Management Journal* 51, no. 2 (2008), pp. 259–276; T. M. Probst, S. M. Stewart, M. L. Gruys, and B. W. Tierney, "Productivity, Counterproductivity and Creativity: The Ups and Downs of Job Insecurity," *Journal of Occupational and Organizational Psychology* 80, no. 3 (2007), pp. 479–497; and C. P. Maertz, J. W. Wiley, C. LeRouge, and M. A. Campion, "Downsizing Effects on Survivors: Layoffs, Offshoring, and Outsourcing," *Industrial Relations* 49, no. 2 (2010), pp. 275–285.

32. C. D. Zatzick, and R. D. Iverson, "High-Involvement Management and Workforce Reduction: Competitive Advantage or Disadvantage?" *Academy of Management Journal* 49, no. 5 (2006), pp. 999–1015; A. Travaglione, and B. Cross, "Diminishing the Social Network in Organizations: Does There Need to Be Such a Phenomenon as 'Survivor Syndrome' After Downsizing?" *Strategic Change* 15, no. 1 (2006), pp. 1–13; and J. D. Kammeyer-Mueller, H. Liao, and R. D. Arvey, "Downsizing and Organizational Performance: A Review of the Literature from a Stakeholder Perspective," *Research in Personnel and Human Resources Management* 20 (2001), pp. 269–329.

33. T. Burns and G. M. Stalker, *The Management of Innovation* (London: Tavistock, 1961); and J. A. Courtright, G. T. Fairhurst, and L. E. Rogers, "Interaction Patterns in Organic and Mechanistic Systems," *Academy of Management Journal* (December 1989), pp. 773–802.

34. This analysis is referred to as a contingency approach to organization design. See, for instance, J. M. Pennings, "Structural Contingency Theory: A Reappraisal," in B. M. Staw and L. L. Cummings (eds.), *Research in Organizational Behavior* 14 (Greenwich, CT: JAI Press, 1992), pp. 267–309; J. R. Hollenbeck, H. Moon, A. P. J. Ellis, B. J. West, D. R. Ilgen, L. Sheppard, C. O. L. H. Porter, and J. A. Wagner III, "Structural Contingency Theory and Individual Differences: Examination of External and Internal Person–Team Fit," *Journal of Applied Psychology* (June 2002), pp. 599–606; and A. Drach-Zahavy and A. Freund, "Team Effectiveness Under Stress: A Structural Contingency Approach," *Journal of Organizational Behavior* 28, no. 4 (2007), pp. 423–450.

35. The strategy–structure thesis was originally proposed in A. D. Chandler Jr., *Strategy and Structure: Chapters in the History of the Industrial Enterprise* (Cambridge, MA: MIT Press, 1962). For more analysis, see T. L. Amburgey and T. Dacin, "As the Left Foot Follows the Right? The Dynamics of Strategic and Structural Change," *Academy of Management Journal* (December 1994), pp. 1427–1452.

36. See R. E. Miles and C. C. Snow, *Organizational Strategy, Structure, and Process* (New York: McGraw-Hill, 1978); D. C. Galunic and K. M. Eisenhardt, "Renewing the Strategy–Structure–Performance Paradigm," in B. M. Staw and L. L. Cummings (eds.), *Research in Organizational Behavior* 16 (Greenwich, CT: JAI Press, 1994), pp. 215–255; and S. M. Toh, F. P. Morgeson, and M. A. Campion, "Human Resource Configurations: Investigating Fit with the Organizational Context," *Journal of Applied Psychology* 93, no. 4 (2008), pp. 864–882.

37. Staff reporter, "Most Innovative Companies of 2015" *Canadian Business*, March 19, 2015, accessed September 2015 at http://www.canadianbusiness.com/innovation/most-innovative-companies-2015-slideshow/image/4.

38. See C. Perrow, "A Framework for the Comparative Analysis of Organizations," *American Sociological Review* (April 1967), pp. 194–208; J. Hage and M. Aiken, "Routine Technology, Social Structure, and Organizational Goals," *Administrative Science Quarterly* (September 1969), pp. 366–377; C. C. Miller, W. H. Glick, Y. Wang, and G. P. Huber, "Understanding Technology–Structure Relationships: Theory Development and Meta-analytic Theory Testing," *Academy of Management Journal* (June 1991), pp. 370–399; and W. D. Sine, H. Mitsuhashi, and D. A. Kirsch, "Revisiting Burns and Stalker: Formal Structure and New Venture Performance in Emerging Economic Sectors," *Academy of Management Journal* 49, no. 1 (2006), pp. 121–132.

39. G. G. Dess and D. W. Beard, "Dimensions of Organizational Task Environments," *Administrative Science Quarterly* (March 1984), pp. 52–73; E. A. Gerloff, N. K. Muir, and W. D. Bodensteiner, "Three Components of Perceived Environmental Uncertainty: An Exploratory Analysis of the Effects of Aggregation," *Journal of Management* (December 1991), pp. 749–768; and O. Shenkar, N. Aranya, and T. Almor, "Construct Dimensions in the Contingency Model: An Analysis Comparing Metric and Non-metric Multivariate Instruments," *Human Relations* (May 1995), pp. 559–580.

40. C. S. Spell and T. J. Arnold, "A Multi-level Analysis of Organizational Justice and Climate, Structure, and Employee Mental Health," *Journal of Management* 33, no. 5 (2007), pp. 724–751; and M. L. Ambrose and M. Schminke, "Organization Structure as a Moderator of the Relationship Between Procedural Justice, Interactional Justice, Perceived Organizational Support, and Supervisory Trust," *Journal of Applied Psychology* 88, no. 2 (2003), pp. 295–305.

41. See, for instance, Spell and Arnold, "A Multi-level Analysis of Organizational Justice and Climate, Structure, and Employee Mental Health"; J. D. Shaw and N. Gupta, "Job Complexity, Performance, and Well-Being: When Does Supplies–Values Fit Matter?" *Personnel Psychology* 57, no. 4 (2004), 847–879; and C. Anderson and C. E. Brown, "The Functions and Dysfunctions of Hierarchy," *Research in Organizational Behavior* 30 (2010), pp. 55–89.

42. T. Martin, "Pharmacies Feel More Heat," *The Wall Street Journal* (March 16–17, 2013), p. A3.

43. G. Hofstede, G. Hofstede, M. Minkov, *Cultures and Organizations: Software of the Mind* (New York: McGraw Hill, 2010).

44. See, for instance, R. E. Ployhart, J. A. Weekley, and K. Baughman, "The Structure and Function of Human Capital Emergence: A Multilevel Examination of the Attraction–Selection–Attrition Model," *Academy of Management Journal* 49, no. 4 (2006), pp. 661–677.

45. J. B. Stewart, "A Place to Play for Google Staff," *The New York Times* (March 16, 2013), p. B1.

Chapter 16

1. See, for example, E. H. Schein, "Culture: The Missing Concept in Organization Studies," *Administrative Science Quarterly* 41, no. 2 (1996), pp. 229–240.

2. This seven-item description is based on C. A. O'Reilly III, J. Chatman, and D. F. Caldwell, "People and Organizational Culture: A Profile Comparison Approach to Assessing Person–Organization Fit," *Academy of Management Journal* (September 1991), pp. 487–516; and J. A. Chatman and K. A. Jehn, "Assessing the Relationship Between Industry Characteristics and Organizational Culture: How Different Can You Be?" *Academy of Management Journal* (June 1994), pp. 522–553.

3. The view that there will be consistency among perceptions of organizational culture has been called the "integration"

perspective. For a review of this perspective and conflicting approaches, see D. Meyerson and J. Martin, "Cultural Change: An Integration of Three Different Views," *Journal of Management Studies* (November 1987), pp. 623–647; and P. J. Frost, L. F. Moore, M. R. Louis, C. C. Lundberg, and J. Martin (eds.), *Reframing Organizational Culture* (Newbury Park, CA: Sage, 1991).

4. See J. M. Jermier, J. W. Slocum Jr., L. W. Fry, and J. Gaines, "Organizational Subcultures in a Soft Bureaucracy: Resistance Behind the Myth and Facade of an Official Culture," *Organization Science* (May 1991), pp. 170–194; and P. Lok, R. Westwood, and J. Crawford, "Perceptions of Organisational Subculture and Their Significance for Organisational Commitment," *Applied Psychology: An International Review* 54, no. 4 (2005), pp. 490–514.

5. D. A. Hoffman and L. M. Jones, "Leadership, Collective Personality, and Performance," *Journal of Applied Psychology* 90, no. 3 (2005), pp. 509–522.

6. T. Hsieh, "Zappos's CEO on Going to Extremes for Customers," *Harvard Business Review* (July/August 2010), pp. 41–45.

7. See, for example, G. G. Gordon and N. DiTomaso, "Predicting Corporate Performance from Organizational Culture," *Journal of Management Studies* (November 1992), pp. 793–798; J. B. Sorensen, "The Strength of Corporate Culture and the Reliability of Firm Performance," *Administrative Science Quarterly* (March 2002), pp. 70–91; and J. Rosenthal and M. A. Masarech, "High-Performance Cultures: How Values Can Drive Business Results," *Journal of Organizational Excellence* (Spring 2003), pp. 3–18.

8. Y. Wiener, "Forms of Value Systems: A Focus on Organizational Effectiveness and Cultural Change and Maintenance," *Academy of Management Review* (October 1988), p. 536; and B. Schneider, A. N. Salvaggio, and M. Subirats, "Climate Strength: A New Direction for Climate Research," *Journal of Applied Psychology* 87 (2002), pp. 220–229.

9. R. T. Mowday, L. W. Porter, and R. M. Steers, *Employee Linkages: The Psychology of Commitment, Absenteeism, and Turnover* (New York: Academic Press, 1982); C. Vandenberghe, "Organizational Culture, Person–Culture Fit, and Turnover: A Replication in the Health Care Industry," *Journal of Organizational Behavior* (March 1999), pp. 175–184; and M. Schulte, C. Ostroff, S. Shmulyian, and A. Kinicki, "Organizational Climate Configurations: Relationships to Collective Attitudes, Customer Satisfaction, and Financial Performance," *Journal of Applied Psychology* 94, no. 3 (2009), pp. 618–634.

10. J. W. Grizzle, A. R. Zablah, T. J. Brown, J. C. Mowen, and J. M. Lee, "Employee Customer Orientation in Context: How the Environment Moderates the Influence of Customer Orientation on Performance Outcomes," *Journal of Applied Psychology* 94, no. 5 (2009), pp. 1227–1242.

11. M. R. Bashshur, A. Hernández, and V. González-Romá, "When Managers and Their Teams Disagree: A Longitudinal Look at the Consequences of Differences in Perceptions of Organizational Support," *Journal of Applied Psychology* 96, no. 3 (2011), pp. 558–573.

12. S. L. Dolan and S. Garcia, "Managing by Values: Cultural Redesign for Strategic Organizational Change at the Dawn of the Twenty-First Century," *Journal of Management Development* 21, no. 2 (2002), pp. 101–117.

13. See C. A. O'Reilly and J. A. Chatman, "Culture as Social Control: Corporations, Cults, and Commitment," in B. M. Staw and L. L. Cummings (eds.), *Research in Organizational Behavior* 18 (Greenwich, CT: JAI Press, 1996), pp. 157–200. See also M. Pinae Cunha, "The 'Best Place to Be': Managing Control and Employee Loyalty in a Knowledge-Intensive Company," *Journal of Applied Behavioral Science* (December 2002), pp. 481–495.

14. Y. Ling, Z. Simsek, M. H. Lubatkin, and J. F. Veiga, "Transformational Leadership's Role in Promoting Corporate

Entrepreneurship: Examining the CEO-TMT Interface," *Academy of Management Journal* 51, no. 3 (2008), pp. 557–576; and A. Malhotra, A. Majchrzak, and B. Rosen, "Leading Virtual Teams," *Academy of Management Perspectives* 21, no. 1 (2007), pp. 60–70.

15. D. Denison, "What Is the Difference Between Organizational Culture and Organizational Climate? A Native's Point of View on a Decade of Paradigm Wars," *Academy of Management Review* 21 (1996), pp. 519–654; and L. R. James, C. C. Choi, C. E. Ko, P. K. McNeil, M. K. Minton, M. A. Wright, and K. Kim, "Organizational and Psychological Climate: A Review of Theory and Research," *European Journal of Work and Organizational Psychology* 17, no. 1 (2008), pp. 5–32.

16. J. Z. Carr, A. M. Schmidt, J. K. Ford, and R. P. DeShon, "Climate Perceptions Matter: A Meta-analytic Path Analysis Relating Molar Climate, Cognitive and Affective States, and Individual Level Work Outcomes," *Journal of Applied Psychology* 88, no. (2003), pp. 605–619.

17. Schulte, Ostroff, Shmulyian, and Kinicki, "Organizational Climate Configurations."

18. S. D. Pugh, J. Dietz, A. P. Brief, and J. W. Wiley, "Looking Inside and Out: The Impact of Employee and Community Demographic Composition on Organizational Diversity Climate," *Journal of Applied Psychology* 93, no. 6 (2008), pp. 1422–1428; K. H. Ehrhart, L. A. Witt, B. Schneider, and S. J. Perry, "Service Employees Give as They Get: Internal Service as a Moderator of the Service Climate–Service Outcomes Link," *Journal of Applied Psychology* 96, no. 2 (2011), pp. 423–431; and A. Simha and J. B. Cullen, "Ethical Climates and Their Effects on Organizational Outcomes: Implications from the Past and Prophecies for the Future," *Academy of Management Perspectives* (November 2011), pp. 20–34.

19. J. C. Wallace, P. D. Johnson, K. Mathe, and J. Paul, "Structural and Psychological Empowerment Climates, Performance, and the Moderating Role of Shared Felt Accountability: A Managerial Perspective," *Journal of Applied Psychology* 96, no. 3 (2011), pp. 840–850.

20. J. M. Beus, S. C. Payne, M. E. Bergman, and W. Arthur, "Safety Climate and Injuries: An Examination of Theoretical and Empirical Relationships," *Journal of Applied Psychology* 95, no. 4 (2010), pp. 713–727.

21. R. King, "Canada's Military Chief Says Military Sexual Harassment Due to Biological Wiring in CBC Interview," *Toronto Star* (2015), accessed September 30, 2015 at http://www.thestar.com/news/canada/2015/06/16/canadas-military-chief-says-military-sex-harassment-due-to-biological-wiring-in-cbc-interview.html.

22. R. L. Jepperson, "Institutions, Institutional Effects, and Institutionalism," in W. W. Powell and P. J. DiMaggio (eds.), *The New Institutionalism in Organizational Analysis* (Chicago: University of Chicago Press, 1991), pp. 143–163; G. F. Lanzara and G. Patriotta, "The Institutionalization of Knowledge in an Automotive Factory: Templates, Inscriptions, and the Problems of Durability," *Organization Studies* 28, no. 5 (2007), pp. 635–660; and T. B. Lawrence, M. K. Mauws, B. Dyck, and R. F. Kleysen, "The Politics of Organizational Learning: Integrating Power into the 4I Framework," *Academy of Management Review* (January 2005), pp. 180–191.

23. J. B. Sorensen, "The Strength of Corporate Culture and the Reliability of Firm Performance," *Administrative Science Quarterly* (March 2002), pp. 70–91.

24. See T. Cox Jr., *Cultural Diversity in Organizations: Theory, Research & Practice* (San Francisco: Berrett-Koehler, 1993), pp. 162–170; L. Grensing-Pophal, "Hiring to Fit Your Corporate Culture," *HR Magazine* (August 1999), pp. 50–54; and D. L. Stone, E. F. Stone-Romero, and K. M. Lukaszewski, "The Impact of Cultural Values on the Acceptance and

Effectiveness of Human Resource Management Policies and Practices," *Human Resource Management Review* 17, no. 2 (2007), pp. 152–165.

25. S. Cartwright and C. L. Cooper, "The Role of Culture Compatibility in Successful Organizational Marriages," *Academy of Management Executive* (May 1993), pp. 57–70; R. A. Weber and C. F. Camerer, "Cultural Conflict and Merger Failure: An Experimental Approach," *Management Science* (April 2003), pp. 400–412; and I. H. Gleibs, A. Mummendey, and P. Noack, "Predictors of Change in Postmerger Identification During a Merger Process: A Longitudinal Study," *Journal of Personality and Social Psychology* 95, no. 5 (2008), pp. 1095–1112.

26. P. Gumbel, "Return of the Urge to Merge," *Time Europe Magazine* (July 13, 2003), http://www.time.com/time/europe/magazine/article/0,13005,901030721-464418,00.html.

27. E. H. Schein, "The Role of the Founder in Creating Organizational Culture," *Organizational Dynamics* (Summer 1983), pp. 13–28; and Y. L. Zhao, O. H. Erekson, T. Wang, and M. Song, "Pioneering Advantages and Entrepreneurs' First-Mover Decisions: An Empirical Investigation for the United States and China," *Journal of Product Innovation Management* (December 2012), pp. 190–210.

28. E. H. Schein, "Leadership and Organizational Culture," in F. Hesselbein, M. Goldsmith, and R. Beckhard (eds.), *The Leader of the Future* (San Francisco: Jossey-Bass, 1996), pp. 61–62.

29. See, for example, J. R. Harrison and G. R. Carroll, "Keeping the Faith: A Model of Cultural Transmission in Formal Organizations," *Administrative Science Quarterly* (December 1991), pp. 552–582; and D. E. Bowen and C. Ostroff, "The 'Strength' of the HRM System, Organizational Climate Formation, and Firm Performance," *Academy of Management Review* 29 (2004), pp. 203–221.

30. B. Schneider, H. W. Goldstein, and D. B. Smith, "The ASA Framework: An Update," *Personnel Psychology* (Winter 1995), pp. 747–773; D. M. Cable and T. A. Judge, "Interviewers' Perceptions of Person–Organization Fit and Organizational Selection Decisions," *Journal of Applied Psychology* (August 1997), pp. 546–561; M. L. Verquer, T. A. Beehr, and S. H. Wagner, "A Meta-analysis of Relations Between Person–Organization Fit and Work Attitudes," *Journal of Vocational Behavior* (December 2003), pp. 473–489; and W. Li, Y. Wang, P. Taylor, K. Shi, and D. He, "The Influence of Organizational Culture on Work-Related Personality Requirement Ratings: A Multilevel Analysis," *International Journal of Selection and Assessment* 16, no. 4 (2008), pp. 366–384.

31. "100 Best Companies to Work For," *Fortune* (2013), accessed June 28, 2013 at http://money.cnn.com/magazines/fortune/best-companies/2013/snapshots/5.html.

32. D. C. Hambrick and P. A. Mason, "Upper Echelons: The Organization as a Reflection of Its Top Managers," *Academy of Management Review* (April 1984), pp. 193–206; M. A. Carpenter, M. A. Geletkanycz, and W. G. Sanders, "Upper Echelons Research Revisited: Antecedents, Elements, and Consequences of Top Management Team Composition," *Journal of Management* 30, no. 6 (2004), pp. 749–778, and H. Wang, A. S. Tsui, and K. R. Xin, "CEO Leadership Behaviors, Organizational Performance, and Employees' Attitudes," *The Leadership Quarterly* 22, no. 1 (2011), pp. 92–105.

33. APTN Corporate website, accessed October 1, 2015 at http://aptn.ca/corporate/senior-management.php.

34. Economic Development Winnipeg, accessed Oct. 2, 2015 at http://www.economicdevelopmentwinnipeg.com/uploads/document_file/aptn_company_profile.pdf?t=1397601473.

35. See, for instance, J. P. Wanous, *Organizational Entry*, 2nd ed. (New York: Addison-Wesley, 1992); D. M. Cable and C. K. Parsons, "Socialization Tactics and Person–Organization Fit,"

Personnel Psychology (Spring 2001), pp. 1–23; and T. N. Bauer, T. Bodner, B. Erdogan, D. M. Truxillo, and J. S. Tucker, "Newcomer Adjustment During Organizational Socialization: A Meta-analytic Review of Antecedents, Outcomes, and Methods," *Journal of Applied Psychology* 92, no. 3 (2007), pp. 707–721.

36. G. Kranz, "Training That Starts Before the Job Begins," *Workforce Management Online* (July 2009), http://www.workforce.com.

37. R. E. Silverman, "Companies Try to Make the First Day for New Hires More Fun," *The Wall Street Journal* (May 28, 2013), http://online.wsj.com/article/SB10001424127887323336104578501631475934850.html.

38. D. C. Feldman, "The Multiple Socialization of Organization Members," *Academy of Management Review* (April 1981), p. 310.

39. C. J. Collins, "The Interactive Effects of Recruitment Practices and Product Awareness on Job Seekers' Employer Knowledge and Application Behaviors," *Journal of Applied Psychology* 92, no. 1 (2007), pp. 180–190.

40. J. D. Kammeyer-Mueller and C. R. Wanberg, "Unwrapping the Organizational Entry Process: Disentangling Multiple Antecedents and Their Pathways to Adjustment," *Journal of Applied Psychology* 88 (2003), pp. 779–794; E. W. Morrison, "Longitudinal Study of the Effects of Information Seeking on Newcomer Socialization," *Journal of Applied Psychology* 78 (2003), pp. 173–183; and M. Wangm, Y. Zhan, E. McCune, and D. Truxillo, "Understanding Newcomers' Adaptability and Work-Related Outcomes: Testing the Mediating Roles of Perceived P–E Fit Variables," *Personnel Psychology* 64, no. 1 (2011), pp. 163–189.

41. E. W. Morrison, "Newcomers' Relationships: The Role of Social Network Ties During Socialization," *Academy of Management Journal* 45 (2002), pp. 1149–1160.

42. T. N. Bauer, T. Bodner, B. Erdogan, D. M. Truxillo, and J. S. Tucker, "Newcomer Adjustment During Organizational Socialization: A Meta-analytic Review of Antecedents, Outcomes, and Methods," *Journal of Applied Psychology* 92, no. 3 (2007), pp. 707–721.

43. W. R. Boswell, A. J. Shipp, S. C., Payne, and S. S. Culbertson, "Changes in Newcomer Job Satisfaction over Time: Examining the Pattern of Honeymoons and Hangovers," *Journal of Applied Psychology* 94, no. 4 (2009), pp. 844–858.

44. C. Vandenberghe, A. Panaccio, K. Bentein, K. Mignonac, and P. Roussel, "Assessing Longitudinal Change of and Dynamic Relationships Among Role Stressors, Job Attitudes, Turnover Intention, and Well-Being in Neophyte Newcomers," *Journal of Organizational Behavior* 32, no. 4 (2011), pp. 652–671.

45. E. Ransdell, "The Nike Story? Just Tell It!" *Fast Company* (January–February 2000), pp. 44–46; and A. Muccino, "Exclusive Interview with Chuck Eichten," *Liquid Brand Summit Blog* (February 4, 2011), http://blog.liquidbrandsummit.com.

46. D. M. Boje, "The Storytelling Organization: A Study of Story Performance in an Office-Supply Firm," *Administrative Science Quarterly* (March 1991), pp. 106–126; and M. Ricketts and J. G. Seiling, "Language, Metaphors, and Stories: Catalysts for Meaning Making in Organizations," *Organization Development Journal* (Winter 2003), pp. 33–431.

47. A. J. Shipp and K. J. Jansen, "Reinterpreting Time in Fit Theory: Crafting and Recrafting Narratives of Fit in Medias Res," *Academy of Management Review* 36, no. 1 (2011), pp. 76–101.

48. See G. Islam and M. J. Zyphur, "Rituals in Organizations: A Review and Expansion of Current Theory," *Group and Organization Management* 34, no. 1 (2009), pp. 114–139.

49. M. G. Pratt and A. Rafaeli "Artifacts and Organizations: Understanding Our Objective Reality," in A. Rafaeli and M. G. Pratt, *Artifacts and Organizations: Beyond Mere Symbolism* (Mahwah, NJ: Lawrence Erlbaum, 2006), pp. 279–288.

50. From personal interview with D2L CEO conducted by Katherine Breward in May 2003.

51. See B. Victor and J. B. Cullen, "The Organizational Bases of Ethical Work Climates," *Administrative Science Quarterly* (March 1988), pp. 101–125; R. L. Dufresne, "An Action Learning Perspective on Effective Implementation of Academic Honor Codes," *Group & Organization Management* (April 2004), pp. 201–218; and A. Ardichvilli, J. A. Mitchell, and D. Jondle, "Characteristics of Ethical Business Cultures," *Journal of Business Ethics* 85, no. 4 (2009), pp. 445–451.

52. J. P. Mulki, J. F. Jaramillo, and W. B. Locander, "Critical Role of Leadership on Ethical Climate and Salesperson Behaviors," *Journal of Business Ethics* 86, no. 2 (2009), pp. 125–141; M. Schminke, M. L. Ambrose, and D. O. Neubaum, "The Effect of Leader Moral Development on Ethical Climate and Employee Attitudes," *Organizational Behavior and Human Decision Processes* 97, no. 2 (2005), pp. 135–151; and M. E. Brown, L. K. Treviño, and D. A. Harrison, "Ethical Leadership: A Social Learning Perspective for Construct Development and Testing," *Organizational Behavior and Human Decision Processes* 97, no. 2 (2005), pp. 117–134.

53. D. M. Mayer, M. Kuenzi, R. Greenbaum, M. Bardes, and S. Salvador, "How Low Does Ethical Leadership Flow? Test of a Trickle-Down Model," *Organizational Behavior and Human Decision Processes* 108, no. 1 (2009), pp. 1–13.

54. B. Sweeney, D. Arnold, and B. Pierce, "The Impact of Perceived Ethical Culture of the Firm and Demographic Variables on Auditors' Ethical Evaluation and Intention to Act Decisions," *Journal of Business Ethics* 93, no. 4 (2010), pp. 531–551.

55. M. L. Gruys, S. M. Stewart, J. Goodstein, M. N. Bing, and A. C. Wicks, "Values Enactment in Organizations: A Multi-level Examination," *Journal of Management* 34, no. 4 (2008), pp. 806–843.

56. D. L. Nelson and C. L. Cooper (eds.), *Positive Organizational Behavior* (London: Sage, 2007); K. S. Cameron, J. E. Dutton, and R. E. Quinn (eds.), *Positive Organizational Scholarship: Foundations of a New Discipline* (San Francisco: Berrett-Koehler, 2003); and F. Luthans and C. M. Youssef, "Emerging Positive Organizational Behavior," *Journal of Management* (June 2007), pp. 321–349.

57. J. Robison, "Great Leadership Under Fire," *Gallup Leadership Journal* (March 8, 2007), pp. 1–3.

58. R. Wagner and J. K. Harter, *12: The Elements of Great Managing* (New York: Gallup Press, 2006).

59. Barrett, B. (2015) "Putting People First Builds World Class Corporate Culture," *Pique Magazine*, accessed October 3, 2015 at http://www.piquenewsmagazine.com/whistler/putting-people-first-builds-world-class-corporate-culture/Content?oid=2649380.

60. R. Wagner and J. K. Harter, "Performance Reviews Without the Anxiety," *Gallup Leadership Journal* (July 12, 2007), pp. 1–4; and Wagner and Harter, *12: The Elements of Great Managing.*

61. S. Fineman, "On Being Positive: Concerns and Counterpoints," *Academy of Management Review* 31, no. 2 (2006), pp. 270–291.

62. Peter B. Smith, Shaun Dugan, and Fons Trompenaars, "National Culture and the Values of Organizational Employees a Dimensional Analysis Across 43 Nations." *Journal of Cross-cultural Psychology* 27, no. 2 (1996), pp. 231–264.

63. J. Nicas, "American, US Airways Face Challenges in Integration," *The Wall Street Journal* (February 14, 2013), http://online.wsj.com/article/SB10001424127887324432004578304192162931544.html.

64. D. J. McCarthy and S. M. Puffer, "Interpreting the Ethicality of Corporate Governance Decisions in Russia: Utilizing Integrative Social Contracts Theory to Evaluate the Relevance of Agency Theory Norms," *Academy of Management Review* 33, no. 1 (2008), pp. 11–31.

Chapter 17

1. P. G. Audia and S. Brion, "Reluctant to Change: Self-Enhancing Responses to Diverging Performance Measures," *Organizational Behavior and Human Decision Processes* 102 (2007), pp. 255–269.

2. M. Fugate, A. J. Kinicki, and G. E. Prussia, "Employee Coping with Organizational Change: An Examination of Alternative Theoretical Perspectives and Models," *Personnel Psychology* 61, no. 1 (2008), pp. 1–36.

3. J. D. Ford, L. W. Ford, and A. D'Amelio, "Resistance to Change: The Rest of the Story," *Academy of Management Review* 33, no. 2 (2008), pp. 362–377.

4. M. T. Hannan, L. Pólos, and G. R. Carroll, "The Fog of Change: Opacity and Asperity in Organizations," *Administrative Science Quarterly* (September 2003), pp. 399–432.

5. J. P. Kotter and L. A. Schlesinger, "Choosing Strategies for Change," *Harvard Business Review* (March–April 1979), pp. 106–114; and R. K. Smollan, "The Multi-dimensional Nature of Resistance to Change," *Journal of Management & Organization* (November 2011), pp. 828–849.

6. A. E. Rafferty and S. L. D. Restubog, "The Impact of Change Process and Context on Change Reactions and Turnover During a Merger," *Journal of Management* 36, no. 5 (2010), pp. 1309–1338.

7. J. E. Dutton, S. J. Ashford, R. M. O'Neill, and K. A. Lawrence, "Moves That Matter: Issue Selling and Organizational Change," *Academy of Management Journal* (August 2001), pp. 716–736.

8. P. C. Fiss and E. J. Zajac, "The Symbolic Management of Strategic Change: Sensegiving via Framing and Decoupling," *Academy of Management Journal* 49, no. 6 (2006), pp. 1173–1193.

9. Q. N. Huy, "Emotional Balancing of Organizational Continuity and Radical Change: The Contribution of Middle Managers," *Administrative Science Quarterly* (March 2002), pp. 31–69; D. M. Herold, D. B. Fedor, and S. D. Caldwell, "Beyond Change Management: A Multilevel Investigation of Contextual and Personal Influences on Employees' Commitment to Change," *Journal of Applied Psychology* 92, no. 4 (2007), pp. 942–951; and G. B. Cunningham, "The Relationships among Commitment to Change, Coping with Change, and Turnover Intentions," *European Journal of Work and Organizational Psychology* 15, no. 1 (2006), pp. 29–45.

10. R. Peccei, A. Giangreco, and A. Sebastiano, "The Role of Organizational Commitment in the Analysis of Resistance to Change: Co-predictor and Moderator Effects," *Personnel Review* 40, no. 2 (2011), pp. 185–204.

11. J. P. Kotter, "Leading Change: Why Transformational Efforts Fail," *Harvard Business Review* 85 (January 2007), pp. 96–103.

12. K. van Dam, S. Oreg, and B. Schyns, "Daily Work Contexts and Resistance to Organisational Change: The Role of Leader-Member Exchange, Development Climate, and Change Process Characteristics," *Applied Psychology: An International Review* 57, no. 2 (2008), pp. 313–334.

13. S. Oreg and N. Sverdlik, "Ambivalence Toward Imposed Change: The Conflict Between Dispositional Resistance to Change and the Orientation Toward the Change Agent," *Journal of Applied Psychology* 96, no. 2 (2011), pp. 337–349.

14. D. B. Fedor, S. Caldwell, and D. M. Herold, "The Effects of Organizational Changes on Employee Commitment: A Multilevel Investigation," *Personnel Psychology* 59 (2006), pp. 1–29; and R. D. Foster, "Resistance, Justice, and Commitment to Change," *Human Resource Development Quarterly* 21, no. 1 (2010), pp. 3–39.

15. S. Oreg, "Personality, Context, and Resistance to Organizational Change," *European Journal of Work and Organizational Psychology* 15, no. 1 (2006), pp. 73–101.

16. S. M. Elias, "Employee Commitment in Times of Change: Assessing the Importance of Attitudes Toward Organizational Change," *Journal of Management* 35, no. 1 (2009), pp. 37–55.

17. J. W. B. Lang and P. D. Bliese, "General Mental Ability and Two Types of Adaptation to Unforeseen Change: Applying Discontinuous Growth Models to the Task-Change Paradigm," *Journal of Applied Psychology* 94, no. 2 (2009), pp. 411–428.

18. C. O. L. H. Porter, J. W. Webb, and C. I. Gogus, "When Goal Orientations Collide: Effects of Learning and Performance Orientation on Team Adaptability in Response to Workload Imbalance," *Journal of Applied Psychology* 95, no. 5 (2010), pp. 935–943.

19. K. Lewin, *Field Theory in Social Science* (New York: Harper & Row, 1951).

20. P. G. Audia, E. A. Locke, and K. G. Smith, "The Paradox of Success: An Archival and a Laboratory Study of Strategic Persistence Following Radical Environmental Change," *Academy of Management Journal* (October 2000), pp. 837–853; and P. G. Audia and S. Brion, "Reluctant to Change: Self-Enhancing Responses to Diverging Performance Measures," *Organizational Behavior and Human Decision Processes* 102, no. 2 (2007), pp. 255–269.

21. J. B. Sorensen, "The Strength of Corporate Culture and the Reliability of Firm Performance," *Administrative Science Quarterly* (March 2002), pp. 70–91.

22. J. Amis, T. Slack, and C. R. Hinings, "The Pace, Sequence, and Linearity of Radical Change," *Academy of Management Journal* (February 2004), pp. 15–39; and E. Autio, H. J. Sapienza, and J. G. Almeida, "Effects of Age at Entry, Knowledge Intensity, and Imitability on International Growth," *Academy of Management Journal* (October 2000), pp. 909–924.

23. J. P. Kotter, "Leading Changes: Why Transformation Efforts Fail," *Harvard Business Review* (March–April 1995), pp. 59–67; and J. P. Kotter, *Leading Change* (Harvard Business School Press, 1996).

24. For a sampling of various OD definitions, see H. K. Sinangil and F. Avallone, "Organizational Development and Change," in N. Anderson, D. S. Ones, H. K. Sinangil, and C. Viswesvaran (eds.), *Handbook of Industrial, Work and Organizational Psychology* 2 (Thousand Oaks, CA: Sage, 2001), pp. 332–335; and R. J. Marshak and D. Grant, "Organizational Discourse and New Organization Development Practices," *British Journal of Management* 19, no. 1 (2008), pp. S7–S19.

25. See, for instance, R. Lines, "Influence of Participation in Strategic Change: Resistance, Organizational Commitment and Change Goal Achievement," *Journal of Change Management* (September 2004), pp. 193–215.

26. J. E. Edwards and M. D. Thomas, "The Organizational Survey Process: General Steps and Practical Considerations," in P. Rosenfeld, J. E. Edwards, and M. D. Thomas (eds.), *Improving Organizational Surveys: New Directions, Methods, and Applications* (Newbury Park, CA: Sage, 1993), pp. 3–28; and T. Fauth, K. Hattrub, K. Mueller, and B. Roberts, "Nonresponse in Employee Attitude Surveys: A Group-Level Analysis," *Journal of Business and Psychology* (March 2013), pp. 1–16.

27. F. J. Lambrechts, R. Bouwen, S. Grieten, J. P. Huybrechts, and E. H. Schein, "Learning to Help Through Humble Inquiry and Implications for Management Research, Practice, and Education: An Interview with Edgar H. Schein," *Academy of Management Learning & Education* (March 2011), pp. 131–148; E. H. Schein, *Process Consultation: Its Role in Organizational Development*, 2nd ed. (Reading, MA: Addison-Wesley, 1988), p. 9; and E. H. Schein, *Process Consultation Revisited: Building Helpful Relationships* (Reading, MA: Addison-Wesley, 1999).

28. Schein, *Process Consultation.*

29. W. W. G. Dyer, W. G. Dyer, and J. H. Dyer, *Team Building: Proven Strategies for Improving Team Performance* (Hoboken, NJ: Jossey-Bass, 2007).

30. U. Wagner, L. Tropp, G. Finchilescu, and C. Tredoux (eds.), *Improving Intergroup Relations* (New York: Wiley-Blackwell, 2008).

31. See, for example, R. Fry, F. Barrett, J. Seiling, and D. Whitney (eds.), *Appreciative Inquiry & Organizational Transformation: Reports from the Field* (Westport, CT: Quorum, 2002); J. K. Barge and C. Oliver, "Working with Appreciation in Managerial Practice," *Academy of Management Review* (January 2003), pp. 124–142; and D. van der Haar and D. M. Hosking, "Evaluating Appreciative Inquiry: A Relational Constructionist Perspective," *Human Relations* (August 2004), pp. 1017–1036.

32. A. Harrington, "Who's Afraid of a New Product?" *Fortune* (November 10, 2003), pp. 189–192; and C. C. Manz, F. Shipper, and G. L. Stewart, "Everyone a Team Leader: Shared Influence at W. L. Gore and Associates," *Organizational Dynamics* 38, no. 3 (2009), pp. 239–244.

33. See, for instance, R. M. Kanter, "When a Thousand Flowers Bloom: Structural, Collective and Social Conditions for Innovation in Organizations," in B. M. Staw and L. L. Cummings (eds.), *Research in Organizational Behavior* 10 (Greenwich, CT: JAI Press, 1988), pp. 169–211.

34. L. Widdicombe, "The End of Food," *The New Yorker* (May 12, 2014), http://www.newyorker.com/reporting/2014/05/12/140512fa_fact_widdicombe?currentPage=all.

35. F. Damanpour, "Organizational Innovation: A Meta-analysis of Effects of Determinants and Moderators," *Academy of Management Journal* (September 1991), p. 557; and H. W. Volberda, F. A. J. Van den Bosch, and C. V. Heij, "Management Innovation: Management as Fertile Ground for Innovation," *European Management Review* (Spring 2013), pp. 1–15.

36. Damanpour, "Organizational Innovation," pp. 555–590; and G. Westerman, F. W. McFarlan, and M. Iansiti, "Organization Design and Effectiveness over the Innovation Life Cycle," *Organization Science* 17, no. 2 (2006), pp. 230–238.

37. See P. R. Monge, M. D. Cozzens, and N. S. Contractor, "Communication and Motivational Predictors of the Dynamics of Organizational Innovation," *Organization Science* (May 1992), pp. 250–274; P. Schepers and P. T. van den Berg, "Social Factors of Work-Environment Creativity," *Journal of Business and Psychology* 21, no. 3 (2007), pp. 407–428.

38. D. L. Day, "Raising Radicals: Different Processes for Championing Innovative Corporate Ventures," *Organization Science* (May 1994), pp. 148–172; and M. E. Mullins, S. W. J. Kozlowski, N. Schmitt, and A. W. Howell, "The Role of the Idea Champion in Innovation: The Case of the Internet in the Mid-1990s," *Computers in Human Behavior* 24, no. 2 (2008), pp. 451–467.

39. J. M. Howell and C. A. Higgins, "Champions of Change: Identifying, Understanding, and Supporting Champions of Technological Innovations," *Organizational Dynamics* 19, (1990), pp. 40–55; and S. C. Parker, "Intrapreneurship or Entrepreneurship?" *Journal of Business Venturing* (January 2011), pp. 19–34.

40. M. Cerne, M. Jaklic, and M. Skerlavaj, "Decoupling Management and Technological Innovations: Resolving the Individualism-Collectivism Controversy," *Journal of International Management* (June 2013), pp. 103–117; and S. Shane, S. Venkataraman, and I. MacMillan, "Cultural Differences in Innovation Championing Strategies," *Journal of Management* 21, no. 5 (1995), pp. 931–952.

41. See, for instance, S. Armour, "Rising Job Stress Could Affect Bottom Line," *USA Today* (July 29, 2003), p. 1B; and J. Schramm, "Work/Life on Hold," *HR Magazine* 53 (October 2008), p. 120.

42. B. Mirza, "Workplace Stress Hits Three-Year High," *HR Magazine* (April 2012), p. 15.

43. Adapted from R. S. Schuler, "Definition and Conceptualization of Stress in Organizations," *Organizational Behavior and Human Performance* (April 1980), p. 189. For an updated review of definitions, see C. L. Cooper, P. J. Dewe, and M. P. O'Driscoll, *Organizational Stress: A Review and Critique of Theory, Research, and Applications* (Thousand Oaks, CA: Sage, 2002).

44. See, for instance, M. A. Cavanaugh, W. R. Boswell, M. V. Roehling, and J. W. Boudreau, "An Empirical Examination of Self-Reported Work Stress Among U.S. Managers," *Journal of Applied Psychology* (February 2000), pp. 65–74.

45. S. Shellenbarger, "When Stress Is Good for You," *The Wall Street Journal* (January 24, 2012), pp. D1, D5.

46. Ibid.

47. N. P. Podsakoff, J. A. LePine, and M. A. LePine, "Differential Challenge-Hindrance Stressor Relationships with Job Attitudes, Turnover Intentions, Turnover, and Withdrawal Behavior: A Meta-analysis," *Journal of Applied Psychology* 92, no. 2 (2007), pp. 438–454; and J. A. LePine, M. A. LePine, and C. L. Jackson, "Challenge and Hindrance Stress: Relationships with Exhaustion, Motivation to Learn, and Learning Performance," *Journal of Applied Psychology* (October 2004), pp. 883–891.

48. L. W. Hunter and S. M. B. Thatcher, "Feeling the Heat: Effects of Stress, Commitment, and Job Experience on Job Performance," *Academy of Management Journal* 50, no. 4 (2007), pp. 953–968.

49. J. C. Wallace, B. D. Edwards, T. Arnold, M. L. Frazier, and D. M. Finch, "Work Stressors, Role-Based Performance, and the Moderating Influence of Organizational Support," *Journal of Applied Psychology* 94, no. 1 (2009), pp. 254–262.

50. N. W. Van Yperen and O. Janssen, "Fatigued and Dissatisfied or Fatigued but Satisfied? Goal Orientations and Responses to High Job Demands," *Academy of Management Journal* (December 2002), pp. 1161–1171; and N. W. Van Yperen and M. Hagedoorn, "Do High Job Demands Increase Intrinsic Motivation or Fatigue or Both? The Role of Job Control and Job Social Support," *Academy of Management Journal* (June 2003), pp. 339–348.

51. J. de Jonge and C. Dormann, "Stressors, Resources, and Strain at Work: A Longitudinal Test of the Triple-Match Principle," *Journal of Applied Psychology* 91, no. 5 (2006), pp. 1359–1374.

52. J. Schaubroeck, J. R. Jones, and J. L. Xie, "Individual Differences in Utilizing Control to Cope with Job Demands: Effects on Susceptibility to Infectious Disease," *Journal of Applied Psychology* (April 2001), pp. 265–278.

53. M. Kivimäki, J. Head, J. E. Ferrie, E. Brunner, M. G. Marmot, J. Vahtera, and M. J. Shipley, "Why Is Evidence on Job Strain and Coronary Heart Disease Mixed? An Illustration of Measurement Challenges in the Whitehall II Study," *Psychosomatic Medicine* 68, no. 3 (2006), pp. 398–401.

54. M. Borritz, K. B. Christensen, U. Bültmann, R. Rugulies, T. Lund, I. Andersen, E. Villadsen, F. Didreichsen, and T. S. Krisensen, "Impact on Burnout and Psychosocial Work Characteristics on Future Long-Term Sickness Absence, Prospective Results of the Danish PUMA Study Among Human Service Workers," *Journal of Occupational and Environmental Medicine* 52, no. 10 (2010), pp. 964–970.

55. R. Ilies, N. Dimotakis, and I. E. DePater, "Psychological and Physiological Reactions to High Workloads: Implications for Well-Being," *Personnel Psychology* 63, no. 2 (2010), pp. 407–463.

56. D. Örtqvist and J. Wincent, "Prominent Consequences of Role Stress: A Meta-analytic Review," *International Journal of Stress Management*, 13, no. 4 (2006), pp. 399–422.

57. J. R. Hackman and G. R. Oldham, "Development of the Job Diagnostic Survey," *Journal of Applied Psychology* (April 1975), pp. 159–170; J. J. Hakanen, A. B. Bakker, and M. Jokisaari, "A 35-Year Follow-Up Study on Burnout among Finnish Employees," *Journal of Occupational Health Psychology* 16, no. 3 (2011), pp. 345–360; Crawford, LePine, and Rich, "Linking Job Demands and Resources to Employee Engagement and Burnout"; and G. A. Chung-Yan, "The Nonlinear Effects of Job Complexity and Autonomy on Job Satisfaction, Turnover, and Psychological Well-Being," *Journal of Occupational Health Psychology* 15, no. 3 (2010), pp. 237–251.

58. L. L. Meier, N. K. Semmer, A. Elfering, and N. Jacobshagen, "The Double Meaning of Control: Three-Way Interactions Between Internal Resources, Job Control, and Stressors at Work," *Journal of Occupational Health Psychology* 13, no. 3 (2008), pp. 244–258.

59. E. M. de Croon, J. K. Sluiter, R. W. B. Blonk, J. P. J. Broersen, and M. H. W. Frings-Dresen, "Stressful Work, Psychological Job Strain, and Turnover: A 2-Year Prospective Cohort Study of Truck Drivers," *Journal of Applied Psychology* (June 2004), pp. 442–454; R. Cropanzano, D. E. Rupp, and Z. S. Byrne, "The Relationship of Emotional Exhaustion to Work Attitudes, Job Performance, and Organizational Citizenship Behaviors," *Journal of Applied Psychology* (February 2003), pp. 160–169; and S. Diestel and K. Schmidt, "Costs of Simultaneous Coping with Emotional Dissonance and Self-Control Demands at Work: Results from Two German Samples," *Journal of Applied Psychology* 96, no. 3 (2011), pp. 643–653.

60. The following discussion has been influenced by J. M. Ivancevich, M. T. Matteson, S. M. Freedman, and J. S. Phillips, "Worksite Stress Management Interventions," *American Psychologist* (February 1990), pp. 252–261; R. Schwarzer, "Manage Stress at Work Through Preventive and Proactive Coping," in E. A. Locke (ed.), *Handbook of Principles of Organizational Behavior* (Malden, MA: Blackwell, 2004), pp. 342–355; and K. M. Richardson and H. R. Rothstein, "Effects of Occupational Stress Management Intervention Programs: A Meta-analysis," *Journal of Occupational Health Psychology* 13, no. 1 (2008), pp. 69–93.

61. T. H. Macan, "Time Management: Test of a Process Model," *Journal of Applied Psychology* (June 1994), pp. 381–391; and B. J. C. Claessens, W. Van Eerde, C. G. Rutte, and R. A. Roe, "Planning Behavior and Perceived Control of Time at Work," *Journal of Organizational Behavior* (December 2004), pp. 937–950.

62. See, for example, G. Lawrence-Ell, *The Invisible Clock: A Practical Revolution in Finding Time for Everyone and Everything* (Seaside Park, NJ: Kingsland Hall, 2002); and B. Tracy, *Time Power* (New York: AMACOM, 2004).

63. R. W. Renn, D. G. Allen, and T. M. Huning, "Empirical Examination of Individual-Level Personality-Based Theory of Self-Management Failure," *Journal of Organizational Behavior* 32, no. 1 (2011), pp. 25–43; and P. Gröpel and P. Steel, "A Mega-trial Investigation of Goal Setting, Interest Enhancement, and Energy on Procrastination," *Personality and Individual Differences* 45, no. 5 (2008), pp. 406–411.

64. P. Salmon, "Effects of Physical Exercise on Anxiety, Depression, and Sensitivity to Stress: A Unifying Theory," *Clinical Psychology Review* 21, no. 1 (2001), pp. 33–61.

65. K. M. Richardson and H. R. Rothstein, "Effects of Occupational Stress Management Intervention Programs: A Meta-analysis," *Journal of Occupational Health Psychology* 13, no. 1 (2008), pp. 69–93.

66. V. C. Hahn, C. Binnewies, S. Sonnentag, and E. J. Mojza, "Learning How to Recover from Job Stress: Effects of a Recovery Training Program on Recovery, Recovery-Related Self-Efficacy, and Well-Being," *Journal of Occupational Health Psychology* 16, no. 2 (2011), pp. 202–216; and C. Binnewies, S. Sonnentag, and E. J. Mojza, "Recovery During the Weekend and Fluctuations in Weekly Job Performance: A Week-Level Study Examining Intra-individual Relationships," *Journal of Occupational and Organizational Psychology* 83, no. 2 (2010), pp. 419–441.

67. E. R. Greenglass and L. Fiksenbaum, "Proactive Coping, Positive Affect, and Well-Being: Testing for Mediation Using Path Analysis," *European Psychologist* 14, no. 1 (2009), pp. 29–39; and P. Miquelon and R. J. Vallerand, "Goal Motives, Well-Being, and Physical Health: Happiness and Self-Realization as Psychological Resources under Challenge," *Motivation and Emotion* 30, no. 4 (2006), pp. 259–272.

68. M. M. Butts, R. J. Vandenberg, D. M. DeJoy, B. S. Schaffer, and M. G. Wilson, "Individual Reactions to High Involvement Work Processes: Investigating the Role of Empowerment and Perceived Organizational Support," *Journal of Occupational Health Psychology* 14, no. 2 (2009), pp. 122–136.

69. L. Blue, "Making Good Health Easy," *Time* (November 12, 2009), http://www.time.com; and M. Andrews, "America's Best Health Plans," *US News and World Report* (November 5, 2007), pp. 54–60.

70. K. M. Richardson and H. R. Rothstein, "Effects of Occupational Stress Management Intervention Programs: A Meta-analysis," *Journal of Occupational Health Psychology* 13, no. 1 (2008), pp. 69–93.

Glossary

ability An individual's capacity to perform the various tasks in a job.

accommodating The willingness of one party in a conflict to put the opponent's interests above his or her own.

accommodation This term is used in the context of working with people with varied needs, such as people with disabilities. It refers to the provision of devices, support, and policies that enable people to work to their maximum capacity.

adjourning stage The final stage in group development for temporary groups, characterized by concern with wrapping up activities rather than task performance.

affect A broad range of feelings that people experience.

affect intensity Experiencing the same emotions with different intensities; affectively intense people experience both positive and negative emotions more deeply.

affective component The emotional or feeling segment of an attitude.

affective events theory (AET) A model that demonstrates employees react emotionally to things at work, which influences their job performance and satisfaction.

agreeableness A personality dimension that describes someone who is good-natured, cooperative, and trusting.

anchoring bias A tendency to fixate on initial information, from which one then fails to adequately adjust for subsequent information.

anthropology The study of societies for the purpose of learning about human beings and their activities.

appreciative inquiry (AI) An approach that seeks to identify the unique qualities and special strengths of an organization, which can then be built on to improve performance.

approach–avoidance framework Personality framework that casts personality traits as motivations.

attitudes Evaluative statements, favourable or unfavourable, concerning objects, people, or events.

attribution theory An attempt to determine whether an individual's behaviour is internally or externally caused.

attribution theory of leadership A leadership theory that says that leadership is merely an attribution that people make about other individuals.

authentic leaders Leaders who know who they are, know what they believe in and value, and act on those values and beliefs openly and candidly; their followers would consider them to be ethical people.

authority The rights inherent in a managerial position to give orders and to expect the orders to be obeyed.

automatic processing A relatively superficial consideration of evidence and information making use of heuristics.

autonomy The degree to which a job provides substantial freedom and discretion to the individual in scheduling the work and in determining the procedures to be used in carrying it out.

availability bias The tendency for people to base their judgments on information that is readily available to them.

avoiding The desire to withdraw from or suppress a conflict.

BATNA The best alternative to a negotiated agreement; the least the individual should accept.

behavioural component An intention to behave in a certain way toward someone or something.

behavioural ethics An area of study that analyzes how people behave in ethical dilemmas.

behavioural theories of leadership Theories proposing that specific behaviours differentiate leaders from non-leaders.

Big Five Model A personality assessment model that taps five basic dimensions.

biographical characteristics Personal characteristics—such as age, gender, race, and length of tenure—that are objective and easily obtained from personnel records. These characteristics are representative of surface-level diversity.

bonus A way to reward employees for recent performance rather than historical performance.

boundaryless organization An organization that seeks to eliminate the chain of command, have limitless spans of control, and replace departments with empowered teams.

bounded rationality A process of making decisions by constructing simplified models that extract the essential features from problems without capturing all their complexity.

brainstorming An idea-generation process that specifically encourages any and all alternatives while withholding any criticism of those alternatives.

bureaucracy An organization structure with highly routine operating tasks achieved through specialization, very formalized rules and regulations, tasks that are grouped into functional departments, centralized authority, narrow spans of control, and decision making that follows the chain of command.

centralization The degree to which decision making is concentrated at a single point in an organization.

chain of command The unbroken line of authority that extends from the top of the organization to the lowest echelon and clarifies who reports to whom.

challenge stressors Stressors associated with workload, pressure to complete tasks, and time urgency.

channel richness The degree to which a communication channel can handle multiple cues simultaneously, facilitate feedback, and be personal.

charismatic leadership theory A leadership theory that states that followers make attributions of heroic or extraordinary leadership abilities when they observe certain behaviours and give these leaders power.

coercive power A power base that is dependent on fear of the negative results from failing to comply.

cognitive component The opinion or belief segment of an attitude.

cognitive dissonance Any incompatibility between two or more attitudes or between behaviour and attitudes.

cognitive evaluation theory A version of self-determination theory that holds that allocating extrinsic rewards for behaviour that previously had been intrinsically rewarding tends to decrease the overall level of motivation if the rewards are seen as controlling.

cohesiveness The degree to which group members are attracted to each other and motivated to stay in the group.

collaborating A situation in which the parties to a conflict each desire to satisfy fully the concerns of all parties.

collectivism A tight social framework in which people expect others in groups of which they are a part to look after them and protect them.

communication The imparting of news, information, and emotional states through speaking, writing, reading, and other signallers such as body language.

communication apprehension Undue tension and anxiety about oral communication, written communication, or both.

communication process The steps between a sender and a receiver that result in the transfer and understanding of meaning.

competing A desire to satisfy one's interests, regardless of the impact on the other party to the conflict.

compromising A situation in which each party to a conflict is willing to give up something.

confirmation bias The tendency to seek out information that reaffirms past choices and to discount information that contradicts past judgments.

conflict A process that begins when one party perceives that another party has negatively affected, or is about to negatively affect, something that the first party cares about.

conflict management The use of resolution and stimulation techniques to achieve the desired level of conflict.

conflict process A process that has five stages: potential opposition or incompatibility, cognition and personalization, intentions, behaviour, and outcomes.

conformity Being one of the group and therefore avoiding being visibly different.

conscientiousness A personality dimension that describes someone who is responsible, dependable, persistent, and organized.

consideration The extent to which a person is likely to have job relationships that are characterized by mutual trust, respect for employees' ideas, and regard for their feelings.

contingency variables Situational factors: variables that moderate the relationship between two or more other variables.

contrast effect Evaluation of a person's characteristics that is affected by comparisons with other people recently encountered who rank higher or lower on the same characteristics.

controlled processing A detailed consideration of evidence and information relying on facts, figures, and logic.

core self-evaluation (CSE) The degree to which an individual likes or dislikes himself or herself, whether the person sees himself or herself as capable and effective, and whether the person feels in control of his or her environment or powerless over the environment; bottom-line conclusions individuals have about their capabilities, competence, and worth as a person.

core values Strongly held values.

cost-minimization strategy A strategy that emphasizes tight cost controls, avoidance of unnecessary innovation or marketing expenses, and price cutting.

creativity The ability to produce novel and useful ideas.

cross-functional teams Employees from about the same hierarchical level, but from different work areas, who come together to accomplish a task.

Dark Triad The traits of Machiavellianism, narcissism, and psychopathy.

decisions Choices made from among two or more alternatives.

deep acting Trying to modify one's true inner feelings based on display rules.

deep-level diversity Differences in values, personality, and work preferences that become progressively more important for determining similarity as people get to know one another better.

defensive behaviours Reactive and protective behaviours to avoid action, blame, or change.

demands Responsibilities, pressures, obligations, and even uncertainties that individuals face in the workplace.

departmentalization The basis by which jobs are grouped together.

dependence B's relationship to A when A possesses something that B requires.

deviant workplace behaviour Voluntary behaviour that violates significant organizational norms and, in so doing, threatens the well-being of the organization or its members. Also called *antisocial behaviour* or *workplace incivility*.

discrimination The noting of a difference between things; often we refer to unfair discrimination, which means making judgments about individuals based on stereotypes regarding their demographic group.

displayed emotions The emotions that the organization requires workers to show and consider appropriate in a given job.

distributive bargaining Negotiation that seeks to divide up a fixed amount of resources; a win–lose situation.

distributive justice Perceived fairness of the amount and allocation of rewards among individuals.

diversity The degree to which members of the group are similar to, or different from, one another.

diversity management The process and programs by which managers make everyone more aware of and sensitive to the needs and differences of others.

dominant culture A culture that expresses the core values that are shared by a majority of the organization's members.

driving forces Forces that direct behaviour away from the status quo.

dyadic conflict Conflict between two people.

dysfunctional conflict Conflict that hinders group performance.

emotional contagion The process by which people's emotions are caused by the emotions of others.

emotional dissonance Inconsistencies between the emotions people feel and the emotions they project.

emotional intelligence (EI) One's ability to be self-aware, detect emotions in others, and manage emotional cues and information.

emotional labour An employee's expression of organizationally desired emotions during interpersonal transactions at work.

emotional stability A personality dimension that characterizes someone as calm, self-confident, secure (positive) versus nervous, depressed, and insecure (negative).

emotions Intense feelings directed at someone or something.

employee engagement An individual's involvement with, satisfaction with, and enthusiasm for the work they do.

employee involvement A participative process that uses the employees' input and is intended to increase employee commitment to an organization's success.

employee-oriented leader A leader who emphasizes interpersonal relations, takes a personal interest in the needs of employees, and accepts individual differences among members.

employee stock ownership plan (ESOP) A company-established benefit plan in which employees acquire stock, often at below-market prices, as part of their benefits.

encounter stage The stage in the socialization process in which a new employee sees what the organization is really like and confronts the possibility that expectations and reality may diverge.

environment Institutions or forces outside an organization that potentially affect the organization's performance.

equity theory A theory that says that individuals compare their job inputs and outcomes with those of others and then respond to eliminate any inequities.

escalation of commitment An increased commitment to a previous decision in spite of negative information.

ethical choices Decisions made on the basis of ethical criteria, including the outcomes of the decision, the rights of those affected, and the equitable distribution of benefits and costs.

ethical dilemmas Situations in which members of organizations are required to define right and wrong conduct.

evidence-based management (EBM) The basing of managerial decisions on the best available scientific evidence.

exit response One of the four responses to the exit–voice–loyalty–neglect framework that directs behaviour toward leaving the organization, including looking for a new position as well as resigning.

expectancy theory A theory that says that the strength of a tendency to act in a certain way depends on the strength of the expectation that the act will be followed by a given outcome and on the attractiveness of that outcome to the individual.

expert power Influence based on expertise, special skills, or knowledge.

extraversion A personality dimension describing someone who is sociable, gregarious, and assertive.

faultlines Perceived divisions that split groups into two or more subgroups based on individual differences.

feedback The degree to which carrying out the work activities required by a job results in the individual obtaining direct and clear information about the effectiveness of his or her performance.

felt conflict Emotional involvement in a conflict that creates anxiety, tenseness, frustration, or hostility.

felt emotions An individual's actual emotions.

femininity A national culture attribute that indicates little differentiation between male and female roles; a high rating indicates that women are treated as the equals of men in all aspects of the society.

Fiedler contingency model The theory that effective groups depend on a proper match between a leader's style of interacting with subordinates and the degree to which the situation gives control and influence to the leader.

filtering A sender's purposely manipulating information so the receiver will see it more favourably.

five-stage group-development model The five distinct stages groups go through: forming, storming, norming, performing, and adjourning.

fixed pie The belief that there is only a set amount of goods or services to be divvied up between the parties.

flexible benefits A benefits plan that allows each employee to put together a benefits package individually tailored to his or her own needs and situation.

flextime Flexible schedule in which employees must work a specific number of hours per week but may vary their hours.

formal channels Communication channels established by an organization to transmit messages related to the professional activities of members.

formal group A designated work group defined by an organization's structure.

formalization The degree to which jobs within an organization are standardized.

forming stage The first stage in group development, characterized by much uncertainty.

functional conflict Conflict that supports the goals of the group and improves its performance.

fundamental attribution error The tendency to underestimate the influence of external factors and overestimate the influence of internal factors when making judgments about the behaviour of others.

gainsharing A formula-based group incentive plan based on improvements in group productivity.

general mental ability (GMA) An overall factor of intelligence, as suggested by the positive correlations among specific intellectual ability dimensions.

goal-setting theory A theory that says that specific and difficult goals, with feedback, lead to higher performance.

grapevine An organization's informal communication network.

group Two or more individuals, interacting and interdependent, who have come together to achieve particular objectives.

groupshift A change in decision risk between a group's decision and an individual decision that a member within that group would make; the shift can be toward either conservatism or greater risk, interacting and interdependent, who have come together to achieve particular objectives.

groupthink A phenomenon in which the norm for consensus overrides the realistic appraisal of alternative courses of action.

halo effect The tendency to draw a general impression about an individual on the basis of a single characteristic.

heredity Factors determined at conception—one's biological, physiological, and inherent psychological makeup.

hierarchy of needs Abraham Maslow's hierarchy of five needs—physiological, safety, social, esteem, and self-actualization—in which, as each need is substantially satisfied, the next need becomes dominant.

high-context cultures Cultures that rely heavily on nonverbal and subtle situational cues in communication.

hindrance stressors Stressors that keep you from reaching your goals (for example, red tape, office politics, confusion over job responsibilities).

hindsight bias The tendency for us to believe falsely, after an outcome is actually known, that we would have accurately predicted the outcome.

hygiene factors Factors—such as company policy and administration, supervision, and salary—that, when adequate in a job, placate workers. When these factors are adequate, people will not be dissatisfied or satisfied.

idea champions People who actively and enthusiastically promote the idea, build support, overcome resistance, and ensure that the innovation is implemented.

idea evaluation The process of creative behaviour in which we evaluate potential solutions to identify the best one.

idea generation The process of creative behaviour in which potential solutions are evaluated.

illusory correlation The tendency of people to correlate two events when in reality there is no connection.

imitation strategy A strategy that seeks to move into new products or new markets only after their viability has already been proven.

impression management (IM) The process by which individuals attempt to control the impression others form of them.

individualism The degree to which people prefer to act as individuals rather than as members of groups and believe in individual rights above all else.

informal channels Communication channels that are created spontaneously and that emerge as responses to individual choices.

informal group A group that is neither formally structured nor organizationally determined.

information gathering The stage of creative behaviour when possible solutions to a problem are sought.

informational justice A perception of whether managers provide employees with explanations for key decisions and keep them informed.

initiating structure The extent to which a leader is likely to define and structure his or her role and those of subordinates in the search for goal attainment.

innovation A new idea applied to initiating or improving a product, process, or service.

innovation strategy A strategy that emphasizes the introduction of major new products and services.

institutionalization A condition that occurs when an organization takes on a life of its own, apart from any of its members, and acquires immortality.

instrumental values Preferable modes of behaviour or means of achieving one's terminal values.

integrative bargaining Negotiation that seeks one or more settlements that can create a win–win solution.

intellectual abilities The capacity to do mental activities—thinking, reasoning, and problem solving.

intentions Decisions to act in a given way.

interacting groups Typical groups in which members interact with each other face to face.

interactionist view of conflict The belief that conflict is not only a positive force in a group but also an absolute necessity for a group to perform effectively.

intergroup conflict Conflict between groups or teams.

intergroup development OD efforts to change the attitudes, stereotypes, and perceptions that groups have of each other.

interpersonal justice A perception of whether employees are treated with dignity and respect.

intragroup conflict Conflict that occurs within a group or team.

intuition A gut feeling not necessarily supported by research.

intuitive decision making An unconscious process created out of distilled experience.

job characteristics model (JCM) A model that proposes that any job can be described in terms of five core job dimensions: skill variety, task identity, task significance, autonomy, and feedback.

job design The way the elements in a job are organized.

job engagement The investment of an employee's physical, cognitive, and emotional energies into job performance.

job enrichment The vertical expansion of jobs, which increases the degree to which the worker controls the planning, execution, and evaluation of the work.

job involvement The degree to which a person identifies with a job, actively participates in it, and considers performance important to self-worth.

job rotation The periodic shifting of an employee from one task to another with similar skill requirements at the same organizational level.

job satisfaction A positive feeling about one's job resulting from an evaluation of its characteristics.

job sharing An arrangement that allows two or more individuals to split a traditional 40-hour-a-week job.

leader–member relations The degree of confidence, trust, and respect subordinates have in their leader.

leadership The ability to influence a group toward the achievement of a vision or set of goals.

least preferred co-worker (LPC) questionnaire An instrument that purports to measure whether a person is task- or relationship-oriented.

legitimate power The power a person receives as a result of his or her position in the formal hierarchy of an organization.

long-term orientation A national culture attribute that emphasizes the future, thrift, and persistence.

low-context cultures Cultures that rely heavily on words to convey meaning in communication.

loyalty response One of the four responses to the exit–voice–loyalty–neglect framework that means passively but optimistically waiting for conditions to improve, including speaking up for the organization in the face of external criticism and trusting the organization and its management to "do the right thing."

Machiavellianism The degree to which an individual is pragmatic, maintains emotional distance, and believes that ends can justify means.

management by objectives (MBO) A program that encompasses specific goals, participatively set, for an explicit time period, with feedback on goal progress.

masculinity A national culture attribute describing the extent to which the culture favours traditional masculine work roles of achievement.

material symbols Objects that serve as signals of an organization's culture, including the size of offices, executive perks, and attire.

matrix structure A structure that creates dual lines of authority and combines functional and product departmentalization.

McClelland's theory of needs A theory that states achievement, power, and affiliation are three important needs that help explain motivation.

mechanistic model A structure characterized by extensive departmentalization, high formalization, a limited information network, and centralization.

mental models Team members' organized mental representations of how the work gets done by the team.

mentor A senior employee who sponsors and supports a less experienced employee.

merit-based pay plan A pay plan based on performance appraisal ratings.

metamorphosis stage The stage in the socialization process in which a new employee changes and adjusts to the job, work group, and organization.

model An abstraction of reality; a simplified representation of some real-world phenomenon.

moods Feelings that tend to be less intense than emotions and that lack a contextual stimulus.

motivation The process that accounts for an individual's intensity, direction, and persistence of effort toward attaining a goal.

movement A change process that transforms the organization from the status quo to a desired end state.

multiteam systems Systems in which different teams need to coordinate their efforts to produce a superordinate goal.

Myers-Briggs Type Indicator (MBTI) A personality test that taps four characteristics and classifies people into one of 16 personality types.

narcissism The tendency to be arrogant, have a grandiose sense of self-importance, require excessive admiration, and have a sense of entitlement.

need for achievement (nAch) The drive to excel, to achieve in relationships to a set of standards, and to strive to succeed.

need for affiliation (nAff) The desire for friendly and close interpersonal relationships.

need for power (nPow) The need to make others behave in a way in which they would not have behaved otherwise.

negative affect A mood dimension that consists of emotions such as nervousness, stress, and anxiety at the high end and contentedness, calmness, and serenity at the low end.

neglect response One of the four responses to the exit–voice–loyalty–neglect framework that passively allows conditions to worsen and includes chronic absenteeism or lateness, reduced effort, and increased error rate.

negotiation A process in which two or more parties decide how to allocate scarce resources.

neutralizers Attributes that make it impossible for leader behaviour to make any difference to follower outcomes.

nominal group technique A group decision-making method in which individuals meet face to face to pool their judgments in a systematic but independent fashion.

norming stage The third stage in group development, characterized by close relationships and cohesiveness.

norms Acceptable standards of behaviour that are shared by the group's members.

openness to experience A personality dimension that characterizes someone in terms of imagination, sensitivity, and curiosity.

organic model A structure that is flat, uses cross-hierarchical and cross-functional teams, has low formalization, possesses a comprehensive information network, and relies on participative decision making.

organizational behaviour (OB) A field of study that investigates the impact that individuals, groups, and structures have on a behaviour within organizations, for the purpose of applying such knowledge toward improving an organization's effectiveness.

organizational climate The shared perceptions organizational members have about their organization and work environment.

organizational commitment The degree to which an employee identifies with a particular organization and its goals and wishes to maintain membership in the organization.

organizational culture A system of shared meaning held by members that distinguishes the organization from other organizations.

organizational demography The degree to which members of a work unit share a common demographic attribute, such as age, sex, race, educational level, or length of service in an organization.

organizational development (OD) A collection of change methods that try to improve organizational effectiveness and employee well-being.

organizational justice An overall perception of what is fair in the workplace, composed of distributive, procedural, and interactional justice.

organizational structure How job tasks are formally divided, grouped, and coordinated.

participative management A process in which subordinates share a significant degree of decision-making power with their immediate superiors.

path-goal theory The theory that effective leaders clarify followers' paths to their work goals and reduce work blocks.

perceived conflict Awareness by one or more parties of the existence of conditions that create opportunities for conflict to arise.

perceived organizational support (POS) The degree to which employees believe the organization values their contributions and cares about their well-being.

perception A process by which individuals organize and interpret their sensory impressions to give meaning to their environment.

performing The fourth stage of the five-stage group development model where group energy has advanced from understanding each other to performing the task at hand.

personality The sum total of ways in which an individual reacts to and interacts with others.

personality–job fit theory A theory that identifies six personality types and proposes that the fit between personality type and occupational environment determines satisfaction and turnover.

personality traits Enduring characteristics that describe an individual's behaviour.

physical abilities The capacity to do tasks that demand stamina, dexterity, strength, and similar characteristics.

piece-rate pay plan A plan in which employees are paid fixed sum for each unit of production completed.

political behaviour Activities that are not required as part of one's formal role in the organization but that influence, or attempt to influence, the distribution of advantages and disadvantages within the organization.

political skill People's ability to influence others to enhance their own objectives.

position power Influence derived from one's formal structural position in the organization; includes power to hire, fire, discipline, promote, and give salary increases.

positive affect A mood dimension consisting of positive emotions such as excitement, enthusiasm, and elation on the high end and boredom, depression, and fatigue at the low end.

positive organizational culture A culture that emphasizes building on employee strengths, rewards more than punishes, and emphasizes individual vitality and growth.

positive organizational scholarship The study of how organizations develop human strengths, foster vitality and resilience, and unlock potential.

positivity offset The tendency of most individuals to experience a mildly positive mood at zero input (when nothing in particular is going on).

power The capacity that A has to influence the behaviour of B so that B acts in accordance with A's wishes.

power distance Degree to which people in a country accept that power in institutions and organizations is distributed unequally.

power tactics Ways in which individuals translate power bases into specific actions.

prearrival stage The period of learning in the socialization process that occurs before a new employee joins the organization.

prevention focus In goal-setting theory, the tendency for some people to strive to fulfill duties and obligations and avoid conditions that pull them away from desired goals.

proactive personality People who identify opportunities, show initiative, take action, and persevere until meaningful change occurs.

problem A discrepancy between the current state of affairs and some desired state.

problem formulation The stage of creative behaviour in which we identify a problem or opportunity which has no known solution.

problem-solving teams Groups of 5 to 12 employees from the same department who meet for a few hours each week to discuss ways of improving quality, efficiency, and the work environment.

procedural justice The perceived fairness of the process used to determine the distribution of rewards.

process conflict Conflict over how work gets done.

process consultation (PC) A meeting in which a consultant assists a client in understanding process events with which he or she must deal and identifying processes that need improvement.

production-oriented leader A leader who emphasizes technical or task aspects of the job.

profit-sharing plan Organization-wide program that distributes compensation based on some established formula designed around a company's profitability.

promotion focus In goal-setting theory, the tendency in some people to strive for advancement and accomplishment.

psychological empowerment Employees' belief in the degree to which they affect their work environments, their competence, the meaningfulness of their jobs, and the perceived autonomy in their work.

psychology The science that seeks to measure, explain, and sometimes change the behaviour of humans and other animals.

psychopathy A lack of concern for others, and a lack of guilt or remorse for causing harm.

punctuated-equilibrium model A set of phases that temporary groups go through that involves transitions between inertia and activity.

rational Characterized by making consistent, value-maximizing choices within specified constraints.

rational decision-making model A decision-making model that describes how individuals should behave in order to maximize some outcome.

reference groups Important groups to which individuals belong or hope to belong and with whose norms individuals are likely to conform.

referent power Influence based on identification with a person who has desirable resources or personal traits.

reflexivity A team characteristic of reflecting on and adjusting the master plan when necessary.

refreezing Stabilizing a change intervention by balancing and restraining forces.

relationship conflict Conflict based on interpersonal relationships.

representative participation A system in which workers participate in organizational decision making through a small group of representative employees.

resources Things within an individual's control that can be used to resolve demands.

restraining forces Forces that hinder movement from the existing equilibrium.

reward power Compliance achieved based on the ability to distribute rewards that others view as valuable.

risk aversion The tendency to prefer a sure gain of a moderate amount over a riskier outcome, even if the riskier outcome might have a higher expected payoff.

rituals Repetitive sequences of activities that express and reinforce the key values of the organization.

role A set of expected behaviour patterns attributed to someone occupying a given position in a social unit.

role conflict When an individual finds that compliance with one role requirement may make it difficult to comply with another.

role expectations How others believe a person should act in a given situation.

role perception An individual's view of how he or she is supposed to act in a given situation.

scientific study A methodology used to generate and confirm knowledge. It consists of generating hypotheses and empirically testing them using methods that ensure the objective reliability and validity of the results.

selective perception Any characteristic that makes a person, object, or event stand out will increase the probability that it will be perceived.

self-concordance The degree to which peoples' reasons for pursuing goals are consistent with their interests and core values.

self-determination theory A theory of motivation that proposes that people prefer to feel they have control over their actions.

self-efficacy theory An individual's belief that he or she is capable of performing a task; the higher your self-efficacy, the more confidence you have in your ability to succeed. Also known as *social cognitive theory* or *social learning theory*.

self-managed work teams Groups of 10 to 15 people who perform highly related or interdependent jobs and take on some supervisory responsibilities.

self-monitoring A personality trait that measures an individual's ability to adjust his or her behaviour to external situational factors.

self-serving bias The tendency of individuals to attribute their own successes to internal factors and put the blame for failures on external factors.

servant leadership A leadership style marked by going beyond the leader's own self-interest and instead focusing on opportunities to help followers grow and develop.

short-term orientation A national culture attribute that emphasizes the present.

simple structure An organization structure characterized by a low degree of departmentalization, wide spans of control, authority centralized in a single person, and little formalization.

situation strength theory Theoretical framework that proposes the way that personality transfers into behaviour depends on the strength of the situation.

situational leadership theory (SLT) The leadership theory that successful leadership depends on the followers.

skill-based pay A pay plan that sets pay levels on the basis of how many skills employees have or how many jobs they can do.

skill variety The degree to which a job requires a variety of different activities.

social loafing The tendency for individuals to expend less effort when working collectively than when working individually.

social psychology Focuses on people's influences on one another.

socialization A process that adapts employees to the organization's culture.

sociology The study of people in relation to their social environment or culture.

span of control The number of subordinates a manager directs.

status A socially defined position or rank given to groups or group members by others.

status characteristics theory A theory that states that differences in status characteristics create status hierarchies within groups.

stereotyping When we judge someone on the basis of our perception of the group to which he or she belongs.

storming stage The second stage in group development, characterized by intragroup conflict.

stress A dynamic condition in which an individual is confronted with an opportunity, a demand, or a resource related to what the individual desires and for which the outcome is perceived to be both uncertain and important.

strong culture A culture in which the core values are intensely held and widely shared.

subcultures Minicultures within an organization, typically defined by department designations and geographical separation.

substitutes Attributes, such as experience and training, that can replace the need for leadership behaviour.

surface acting Hiding one's inner feelings and foregoing emotional expressions in response to display rules.

surface-level diversity Differences in easily perceived characteristics, such as gender, race, ethnicity, age, or disability, that do not necessarily reflect the ways people think or feel but that may activate certain stereotypes.

survey feedback The use of questionnaires to identify discrepancies among member perceptions; discussion follows and remedies are suggested.

task conflict Conflict over content and goals of the work.

task identity The degree to which a job requires completion of a whole and identifiable piece of work.

task significance The degree to which a job has a substantial impact on the lives or work of other people.

task structure The degree to which the job assignments are proceduralized.

team building High interaction among team members to increase trust and openness.

technology The way in which an organization transfers its inputs into outputs.

telecommuting Working from home at least two days a week on a computer that is linked to the employer's office.

terminal values Desirable end-states of existence; the goals a person would like to achieve during his or her lifetime.

theory X The assumption that employees dislike work, are lazy, dislike responsibility, and must be coerced to perform.

theory Y The assumption that employees like work, are creative, seek responsibility, and can exercise self-direction.

three-stage model of creativity A model which details the causes and effects of creative behaviour.

traditional view of conflict The belief that all conflict is harmful and must be avoided.

trait activation theory (TAT) The theory that some situations, events, or interventions activate a trait more than others.

trait theories of leadership Theories that consider personal qualities and characteristics that differentiate leaders from non-leaders.

transactional leaders Leaders who guide or motivate their followers in the direction of established goals by clarifying role and task requirements.

transformational leaders Leaders who inspire followers to transcend their own self-interests and who are capable of having a profound and extraordinary effect on followers.

trust A positive expectation that another will not act opportunistically.

two-factor theory A theory that relates intrinsic factors to job satisfaction and associates extrinsic factors with dissatisfaction. Also called *motivation-hygiene theory*.

uncertainty avoidance A national culture attribute that describes the extent to which a society feels threatened by uncertain and ambiguous situations and tries to avoid them.

unfreezing Changing to overcome the pressures of both individual resistance and group conformity.

unity of command The idea that a subordinate should have only one superior to whom he or she is directly responsible.

utilitarianism A system in which decisions are made solely on the basis of their outcomes or consequences and to provide the greatest good for the greatest number.

values Basic convictions that a specific mode of conduct or endstate of existence is personally or socially preferable to an opposite or converse mode of conduct or end-state of existence.

variable-pay program A pay plan that bases a portion of an employee's pay on some individual and/or organizational measure of performance.

virtual organization A small, core organization that outsources major business functions.

virtual teams Teams that use computer technology to tie together physically dispersed members in order to achieve a common goal.

vision A long-term strategy for attaining a goal or goals by linking the present with a better future for the organization.

vision statement A formal articulation of an organization's vision or mission.

voice response One of the four responses to the exit–voice–loyalty–neglect framework that includes actively and constructively attempting to improve conditions, including suggesting improvements, discussing problems with superiors, and undertaking some forms of union activity.

wellness programs Organizationally supported programs that focus on the employee's total physical and mental condition.

whistle-blowers Individuals who report unethical or illegal practices by their employers to outsiders.

workforce diversity The concept that organizations are becoming more heterogeneous in terms of gender, age, race, ethnicity, sexual orientation, and inclusion of other diverse groups.

work group A group that interacts primarily to share information and to make decisions to help each group member perform within his or her area of responsibility.

work specialization The degree to which tasks in an organization are subdivided into separate jobs.

work team A group whose individual efforts result in performance that is greater than the sum of the individual inputs.

zero-sum approach An approach to negotiation that implies that gains on one side always require losses on the other side. This is often contrasted with mutual gain, or win-win styles of negotiation.

Note: Page references with "e" refer to exihibits.

A

A. T. Kearney, 314
ABB, 295
ability, 34, 193–194
Aboriginal cultures, 101
Aboriginal peoples, 20, 28, 38–39, 120, 154, 180, 282
Aboriginal Peoples Television Network, 315
Aboriginal values, 101
absenteeism, 57, 152–153
accommodating, 272, 273
accountability, 239
acculturation, 101
acquisitions, 313–314
adjourning stage, 167
Admiral, 322
affect, 64, 64e
affect intensity, 67
affective component, 47
affective events theory (AET), 72–73, 72e
affirmative action, 40–41
age, 24–26, 24e
    discrimination, 27
    and effective communication, 215
    and moods and emotions, 68
aggressiveness, 310
agreeableness, 85, 280
Air Canada, 323
AirAsia, 323
Albert, Sylvie, 2
Alberta Dairy Pool v. Alberta Human Rights Commission, 32
all-channel, 206–207
alternative work arrangements, 151–155
    flextime, 151–153, 152e
    job sharing, 153
    telecommuting, 153–155
ambiguous responsibility, 178
America Online (AOL), 314
American Airlines, 323
anchoring bias, 114–115
Andersson, Bo, 299
anger, 280
Anglophone Canadians, 98
Anthony, Carmelo, 197
anthropology, 6
antisocial behaviour, 172
    see also deviant workplace behaviour
anxiety, 281
AOL Time Warner, 314
apologies, 257e
appearance norms, 170

Apple, 298
appreciative inquiry (AI), 335
approach–avoidance framework, 90
ARA (accountability, responsibility, and authority), 216
arousal, 136
Asch, Solomon, 171, 171e, 179
Ash, Mary Kay, 229
Assembly of First Nations, 315
assertive IM technique, 258e
assertiveness, 272
AT&T, 298
attention to detail, 310
attitudes, 46
    affective component, 47
    and behaviour, 48–49
    behavioural component, 47
    cognitive component, 47
    components of, 47, 47e
    major job attitudes, 49–52
    moderating variables, 49
attribution theory, 107–109, 108e
attribution theory of leadership, 238–239
Auglaize Provico, 320
Australia, 51–52, 98
Austria, 98
authentic leaders, 235
authentic leadership, 235–237
authority, 291
automatic processing, 213
autonomy, 148, 303
availability bias, 115
avoiding, 273

B

Balsillie, Jim, 159
Bandura, Albert, 135, 136
bargaining strategies, 275–278
barriers to change, 313
barriers to effective communication, 214–217
    communication apprehension, 216–217
    cultural barriers, 217–218
    emotions, 215
    filtering, 214
    information overload, 215
    language, 215–216
    lying, 217
    selective perception, 215
    silence, 216
    social anxiety, 216–217

bases of power, 246–248
basic emotions, 64–65
basic moods, 65
Bates, Paul, 264
BATNA, 279
behaviour
    and attitudes, 48–49
    conflict process, 273–274
    externally caused behaviour, 108
    internally caused behaviours, 108
    organizational behaviour (OB) See organizational behaviour (OB)
    and organizational design, 302–304
behavioural component, 47
behavioural ethics, 118–119
behavioural symptoms of stress, 339
behavioural theories of leadership, 224–226
Belgium, 72, 152
benefit package, 39
benefits, 160–161
Benioff, Marc, 50
Bennett, John, 119
best alternative to a negotiated agreement (BATNA), 279
Best Buy, 154
biases and errors
    anchoring bias, 114–115
    availability bias, 115
    confirmation bias, 115
    in decision making, 113–116
    escalation of commitment, 115
    fundamental attribution error, 109
    hindsight bias, 116
    overconfidence bias, 113–114
    reducing biases and errors, 114e
    risk aversion, 115–116
    self-serving bias, 109
biculturalism, 101
big data, 4
Big Five Model, 85–87, 87e, 224
Bill 125, 31
biographical characteristics, 24
    ability, 34
    age, 24–25, 24e
    cultural identity, 31
    disabilities, 31–33
    ethnicity, 28
    gender, 26–27
    gender identity, 27
    immigration status, 28–30
    race, 27–28
    religion, 33
    sexual orientation, 27

bisexual, 27
Blockbuster, 116
blood sugar levels, 71
BMW, 190, 295
board representatives, 156
body language, 210
body movement, 210
Boeing, 295, 298
bona fide occupational requirements
    (BFOR), 32
bonus, 159
Booz Allen Hamilton, 315
bossless work environment, 239
boundary spanners, 191
boundaryless organization, 297–298
bounded rationality, 112–113
Bowerman, Bill, 318
brainstorming, 180
Brandon Police Services, 43–44
Brazil, 225
Broadwater, Gene, 132
Brynaert, Didier, 321
buck passing, 256e
buffing, 256e
bureaucracy, 294–295
bureaucratic specialization, 295
bureaupathologies, 296

C
Canada, 130, 152, 160, 161, 171, 175,
    210, 250, 282, 322
Canada's Food Guide, 184–185
Canadian Association of Oilwell Drilling
    Contractors, 299
Canadian Business, 301
Canadian Charter of Rights and
    Freedoms, 31, 33, 118
Canadian culture, 100e, 322
Canadian Football League, 190
Canadian Human Resources Centre, 126
Canadian military, 188
Canadian National Railway Co., 159
Canadian Special Forces, 316
Canadian Tire, 290
Canadian workforce
    biographical characteristics, 24–34
    demographic characteristics, 20–23
capacity, 302
Carbee, Marshall, 119
Carnegie School, 7
Casmir, Fred, 218–219
Caterpillar, 51, 301
Cavalli-Sforza, L.L., 27
CBC, 145–146
cellphones, 209e
centralization, 292–293, 303
chain, 206
chain of command, 291
challenge stressors, 338
change, 6
    see also change management

culture for change, 355–357
fair implementation of, 331
forces for change, 327–329
resistance to change, 329–332
change barriers, 313
change management
    Kotter's eight-step plan for imple-
      menting change, 333–334, 333e
    Lewin's three-step model,
      332–333, 332e
    organizational development (OD),
      334–335
channel richness, 211, 211e, 212
charismatic leadership, 229–232, 230e, 234
charismatic leadership theory, 230
Chile, 130
China, 51, 65, 98, 175, 210, 218, 225, 234,
    250, 259, 275, 281, 298, 322
Chrysler, 190
CIBC, 291
Cisco Systems, 190
citizenship behaviour, 57
    see also organizational citizenship
      behaviour (OCB)
clarification, 279
clarity, 92
Clear Channel Communications, 316
client relationships, 150
closure, 280
cloud computing, 213
cloud-based electronic data storage, 213
coalition tactics, 250
coalitions, 249
coercion, 332
coercive power, 247
cognition, and conflict, 271–272
cognitive component, 47
cognitive dissonance, 49, 71
cognitive evaluation theory, 131
cohesiveness, 175–176
collaborating, 272–273
collectivism, 97, 140, 171, 175, 218,
    234, 275
Columbia, 171
common-law partners, 27
communication, 204
    barriers to effective communication,
      214–217
    communication channels,
      211–213, 211e
    communication process, 204, 204e
    conflict and, 271
    direction of communication, 204–206
    downward communication, 205
    electronic communication, 208, 209e
    formal organizational
      communication, 341
    formal small-group networks,
      206–207, 206e
    global implications, 217–219
    grapevine, 207–208

information security, 213
intercultural communications,
    217–219
lateral communication, 205–206
modes of communication, 208–211
non-routine communications, 212
nonverbal communication, 210–211
oral communication, 208, 212
organizational communication,
    206–208
persuasive communication, 213–214
and resistance to change, 330
small-group networks, 206–207,
    206e, 207e
technology-mediated professional
    communication guidelines, 209e
upward communication, 205
written communication, 208, 212
communication apprehension, 216–217
communication channels, 211–213, 211e
communication process, 204, 204e
compensation. *See* pay
competency-based pay, 159
competing, 272
competition, 328
complexity, 302
compromise, 278
compromising, 273
Conchie, Barry, 320
confirmation bias, 115
conflict, 196–197, 267
    see also specific types of conflict
    and communication, 271
    conflict process, 270–275, 271e
    interactionist view of conflict, 267
    loci of conflict, 269–270
    and personal variables, 271
    sources of, 271
    and structure, 271
    and teams, 196–197
    traditional view of conflict, 267
    types of conflict, 268–269
conflict management, 274
conflict process, 270–275, 271e
    behaviour, 273–274
    cognition and personalization,
      271–272
    intentions, 272–273
    outcomes, 274–275
    potential opposition or
      incompatibility, 271
conflict resolution, 218
conflict-intensity continuum, 274e
conformity, 170–172, 257e, 258
conformity pressures, 178
confrontation, 334
conscientiousness, 86, 195, 224
consensus, 108
consequences, 93
consideration, 225
consistency, 92–93, 108

constraints, 93
consultation, 249
contemporary theories of motivation, 131–142
context, 107, 215
contingency theories, 226–229, 303
contingency variables, 8
contingent reward leadership, 233
contrast effect, 110
controlled processing, 213
cooperativeness, 272
cooptation, 331
core self-evaluation (CSE), 55, 91
core values, 310–311
cost-minimization strategy, 301
counterproductive behaviour, 58
Coupland, Michael, 190
creative personality, 120
creativity, 87, 119, 178, 234
    causes, 119
    causes of creative behaviour, 120–121
    creative behaviour, 119–120
    creative outcomes, 121
    effects, 119
    free flow of ideas, 121
    and moods and emotions, 76
    and motivation, 120–121
    in organizations, 119–121
    three-stage model of creativity, 119, 119e
cross-functional teams, 189–190
Cuban, Mark, 120
cultural context, 218
cultural differences, 140
cultural dimensions, 98–99, 99e
cultural factors, 215
cultural identity, 31
cultural norms, 12, 31
culture. See national culture; organizational culture
culture clash, 314
customer markets, 291
customer satisfaction, 57
customer service, 12, 77

D

Dallas Mavericks, 120
Dark Triad, 88–90
day of the week, 68, 70e
decentralization, 292–293
deception, 217
decision making, 75–76
    bounded rationality, 112–113
    common biases and errors, 113–116
    and ethics, 117–119
    group decision making. See group decision making
    individual decision making, 111–112
    intuitive decision making, 113
    organizational constraints, 116–117

organizational decision making, 112–113
    rational decision making, 112
decisions, 111
decoding, 204
deep acting, 71, 280
deep-level diversity, 23
defensive behaviours, 256, 256e
defensive IM technique, 257e
degree of routineness, 302
DeGroote School of Business, 264
demands, 338
demographic characteristics, 20–23
demographic diversity, 40
departmentalization, 290–291
dependence, 245–246
Desire2Learn (D2L), 301, 316, 319
deviant workplace behaviour, 58, 78, 172–173, 173e
direction, 127
disabilities, 22, 31–33, 36
disability-based discrimination, 43–44
disappointment, 281
discrimination, 31, 36–38
    age discrimination, 27
    disability-based discrimination, 43–44
    forms of, 37e
    gender-based employment discrimination, 20–22
displayed emotions, 71
dissatisfaction, 55–56, 55e
    see also job satisfaction
dissatisfiers, 129e
distinctiveness, 108
distributive bargaining, 276–277, 276e
distributive justice, 138–139
diversity, 19–20, 38, 176
    see also diversity management
    barriers to diversity, 313
    biographical characteristics of workforce, 24–34
    in Canadian context, 20
    deep-level diversity, 23
    demographic characteristics of workforce, 20–23
    demographic diversity, 40
    faultlines, 177
    group diversity, 40, 176–177
    intellectual abilities, 34–35, 35e
    levels of diversity, 23
    multiculturalism, 20
    physical abilities, 36–38, 36e
    surface-level diversity, 23, 176
    of team members, 194–195
    workplace diversity, 12, 38
diversity management, 38
    see also diversity
    effective diversity programs, 40–41
    group performance, 40
    recruitment of diverse employees, 38–40

division of labour, 289
D2L. See Desire2Learn (D2L)
Docken, Dwayne, 85
Dollo, Christian, 284–285
dominant culture, 310–311
Don Jagoda Associates, 249
downsizing, 298–300
downward communication, 205
driving forces, 332
Drucker, Peter, 320
Dunning, Kitty, 249
duty to accommodate, 32
Duxbury, Linda, 326
dyadic conflict, 269–270
Dynegy, 319
dysfunctional conflict, 267
dysfunctional outcomes, 274

E

early theories of motivation, 127–131
East Asia, 280
Eastern Europe, 225
Eco Safety Products, 119
Economic Participation and Opportunity Sub-Index, 22
economic pressures, 11
economic-class immigrants, 29
education
    gender gap and, 21–22e
    and resistance to change, 330
effective leaders, 240
effective teams, 192–197
effectiveness, 178, 181e, 207
efficiency, 178
effort–performance relationship, 141
Eiffel tower cultures, 322–323
electronic communication, 208, 209e
Ellison, Larry, 89
e-mail, 209e
emotion regulation, 74–75
emotional contagion, 77, 80–81
emotional dissonance, 71
emotional intelligence (EI), 73–74, 74e
emotional labour, 71–72, 79–80
emotional stability, 86
emotions, 64, 64e
    as barrier to effective communication, 215
    the basic emotions, 64–65
    and ethics, 66–67
    experiencing emotions, 65–66
    function of, 66–67
    and irrationality, 66
    negotiation, 77, 280–281
    OB applications of, 75–78
    potential influences on, 67–71
    sources of, 67–71
empathy, 280
employee assistance programs (EAPs), 337
employee engagement, 51–52

employee involvement, 155–156
employee motivation. *See* motivation
employee recognition programs, 161–162
employee stock ownership plan
 (ESOP), 160
employee strengths, 320
employee well-being, 13
employee withdrawal, 58
employee-oriented leader, 225
employment, gender gap and, 21–22e
Employment Equity Act, 31
employment equity programs, 41
employment options, 9–10e
empowerment, 234
enactive mastery, 135
encounter stage, 316
Energizer, 291, 295
enhancement, 257e
Enron, 232
entry socialization options, 317e
Environics Institute for Survey
 Research, 100
environment, 302
Equitable, 290
equity theory, 136–140, 137e
errors. *See* biases and errors
escalation of commitment, 115
esteem needs, 128
ethical behaviour
 see also ethics
 and emotions, 66–67
 improvement of, 14
 top management, and ESOPs, 160
ethical dilemmas, 14
ethical leadership, 235
ethical organizational culture, 319–320
ethics
 see also ethical behaviour
 authentic leadership, 235–237
 behavioural ethics, 118–119
 in decision making, 117–119
 ethical choices, 14
 ethical decision criteria, 118–119
 of political behaviour, 259–260
 utilitarianism, 118
ethnicity, 28
Etsy, 39
Europe, 158, 218, 280
evidence-based management (EBM), 3–4
exchange, 249
exclusion, 37e
excuses, 257e
exemplification, 258e
exercise, 70
exit response, 56
expectancy theory, 141–142, 141e
expert power, 247–248
expertise, 120
explicit deadlines, 117
external equity, 157
externally caused behaviour, 108

extraversion, 85, 86–87, 224
extraverted (E), 84
extrinsic rewards, 131–132, 198

F

Facebook, 159, 316
face-to-face conversation, 211
facial expressions, 210
Fairmont Group, 161
family cultures, 322
family-class immigrants, 29
Farrows, 298
faultlines, 177
favours, 257e, 258
feedback, 133, 148, 204
feedback channels, 150
feeling (F), 84
felt conflict, 272
felt emotions, 71
femininity, 98
Festinger, Leon, 48–49
FHRITP phenomenon, 183
Fiedler, Fred, 226
 see also Fiedler contingency model
Fiedler contingency model,
 226–228, 227e
filtering, 214
Fiserv, 140
five-stage group-development model,
 167–168
fixed pie, 276–277
flattery, 258, 258e
flexible benefits, 161
flextime, 151–153, 152e
Food Guide Advisory Committee, 184
forces for change, 327–329
Ford, Henry, 289
Ford, Henry II, 318
Ford Motor Company, 190, 301, 318
foreign assignment, 11
formal channel, 204
formal group, 167
formal organizational
 communication, 341
formal power, 247
formal regulations, 117
formal small-group networks,
 206–207
formalization, 293, 311
format regulations, 117
forming stage, 167
France, 152, 210, 225, 323
Francophone Canadians, 98
Free the Children, 314
full range of leadership model,
 233, 233e
functional conflict, 267, 275
functional departmentalization,
 290, 291, 295
functional outcomes, 274
fundamental attribution error, 109

G

gainsharing, 160
Gallup, 142, 320
Gates, Bill, 314
gay, 27
gender, 26–27
 and discrimination, 20–22
 and negotiations, 282
gender gap, 21–22e
gender identity, 27
gender role congruency effects, 249–250
gender role stereotypes, 259
gender-based employment discrimination,
 20–22
General Electric (GE), 134, 297–298
General Foods, 186
general mental ability (GMA), 35
General Motors (GM), 117, 190
generational differences, 208
geographic departmentalization, 290
Germany, 152, 153, 225, 323
Gestion Bernard Belanger, 284–285
Gino, Francesca, 316
GitHub, 239
Gladwell, Malcolm, 116
Glassdoor, 140
global implications
 communication, 217–219
 organizational culture, 322–323
Global Leadership and Organizational
 Behaviour Effectiveness
 (GLOBE). *See* GLOBE
 Framework
globalization, 11–12
GLOBE Framework, 99–100, 225, 234
goal commitment, 133
goal setting, 136e, 340
goals, specific, 196
goal-setting theory, 132–134, 134e
Google, 39, 316
Gorky Automobile Factory (GAZ), 299
Górska-Kolodziejczyk, Elzbieta, 321
grapevine, 207–208
Great Britain, 98, 130, 259
Great-West, 290
Greece, 98
Greene, John, 50, 51
Gretzky, Wayne, 229
ground rules, 279
group, 167
 classroom diversity and groups,
 44–45
 cohesiveness, 175–176
 diversity, 40, 176–177
 effectiveness, 178, 181e
 efficiency, 178
 five-stage group-development model,
 167–168
 formal group, 167
 informal group, 167
 interacting groups, 180

interaction and status, 174
norms, 170–173
punctuated-equilibrium model, 168–169, 168e
reference groups, 172
roles, 169
size, 174–175
social loafing, 174, 175
stages of group development, 167e
status, 173–174
temporary groups with deadlines, 168–169
vs. team, 187, 188e, 198
work attitudes, 175
group decision making, 177–180
brainstorming, 180
groupshift, 178, 179–180
groupthink, 178, 179
nominal group technique, 180–181
strengths of, 177–178
techniques, 180–181
weaknesses of, 178
group diversity, 40, 176–177
group norms, 170–173
group polarization, 179–180
group roles, 169
group size, 174–175
group status, 173–174
groupshift, 178, 179–180
groupthink, 178, 179
growth, 321
Guatemala, 98
guided missile cultures, 322

H

Hackman, J. Richard, 148, 192
Hackman Criteria, 192
Hallmark Cards Inc., 198
halo effect, 110
Hammond, Larry, 320
"hangovers," 317
Harper, Stephen, 28
Harris, Rothenberg International, 337
Harvard, 316
Hawthorne Electrical Company, 7
Hawthorne studies, 7, 170
"headline" approach, 205
Health Canada, 184
HealthSouth, 232
heredity, 83
HeroX, 120
Herzberg, Frederick, 129–130
heuristics, 110
Hewlett-Packard, 298, 301
hierarchy of needs, 127–128, 128e
high-ability teams, 194–195
high-context cultures, 218, 281
high-Mach perspective, 88
hijab, 28
hindrance stressors, 338
hindsight bias, 116

historical precedents, 117
history of organizational behaviour (OB), 7
Hitler, Adolph, 225
Hoa's Tool Shop, 119
Hofstede, Geert, 97, 98, 99, 100, 322
Hofstede Centre, 8
Hofstede's framework, 97–99, 99e, 100
Holland, John, 95–96, 96e
Honda, 190
"honeymoons," 317
Hong Kong, 98, 160, 259
House, Robert, 229, 230
human capital, 58
Human Resources Professional Association (HRPA), 23
Human Rights Act, 31, 33
Human rights tribunals, 118
humanitarian-class immigrants, 28–29
Hunt, Shauna, 183–184
Husky Energy, 299
Hydro Ontario, 183
hygiene factors, 129
Hyundai, 314

I

IBM, 98, 295
idea champions, 336–337
idea evaluation, 120
idea generation, 119–120
idealized influence, 233
IKEA, 314
Ille, Monika, 315
illusion of unanimity, 179
illusory correlation, 68
IM technique, 257e
imitation strategy, 301
immigrants, and values, 101
immigration status, 28–30, 29e, 30e
implementation, 280
implicit association test, 38
impression management (IM), 256–259, 257e, 258e
incentives, team, 198
incivility, 37e
Incubator cultures, 322
India, 97, 322
individual decision making, 111–112
individualism, 97, 140, 171, 218, 275
individualized consideration, 233
influence tactics, 249–250
informal channel, 204
informal group, 167
information gathering, 119
information overload, 215
information security, 213
informational justice, 139
ingratiation, 249, 257e, 258
initiating structure, 225
injury, 78
innovation, 121, 310, 336–337

innovation strategy, 301
inspirational appeals, 249
inspirational motivation, 233
institutional practices, 316–317
institutionalization, 313
instrumental values, 95
insults, 37e
integrative bargaining, 276e, 277–278
intellectual abilities, 34–35, 35e
intellectual stimulation, 233
intelligence, 120
intensity, 127
intentions, 272–273
interacting groups, 180
interactionist view of conflict, 267
intercultural communications, 217–219
intergroup conflict, 269–270
intergroup development, 335
internal equity, 157
internally caused behaviours, 108
international joint ventures (IJVs), 298
International Paper, 321
international values, 97–101
    GLOBE Framework, 99–100
    Hofstede's framework, 97–99, 99e, 100
interpersonal justice, 139–140
interpersonal skills, 1–2
intersectionality, 29
intimidation, 37e
intragroup conflict, 269–270
intrinsic rewards, 161–162, 198
introverted (I), 84
intuition, 3–4, 73, 113
intuitive decision making, 113
intuitive (N), 84
IQ (intelligence quotient) tests, 34
Iran, 171
Ireland, 322
irrationality, 66
Islam, 33
Israel, 175, 322

J

Japan, 98, 153, 218, 275
JCPenney, 329
Jiang, Ping, 246
job attitudes, 49–52
    distinctiveness of, 52
    employee engagement, 51–52
    groups, and social loafing, 175
    job involvement, 50
    job satisfaction, 50
    and moods and emotions, 77–78
    organizational commitment, 50
    perceived organizational support (POS), 50–51
job characteristics model (JCM), 148–149, 149e
job design, 148
job dissatisfaction, 339

job engagement, 51–52, 142–143
job enrichment, 150–151, 150e
job evaluation, 157
job involvement, 50
job losses, 11
job performance, 56–57
job redesign, 149–151, 340–341
	job enrichment, 150–151, 150e
	job rotation, 149–150
	relational job design, 151
job rotation, 149–150
job satisfaction, 50, 52, 303
	and absenteeism, 57
	and bottom line, 58
	causes of, 54–55
	and customer satisfaction, 57
	impact of satisfied and dissatisfied
		employees, 55–58
	and job performance, 56–57
	job satisfaction curve, 26e
	levels of, 53–54, 53e, 54e
	and management, 58
	measurement of, 52–53
	and organizational citizenship
		behaviour, 57
	responses to dissatisfaction,
		55–56, 55e
	and turnover, 57–58
	and workplace deviance, 58
job sharing, 153
job specification, and disabilities, 36
Jobs, Steven, 229
judging (J), 84
judgment of others. See social perception
justification, 279
justifying, 256e
Ju-Yung, Chung, 314

K
Kamprad, Ingvar, 314
Kelleher, Herb, 314
KFC, 58
Kielburger, Craig, 314
knowledge-based pay, 159
Korea, 218
Kotter, John, 333
Kotter's eight-step plan for implementing
	change, 333–334, 333e
Kraft Foods Inc., 189

L
laissez-faire, 233
language, 215–216, 319
Laninge, Niklas, 119
Larger Than life, 145–146
lateral communication, 205–206
Latin America, 158, 259
layoffs, 11
Lazear, Ed, 160
leader–member exchange (LMX), 229

leader–member relations, 227
leadership, 223–224
	attribution theory of leadership,
		238–239
	authentic leadership, 235–237
	behavioural theories of leadership,
		224–226
	challenges to the leadership
		construct, 238–239
	charismatic leadership, 229–232,
		230e, 234
	contingency theories, 226–229
	effective leaders, 240
	ethical leadership, 235
	Fiedler contingency model,
		226–228, 227e
	full range of leadership model,
		233, 233e
	leadership style, 226–227
	mentoring, 237–238
	and moods and emotions, 76–77
	neutralizers, 239, 239e
	path–goal theory, 229
	selection, 240
	servant leadership, 235–236
	situational leadership theory
		(SLT), 228
	substitutes, 239, 239e
	and team effectiveness, 193
	training, 240
	trait theories of leadership,
		224, 226
	transactional leaders,
		232, 232e
	transformational leaders,
		232–234, 232e
	vs. power, 246
leadership style, 226–227
lean organizations, 298–300
least preferred co-worker (LPC)
		questionnaire, 226–228
legitimacy, 249
legitimate power, 247
lesbian, 27
Lescornez, Philippe, 321
Lewin, Kurt, 332
Lewin's three-step model,
		332–333, 332e
liability, culture as, 313–314
Liz Claiborne, 328
Loblaws, 301
Locke, Edwin, 132
Lockheed Martin, 27
long-term orientation, 98
LoveMachine, 297
low Machs, 88
low-context cultures, 218, 281
low-cost labour, 11–12
loyalty response, 56
Lumenpulse, 301
lying, 217

M
Machiavellianism, 88, 253
Malaysia, 98, 250, 323
management by exception, 233
management by objectives (MBO), 134
managerial communication, 206–208
manipulation, 331
Manitoba Human Rights Commission,
		43–44
Manpower Business Solutions, 212
Marshall, David, 306
masculinity, 98, 275
Maslow, Abraham, 127–128
MasterFoods, 321
material symbols, 318–319
materialistic cultures, 140
matrix structure, 295–296, 295e
Mayer, Marissa, 154
McClelland, David, 130–131
McClelland's theory of needs, 130–131
McDaniel, Jonathan, 58
McGregor, Douglas, 128, 129
McMaster University, 264
mechanistic model, 300, 300e
Menozzi, P., 27
mental models, 196
mentor, 237
mentoring, 237–238
mergers, 313–314
merit-based pay plan, 158
Merrill Lynch, 188
metamorphosis stage, 316–317
Mexico, 171
Microsoft, 291, 314
Middle East, 259
mindfulness, 72
mini cases
	Accepting new norms? A harassed
		reporter fights back, 183–184
	Canada's (biased?) guide to healthy
		eating, 184–185
	Career planning as decision making,
		124–125
	Classroom diversity and groups,
		44–45
	Coming back from conflict, 285–287
	Culture change at the RCMP,
		325–326
	Developing and maintaining a safety
		culture, 325
	Disability-based discrimination,
		43–44
	Emotional contagion unleashed,
		80–81
	Emotional labour at the call centre,
		79–80
	Enriching jobs at the construction
		site, 165
	Getting the best from your
		salesforce, 163–164
	Goals, revisited, 145–146

Hiring school bus drivers, 123–124
The informal communication
network, 221
Interview expectations and cultural
confusion, 104–105
Lifelong learning and teamwork,
200–201
Make way for innovation, 344
Managing group behaviour without
formal power, 16–17
The people side of Target's Canadian
catastrophe, 17–18
The personality problem, 103–104
Power abused—celebrity and
harassment, 263
Power in academe, 264
The promotion, 60–61
Situational leadership comes clean,
243–244
Stressed in software, 342–343
Structured for service, 305–306
Structuring for multiple purposes—
finding the right balance,
306–308
A study of leadership style, 242
Team incentives and unintended
consequences, 201–202
Voicing and being a "team player,"
221–222
What does "fair" mean, 144–145
Win-lose negotiation tactics lead to
corporate humiliation, 284–285
Work attitudes, recognition,
feedback, and fairness, 61–62
misrepresenting, 256e
MNP LLP, 120
mockery, 37e
model, 14
see also OB model
modular organization, 296
Molson Coors, 51
moods, 64, 64e
the basic moods, 65
experiencing moods, 65–66
function of, 66–67
negotiation, 77, 280–281
OB applications of, 75–78
potential influences on, 67–71
sources of, 67–71
motivation, 127
see also motivation theories
alternative work arrangements,
151–155
benefits, 160–161
creative environment, 120–121
creative outcomes, 121
creative potential, 120
and creativity, 120–121
employee involvement, 155–156
fostering workplace motivation,
142–143

intrinsic rewards, 161–162
job characteristics model (JCM),
148–149, 149e
by job design, 148–149
job engagement, 142–143
and moods and emotions, 76
and pay, 156–160
motivation theories
see also motivation
contemporary theories, 131–142
early theories of motivation,
127–131
and employee involvement
programs, 156
equity theory, 136–140, 137e
expectancy theory, 141–142, 141e
goal-setting theory, 132–134, 134e
hierarchy of needs, 127–128, 128e
McClelland's theory of needs,
130–131
self-determination theory, 131–132
self-efficacy theory, 135–136
Theory X, 128, 156
Theory Y, 128, 156
two-factor theory, 129–130
motivation-hygiene theory, 129–130
Motorola, 298
movement, 332, 333
movie-making organizations, 296
multiculturalism, 19, 20
Multiculturalism Act, 20
Multiculturalism Policy of Canada
(1971), 20
multiteam systems, 191
Myers-Briggs Type Indicator (MBTI),
84–85

N

nAch, 130
Nachuk, Billy-Jo, 43–44
nAff, 130
narcissism, 88
national culture, 133
adaptation to differing cultural
norms, 12
barriers to effective communication,
217–218
cultural context, 218
cultural differences, 140
day-of-week mood effects, 70e
high-context cultures, 218, 281
intercultural communications,
217–219
international values, 97–101
low-context cultures, 218, 281
and negotiation, 281–282
working with people from different
cultures, 11
natural work units, 150
nature, 94
NEC Corporation, 298

need for achievement (nAch), 130
need for affiliation (nAff), 130
need for cognition, 214
need for power (nPow), 130
negative affect, 65
neglect response, 56
negotiation, 275–278
bargaining strategies, 275–278
and culture, 281–282
emotions, 77, 280–281
gender differences, 282
individual differences in negotiation
effectiveness, 280–282
moods, 77, 280–281
negotiation process, 278–280, 279e
personality traits, 280
negotiation process, 278–280, 279e
clarification, 279
closure, 280
ground rules, 279
implementation, 280
justification, 279
preparation and planning, 278–279
problem solving, 280
steps in, 278–280
Netflix, 116
Netherlands, 72, 152
network organizations, 13, 296
neuroscience, 7
neutralizers, 239, 239e
New Zealand, 98
Newman, Paul, 297
Newman's Own, 297
Nike, 318
Nisichawayasihk Cree Nation, 172
Nissan, 190
noise, 204
Nokia, 205
nominal group technique, 180–181
non-routine communications, 212
nonverbal communication, 210–211
nonverbal cues, 210
norming stage, 167
norms, 170–173, 174
North America, 218
nPow, 130
nurture, 94
Nygard, 145–146
Nygard, Peter, 145–146

O

OB. See organizational behaviour (OB)
OB model
basic OB model, 15e
development of, 14–15
OCB. See organizational citizenship
behaviour (OCB)
official languages, 20
Ohio State Studies, 224–225, 225
Oldham, Greg, 148
onboarding, 316

1-800-GOT-JUNK, 321
Ontarians with Disability Act, 31–32
Ontario Human Rights Commission, 31–32
openness to experience, 86, 120, 224
oral agreements, 218
oral communication, 208, 212
oral-communication apprehensives, 217
organic model, 300, 300e
organization size, 301
organizational behaviour (OB), 2–3
    challenges for, 9–14
    developing an OB model, 14–15
    disciplines that contribute to, 4–7
    emotions, OB applications of, 75–78
    few absolutes in, 7–8
    history of OB, 7
    moods, OB applications of, 75–78
    opportunities for, 9–14
    systematic study of, 3–4
    toward an OB discipline, 5e
organizational citizenship behaviour (OCB), 57, 236
organizational climate, 312–313
organizational commitment, 50
organizational communication, 206–208
    see also communication
    formal small-group networks, 206–207, 206e
    grapevine, 207–208
    small-group networks, 206–207, 206e, 207e
organizational constraints on decision making, 116–117
organizational culture, 76–77, 309, 310
    change, culture for, 355–357
    and climate, 312–313
    as descriptive term, 310
    employee strengths, 320
    ethical organizational culture, 319–320
    formation of, 314, 317–318
    function of cultures, 311–312
    global implications, 322–323
    growth, 321
    language, 319
    as liability, 313–314
    positive organizational culture, 320–322
    rewards vs. punishments, 321
    rituals, 318
    "small" stuff, value of, 321
    stories, 318
    strong vs. weak cultures, 311
    sustaining, 314–317
    symbols, 318–319
    transmission to employees, 318–319
    Trompenaars's four types of organizational cultures, 322, 322e
    uniform cultures, 310–311

vitality, 321
    vs. formalization, 311
organizational decision making, 112–113
organizational demography, 194
organizational designs
    see also organizational structure
    boundaryless organization, 297–298
    bureaucracy, 294–295
    common organizational designs, 293–296
    and employee behaviour, 302–304
    lean organizations, 298–300
    matrix structure, 295–296, 295e
    mechanistic model, 300, 300e
    new design options, 296–300
    organic model, 300, 300e
    simple structure, 293–294
    virtual organization, 296–297, 297e
organizational development (OD), 334–335
organizational goals, 127
organizational justice, 136–140, 138e
organizational politics, 252
    see also political behaviour; politics
organizational strategies, 301
organizational structure, 289
    see also organizational designs
    and environment, 302
    centralization, 292–293
    chain of command, 291
    decentralization, 292–293
    departmentalization, 290–291
    differences, 300–302
    formalization, 293
    key design questions and answers, 289e
    and organizational size, 301
    organizational strategies, 301
    span of control, 291–292, 292e
    and technology, 301–302
    work specialization, 289–290, 290e
outcome orientation, 310
outcomes, 118
Outward Bound program, 240
overconfidence bias, 113–114
overconforming, 256e

P
Pakistan, 98, 322
participation, 330, 334
participative management, 155–156
path–goal theory, 229
patriarchal privilege, 183
Paulson, Bob, 326
pay
    how to pay, 157–160
    and motivation, 156–160
    pay structure, 157
    variable-pay programs, 157–160
    what to pay, 157
Penn West Petroleum, 299

people orientation, 310
people skills, 12–13
Pepsi, 302
perceived conflict, 271–272
perceived organizational support (POS), 50–51
perceiving (P), 84
perception, 107
    and individual decision making, 111–112
    influencing factors, 107
    social perception, 107–111
performance appraisal, 158
performance evaluation, 116–117, 193, 254
performance norm, 170
performance–reward relationship, 141
performing, 167
persistence, 127
personal appeals, 249
personal best, 13
personal power, 247–248
personality, 83
    see also personality frameworks
    and acceptance of change, 331–332
    creative personality, 120
    determinants of, 83–84
    measurement of, 83
    and moods and emotions, 67
    personality traits, 84, 90–92, 280
    and persuasive communication, 214
    and situations, 92–94
    of team members, 194
    and values, 95–97
    vs. emotional intelligence, 73–74
personality frameworks
    approach–avoidance framework, 90
    Big Five Model, 85–87, 87e
    Dark Triad, 88–90
    Myers-Briggs Type Indicator (MBTI), 84–85
personality traits, 84, 90–92, 280
personality–job fit theory, 95–96
personalization, and conflict, 271–272
person–organization fit, 97
persuasive communication, 213–214
    automatic processing, 213
    controlled processing, 213
    interest level, 213
    message characteristics, 214
    and personality, 214
    prior knowledge, 214
Peru, 171
physical abilities, 36–38, 36e
physical distance, 210–211
physical exercise, 340
physiological needs, 127
physiological symptoms of stress, 338–339
Piazza, A., 27
piece-rate pay plan, 158
placement, 340